Krajewski • Ritzman • Malhotra

Operations Management
Processes and Supply Chains
MAN 3504

Second Custom Edition for University of North Florida

D1368698

Taken from:
Operations Management: Processes and Supply Chains, Tenth Edition
by Lee J. Krajewski, Larry P. Ritzman, and Manoj K. Malhotra

Cover Art: Courtesy of Photodisc/GettyImages.

Taken from:

Operations Management: Processes and Supply Chains, Tenth Edition
by Lee J. Krajewski, Larry P. Ritzman, and Manoj K. Malhotra
Copyright © 2013, 2010, 2007, 2005, 2002 by Pearson Education, Inc.
Published by Prentice Hall
Upper Saddle River, New Jersey 07458

This special edition published in cooperation with Pearson Learning Solutions.

Pearson Learning Solutions, 501 Boylston Street, Suite 900, Boston, MA 02116
A Pearson Education Company
www.pearsoned.com

Printed in the United States of America

10   16

000200010271895497

ML

ISBN 10: 1-269-90036-6
ISBN 13: 978-1-269-90036-2

Dedicated with love to our families.

■

Judie Krajewski
Gary and Christine; Gabrielle
Lori and Dan; Aubrey, Madeline, Amelia, and Marianna
Carrie and Jon; Jordanne, Alaina, and Bradley
Selena and Jeff; Alex
Virginia and Jerry
Virginia and Larry

■

Barbara Ritzman
Karen and Matt; Kristin and Alayna
Todd; Cody, Cole, Taylor, and Clayton
Kathryn and Paul
Mildred and Ray

■

Maya Malhotra
Vivek, Pooja, and Neha
Santosh and Ramesh Malhotra
Indra and Prem Malhotra; Neeti and Neil Ardeshna, and Deeksha
Sadhana Malhotra
Leela and Mukund Dabholkar
Aruna and Harsha Dabholkar; Aditee
Mangala and Pradeep Gandhi; Priya and Medha

About the Authors

Lee J. Krajewski is Professor Emeritus at The Ohio State University and Professor Emeritus at the University of Notre Dame. While at The Ohio State University, he received the University Alumni Distinguished Teaching Award and the College of Business Outstanding Faculty Research Award. He initiated the Center for Excellence in Manufacturing Management and served as its director for 4 years. In addition, he received the National President's Award and the National Award of Merit of the American Production and Inventory Control Society. He served as president of the Decision Sciences Institute and was elected a fellow of the institute in 1988. He received the Distinguished Service Award in 2003.

Lee received his PhD from the University of Wisconsin. Over the years, he has designed and taught courses at both graduate and undergraduate levels on topics such as operations strategy, introduction to operations management, operations design, project management, and manufacturing planning and control systems.

Lee served as the editor of *Decision Sciences*, was the founding editor of the *Journal of Operations Management*, and has served on several editorial boards. Widely published himself, Lee has contributed numerous articles to such journals as *Decision Sciences*, *Journal of Operations Management*, *Management Science*, *Production and Operations Management*, *International Journal of Production Research*, *Harvard Business Review*, and *Interfaces*, to name just a few. He has received five best-paper awards. Lee's areas of specialization include operations strategy, manufacturing planning and control systems, supply chain management, and master production scheduling.

Larry P. Ritzman is Professor Emeritus at The Ohio State University and Professor Emeritus at Boston College. While at The Ohio State University, he served as department chairman and received several awards for both teaching and research, including the Pace Setters' Club Award for Outstanding Research. While at Boston College, he held the Thomas J. Galligan, Jr. chair and received the Distinguished Service Award from the School of Management. He received his doctorate at Michigan State University, having had prior industrial experience at the Babcock and Wilcox Company. Over the years, he has been privileged to teach and learn more about operations management with numerous students at all levels—undergraduate, MBA, executive MBA, and doctorate.

Particularly active in the Decision Sciences Institute, Larry has served as council coordinator, publications committee chair, track chair, vice president, board member, executive committee member, doctoral consortium coordinator, and president. He was elected a fellow of the institute in 1987 and earned the Distinguished Service Award in 1996. He has received three best-paper awards. He has been a frequent reviewer, discussant, and session chair for several other professional organizations.

Larry's areas of particular expertise are service processes, operations strategy, production and inventory systems, forecasting, multistage manufacturing, and layout. An active researcher, Larry's publications have appeared in such journals as *Decision Sciences*, *Journal of Operations Management*, *Production and Operations Management*, *Harvard Business Review*, and *Management Science*. He has served in various editorial capacities for several journals.

Manoj K. Malhotra is the Jeff B. Bates Professor in the Moore School of Business, and has served as the chairman of the Management Science Department at the University of South Carolina (USC), Columbia, since 2000. He is the founding director of the Center for Global Supply Chain and Process Management (GSCPM), which has been in operation since 2005. He earned an engineering undergraduate degree from the Indian Institute of Technology (IIT), Kanpur, India, in 1983, and a PhD in operations management from The Ohio State University in 1990. He is a fellow of the Decision Sciences Institute and is certified as a fellow of the American Production and Inventory Management Society (CFPIM). Manoj has conducted seminars and consulted with firms such as Cummins Turbo Technologies, John Deere, Metso Paper, Palmetto Health Richland, Phelps Dodge, Sonoco, UCB Chemicals, Verizon, Walmart Global Logistics, and Westinghouse Nuclear Fuels Division, among others.

Apart from teaching operations management, supply chain management, and global business issues at USC, Manoj has also taught at the Terry School of Business, University of Georgia; Wirtschaftsuniversität Wien in Austria; and the Graduate School of Management at Macquarie University, Australia. His research has thematically focused on the deployment of flexible resources in manufacturing and service firms, and on the interface between operations and supply chain management and other functional areas of business. His work on these and related issues has been published in refereed journals such as *Decision Sciences, European Journal of Operational Research, IIE Transactions, International Journal of Production Research, Journal of Operations Management, OMEGA,* and *Production and Operations Management Journal.* He is a recipient of the Decision Sciences Institute's Outstanding Achievement Award for the best application paper in 1990, and the Stan Hardy Award in 2002 and 2006 for the best paper published in the field of operations management. In 2007, his co-authored study on the evolution of manufacturing planning systems was a finalist for the best paper award in the *Journal of Operations Management.* In 2007, Manoj won the University of South Carolina Educational Foundation Award for Professional Schools, which is the university's most prestigious annual prize for innovative research, scholarship, and creative achievement. More recently, he received the *Decision Sciences* journal best paper award for the year 2011.

Manoj has won several teaching awards, including the Michael J. Mungo Outstanding Graduate Teaching Award in 2006 from the University of South Carolina and the Alfred G. Smith Jr. Excellence in Teaching Award in 1995 from the Moore School of Business. He was voted by the students as an outstanding professor in the international MBA program by the classes of 1997, 1998, 1999, 2000, 2005, and 2008; and as the outstanding professor in the IMBA-Vienna program by the classes of 1998 and 2004. He was designated as one of the first "Master Teachers" in the Moore School of Business in 1998, and has been listed in "Who's Who among America's Teachers" in 1996 and 2000.

Manoj is an associate editor of *Decision Sciences* and senior editor for the *POMS* journal. He has served as the past area editor for *POMS* journal (2000–2003) and an associate editor for the *Journal of Operations Management* (2001–2010). He is an active referee for several other journals in the field, and has served as the co-editor for special focus issues of *Decision Sciences* (1999) and *Journal of Operations Management* (2002). He was the program chair for the 36th International Meeting of the Decision Sciences Institute (DSI) in San Francisco in 2005, and has also served as an associate program chair for the POMS national meeting. He has been involved in the Mid-Carolina chapter of APICS as its past president, executive board member, and as an instructor of professional level CPIM certification courses. He is a founding board member of Shingo Prize for Lean Excellence in South Carolina.

Brief Contents

Contents

4 OPERATIONS PLANNING AND SCHEDULING 105

5 RESOURCE PLANNING 141

6 SUPPLY CHAIN INVENTORY MANAGEMENT 185

Preface

Creating Value through Operations Management

Operations management is a vital topic that every business student needs to understand because it is at the heart of the creation of wealth for businesses and the improvement in the living standard of citizens of all countries. Operations managers are responsible for the production of services and products in an ethical and environmentally responsible way while being responsive to the market. Sound like a challenge? Add to it the need to manage supply chains of materials, information, and funds reaching to all areas of the world. While challenging, there are concepts, tools and methods that managers use to deal with operating problems in a global environment. The mission of this text is to provide you with a comprehensive framework for addressing operational and supply chain issues. We accomplish this mission by using a systemized approach while focusing on issues of current interest to you. It is important to be efficient and capable with respect to internal processes; however, it is critical for organizations to be able to link those processes to those of their customers and their suppliers to provide competitive supply chains. This text is unique in that it builds the concept of a supply chain from the ground up. Starting with the analysis of business processes and how they relate to the overall operational goals of a firm, our text proceeds to show how these processes are integrated to form supply chains and how they can be managed to obtain efficient flows of materials, information, and funds. This approach reinforces the concept that supply chains are only as good as the processes within and across each firm in them.

This text has been thoroughly revised to meet your needs regardless of your major. Any manager needs to know the global implications of supply chains and how to make decisions in a dynamic environment. We address these contemporary issues of interest through opening vignettes and managerial practices in each chapter. We show you the essential tools you will need to improve process performance. Irrespective of the industry in which you are seeking a career, processes and supply chains are analyzed from the perspective of service as well as manufacturing firms. Our philosophy is that you will learn by doing; consequently, the text has ample opportunities for you to experience the role of a manager with challenging problems, cases, a library of videos customized to the individual chapters, simulations, experiential exercises, and tightly integrated online computer resources. With this text, you will develop the capability to analyze problems and support managerial decisions.

Helping You Learn

Key Features

Several new additions and changes have been made to the book to retain and enhance its theme of processes and supply chains and to expand these themes through new content, Managerial Practices, Examples, and End-of-Chapter Problems and Cases. Several key features designed to help aid in the learning process are highlighted next:

Chapter Opening Vignettes engage and stimulate student interest by profiling how real companies apply specific operational issues addressed in each chapter.

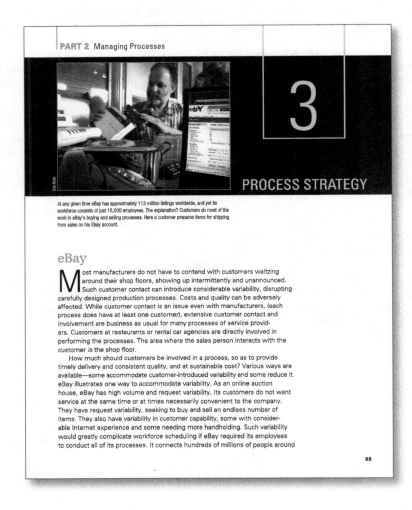

Managerial Practices provide current examples of how companies deal—either successfully or unsuccessfully—with process and supply chain issues facing them as they run their operations.

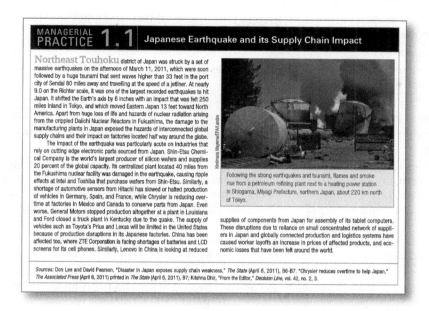

Examples demonstrate how to apply what students have learned and walk them through the solution process modeling good problem-solving techniques. These examples always close with a unique feature called **Decision Point**, which focuses students on the decision implications for managers.

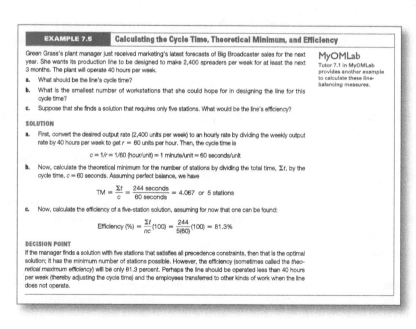

End of Chapter Resources

- **Learning Goals in Review** for review purposes.
- **MyOMLab Resources** lists the resources found in MyOMLab and how those resources relate back to the topics and discussions in the chapter.
- **Key Equations** for review purposes.
- **Key Terms** for review purposes, the page references highlight where the concept was first discussed.
- **Solved Problems** reinforce and help students prepare their homework assignments by detailing how to solve model problems with the appropriate techniques presented in the chapter.
- **Discussion Questions** test student comprehension of the concepts through the use of short scenarios.
- **Problems** sharpen students' quantitative skills by providing a bridge between chapter materials with a wide selection of homework material. Advanced problems are also included to increase the level of difficulty. Most of the homework problems can be done manually, or students can utilize a variety of software tools through MyOMLab, which is discussed in a later section.
- **Active Model Exercises** enable students to use pre-created spreadsheets to do "what-if" analysis of examples presented in the text to see what would happen if certain parameters were changed.
- **Video Cases** provide a summary of content covered in a series of on-location video profiles of real-world service and manufacturing companies and challenges they face in their operations. Questions are included for classroom discussion or assignment purposes.
- **Cases** challenge students to grapple with a capstone problem that can be used as an in-class exercise or a homework assignment or team project.
- **Experiential Learning** forms students into teams who work both in and out of class on exercises that actively involve them in team-based discussion questions and decisions. The six exercises reinforce student learning. Each exercise has been thoroughly tested in class and proven to be a valuable learning tool.
- A **Video Library** of 23 cases in MyOMLab (including 3 tutorials) offers at least one video customized for each chapter, which make for excellent class discussion and learning.

Teaching and Learning Support

MyOMLab

MyOMLab A key capability of MyOMLab is as an online homework and assessment tool designed to help students practice operations management problems and improve their understanding of course concepts, and to give their instructors feedback on their performance. This online product expands the student's learning experience with out-of-class quizzes that are automatically graded and tutorials to guide the problem solving process, keeping students up to date, and freeing instructors for more creative use of class time.

MyOMLab lets you teach your course your way. Use MyOMLab as an out-of-the-box resource for students who need extra help, or take full advantage of its advanced customization options.

For Instructors

Instructor's Resource Center—Reached through a link at **www.pearsonhighered.com/krajewski**, the Instructor's Resource Center contains the electronic files for the complete Instructor's Solutions Manual, PowerPoint lecture presentations, the Image Library, and the Test Item File.

- **Register, redeem, log in** at **www.pearsonhighered.com/irc**, instructors can access a variety of print, media, and presentation resources that are available with this book in downloadable digital format. Resources are also available for course management platforms such as Blackboard, WebCT, and CourseCompass.
- **Need help?** Pearson Education's dedicated technical support team is ready to assist instructors with questions about the media supplements that accompany this text. Visit **http://247pearsoned.com** for answers to frequently asked questions and toll-free user support phone numbers. The supplements are available to adopting instructors. Detailed descriptions are provided at the Instructor's Resource Center.

Instructor's Solutions Manual (0-13-280741-6)—Prepared by John Jensen at The University of South Carolina, this resource begins with the video notes and solutions. They are followed by the instructor notes, and the solutions, and answers to end-of-chapter questions, problems, and cases. This manual is available for download by visiting **www.pearsonhighered.com/krajewski**.

Instructor's Resource Manual—Prepared by John Jensen at The University of South Carolina, this resource begins with sample syllabi for the course suited to various situations: with or without MyOMLab, quarter vs. 7-week course, undergraduate vs. MBA, quantitative vs. qualitative orientation, and process vs. supply chain orientation. It then offers generic (in both Word and PDF versions) Instructor and Student Notes. Both must be revised to reflect the instructor's approach to the course. The Student Notes can be handed out or posted so that the students can have them during class to simplify note taking and concentrate more on what is being said. The Image Library provides possible inserts to the Student Notes. The Instructor Notes offer a course outline, chapter outlines, teaching notes, sample course syllabi, and solutions to the videos. This manual is available for download by visiting **www.pearsonhighered.com/krajewski**.

PowerPoint lecture slides in chapter-by-chapter files for classroom presentation purposes are available for download by visiting **www.pearsonhighered.com/krajewski**. PowerPoints can be customized by the instructor, including inserts from Image Library, just as with the Student Notes.

Image Library—most of the images and illustrations featured in the text are available for download by visiting **www.pearsonhighered.com/krajewski**.

Test Item File—this resource offers an array of questions and problems ranging from easy to difficult. This resource includes true/false and multiple choice questions, which can be accessed by MyOMLab, and short answer, and essay questions. These files are available for download by visiting **www.pearsonhighered.com/krajewski**.

TestGen EQ—Pearson Education's test-generating software is available from **www .pearsonhighered.com/irc**. The software is PC/MAC compatible and preloaded with all of the Test Item File questions. You can manually or randomly view test questions and drag and drop to create a test. You can add or modify test-bank questions as needed.

For Students

Besides having access to study plans and tutorial resources in MyOMLab, students can utilize the following additional course resources within MyOMLab:

OM Explorer a text-specific software tool consisting of Excel worksheets and including tutors, additional exercises, and solvers.

- **Tutors** provide coaching for more than 60 analytical techniques presented in the text. The tutors also provide additional examples for learning and practice.
- **Additional Exercises** pose questions and can be answered with one or more of the tutor applications.
- **Solvers** provide powerful general purpose routines often encountered in practice. These are great for experiential exercises and homework problems.

POM for Windows an easy-to-use software program that covers over 25 common OM techniques.

Active Models include 29 spreadsheets requiring students to evaluate different situations based on problem scenarios.

Download page offers access to software (such as OM Explorer, POM for Windows, SimQuick, and Active Models), and links to free trial of software (such as MS Project, MS MapPoint, and SmartDraw).

CourseSmart

CourseSmart eTextbooks were developed for students looking to save on required or recommended textbooks. Students simply select their eText by title or author and purchase immediate access to the content for the duration of the course using any major credit card. With a CourseSmart eText, students can search for specific keywords or page numbers, take notes online, print out reading assignments that incorporate lecture notes, and bookmark important passages for later review. For more information or to purchase a CourseSmart eTextbook, visit **www.coursesmart.com**.

Acknowledgments

No book is just the work of the authors. We greatly appreciate the assistance and valuable contributions by several people who made this edition possible. Thanks to Beverly Amer of Aspenleaf Productions for her efforts in filming and putting together the new video segments for this edition; and Annie Puciloski for her diligent work of accuracy checking the book and ancillary materials. Special thanks are due to Howard Weiss, of Temple University, whose expertise in upgrading the software for this edition was greatly appreciated.

Many colleagues at other colleges and universities provided valuable comments and suggestions for this and previous editions. We would also like to thank the following faculty members who gave extensive written feedback and commentary to us:

Harold P. Benson, *University of Florida*

James P. McGuire, *Rhode Island College*

David L. Bakuli, *Westfield State College*

David Levy, *Bellevue University*

Tobin Porterfield, *Towson University*

Anil Gulati, Western *New England College*

Linda C. Rodriguez, *University of South Carolina–Aiken*

Kathryn Marley, *Duquesne University*

Qingyu Zhang, *Arkansas State University*

Ching-Chung Kuo, *University of North Texas*

We would like to thank the people at Pearson Prentice Hall, including Chuck Synovec, Mary Kate Murray, Ashlee Bradbury, Anne Fahlgren, Judy Leale, Sarah Petersen, and Lauren McFalls and Haylee Schwenk at PreMediaGlobal. Without their hard work, dedication, and guidance this book would not have been possible.

At the University of Notre Dame Mendoza College of Business, we want to thank Jerry Wei, Sarv Devaraj, Dave Hartvigsen, Carrie Queenan, Xuying Zhao and Daewon Sun for their constant encouragement and for their willingness to share their teaching secrets. At the University of South Carolina, we thank Sanjay Ahire, Jack Jensen, and Ashley Metcalf for contributing their thoughts and insights on classroom pedagogical issues to this text. In particular, we gratefully acknowledge Jack Jensen for the stellar contributions he has made to the development of ISM and MyOMLab. Thanks go to colleagues at The Ohio State University for their encouragement and ideas on text revision.

Finally, we thank our families for supporting us during this project involving multiple teleconference calls and long periods of seclusion. Our wives, Judie, Barb, and Maya, have provided the love, stability, and encouragement that sustained us while we transformed the ninth edition into the tenth.

Bizuayehu Tesfaye/AP Photos

USING OPERATIONS TO COMPETE

The seventh novel in the Harry Potter series was released on July 21, 2007 and became an instant best seller around the globe. Because the book had to be delivered in a tight time window to the customers, Scholastic coordinated its publishing and distribution processes in USA months in advance of the release date.

Scholastic and Harry Potter

Scholastic is the world's largest publisher and distributor of children's books and educational materials. Founded in 1920, it had $1.9 billion in revenues in fiscal 2011 with offices in 16 countries including North America, Europe, Southeast Asia, Latin America, the Middle East, Australia, New Zealand, and Africa. Scholastic started planning in early 2007 for the worldwide release of the eagerly awaited seventh book *Harry Potter and the Deathly Hallows* in the acclaimed series by J.K. Rowling on the boy wizard. When the author finished the book in spring 2007, Scholastic's printers R.R. Donnelly & Sons and Quebecor World worked around the clock to make sure that the book would be ready by the release date. To save time in loading and unloading, Scholastic bypassed its own warehouses and required its truckers, Yellow Transportation and JB Hunt Transport Services, to use the same size trailers and pallets to ship books directly from six printing sites to big retailers like Barnes & Noble and Amazon.com. This fleet of trucks, if lined up bumper-to-bumper, would stretch for 15 miles. GPS transponders were used to alert Scholastic by e-mail if the driver or the trailer veered off the designated routes. The timing was particularly tricky for e-tailers, who had to directly ship books in advance for individual orders to arrive simultaneously around the country in order to minimize the risk of someone leaking the book's ending.

Since close to 90 percent of sales of such special books occur in the first week, they get special treatment to save time, money, space, and work. Scholastic had to customize, coordinate, and synchronize its operations and supply chain processes across multiple partners at the printing, warehousing, distribution, and retailing locations to ensure that the last book in the Harry Potter series reached the final customers no more than a few hours before the scheduled July 21, 12:01 A.M. release deadline. Not bad for a bunch of Muggles who transported 12 million copies in a short time window without the magical floo powder, portkeys, and broomsticks!

Source: Dean Foust, "Harry Potter and the Logistical Nightmare," *Business Week* (August 6, 2007), p. 9; Michelle Regenold, "Shipping Harry Potter: How Do They Do That?" **www.go-explore-trans.org/2007/mar-apr/shipping_HP.cfm; www.scholastic.com,** 2011.

LEARNING GOALS *After reading this chapter, you should be able to:*

1 Describe operations and supply chains in terms of inputs, processes, outputs, information flows, suppliers, and customers.

2 Define an operations strategy and its linkage to corporate strategy, as well as the role it plays as a source of competitive advantage in a global marketplace.

3 Identify nine competitive priorities used in operations strategy, and their linkage to marketing strategy.

4 Explain how operations can be used as a competitive weapon.

5 Identify the global trends and challenges facing operations management.

---

operations management

The systematic design, direction, and control of processes that transform inputs into services and products for internal, as well as external, customers.

process

Any activity or group of activities that takes one or more inputs, transforms them, and provides one or more outputs for its customers.

operation

A group of resources performing all or part of one or more processes.

supply chain

An interrelated series of processes within and across firms that produces a service or product to the satisfaction of customers.

supply chain management

The synchronization of a firm's processes with those of its suppliers and customers to match the flow of materials, services, and information with customer demand.

Operations management refers to the systematic design, direction, and control of processes that transform inputs into services and products for internal, as well as external customers.

This book deals with managing those fundamental activities and processes that organizations use to produce goods and services that people use every day. A **process** is any activity or group of activities that takes one or more inputs, transforms them, and provides one or more outputs for its customers. For organizational purposes, processes tend to be clustered together into operations. An **operation** is a group of resources performing all or part of one or more processes. Processes can be linked together to form a **supply chain**, which is the interrelated series of processes within a firm and across different firms that produce a service or product to the satisfaction of customers.[1] A firm can have multiple supply chains, which vary by the product or service provided. **Supply chain management** is the synchronization of a firm's processes with those of its suppliers and customers to match the flow of materials, services, and information with customer demand. For example, Scholastic must schedule the printing of a very large quantity of books in a timely fashion, receive orders from its largest customers, directly load and dispatch a fleet of trucks by specific destination while bypassing regular warehouses, keep track of their progress using technology, and finally, bill their customers and collect payment. The operational planning at Scholastic, along with internal and external coordination within its supply chain, provides one example of designing customized processes for competitive operations.

Operations and Supply Chain Management across the Organization

Broadly speaking, operations and supply chain management underlie all departments and functions in a business. Whether you aspire to manage a department or a particular process within it, or you just want to understand how the process you are a part of fits into the overall fabric of the business, you need to understand the principles of operations and supply chain management.

Operations serve as an excellent career path to upper management positions in many organizations. The reason is that operations managers are responsible for key decisions that affect the success of the organization. In manufacturing firms, the head of operations usually holds the

---

[1]The terms *supply chain* and *value chain* are sometimes used interchangeably.

title chief operations officer (COO) or vice president of manufacturing (or of production or operations). The corresponding title in a service organization might be COO or vice president (or director) of operations. Reporting to the head of operations are the managers of departments, such as customer service, production and inventory control, and quality assurance.

Figure 1.1 shows operations as one of the key functions within an organization. The circular relationships in Figure 1.1 highlight the importance of the coordination among the three mainline functions of any business, namely, (1) operations, (2) marketing, and (3) finance. Each function is unique and has its own knowledge and skill areas, primary responsibilities, processes, and decision domains. From an external perspective, finance generates resources, capital, and funds from investors and sales of its goods and services in the marketplace. Based on business strategy, the finance and operations functions then decide how to invest these resources and convert them into physical assets and material inputs. Operations subsequently transforms these material and service inputs into product and service outputs. These outputs must match the characteristics that can be sold in the selected markets by marketing. Marketing is responsible for producing sales revenue of the outputs, which become returns to investors and capital for supporting operations. Functions such as accounting, information systems, human resources, and engineering make the firm complete by providing essential information, services, and other managerial support.

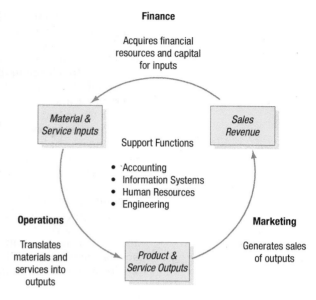

▲ FIGURE 1.1
Integration between Different Functional Areas of a Business

These relationships provide direction for the business as a whole, and are aligned to the same strategic intent. It is important to understand the entire circle, and not just the individual functional areas. How well these functions work together determines the effectiveness of the organization. Functions should be integrated and should pursue a common strategy. Success depends on how well they are able to do so. No part of this circle can be dismissed or minimized without loss of effectiveness, and regardless of how departments and functions are individually managed, they are always linked together through processes. Thus, a firm competes not only by offering new services and products, creative marketing, and skillful finance, but also through its unique competencies in operations and sound management of core processes.

Historical Evolution of Operations and Supply Chain Management

The history of modern operations and supply chain management is rich and over two hundred years old, even though its practice has been around in one form or another for centuries. James Watt invented the steam engine in 1785. The subsequent establishment of railroads facilitated efficient movement of goods throughout Europe, and eventually even in distant colonies such as India. With the invention of the cotton gin in 1794, Eli Whitney introduced the concept of interchangeable parts. It revolutionized the art of machine-based manufacturing, and coupled with the invention of the steam engine, lead to the great industrial revolution in England and the rest of Europe. The textile industry was one of the earliest industries to be mechanized. The industrial revolution gradually spread to the United States and the rest of the world in the nineteenth century, and was accompanied by such great innovations as the internal combustion engine, steam-powered ships, metallurgy of iron making, large-scale production of chemicals, and invention of machine tools, among others. The foundations of modern manufacturing and technological breakthroughs were also inspired by the creation of a mechanical computer

Henry Ford with a Model T in Buffalo, New York, in 1921. The Ford Motor Company, founded in 1903, produced about one million Model T's in 1921.

by Charles Babbage in the early part of the nineteenth century. He also pioneered the concept of division of labor, which laid the foundation for scientific management of operations and supply chain management that was further improved upon by Frederick Taylor in 1911.

Three other landmark events from the twentieth century define the history of operations and supply chain management. First is the invention of the assembly line for the Model T car by Henry Ford in 1909. The era of mass production was born, where complex products like automobiles could be manufactured in large numbers at affordable prices through repetitive manufacturing. Second, Alfred Sloan in the 1930s introduced the idea of strategic planning for achieving product proliferation and variety, with the newly founded General Motors Corporation offering "a car for every purse and purpose." Finally, with the publication of the Toyota Production System in 1978, Taiichi Ohno laid the groundwork for removing wasteful activities from an organization, a concept that we explore further in this book while learning about lean systems.

The recent history of operations and supply chains over the past three decades has been steeped in technological advances. The 1980s were characterized by wide availability of computer aided design (CAD), computer aided manufacturing (CAM), and automation. Information technology applications started playing an increasingly important role in 1990s, and started connecting the firm with its extended enterprise through Enterprise Resource Planning Systems and outsourced technology hosting for supply chain solutions. Service organizations like Federal Express, United Parcel Service (UPS), and Walmart also became sophisticated users of information technology in operations, logistics, and management of supply chains. The new millennium has seen an acceleration of this trend, along with an increased focus on sustainability and the natural environment. We cover all these ideas and topical areas in greater detail throughout this book.

A Process View

You might wonder why we begin by looking at processes, rather than at departments or even the firm. The reason is that a process view of the firm provides a much more relevant picture of the way firms actually work. Departments typically have their own set of objectives, a set of resources with capabilities to achieve those objectives, and managers and employees responsible for performance. Some processes, such as billing, may be so specific that they are contained wholly within a single department, such as accounting.

The concept of a process, however, can be much broader. A process can have its own set of objectives, involve a work flow that cuts across departmental boundaries, and require resources from several departments. You will see examples throughout this text of companies that discovered how to use their processes to gain a competitive advantage. You will notice that the key to success in many organizations is a keen understanding of how their processes work, since an organization is only as effective as its processes. Therefore, operations management is relevant and important for all students, regardless of major, because all departments have processes that must be managed effectively to gain a competitive advantage.

How Processes Work

Figure 1.2 shows how processes work in an organization. Any process has inputs and outputs. Inputs can include a combination of human resources (workers and managers), capital (equipment and facilities), purchased materials and services, land, and energy. The numbered circles in Figure 1.2 represent operations through which services, products, or customers pass and where processes are performed. The arrows represent flows, and can cross because one job or customer can have different requirements (and thus a different flow pattern) than the next job or customer.

Processes provide outputs to customers. These outputs may often be services (that can take the form of information) or tangible products. Every process and every person in an organization has customers. Some are **external customers**, who may be end users or intermediaries (e.g., manufacturers, financial institutions, or retailers) buying the firm's finished services or products. Others are **internal customers**, who may be employees in the firm whose process inputs are actually the outputs of earlier processes managed within the firm. Either way, processes must be managed with the customer in mind.

In a similar fashion, every process and every person in an organization relies on suppliers. **External suppliers** may be other businesses or individuals who provide the resources, services, products, and materials for the firm's short-term and long-term needs. Processes also have **internal suppliers**, who may be employees or processes that supply important information or materials.

---

external customers

A customer who is either an end user or an intermediary (e.g., manufacturers, financial institutions, or retailers) buying the firm's finished services or products.

internal customers

One or more employees or processes that rely on inputs from other employees or processes in order to perform their work.

external suppliers

The businesses or individuals who provide the resources, services, products, and materials for the firm's short-term and long-term needs.

internal suppliers

The employees or processes that supply important information or materials to a firm's processes.

▼ FIGURE 1.2
Processes and Operations

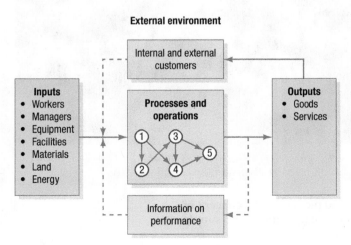

Inputs and outputs vary depending on the service or product provided. For example, inputs at a jewelry store include merchandise, the store building, registers, the jeweler, and customers; outputs to external customers are services and sold merchandise. Inputs to a factory manufacturing blue jeans include denim, machines, the plant, workers, managers, and services provided by outside consultants; outputs are clothing and supporting services. The fundamental role of inputs, processes, and customer outputs holds true for processes at all organizations.

Figure 1.2 can represent a whole firm, a department, a small group, or even a single individual. Each one has inputs and uses processes at various operations to provide outputs. The dashed lines represent two special types of input: participation by customers and information on performance from both internal and external sources. Participation by customers occurs not only when they receive outputs, but also when they take an active part in the processes, such as when students participate in a class discussion. Information on performance includes internal reports on customer service or inventory levels and external information from market research, government reports, or telephone calls from suppliers. Managers need all types of information to manage processes most effectively.

Nested Processes

Processes can be broken down into subprocesses, which in turn can be broken down further into still more subprocesses. We refer to this concept of a process within a process as a **nested process**. It may be helpful to separate one part of a process from another for several reasons. One person or one department may be unable to perform all parts of the process, or different parts of the process may require different skills. Some parts of the process may be designed for routine work while other parts may be geared for customized work. The concept of nested processes is illustrated in greater detail in Chapter 8, "Process Analysis," where we reinforce the need to understand and improve activities within a business and each process's inputs and outputs.

nested process
The concept of a process within a process.

Service and Manufacturing Processes

Two major types of processes are (1) service and (2) manufacturing. Service processes pervade the business world and have a prominent place in our discussion of operations management. Manufacturing processes are also important; without them the products we enjoy as part of our daily lives would not exist. In addition, manufacturing gives rise to service opportunities.

Differences   Why do we distinguish between service and manufacturing processes? The answer lies at the heart of the design of competitive processes. While Figure 1.3 shows several distinctions between service and manufacturing processes along a continuum, the two key differences that we discuss in detail are (1) the nature of their output and (2) the degree of customer contact. In general, manufacturing processes also have longer response times, are more capital intensive, and their quality can be measured more easily than those of service processes.

Manufacturing processes convert materials into goods that have a physical form we call products. For example, an assembly line produces a 350 Z sports car, and a tailor produces an outfit for the rack of an upscale clothing store. The transformation processes change the materials on one or more of the following dimensions:

1. Physical properties

2. Shape

3. Size (e.g., length, breadth, and height of a rectangular block of wood)

4. Surface finish

5. Joining parts and materials

- Physical, durable output
- Output can be inventoried
- Low customer contact
- Long response time
- Capital intensive
- Quality easily measured

- Intangible, perishable output
- Output cannot be inventoried
- High customer contact
- Short response time
- Labor intensive
- Quality not easily measured

▲ **FIGURE 1.3**
Continuum of Characteristics of Manufacturing and Service Processes

The outputs from manufacturing processes can be produced, stored, and transported in anticipation of future demand.

If a process does not change the properties of materials on at least one of these five dimensions, it is considered a service (or nonmanufacturing) process. Service processes tend to produce intangible, perishable outputs. For example, the output from the auto loan process of a bank would be a car loan, and an output of the order fulfillment process of the U.S. Postal Service is the delivery of your letter. The outputs of service processes typically cannot be held in a finished goods inventory to insulate the process from erratic customer demands.

A second key difference between service processes and manufacturing processes is degree of customer contact. Service processes tend to have a higher degree of customer contact. Customers may take an active role in the process itself, as in the case of shopping in a supermarket, or they may be in close contact with the service provider to communicate specific needs, as in the case of a medical clinic. Manufacturing processes tend to have less customer contact. For example, washing machines are ultimately produced to meet retail forecasts. The process requires little information from the ultimate consumers (you and me), except indirectly through market surveys and market focus groups. Even though the distinction between service and manufacturing processes on the basis of customer contact is not perfect, the important point is that managers must recognize the degree of customer contact required when designing processes.

Similarities   At the level of the firm, service providers do not just offer services and manufacturers do not just offer products. Patrons of a restaurant expect good service and good food. A customer purchasing a new computer expects a good product as well as a good warranty, maintenance, replacement, and financial services.

Further, even though service processes do not keep finished goods inventories, they do inventory their inputs. For example, hospitals keep inventories of medical supplies and materials needed for day-to-day operations. Some manufacturing processes, on the other hand, do not inventory their outputs because they are too costly. Such would be the case with low-volume customized products (e.g., tailored suits) or products with short shelf lives (e.g., daily newspapers).

When you look at what is being done at the process level, it is much easier to see whether the *process* is providing a service or manufacturing a product. However, this clarity is lost when the whole company is classified as either a manufacturer or a service provider because it often performs both types of processes. For example, the process of cooking a hamburger at a McDonald's is a manufacturing process because it changes the material's physical properties (dimension 1), as is the process of assembling the hamburger with the bun (dimension 5). However, most of the other processes visible or invisible to McDonald's customers are service processes. You can debate whether to call the whole McDonald's organization a service provider or a manufacturer, whereas classifications at the process level are much less ambiguous.

The Supply Chain View

Most services or products are produced through a series of interrelated business activities. Each activity in a process should add value to the preceding activities; waste and unnecessary cost should be eliminated. Our process view of a firm is helpful for understanding how services or products are produced and why cross-functional coordination is important, but it does not shed any light on the strategic benefits of the processes. The missing strategic insight is that processes must add value for customers throughout the supply chain. The concept of supply chains reinforces the link between processes and performance, which includes a firm's internal processes as well as those of its external customers and suppliers. It also focuses attention on the two main types of processes in the supply chain, namely (1) core processes and (2) support processes. Figure 1.4 shows the links between the core and support processes in a firm and a firm's external customers and suppliers within its supply chain.

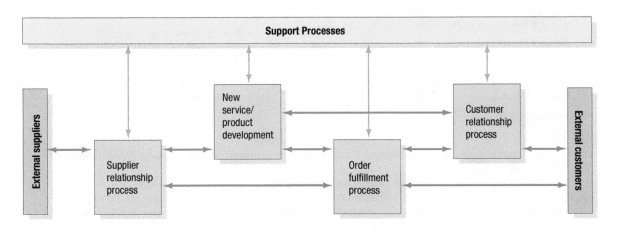

▲ **FIGURE 1.4**
Supply Chain Linkages Showing Work and Information Flows

Core Processes

A **core process** is a set of activities that delivers value to external customers. Managers of these processes and their employees interact with external customers and build relationships with them, develop new services and products, interact with external suppliers, and produce the service or product for the external customer. Examples include a hotel's reservation handling, a new car design for an auto manufacturer, or Web-based purchasing for an online retailer like amazon.com. Of course, each of the core processes has nested processes within it.

In this text we focus on four core processes:

1. *Supplier Relationship Process.* Employees in the **supplier relationship process** select the suppliers of services, materials, and information and facilitate the timely and efficient flow of these items into the firm. Working effectively with suppliers can add significant value to the services or products of the firm. For example, negotiating fair prices, scheduling on-time deliveries, and gaining ideas and insights from critical suppliers are just a few of the ways to create value.

2. *New Service/Product Development Process.* Employees in the **new service/product development process** design and develop new services or products. The services or products may be developed to external customer specifications or conceived from inputs received from the market in general.

3. *Order Fulfillment Process.* The **order fulfillment process** includes the activities required to produce and deliver the service or product to the external customer.

4. *Customer Relationship Process,* sometimes referred to as *customer relationship management.* Employees involved in the **customer relationship process** identify, attract, and build relationships with external customers, and facilitate the placement of orders by customers. Traditional functions, such as marketing and sales, may be a part of this process.

Support Processes

A **support process** provides vital resources and inputs to the core processes and is essential to the management of the business. Firms have many support processes. Examples include budgeting, recruiting, and scheduling. Support processes provide key resources, capabilities, or other inputs that allow the core processes to function.

The Human Resources function in an organization provides many support processes such as recruiting and hiring workers who are needed at different levels of the organization, training the workers for skills and knowledge needed to properly execute their assigned responsibilities, and establishing incentive and compensation plans that reward employees for their performance. The legal department puts in place support processes that ensure that the firm is in compliance with the rules and regulations under which the business operates. The Accounting function supports processes that track how the firm's financial resources are being created and allocated over time, while the Information Systems function is responsible for the movement and processing of data and information needed to make business decisions. Support processes from different functional areas like Accounting, Engineering, Human Resources, and Information Systems are therefore vital to the execution of core processes highlighted in Figure 1.4.

Operations Strategy

Operations strategy specifies the means by which operations implements corporate strategy and helps to build a customer-driven firm. It links long-term and short-term operations decisions to corporate strategy and develops the capabilities the firm needs to be competitive. It is at the heart of managing processes and supply chains. A firm's internal processes are only building blocks: They need to be organized to ultimately be effective in a competitive environment. Operations strategy is the linchpin that brings these processes together to form supply chains that extend beyond the walls of the firm, encompassing suppliers as well as customers. Since customers constantly desire change, the firm's operations strategy must be driven by the needs of its customers.

Developing a customer-driven operations strategy begins with *corporate strategy*, which, as shown in Figure 1.5, coordinates the firm's overall goals with its core processes. It determines the markets the firm will serve and the responses the firm will make to changes in the environment. It provides the resources to develop the firm's core competencies and core processes, and it identifies the strategy the firm will employ in international markets. Based on corporate strategy, a *market analysis* categorizes the firm's customers, identifies their needs, and assesses competitors' strengths. This information is used to develop *competitive priorities*. These priorities help managers develop the services or products and the processes needed to be competitive in the

---

core process

A set of activities that delivers value to external customers.

supplier relationship process

A process that selects the suppliers of services, materials, and information and facilitates the timely and efficient flow of these items into the firm.

new service/product development process

A process that designs and develops new services or products from inputs received from external customer specifications or from the market in general through the customer relationship process.

order fulfillment process

A process that includes the activities required to produce and deliver the service or product to the external customer.

customer relationship process

A process that identifies, attracts, and builds relationships with external customers, and facilitates the placement of orders by customers, sometimes referred to as *customer relationship management.*

support process

A process that provides vital resources and inputs to the core processes and therefore is essential to the management of the business.

operations strategy

The means by which operations implements the firm's corporate strategy and helps to build a customer-driven firm.

▶ **FIGURE 1.5**
Connection Between
Corporate Strategy and Key
Operations Management
Decisions

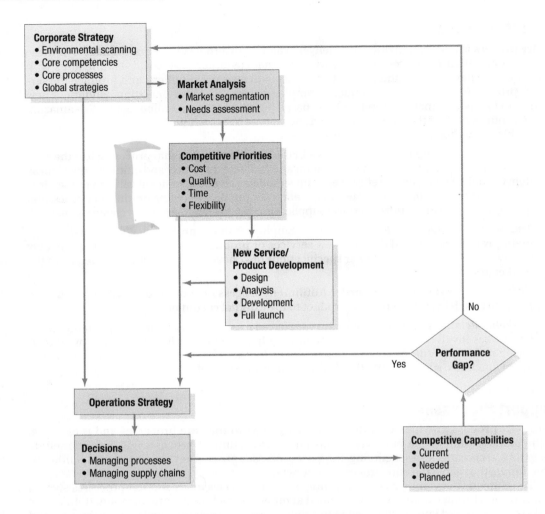

marketplace. Competitive priorities are important to the design of existing as well as new services or products, the processes that will deliver them, and the operations strategy that will develop the firm's capabilities to fulfill them. Developing a firm's operations strategy is a continuous process because the firm's capabilities to meet the competitive priorities must be periodically checked and any gaps in performance must be addressed in the operations strategy.

Corporate Strategy

Corporate strategy provides an overall direction that serves as the framework for carrying out all the organization's functions. It specifies the business or businesses the company will pursue, isolates new opportunities and threats in the environment, and identifies growth objectives.

Developing a corporate strategy involves four considerations: (1) monitoring and adjusting to changes in the business environment, (2) identifying and developing the firm's core competencies, (3) developing the firm's core processes, and (4) developing the firm's global strategies.

Environmental Scanning The external business environment in which a firm competes changes continually and an organization needs to adapt to those changes. Adaptation begins with *environmental scanning*, the process by which managers monitor trends in the environment (e.g., the industry, the marketplace, and society) for potential opportunities or threats. A crucial reason for environmental scanning is to stay ahead of the competition. Competitors may be gaining an edge by broadening service or product lines, improving quality, or lowering costs. New entrants into the market or competitors that offer substitutes for a firm's service or product may threaten continued profitability. Other important environmental concerns include economic trends, technological changes, political conditions, social changes (i.e., attitudes toward work), and the availability of vital resources. For example, car manufacturers recognize that dwindling oil reserves will eventually require alternative fuels for their cars. Consequently, they have designed prototype cars that use hydrogen or electric power as supplements to gasoline as a fuel.

Developing Core Competencies   Good managerial skill alone cannot overcome environmental changes. Firms succeed by taking advantage of what they do particularly well—that is, the organization's unique strengths. **Core competencies** are the unique resources and strengths that an organization's management considers when formulating strategy. They reflect the collective learning of the organization, especially in how to coordinate processes and integrate technologies. These competencies include the following:

1. *Workforce.* A well-trained and flexible workforce allows organizations to respond to market needs in a timely fashion. This competency is particularly important in service organizations, where customers come in direct contact with employees.

2. *Facilities.* Having well-located facilities (offices, stores, and plants) is a primary advantage because of the long **lead time** needed to build new ones. In addition, flexible facilities that can handle a variety of services or products at different levels of volume provide a competitive advantage.

3. *Market and Financial Know-How.* An organization that can easily attract capital from stock sales, market and distribute its services or products, or differentiate them from similar services or products on the market has a competitive edge.

4. *Systems and Technology.* Organizations with expertise in information systems have an edge in industries that are data intensive, such as banking. Particularly advantageous is expertise in Internet technologies and applications, such as business-to-consumer and business-to-business systems. Having the patents on a new technology is also a big advantage.

core competencies
The unique resources and strengths that an organization's management considers when formulating strategy.

lead time
The elapsed time between the receipt of a customer order and filling it.

Developing Core Processes   A firm's core competencies should drive its core processes: customer relationship, new service/product development, order fulfillment, and supplier relationship. Many companies have all four processes, while others focus on a subset of them to better match their core competencies, since they find it difficult to be good at all four processes and still be competitive. For instance, in the credit card business within the banking industry, some companies primarily specialize in finding customers and maintaining relationships with them. American Airlines's credit card program reaches out and achieves a special affinity to customers through its marketing database. On the other hand, specialized credit card companies, such as CapitalOne, focus on service innovation by creating new features and pricing programs. Finally, many companies are taking over the order fulfillment process by managing the processing of credit card transactions and call centers. The important point is that every firm must evaluate its core competencies and choose to focus on those processes that provide it the greatest competitive strength.

Global Strategies   Identifying opportunities and threats today requires a global perspective. A global strategy may include buying foreign services or parts, combating threats from foreign competitors, or planning ways to enter markets beyond traditional national boundaries. Although warding off threats from global competitors is necessary, firms should also actively seek to penetrate foreign markets. Two effective global strategies are (1) strategic alliances and (2) locating abroad.

One way for a firm to open foreign markets is to create a *strategic alliance.* A strategic alliance is an agreement with another firm that may take one of three forms. One form of strategic alliance is the *collaborative effort,* which often arises when one firm has core competencies that another needs but is unwilling (or unable) to duplicate. Such arrangements commonly arise out of buyer–supplier

The popular smiling red bee, the mascot of Jollibee, welcomes customers at an outlet in Manila. What began from a two ice cream parlors in Manila in 1975, Jollibee has grown into the biggest Philippines fast-food company employing over 26,000 people in over 1,000 stores in seven countries. By catering to local tastes and preferences, Jollibee took 65 percent of the fiercely competitive Philippine fast-food market, pushing the world giant McDonald's into second place.

Romeo Gacad/AFP/Getty Images/Newscom

relationships. Another form of strategic alliance is the *joint venture,* in which two firms agree to produce a service or product jointly. This approach is often used by firms to gain access to foreign markets. For example, to get access to the large Chinese market, General Motors (GM) and Volkswagen (VW) each developed joint ventures with Shanghai Automotive Industry Corporation or SAIC.[2] The Chinese partner is a large manufacturer of automobiles, producing more than 600,000 cars with GM and VW. In 2010, SAIC upped its total share to 51% in Shanghai GM, which is now among the top three passenger vehicle producers in mainland China. Finally, *technology licensing* is a form of strategic alliance in which one company licenses its service or production methods to another. Licenses may be used to gain access to foreign markets.

Another way to enter global markets is to locate operations in a foreign country. However, managers must recognize that what works well in their home country might not work well elsewhere. The economic and political environment or customers' needs may be significantly different. For example, the family-owned chain Jollibee Foods Corporation has become the dominant fast-food chain in the Philippines by catering to a local preference for sweet and spicy flavors, which it incorporates into its fried chicken, spaghetti, and burgers. Jollibee's strength is its creative marketing programs and an understanding of local tastes and claims that its burger is similar to the one a Filipino would cook at home. McDonald's responded by introducing its own Filipino-style spicy burger, but competition is stiff. This example shows that to be successful, corporate strategies must recognize customs, preferences, and economic conditions in other countries.

Market Analysis

One key to successfully formulating a customer-driven operations strategy for both service and manufacturing firms is to understand what the customer wants and how to provide it. A *market analysis* first divides the firm's customers into market segments and then identifies the needs of each segment. In this section, we examine the process of market analysis and we define and discuss the concepts of market segmentation and needs assessment.

Market Segmentation   *Market segmentation* is the process of identifying groups of customers with enough in common to warrant the design and provision of services or products that the group wants and needs. To identify market segments, the analyst must determine the characteristics that clearly differentiate each segment. The company can then develop a sound marketing program and an effective operating strategy to support it. For instance, The Gap, Inc., a major provider of casual clothes, targets teenagers and young adults while the parents or guardians of infants through 12-year-olds are the primary targets for its GapKids stores. At one time, managers thought of customers as a homogeneous mass market, but now realize that two customers may use the same product for different reasons. Identifying the key factors in each market segment is the starting point in devising a customer-driven operations strategy.

Needs Assessment   The second step in market analysis is to make a *needs assessment,* which identifies the needs of each segment and assesses how well competitors are addressing those needs. Each market segment's needs can be related to the service or product and its supply chain. Market needs should include both the tangible and intangible attributes and features of products and services that a customer desires. Market needs may be grouped as follows:

- *Service or Product Needs.* Attributes of the service or product, such as price, quality, and degree of customization.
- *Delivery System Needs.* Attributes of the processes and the supporting systems, and resources needed to deliver the service or product, such as availability, convenience, courtesy, safety, accuracy, reliability, delivery speed, and delivery dependability.
- *Volume Needs.* Attributes of the demand for the service or product, such as high or low volume, degree of variability in volume, and degree of predictability in volume.
- *Other Needs.* Other attributes, such as reputation and number of years in business, after-sale technical support, ability to invest in international financial markets, and competent legal services.

---

[2]Alex Taylor, "Shanghai Auto Wants to Be the World's Next Great Car Company," *Fortune* (October 4, 2004), pp. 103–110.

Competitive Priorities and Capabilities

A customer-driven operations strategy requires a cross-functional effort by all areas of the firm to understand the needs of the firm's external customers and to specify the operating capabilities the firm requires to outperform its competitors. Such a strategy also addresses the needs of internal customers because the overall performance of the firm depends upon the performance of its core and supporting processes, which must be coordinated to provide the overall desirable outcome for the external customer.

Competitive priorities are the critical operational dimensions a process or supply chain must possess to satisfy internal or external customers, both now and in the future. Competitive priorities are planned for processes and the supply chain created from them. They must be present to maintain or build market share or to allow other internal processes to be successful. Not all competitive priorities are critical for a given process; management selects those that are most important. **Competitive capabilities** are the cost, quality, time, and flexibility dimensions that a process or supply chain actually possesses and is able to deliver. When the capability falls short of the priority attached to it, management must find ways to close the gap or else revise the priority.

We focus on nine broad competitive priorities that fall into the four capability groups of cost, quality, time, and flexibility. Table 1.1 provides definitions and examples of these competitive priorities, as well as how firms achieve them at the process level.

At times, management may emphasize a cluster of competitive priorities together. For example, many companies focus on the competitive priorities of delivery speed and development speed for their processes, a strategy called **time-based competition**. To implement the strategy, managers carefully define the steps and time needed to deliver a service or produce a product and then critically analyze each step to determine whether they can save time without hurting quality.

To link to corporate strategy, management assigns selected competitive priorities to each process (and the supply chains created from them) that are consistent with the needs of external as well as internal customers. Competitive priorities may change over time. For example, consider a high-volume standardized product, such as color ink-jet desktop printers. In the early stages of the ramp-up period when the printers had just entered the mass market, the manufacturing processes required consistent quality, delivery speed, and volume flexibility. In the later stages of the ramp-up when demand was high, the competitive priorities became low-cost operations, consistent quality, and on-time delivery. Competitive priorities must change and evolve over time along with changing business conditions and customer preferences.

The lavish interior lobby decor of the Ritz Carlton resort in Palm Beach, Florida, USA

Order Winners and Qualifiers

Competitive priorities focus on what operations can do to help a firm be more competitive, and are in response to what the market wants. Another useful way to examine a firm's ability to be successful in the marketplace is to identify the order winners and order qualifiers. An **order winner** is a criterion that customers use to differentiate the services or products of one firm from those of another. Order winners can include price (which is supported by low-cost operations) and other dimensions of quality, time, and flexibility. However, order winners also include criteria not directly related to the firm's operations, such as after-sale support (Are maintenance service contracts available? Is there a return policy?); technical support (What help do I get if something goes wrong? How knowledgeable are the technicians?); and reputation (How long has this company been in business? Have other customers been satisfied with the service or product?). It may take good performance on a subset of the order-winner criteria, cutting across operational as well as nonoperational criteria, to make a sale.

Order winners are derived from the considerations customers use when deciding which firm to purchase a service or product from in a given market segment. Sometimes customers demand a certain level of demonstrated performance before even contemplating a service or product.

competitive priorities
The critical dimensions that a process or supply chain must possess to satisfy its internal or external customers, both now and in the future.

competitive capabilities
The cost, quality, time, and flexibility dimensions that a process or supply chain actually possesses and is able to deliver.

time-based competition
A strategy that focuses on the competitive priorities of delivery speed and development speed.

order winner
A criterion customers use to differentiate the services or products of one firm from those of another.

TABLE 1.1 | DEFINITIONS, PROCESS CONSIDERATIONS, AND EXAMPLES OF COMPETITIVE PRIORITIES

Cost	Definition	Processes Considerations	Example
1. **Low-cost operations**	Delivering a service or a product at the lowest possible cost to the satisfaction of external or internal customers of the process or supply chain	To reduce costs, processes must be designed and operated to make them efficient using rigorous process analysis that addresses workforce, methods, scrap or rework, overhead, and other factors, such as investments in new automated facilities or technologies to lower the cost per unit of the service or product.	**Costco** achieves low costs by designing all processes for efficiency, stacking products on pallets in warehouse-type stores, and negotiating aggressively with their suppliers. Costco can provide low prices to its customers because they have designed operations for low cost.
Quality			
2. **Top quality**	Delivering an outstanding service or product	To deliver top quality, a service process may require a high level of customer contact, and high levels of helpfulness, courtesy, and availability of servers. It may require superior product features, close tolerances, and greater durability from a manufacturing process.	**Rolex** is known globally for creating precision timepieces.
3. **Consistent quality**	Producing services or products that meet design specifications on a consistent basis	Processes must be designed and monitored to reduce errors, prevent defects, and achieve similar outcomes over time, regardless of the "level" of quality.	**McDonald's** standardizes work methods, staff training processes, and procurement of raw materials to achieve the same consistent product and process quality from one store to the next.
Time			
4. **Delivery speed**	Quickly filling a customer's order	Design processes to reduce lead time (elapsed time between the receipt of a customer order and filling it) through keeping backup capacity cushions, storing inventory, and using premier transportation options.	**Dell** engineered its customer relationship, order fulfillment, and supplier relationship processes to create an integrated and an agile supply chain that delivers reliable and inexpensive computers to its customers with short lead times.
5. **On-time delivery**	Meeting delivery-time promises	Along with processes that reduce lead time, planning processes (forecasting, appointments, order promising, scheduling, and capacity planning) are used to increase percent of customer orders shipped when promised (95% is often a typical goal).	**United Parcel Services (UPS)** uses its expertise in logistics and warehousing processes to deliver a very large volume of shipments on-time across the globe.
6. **Development speed**	Quickly introducing a new service or a product	Processes aim to achieve cross-functional integration and involvement of critical external suppliers in the service or product development process.	**Zara** is known for its ability to bring fashionable clothing designs from the runway to market quickly.
Flexibility			
7. **Customization**	Satisfying the unique needs of each customer by changing service or product designs	Processes with a customization strategy typically have low volume, close customer contact, and an ability to reconfigure processes to meet diverse types of customer needs.	**Ritz Carlton** customizes services to individual guest preferences.
8. **Variety**	Handling a wide assortment of services or products efficiently	Processes supporting variety must be capable of larger volumes than processes supporting customization. Services or products are not necessarily unique to specific customers and may have repetitive demands.	**Amazon.com** uses information technology and streamlined customer relationship and order fulfillment processes to reliably deliver a vast variety of items to its customers.
9. **Volume flexibility**	Accelerating or decelerating the rate of production of services or products quickly to handle large fluctuations in demand	Processes must be designed for excess capacity and excess inventory to handle demand fluctuations that can vary in cycles from days to months. This priority could also be met with a strategy that adjusts capacity without accumulation of inventory or excess capacity.	**The United States Post Office (USPS)** can have severe demand peak fluctuations at large postal facilities where processes are flexibly designed for receiving, sorting, and dispatching mail to numerous branch locations.

Minimal level required from a set of criteria for a firm to do business in a particular market segment is called an **order qualifier**. Fulfilling the order qualifier will not ensure competitive success; it will only position the firm to compete in the market. From an operations perspective, understanding which competitive priorities are order qualifiers and which ones are order winners is important for the investments made in the design and management of processes and supply chains.

Figure 1.6 shows how order winners and qualifiers are related to achieving the competitive priorities of a firm. If a minimum threshold level is not met for an order-qualifying dimension (consistent quality, for example) by a firm, then it would get disqualified from even being considered further by its customers. For example, there is a level of quality consistency that is minimally tolerable by customers in the auto industry. When the subcompact car Yugo built by Zastava Corporation could not sustain the minimal level of quality, consistency, and reliability expected by customers, it had to exit the U.S. car market in 1991 despite offering very low prices (order winner) of under $4,000. However, once the firm qualifies by attaining consistent quality beyond the threshold, it may only gain additional sales at a very low rate by investing further in improving that order-qualifying dimension. In contrast, for an order-winning dimension (i.e., low price driven by low-cost operations), a firm can reasonably expect to gain appreciably greater sales and market share by continuously lowering its prices as long as the order qualifier (i.e., consistent quality) is being adequately met. Toyota Corolla and Honda Civic have successfully followed this route in the marketplace to become leaders in their target market segment.

Order winners and qualifiers are often used in competitive bidding. For example, before a buyer considers a bid, suppliers may be required to document their ability to provide consistent quality as measured by adherence to the design specifications for the service or component they are supplying (order qualifier). Once qualified, the supplier may eventually be selected by the buyer on the basis of low prices (order winner) and the reputation of the supplier (order winner).

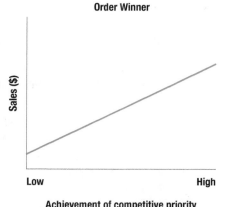

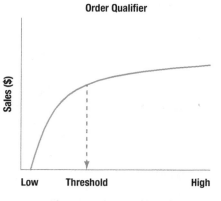

order qualifier
Minimal level required from a set of criteria for a firm to do business in a particular market segment.

▲ **FIGURE 1.6**
Relationship of Order Winners and Order Qualifiers to Competitive Priorities

Using Competitive Priorities: An Airline Example

To get a better understanding of how companies use competitive priorities, let us look at a major airline. We will consider two market segments: (1) first-class passengers and (2) coach passengers. Core services for both market segments are ticketing and seat selection, baggage handling, and transportation to the customer's destination. The peripheral services are quite different across the two market segments. First-class passengers require separate airport lounges; preferred treatment during check-in, boarding, and deplaning; more comfortable seats; better meals and beverages; more personal attention (cabin attendants who refer to customers by name); more frequent service from attendants; high levels of courtesy; and low volumes of passengers (adding to the feeling of being special). Coach passengers are satisfied with standardized services (no surprises), courteous flight attendants, and low prices. Both market segments expect the airline to hold to its schedule. Consequently, we can say that the competitive priorities for the

One of the competitive priorities of airline companies is on-time delivery of their services. Being able to repair and maintain planes rapidly to avoid delays is a crucial aspect of this.

first-class segment are *top quality* and *on-time delivery*, whereas the competitive priorities for the coach segment are *low-cost operations, consistent quality*, and *on-time delivery*.

The airline knows what its collective capabilities must be as a firm, but how does that get communicated to each of its core processes? Let us focus on the four core processes: (1) customer relationship, (2) new service/product development, (3) order fulfillment, and (4) supplier relationship. Competitive priorities are assigned to each core process to achieve the service required to provide complete customer satisfaction. Table 1.2 shows some possible assignments, just to give you an idea of how this works.

TABLE 1.2 | COMPETITIVE PRIORITIES ACROSS DIFFERENT CORE PROCESSES FOR AN AIRLINE

	CORE PROCESSES			
Priority	**Supplier Relationship**	**New Service Development**	**Order Fulfillment**	**Customer Relationship**
Low Cost Operations	Costs of acquiring inputs must be kept to a minimum to allow for competitive pricing.		Airlines compete on price and must keep operating costs in check.	
Top Quality		New services must be carefully designed because the future of the airline industry depends on them.	High quality meal and beverage service delivered by experienced cabin attendants ensures that the service provided to first-class passengers is kept top notch.	High levels of customer contact and lounge service for the first-class passengers.
Consistent Quality	Quality of the inputs must adhere to the required specifications. In addition, information provided to suppliers must be accurate.		Once the quality level is set, it is important to achieve it every time.	The information and service must be error free.
Delivery Speed				Customers want immediate information regarding flight schedules and other ticketing information.
On time delivery	Inputs must be delivered to tight schedules.		The airline strives to arrive at destinations on schedule, otherwise passengers might miss connections to other flights.	
Development Speed		It is important to get to the market fast to preempt the competition.		
Customization		The process must be able to create unique services.		
Variety	Many different inputs must be acquired, including maintenance items, meals and beverages.		Maintenance operations are required for a variety of aircraft models.	The process must be capable of handling the service needs of all market segments and promotional programs.
Volume Flexibility	The process must be able to handle variations in supply quantities efficiently.			

Operations Strategy as a Pattern of Decisions

Operations strategy translates service or product plans and competitive priorities for each market segment into decisions affecting the supply chains that support those market segments. Even if it is not formally stated, the current operations strategy for any firm is really the pattern of decisions that have been made for its processes and supply chains. As we have previously seen in Figure 1.5, corporate strategy provides the umbrella for key operations management decisions that contribute to the development of the firm's ability to compete successfully in the marketplace. Once managers determine the competitive priorities for a process, it is necessary to assess the *competitive capabilities* of the process. Any gap between a competitive priority and the capability to achieve that competitive priority must be closed by an effective operations strategy.

Developing capabilities and closing gaps is the thrust of operations strategy. To demonstrate how this works, suppose the management of a bank's credit card division decides to embark on a marketing campaign to significantly increase its business, while keeping costs low. A key process in this division is billing and payments. The division receives credit transactions from the merchants, pays the merchants, assembles and sends the bills to the credit card holders, and processes payments. The new marketing effort is expected to significantly increase the volume of bills and payments. In assessing the capabilities, the process must have to serve the bank's customers and to meet the challenges of the new market campaign; management assigns the following competitive priorities for the billing and payments process:

- *Low-Cost Operations.* It is important to maintain low costs in the processing of the bills because profit margins are tight.
- *Consistent Quality.* The process must consistently produce bills, make payments to the merchants, and record payments from the credit card holders accurately.
- *Delivery Speed.* Merchants want to be paid for the credit purchases quickly.
- *Volume Flexibility.* The marketing campaign is expected to generate many more transactions in a shorter period of time.

Management assumed that customers would avoid doing business with a bank that could not produce accurate bills or payments. Consequently, consistent quality is an order qualifier for this process.

Is the billing and payment process up to the competitive challenge? Table 1.3 shows how to match capabilities to priorities and uncover any gaps in the credit card division's operations strategy. The procedure for assessing an operations strategy begins with identifying good measures for each priority. The more quantitative the measures are, the better. Data are gathered for each measure to determine the current capabilities of the process. Gaps are identified by comparing each capability to management's target values for the measures, and unacceptable gaps are closed by appropriate actions.

The credit card division shows significant gaps in the process's capability for low-cost operations. Management's remedy is to redesign the process in ways that reduce costs but will not impair the other competitive priorities. Likewise, for volume flexibility, management realized that a high level of utilization is not conducive for processing quick surges in volumes while maintaining delivery speed. The recommended actions will help build a capability for meeting more volatile demands.

TABLE 1.3 | OPERATIONS STRATEGY ASSESSMENT OF THE BILLING AND PAYMENT PROCESS

Competitive Priority	Measure	Capability	Gap	Action
Low-cost operations	■ Cost per billing statement ■ Weekly postage	■ $0.0813 ■ $17,000	■ Target is $0.06 ■ Target is $14,000	■ Eliminate microfilming and storage of billing statements ■ Develop Web-based process for posting bills
Consistent quality	■ Percent errors in bill information ■ Percent errors in posting payments	■ 0.90% ■ 0.74%	■ Acceptable ■ Acceptable	■ No action ■ No action
Delivery speed	■ Lead time to process merchant payments	■ 48 hours	■ Acceptable	■ No action
Volume flexibility	■ Utilization	■ 98%	■ Too high to support rapid increase in volumes	■ Acquire temporary employees ■ Improve work methods

Trends in Operations Management

Several trends are currently having a great impact on operations management: productivity improvement; global competition; and ethical, workforce diversity, and environmental issues. Accelerating change in the form of information technology, e-commerce, robotics, and the Internet is dramatically affecting the design of new services and products as well as a firm's sales, order fulfillment, and purchasing processes. In this section, we look at these trends and their challenges for operations managers.

Productivity Improvement

Productivity is a basic measure of performance for economies, industries, firms, and processes. Improving productivity is a major trend in operations management because all firms face pressures to improve their processes and supply chains so as to compete with their domestic and foreign competitors. **Productivity** is the value of outputs (services and products) produced divided by the values of input resources (wages, cost of equipment, and so on) used:

productivity

The value of outputs (services and products) produced divided by the values of input resources (wages, costs of equipment, and so on).

$$\text{Productivity} = \frac{\text{Output}}{\text{Input}}$$

Manufacturing employment peaked at just below 20 million in mid-1979, and shrunk by nearly 8 million from 1979 to 2011.[3] However, the manufacturing productivity in the United States has climbed steadily, as more manufacturing capacity and output has been achieved efficiently with a leaner work force. It is interesting and even surprising to compare productivity improvements in the service and manufacturing sectors. In the United States, employment in the service sector has grown rapidly, outstripping the manufacturing sector. It now employs about 90 percent of the workforce. But service-sector productivity gains have been much lower. If productivity growth in the service sector stagnates, so does the overall standard of living regardless of which part of the world you live in. Other major industrial countries, such as Japan and Germany, are experiencing the same problem. Yet, signs of improvement are appearing. The surge of investment across national boundaries can stimulate productivity gains by exposing firms to greater competition. Increased investment in information technology by service providers also increases productivity.

Measuring Productivity   As a manager, how do you measure the productivity of your processes? Many measures are available. For example, value of output can be measured by what the customer pays or simply by the number of units produced or customers served. The value of inputs can be judged by their cost or simply by the number of hours worked.

Managers usually pick several reasonable measures and monitor trends to spot areas needing improvement. For example, a manager at an insurance firm might measure office productivity as the number of insurance policies processed per employee per week. A manager at a carpet company might measure the productivity of installers as the number of square yards of carpet installed per hour. Both measures reflect *labor productivity*, which is an index of the output per person or per hour worked. Similar measures may be used for *machine productivity*, where the denominator is the number of machines. Accounting for several inputs simultaneously is also possible. *Multifactor productivity* is an index of the output provided by more than one of the resources used in production; it may be the value of the output divided by the sum of labor, materials, and overhead costs. Here is an example:

EXAMPLE 1.1	**Productivity Calculations**

MyOMLab

Tutor 1.1 in MyOMLab provides a new example for calculating productivity.

Calculate the productivity for the following operations:

a.   Three employees process 600 insurance policies in a week. They work 8 hours per day, 5 days per week.

b.   A team of workers makes 400 units of a product, which is sold in the market for $10 each. The accounting department reports that for this job the actual costs are $400 for labor, $1,000 for materials, and $300 for overhead.

---

[3] Paul Wiseman, "Despite China's Might, US Factories Maintain Edge," *The State* and *The Associated Press* (January 31, 2011).

SOLUTION

a.   Labor productivity $= \dfrac{\text{Policies processed}}{\text{Employee hours}}$

$\qquad\qquad\qquad\quad = \dfrac{600 \text{ policies}}{(3 \text{ employees}) (40 \text{ hours/employee})} = 5 \text{ policies/hour}$

b.   Multifactor productivity $= \dfrac{\text{Value of output}}{\text{Labor cost } + \text{ Materials cost } + \text{ Overhead cost}}$

$\qquad\qquad\qquad\qquad\qquad = \dfrac{(400 \text{ units}) (\$10/\text{unit})}{\$400 + \$1,000 + \$300} = \dfrac{\$4,000}{\$1,700} = 2.35$

DECISION POINT

We want multifactor productivity to be as high as possible. These measures must be compared with performance levels in prior periods and with future goals. If they do not live up to expectations, the process should be investigated for improvement opportunities.

The Role of Management   The way processes are managed plays a key role in productivity improvement. Managers must examine productivity from the level of the supply chain because it is the collective performance of individual processes that makes the difference. The challenge is to increase the value of output relative to the cost of input. If processes can generate more output or output of better quality using the same amount of input, productivity increases. If they can maintain the same level of output while reducing the use of resources, productivity also increases.

Global Competition

Most businesses realize that, to prosper, they must view customers, suppliers, facility locations, and competitors in global terms. Firms have found that they can increase their market penetration by locating their production facilities in foreign countries because it gives them a local presence that reduces customer aversion to buying imports. Globalization also allows firms to balance cash flows from other regions of the world when economic conditions are less robust in the home country. Sonoco, a $4-billion-a-year industrial and consumer packaging company in Hartsville, South Carolina, has 335 locations worldwide in Australia, China, Europe, Mexico, New Zealand, and Russia, with 41 industrial product manufacturing facilities and 6 paper mills in Europe alone. These global operations resulted in international sales and income growth even as domestic sales were stumbling during 2007. How did Sonoco do it?[4] Locating operations in countries with favorable tax laws is one reason. Lower tax rates in Italy and Canada helped in padding the earnings margin. Another reason was a weak dollar, whereby a $46 million boost came from turning foreign currencies into dollars as Sonoco exported such items as snack bag packaging, and tubes and cores used to hold tape and textiles, to operations it owned in foreign countries. The exchange

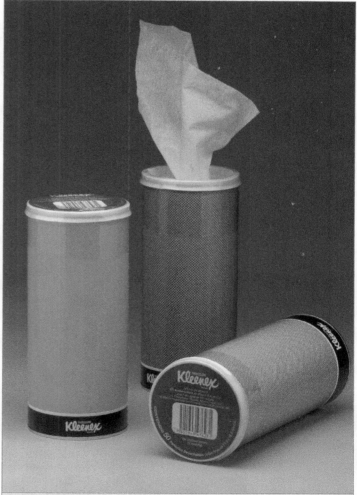

Sonoco is a leading global manufacturer of industrial and consumer packaging goods with more than 300 locations in 35 countries serving 85 nations.

PR Newswire/Associated Press

---

[4] Ben Werner, "Sonoco Holding Its Own," *The State* (February 7, 2008); **www.sonoco.com**, 2008.

rate difference was more than enough to counter the added expense of increased raw materials, shipping, and energy costs in the United States.

Most products today are composites of materials and services from all over the world. Your Gap polo shirt is sewn in Honduras from cloth cut in the United States. Sitting in a Cineplex theater (Canadian), you munch a Nestle's Crunch bar (Swiss) while watching a Columbia Pictures movie (Japanese). Five developments spurred the need for sound global strategies: (1) improved transportation and communications technologies, (2) loosened regulations on financial institutions, (3) increased demand for imported services and goods, (4) reduced import quotas and other international trade barriers due to the formation of regional trading blocks, such as the European Union (EU) and the North American Free Trade Agreement (NAFTA), and (5) comparative cost advantages.

Comparative Cost Advantages   China and India have traditionally been the sources for low-cost, but skilled, labor, even though the cost advantage is diminishing as these countries become economically stronger. In the late 1990s, companies manufactured products in China to grab a foothold in a huge market, or to get cheap labor to produce low-tech products despite doubts about the quality of the workforce and poor roads and rail systems. Today, however, China's new factories, such as those in the Pudong industrial zone in Shanghai, produce a wide variety of products that are sold overseas in the United States and other regions of the world. U.S. manufacturers have increasingly abandoned low profit margin sectors like consumer electronics, shoes, and toys to emerging nations such as China and Indonesia. Instead, they are focusing on making expensive goods like computer chips, advanced machinery, and health care products that are complex and which require specialized labor.

Foreign companies have opened tens of thousands of new facilities in China over the past decade. Many goods the United States imports from China now come from foreign-owned companies with operations there. These companies include telephone makers, such as Nokia and Motorola, and nearly all of the big footwear and clothing brands. Many more major manufacturers are there as well. The implications for competition are enormous. Companies that do not have operations in China are finding it difficult to compete on the basis of low prices with companies that do. Instead, they must focus on speed and small production runs.

What China is to manufacturing, India is to service. As with the manufacturing companies, the cost of labor is a key factor. Indian software companies have grown sophisticated in their applications and offer a big advantage in cost. The computer services industry is also affected. Back-office operations are affected for the same reason. Many firms are using Indian companies for accounting and bookkeeping, preparing tax returns, and processing insurance claims. Many tech companies, such as Intel and Microsoft, are opening significant research and development (R&D) operations in India.

Disadvantages of Globalization   Of course, operations in other countries can have disadvantages. A firm may have to relinquish proprietary technology if it turns over some of its component manufacturing to offshore suppliers or if suppliers need the firm's technology to achieve desired quality and cost goals. Political risks may also be involved. Each nation can exercise its sovereignty over the people and property within its borders. The extreme case is nationalization, in which a government may take over a firm's assets without paying compensation. Exxon and other large multinational oil firms are scaling back operations in Venezuela due to nationalization concerns. Further, a firm may actually alienate customers back home if jobs are lost to offshore operations.

Employee skills may be lower in foreign countries, requiring additional training time. South Korean firms moved much of their sports shoe production to low-wage Indonesia and China, but they still manufacture hiking shoes and in-line roller skates in South Korea because of the greater

Shortage of components from suppliers prevented Nintendo from meeting the customer demand for its popular Wii game system.

MANAGERIAL PRACTICE 1.1   Japanese Earthquake and its Supply Chain Impact

Northeast Touhoku district of Japan was struck by a set of massive earthquakes on the afternoon of March 11, 2011, which were soon followed by a huge tsunami that sent waves higher than 33 feet in the port city of Sendai 80 miles away and travelling at the speed of a jetliner. At nearly 9.0 on the Richter scale, it was one of the largest recorded earthquakes to hit Japan. It shifted the Earth's axis by 6 inches with an impact that was felt 250 miles inland in Tokyo, and which moved Eastern Japan 13 feet toward North America. Apart from huge loss of life and hazards of nuclear radiation arising from the crippled Daiichi Nuclear Reactors in Fukushima, the damage to the manufacturing plants in Japan exposed the hazards of interconnected global supply chains and their impact on factories located half way around the globe.

The impact of the earthquake was particularly acute on industries that rely on cutting edge electronic parts sourced from Japan. Shin-Etsu Chemical Company is the world's largest producer of silicon wafers and supplies 20 percent of the global capacity. Its centralized plant located 40 miles from the Fukushima nuclear facility was damaged in the earthquake, causing ripple effects at Intel and Toshiba that purchase wafers from Shin-Etsu. Similarly, a shortage of automotive sensors from Hitachi has slowed or halted production of vehicles in Germany, Spain, and France, while Chrysler is reducing overtime at factories in Mexico and Canada to conserve parts from Japan. Even worse, General Motors stopped production altogether at a plant in Louisiana and Ford closed a truck plant in Kentucky due to the quake. The supply of vehicles such as Toyota's Prius and Lexus will be limited in the United States because of production disruptions in its Japanese factories. China has been affected too, where ZTE Corporation is facing shortages of batteries and LCD screens for its cell phones. Similarly, Lenovo in China is looking at reduced

Kimimasa Mayama/EPA/Landov

Following the strong earthquakes and tsunami, flames and smoke rise from a petroleum refining plant next to a heating power station in Shiogama, Miyagi Prefecture, northern Japan, about 220 km north of Tokyo.

supplies of components from Japan for assembly of its tablet computers. These disruptions due to reliance on small concentrated network of suppliers in Japan and globally connected production and logistics systems have caused worker layoffs an increase in prices of affected products, and economic losses that have been felt around the world.

Sources: Don Lee and David Pearson, "Disaster in Japan exposes supply chain weakness," *The State* (April 8, 2011), B6-B7; "Chrysler reduces overtime to help Japan," *The Associated Press* (April 8, 2011) printed in *The State* (April 6, 2011), B7; Krishna Dhir, "From the Editor," *Decision Line*, vol. 42, no. 2, 3.

skills required. In addition, when a firm's operations are scattered globally, customer response times can be longer. Coordinating components from a wide array of suppliers can be challenging, as Nintendo found out in the production and worldwide distribution of its Wii game systems.[5] Despite twice increasing capacity since April 2007 to 1.8 million Wii's a month, Nintendo could only ship the completed units to retailers like Best Buy, Costco, and Circuit City in limited quantities that did not meet the large demand through the 2007 holiday season and beyond. In addition, as Managerial Practice 1.1 shows, catastrophic events such as the Japanese earthquake affect production and operations in Europe and United States because connected supply chains can spread disruptions rapidly and quickly across international borders.

Strong global competition affects industries everywhere. For example, U.S. manufacturers of steel, appliances, household durable goods, machinery, and chemicals have seen their market share decline in both domestic and international markets. With the value of world trade in services now at more than $2 trillion per year, banking, data processing, airlines, and consulting services are beginning to face many of the same international pressures. Regional trading blocs, such as EU and NAFTA, further change the competitive landscape in both services and manufacturing. Regardless of which area of the world you live in, the challenge is to produce services or products that can compete in a global market, and to design the processes that can make it happen.

Ethical, Workforce Diversity, and Environmental Issues

Businesses face more ethical quandaries than ever before, intensified by an increasing global presence and rapid technological change. As companies locate new operations and acquire more

---

[5] Peter Svensson, "GameStop to Sell Rain Checks for Wii," *The State* (December 18, 2007).

A Chinese consumer looks at Timberland products at a department store in Shanghai, China, November 11, 2010. Timberland seeks to benefit from rising incomes in the worlds fastest-growing major economy, and will also invest in its Hong Kong shops.

Weng lei/AP Photos

suppliers and customers in other countries, potential ethical dilemmas arise when business is conducted by different rules. Some countries are more sensitive than others about conflicts of interest, bribery, discrimination against minorities and women, minimum-wage levels, and unsafe workplaces. Managers must decide whether to design and operate processes that do more than just meet local standards. In addition, technological change brings debates about data protection and customer privacy. In an electronic world, businesses are geographically far from their customers, so a reputation of trust is paramount.

In the past, many people viewed environmental problems, such as toxic waste, poisoned drinking water, poor air quality, and climate change as quality-of-life issues; now, many people and businesses see them as survival issues. The automobile industry has seen innovation in electric and hybrid cars in response to environmental concerns and economic benefits arising from using less expensive fuels. Industrial nations face a particular burden because their combined populations consume proportionally much larger resources. Just seven nations, including the United States and Japan, produce almost half of all greenhouse gases. Now China and India have added to that total carbon footprint because of their vast economic and manufacturing expansion over the past decade.

Apart from government initiatives, large multinational companies have a responsibility as well for creating environmentally conscious practices, and can do so profitably. For instance, Timberland has over 110 stores in China because of strong demand for its boots, shoes, clothes, and outdoor gear in that country. It highlights its environmental credentials and corporate social responsibility through investments such as the reforestation efforts in northern China's Horqin Desert. Timberland hopes to double the number of stores over the next 3 years by environmentally differentiating itself from the competition.

The challenge is clear: Issues of ethics, workforce diversity, and the environment are becoming part of every manager's job. When designing and operating processes, managers should consider integrity, respect for the individual, and customer satisfaction along with more conventional performance measures such as productivity, quality, cost, and profit.

Operations Management as a Set of Decisions

In this text, we cover the major decisions operations managers make in practice. At the strategic level, operations managers are involved in the development of new capabilities and the maintenance of existing capabilities to best serve the firm's external customers. Operations managers design new processes that have strategic implications, and they are deeply involved in the development and organization of supply chains that link external suppliers and external customers to the firm's internal processes. Operations managers are often responsible for key performance measures such as cost and quality. These decisions have strategic impact because they affect the processes the firm uses to gain a competitive edge.

The operations manager's decisions should reflect corporate strategy. Plans, policies, and actions should be linked to those in other functional areas to support the firm's overall goals and objectives. These links are facilitated by taking a process view of a firm. Regardless of whether you aspire to be an operations manager, or you just want to use the principles of operations management to become a more effective manager, remember that effective management of people, capital, information, and materials is critical to the success of any process and any supply chain.

As you study operations management, keep two principles in mind:

1. Each part of an organization, not just the operations function, must design and operate processes that are part of a supply chain and deal with quality, technology, and staffing issues.

2. Each function of an organization has its own identity and yet is connected with operations through shared processes.

Great strategic decisions lead nowhere if the tactical decisions that support them are wrong. Operations managers are also involved in tactical decisions, including process improvement and performance measurement, managing and planning projects, generating production and staffing plans, managing inventories, and scheduling resources. You will find numerous examples of these decisions, and the implications of making them, throughout this text. You will also learn about the decision-making tools practicing managers use to recognize and define the problem and then choose the best solution.

Computerized Decision-Making Tools

MyOMLab contains a unique set of decision tools we call OM Explorer. This package contains powerful Excel-based computer routines to solve problems often encountered in practice. OM Explorer also has several tutors that provide coaching for all of the difficult analytical techniques in this text, and can be accessed from the drop-down menu. MyOMLab also contains POM for Windows, which is an extensive set of useful decision-making tools to complete your arsenal for solving operations problems, many Active Models (spreadsheets designed to help you learn more about important decision-making techniques), and a spreadsheet-based simulation package called SimQuick.

MyOMLab

Addressing the Challenges in Operations Management

How can firms meet challenges today and in the future? One way is to recognize challenges as opportunities to improve existing processes and supply chains or to create new, innovative ones. The management of processes and supply chains goes beyond designing them; it requires the ability to ensure they achieve their goals. Firms should manage their processes and supply chains to maximize their competitiveness in the markets they serve. We share this philosophy of operations management, as illustrated in Figure 1.7. We use this figure at the start of each chapter to show how the topic of the chapter fits into our philosophy of operations management. In addition, this text also contains several chapter supplements that are not explicitly shown in Figure 1.7.

The figure shows that all effective operations decisions follow from a sound operations strategy. Consequently, our text has three major parts: "Creating Value through Operations Management," "Managing Processes," and "Managing Supply Chains." The flow of topics reflects our approach of first understanding how a firm's operations can help provide a solid foundation for competitiveness before tackling the essential process design decisions that will support its strategies. Each part begins with a strategy discussion to support the decisions in that part. Once it is clear how firms design and improve processes, and how they implement those designs, we examine the design and operation of supply chains that link processes, whether they are internal or external to the firm. The performance of the supply chains determines the firm's outcomes, which include the services or products the firm produces, the financial results, and feedback from the firm's customers. These outcomes, which are considered in the firm's strategic plan, are discussed throughout this text.

Creating Value through Operations Management

The concluding chapter of "Creating Value through Operations Management" is a discussion of the methods and tools of project management. Project management is an effective approach to implementing operations strategy through the introduction of new services or products as well as any changes to a firm's processes or supply chains. Supplement A, "Decision Making," follows this chapter and covers some basic decision techniques that apply to multiple chapters.

Managing Processes

In "Managing Processes," we focus on analyzing processes and how they can be improved to meet the goals of the operations strategy. We begin by addressing the strategic aspects of process design and then present a six-step systematic approach to process analysis. Each chapter in this part deals with some aspect of that approach. We discuss the tools that help managers analyze processes, and we reveal the methods firms use to measure process performance and quality. These methods provide the foundation for programs such as Six Sigma and total quality management.

Determining the best process capacity with effective constraint management and making processes "lean" by eliminating activities that do not add value while improving those that do are also key decisions in the redesign of processes. The activities involved in managing processes are

Creating Value through Operations Management

Using Operations to Compete
Project Management

Managing Processes

Process Strategy
Process Analysis
Quality and Performance
Capacity Planning
Constraint Management
Lean Systems

Managing Supply Chains

Supply Chain Inventory Management
Supply Chain Design
Supply Chain Location Decisions
Supply Chain Integration
Supply Chain Sustainability and Humanitarian Logistics
Forecasting
Operations Planning and Scheduling
Resource Planning

▲ **FIGURE 1.7**
Managing Processes and Supply Chains

essential for providing significant benefits to the firm. Effective management of its processes can allow a firm to reduce its costs and also increase customer satisfaction.

Managing Supply Chains

The management of supply chains is based upon process management and operations strategy. In "Managing Processes," we focus on individual processes. The focus of Managing Supply Chains, however, is on supply chains involving processes both internal and external to the firm and the tools that enhance their execution. We begin this part with a look at managing inventory in supply chains. We follow that with understanding how the design of supply chains and major strategic decisions, such as outsourcing, inventory placement, and locating facilities affect performance. We also look at contemporary issues surrounding supply chain integration and the impact of supply chains on the environment. We follow that with chapters focused on three key planning activities for the effective operation of supply chains: (1) forecasting, (2) operations planning and scheduling, and (3) resource planning.

Adding Value with Process Innovation in Supply Chains

It is important to note that the effective operation of a firm and its supply chain is as important as the design and implementation of its processes. Process innovation can make a big difference even in a low-growth industry. Examining processes from the perspective of the value they add is an important part of a successful manager's agenda, as is gaining an understanding of how core processes and related supply chains are linked to their competitive priorities, markets, and the operations strategy of a firm. As illustrated by Progressive Insurance in Managerial Practice 1.2, who says operations management does not make a difference?

MANAGERIAL PRACTICE 1.2   Operational Innovation Is a Competitive Weapon at Progressive Insurance

Progressive Insurance, an automobile insurer that started business in 1937, had approximately $1.3 billion in sales in 1991. By 2011, it was one of the largest U.S. private passenger auto insurance groups with annual premiums in excess of $14 billion. How did it accomplish this amazing growth rate in a 100-year-old industry that traditionally does not experience that sort of growth?

The answer is simple but the implementation was challenging: offer low prices, better service, and more value to customers through operational innovation. *Operational innovation* means designing entirely new processes by dramatically changing the way work is done. For example, Progressive reinvented claims processing to lower costs and increase customer satisfaction and retention. Progressive's agency-dedicated Web site, ForAgentsOnly.com (FAO), lets agents quickly, easily, and securely access payments; view policy, billing, and claims information; and send quote information directly to customers via e-mail. Customers are encouraged to go online to perform routine tasks such as address changes or simple billing inquiries. In addition, Immediate Response Claims Handling allows a claimant to now reach a Progressive representative by telephone 24 hours a day. The representative immediately sends a claims adjuster to inspect the damaged vehicle. The adjuster drives to the vehicle accident site in a mobile claims van, examines the vehicle, prepares an onsite estimate of damage, and if possible, writes a check on the spot. It now takes only 9 hours to complete the cycle, compared with 7–10 days before the changes were made.

The operational innovations to the processes in the customer relationship–order fulfillment supply chain for claims processing produced several benefits. First, claimants received faster service with less hassle, which helped retain them as customers. Second, the shortened cycle time significantly reduced costs. The costs of storing a damaged vehicle and providing a rental car can often wipe out the expected underwriting profit for

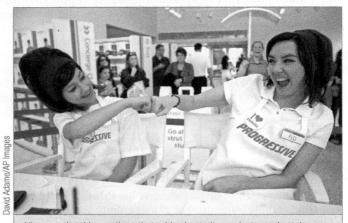

David Adame/AP Images

Via operational innovations that add value to its products, and catchy promotional advertisements, Progressive Insurance has been able to achieve amazing growth in a low-growth industry.

a six-month policy. This cost becomes significant when you realize that the company processes more than 10,000 claims a day. Third, the new supply chain design requires fewer people for handling the claim, which reduces operational costs. Finally, the operational innovations improved Progressive's ability to detect fraud by arriving on the accident scene quickly and helped to reduce payouts because claimants often accept less money if the payout is quick and hassle-free. Progressive Insurance found a way to differentiate itself in a low-growth industry without compromising profitability, and it accomplished that feat with operational innovation.

Source: Michael Hammer, "Deep Change: How Operational Innovation Can Transform Your Company," *Harvard Business Review* (April 2004), pp. 85–93; http://www.progressive.com/about-progressive-insurance.aspx, 2011.

The topics in this text will help you meet operations challenges and achieve operational innovation regardless of your chosen career path.

LEARNING GOALS IN REVIEW

1 **Describe operations and supply chains in terms of inputs, processes, outputs, information flows, suppliers, and customers.** Review Figure 1.4 for the important supply chain linkage and information flows. The section "Operations and Supply Chain Management Across the Organization," pp. 2–3, shows how different functional areas of business come together to create value for a firm.

2 **Define an operations strategy and its linkage to corporate strategy, as well as the role it plays as a source of competitive advantage in a global marketplace.** See the sections on "Operations Strategy" and "Corporate Strategy," pp. 7–10, and review Figure 1.5.

3 **Identify nine competitive priorities used in operations strategy, and their linkage to marketing strategy.** The section "Competitive Priorities and Capabilities," pp. 11–14, discusses the important concept of order winners and qualifiers. Review Table 1.1 for

important illustrations and examples of how leading edge firms implemented different competitive priorities to create a unique positioning in the marketplace.

4 **Explain how operations can be used as a competitive weapon.** The section "Operations Strategy as a Pattern of Decisions," p. 15, shows how firms must identify gaps in their competitive priorities and build capabilities through related process and operational changes. Make sure that you review Table 1.3 that provides a nice illustrative example.

5 **Identify the global trends and challenges facing operations management.** The section "Trends in Operations Management," pp. 16–20, describes the pressures managers face for achieving productivity improvements, along with managing sustainability and work force diversity related issues in the face of global competition.

MyOMLab helps you develop analytical skills and assesses your progress with multiple problems on labor and multifactor productivity.

MyOMLab Resources	Titles	Link to the Book
Video	*Operations as a Competitive Weapon at Starwood*	A Process View; Operations Strategy as a Pattern of Decisions
Active Model Exercise	1.1 Productivity	Trends in Operations Management; Example 1.1 (pp. 16–17); Solved Problem 1 (p. 24); Solved Problem 2 (pp. 24–25)
OM Explorer Tutors	1.1 Productivity Measures	Trends in Operations Management; Example 1.1 (pp. 16–17); Solved Problem 1 (p. 24); Solved Problem 2 (p. 24–25)
Tutor Exercises	1.1 Ticket sales	Example 1.1 (pp. 16–17); Solved Problem 1 (p. 24); Solved Problem 2 (pp. 24–25)
Virtual Tours	L'Oréal Cosmetics EDS Industries EDS Services	The Supply Chain View; Trends in Operations Management A Process View; The Supply Chain View A Process View; The Supply Chain View
Internet Exercises	1. Coca-Cola and Nestlé 2. Xerox 3. L'Oréal 4. Environment, Health, and Safety at Xerox	The Supply Chain View; Operations Strategy as a Pattern of Decisions The Supply Chain View; Competitive Priorities and Capabilities A Process View; Trends in Operations Management Trends in Operations Management
Additional Cases	BSB, Inc., The Pizza Wars Come to Campus	A Process View; The Supply Chain View; Competitive Priorities and Capabilities
Key Equations		
Image Library		

Key Equation

1. Productivity is the ratio of output to input:

$$\text{Productivity} = \frac{\text{Output}}{\text{Input}}$$

Key Terms

competitive capabilities 11
competitive priorities 11
consistent quality 12
core competencies 9
core process 7
customer relationship process 7
customization 12
delivery speed 12
development speed 12
external customers 4
external suppliers 4
internal customers 4

internal suppliers 4
lead time 9
low-cost operations 12
nested process 5
new service/product development
    process 7
on-time delivery 12
operation 2
operations management 2
operations strategy 7
order fulfillment process 7
order qualifier 13

order winner 11
process 2
productivity 16
supplier relationship process 7
supply chain 2
supply chain management 2
support process 7
time-based competition 11
top quality 12
variety 12
volume flexibility 12

Solved Problem 1

Student tuition at Boehring University is $150 per semester credit hour. The state supplements school revenue by $100 per semester credit hour. Average class size for a typical 3-credit course is 50 students. Labor costs are $4,000 per class, materials costs are $20 per student per class, and overhead costs are $25,000 per class.

a. What is the *multifactor* productivity ratio for this course process?

b. If instructors work an average of 14 hours per week for 16 weeks for each 3-credit class of 50 students, what is the *labor* productivity ratio?

SOLUTION

a. Multifactor productivity is the ratio of the value of output to the value of input resources.

$$\text{Value of output} = \left(\frac{50 \text{ students}}{\text{class}}\right)\left(\frac{3 \text{ credit hours}}{\text{students}}\right)\left(\frac{\$150 \text{ tuition} + \$100 \text{ state support}}{\text{credit hour}}\right)$$

$$= \$37,500/\text{class}$$

$$\text{Value of inputs} = \text{Labor} + \text{Materials} + \text{Overhead}$$

$$= \$4,000 + (\$20/\text{student} \times 50 \text{ students}/\text{class}) + \$25,000$$

$$= \$30,000/\text{class}$$

$$\text{Multifactor productivity} = \frac{\text{Output}}{\text{Input}} = \frac{\$37,500/\text{class}}{\$30,000/\text{class}} = 1.25$$

b. Labor productivity is the ratio of the value of output to labor hours. The value of output is the same as in part (a), or $37,500/class, so

$$\text{Labor hours of input} = \left(\frac{14 \text{ hours}}{\text{week}}\right)\left(\frac{16 \text{ weeks}}{\text{class}}\right) = 224 \text{ hours}/\text{class}$$

$$\text{Labor productivity} = \frac{\text{Output}}{\text{Input}} = \frac{\$37,500/\text{class}}{224 \text{ hours}/\text{class}}$$

$$= \$167.41/\text{hour}$$

Solved Problem 2

Natalie Attire makes fashionable garments. During a particular week, employees worked 360 hours to produce a batch of 132 garments, of which 52 were "seconds" (meaning that they were flawed). Seconds are sold for $90 each at Attire's Factory Outlet Store. The remaining 80 garments are sold to retail distribution at $200 each. What is the *labor* productivity ratio of this manufacturing process?

SOLUTION

$$\text{Value of output} = (52 \text{ defective} \times 90/\text{defective}) + (80 \text{ garments} \times 200/\text{garment})$$

$$= \$20,680$$

Labor hours of input = 360 hours

$$\text{Labor productivity} = \frac{\text{Output}}{\text{Input}} = \frac{\$20,680}{360 \text{ hours}}$$

$$= \$57.44 \text{ in sales per hour}$$

Discussion Questions

1. Consider your last (or current) job.

   a. What activities did you perform?

   b. Who were your customers (internal and external), and how did you interact with them?

   c. How could you measure the customer value you were adding by performing your activities?

   d. Was your position in accounting, finance, human resources, management information systems, marketing, operations, or other? Explain.

2. Consider amazon.com, whose Web site enjoys millions of "hits" each day and puts customers in touch with millions of services and products. What are amazon.com's competitive priorities and what should its operations strategy focus on?

3. A local hospital declares that it is committed to provide *care* to patients arriving at the emergency unit in less than 15 minutes and that it will never turn away patients who need to be hospitalized for further medical care. What implications does this commitment have for strategic operations management decisions (i.e., decisions relating to capacity and workforce)?

4. FedEx built its business on quick, dependable delivery of items being shipped by air from one business to another. Its early advantages included global tracking of shipments using Web technology. The advancement of Internet technology enabled competitors to become much more sophisticated in order tracking. In addition, the advent of Web-based businesses put pressure on increased ground transportation deliveries. Explain how this change in the environment has affected FedEx's operations strategy, especially relative to UPS, which has a strong hold on the business-to-consumer ground delivery business.

5. Suppose that you were conducting a market analysis for a new textbook about technology management. What would you need to know to identify a market segment? How would you make a needs assessment? What should be the collection of services and products?

6. Although all nine of the competitive priorities discussed in this chapter are relevant to a company's success in the marketplace, explain why a company should not necessarily try to excel in all of them. What determines the choice of the competitive priorities that a company should emphasize for its key processes?

7. Choosing which processes are core to a firm's competitive position is a key strategic decision. For example, Nike, a popular sports shoe company, focuses on the customer relationship, new product development, and supplier relationship processes and leaves the order fulfillment process to others. Allen Edmonds, a top-quality shoe company, considers all four processes to be core processes. What considerations would you make in determining which processes should be core to your manufacturing company?

8. A local fast-food restaurant processes several customer orders at once. Service clerks cross paths, sometimes nearly colliding, while they trace different paths to fill customer orders. If customers order a special combination of toppings on their hamburgers, they must wait quite some time while the special order is cooked. How would you modify the restaurant's operations to achieve competitive advantage? Because demand surges at lunchtime, volume flexibility is a competitive priority in the fast-food business. How would you achieve volume flexibility?

9. Kathryn Shoemaker established Grandmother's Chicken Restaurant in Middlesburg 5 years ago. It features a unique recipe for chicken, "just like grandmother used to make." The facility is homey, with relaxed and friendly service. Business has been good during the past 2 years, for both lunch and dinner. Customers normally wait about 15 minutes to be served, although complaints about service delays have increased recently. Shoemaker is currently considering whether to expand the current facility or open a similar restaurant in neighboring Uniontown, which has been growing rapidly.

   a. What types of strategic plans must Shoemaker make?

   b. What environmental forces could be at work in Middlesburg and Uniontown that Shoemaker should consider?

   c. What are the possible distinctive competencies of Grandmother's?

10. Wild West, Inc., is a regional telephone company that inherited nearly 100,000 employees and 50,000 retirees from AT&T. Wild West has a new mission: to diversify. It calls for a 10-year effort to enter the financial services, real estate, cable TV, home shopping, entertainment, and cellular communication services markets—and to compete with other telephone companies. Wild West plans to provide cellular and fiber-optic communications services in markets with established competitors, such as the United Kingdom, and in markets with essentially no competition, such as Russia and former Eastern Bloc countries.

    a. What types of strategic plans must Wild West make? Is the "do-nothing" option viable? If Wild West's mission appears too broad, which businesses would you trim first?

    b. What environmental forces could be at work that Wild West should consider?

    c. What are the possible core competencies of Wild West? What weaknesses should it avoid or mitigate?

11. You are designing a grocery delivery business. Via the Internet, your company will offer staples and frozen foods in a large metropolitan area and then deliver them within a customer-defined window of time. You plan to partner with two major food stores in the area. What should be your competitive priorities and what capabilities do you want to develop in your core and support processes?

Problems

The OM Explorer and POM for Windows software is available to all students using the 10th edition of this textbook. Go to **www.pearsonhighered.com/krajewski** to download these computer packages. If you purchased MyOMLab, you also have access to Active Models software and significant help in doing the following problems. Check with your instructor on how best to use these resources. In many cases, the instructor wants you to understand how to do the calculations by hand. At the least, the software provides a check on your calculations. When calculations are particularly complex and the goal is interpreting the results in making decision, the software entirely replaces the manual calculations.

1. (Refer to Solved Problem 1.) Coach Bjourn Toulouse led the Big Red Herrings to several disappointing football seasons. Only better recruiting will return the Big Red Herrings to winning form. Because of the current state of the program, Boehring University fans are unlikely to support increases in the $192 season ticket price. Improved recruitment will increase overhead costs to $30,000 per class section from the current $25,000 per class section. The university's budget plan is to cover recruitment costs by increasing the average class size to 75 students. Labor costs will increase to $6,500 per 3-credit course. Material costs will be about $25 per student for each 3-credit course. Tuition will be $200 per semester credit, which is supplemented by state support of $100 per semester credit.

    a. What is the multifactor productivity ratio? Compared to the result obtained in Solved Problem 1, did productivity increase or decrease for the course process?

    b. If instructors work an average of 20 hours per week for 16 weeks for each 3-credit class of 75 students, what is the *labor* productivity ratio?

2. Suds and Duds Laundry washed and pressed the following numbers of dress shirts per week.

Week	Work Crew	Total Hours	Shirts
1	Sud and Dud	24	68
2	Sud and Jud	46	130
3	Sud, Dud, and Jud	62	152
4	Sud, Dud, and Jud	51	125
5	Dud and Jud	45	131

    a. Calculate the *labor* productivity ratio for each week.

    b. Explain the labor productivity pattern exhibited by the data.

3. CD players are produced on an automated assembly line process. The standard cost of CD players is $150 per unit (labor, $30; materials, $70; and overhead, $50). The sales price is $300 per unit.

    a. To achieve a 10 percent multifactor productivity improvement by reducing materials costs only, by what percentage must these costs be reduced?

    b. To achieve a 10 percent multifactor productivity improvement by reducing labor costs only, by what percentage must these costs be reduced?

    c. To achieve a 10 percent multifactor productivity improvement by reducing overhead costs only, by what percentage must these costs be reduced?

4. The output of a process is valued at $100 per unit. The cost of labor is $50 per hour including benefits. The accounting department provided the following information about the process for the past four weeks:

	Week 1	Week 2	Week 3	Week 4
Units Produced	1,124	1,310	1,092	981
Labor ($)	12,735	14,842	10,603	9,526
Material ($)	21,041	24,523	20,442	18,364
Overhead ($)	8,992	10,480	8,736	7,848

    a. Use the multifactor productivity ratio to see whether recent process improvements had any effect and, if so, when the effect was noticeable.

    b. Has labor productivity changed? Use the labor productivity ratio to support your answer.

5. Alyssa's Custom Cakes currently sells 5 birthday, 2 wedding, and 3 specialty cakes each month for $50, $150, and $100 each, respectively. The cost of labor is $50 per hour including benefits. It takes 90 minutes to produce a birthday cake, 240 minutes to produce a wedding cake, and 60 minutes to produce a specialty cake. Alyssa's current multifactor productivity ratio is 1.25.

    a. Use the multifactor productivity ratio provided to calculate the average cost of the cakes produced.

    b. Calculate Alyssa's labor productivity ratio in dollars per hour for each type of cake.

    c. Based solely on the labor productivity ratio, which cake should Alyssa try to sell the most?

    d. Based on your answer in part (a), is there a type of cake Alyssa should stop selling?

Advanced Problems

6. The Big Black Bird Company (BBBC) has a large order for special plastic-lined military uniforms to be used in an urgent military operation. Working the normal two shifts of 40 hours each per week, the BBBC production process usually produces 2,500 uniforms per week at a standard cost of $120 each. Seventy employees work the first shift and 30 employees work the second. The contract price is $200 per uniform. Because of the urgent need, BBBC is authorized to use around-the-clock production, 6 days per week. When each of the two shifts works 72 hours per week, production increases to 4,000 uniforms per week but at a cost of $144 each.

   a. Did the multifactor productivity ratio increase, decrease, or remain the same? If it changed, by what percentage did it change?

   b. Did the labor productivity ratio increase, decrease, or remain the same? If it changed, by what percentage did it change?

   c. Did weekly profits increase, decrease, or remain the same?

7. Mack's guitar fabrication shop produces low-cost, highly durable guitars for beginners. Typically, out of the 100 guitars that begin production each month, only 80 percent are considered good enough to sell. The other 20 percent are scrapped due to quality problems that are identified after they have completed the production process. Each guitar sells for $250. Because some of the production process is automated, each guitar only requires 10 labor hours. Each employee works an average 160 hours per month. Labor is paid at $10/hour, materials cost is $40/guitar, and overhead is $4,000.

   a. Calculate the labor and multifactor productivity ratios.

   b. After some study, the operations manager Darren Funk recommends three options to improve the company's multifactor productivity: (1) increase the sales price by 10 percent, (2) improve quality so that only 10 percent are defective, or (3) reduce labor, material, and overhead costs by 10 percent. Which option has the greatest impact on the multifactor productivity measure?

8. Mariah Enterprises makes a variety of consumer electronic products. Its camera manufacturing plant is considering choosing between two different processes, named Alpha and Beta, which can be used to make a component part. To make the correct decision, the managers would like to compare the labor and multifactor productivity of process Alpha with that of process Beta. The value of process output for Alpha and Beta is $175 and $140 per unit, and the corresponding overhead costs are $6,000 and $5,000, respectively.

	PROCESS ALPHA		PROCESS BETA	
Product	A	B	A	B
Output (units)	50	60	30	80
Labor ($)	$1,200	$1,400	$1,000	$2,000
Material ($)	$2,500	$3,000	$1,400	$3,500

   a. Which process, Alpha or Beta, is more productive?

   b. What conclusions can you draw from your analysis?

9. The Morning Brew Coffee Shop sells Regular, Cappuccino, and Vienna blends of coffee. The shop's current daily labor cost is $320, the equipment cost is $125, and the overhead cost is $225. Daily demands, along with selling price and material costs per beverage, are given below.

	Regular Coffee	Cappuccino	Vienna coffee
Beverages sold	350	100	150
Price per beverage	$2.00	$3.00	$4.00
Material ($)	$0.50	$0.75	$1.25

Harald Luckerbauer, the manager at Morning Brew Coffee Shop, would like to understand how adding Eiskaffee (a German coffee beverage of chilled coffee, milk, sweetener, and vanilla ice cream) will alter the shop's productivity. His market research shows that Eiskaffee will bring in new customers and not cannibalize current demand. Assuming that the new equipment is purchased before Eiskaffee is added to the menu, Harald has developed new average daily demand and cost projections. The new equipment cost is $200, and the overhead cost is $350. Modified daily demands, as well as selling price and material cost per beverage for the new product line, are given below.

	Regular Coffee	Cappuccino	Vienna cofee	Eiskaffee
Beverages sold	350	100	150	75
Price per beverage	$2.00	$3.00	$4.00	$5.00
Material ($)	$0.50	$0.75	$1.25	$1.50

   a. Calculate the change in labor and multifactor productivity if Eiskaffee is added to the menu.

   b. If everything else remains unchanged, how many units of Eiskaffee would have to be sold to ensure that the multifactor productivity increases from its current level?

Active Model Exercise

This Active Model appears in MyOMLab. It allows you to evaluate the important elements of labor productivity.

QUESTIONS

1. If the insurance company can process 60 (10 percent) more policies per week, by what percentage will the productivity measure rise?

2. Suppose the 8-hour day includes a 45-minute lunch. What is the revised productivity measure, excluding lunch?

3. If an employee is hired, what will be the weekly number of policies processed if the productivity of five policies per hour is maintained?

4. Suppose that, during the summer, the company works for only 4 days per week. What will be the weekly number of policies processed if the productivity of five policies per hour is maintained?

▶ **ACTIVE MODEL 1.1**
Labor Productivity Using Data from Example 1.1

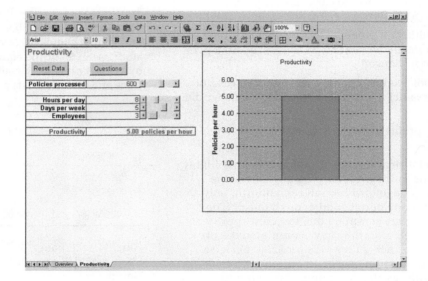

VIDEO CASE | Operations as a Competitive Weapon at Starwood

Starwood is one of the world's largest hotel companies, with more than 750 owned, managed, and franchised properties in more than 80 countries. The company's lodging brands include The Luxury Collection, St. Regis, Sheraton, Westin, Four Points, and W Hotels. Its hotels regularly appear on lists of top hotels around the world. On any given night, guests in the hotels may be individual leisure travelers, independent business guests, or part of a meeting or convention.

In 2002, Starwood standardized its operating processes so that it could measure, improve, and ultimately grow its convention business. Each meeting is assigned a Star Meeting Concierge who works closely with meeting planners.

When guests stay at a Starwood property as part of a meeting or convention, arrangements are typically made by a meeting planner. The meeting planner works with a location to arrange meeting facilities, banquet rooms, lodging, and events for participants. Prior to 2002, the company's individual properties had their own approaches to convention planning, yet no consistent, coordinated program within or across brands made it easy for meeting planners to do business with Starwood. For example, paperwork for confirming program details, rooms, and food and beverage requirements differed between properties and brands. Some hotels had diagrams of meeting space, while others did not. Technology available for meeting rooms varied widely, and a hotel liaison was not always immediately available during the event in case a need arose.

Recognizing that Starwood's future growth and success relied heavily on its relationships with meeting planners, the company held focus groups to gather information about their needs and expectations. One clear priority emerged: consistency in the meeting planning process, whether that meeting was held at the Sheraton in New York, the Westin Kierland in Phoenix, or the W Hotel in Lakeshore, Chicago. Such a program could create consistency across all brands, and generate loyalty and increased revenues from those meeting planners who drive large volumes of business to Starwood properties annually.

As a result of the meetings, Starwood created the Starwood Preferred Planner program. Every hotel property now has the same paperwork for the meeting planning process, and shares that paperwork electronically across properties and brands. Contracts were standardized and new standards created to recognize and reward frequent VIP meeting planners. Each meeting is assigned a "Star Meeting Concierge" whose sole responsibility is to anticipate and fulfill any needs of the meeting planner during the event. Handheld Nextel radio phones are now issued at check-in to the meeting planners at no extra charge so that they have 24-hour access to the concierge.

To measure the performance of the new process, Starwood set high internal targets for scores on the surveys given to meeting planners after their events concluded. For instance, at the Luxury Collection and St. Regis brands, individual meeting scores must be 4.55 on a 5-point scale. At the Westin and W Hotels, scores must be above 4.35 on the 5-point scale. Scores from Sheraton properties must exceed 4.30, and Four Points hotels have a target of 4.25 on the 5-point scale. Because the expectations for an airport location one-day meeting (not held at the St. Regis or Luxury Collection) differ from a multiday resort experience, the targets reflect those expectations.

QUESTIONS

1. What are the key inputs and outputs associated with Starwood's new meeting planning process?

2. How does the meeting planning process at Starwood interact with the following core processes in their hotels?
   a. Customer relationship (internal and external)
   b. New service or product development
   c. Order fulfillment
   d. Supplier relationship

CASE | Chad's Creative Concepts

Chad's Creative Concepts designs and manufactures wood furniture. Founded by Chad Thomas on the banks of Lake Erie in Sandusky, Ohio, the company began by producing custom-made wooden furniture for vacation cabins located along the coast of Lake Erie and on nearby Kelly's Island and Bass Island. Being an "outdoors" type himself, Thomas originally wanted to bring "a bit of the outdoors" inside. Chad's Creative Concepts developed a solid reputation for creative designs and high-quality workmanship. Sales eventually encompassed the entire Great Lakes region. Along with growth came additional opportunities.

Traditionally, the company focused entirely on custom-made furniture, with the customer specifying the kind of wood from which the piece would be made. As the company's reputation grew and sales increased, the sales force began selling some of the more popular pieces to retail furniture outlets. This move into retail outlets led Chad's Creative Concepts into the production of a more standard line of furniture. Buyers of this line were much more price-sensitive and imposed more stringent delivery requirements than did clients for the custom line. Custom-designed furniture, however, continued to dominate sales, accounting for 60 percent of volume and 75 percent of dollar sales. Currently, the company operates a single manufacturing process in Sandusky, where both custom furniture and standard furniture are manufactured. The equipment is mainly general purpose in nature to provide the flexibility needed for producing custom pieces of furniture. The layout puts together saws in one section of the facility, lathes in another, and so on. The quality of the finished product reflects the quality of the wood chosen and the craftsmanship of individual workers. Both custom and standard furniture compete for processing time on the same equipment by the same craftspeople.

During the past few months, sales of the standard line steadily increased, leading to more regular scheduling of this product line. However, when scheduling trade-offs had to be made, custom furniture was always given priority because of its higher sales and profit margins. Thus, scheduled lots of standard furniture pieces were left sitting around the plant in various stages of completion.

As he reviews the progress of Chad's Creative Concepts, Thomas is pleased to note that the company has grown. Sales of custom furniture remain strong, and sales of standard pieces are steadily increasing. However, finance and accounting indicate that profits are not what they should be. Costs associated with the standard line are rising. Dollars are being tied up in inventory, both in raw materials and work-in-process. Expensive public ware-

house space has to be rented to accommodate the inventory volume. Thomas also is concerned with increased lead times for both custom and standard orders, which are causing longer promised delivery times. Capacity is being pushed, and no space is left in the plant for expansion. Thomas begins a careful assessment of the overall impact that the new standard line is having on his manufacturing process.

QUESTIONS

1. What types of decisions must Chad Thomas make daily for his company's operations to run effectively? Over the long run?

2. How did sales and marketing affect operations when they began to sell standard pieces to retail outlets?

3. How has the move to producing standard furniture affected the company's financial structure?

4. What might Chad Thomas have done differently to avoid some of the problems he now faces?

Source: This case was prepared by Dr. Brooke Saladin, Wake Forest University, as a basis for classroom discussion. Copyright © Brooke Saladin. Used with permission.

Selected References

Chase, Richard B., and Uday M. Apte. "A History of Research in Service Operations: What's the Big Idea?" *Journal of Operations Management*, vol. 25, no. 2 (2007), pp. 375–386.

Collis, David J. and Michael G. Rukstad. "Can You Say What Your Strategy Is?" *Harvard Business Review*, vol. 86, no. 4 (2008), pp. 82–90.

Fitzsimmons, James A., and Mona Fitzsimmons. *Service Management*. New York: McGraw-Hill, 2005.

Gaimon, Cheryl. "The Management of Technology: A Production and Operations Management Perspective." *Production and Operations Management*, vol. 17, no. 1 (2008), pp. 1–11.

Hammer, Michael. "Deep Change: How Operational Innovation Can Transform Your Company." *Harvard Business Review* (April 2004), pp. 85–93.

Heineke, Janelle, and Mark Davis. "The Emergence of Service Operations as an Academic Discipline." *Journal of Operations Management*, vol. 25, no. 2 (2007), pp. 364–374.

Hill, Terry. *Manufacturing Strategy: Text and Cases*, 3rd ed. Homewood, IL: Irwin/McGraw-Hill, 2000.

Huckman, Robert S., and Darren E. Zinner. "Does Focus Improve Operational Performance? Lessons from the Management of Clinical Trials." *Strategic Management Journal*, vol. 29 (2008), pp. 173–193.

Karmarkar, Uday. "Will You Survive the Services Revolution?" *Harvard Business Review*, vol. 82 (2004), pp. 100–108.

Kaplan, Robert S., and David P. Norton. *Balanced Scoreboard*. Boston, MA: Harvard Business School Press, 1997.

King Jr., Neil. "A Whole New World." *Wall Street Journal* (September 27, 2004).

Meyer, Christopher and Andre Schwager. "Understanding customer experience." *Harvard Business Review*, vol. 85 (2007), pp. 116–126.

Neilson, Gary L., Karla L. Martin, and Elizabeth Powers. "The secrets to successful strategy execution." *Harvard Business Review*, vol. 86, no. 6 (2008), pp. 60–70.

Pande, Peter S., Robert P. Neuman, and Roland R. Cavanagh. *The Six Sigma Way*. New York: McGraw-Hill, 2000.

Porter, Michael. *Competitive Advantage*. New York: The Free Press, 1987.

Porter, Michael E., and Mark R. Kramer. "Strategy and Society: The Link Between Competitive Advantage and Corporate Social Responsibility." *Harvard Business Review*, vol. 84, no. 12 (2006), pp. 78–92.

Powell, Bill. "It's All Made in China Now." *Fortune* (March 4, 2002), pp. 121–128.

Safizadeh, M. Hossein, Larry P. Ritzman, Deven Sharma, and Craig Wood. "An Empirical Analysis of the Product–Process Matrix." *Management Science*, vol. 42, no. 11 (1996), pp. 1576–1591.

Skinner, Wickham. "Manufacturing—Missing Link in Corporate Strategy." *Harvard Business Review* (May–June 1969), pp. 136–145.

Svensson, Peter. "GameStop to Sell Rain Checks for Wii." *The State* (December 18, 2007).

Voss, Chris, Aleda Roth, and Richard Chase. "Experience, Service Operations Strategy, and Services as Destinations: Foundations and Exploratory Investigation" *Production and Operations Management*, vol. 17, no. 3 (2008), pp. 247–266.

Ward, Peter T., and Rebecca Duray. "Manufacturing Strategy in Context: Environment, Competitive Strategy and Manufacturing Strategy." *Journal of Operations Management*, vol. 18 (2000), pp. 123–138.

Wiseman, Paul. "Despite China's might, US factories maintain edge," *The State* and *The Associated Press* (January 31, 2011).

Womack, James P., Daniel T. Jones, and Daniel Roos. *The Machine That Changed the World*. New York: HarperPerennial, 1991.

At any given time eBay has approximately 113 million listings worldwide, and yet its workforce consists of just 15,000 employees. The explanation? Customers do most of the work in eBay's buying and selling processes. Here a customer prepares items for shipping from sales on his Ebay account.

eBay

Most manufacturers do not have to contend with customers waltzing around their shop floors, showing up intermittently and unannounced. Such customer contact can introduce considerable variability, disrupting carefully designed production processes. Costs and quality can be adversely affected. While customer contact is an issue even with manufacturers, (each process does have at least one customer), extensive customer contact and involvement are business as usual for many processes of service providers. Customers at restaurants or rental car agencies are directly involved in performing the processes. The area where the sales person interacts with the customer *is* the shop floor.

How much should customers be involved in a process, so as to provide timely delivery and consistent quality, and at sustainable cost? Various ways are available—some accommodate customer-introduced variability and some reduce it. eBay illustrates one way to accommodate variability. As an online auction house, eBay has high volume and request variability. Its customers do not want service at the same time or at times necessarily convenient to the company. They have request variability, seeking to buy and sell an endless number of items. They also have variability in customer capability, some with considerable Internet experience and some needing more handholding. Such variability would greatly complicate workforce scheduling if eBay required its employees to conduct all of its processes. It connects hundreds of millions of people around the world every day. It has a global presence in 39 markets, with revenue of $9.2 billion in more than 50,000 categories—and only with 15,500 employees. This relatively small workforce is possible in the face of customer-induced variability because its customers perform virtually all of the selling and buying processes through the eBay Web site. When the customer is responsible for much of the work, the right labor is provided at the right moment.

Source: Frances X. Frei, "Breaking the Trade-Off between Efficiency and Service," *Harvard Business Review* (November 2006), pp. 93–101; **http://en.wikipedia.org/wiki/Ebay** (March 19, 2011).

process strategy
The pattern of decisions made in managing processes so that they will achieve their competitive priorities.

LEARNING GOALS *After reading this chapter, you should be able to:*

1 Explain why processes exist everywhere in all organizations.

2 Discuss the four major process decisions.

3 Position a process on the customer-contact matrix or product-process matrix.

4 Configure operations into layouts.

5 Define customer involvement, resource flexibility, capital intensity, and economies of scope.

6 Discuss how process decisions should fit together.

7 Define process reengineering and process improvement.

Creating Value through Operations Management

Using Operations to Compete
Project Management

Managing Processes

Process Strategy
Process Analysis
Quality and Performance
Capacity Planning
Constraint Management
Lean Systems

Managing Supply Chains

Supply Chain
Inventory Management
Supply Chain Design
Supply Chain Location Decisions
Supply Chain Integration
Supply Chain Sustainability and Humanitarian Logistics
Forecasting
Operations Planning and Scheduling
Resource Planning

Process decisions, such as the amount of customer involvement allowed at eBay, are strategic in nature: As we saw in Chapter 1, they should further a company's long-term competitive goals. In making process decisions, managers focus on controlling such competitive priorities as quality, flexibility, time, and cost. Process management is an ongoing activity, with the same principles applying to both first-time and redesign choices.

In this chapter, we focus on **process strategy**, which specifies the pattern of decisions made in managing processes so that the processes will achieve their competitive priorities. Process strategy guides a variety of process decisions, and in turn is guided by operations strategy and the organization's ability to obtain the resources necessary to support them. We begin by defining four basic process decisions: (1) process structure (including layout), (2) customer involvement, (3) resource flexibility, and (4) capital intensity. We discuss these decisions for both service and manufacturing processes. We pay particular attention to ways in which these decisions fit together, depending on factors such as competitive priorities, customer contact, and volume. We conclude with two basic change strategies for analyzing and modifying processes: (1) process reengineering and (2) process improvement.

Three principles concerning process strategy are particularly important:

1. The key to successful process decisions is to make choices that fit the situation and that make sense together. They should not work at cross-purposes, with one process optimized at the expense of other processes. A more effective process is one that matches key process characteristics and has a close *strategic fit*.

2. Although this section of the text focuses on individual processes, they are the building blocks that eventually create the firm's whole supply chain. The cumulative effect on customer satisfaction and competitive advantage is huge.

3. Whether processes in the supply chain are performed internally or by outside suppliers and customers, management must pay particular attention to the interfaces between processes. Dealing with these interfaces underscores the need for cross-functional coordination.

Process Strategy across the Organization

As we explained in Chapter 1, processes are everywhere and are the basic unit of work. Consider the following two major points: (1) supply chains have processes and (2) processes are found throughout the whole organization, and not just in operations.

Supply Chains Have Processes

If you infer that Managing Processes and Managing Supply Chains are essential aspects of operations management, you are correct. If you also infer that only Managing Processes deals with processes, you would be wrong. The correct conclusion is that Managing supply processes, which are business processes that have external customers or suppliers. Table 2.1 illustrates some common supply chain processes.

supply chain processes
Business processes that have external customers or suppliers.

TABLE 2.1 | SUPPLY CHAIN PROCESS EXAMPLES

Process	Description	Process	Description
Outsourcing	Exploring available suppliers for the best options to perform processes in terms of price, quality, delivery time, environmental issues	Customer Service	Providing information to answer questions or resolve problems using automated information services as well as voice-to-voice contact with customers
Warehousing	Receiving shipments from suppliers, verifying quality, placing in inventory, and reporting receipt for inventory records	Logistics	Selecting transportation mode (train, ship, truck, airplane, or pipeline) scheduling both inbound and outbound shipments, and providing intermediate inventory storage
Sourcing	Selecting, certifying and evaluating suppliers and managing supplier contracts	Cross-docking	Packing of products of incoming shipments so they can be easily sorted more economically at intermediate warehouses for outgoing shipments to their final destination

These supply chain processes should be documented and analyzed for improvement, examined for quality improvement and control, and assessed in terms of capacity and bottlenecks. Supply chain processes will be only as good as the processes within the organization that have only internal suppliers and customers. Each process in the chain, from suppliers to customers, must be designed to achieve its competitive priorities and add value to the work performed.

Processes Are Not Just in Operations

Processes are found in accounting, finance, human resources, management information systems, and marketing. Organizational structure throughout the many diverse industries varies, but for the most part, all organizations perform similar business processes. Table 2.2 lists a sample of them that are outside the operations area. All of these processes must be managed.

TABLE 2.2 | ILLUSTRATIVE BUSINESS PROCESSES OUTSIDE OF OPERATIONS

Activity based costing	Employee-development	Payroll
Asset management	Employee-recruiting	Records management
Billing budget	Employee-training	Research and development
Complaint handling	Engineering	Sales
Credit management	Environment	Help desks
Customer-satisfaction	External communications	Disaster recovery
Employee-benefits	Finance	Waste management
Employee-compensation	Security management	Warranty

Managers of these processes must make sure that they are adding as much customer value as possible. They must understand that many processes cut across organizational lines, regardless of whether the firm is organized along functional, product, regional, or process lines.

Process Strategy Decisions

A process involves the use of an organization's resources to provide something of value. No service can be provided and no product can be made without a process, and no process can exist without at least one service or product. One recurring question in managing processes is

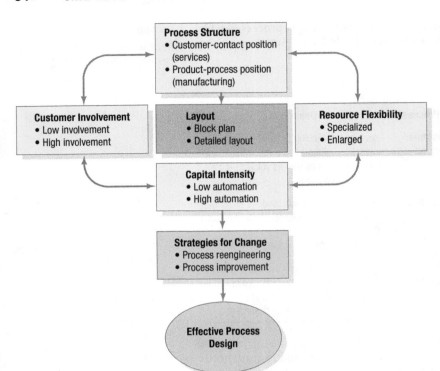

▲ **FIGURE 2.1**
Major Decisions for Effective
Processes

process structure

The process type relative to
the kinds of resources needed,
how resources are partitioned
between them, and their key
characteristics.

layout

The physical arrangement of
operations created by the various
processes.

customer involvement

The ways in which customers become part of the process and the
extent of their participation.

resource flexibility

The ease with which employees
and equipment can handle a wide
variety of products, output levels,
duties, and functions.

capital intensity

The mix of equipment and human
skills in a process.

deciding *how* to provide services or make products. Many different choices are available in
selecting human resources, equipment, outsourced services, materials, work flows, and
methods that transform inputs into outputs.
Another choice is which processes are to be
done in-house, and which processes are to be
outsourced—that is, done outside the firm and
purchased as materials and services. This decision helps to define the supply chain, and is covered more fully in subsequent chapters.

Process decisions directly affect the process itself and indirectly the services and the
products that it provides. Whether dealing
with processes for offices, service providers, or
manufacturers, operations managers must consider four common process decisions. Figure 2.1
shows that they are all important steps toward
an effective process design. These four decisions
are best understood at the process or subprocess level, rather than at the firm level.

- **Process structure** determines the process type relative to the kinds of resources
  needed, how resources are partitioned between them, and their key characteristics. A
layout, which is the physical arrangement of operations created from the various processes,
puts these decisions into tangible form.

- **Customer involvement** reflects the ways in which customers become part of the process and
  the extent of their participation.

- **Resource flexibility** is the ease with which employees and equipment can handle a wide variety of products, output levels, duties, and functions.

- **Capital intensity** is the mix of equipment and human skills in a process. The greater the relative cost of equipment, the greater is the capital intensity.

The concepts that we develop around these four decisions establish a framework within which
we can address the appropriate process design in every situation. There is no "how to" element
here in this chapter. Instead, we establish the patterns of choices that create a good fit between
the four decisions. For example, if you walk through a manufacturing facility where materials flow
smoothly from one work station to the next (which we will define later to be a *line* process), you
would be tempted to conclude that all processes should be line processes. They seem so efficient
and organized. However, if volumes are low and the products made are customized, converting
to a line process would be a big mistake. When volumes are low and products are customized,
resources must be more flexible to handle a variety of products. The result is a more disorganized
appearance with jobs crisscrossing in many different directions depending on the product being
made. Despite appearances, this process is the best choice.

Process Structure in Services

One of the first decisions a manager makes in designing a well-functioning process is to choose a
process type that best achieves the competitive priorities for that process. Strategies for designing
processes can be quite different, depending on whether a service is being provided or a product is
being manufactured. We begin with service processes, given their huge implication for workforce
resources in industrialized countries.

Nature of Service Processes: Customer Contact

A process strategy that gets customers in and out of a fast-food restaurant quickly would not be
the right process strategy for a five-star restaurant, where customers seek a leisurely dining experience. To gain insights, we must start at the process level and recognize key contextual variables associated with the process. A good process strategy for a service process depends first and foremost

on the type and amount of customer contact. **Customer contact** is the extent to which the customer is present, is actively involved, and receives personal attention during the service process. Face-to-face interaction, sometimes called a *moment of truth* or *service encounter*, brings the customer and service providers together. At that time, customer attitudes about the quality of the service provided are shaped. Table 2.3 shows several dimensions of customer contact. Many levels are possible on each of the five dimensions. The nested-process concept applies to customer contact, because some parts of a process can have low contact and other parts of a process can have high contact.

TABLE 2.3 | DIMENSIONS OF CUSTOMER CONTACT IN SERVICE PROCESSES

Dimension	High Contact	Low Contact
Physical presence	Present	Absent
What is processed	People	Possessions or information
Contact intensity	Active, visible	Passive, out of sight
Personal attention	Personal	Impersonal
Method of delivery	Face-to-face	Regular mail or e-mail

Customer-Contact Matrix

The customer-contact matrix, shown in Figure 2.2, brings together three elements: (1) the degree of customer contact, (2) customization, and (3) process characteristics. The matrix is the starting point for evaluating and improving a process.

customer contact

The extent to which the customer is present, is actively involved, and receives personal attention during the service process.

Customer Contact and Customization   The horizontal dimension of the matrix represents the service provided to the customer in terms of customer contact and competitive priorities. A key competitive priority is how much customization is needed. Positions on the left side of the matrix represent high customer contact and highly customized services. The customer is more likely to be present and active. The process is more likely to be visible to the customer, who receives more personal attention. The right side of the matrix represents low customer contact, passive involvement, less personalized attention, and a process out of the customer's sight.

Process Divergence and Flow   The vertical dimension of the customer-contact matrix deals with two characteristics of the process itself: (1) process divergence and (2) flow. Each process can be analyzed on these two dimensions.

Process divergence is the extent to which the process is highly customized with considerable latitude as to how its tasks are performed. If the process changes with each customer, virtually every performance of the service is unique. Examples of highly divergent service processes where many steps in them change with each customer are found in consulting, law, and architecture. A service with low divergence, on the other hand, is repetitive and standardized. The work is performed exactly the same with all customers, and tends to be less complex. Certain hotel services and telephone services are highly standardized to assure uniformity.

Closely related to divergence is how the customer, object, or information being processed flows through the service facility. Work progresses through the sequence of steps in a process, which could range from highly diverse to linear. When divergence is considerable, the work flow tends to be more flexible. A **flexible flow** means that the customers, materials, or information move in diverse ways,

process divergence

The extent to which the process is highly customized with considerable latitude as to how its tasks are performed.

flexible flow

The customers, materials, or information move in diverse ways, with the path of one customer or job often crisscrossing the path that the next one takes.

◀ FIGURE 2.2
Customer-Contact Matrix for Service Processes

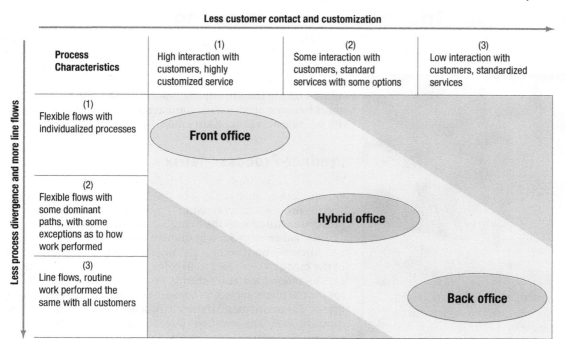

A financial consultant discusses options with a young couple at their home. This process scores high on customer contact, because the customers are present, take an active part in creating the service, receive personal attention, and have face-to-face contact.

with the path of one customer or job often criss-crossing the path that the next one takes. Each one can follow a carefully preplanned path, even though the first impression is one of disorganized, jumbled flows. Such an appearance goes naturally with high process divergence. A **line flow** means that the customers, materials, or information move linearly from one operation to the next, according to a fixed sequence. When diversity is low and the process standardized, line flows are a natural consequence.

Service Process Structuring

Figure 2.2 shows several desirable positions in the matrix that effectively connect the service product with the process. The manager has three process structures, which form a continuum, to choose from: (1) front office, (2) hybrid office, and (3) back office. It is unlikely that a process can be a top performer if a process lies too far from one of these diagonal positions, occupying instead one of the extreme positions represented by the light blue triangles in the matrix (refer to Figure 2.2). Such positions represent too much of a disconnect between the service provided and process characteristics.

line flow

The customers, materials, or information move linearly from one operation to the next, according to a fixed sequence.

front office

A process with high customer contact where the service provider interacts directly with the internal or external customer.

hybrid office

A process with moderate levels of customer contact and standard services with some options available.

back office

A process with low customer contact and little service customization.

Front Office   A **front-office** process has high customer contact where the service provider interacts directly with the internal or external customer. Because of the customization of the service and variety of service options, many of the steps in it have considerable divergence. Work flows are flexible, and they vary from one customer to the next. The high-contact service process tends to be adapted or tailored to each customer.

Hybrid Office A hybrid office tends to be in the middle of the five dimensions in Table 2.3, or perhaps high on some contact measures and low on others. A **hybrid-office** process has moderate levels of customer contact and standard services, with some options available from which the customer chooses. The work flow progresses from one workstation to the next, with some dominant paths apparent.

Back Office   A **back-office** process has low customer contact and little service customization. The work is standardized and routine, with line flows from one service provider to the next until the service is completed. Preparing the monthly client fund balance reports in the financial services industry is a good example. It has low customer contact, low divergence, and a line flow.

Process Structure in Manufacturing

Many processes at a manufacturing firm are actually services to internal or external customers, and so the previous discussion on services applies to them. Similarly, manufacturing processes can be found in service firms. Clarity comes when viewing work at the process level, rather than the organizational level. Here we focus instead on the manufacturing processes. Because of the differences between service and manufacturing processes, we need a different view on process structure.

Product-Process Matrix

The product-process matrix, shown in Figure 2.3, brings together three elements: (1) volume, (2) product customization, and (3) process characteristics. It synchronizes the product to be manufactured with the manufacturing process itself.

A good strategy for a manufacturing process depends first and foremost on volume. Customer contact, a primary feature of the customer-contact matrix for services, normally is not a consideration for manufacturing processes (although it *is* a factor for the many service processes throughout manufacturing firms). For many manufacturing processes, high product customization means lower volumes for many of the steps in the process. The vertical dimension of the product-process matrix

An employee discusses work with her supervisor. Each employee in this series of work stations are in a back office, because they have low customer contact and little service customization.

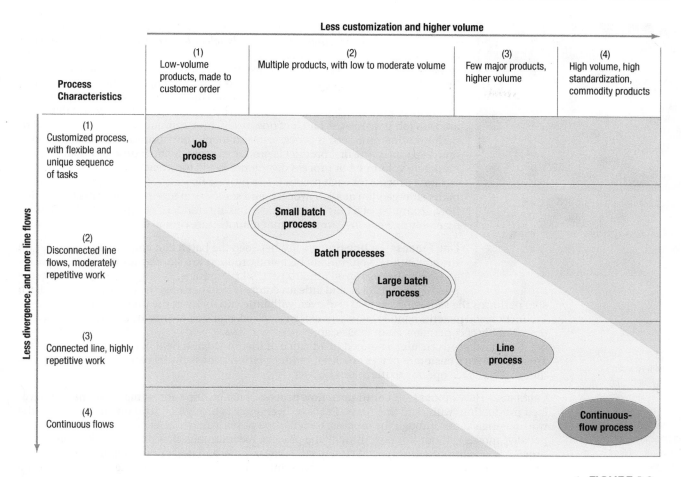

Less customization and higher volume →

	(1) Low-volume products, made to customer order	(2) Multiple products, with low to moderate volume	(3) Few major products, higher volume	(4) High volume, high standardization, commodity products

Process Characteristics

Less divergence, and more line flows ↓

(1) Customized process, with flexible and unique sequence of tasks — **Job process**

(2) Disconnected line flows, moderately repetitive work — **Small batch process**, **Batch processes**, **Large batch process**

(3) Connected line, highly repetitive work — **Line process**

(4) Continuous flows — **Continuous-flow process**

▲ **FIGURE 2.3**
Product-Process Matrix for Manufacturing Processes

deals with the same two characteristics in the customer-contact matrix: process divergence and flow. Each manufacturing process should be analyzed on these two dimensions, just as was done for a service process.

Manufacturing Process Structuring

Figure 2.3 shows several desirable positions (often called *process choices*) in the product-process matrix that effectively connect the manufactured product with the process. **Process choice** is the way of structuring the process by organizing resources around the process or organizing them around the products. Organizing around the process means, for example, that all milling machines are grouped together and process all products or parts needing that kind of transformation. Organizing around the product means bringing together all the different human resources and equipment needed for a specific product and dedicating them to producing just that product. The manager has four process choices, which form a continuum, to choose from: (1) job process, (2) batch process, (3) line process, and (4) continuous-flow process. As with the customer-contact matrix, it is unlikely that a manufacturing process can be a top performer if its position is too far from the diagonal. The fundamental message in Figure 2.3 is that the best choice for a manufacturing process depends on the volume and degree of customization required of the process. The process choice might apply to an entire manufacturing process or just one subprocess nested within it.

Job Process   A **job process** creates the flexibility needed to produce a wide variety of products in significant quantities, with considerable divergence in the steps performed. Customization is high and volume for any one product is low. The workforce and equipment are flexible to handle considerable task divergence. Companies choosing job processes often bid for work. Typically, they make products to order and do not produce them ahead of time. Each new order is handled as a single unit—as a job. Examples are machining a metal casting for a customized order or producing customized cabinets.

With a job process, all equipment and workers capable of certain types of work are located together. Because customization is high and most jobs have a different sequence of steps, this process choice creates flexible flows through the operations rather than a line flow.

process choice

A way of structuring the process by organizing resources around the process or organizing them around the products.

job process

A process with the flexibility needed to produce a wide variety of products in significant quantities, with considerable divergence in the steps performed.

A batch of apple fritters roll off one of the pastry lines at the King Soopers's Bakery in Denver to be packaged for transportation. The pastry line is a batch process, and a different kind of pastry will be made next.

batch process

A process that differs from the job process with respect to volume, variety, and quantity.

line process

A process that lies between the batch and continuous processes on the continuum; volumes are high and products are standardized, which allows resources to be organized around particular products.

continuous flow process

The extreme end of high-volume standardized production and rigid line flows, with production not starting and stopping for long time intervals.

make-to-order strategy

A strategy used by manufacturers that make products to customer specifications in low volumes.

assemble-to-order strategy

A strategy for producing a wide variety of products from relatively few subassemblies and components after the customer orders are received.

postponement

The strategy of delaying final activities in the provision of a product until the orders are received.

Batch Process   The batch process is by far the most common process choice found in practice, leading to terms such as *small batch* or *large batch* to further distinguish one process choice from another. A **batch process** differs from the job process with respect to volume, variety, and quantity. The primary difference is that volumes are higher because the same or similar products or parts going into them are produced repeatedly. Some of the components going into the final product may be processed in advance. Production lots are handled in larger quantities (or *batches*) than they are with job processes. A batch of one product (or component part going into it or perhaps other products) is processed, and then production is switched to the next one. Eventually, the first product is produced again. A batch process has average or moderate volumes, but process divergence is still too great to warrant dedicating a separate process for each product. The process flow is flexible, but more dominant paths emerge than at a job process, and some segments of the process have a line flow. Examples of a batch process are making standard components that feed an assembly line or some processes that manufacture capital equipment.

Line Process   A **line process** lies between the batch and continuous processes on the continuum; volumes are high and products are standardized, which allows resources to be organized around particular products. Divergence is minimal in the process or line flows, and little inventory is held between the processing steps. Each step performs the same process over and over, with little variability in the products manufactured. Production and material handling equipment is specialized. Products created by a line process include the assembly of computers, automobiles, appliances, and toys.

Standard products are produced in advance of their need and held in inventory so that they are ready when a customer places an order. Product variety is possible by careful control of the addition of standard options to the main product.

Continuous Flow Process   A **continuous flow process** is the extreme end of high-volume standardized production, with rigid line flows. Process divergence is negligible. Its name derives from the way materials move through the process. Usually, one primary material (such as a liquid, a gas, or a powder) moves without stopping through the process. A continuous-flow process differs from a line process in one important respect: Materials (be they undifferentiated or discrete) flow through the process without stopping until the whole batch is finished. The time span can be several shifts or even several months. Examples of a continuous flow process are petroleum refining; chemical processes; and processes making steel, soft drinks, and food (such as Borden's huge pasta-making plant).

Production and Inventory Strategies

Strategies for manufacturing processes differ from those in services, not only because of low customer contact and involvement, but also because of the ability to use inventories[1]. Make-to-order, assemble-to-order, and make-to-stock strategies are three approaches to inventory that should be coordinated with process choice.

Make-to-Order Strategy   Manufacturers that make products to customer specifications in low volumes tend to use the **make-to-order strategy**, coupling it with job or small batch processes. It is a more complex process than assembling a final product from standard components. This strategy provides a high degree of customization and typically uses job or small batch processes. The processes have high divergence. Specialized medical equipment, castings, and expensive homes are suited to the make-to-order strategy.

Assemble-to-Order Strategy   The **assemble-to-order strategy** is an approach to producing a wide variety of products from relatively few subassemblies and components after the customer orders are received. Typical competitive priorities are variety and fast delivery times. The assemble-to-order strategy often involves a line process for assembly and a batch process for fabrication. Because they are devoted to manufacturing standardized components and subassemblies in high volumes, the fabrication processes focus on creating appropriate amounts of component inventories for the assembly processes. Once the specific order from the customer is received, the assembly processes create the product from standardized components and subassemblies produced by the fabrication processes.

Stocking finished products would be economically prohibitive because the numerous possible options make forecasting relatively inaccurate. Thus, the principle of **postponement** is applied, whereby the final activities in the provision of a product are delayed until the orders are

---

[1]Service firms also hold inventories, but only as purchased material. Manufacturing firms have the additional flexibility of holding inventories as subassemblies or finished products.

received. The assemble-to-order strategy is also linked to **mass customization**, where highly divergent processes generate a wide variety of customized products at reasonably low costs.

Make-to-Stock Strategy   Manufacturing firms that hold items in stock for immediate delivery, thereby minimizing customer delivery times, use a **make-to-stock strategy**. This strategy is feasible for standardized products with high volumes and reasonably accurate forecasts. It is the inventory strategy of choice for line or continuous-flow processes. Examples of products produced with a make-to-stock strategy include garden tools, electronic components, soft drinks, and chemicals.

Combining a line process with the make-to-stock strategy is sometimes called **mass production**. It is what the popular press commonly envisions as the classical manufacturing process, because the environment is stable and predictable, with workers repeating narrowly defined tasks with low divergence.

A Chinese manufacturing firm using the make-to-stock strategy has considerable inventory stacked on pallets with rows of shelving racks in the background.

Layout

Selecting process structures for the various processes housed in a facility is a strategic decision, but must be followed by a more tactical decision—creating a layout. A *layout* is the physical arrangement of operations (or departments) created from the various processes and puts them in tangible form. For organizational purposes, processes tend to be clustered together into operations or departments. An *operation* is a group of human and capital resources performing all or part of one or more processes. For example, an operation could be several customer service representatives in a customer reception area; a group of machines and workers producing cell phones; or a marketing department. Regardless of how processes are grouped together organizationally, many of them cut across departmental boundaries. The flows across departmental lines could be informational, services, or products. Process structures that create more flows across departmental lines, as with job or batch processes, are the most challenging layout problems.

Here we demonstrate an approach to layout design that positions those departments close together that have strong interactions between them. It involves three basic steps, whether the design is for a new layout or for revising an existing layout: (1) gather information, (2) develop a block plan, and (3) design a detailed layout. We illustrate these steps with the Office of Budget Management (OBM), which is a major division in a large state government.

Gather Information

OBM consists of 120 employees assigned to six different departments. Workloads have expanded to the extent that 30 new employees must be hired and somehow housed in the space allocated to OBM. The goal is to improve communication among people who must interact with each other effectively, creating a good work environment.

Three types of information are needed to begin designing the revised layout for OBM: (1) space requirements by center, (2) available space, and (3) closeness factors. OBM has grouped its processes into six different departments: (1) administration, (2) social services, (3) institutions, (4) accounting, (5) education, and (6) internal audit. The exact space requirements of each department, in square feet, are as follows:

Department	Area Needed (ft²)
1. Administration	3,500
2. Social services	2,600
3. Institutions	2,400
4. Accounting	1,600
5. Education	1,500
6. Internal audit	3,400
	Total 15,000

mass customization

The strategy that uses highly divergent processes to generate a wide variety of customized products at reasonably low costs.

make-to-stock strategy

A strategy that involves holding items in stock for immediate delivery, thereby minimizing customer delivery times.

mass production

A term sometimes used in the popular press for a line process that uses the make-to-stock strategy.

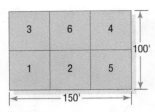

▲ FIGURE 2.4
Current Block Plan for the
Office of Budget Management

block plan

A plan that allocates space and
indicates placement of each
operation.

closeness matrix

A table that gives a measure of
the relative importance of each
pair of operations being located
close together.

Management must tie space requirements to capacity and staffing plans; calculate the specific equipment and space needs for each center; and allow circulation space, such as aisles and the like. At OBM, a way must be found to include all 150 employees in its assigned area. Consulting with the managers and employees involved can help avoid excessive resistance to change and make the transition smoother.

A **block plan** allocates space and indicates placement of each operation. To describe a new facility layout, the plan need only provide the facility's dimensions and space allocations. When an existing facility layout is being modified, the current block plan is also needed. OBM's available space is 150 feet by 100 feet, or 15,000 square feet. The designer could begin the design by dividing the total amount of space into six equal blocks (2,500 square feet each). The equal-space approximation shown in Figure 2.4 is sufficient until the detailed layout stage, when larger departments (such as administration) are assigned more space than smaller departments.

The layout designer must also know which operations need to be located close to one another. The table below shows OBM's **closeness matrix**, which gives a measure of the relative importance of each pair of operations being located close together. The metric used depends on the type of processes involved and the organizational setting. It can be a qualitative judgment on a scale from 0 to 10 that the manager uses to account for multiple performance criteria, as in the OBM's case. Only the right-hand portion of the matrix is used. The closeness factors are indicators of the need for proximity based on an analysis of information flows and the need for face-to-face meetings. They give clues as to which departments should be located close together. For example, the most important interaction is between the administration and internal audit departments for OBM, with a score of 10. This closeness factor is given in the first row and last column. Thus, the designer should locate departments 1 and 6 close together, which is not the arrangement in the current layout. Entries in both the columns and rows result in five factor scores for each department.

CLOSENESS FACTORS						
Department	**1**	**2**	**3**	**4**	**5**	**6**
1. Administration	—	3	6	5	6	10
2. Social services		—	8	1	1	
3. Institutions			—	3	9	
4. Accounting				—	2	
5. Education					—	1
6. Internal audit						—

At a manufacturing plant, the closeness factor could be the number of trips (or some other measure of materials movement) between each pair of operations per day. This information can be gleaned by conducting a statistical sampling, polling supervisors and materials handlers, or using the routings and ordering frequencies for typical items made at the plant.

Finally, the information gathered for OBM includes performance criteria that depend not on the relative location of department pairs, but the *absolute* location of a single department. OBM has two such criteria.

1. Education (department 5) should remain where it is because it is next to the office library.

2. Administration (department 1) should remain where it is because that location has the largest conference room, which administration uses often. Relocating the conference room would be costly.

Develop a Block Plan

Having gathered the needed information, the next step is to develop a block plan that best satisfies performance criteria and area requirements. The most elementary way to do so is by trial and error. Because success depends on the designer's ability to spot patterns in the data, this approach does not guarantee the selection of the best or even a nearly best solution. When supplemented by the use of a computer to evaluate solutions, however, research shows that such an approach compares quite favorably with more sophisticated computerized techniques.

Applying the Weighted-Distance Method

weighted-distance method

A mathematical model used to
evaluate layouts (of facility locations) based on closeness factors.

When *relative* locations are a primary concern, such as for effective information flow, communication, material handling, and stockpicking, the weighted-distance method can be used to compare alternative block plans. The **weighted-distance method** is a mathematical model used to evaluate layouts based on closeness factors. A similar approach, sometimes called the *load-distance method*, can be used to evaluate facility locations. The objective is to select a layout (or facility location) that minimizes the total weighted distances. The distance between two points is expressed by assigning the points to grid coordinates on a block diagram or map. An alternative approach is to use time rather than distance.

For a rough calculation, which is all that is needed for the weighted-distance method, either a Euclidean or rectilinear distance measure may be used. **Euclidean distance** is the straight-line distance, or shortest possible path, between two points. To calculate this distance, we create a graph. The distance between two points, say, points A and B, is

$$d_{AB} = \sqrt{(x_A - x_B)^2 + (y_A - y_B)^2}$$

where

$d_{AB} =$ distance between points A and B
$x_A = x$-coordinate of point A
$y_A = y$-coordinate of point A
$x_B = x$-coordinate of point B
$y_B = y$-coordinate of point B

Rectilinear distance measures the distance between two points with a series of 90-degree turns, as along city blocks. The distance traveled in the x-direction is the absolute value of the difference between the x-coordinates. Adding this result to the absolute value of the difference between the y-coordinates gives

$$d_{AB} = |x_A - x_B| + |y_A - y_B|$$

For assistance in calculating distances using either measure, see Tutor 2.1 in OM Explorer.

The layout designer seeks to minimize the weighted-distance (*wd*) score by locating centers that have high-closeness ratings close together. To calculate a layout's *wd* score, we use either of the distance measures and simply multiply the proximity scores by the distances between centers. The sum of those products becomes the layout's final *wd* score—the lower the better. The location of a center is defined by its x-coordinate and y-coordinate.

Euclidean distance

The straight-line distance, or shortest possible path, between two points.

rectilinear distance

The distance between two points with a series of 90-degree turns, as along city blocks.

MyOMLab

Tutor 2.1 in MyOMLab provides an example to calculate both Euclidean and rectilinear distance measures.

EXAMPLE 2.1	**Calculating the Weighted-Distance Score**

The block plan in Figure 2.5 was developed using trial and error. A good place to start was to fix Departments 1 and 5 in their current locations. Then, the department pairs that had the largest closeness factors were located. The rest of the layout fell into place rather easily.

How much better, in terms of the *wd* score, is the proposed block plan shown in Figure 2.5 than the current plan shown in Figure 2.4? Use the rectilinear distance measure.

SOLUTION

The accompanying table lists each pair of departments that has a nonzero closeness factor in the closeness matrix. For the third column, calculate the rectilinear distances between the departments in the current layout. For example, departments 3 and 5 in the current plan are in the upper-left corner and bottom-right corner of the building, respectively. The distance between the centers of these blocks is three units (two horizontally and one vertically). For the fourth column, we multiply the weights (closeness factors) by the distances, and then add the results for a total *wd* score of 112 for the current plan. Similar calculations for the proposed plan produce a *wd* score of only 82. For example, between departments 3 and 5 is just one unit of distance (one vertically and zero horizontally).

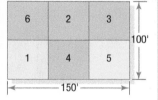

▲ **FIGURE 2.5**
Proposed Block Plan

MyOMLab

Active Model 2.1 in MyOMLab allows evaluation of the impact of swapping OBM departmental positions.

Current Plan

3	6	4
1	2	5

Proposed Plan

6	2	3
1	4	5

Department Pair	Closeness Factor (*w*)	CURRENT PLAN		PROPOSED PLAN	
		Distance (*d*)	Weighted-Distance Score (*wd*)	Distance (*d*)	Weighted-Distance Score (*wd*)
1, 2	3	1	3	2	6
1, 3	6	1	6	3	18
1, 4	5	3	15	1	5
1, 5	6	2	12	2	12
1, 6	10	2	20	1	10
2, 3	8	2	16	1	8
2, 4	1	2	2	1	1

Department Pair	Closeness Factor (w)	CURRENT PLAN		PROPOSED PLAN	
		Distance (d)	Weighted-Distance Score (wd)	Distance (d)	Weighted-Distance Score (wd)
2, 5	1	1	1	2	2
3, 4	3	2	6	2	6
3, 5	9	3	27	1	9
4, 5	2	1	2	1	2
5, 6	1	2	2	3	3
			Total 112		Total 82

To be exact, we could multiply the two wd total scores by 50 because each unit of distance represents 50 feet. However, the relative difference between the two totals remains unchanged.

DECISION POINT
The wd score for the proposed layout makes a sizeable drop from 112 to 82, but management is not sure the improvement outweighs the cost of relocating four of the six departments (i.e., all departments but 1 and 5).

⦿ Rectilinear Distances ◯ Euclidean Distances

Department Pair	Closeness Factor	Distance	Score
1, 6	10	1	10
3, 5	9	1	9
2, 3	8	1	8
1, 3	6	1	6
1, 5	6	2	12
1, 4	5	3	15
1, 2	3	2	6
3, 4	3	2	6
4, 5	2	1	2
2, 4	1	1	1
2, 5	1	2	2
5, 6	1	3	3
		Total	80

6	2	4
1	3	5

▲ **FIGURE 2.6**
Second Proposed Block Plan (Analyzed with *Layout* Solver)

Although the wd score for the proposed layout in Example 2.1 represents an almost 27 percent improvement, the designer may be able to improve on this solution. Furthermore, the manager must determine whether the revised layout is worth the cost of relocating four of the six departments. If relocation costs are too high, a less-expensive proposal must be found.

OM Explorer and POM for Windows can help identify some even more attractive proposals. For example, one option is to modify the proposed plan by switching the locations of departments 3 and 4. OM Explorer's output in Figure 2.6 shows that the wd score for this second revision not only drops to 80, but requires that only three departments be relocated compared with the original layout in Figure 2.4. Perhaps this second proposed plan is the best solution.

Design a Detailed Layout

After finding a satisfactory block plan, the final step translates it into a detailed representation, showing the exact size and shape of each center; the arrangement of elements (e.g., desks, machines, and storage areas); and the location of aisles, stairways, and other service space. These visual representations can be two-dimensional drawings, three-dimensional models, or computer-aided graphics. This step helps decision makers discuss the proposal and problems that might otherwise be overlooked. Such visual representations can be particularly important when evaluating high customer-contact processes.

Customer Involvement

Having covered process structure decisions and how they are translated into a layout, we now turn to a second major decision—customer involvement—shown in Figure 2.1. Customer involvement reflects the ways in which customers become part of the process and the extent of their participation. It is especially important for many service processes, particularly if customer contact is (or should be) high.

While eBay devised one way to accommodate the variability created by customer involvement, Starbucks faces a different kind of customer variability. The coffee shop chain allows customers to choose among many permutations of sizes, flavors, and preparation techniques in its beverages.

In order to fill orders accurately and efficiently, Starbucks trains its counter clerks to call out orders to beverage makers in a particular sequence. It is even better when customers themselves can do so. Starbucks attempts to teach customers its ordering protocol. First, it provides a "guide-to-ordering pamphlet" for customers to look over. Second, it trains clerks to repeat the order in the correct sequence for the beverage makers, which may not be how the customer presented it. This process not only makes it easier for the beverage makers, but also indirectly "trains" the customers in how to place their orders.

Possible Disadvantages

Customer involvement is not always a good idea. In some cases, giving the customer more active contact in a service process will just be disruptive, making the process less efficient. Managing the timing and volume of customer demands becomes more challenging if the customer is physically present and expects prompt delivery. Exposing the facilities and employees to the customer can have important quality implications (favorable or unfavorable). Such changes make interpersonal skills a prerequisite to the service provider's job, but higher skill levels come at a cost. Revising the facility layout might be a necessary investment, now that managing customer perceptions becomes an important part of the process. It also might mean having many smaller decentralized facilities closer to the various customer concentration areas if the customer comes to the service providers.

The detailed layout becomes a reality. Shown here is part of the office in one of the ABB facilities, a global leader in power and automation technologies. Here the workstations are small and semiprivate, but "outposts" are available. This common area has easy chairs fitted with arms that provide a surface for writing or laptops. People meet comfortably for face-to-face talks, rather than communicating by e-mail.

ABB, Inc.

Possible Advantages

Despite these possible disadvantages, the advantages of a more customer-focused process might increase the net value to the customer. Some customers seek active participation in and control over the service process, particularly if they will enjoy savings in both price and time. The manager must assess whether advantages outweigh disadvantages, judging them in terms of the competitive priorities and customer satisfaction. More customer involvement can mean better quality, faster delivery, greater flexibility, and even lower cost.

Self-service is the choice of many retailers, such as gasoline stations, supermarkets, and bank services. Manufacturers of products (such as toys, bicycles, and furniture) may also prefer to let the customer perform the final assembly because product, shipping, and inventory costs frequently are lower. Customer involvement can also help coordinate across the supply chain. Emerging technologies allow companies to engage in an active dialogue with customers and make them partners in creating value and forecasting future demand. Companies can also revise some of their traditional processes, such as pricing and billing systems, to account for their customers' new role. For example, in business-to-business relationships, the Internet changes the roles that companies play with other businesses. Suppliers to automobile companies can be close collaborators in the process of developing new vehicles and no longer are passive providers of materials and services. The same is true for distributors. Walmart does more than just distribute Procter & Gamble's products: It shares daily sales information and works with Procter & Gamble in managing inventories and warehousing operations.

A customer at Starbucks, a large coffee shop chain, places his order in the correct way. By structuring the ordering process for counter clerks and customers, Starbucks can deal efficiently with the variety in products offered, and with no hit on the service experience.

Ramin Talaie/Corbis

Technicians in the parts repair department of this ABB facility must be flexible enough to repair many different parts for automation equipment installed at customer locations in the field. This operation has 30 different workstations configured to perform different types of processes. Workers are cross-trained to move from one station to another, depending on what needs to be done.

Resource Flexibility

Just as managers must account for customer contact when making customer involvement decisions, so must they account for process divergence and diverse process flows when making resource flexibility decisions in Figure 2.1. High task divergence and flexible process flows require more flexibility of the process's resources—its employees, facilities, and equipment. Employees need to perform a broad range of duties, and equipment must be general purpose. Otherwise, resource utilization will be too low for economical operations.

Workforce

Operations managers must decide whether to have a **flexible workforce**. Members of a flexible workforce are capable of doing many tasks, either at their own workstations or as they move from one workstation to another. However, such flexibility often comes at a cost, requiring greater skills and thus more training and education. Nevertheless, benefits can be large: Worker flexibility can be one of the best ways to achieve reliable customer service and alleviate capacity bottlenecks. Resource flexibility helps to absorb the feast-or-famine workloads in individual operations that are caused by low-volume production, divergent tasks, flexible flows, and fluid scheduling.

flexible workforce

A workforce whose members are capable of doing many tasks, either at their own workstations or as they move from one workstation to another.

The type of workforce required also depends on the need for volume flexibility. When conditions allow for a smooth, steady rate of output, the likely choice is a permanent workforce that expects regular full-time employment. If the process is subject to hourly, daily, or seasonal peaks and valleys in demand, the use of part-time or temporary employees to supplement a smaller core of full-time employees may be the best solution. However, this approach may not be practical if knowledge and skill requirements are too high for a temporary worker to grasp quickly.

MyOMLab

Tutor 2.2 in MyOMLab demonstrates how to do break-even analysis for equipment selection.

Equipment

Low volumes mean that process designers should select flexible, general-purpose equipment. Figure 2.7 illustrates this relationship by showing the total cost lines for two different types of equipment that can be chosen for a process. Each line represents the total annual cost of the process at different volume levels. It is the sum of fixed costs and variable costs. When volumes are low (because customization is high), process 1 is the better choice. It calls for inexpensive general-purpose equipment, which keeps investment in equipment low and makes fixed costs (F_1) small. Its variable unit cost is high, which gives its total cost line a relatively steep slope. Process 1 does the job, but not at peak efficiency.

Conversely, process 2 is the better choice when volumes are high and customization is low. Its advantage is low variable unit cost, as reflected in the flatter total cost line. This efficiency is possible when customization is low because the equipment can be designed for a narrow range of products or tasks. Its disadvantage is high equipment investment and, thus, high fixed costs (F_2). When annual volume produced is high enough, spreading these fixed costs over more units produced, the advantage of low variable costs more than compensates for the high fixed costs.

The break-even quantity in Figure 2.7 is the quantity at which the total costs for the two alternatives are equal. At quantities beyond this point, the cost of process 1 exceeds that of process 2. Unless the firm expects to sell more than the break-even amount, which is unlikely with high customization and low volume, the capital investment of process 2 is not warranted.

Capital Intensity

Capital intensity is the mix of equipment and human skills in the process; the greater the relative cost of equipment, the greater is the capital intensity. As the capabilities of technology increase and its costs decrease, managers face an ever-widening range of choices, from

▼ **FIGURE 2.7**
Relationship Between Process Costs and Product Volume

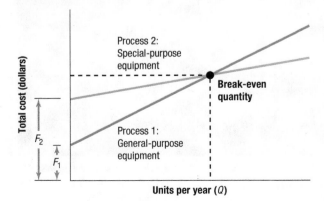

operations utilizing very little automation to those requiring task-specific equipment and little human intervention. **Automation** is a system, process, or piece of equipment that is self-acting and self-regulating. Although automation is often thought to be necessary to gain competitive advantage, it has both advantages and disadvantages. Thus, the automation decision requires careful examination.

Automating Manufacturing Processes

Substituting labor-saving capital equipment and technology for labor has been a classic way of improving productivity and quality consistency in manufacturing processes. If investment costs are large, automation works best when volume is high, because more customization typically means reduced volume. Gillette, for example, spent $750 million on the production lines and robotics that gave it a capacity to make 1.2 billion razor cartridges a year. The equipment is complicated and expensive. Only with such high volumes could this line process produce the product at a price low enough that consumers could afford to buy it.

One big disadvantage of capital intensity can be the prohibitive investment cost for low-volume operations (see Figure 2.7). Generally, capital-intensive operations must have high utilization to be justifiable. Also, automation does not always align with a company's competitive priorities. If a firm offers a unique product or high-quality service, competitive priorities may indicate the need for hand labor and individual attention rather than new technology. A case in point is the downstream processes in Gillette's supply chain that package and store the razor cartridges. It customizes the packaging for different regions of the world, so that volumes for any one type of package are much lower. As a result of the low volumes, Gillette does not use expensive automation for these processes. In fact, it outsources them. Producing razor cartridges to stock using highly automated processes, and then packaging them in customized fashion at remote locations on demand, is also a good example of the principle of postponement.

Volkswagen aspires to become a full-line manufacturer of cars ranging from the smallest compacts to the largest luxury models. In the United States, for example, it offers the Jetta, GTI, Golf, Passat, CC, Routan, Tiguan, Touareg and Eos. The new VW Phaeton is the latest example of the brand's higher end. It uses a line process dedicated strictly to Phaeton cars. Because of its focus on Phaetons, which are made nowhere else, it enjoys high volumes. This volume justifies the high automation invested in this $208 million plant. The building is located in the heart of Dresden, a city known for its arts and craftsmanship. Its walls are made almost exclusively of glass, and it floors are covered entirely in Canadian maple. There are no smokestacks, no noises, and no toxic byproducts. Parts arrive and luxury cars depart. Of course, such a plant is not always possible, as with a steel mill or foundry. Shown in the photo is the arrival of the body structure that is painted in a plant about 60 miles from Dresden. It is what it looks like when it arrives, before the Phaeton assembly begins. For a photo tour, see **http://forums.vwvortex.com/showthread.php?1837641**.

Fixed Automation   Manufacturers use two types of automation: (1) fixed and (2) flexible (or programmable). Particularly appropriate for line and continuous-flow process choices, **fixed automation** produces one type of part or product in a fixed sequence of simple operations. Operations managers favor fixed automation when demand volumes are high, product designs are stable, and product life cycles are long. These conditions compensate for the process's two primary drawbacks: (1) large initial investment cost and (2) relative inflexibility. However, fixed automation maximizes efficiency and yields the lowest variable cost per unit if volumes are high.

Flexible Automation   **Flexible (or programmable) automation** can be changed easily to handle various products. The ability to reprogram machines is useful for both low-customization and high-customization processes. In the case of high customization, a machine that makes a variety of products in small batches can be programmed to alternate between products. When a machine has been dedicated to a particular product or family of products, as in the case of low customization and a line flow, and the product is at the end of its life cycle, the machine can simply be reprogrammed with a new sequence of tasks for a new product. An **industrial robot**, which is a versatile, computer-controlled machine programmed to perform various tasks, is a classic example of flexible automation. These "steel-collar" workers operate independently of human control. A robot's arm has up to six standard movements. The robot's "hand" actually does the work. The hand can be changed to perform different tasks, such as materials handling, assembly, and testing. Managerial Practice 2.1 describes how R.R. Donnelley benefits from more flexible automation, allowing for quick changeovers from one customer order to the next.

Automating Service Processes

Using capital inputs as a labor-saving device is also possible for service processes. In educational services, for example, long-distance learning technology now can supplement or even replace the traditional classroom experience by using books, computers, Web sites, and videos as facilitating goods that go with the service. Justifying technology need not be limited to cost reduction. Sometimes, it can actually allow more task divergence by making available a wide menu of choices to the customer.

automation

A system, process, or piece of equipment that is self-acting and self-regulating.

fixed automation

A manufacturing process that produces one type of part or product in a fixed sequence of simple operations.

flexible (or programmable) automation

A manufacturing process that can be changed easily to handle various products.

industrial robot

Versatile, computer-controlled machine programmed to perform various tasks.

Flexible Automation at Just Born, Inc., a candy company in Pennsylvania (**www.justborn.com**).

On the left, a robot picks up the PEEPS® brand marshmallow yellow bunnies with great speed in groups of four and places them into preformed trays, which then move to automatic shrink-wrapping machines. The trays are then boxed into cases for shipment. Upstream in this line process, the bunnies were extruded in shape on a belt with about 1/2 inch of sugar on it and then cooled as the conveyor moves along. The robot is regularly reprogrammed based on the marshmallow configuration being produced.

On the right, the robot using vacuum cups on the "hand" of its arm picks up boxes of five-pound MIKE AND IKE® bags that are packaged with six bags in a box. The robot reads the bar code, knows the pallet configuration, picks up and places the pallet and a thin cardboard liner on the conveyor, and stacks the boxes until complete. The pallet then comes toward the camera to be picked off the line by a fork truck, and then shrink-wrapped (automatically) and loaded into a 54-foot trailer. PEEPS® and MIKEANDIKE® are registered trademarks of Just Born, Inc. Used with permission.

Technology in the future will surely make possible even a greater degree of customization and variety in services that currently only human providers can now deliver. Beyond cost and variety considerations, management must understand the customer and how much close contact is valued. If the customers seek a visible presence and personal attention, technologies reduced to sorting through a variety of options on the Internet or over the telephone might be a poor choice.

The need for volume to justify expensive automation is just as valid for service processes as for manufacturing processes. Increasing the volume lowers the cost per dollar of sales. Volume is essential for many capital-intensive processes in the transportation, communications, and utilities industries.

Economies of Scope

economies of scope

Economies that reflect the ability to produce multiple products more cheaply in combination than separately.

If capital intensity is high, resource flexibility usually is low. In certain types of manufacturing operations, such as machining and assembly, programmable automation breaks this inverse relationship between resource flexibility and capital intensity. It makes possible both high capital intensity and high resource flexibility, creating economies of scope. **Economies of scope** reflect the ability to produce multiple products more cheaply in combination than separately. In such situations, two conflicting competitive priorities—customization and low price—become more compatible. However, taking advantage of economies of scope requires that a family of parts or products have enough collective volume to utilize equipment fully.

Economies of scope also apply to service processes. Consider, for example, Disney's approach to the Internet. When the company's managers entered the volatile Internet world, their businesses were only weakly tied together. Disney's Infoseek business, in fact, was not even fully owned. However, once its Internet markets became more crystallized, managers at Disney moved to reap the benefits of economies of scope. They aggressively linked their Internet processes with one another and with other parts of Disney. A flexible technology that handles many services together can be less expensive than handling each one separately, particularly when the markets are not too volatile.

Strategic Fit

The manager should understand how the four major process decisions tie together, so as to spot ways of improving poorly designed processes. The choices should fit the situation and each other. When the fit is more *strategic*, the process will be more effective. We examine services and manufacturing processes, looking for ways to test for strategic fit.

MANAGERIAL PRACTICE 2.1 | Flexible Automation at R.R. Donnelley

R.R. Donnelley & Sons Company is the largest commercial printer in the United States and the number one printer of books. The industry makes huge capital investments in its printing presses to help drive down the variable unit cost of a book (see Figure 2.7). Its uses a make-to-order strategy, with customers such as book publishers placing new orders as their inventories became too low. However, the "make-ready" time to prepare for the new order and change over the presses for the next customer order was time-consuming. Keeping such expensive equipment idle for change-overs is costly. These high costs force customers, such as book publishers, to make large, infrequent orders for their books.

Flexible automation at its Roanoke, Virginia, plant allows R.R. Donnelley to take a different course, and it is reaping big rewards. The new process begins when the contents of a book arrive via the Internet as a PDF (portable document format) file and go to the plant's prepress department. The intricate manual operations required to prepare text and pictures for printing traditionally caused the biggest bottlenecks. Roanoke now makes its plates digitally instead of from photographic film. With the elimination of steps, such as duplicating and cleaning the file, a job that once took hours can now be completed in 12 minutes. The all-digital workflow also makes possible the creation of electronic instructions, known as ink presets, which improve productivity and quality. Cleaner and sharper plates are created for the presses because, unlike film, electronic type does not have to be repeatedly handled.

With more flexible automation, the Roanoke plant produces 75 percent of its titles in 2 weeks or less, compared with 4 to 6 weeks for a 4-color book using traditional technology. Management created a culture of continuous improvement at the plant, home of some 300 workers. Overall, Roanoke increased throughput by 20 percent without having to buy an additional press

R.R. Donnelly has been able to achieve flexible automation by receiving books digitally and preparing them to go on press electronically. This allows the company to put books on press more quickly and print smaller, more manageable quantities in a single print run.

and binding line, a savings of $15 million. Its presses run around the clock producing 3.5 million books a month; productivity rose 20 percent, and service improved. Book publishers now enjoy a just-in-time product when they want it.

Decision Patterns for Service Processes

After analyzing a process and determining its position on the customer-contact matrix in Figure 2.2, it may be apparent that it is improperly positioned, either too far to the left or right, or too far to the top or bottom. Opportunities for improvement become apparent. Perhaps, more customization and customer contact is needed than the process currently provides. Perhaps, instead, the process is too divergent, with unnecessarily flexible flows. Reducing divergence might reduce costs and improve productivity.

The process should reflect its desired competitive priorities. Front offices generally emphasize top quality and customization, whereas back offices are more likely to emphasize low-cost operation, consistent quality, and on-time delivery. The process structure selected then points the way to appropriate choices on customer involvement, resource flexibility, and capital intensity. Figure 2.8 shows how these key process decisions are tied to customer contact. High customer contact at a front-office service process means:

1. *Process Structure.* The customer (internal or external) is present, actively involved, and receives personal attention. These conditions create processes with high divergence and flexible process flows.

2. *Customer Involvement.* When customer contact is high, customers are more likely to become part of the process. The service created for each customer is unique.

3. *Resource Flexibility.* High process divergence and flexible process flows fit with more flexibility from the process's resources—its workforce, facilities, and equipment.

4. *Capital Intensity.* When volume is higher, automation and capital intensity are more likely. Even though higher volume is usually assumed to be found in the back office, it is just as likely to be in the front office for financial services. Information technology is a major type of automation at many service processes, which brings together both resource flexibility and automation.

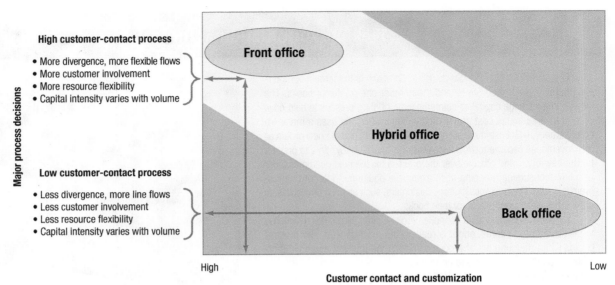

High customer-contact process

- More divergence, more flexible flows
- More customer involvement
- More resource flexibility
- Capital intensity varies with volume

Low customer-contact process

- Less divergence, more line flows
- Less customer involvement
- Less resource flexibility
- Capital intensity varies with volume

Major process decisions

Front office

Hybrid office

Back office

High   Low

Customer contact and customization

FIGURE 2.8 ▶
Decision Patterns for
Service Processes

Of course, this list provides general tendencies rather than rigid prescriptions. Exceptions can be found, but these relationships provide a way of understanding how service process decisions can be linked coherently.

Decision Patterns for Manufacturing Processes

Just as a service process can be repositioned in the customer-contact matrix, a manufacturing process can also be moved in the product-process matrix. Changes can be made either in the horizontal direction of Figure 2.3 by changing the degree of customization and volume, or they can be moved in the vertical direction by changing process divergence. The production and inventory strategy can also be changed. Competitive priorities must be considered when translating strategy into specific manufacturing processes. Figure 2.9 shows some usual tendencies found in practice. Job and small batch processes are usual choices if top quality, on-time delivery, and flexibility (customization, variety, and volume flexibility) are given primary emphasis. Large batch, line, and continuous-flow processes match up with an emphasis on low-cost operations, consistent quality, and delivery speed.

For production and inventory strategies, the make-to-order strategy matches up with flexibility (particularly customization) and top quality. Because delivery speed is more difficult, meeting due dates and on-time delivery get the emphasis on the time dimension. The assemble-to-order strategy allows delivery speed and flexibility (particularly variety) to be achieved, whereas the make-to-stock strategy is the usual choice if delivery speed and low-cost operations are emphasized. Keeping an item in stock assures quick delivery because it is generally available when needed, without delays in producing it. High volumes open up opportunities to reduce costs.

The process structure selected once again points the way to appropriate choices on customer involvement, resource flexibility, and capital intensity. Figure 2.10 summarizes the relationships between volume and the four key process decisions. High volumes per part type at a manufacturing process typically mean:

1. *Process Structure.* High volumes, combined with a standard product, make a line flow possible. It is just the opposite where a job process produces to specific customer orders.

2. *Customer Involvement.* Customer involvement is not a factor in most manufacturing processes, except for choices made on product variety and customization. Less discretion is allowed with line or continuous-flow processes in order to avoid the unpredictable demands required by customized orders.

▼ FIGURE 2.9
Links of Competitive Priorities
with Manufacturing Strategy

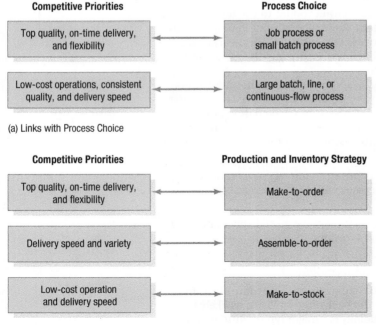

Competitive Priorities   **Process Choice**

Top quality, on-time delivery, and flexibility	◄──►	Job process or small batch process
Low-cost operations, consistent quality, and delivery speed	◄──►	Large batch, line, or continuous-flow process

(a) Links with Process Choice

Competitive Priorities   **Production and Inventory Strategy**

Top quality, on-time delivery, and flexibility	◄──►	Make-to-order
Delivery speed and variety	◄──►	Assemble-to-order
Low-cost operation and delivery speed	◄──►	Make-to-stock

(b) Links with Production and Inventory Strategy

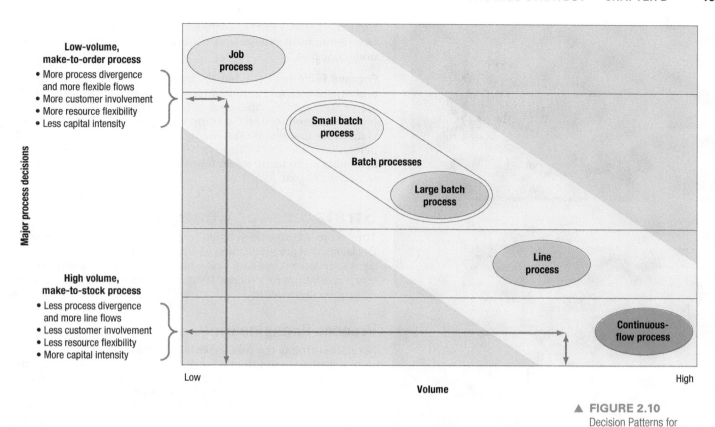

▲ **FIGURE 2.10**
Decision Patterns for
Manufacturing Processes

3. *Resource Flexibility.* When volumes are high and process divergence is low, flexibility is not needed to utilize resources effectively, and specialization can lead to more efficient processes.

4. *Capital Intensity.* High volumes justify the large fixed costs of an efficient operation. The King Soopers's bread line (see *The Big Picture* and the video in MyOMLab) is capital-intensive. It is automated from dough mixing to placement of the product on shipping racks. Expanding this process would be expensive. By way of contrast, the King Soopers's custom cake process is labor-intensive and requires little investment to equip the workers.

MyOMLab

Gaining Focus

In the past, new services or products often were added to a facility in the name of better utilizing fixed costs and keeping everything under the same roof. The result was a jumble of competitive priorities, process structures, and technologies. In the effort to do everything, nothing was done well.

Focus by Process Segments   A facility's operations often can neither be characterized nor actually designed for one set of competitive priorities and one process choice. King Soopers (see *The Big Picture* and video in MyOMLab) had three processes under one roof, but management segmented them into three separate operations that were relatively autonomous. At a services facility, some parts of the process might seem like a front office and other parts like a back office. Such arrangements can be effective, provided that sufficient focus is given to each process.

MyOMLab

Plants within plants (PWPs) are different operations within a facility with individualized competitive priorities, processes, and workforces under the same roof. Boundaries for PWPs may be established by physically separating subunits or simply by revising organizational relationships. At each PWP, customization, capital intensity volume, and other relationships are crucial and must be complementary. The advantages of PWPs are fewer layers of management, greater ability to rely on team problem solving, and shorter lines of communication between departments.

plants within plants (PWPs)

Different operations within a facility with individualized competitive priorities, processes, and workforces under the same roof.

Focused Service Operations   Service industries also implement the concepts of focus and PWPs. Specialty retailers opened stores with smaller, more accessible spaces. These focused facilities generally chipped away at the business of large department stores. Using the same philosophy,

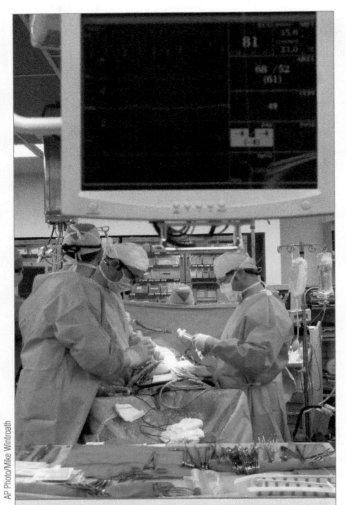

AP Photo/Mike Wintroath

Focused factories are not just found in manufacturing. This single-speciality facility focuses just on heart surgery and has all of the advanced resources needed that cannot be provided by a general hospital. Another example is the Toronto-based Shouldice Clinic, which focuses just on hernias.

some department stores now focus on specific customers or products. Remodeled stores create the effect of many small boutiques under one roof.

Focused Factories   Hewlett-Packard, Rolls-Royce, Japan's Ricoh and Mitsubishi, and Britain's Imperial Chemical Industries PLC are some of the firms that created **focused factories**, splitting large plants that produced all the company's products into several specialized smaller plants. The theory is that narrowing the range of demands on a facility will lead to better performance because management can concentrate on fewer tasks and lead a workforce toward a single goal.

Strategies for Change

The four major process decisions represent broad, strategic issues. Decisions that are made must be translated into actual process designs or redesigns. We conclude with two different but complementary philosophies for process design: (1) process reengineering and (2) process improvement.

Process Reengineering

Reengineering is the fundamental rethinking and radical redesign of processes to improve performance dramatically in terms of cost, quality, service, and speed. Process reengineering is about reinvention, rather than incremental improvement. It is strong medicine and not always needed or successful. Pain, in the form of layoffs and large cash outflows for investments in information technology, almost always accompanies massive change. However, reengineering processes can have big payoffs. Table 2.4 lists the key elements of the overall approach.

Reengineering has led to many successes and will continue to do so. However, it is not simple or easily done, nor is it appropriate for all processes or all organizations. The best understanding of a process, and how to improve it, often lies with the people who perform the work each day, not with cross-functional teams or top management.

focused factories

The result of a firm's splitting large plants that produced all the company's products into several specialized smaller plants.

reengineering

The fundamental rethinking and radical redesign of processes to improve performance dramatically in terms of cost, quality, service, and speed.

TABLE 2.4 | KEY ELEMENTS OF REENGINEERING

Element	Description
Critical processes	The emphasis of reengineering should be on core business processes. Normal process-improvement activities can be continued with the other processes.
Strong leadership	Senior executives must provide strong leadership for reengineering to be successful. Otherwise, cynicism, resistance ("we tried that before"), and boundaries between departments can block radical changes.
Cross-functional teams	A team, consisting of members from each functional area affected by the process change, is charged with carrying out a reengineering project. Self-managing teams and employee empowerment are the rule rather than the exception.
Information technology	Information technology is a primary enabler of process engineering. Most reengineering projects design processes around information flows, such as customer order fulfillment.
Clean-slate philosophy	Reengineering requires a "clean-slate" philosophy—that is, starting with the way the customer wants to deal with the company. To ensure a customer orientation, teams begin with internal and external customer objectives for the process.
Process analysis	Despite the clean-slate philosophy, a reengineering team must understand things about the current process: what it does, how well it performs, and what factors affect it. The team must look at every procedure involved in the process throughout the organization.

Process Improvement

Process improvement is the systematic study of the activities and flows of each process to improve it. Its purpose is to "learn the numbers," understand the process, and dig out the details. Once a process is really understood, it can be improved. The relentless pressure to provide better quality at a lower price means that companies must continually review all aspects of their operations. Process improvement goes on, whether or not a process is reengineered. There is always a better way.

An individual or a whole team examines the process, using the tools described in the next chapter. One must look for ways to streamline tasks, eliminate whole processes entirely, cut expensive materials or services, improve the environment, or make jobs safer. One must find the ways to trim costs and delays and to improve customer satisfaction.

process improvement
The systematic study of the activities and flows of each process to improve it.

LEARNING GOALS IN REVIEW

1 **Explain why processes exist everywhere in all organizations.** The "Process Strategy Across the Organization" section, pp. 32–33, demonstrates that supply chain process exist throughout the supply chain and actually exist in all places throughout the organization. Pay particular attention to Tables 2.1 and 2.2.

2 **Discuss the four major process decisions.** The "Process Strategy Decisions" section, pp. 33–34, identifies the four key decisions around which we develop a vocabulary for understanding operations. Figure 2.1 shows how they interact in creating an effective process design.

3 **Position a process on the customer-contact matrix or product-process matrix.** The Customer-Contact Matrix for service processes in Figure 2.2 shows how the degree of customer contact and customization are linked with process divergence and line flows. Three natural positions emerge: the front office, hybrid office, and back office. In manufacturing, the key drivers are customization and volume, which are linked with line flows and the extent of repetitive work. Figure 2.3 shows these relationships in the form of the Product-Process Matrix, with natural positions ranging from the job process to the continuous flow process.

4 **Configure operations into layouts.** The "Layout" section, pp. 39–42, puts the process structure into a physical form by showing here each operation is located within the facility.

Example 2.1 shows how to develop a block plan, and evaluate it with the help of the *Layout* Solver of OM Explorer. See Solved Problem 2.1 for another example.

5 **Define customer involvement, resource flexibility, capital intensity, and economies of scope.** These topics are covered in the "Customer Involvement," "Resource Flexibility," "Capital Intensity," and "Economies of Scope" sections on pp. 42–46. Note that customer involvement has advantages and disadvantages, resource flexibility applies to both workforce and equipment, and economies of scope in certain situations can break the inverse relationship between resource flexibility and capital intensity.

6 **Discuss how process decisions should fit together.** The "Strategic Fit" section, pp. 46–50, describes how the four major process decisions should tie together. Figures 2.8 and 2.9 show the decision patterns in pictorial form. The section concludes with a way to achieve these patterns by gaining focus, either with focused factories or gaining focus by process segments.

7 **Define process reengineering and process improvement.** The "Strategies for Change," pp. 50–51, describe both approaches to finding better process designs. Table 2.4 gives the key elements of reengineering. Process improvement is more of an incremental approach which uses the tools described in the next chapter.

MyOMLab helps you develop analytic skills and assesses your progress with multiple problems on the break-even analysis in choosing between two different processes, the weighted-distance method, and layout.

MyOMLab Resources	Titles	Link to the Book
Videos	*King Soopers Bakery: Process Choice*	Manufacturing Process Structuring
	Process Choice: Pearson Education Information Technology	Capital Intensity
OM Explorer Solver	Layout	Layout
OM Explorer Tutors	2.1 Distance Measures	Applying the Weighted-Distance Method Example 2.1 (pp. 41–42)
	2.2 Breakeven for Equipment Selection	Resource Flexibility Figure 2.7 (p. 44)
POM for Windows: Layout	Layout	Example 2.1 (pp. 41–42)

MyOMLab Resources	Titles	Link to the Book
Tutor Exercises	2.1—Mt. Mudge	Applying the Weighted-Distance Method Example 2.1 (pp. 41–42)
	2.2—Break-Even for Equipment Selection	Resource Flexibility Figure 2.7 (p. 44)
SmartDraw	Often used to prepare detailed layouts and floor plans	Detailed Layout
Virtual Tours	1. Leannie Company Doll Factory 2. LA Aluminum Casting Company	Process Choice; Production and Inventory Strategy Process Choice; Production and Inventory Strategy
Internet Exercises	2.1—United Parcel Service 2.2—Carnival and Twilight 2.3—Timbuk2	Service Strategy; Customer Involvement
Advanced Problems	2.1 CCI Electronics 2.2 Getwell Hospital	Layout Layout
Additional Cases	Car Lube Operations Hightech, Inc. The Pizza Connection Bill's Hardware The Big Picture: Process Choice at King Soopers Bakery	Layout Layout Design a Detailed layout Capital Intensity Manufacturing Process Structuring
Key Equations		
Image Library		

Key Equations

1. Euclidean distance: $d_{AB} = \sqrt{(x_A - x_B)^2 + (y_A - y_B)^2}$
2. Rectilinear distance: $d_{AB} = |x_A - x_B| + |y_A - y_B|$

Key Terms

assemble-to-order strategy 38
automation 45
back office 36
batch process 38
block plan 40
capital intensity 34
closeness matrix 40
continuous flow process 38
customer contact 35
customer involvement 34
economies of scope 46
Euclidean distance 41
fixed automation 45
flexible (or programmable) automation 45
flexible flow 35

flexible workforce 44
focused factories 50
front office 36
hybrid office 36
industrial robot 45
job process 37
layout 34
line flow 36
line process 38
make-to-order strategy 38
make-to-stock strategy 39
mass customization 39
mass production 39

plants within plants (PWPs) 49
postponement 38
process choice 37
process divergence 35
process improvement 51
process strategy 32
process structure 34
rectilinear distance 41
reengineering 50
resource flexibility 34
supply chain processes 33
weighted-distance method 40

Solved Problem 1

A defense contractor is evaluating its machine shop's current layout. Figure 2.11 shows the current layout, and the table shows the closeness matrix for the facility measured as the number of trips per day between department pairs. Safety and health regulations require departments E and F to remain at their current locations.

	TRIPS BETWEEN DEPARTMENTS					
Department	**A**	**B**	**C**	**D**	**E**	**F**
A	—	8	3		9	5
B		—		3		
C			—		8	9
D				—		3
E					—	3
F						—

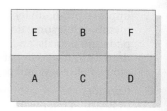

▲ FIGURE 2.11
Current Layout

a. Use trial and error to find a better layout.

b. How much better is your layout than the current layout in terms of the *wd* score? Use rectilinear distance.

SOLUTION

a. In addition to keeping departments E and F at their current locations, a good plan would locate the following department pairs close to each other: A and E, C and F, A and B, and C and E. Figure 2.12 was worked out by trial and error and satisfies all these requirements. Start by placing E and F at their current locations. Then, because C must be as close as possible to both E and F, put C between them. Place A below E, and B next to A. All of the heavy traffic concerns have now been accommodated. Department D, located in the remaining space, does not need to be relocated.

▲ FIGURE 2.12
Proposed Layout

Department Pair	Number of Trips (1)	CURRENT PLAN		PROPOSED PLAN	
		Distance (2)	*wd* Score (1) × (2)	Distance (3)	*wd* Score (1) × (3)
A, B	8	2	16	1	8
A, C	3	1	3	2	6
A, E	9	1	9	1	9
A, F	5	3	15	3	15
B, D	3	2	6	1	3
C, E	8	2	16	1	8
C, F	9	2	18	1	9
D, F	3	1	3	1	3
E, F	3	2	6	2	6
			wd = 92		*wd* = 67

b. The table reveals that the *wd* score drops from 92 for the current plan to 67 for the revised plan, a 27 percent reduction.

Discussion Questions

1. What processes at manufacturing firms are really service processes that involve considerable customer contact? Can customer contact be high, even if the process only has internal customers?

2. Consider this sign seen in a local restaurant: "To-go orders do NOT include complimentary chips and salsa. If you have any questions, see our management, NOT our employees." What impact does this message have on its employees, their service processes, and customer satisfaction? Contrast this approach with the one taken by a five-star restaurant. Are the differences primarily due to different competitive priorities?

3. How do the process strategies of eBay and McDonald's differ, and how do their choices relate to customer-introduced variability?

4. Medical technology can outfit a patient with an artificial heart, or cure vision defects with the touch of a laser. However, hospitals still struggle with their back-office processes, such as getting X-ray files from radiology on the fourth floor to the first-floor view boxes in the emergency room without having to send a runner. More than 90 percent of the estimated 30 billion health transactions each year are conducted by telephone, fax, or mail. To what extent, and how, can information technology

improve productivity and quality for such processes? Remember that some doctors are not ready to give up their pads and pencils, and many hospitals have strong lines drawn around its departments, such as pharmacy, cardiology, radiology, and pediatrics.

5. Consider the range of processes in the financial services industry. What position on the customer-contact matrix would the process of selling financial services to municipalities occupy? The process of preparing monthly fund balance reports? Explain why they would differ.

6. Performance criteria important in creating a layout can go well beyond communication and materials handling. Identify the types of layout performance criteria that might be most important in the following settings.

   a. Airport

   b. Bank

   c. Classroom

   d. Product designers' office

   e. Law firm

7. Rate operators at a call center, who respond to queries from customers who call in about the company's product, on each of the five dimensions of customer contact in Table 2.3. Use a seven-point scale, where 1 = very low and 7 = very high. For example, the operators newer are physically present with the customer, and so they would get a score of 1 for physical presence. Explain your ratings, and then calculate a combined score for the overall customer contact. Did you use equal weights in calculating the combined score? Why or why not? Where is your process positioned on the customer-contact matrix? Is it properly aligned? Why or why not?

8. Select one of the three processes shown in the MyOMLab's video for King Soopers (bread, pastry, or custom cakes). What kind of transformation process, process choice, and inventory strategy are involved? Is the process properly aligned? Explain.

Problems

The OM Explorer and POM for Windows software is available to all students using the 10th edition of this textbook. Go to **www.pearsonhighered.com/krajewski** to download these computer packages. If you purchased MyOMLab, you also have access to Active Models software and significant help in doing the following problems. Check with your instructor on how best to use these resources. In many cases, the instructor wants you to understand how to do the calculations by hand. At the least, the software provides a check on your calculations. When calculations are particularly complex and the goal is interpreting the results in making decision, the software entirely replaces the manual calculations.

Problems 1 and 2 apply break-even analysis to process decisions.

1. Dr. Gulakowicz is an orthodontist. She estimates that adding two new chairs will increase fixed costs by $150,000, including the annual equivalent cost of the capital investment and the salary of one more technician. Each new patient is expected to bring in $3,000 per year in additional revenue, with variable costs estimated at $1,000 per patient. The two new chairs will allow Dr. Gulakowicz to expand her practice by as many as 200 patients annually. How many patients would have to be added for the new process to break even?

2. Two different manufacturing processes are being considered for making a new product. The first process is less capital-intensive, with fixed costs of only $50,000 per year and variable costs of $700 per unit. The second process has fixed costs of $400,000, but has variable costs of only $200 per unit.

   a. What is the break-even quantity, beyond which the second process becomes more attractive than the first?

   b. If the expected annual sales for the product is 800 units, which process would you choose?

3. Baker Machine Company is a job shop that specializes in precision parts for firms in the aerospace industry. Figure 2.13 shows the current block plan for the key manufacturing centers of the 75,000-square-foot facility. Refer to the following closeness matrix and use rectilinear

distance (the current distance from inspection to shipping and receiving is three units) to calculate the change in the weighted distance, wd, score if Baker exchanges the locations of the tool crib and inspection.

CLOSENESS MATRIX

Department	Trips Between Departments					
	1	2	3	4	5	6
1. Burr and grind	—	8	3		9	5
2. Numerically controlled (NC) equipment		—	3			
3. Shipping and receiving			—		8	9
4. Lathes and drills				—		3
5. Tool crib					—	3
6. Inspection						—

3	4	2
1	5	6

◀ **FIGURE 2.13**
Current Layout

4. Baker Machine (see Problem 3) is considering two alternative layouts. Compare the wd scores using rectilinear distance of the following two block plans to determine which alternative layout is better.

3	6	4
5	1	2

◀ **FIGURE 2.13(a)**
Alternative Layout 1

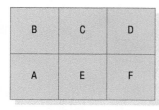

FIGURE 2.13(b)
Alternative Layout 2

5. The head of the information systems group at Conway Consulting must assign six new analysts to offices. The following closeness matrix shows the expected frequency of contact between analysts. The block plan in Figure 2.14 shows the available office locations (1–6) for the six analysts (A–F). Assume equal-sized offices and rectilinear distance.

CLOSENESS MATRIX

Analyst		Contacts Between Analysts				
	A	B	C	D	E	F
Analyst A	—		6			
Analyst B		—	12			
Analyst C			—	2	7	
Analyst D				—		4
Analyst E					—	
Analyst F						—

FIGURE 2.14
Conway Consulting's Block Plan

Evaluate the *wd* scores of the following three alternative layouts, again assuming rectilinear distance, and determine which is best.

FIGURE 2.14(a)
Alternative Layout 1

FIGURE 2.14(b)
Alternative Layout 2

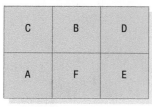

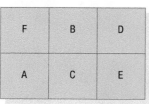

FIGURE 2.14(c)
Alternative Layout 3

6. Richard Garber is the head designer for Matthews and Novak Design Company. Garber has been called in to design the layout for a newly constructed office building. From statistical samplings over the past three months, Garber developed the following closeness matrix for daily trips between the department's offices.

CLOSENESS MATRIX

Department		Trips Between Departments				
	A	B	C	D	E	F
A	—	25	90			185
B		—			105	
C			—		125	125
D				—	25	
E					—	105
F						—

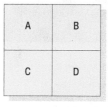

FIGURE 2.15
Alternative Block Plan

a. If other factors are equal, which two offices should be located closest together?

b. Figure 2.15 shows an alternative layout for the department. What is the total weighted-distance score for this plan based on rectilinear distance and assuming that offices A and B are three units of distance apart?

c. Use the explicit enumeration method of the POM for Windows software to find the block plan that minimize the total weighted-distance score.

7. A firm with four departments has the following closeness matrix and the current block plan shown in Figure 2.16.

a. What is the weighted-distance score for the current layout (assuming rectilinear distance)?

CLOSENESS MATRIX

Department		Trips Between Departments		
	A	B	C	D
A	—	12	10	8
B		—	20	6
C			—	0
D				—

FIGURE 2.16
Current Block Plan

b. Develop a better layout. What is its total weighted-distance score?

8. The department of engineering at a university in New Jersey must assign six faculty members to their new offices. The following closeness matrix indicates the expected number of contacts per day between professors. The available office spaces (1–6) for the six faculty members are shown in Figure 2.17. Assume equal-sized offices. The distance between offices 1 and 2 (and between offices 1 and 3) is 1 unit, whereas the distance between offices 1 and 4 is 2 units.

CLOSENESS MATRIX

Professor	Contacts Between Professors					
	A	B	C	D	E	F
A	—		4			
B		—	12			10
C			—	2	7	
D				—		4
E					—	
F						—

a. Because of their academic positions, Professor A must be assigned to office 1, Professor C must be assigned to office 2, and Professor D must be assigned to office 6. Which faculty members should be assigned to offices 3, 4, and 5, respectively, to minimize the total weighted-distance score (assuming rectilinear distance)?

b. What is the weighted-distance score of your solution?

◀ **FIGURE 2.17**
Available Space

Active Model Exercise

This Active Model for Example 2.1 appears in MyOMLab. It allows you to see the effects of performing paired swaps of departments.

QUESTIONS

1. What is the current total weighted-distance score?

2. Use the swap button one swap at a time. If the swap helps, move to the next pair. If the swap does not help, hit the swap button once again to put the departments back. What is the minimum weighted-distance score after all swaps have been tried?

3. Look at the two data tables, and use the yellow-shaded column to put departments in spaces. What space assignments lead to the minimum cost? What is this cost?

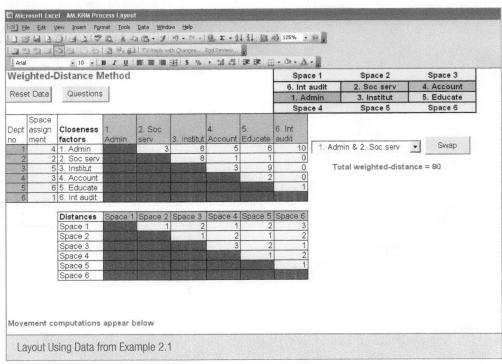

Layout Using Data from Example 2.1

CASE | Custom Molds, Inc.

Custom Molds, Inc., manufactures custom-designed molds for plastic parts and produces custom-made plastic connectors for the electronics industry. Located in Tucson, Arizona, Custom Molds was founded by the father-and-son-team of Tom and Mason Miller in 1987. Tom Miller, a mechanical engineer, had more than 20 years of experience in the connector industry with AMP, Inc., a large multinational producer of electronic connectors. Mason Miller graduated from the Arizona State University in 1986 with joint degrees in chemistry and chemical engineering.

The company was originally formed to provide manufacturers of electronic connectors with a source of high-quality, custom-designed molds for producing plastic parts. The market consisted mainly of the product design and development divisions of those manufacturers. Custom Molds worked closely with each customer to design and develop molds to be used in the customer's product development processes. Thus, virtually every mold had to meet exacting standards and was somewhat unique. Orders for multiple molds would arrive when customers moved from the design and pilot-run stage of development to large-scale production of newly designed parts.

As the years went by, Custom Molds's reputation grew as a designer and fabricator of precision molds. Building on this reputation, the Millers decided to expand into the limited manufacture of plastic parts. Ingredient-mixing facilities and injection-molding equipment were added, and by the mid-1990s, Custom Molds developed its reputation to include being a supplier of high-quality plastic parts. Because of limited capacity, the company concentrated its sales efforts on supplying parts that were used in limited quantities for research and development efforts and in preproduction pilot runs.

Production Processes

By 2000, operations at Custom Molds involved two distinct processes: one for fabricating molds and one for producing plastic parts. Although different, in many instances these two processes were linked, as when a customer would have Custom Molds both fabricate a mold and produce the necessary parts to support the customer's research and design efforts. All fabrication and production operations were housed in a single facility. The layout was characteristic of a typical job shop, with like processes and similar equipment grouped in various places in the plant. Figure 2.18 shows a layout of the plant floor. Multiple pieces of various types of high-precision machinery,

Dock		Dock
Receiving raw materials inventory	Lunch room	Packing and shipping finished goods inventory
Dry mix	Cut and trim	
Wet mix		Testing and inspection
Assembly	Injection machines	
Offices	Mold fabrication	

▲ **FIGURE 2.18**
Plant Layout

including milling, turning, cutting, and drilling equipment, were located in the mold-fabrication area.

Fabricating molds is a skill-oriented, craftsman-driven process. When an order is received, a design team, comprising a design engineer and one of 13 master machinists, reviews the design specifications. Working closely with the customer, the team establishes the final specifications for the mold and gives them to the master machinist for fabrication. It is always the same machinist who was assigned to the design team. At the same time, the purchasing department is given a copy of the design specifications, from which it orders the appropriate raw materials and special tooling. The time needed to receive the ordered materials is usually three to four weeks. When the materials are received for a particular mold, the plant master scheduler reviews the workload of the assigned master machinist and schedules the mold for fabrication.

Fabricating a mold takes from two to four weeks, depending on the amount of work the machinist already has scheduled. The fabrication process itself takes only three to five days. Upon completion, the mold is sent to the testing and inspection area, where it is used to produce a small number of parts on one of the injection molding machines. If the parts meet the design specifications established by the design team, the mold is passed on to be cleaned and polished. It is then packed and shipped to the customer. One day is spent inspecting and testing the mold and a second day cleaning, polishing, packing, and shipping it to the customer. If the parts made by the mold do not meet design specifications, the mold is returned to the master machinist for retooling and the process starts over. Currently, Custom Molds has a published lead time of nine weeks for delivery of custom-fabricated molds.

The manufacturing process for plastic parts is somewhat different from that for mold fabrication. An order for parts may be received in conjunction with an order for a mold to be fabricated. In instances where Custom Molds has previously fabricated the mold and maintains it in inventory, an order may be just for parts. If the mold is already available, the order is reviewed by a design engineer, who verifies the part and raw material specifications. If the design engineer has any questions concerning the specifications, the customer is contacted and any revisions to specifications are mutually worked out and agreed upon.

Upon acceptance of the part and raw material specifications, raw material orders are placed and production is scheduled for the order. Chemicals and compounds that support plastic-parts manufacturing are typically ordered and received within one week. Upon receipt, the compounds are first dry-mixed and blended to achieve the correct composition. Then, the mixture is wet-mixed to the desired consistency (called *slurry*) for injection into molding machines. When ready, the slurry is transferred to the injection molding area by an overhead pipeline and deposited in holding tanks adjacent to the injection machines. The entire mixing process takes only one day.

When the slurry is staged and ready, the proper molds are secured—from inventory or from the clean and polish operation if new molds were fabricated for the order—and the parts are manufactured. Although different parts require different temperature and pressure settings, the time to produce a part is relatively constant. Custom Molds has the capacity to produce 5,000 parts per day in the injection-molding department; historically, however, the lead time for handling orders in this department has averaged one week. Upon completion of molding, the parts are taken to the cut and trim operation, where they are disconnected and leftover flashing is removed. After being inspected, the parts may be taken to assembly or transferred to the packing and shipping area for shipment to the customer. If assembly of the final parts is not required, the parts can be on their way to the customer two days after being molded.

Sometimes, the final product requires some assembly. Typically, this entails attaching metal leads to plastic connectors. If assembly is necessary, an additional three days are needed before the order can be shipped. Custom Molds is currently quoting a three-week lead time for parts not requiring fabricated molds.

The Changing Environment

In early 2009, Tom and Mason Miller began to realize that the electronics industry they supplied, along with their own business, was changing. Electronics manufacturers had traditionally manufactured their own component parts to reduce costs and ensure a timely supply of parts. By the 1990s, this trend had changed. Manufacturers were developing strategic partnerships with parts suppliers to ensure the timely delivery of high-quality, cost-effective parts. This approach allowed funds to be diverted to other uses that could provide a larger return on investment.

The impact on Custom Molds could be seen in sales figures over the past three years. The sales mix was changing. Although the number of orders per year for mold fabrication remained virtually constant, orders for multiple molds were declining, as shown in the following table:

	NUMBER OF ORDERS		
Order Size	**Molds 2006**	**Molds 2007**	**Molds 2008**
1	80	74	72
2	60	70	75
3	40	51	55
4	5	6	5
5	3	5	4
6	4	8	5
7	2	0	1
8	10	6	4
9	11	8	5
10	15	10	5
Total orders	230	238	231

The reverse was true for plastic parts, for which the number of orders per year had declined, but for which the order sizes were becoming larger, as illustrated in the following table:

	NUMBER OF ORDERS		
Order Size	**Parts 2006**	**Parts 2007**	**Parts 2008**
50	100	93	70
100	70	72	65
150	40	30	35
200	36	34	38
250	25	27	25
500	10	12	14
750	1	3	5
1,000	2	2	8
3,000	1	4	9
5,000	1	3	8
Total orders	286	280	277

During this same period, Custom Molds began having delivery problems. Customers were complaining that parts orders were taking four to five weeks instead of the stated three weeks and that the delays were disrupting production schedules. When asked about the situation, the master scheduler said that determining when a particular order could be promised for delivery was difficult. Bottlenecks were occurring during the production process, but where or when they would occur could not be predicted. The bottlenecks always seemed to be moving from one operation to another.

Tom Miller thought that he had excess labor capacity in the mold-fabrication area. So, to help push through those orders that were behind schedule, he assigned one of the master machinists the job of identifying and expediting those late orders. However, that tactic did not seem to help much. Complaints about late deliveries were still being received. To add to the problems, two orders had been returned recently because of the number of defective parts. The Millers knew that something had to be done. The question was "What?"

QUESTIONS

1. What are the major issues facing Tom and Mason Miller?
2. What are the competitive priorities for Custom Molds's processes and the changing nature of the industry?
3. What alternatives might the Millers pursue? What key factors should they consider as they evaluate these alternatives?

Source: This case was prepared by Dr. Brooke Saladin, Wake Forest University, as a basis for classroom discussion. Copyright © Brooke Saladin. Used with permission.

Selected References

Brink, Harold, Senthiah, and Rajan Naik. "A Better Way to Automate Service Operations." *McKinsey on Business Technology*, no. 20 (Summer, 2010), pp. 1–10.

Baghai, Ramin, Edward H. Levine, and Saumya S. Sutaria. "Service-Line Strategies for US Hospitals." *The McKinsey Quarterly* (July 2008), pp. 1–9.

Booth, Alan. "The Management of Technical Change: Automation in the UK and USA since 1950." *The Economic History Review*, vol. 62, no. 2 (May 2009), pp. 493–494.

Chase, Richard B. and Uday M. Apte. "A History of Research in Service Operations: What's the Big Idea?" *Journal of Operations Management*, vol. 25 (2007), pp. 375–386.

Fisher, Marshall L. "Bob Hayes: Forty Years of Leading Operations Management Into Uncharted Waters." *Production and Operations Management*, vol. 16, no. 2, (March–April 2007), pp. 159–168.

Grover, Varun, and Manoj K. Malhotra. "Business Process Reengineering: A Tutorial on the Concept, Evolution, Method, Technology, and Application." *Journal of Operations Management*, vol. 15, no. 3 (1997), pp. 194–213.

Hayes, Robert. "Operations, Strategy, and Technology: Pursuing the Competitive Edge." *Strategic Direction,* vol. 22, no. 7, (2006).

Johansson, Pontus and Jan Olhger. "Linking Product-Process Matrices for Manufacturing and Industrial Service Operations." *International Journal of Production Economics*, vol. 104 (2006), pp. 615–624.

Hammer, Michael. "Deep Change: How Operational Innovation Can Transform Your Company." *Harvard Business Review*, vol. 82, no. 4 (April 2004), pp. 85–93.

Hill, Terry. *Manufacturing Strategy: Text and Cases*, 3rd ed. Homewood, IL: Irwin/McGraw-Hill, 2000.

Jack, Eric, and John Collis. "Strengthen and Tone: A Flexible Approach to Operations Can Build Some Serious Muscle." *APICS Magazine* (June 2006), pp. 35–38.

Kung, Peter and Claus Hagen. "The Fruits of Business Process Management: An Experience Report from a Swiss Bank." *Business Process Management Journal*, vol. 13, no. 4 (2007), pp. 477–487.

Malhotra, Manoj K., and Larry P. Ritzman. "Resource Flexibility Issues in Multistage Manufacturing." *Decision Sciences*, vol. 21, no. 4 (1990), pp. 673–690.

Metters, Richard, Kathryn King-Metters, and Madeleine Pullman. *Successful Service Operations Management.* Mason, OH: South-Western, 2003.

Prajogo, Daniel. "The Implementation of Operations Management Techniques in Service Organisations." *International Journal of Operations & Production Management*, vol. 26, No. 12 (2006), pp. 1374–1390.

Rayport, Jeffrey F., and Bernard J. Jaworski. "Best Face Forward." *Harvard Business Review*, vol. 82, no. 12 (2003), pp. 47–58.

Safizadeh, M. Hossein, Joy M. Field, and Larry P. Ritzman. "An Empirical Analysis of Financial Services Processes with a Front-Office or Back-Office Orientation." *Journal of Operations Management*, vol. 21, no. 5 (2003), pp. 557–576.

Safizadeh, M. Hossein, Larry P. Ritzman, and Debasish Mallick. "Revisiting Alternative Theoretical Paradigms in Manufacturing." *Production and Operations Management*, vol. 9, no. 2 (2000), pp. 111–127.

Sehgal, Sanjay, B.S. Sahay, and S.K. Goyal. "Reengineering the Supply Chain in a Paint Company." *International Journal of Productivity and Performance Management*, vol. 55, no. 8 (2006), pp. 655–670.

Skinner, Wickham. "Operations Technology: Blind Spot in Strategic Management." *Interfaces*, vol. 14 (January–February 1984), pp. 116–125.

Swink, Morgan and Anand Nair. "Capturing the Competitive Advantages of AMT: Design-Manufacturing Integration as a Complementary Asset." *Journal of Operations Management*, vol. 25 (2007), pp. 736–754.

Zomerdijk, Leonieke G. and Jan de Vries. "Structuring Front Office and Back Office Work in Service Delivery Systems." *International Journal of Operations & Production Management*, vol. 27, no. 1 (2007), pp. 108–131.

A Motorola Droid phone displayed Google's homepage in Washington, D.C. on August 15, 2011. Google Inc. bought the phone manufacturer Motorola Mobility for $12.5 billion. Motorola considerably improved its demand forecasting process, with payoffs in how it managed its supply chain.

Motorola Mobility

Motorola Mobility makes mobile phone handsets, smartphones, tablets, and cable set-top box assets. In the early 2000s, Motorola's leadership and market share were eroding. Motorola realized that it must transform its supply chain, and embarked on a major initiative to tighten communications and collaboration along its supply chain. It put collaborative planning, forecasting, and replenishment (*CPFR*) into action in 2002. The payoff has been significant.

Motorola sells over 120 handset models globally. Forecasting how many of which models to make and sell is difficult, and accurate replenishment of retailers' shelves is critical. If a customer's favorite handset is not in stock, there is a real risk that Motorola loses that customer for life, and not just for the next service contract. Approximately one half of all stockouts result in lost sales. To make matters worse, a phone model can have multiple SKUs, life cycles average little more than a year, and new product introductions are rapid.

Prior to adopting CPFR, Motorola Mobile's sales were highly variable and were not synchronized with customer demand. Motorola had visibility only for its shipments to retailers' distribution centers, but not for shipments from the retailers' distribution centers to the stores. Knowing what retailers are selling is much more valuable information in forecasting future demand than knowing what retailers are buying. Without this information, forecast errors were very high, resulting in excessive stockouts. CPFR enabled Motorola to collaborate with its retailers' distribution centers' customers and increase its ability to forecast effectively. Motorola launched an organization-wide shift to customer-focused operations teams. They shared with their retailers their real-time data and plans, including forecasts, inventories, sales to retailers' shelves, promotions, product plans, and exceptions. Traditionally, suppliers and buyers in most supply chains prepare independent demand forecasts.

Before CPFR, the retailers' forecasts were developed at the end of the second week of each month while Motorola's assembled its sales and operations plan earlier in the second week. Motorola convinced the retailer to move up its planning cycle by just two or three days, which eliminated a seven-week forecast lag resulting from the forecast not being incorporated until the next month's planning cycle. Now, the retailer loads its forecasts for the next month on Monday. On Tuesday, Motorola loads its forecast. During the weekly call on Wednesday, the two teams jointly resolve discrepancies line-by-line. The inclusion of a forecasting analyst means they can immediately resolve issues arising from the discrepancies.

The real key to a successful implementation of CPFR is the forging of a cultural alliance that involves peer-to peer relations and cross-functional teams. Prior to CPFR, retailers sometimes gave Motorola "C," "D," and "F" rating on metrics such as on-time delivery, ease of doing business, and stockouts. After CPFR, they give Motorola "A" ratings. Motorola's CPFR initiative reduced forecast error to a fraction of its previous level, allowed quick reductions in safety stock, cut transportation costs in half because of fewer less-than-truckload shipments, and cut stockouts to less than a third of previous levels. Such success is one reason Google paid big ($12.5 billion) to buy Motorola's cellphone business in August 2011.

Source: Jerold P. Cederlund, Rajiv Kohli, Susan A. Sherer, and Yuliang Yao, "How Motorola Put CPFR into Action," *Supply Chain Management Review* (October 2007), pp. 28–35; Sharyn Leaver, Patrick Connaughton, and Elisse Gaynor, "Case Study: Motorola's Quest for Supply Chain Excellence," *Forrester Research, Inc.* (October, 2006), pp. 1–12, **www .motorola.com**, April 29, 2011; Amir Efrati and Spencer A. Ante, "Google's $12.5 Billion Gamble," *The Wall Street Journal*, August 12, 2011.

LEARNING GOALS *After reading this chapter, you should be able to:*

1 Identify the five basic patterns of most demand time series.

2 Identify the various measures of forecast errors.

3 Use regression to make forecasts with one or more independent variables.

4 Make forecasts using the most common approaches for time-series analysis.

5 Make forecasts using trend projection with regression.

6 Describe a typical forecasting process used by businesses.

7 Explain collaborative planning, forecasting, and replenishment (CPFR).

---

forecast

A prediction of future events used for planning purposes.

Balancing supply and demand begins with making accurate forecasts, and then reconciling them across the supply chain as shown by Motorola Mobility. A **forecast** is a prediction of future events used for planning purposes. Planning, on the other hand, is the process of making management decisions on how to deploy resources to best respond to the demand forecasts. Forecasting methods may be based on mathematical models that use available historical data, or on qualitative methods that draw on managerial experience and judgments, or on a combination of both.

In this chapter, our focus is on demand forecasts. We begin with different types of demand patterns. We examine forecasting methods in three basic categories: (1) judgment, (2) causal, and (3) time-series methods. Forecast errors are defined, providing important clues for making better forecasts. We next consider the forecasting techniques themselves, and then how they can be combined to bring together insights from several sources. We conclude with overall processes for making forecasts and designing the forecasting system.

Forecasts are useful for both managing processes and managing supply chains. At the supply chain level, a firm needs forecasts to coordinate with its customers and suppliers. At the process level, output forecasts are needed to design the various processes throughout the organization, including identifying and dealing with in-house bottlenecks.

Forecasting across the Organization

The organization-wide forecasting process cuts across functional areas. Forecasting overall demand typically originates with marketing, but internal customers throughout the organization depend on forecasts to formulate and execute their plans as well. Forecasts are critical inputs to business plans, annual plans, and budgets. Finance needs forecasts to project cash flows and capital requirements. Human resources uses forecasts to anticipate hiring and training needs. Marketing is an important source for sales forecast information because it is closest to external customers. Operations and supply chain managers need forecasts to plan output levels, purchases of services and materials, workforce and output schedules, inventories, and long-term capacities.

Managers throughout the organization make forecasts on many variables other than future demand, such as competitor strategies, regulatory changes, technological changes, processing times, supplier lead times, and quality losses. Tools for making these forecasts are basically the same tools covered here for demand forecasting: judgment, opinions of knowledgeable people, averages of experience, regression, and time-series techniques. Using these tools, forecasting can be improved. Still, forecasts are rarely perfect. As Samuel Clemens (Mark Twain) said in *Following the Equator*, "Prophesy is a good line of business, but it is full of risks." Smart managers recognize this reality and find ways to update their plans when the inevitable forecast error or unexpected event occurs.

Demand Patterns

Forecasting customer demand is a difficult task because the demand for services and goods can vary greatly. For example, demand for lawn fertilizer predictably increases in the spring and summer months; however, the particular weekends when demand is heaviest may depend on uncontrollable factors such as the weather. Sometimes, patterns are more predictable. Thus, the peak hours of the day for a large bank's call center are from 9:00 A.M. to 12:00 P.M., and the peak day of the week is Monday. For its statement-rendering processes, the peak months are January, April, July, and October, which is when the quarterly statements are sent out. Forecasting demand in such situations requires uncovering the underlying patterns from available information. In this section, we discuss the basic patterns of demand.

The repeated observations of demand for a service or product in their order of occurrence form a pattern known as a **time series**. There are five basic patterns of most demand time series:

1. *Horizontal.* The fluctuation of data around a constant mean.
2. *Trend.* The systematic increase or decrease in the mean of the series over time.
3. *Seasonal.* A repeatable pattern of increases or decreases in demand, depending on the time of day, week, month, or season.
4. *Cyclical.* The less predictable gradual increases or decreases in demand over longer periods of time (years or decades).
5. *Random.* The unforecastable variation in demand.

Cyclical patterns arise from two influences. The first is the business cycle, which includes factors that cause the economy to go from recession to expansion over a number of years. The other influence is the service or product life cycle, which reflects the stages of demand from development through decline. Business cycle demand is difficult to predict because it is affected by national or international events.

The four patterns of demand—horizontal, trend, seasonal, and cyclical—combine in varying degrees to define the underlying time pattern of demand for a service or product. The fifth pattern, random variation, results from chance causes and thus, cannot be predicted. Random variation is an aspect of demand that makes every forecast ultimately inaccurate. Figure 3.1 shows the first four patterns of a demand time series, all of which contain random variations.

Creating Value through Operations Management

Using Operations to Compete
Project Management

Managing Processes

Process Strategy
Process Analysis
Quality and Performance
Capacity Planning
Constraint Management
Lean Systems

Managing Supply Chains

Supply Chain Inventory Management
Supply Chain Design
Supply Chain Location Decisions
Supply Chain Integration
Supply Chain Sustainability and Humanitarian Logistics
Forecasting
Operations Planning and Scheduling
Resource Planning

time series

The repeated observations of demand for a service or product in their order of occurrence.

FIGURE 3.1 ▶
Patterns of Demand

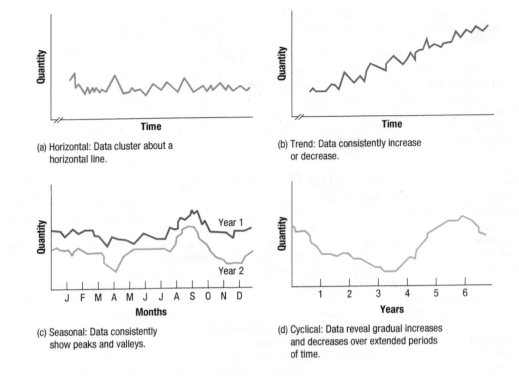

(a) Horizontal: Data cluster about a horizontal line.

(b) Trend: Data consistently increase or decrease.

(c) Seasonal: Data consistently show peaks and valleys.

(d) Cyclical: Data reveal gradual increases and decreases over extended periods of time.

Key Decisions on Making Forecasts

Before using forecasting techniques, a manager must make two decisions: (1) what to forecast, and (2) what type of forecasting technique to select for different items.

Deciding What to Forecast

Although some sort of demand estimate is needed for the individual services or goods produced by a company, forecasting total demand for groups or clusters and then deriving individual service or product forecasts may be easiest. Also, selecting the correct unit of measurement (e.g., service or product units or machine-hours) for forecasting may be as important as choosing the best method.

Level of Aggregation   Few companies err by more than 5 percent when forecasting the annual total demand for all their services or products. However, errors in forecasts for individual items and shorter time periods may be much higher. Recognizing this reality, many companies use a two-tier forecasting system. They first cluster (or "roll up") several similar services or products in a process called **aggregation**, making forecasts for families of services or goods that have similar demand requirements and common processing, labor, and materials requirements. Next, they derive forecasts for individual items, which are sometimes called stock-keeping units. A *stock-keeping unit (SKU)* is an individual item or product that has an identifying code and is held in inventory somewhere along the supply chain, such as in a distribution center.

> **aggregation**
>
> The act of clustering several similar services or products so that forecasts and plans can be made for whole families.

Units of Measurement   Rather than using dollars as the initial unit of measurement, forecasts often begin with service or product units, such as SKUs, express packages to deliver, or customers needing maintenance service or repairs for their cars. Forecasted units can then be translated to dollars by multiplying them by the unit price. If accurately forecasting demand for a service or product is not possible in terms of number of units, forecast the standard labor or machine-hours required of each of the critical resources.

Choosing the Type of Forecasting Technique

> **judgment methods**
>
> A forecasting method that translates the opinions of managers, expert opinions, consumer surveys, and salesforce estimates into quantitative estimates.

Forecasting systems offer a variety of techniques, and no one of them is best for all items and situations. The forecaster's objective is to develop a useful forecast from the information at hand with the technique that is appropriate for the different patterns of demand. Two general types of forecasting techniques are used: judgment methods and quantitative methods. **Judgment methods** translate the opinions of managers, expert opinions, consumer surveys, and salesforce estimates into quantitative estimates. Quantitative methods include causal methods, time-series analysis, and trend projection with regression. **Causal methods** use historical data on independent variables, such as promotional campaigns, economic conditions, and competitors' actions, to predict demand. **Time-series analysis** is a statistical approach that relies heavily on historical demand data to project the future size of demand and recognizes trends and seasonal patterns. **Trend projection using regression** is a hybrid between a time-series technique and the causal method.

Forecast Error

For any forecasting technique, it is important to measure the accuracy of its forecasts. Forecasts almost always contain errors. Random error results from unpredictable factors that cause the forecast to deviate from the actual demand. Forecasting analysts try to minimize forecast errors by selecting appropriate forecasting models, but eliminating all forms of errors is impossible.

Forecast error for a given period t is simply the difference found by subtracting the forecast from actual demand, or

$$E_t = D_t - F_t$$

where

$$E_t = \text{forecast error for period } t$$

$$D_t = \text{actual demand for period } t$$

$$F_t = \text{forecast for period } t$$

This equation (notice the alphabetical order with D_t coming before F_t) is the starting point for creating several measures of forecast error that cover longer periods of time. Figure 3.2 shows the output from the *Error Analysis* routine in Forecasting's dropdown menu of POM for Windows. Part (a) gives a big picture view of how well the forecast has been tracking the actual demand. Part (b) shows the detailed calculations needed to obtain the summary error terms. Finally, Part (c) gives the summary error measures summarized across all 10 time periods, as derived from Part (b).

The **cumulative sum of forecast errors (CFE)** measures the total forecast error:

$$\text{CFE} = \sum E_t$$

CFE is a cumulative sum. Figure 3.3(b) shows that it is the sum of the errors for all 10 periods. For any given period, it would be the sum of errors up through that period. For example, it would be -8 (or $-2-6$) for period 2. CFE is also called the *bias error* and results from consistent mistakes—the forecast is always too high or too low. This type of error typically causes the greatest disruption to planning efforts. For example, if a forecast is consistently lower than actual demand, the value of CFE will gradually get larger and larger. This increasingly large error indicates some systematic deficiency in the forecasting approach. The average forecast error, sometimes called the *mean bias*, is simply

$$\overline{E} = \frac{\text{CFE}}{n}$$

causal methods

A quantitative forecasting method that uses historical data on independent variables, such as promotional campaigns, economic conditions, and competitors' actions, to predict demand.

time-series analysis

A statistical approach that relies heavily on historical demand data to project the future size of demand and recognizes trends and seasonal patterns.

trend projection with regression

A forecasting model that is a hybrid between a time-series technique and the causal method.

forecast error

The difference found by subtracting the forecast from actual demand for a given period.

cumulative sum of forecast errors (CFE)

A measurement of the total forecast error that assesses the bias in a forecast.

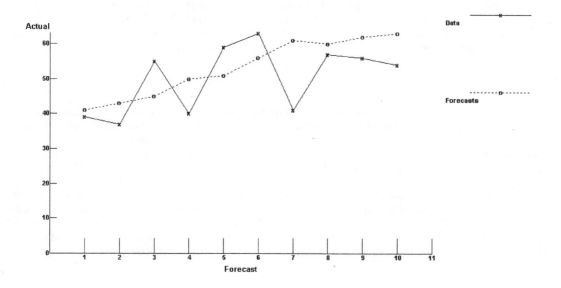

◄ **FIGURE 3.2(a)**
Graph of Actual and Forecast Demand Using *Error Analysis* of Forecasting in POM for Windows

▶ **FIGURE 3.2(b)**
Detailed Calculations of
Forecast Errors

		Forecast	Error	|Error|	Error^2	|Pct Error|
Past period 1	39	41	-2	2	4	5.128%
Past period 2	37	43	-6	6	36	16.216%
Past period 3	55	45	10	10	100	18.182%
Past period 4	40	50	-10	10	100	25%
Past period 5	59	51	8	8	64	13.559%
Past period 6	63	56	7	7	49	11.111%
Past period 7	41	61	-20	20	400	48.78%
Past period 8	57	60	-3	3	9	5.263%
Past period 9	56	62	-6	6	36	10.714%
Past period 10	54	63	-9	9	81	16.667%
TOTALS	501		-31	81	879	170.621%
AVERAGE	50.1		-3.1	8.1	87.9	17.062%
			(Bias)	(MAD)	(MSE)	(MAPE)
				Std dev	29.648	

mean squared error (MSE)

A measurement of the dispersion of forecast errors.

standard deviation (σ)

A measurement of the dispersion of forecast errors.

mean absolute deviation (MAD)

A measurement of the dispersion of forecast errors.

The **mean squared error (MSE)**, **standard deviation of the errors** (σ), and **mean absolute deviation (MAD)** measure the dispersion of forecast errors attributed to trend, seasonal, cyclical, or random effects:

$$MSE = \frac{\sum E_t^2}{n}$$

$$\sigma = \sqrt{\frac{\sum (E_t - \overline{E})^2}{n-1}}$$

$$MAD = \frac{\sum |E_t|}{n}$$

Figure 3.2(b) shows the squared error in period 1 is 4, and MSE is 87.9 for the whole sample. The standard deviation of the errors is calculated using one of the functions available in Excel and is not shown in Figure 3.2(b). The absolute value of the error in period 2 is 6, and MAD is 8.1 across the whole sample.

The mathematical symbol $|\ \ |$ is used to indicate the absolute value—that is, it tells you to disregard positive or negative signs. If MSE, σ, or MAD is small, the forecast is typically close to actual demand; by contrast, a large value indicates the possibility of large forecast errors. The measures do differ in the way they emphasize errors. Large errors get far more weight in MSE and σ because the errors are squared. MAD is a widely used measure of forecast error and is easily understood; it is merely the mean of the absolute forecast errors over a series of time periods, without regard to whether the error was an overestimate or an underestimate.

mean absolute percent error (MAPE)

A measurement that relates the forecast error to the level of demand and is useful for putting forecast performance in the proper perspective.

The **mean absolute percent error (MAPE)** relates the forecast error to the level of demand and is useful for putting forecast performance in the proper perspective:

$$MAPE = \frac{(\sum |E_t|/D_t)\,(100)}{n} \text{ (expressed as a percentage)}$$

For example, an absolute forecast error of 100 results in a larger percentage error when the demand is 200 units than when the demand is 10,000 units. MAPE is the best error measure to use when making comparisons between time series for different SKUs. Looking again at Figure 3.2(b), the percent error in period 2 is 16.22 percent, and MAPE, the average over all 10 periods, is 17.06 percent.

▼ **FIGURE 3.2(c)**
Error Measures

Measure	Value
Error Measures	
CFE (Cumulative Forecast Error)	-31
MAD (Mean Absolute Deviation)	8.1
MSE (Mean Squared Error)	87.9
Standard Deviation of Errors	29.648
MAPE (Mean Absolute Percent	17.062%

Finally, Figure 3.2(c) summarizes the key error terms across all 10 time periods. They are actually found in selected portions of Figure 3.2(b). For example, CFE is -31, which is in the error column of Figure 3.2(b) in the TOTALS row. MAD is 8.1, found in the |Error| column and AVERAGE row. Finally, | | is 17.06%, which is in the |Pct Error| column and AVERAGE row.

EXAMPLE 3.1	Calculating Forecast Error Measures

The following table shows the actual sales of upholstered chairs for a furniture manufacturer and the forecasts made for each of the last 8 months. Calculate CFE, MSE, σ, MAD, and MAPE for this product.

Month, t	Demand, D_t	Forecast, F_t	Error, E_t	Error, Squared, E_t^2	Absolute Error $|E_t|$	Absolute Percent Error, $(|E_t|/D_t)(100)$
1	200	225	−25	625	25	12.5%
2	240	220	20	400	20	8.3
3	300	285	15	225	15	5.0
4	270	290	−20	400	20	7.4
5	230	250	−20	400	20	8.7
6	260	240	20	400	20	7.7
7	210	250	−40	1,600	40	19.0
8	275	240	35	1,225	35	12.7
		Total	−15	5,275	195	81.3%

SOLUTION

Using the formulas for the measures, we get

Cumulative forecast error (bias):

CFE $= -15$ (the bias, or the sum of the errors for all time periods in the time series)

Average forecast error (mean bias):

$$\bar{E} = \frac{\text{CFE}}{n} = \frac{-15}{8} = -1.875$$

Mean squared error:

$$\text{MSE} = \frac{\Sigma E_t^2}{n} = \frac{5,275}{8} = 659.4$$

Standard deviation of the errors:

$$\sigma = \sqrt{\frac{\Sigma [E_t - (-1.875)]^2}{7}} = 27.4$$

Mean absolute deviation:

$$\text{MAD} = \frac{\Sigma |E_t|}{n} = \frac{195}{8} = 24.4$$

Mean absolute percent error:

$$\text{MAPE} = \frac{[\Sigma |E_t|/D_t]100}{n} = \frac{81.3\%}{8} = 10.2\%$$

A CFE of −15 indicates that the forecast has a slight bias to overestimate demand. The MSE, σ, and MAD statistics provide measures of forecast error variability. A MAD of 24.4 means that the average forecast error was 24.4 units in absolute value. The value of σ, 27.4, indicates that the sample distribution of forecast errors has a standard deviation of 27.4 units. A MAPE of 10.2 percent implies that, on average, the forecast error was about 10 percent of actual demand. These measures become more reliable as the number of periods of data increases.

DECISION POINT

Although reasonably satisfied with these forecast performance results, the analyst decided to test out a few more forecasting methods before reaching a final forecasting method to use for the future.

Computer Support

Computer support, such as from OM Explorer or POM for Windows, makes error calculations easy when evaluating how well forecasting models fit with past data. Errors are measured across past data, often called the *history file* in practice. They show the various error measures across the entire history file for each forecasting method evaluated. They also make forecasts into the future, based on the method selected.

Judgment Methods

Forecasts from quantitative methods are possible only when there is adequate historical data, (i.e., the *history file*). However, the history file may be nonexistent when a new product is introduced or when technology is expected to change. The history file might exist but be less useful when certain events (such as rollouts or special packages) are reflected in the past data, or when certain events are expected to occur in the future. In some cases, judgment methods are the only practical way to make a forecast. In other cases, judgment methods can also be used to modify forecasts that are generated by quantitative methods. They may recognize that one or two quantitative models have been performing particularly well in recent periods. Adjustments certainly would be called for if the forecaster has important contextual knowledge. *Contextual knowledge* is knowledge that practitioners gain through experience, such as cause-and-effect relationships, environmental cues, and organizational information that may have an effect on the variable being forecast. Adjustments also could account for unusual circumstances, such as a new sales promotion or unexpected international events. They could also have been used to remove the effect of special one-time events in the history file before quantitative methods are applied. Four of the more successful judgment methods are as follows: (1) salesforce estimates, (2) executive opinion, (3) market research, and (4) the Delphi method.

Salesforce estimates are forecasts compiled from estimates made periodically by members of a company's salesforce. The salesforce is the group most likely to know which services or products customers will be buying in the near future and in what quantities. Forecasts of individual salesforce members can be combined easily to get regional or national sales estimates. However, individual biases of the salespeople may taint the forecast. For example, some people are naturally optimistic, whereas others are more cautious. Adjustments in forecasts may need to be made to account for these individual biases.

Executive opinion is a forecasting method in which the opinions, experience, and technical knowledge of one or more managers or customers are summarized to arrive at a single forecast. All of the factors going into judgmental forecasts would fall into the category of executive opinion. Executive opinion can also be used for **technological forecasting**. The quick pace of technological change makes keeping abreast of the latest advances difficult.

Market research is a systematic approach to determine external consumer interest in a service or product by creating and testing hypotheses through data-gathering surveys. Conducting a market research study includes designing a questionnaire, deciding how to administer it, selecting a representative sample, and analyzing the information using judgment and statistical tools to interpret the responses. Although market research yields important information, it typically includes numerous qualifications and hedges in the findings.

The **Delphi method** is a process of gaining consensus from a group of experts while maintaining their anonymity. This form of forecasting is useful when no historical data are available from which to develop statistical models and when managers inside the firm have no experience on which to base informed projections. A coordinator sends questions to each member of the group of outside experts, who may not even know who else is participating. The coordinator prepares a statistical summary of the responses along with a summary of arguments for particular responses. The report is sent to the same group for another round, and the participants may choose to modify their previous responses. These rounds continue until consensus is obtained.

In the remainder of this chapter, we turn to the commonly used quantitative forecasting approaches.

Causal Methods: Linear Regression

Causal methods are used when historical data are available and the relationship between the factor to be forecasted and other external or internal factors (e.g., government actions or advertising promotions) can be identified. These relationships are expressed in mathematical terms and can be complex. Causal methods are good for predicting turning points in demand and for preparing long-range forecasts. We focus on linear regression, one of the best known and most commonly used causal methods.

In **linear regression**, one variable, called a dependent variable, is related to one or more independent variables by a linear equation. The **dependent variable** (such as demand for door

---

salesforce estimates

The forecasts that are compiled from estimates of future demands made periodically by members of a company's salesforce.

executive opinion

A forecasting method in which the opinions, experience, and technical knowledge of one or more managers are summarized to arrive at a single forecast.

technological forecasting

An application of executive opinion to keep abreast of the latest advances in technology.

market research

A systematic approach to determine external consumer interest in a service or product by creating and testing hypotheses through data-gathering surveys.

Delphi method

A process of gaining consensus from a group of experts while maintaining their anonymity.

linear regression

A causal method in which one variable (the dependent variable) is related to one or more independent variables by a linear equation.

dependent variable

The variable that one wants to forecast.

hinges) is the one the manager wants to forecast. The **independent variables** (such as advertising expenditures and new housing starts) are assumed to affect the dependent variable and thereby "cause" the results observed in the past. Figure 3.3 shows how a linear regression line relates to the data. In technical terms, the regression line minimizes the squared deviations from the actual data.

independent variables

Variables that are assumed to affect the dependent variable and thereby "cause" the results observed in the past.

In the simplest linear regression models, the dependent variable is a function of only one independent variable and, therefore, the theoretical relationship is a straight line:

$$Y = a + bX$$

where

$Y =$ dependent variable

$X =$ independent variable

$a =$ Y-intercept of the line

$b =$ slope of the line

The objective of linear regression analysis is to find values of a and b that minimize the sum of the squared deviations of the actual data points from the graphed line. Computer programs are used for this purpose. For any set of matched observations for Y and X, the program computes the values of a and b and provides measures of forecast accuracy. Three measures commonly reported are (1) the sample correlation coefficient, (2) the sample coefficient of determination, and (3) the standard error of the estimate.

The *sample correlation coefficient, r,* measures the direction and strength of the relationship between the independent variable and the dependent variable. The value of r can range from -1.00 to $+1.00$. A correlation coefficient of $+1.00$ implies that period-by-period changes in direction (increases or decreases) of the independent variable are always accompanied by changes in the same direction by the dependent variable. An r of -1.00 means that decreases in the independent variable are always accompanied by increases in the dependent variable, and vice versa. A zero value of r means no linear relationship exists between the variables. The closer the value of r is to $\pm$ 1.00, the better the regression line fits the points.

The *sample coefficient of determination* measures the amount of variation in the dependent variable about its mean that is explained by the regression line. The coefficient of determination is the square of the correlation coefficient, or r^2. The value of r^2 ranges from 0.00 to 1.00. Regression equations with a value of r^2 close to 1.00 mean a close fit.

The *standard error of the estimate, s_{xy},* measures how closely the data on the dependent variable cluster around the regression line. Although it is similar to the sample standard deviation, it measures the error from the dependent variable, Y, to the regression line, rather than to the mean. Thus, it is the standard deviation of the difference between the actual demand and the estimate provided by the regression equation.

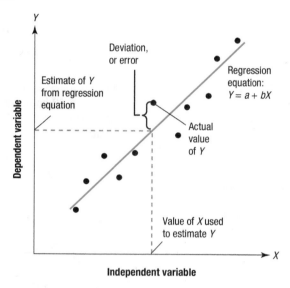

FIGURE 3.3 ▲
Linear Regression Line Relative to Actual Demand

*Regression r
Coefficients
<71*

EXAMPLE 3.2	**Using Linear Regression to Forecast Product Demand**

The supply chain manager seeks a better way to forecast the demand for door hinges and believes that the demand is related to advertising expenditures. The following are sales and advertising data for the past 5 months:

Month	Sales (Thousands of Units)	Advertising (Thousands of $)
1	264	2.5
2	116	1.3
3	165	1.4
4	101	1.0
5	209	2.0

MyOMLab

Active Model 3.1 in MyOMLab provides insight on varying the intercept and slope of the model.

The company will spend $1,750 next month on advertising for the product. Use linear regression to develop an equation and a forecast for this product.

SOLUTION

We used POM for Windows to determine the best values of a, b, the correlation coefficient, the coefficient of determination, and the standard error of the estimate.

$$a = -8.135$$
$$b = 109.229X$$
$$r = 0.980$$
$$r^2 = 0.960$$
$$s_{yx} = 15.603$$

The regression equation is

$$Y = -8.135 + 109.229X$$

and the regression line is shown in Figure 3.4. The sample correlation coefficient, r, is 0.98, which is unusually close to 1.00 and suggests an unusually strong positive relationship exists between sales and advertising expenditures. The sample coefficient of determination, r^2, implies that 96 percent of the variation in sales is explained by advertising expenditures.

FIGURE 3.4 ▶
Linear Regression Line for the Sales and Advertising Data Using POM for Windows

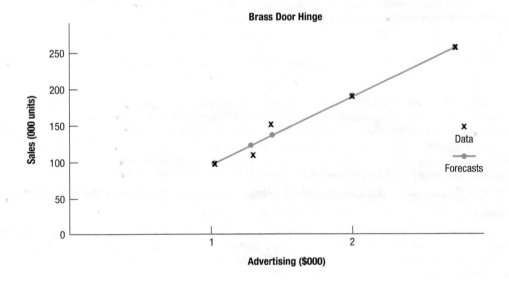

DECISION POINT

The supply chain manager decided to use the regression model as input to planning production levels for month 6. As the advertising expenditure will be $1,750, the forecast for month 6 is $Y = -8.135 + 109.229(1.75) = 183.016$, or 183,016 units.

Often several independent variables may affect the dependent variable. For example, advertising expenditures, new corporation start-ups, and residential building contracts all may be important for estimating the demand for door hinges. In such cases, *multiple regression analysis* is helpful in determining a forecasting equation for the dependent variable as a function of several independent variables. Such models can be analyzed with POM for Windows or OM Explorer and can be quite useful for predicting turning points and solving many planning problems.

Time-Series Methods

Rather than using independent variables for the forecast as regression models do, time-series methods use historical information regarding only the dependent variable. These methods are based on the assumption that the dependent variable's past pattern will continue in the future. Time-series analysis identifies the underlying patterns of demand that combine to produce an observed historical pattern of the dependent variable and then develops a model to replicate it. In this section, we focus on time-series methods that address the horizontal, trend, and seasonal patterns of demand. Before we discuss statistical methods, let us take a look at the simplest time-series method for addressing all patterns of demand—the naïve forecast.

Naïve Forecast

A method often used in practice is the **naïve forecast**, whereby the forecast for the next period (F_{t+1}) equals the demand for the current period (D_t). So if the actual demand for Wednesday is 35 customers, the forecasted demand for Thursday is 35 customers. Despite its name, the naïve forecast can perform well.

The naïve forecast method may be adapted to take into account a demand trend. The increase (or decrease) in demand observed between the last two periods is used to adjust the current demand to arrive at a forecast. Suppose that last week the demand was 120 units and the week before it was 108 units. Demand increased 12 units in 1 week, so the forecast for next week would be $120 + 12 = 132$ units. The naïve forecast method also may be used to account for seasonal patterns. If the demand last July was 50,000 units, and assuming no underlying trend from one year to the next, the forecast for this July would be 50,000 units. The method works best when the horizontal, trend, or seasonal patterns are stable and random variation is small.

naïve forecast

A time-series method whereby the forecast for the next period equals the demand for the current period, or Forecast $= D_t$

Estimating the Average

We begin our discussion of statistical methods of time-series forecasting with demand that has no apparent trend, seasonal, or cyclical patterns. The horizontal pattern in a time series is based on the mean of the demands, so we focus on forecasting methods that estimate the average of a time series of data. The forecast of demand for *any* period in the future is the average of the time series computed in the current period. For example, if the average of past demand calculated on Tuesday is 65 customers, the forecasts for Wednesday, Thursday, and Friday are 65 customers each day.

Consider Figure 3.5, which shows patient arrivals at a medical clinic over the past 28 weeks. Assuming that the time series has only a horizontal and random pattern, one approach is simply to calculate the average of the data. However, this approach has no adaptive quality if there is a trend, seasonal, or cyclical pattern. The statistical techniques that do have an adaptive quality in estimating the average in a time series are (1) simple moving averages, (2) weighted moving averages, and (3) exponential smoothing. Another option is the simple average, but it has no adaptive capability.

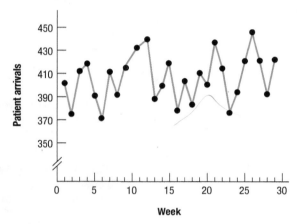

FIGURE 3.5 ▲
Weekly Patient Arrivals at a Medical Clinic

Simple Moving Averages   The **simple moving average method** simply involves calculating the average demand for the *n* most recent time periods and using it as the forecast for future time periods. For the next period, after the demand is known, the oldest demand from the previous average is replaced with the most recent demand and the average is recalculated. In this way, the *n* most recent demands are used, and the average "moves" from period to period.

Specifically, the forecast for period $t + 1$ can be calculated at the end of period t (after the actual demand for period t is known) as

simple moving average method

A time-series method used to estimate the average of a demand time series by averaging the demand for the *n* most recent time periods.

$$F_{t+1} = \frac{\text{Sum of last } n \text{ demands}}{n} = \frac{D_t + D_{t-1} + D_{t-2} + \cdots + D_{t-n+1}}{n}$$

where

$D_t =$ actual demand in period t

$n =$ total number of periods in the average

$F_{t+1} =$ forecast for period $t + 1$

EXAMPLE 3.3	**Using the Moving Average Method to Estimate Average Demand**

a. Compute a *three-week* moving average forecast for the arrival of medical clinic patients in week 4. The numbers of arrivals for the past 3 weeks were as follows:

Week	Patient Arrivals
1	400
2	380
3	411

b. If the actual number of patient arrivals in week 4 is 415, what is the forecast error for week 4?

c. What is the forecast for week 5?

MyOMLab

Active Model 3.2 in MyOMLab provides insight on the impact of varying *n* using the example in Figure 3.5.

MyOMLab

Tutor 3.1 in MyOMLab provides another example to practice making forecasts with the moving average method.

SOLUTION

a. The moving average forecast at the end of week 3 is

$$F_4 = \frac{411 + 380 + 400}{3} = 397.0$$

b. The forecast error for week 4 is

$$E_4 = D_4 - F_4 = 415 - 397 = 18$$

c. The forecast for week 5 requires the actual arrivals from weeks 2 through 4, the 3 most recent weeks of data.

$$F_5 = \frac{415 + 411 + 380}{3} = 402.0$$

DECISION POINT

Thus, the forecast at the end of week 3 would have been 397 patients for week 4, which fell short of actual demand by 18 patients. The forecast for week 5, made at the end of week 4, would be 402 patients. If a forecast is needed now for week 6 and beyond, it would also be for 402 patients.

The moving average method may involve the use of as many periods of past demand as desired. Large values of n should be used for demand series that are stable, and small values of n should be used for those that are susceptible to changes in the underlying average. If n is set to its lowest level (i.e., 1), it becomes the naïve method.

weighted moving average method

A time-series method in which each historical demand in the average can have its own weight; the sum of the weights equals 1.0.

exponential smoothing method

A weighted moving average method that calculates the average of a time series by implicitly giving recent demands more weight than earlier demands.

Weighted Moving Averages   In the simple moving average method, each demand has the same weight in the average—namely, $1/n$. In the **weighted moving average method**, each historical demand in the average can have its own weight. The sum of the weights equals 1.0. For example, in a *three-period* weighted moving average model, the most recent period might be assigned a weight of 0.50, the second most recent might be weighted 0.30, and the third most recent might be weighted 0.20. The average is obtained by multiplying the weight of each period by the value for that period and adding the products together:

$$F_{t+1} = 0.50D_t + 0.30D_{t-1} + 0.20D_{t-2}$$

For a numerical example of using the weighted moving average method to estimate average demand, see Solved Problem 2 and Tutor 3.2 of OM Explorer in MyOMLab.

The advantage of a weighted moving average method is that it allows you to emphasize recent demand over earlier demand. (It can even handle seasonal effects by putting higher weights on prior years in the same season.) The forecast will be more responsive to changes in the underlying average of the demand series than the simple moving average forecast.

Exponential Smoothing   The **exponential smoothing method** is a sophisticated weighted moving average method that calculates the average of a time series by implicitly giving recent demands more weight than earlier demands, all the way back to the first period in the history file. It is the most frequently used formal forecasting method because of its simplicity and the small amount of data needed to support it. Unlike the weighted moving average method, which requires n periods of past demand and n weights, exponential smoothing requires only three items of data: (1) the last period's forecast; (2) the actual demand for this period; and (3) a smoothing parameter, alpha (α), which has a value between 0 and 1.0. The equation for the exponentially smoothed forecast for period $t + 1$ is calculated

$$F_{t+1} = \alpha D_t + (1 - \alpha)F_t$$

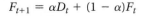

Art Directors & TRIP/Alamy

Unilever—the purveyor of Lipton Tea, Dove, Hellmann's, and hundreds of other brands, must forecast demand around the world. It has a state-of-the-art forecasting system. Using software from Manugistics, the system blends forecasts from time series techniques with judgmental adjustments for planned promotions from its sales teams. Unilever compares point-of-sales data with its own forecasts. The forecasts are reviewed and judgmentally adjusted as needed.

The emphasis given to the most recent demand levels can be adjusted by changing the smoothing parameter. Larger α values emphasize recent levels of demand and result in forecasts more responsive to changes in the underlying average. Smaller α values treat past demand more uniformly and result in more stable forecasts. Smaller α values are analogous to increasing the value of n in the moving average method and giving greater weight to past demand. In practice, various values of α are tried and the one producing the best forecasts is chosen.

Exponential smoothing requires an initial forecast to get started. There are several ways to get this initial forecast. OM Explorer and POM for Windows use as a default setting the actual demand in the first period, which becomes the forecast for the second period. Forecasts and forecast errors then are calculated beginning with period 2. If some historical data are available, the initial forecast can be found by calculating the average of several recent periods of demand. The effect of the initial estimate of the average on successive estimates of the average diminishes over time.

EXAMPLE 3.4	Using Exponential Smoothing to Estimate Average Demand

a. Reconsider the patient arrival data in Example 3.3. It is now the end of week 3, so the actual number of arrivals is known to be 411 patients. Using $\alpha = 0.10$, calculate the exponential smoothing forecast for week 4.

b. What was the forecast error for week 4 if the actual demand turned out to be 415?

c. What is the forecast for week 5?

MyOMLab

Active Model 3.3 in MyOMLab provides insight on the impact of varying α in Figure 3.5.

MyOMLab

Tutor 3.3 in MyOMLab provides a new practice example of how to make forecasts with the exponential smoothing method.

SOLUTION

a. The exponential smoothing method requires an initial forecast. Suppose that we take the demand data for the first 2 weeks and average them, obtaining $(400 + 380)/2 = 390$ as an initial forecast. (POM for Windows and OM Explorer simply use the actual demand for the first week as a default setting for the initial forecast for period 1, and do not begin tracking forecast errors until the second period). To obtain the forecast for week 4, using exponential smoothing with $D_3 = 411$, $\alpha = 0.10$, and $F_3 = 390$, we calculate the forecast for week 4 as

$$F_4 = 0.10(411) + 0.90(390) = 392.1$$

Thus, the forecast for week 4 would be 392 patients.

b. The forecast error for week 4 is

$$E_4 = 415 - 392 = 23$$

c. The new forecast for week 5 would be

$$F_5 = 0.10(415) + 0.90(392.1) = 394.4$$

or 394 patients. Note that we used F_4, not the integer-value forecast for week 4, in the computation for F_5. In general, we round off (when it is appropriate) only the final result to maintain as much accuracy as possible in the calculations.

DECISION POINT

Using this exponential smoothing model, the analyst's forecasts would have been 392 patients for week 4 and then 394 patients for week 5 and beyond. As soon as the actual demand for week 5 is known, then the forecast for week 6 will be updated.

Because exponential smoothing is simple and requires minimal data, it is inexpensive and attractive to firms that make thousands of forecasts for each time period. However, its simplicity also is a disadvantage when the underlying average is changing, as in the case of a demand series with a trend. Like any method geared solely to the assumption of a stable average, exponential smoothing results will lag behind changes in the underlying average of demand. Higher α values may help reduce forecast errors when there is a change in the average; however, the lags will still occur if the average is changing systematically. Typically, if large α values (e.g., > 0.50) are required for an exponential smoothing application, chances are good that another model is needed because of a significant trend or seasonal influence in the demand series.

Trend Projection with Regression

Let us now consider a demand time series that has a trend. A *trend* in a time series is a systematic increase or decrease in the average of the series over time. Where a significant trend is present, forecasts from naïve, moving average, and exponential smoothing approaches are adaptive, but still lag behind actual demand and tend to be below or above the actual demand.

Trend projection with regression is a forecasting model that accounts for the trend with simple regression analysis. To develop a regression model for forecasting the trend, let the dependent variable, Y, be a period's demand and the independent variable, t, be the time period. For the first period, let $t = 1$; for the second period, let $t = 2$; and so on. The regression equation is

$$F_t = a + bt$$

One advantage of the trend projection with regression model is that it can forecast demand well into the future. The previous models project demand just one period ahead, and assume that demand beyond that will remain at that same level. Of course, all of the models (including the trend projection with regression model) can be updated each period to stay current. One *apparent* disadvantage of the trend with regression model is that it is not adaptive. The solution to this problem comes when you answer the following question. If you had the past sales of Ford automobiles since 1920, would you include each year in your regression analysis, giving equal weight to each year's sales, or include just the sales for more recent years? You most likely would decide to include just the more recent years, making your regression model more adaptive. The trend projection with regression model can thus be made more or less adaptive by the selection of historical data periods to include in the same way that moving average (changing n) or exponential smoothing (changing α) models do.

The trend projection with regression model can be solved with either the *Trend Projection with Regression* Solver or the *Time Series Forecasting* Solver in OM Explorer. Both solvers provide the regression coefficients, coefficient of determination r^2, error measures, and forecasts into the future. POM for Windows has an alternative model (we do not cover in the textbook, although a description is provided in MyOMLab) that includes the trend, called the *Trend-Adjusted Smoothing* model.

MyOMLab

The *Trend Projection with Regression* Solver focuses exclusively on trend analysis. Its graph gives a big-picture view of how well the model fits the actual demand. Its sliders allow you to control when the regression begins, how many periods are included in the regression analysis, and how many periods you want forecasted into the future. The *Time Series Forecasting* Solver, on the other hand, covers all time series models, including the trend projection with regression. It also computes a combination forecast, which we cover in a subsequent section on using multiple techniques.

| EXAMPLE 3.5 | Using Trend Projection with Regression to Forecast a Demand Series with a Trend |

MyOMLab

Active Model 3.4 in MyOMLab provides insight on the behavior of the Trend Projetion with Regression model on the Medanalysis data.

Medanalysis, Inc., provides medical laboratory services to patients of Health Providers, a group of 10 family-practice doctors associated with a new health maintenance program. Managers are interested in forecasting the number of blood analysis requests per week. Recent publicity about the damaging effects of cholesterol on the heart has caused a national increase in requests for standard blood tests. The arrivals over the last 16 weeks are given in Table 3.1. What is the forecasted demand for the next three periods?

TABLE 3.1 ARRIVALS AT MEDANALYSIS FOR LAST 16 WEEKS

Week	Arrivals	Week	Arrivals
1	28	9	61
2	27	10	39
3	44	11	55
4	37	12	54
5	35	13	52
6	53	14	60
7	38	15	60
8	57	16	75

SOLUTION

Figure 3.6(a) shows the results using the *Trend Projection with Regression* Solver when all 16 weeks are included in the regression analysis, with Figure 3.6(b) showing the worksheet that goes with it.

Solver - Trend Projection with Regression

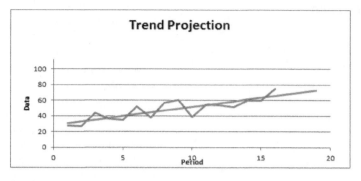

Regression begins in period	1
Error analysis begins in period	1
Number of future forecasts	3

▼ **FIGURE 3.6(a)**
First Model

Trend Projection

a (Y intercept)	28.50
b (slope or trend)	2.35
r2	0.69
CFE	0.00
MAD	6.21
MSE	52.96
MAPE	13.53%
Forecast for period 17	68.375
Forecast for period 18	70.72059
Forecast for period 19	73.06618

▼ **FIGURE 3.6(b)**
Detailed Calculations of Forecast Errors for First Model

					Averages		
				CFE	MSE	MAD	MAPE
				0.000	52.958	6.210	13.53%
	Actual				Error	Absolute	Abs %
Period #	Demand	Forecast	Error	Running CFE	Squared	Error	error
1	28	31	-2.846	-2.846	8.097	2.846	10.16%
2	27	33	-6.191	-9.037	38.331	6.191	22.93%
3	44	36	8.463	-0.574	71.626	8.463	19.23%
4	37	38	-0.882	-1.456	0.779	0.882	2.38%
5	35	40	-5.228	-6.684	27.331	5.228	14.94%
6	53	43	10.426	3.743	108.711	10.426	19.67%
7	38	45	-6.919	-3.176	47.874	6.919	18.21%
8	57	47	9.735	6.559	94.776	9.735	17.08%
9	61	50	11.390	17.949	129.725	11.390	18.67%
10	39	52	-12.956	4.993	167.855	12.956	33.22%
11	55	54	0.699	5.691	0.488	0.699	1.27%
12	54	57	-2.647	3.044	7.007	2.647	4.90%
13	52	59	-6.993	-3.949	48.897	6.993	13.45%
14	60	61	-1.338	-5.287	1.791	1.338	2.23%
15	60	64	-3.684	-8.971	13.571	3.684	6.14%
16	75	66	8.971	0.000	80.471	8.971	11.96%

▼ **FIGURE 3.6(c)**
Second Model

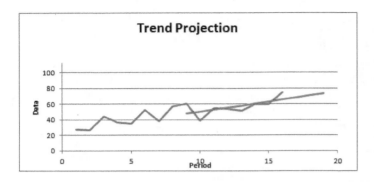

Solver - Trend Projection with Regression

Regression begins in period	9
Error analysis begins in period	9
Number of future forecasts	3

Trend Projection

a (Y intercept)	24.86
b (slope or trend)	2.57
r2	0.39
CFE	0.00
MAD	5.96
MSE	55.29
MAPE	11.10%
Forecast for period 17	68.57143
Forecast for period 18	71.14286
Forecast for period 19	73.71429

Looking at the Results sheet of Figure 3.6(a), we see that the Y intercept of the trend line (a) is 28.50 and the slope of the line (b) is 2.35. Thus, the trend equation is $F_t = a + bt$, where t is the time period for which you are forecasting. The forecast for period 19 is 28.5 + 2.35 (19) = 73. The error terms are CFE = 0 (which is to be expected when the regression begins at the same time that error analysis begins), MAD = 6.21, MSE = 52.96, and MAPE = 13.53 percent. The coefficient of determination r^2 is decent at 0.69. The trend line is rising gently and reaches 73 for period 19. Each period the forecast predicts an increase of 2.35 arrivals per week.

When the number of periods included in the regression analysis is reduced to 9, Figure 3.6(c) shows this second model produces mixed results. The trend line has a steeper slope. MAD and MAPE are better, but r^2 and MSE are worse. The third model in Figure 3.6(d) is the extreme, where only the last four periods are used in building the regression model. It has the best r^2, and all of the error measures are much better than the first two models. Its forecast for period 19 is 93 arrivals. However, this model is based only on the last 4 weeks of data, ignoring all previous data in the history file. For that reason, management decided to split the difference with a forecast of 83 arrivals. It is halfway between the more conservative forecast of 73 in Figure 3.6(a) and Figure 3.6(c), and the optimistic forecast of 93 in Figure 3.6(d).

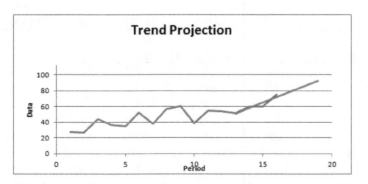

Solver - Trend Projection with Regression

Regression begins in period	13
Error analysis begins in period	13
Number of future forecasts	3

FIGURE 3.6(d) ▶
Third Model

Trend Projection

a (Y intercept)	-38.30
b (slope or trend)	6.90
r2	0.86
CFE	0.00
MAD	2.60
MSE	9.67
MAPE	4.13%
Forecast for period 17	79
Forecast for period 18	85.9
Forecast for period 19	92.8

Seasonal Patterns

Seasonal patterns are regularly repeating upward or downward movements in demand measured in periods of less than one year (hours, days, weeks, months, or quarters). In this context, the time periods are called *seasons*. For example, customer arrivals at a fast-food shop on any day may peak between 11 A.M. and 1 P.M. and again from 5 P.M. to 7 P.M.

An easy way to account for seasonal effects is to use one of the techniques already described, but to limit the data in the time series to those time periods in the same season. For example, for a day-of-the-week seasonal effect, one time series would be for Mondays, one for Tuesdays, and so on. Such an approach accounts for seasonal effects, but has the disadvantage of discarding considerable information on past demand.

Other methods are available that analyze all past data, using one model to forecast demand for all of the seasons. We describe only the **multiplicative seasonal method**, whereby an estimate of average demand is multiplied by seasonal factors to arrive at a seasonal forecast. The four-step procedure presented here involves the use of simple averages of past demand, although more sophisticated methods for calculating averages, such as a moving average or exponential smoothing approach, could be used. The following description is based on a seasonal pattern lasting one year and seasons of one month, although the procedure can be used for any seasonal pattern and season of any length.

multiplicative seasonal method
A method whereby seasonal factors are multiplied by an estimate of average demand to arrive at a seasonal forecast.

1. For each year, calculate the average demand per season by dividing annual demand by the number of seasons per year.

2. For each year, divide the actual demand for a season by the average demand per season. The result is a *seasonal index* for each season in the year, which indicates the level of demand relative to the average demand. For example, a seasonal index of 1.14 calculated for April implies that April's demand is 14 percent greater than the average demand per month.

3. Calculate the average seasonal index for each season, using the results from step 2. Add the seasonal indices for a season and divide by the number of years of data.

4. Calculate each season's forecast for next year. Begin by forecasting next year's annual demand using the naïve method, moving averages, exponential smoothing, or trend projection with regression. Then, divide annual demand by the number of seasons per year to get the average demand per season. Finally, make the seasonal forecast by multiplying the average demand per season by the appropriate seasonal index found in step 3.

EXAMPLE 3.6	Using the Multiplicative Seasonal Method to Forecast the Number of Customers

The manager of the Stanley Steemer carpet cleaning company needs a quarterly forecast of the number of customers expected next year. The carpet cleaning business is seasonal, with a peak in the third quarter and a trough in the first quarter. The manager wants to forecast customer demand for each quarter of year 5, based on an estimate of total year 5 demand of 2,600 customers.

SOLUTION
The following table calculates the seasonal factor for each week.

It shows the quarterly demand data from the past 4 years, as well as the calculations performed to get the average seasonal factor for each quarter.

	YEAR 1		YEAR 2		YEAR 3		YEAR 4		
Quarter	Demand	Seasonal Factor (1)	Demand	Seasonal Factor (2)	Demand	Seasonal Factor (3)	Demand	Seasonal Factor (4)	Average Seasonal Factor [(1+2+3+4+)/4]
1	45	45/250 = 0.18	70	70/300 = 0.23333	100	100/450 = 0.22222	100	100/550 = 0.18182	0.2043
2	335	335/250 = 1.34	370	370/300 = 1.23333	585	585/450 = 1.30	725	725/550 = 1.31818	1.2979
3	520	520/250 = 2.08	590	590/300 = 1.96667	830	830/450 = 1.84444	1160	1160/550 = 2.10909	2.0001
4	100	100/250 = 0.40	170	170/300 = 0.56667	285	285/450 = 0.63333	215	215/550 = 0.39091	0.4977
Total	1,000		1,200		1,800		2,200		
Average	1,000/4 = 250		1,200/4 = 300		1,800 = 450		2,200/4 = 550		

For example, the seasonal factor for quarter 1 in year 1 is calculated by dividing the actual demand (45) by the average demand for the whole year (1000/4 = 250). When this is done for all 4 years, we then can average the seasonal factors for quarter 1 over all 4 years. The result is a seasonal factor of 0.2043 for quarter 1.

Once seasonal factors are calculated for all four seasons (see last column in the table on the previous page), we then turn to making the forecasts for year 5. The manager suggests a forecast of 2,600 customers for the whole year, which seems reasonable given that the annual demand has been increasing by an average of 400 customers each year (from 1,000 in year 1 to 2,200 in year 4, or 1,200/3 = 400. The computed forecast demand is found by extending that trend, and projecting an annual demand in year 5 of 2,200 + 400 = 2,600 customers. (This same result is confirmed using the *Trend Projection with Regression* Solver of OM Explorer.) The quarterly forecasts are straight-forward. First, find the average demand forecast for year 5, which is 2,600/4 = 650. Then multiple this average demand by the average seasonal index, giving us

Quarter	Forecast
1	650 × 0.2043 = 132.795
2	650 × 1.2979 = 843.635
3	650 × 2.0001 = 1,300.065
4	650 × 0.4977 = 323.505

Figure 3.7 shows the computer solution using the *Seasonal Forecasting* Solver in OM Explorer. Figure 3.7(b) confirms all of the calculations made above. Notice in Figure 3.7(a) that a computer demand forecast is provided as a default for year 5. However, there is an option for user-supplied demand forecast that overrides the computer-supplied forecast if the manager wishes to make a judgmental forecast based on additional information.

FIGURE 3.7 ▶
Demand Forecasts Using the
Seasonal Forecasting Solver
of *OM Explorer*

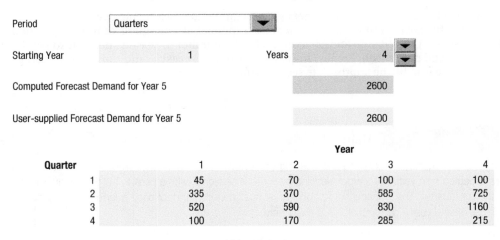

Period	Quarters ▼			
Starting Year	1	Years	4	
Computed Forecast Demand for Year 5			2600	
User-supplied Forecast Demand for Year 5			2600	

		Year		
Quarter	1	2	3	4
1	45	70	100	100
2	335	370	585	725
3	520	590	830	1160
4	100	170	285	215

(a) Inputs sheet

Quarter	Seasonal Index	Forecast
1	0.2043	132.795
2	1.2979	843.635
3	2.0001	1300.065
4	0.4977	323.505

(b) Results

DECISION POINT
Using this seasonal method, the analyst makes a demand forecast as low as 133 customers in the first quarter and as high as 1,300 customers in the third quarter. The season of the year clearly makes a difference.

An alternative to the multiplicative seasonal method is the **additive seasonal method**, whereby seasonal forecasts are generated by adding or subtracting a seasonal constant (say, 50 units) to the estimate of average demand per season. This approach is based on the assumption that the seasonal pattern is constant, regardless of average demand. The amplitude of the seasonal adjustment remains the same regardless of the level of demand.

additive seasonal method

A method in which seasonal forecasts are generated by adding a constant to the estimate of average demand per season.

Choosing a Quantitative Forecasting Method
Criteria for Selecting Time-Series Methods

Forecast error measures provide important information for choosing the best forecasting method for a service or product. They also guide managers in selecting the best values for the parameters needed for the method: n for the moving average method, the weights for the weighted moving average method, α for the exponential smoothing method, and when regression data begins for the trend projection with regression method. The criteria to use in making forecast method and parameter choices include (1) minimizing bias (CFE); (2) minimizing MAPE, MAD, or MSE; (3) maximizing r^2; (4) meeting managerial expectations of changes in the components of demand; and (5) minimizing the forecast errors in recent periods. The first three criteria relate to statistical measures based on historical performance, the fourth reflects expectations of the future that may not be rooted in the past, and the fifth is a way to use whatever method seems to be working best at the time a forecast must be made.

Using Statistical Criteria   Statistical performance measures can be used in the selection of which forecasting method to use. The following guidelines will help when searching for the best time-series models:

1. For projections of more stable demand patterns, use lower α values or larger n values to emphasize historical experience.

2. For projections of more dynamic demand patterns using the models covered in this chapter, try higher α values or smaller n values. When historical demand patterns are changing, recent history should be emphasized.

   Often, the forecaster must make trade-offs between bias (CFE) and the measures of forecast error dispersion (MAPE, MAD, and MSE). Managers also must recognize that the best technique in explaining the past data is not necessarily the best technique to predict the future, and that "overfitting" past data can be deceptive. Such was the case in Example 3.5. All of the forecast error measures suggested that the regression model in Figure 3.5(d) was best, but management was hesitant because it used so little of the time series. A forecasting method may have small errors relative to the history file, but may generate high errors for future time periods. For this reason, some analysts prefer to use a **holdout sample** as a final test (see the two Experiential Learning Exercises at the end of this chapter). To do so, they set aside some of the more recent periods from the time series and use only the earlier time periods to develop and test different models. Once the final models have been selected in the first phase, they are tested again with the holdout sample. Performance measures, such as MAD and CFE, would still be used but they would be applied to the holdout sample. Whether this idea is used or not, managers should monitor future forecast errors, and modify their forecasting approaches as needed. Maintaining data on forecast performance is the ultimate test of forecasting power—rather than how well a model fits past data or holdout samples.

holdout sample

Actual demands from the more recent time periods in the time series that are set aside to test different models developed from the earlier time periods.

Tracking Signals

A **tracking signal** is a measure that indicates whether a method of forecasting is accurately predicting actual changes in demand. The tracking signal measures the number of MADs represented by the cumulative sum of forecast errors, the CFE. The CFE tends to be close to 0 when a correct forecasting system is being used. At any time, however, random errors can cause the CFE to be a nonzero number. The tracking signal formula is

tracking signal

A measure that indicates whether a method of forecasting is accurately predicting actual changes in demand.

$$\text{Tracking signal} = \frac{\text{CFE}}{\text{MAD}} \text{ or } \frac{\text{CFE}}{\text{MAD}_t}$$

   Each period, the CFE and MAD are updated to reflect current error, and the tracking signal is compared to some predetermined limits. The MAD can be calculated in one of two ways: (1) as the simple average of all absolute errors (as demonstrated in Example 3.1) or (2) as a weighted average determined by the exponential smoothing method:

$$\text{MAD}_t = \alpha |E_t| + (1 - \alpha)\text{MAD}_{t-1}$$

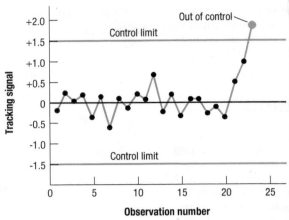

FIGURE 3.8 ▲
Tracking Signal

If forecast errors are normally distributed with a mean of 0, the relationship between σ and MAD is simple:

$$\sigma = (\sqrt{\pi/2})(\text{MAD}) \cong 1.25(\text{MAD})$$

$$\text{MAD} = 0.7978\sigma \cong 0.8\sigma$$

where

$$\pi = 3.1416$$

This relationship allows use of the normal probability tables to specify limits for the tracking signal. If the tracking signal falls outside those limits, the forecasting model no longer is tracking demand adequately. A tracking system is useful when forecasting systems are computerized because it alerts analysts when forecasts are getting far from desirable limits. Figure 3.8 shows tracking signal results for 23 periods plotted on a *control chart*. The control chart is useful for determining whether any action needs to be taken to improve the forecasting model. In the example, the first 20 points cluster around 0, as we would expect if the forecasts are not biased. The CFE will tend toward 0. When the underlying characteristics of demand change but the forecasting model does not, the tracking signal eventually goes out of control. The steady increase after the 20th point in Figure 3.8 indicates that the process is going out of control. The 21st and 22nd points are acceptable, but the 23rd point is not.

Using Multiple Techniques

We described several individual forecasting methods and showed how to assess their forecast performance. However, we need not rely on a single forecasting method. Several different forecasts can be used to arrive at a final forecast. Initial statistical forecasts using several time-series methods and regression are distributed to knowledgeable individuals, such as marketing directors and sales teams, (and sometimes even suppliers and customers) for their adjustments. They can account for current market and customer conditions that are not necessarily reflected in past data. Multiple forecasts may come from different sales teams, and some teams may have a better record on forecast errors than others.

Research during the last two decades suggests that combining forecasts from multiple sources often produces more accurate forecasts. **Combination forecasts** are forecasts that are produced by averaging independent forecasts based on different methods, different sources, or different data. It is intriguing that combination forecasts often perform better over time than even the *best* single forecasting procedure. For example, suppose that the forecast for the next period is 100 units from technique 1 and 120 units from technique 2 and that technique 1 has provided more accurate forecasts to date. The combination forecast for next period, giving equal weight to each technique, is 110 units (or $0.5 \times 100 + 0.5 \times 120$). When this averaging technique is used consistently into the future, its combination forecasts often will be much more accurate than those of any single best forecasting technique (in this example, technique 1). Combining is most effective when the individual forecasts bring different kinds of information into the forecasting process. Forecasters have achieved excellent results by weighting forecasts equally, and this is a good starting point. However, unequal weights may provide better results under some conditions.

OM Explorer and POM for Windows allow you to evaluate several forecasting models, and then you can create combination forecasts from them. In fact, the *Time-Series Forecasting* Solver of OM Explorer automatically computes a combination forecast as a weighted average, using the weights that you supply for the various models that it evaluates. The models include the naïve, moving average, exponential smoothing, and regression projector methods. Alternately, you can create a simple Excel spreadsheet that combines forecasts generated by POM for Windows to create combination forecasts. The *Time Series Forecasting* Solver also allows you evaluate your forecasting process with a holdout sample. The forecaster makes a forecast just one period ahead, and learns of given actual demand. Next the solver computes forecasts and forecast errors for the period. The process continues to the next period in the holdout sample with the forecaster committing to a forecast for the next period. To be informed, the forecaster should also be aware of how well the other forecasting methods have been performing, particularly in the recent past.

combination forecasts

Forecasts that are produced by averaging independent forecasts based on different methods, different sources, or different data.

MANAGERIAL PRACTICE 3.1 — Combination Forecasts and the Forecasting Process

Fiskars Brands, Inc., totally overhauled its forecasting process. It serves 2,000 customers ranging from large discounters to local craft stores providing about 2,300 finished SKUs. Its parent company, Fiskars Corporation, is the second oldest incorporated entity in the world and produces a variety of high-quality products such as garden shears, pruners, hand tools, scissors for preschoolers, ratchet tools, screwdrivers, and the like. Business is highly seasonal and prices quite variable. About 10 percent to 15 percent of the annual revenue comes from one-time promotions, and 25 percent to 35 percent of its products are new every year.

It introduced a statistical-based analysis along with a Web-based business intelligence tool for reporting. It put much more emphasis on combination forecasts. Instead of asking members of the sales staff to provide their own forecasts, forecasts were sent to them, and they were asked for their validation and refinement. Their inputs are most useful relative to additions, deletions, and promotions. Converting multiple forecasts into one number (forecasts from time-series techniques, sales input, and customer input) creates more accurate forecasts by SKU. Fiskars's software has the ability to weigh each input. It gives more weight to a statistical forecast for in-line items, and inputs from the sales staff get much more weight for promoted products and new items.

It also segments SKUs by value and forecastability so as to focus forecasting efforts on SKUs that have the biggest impact on the business. High-value items ("A" items identified with ABC analysis in Chapter 9, "Supply Chain Inventory Management") that also have high forecastability (stable demand with low forecast errors to date) tend to do well with the time-series techniques, and **judgmental adjustments** are made with caution. High-value items with low forecastability get top priority in the forecasting effort, such as with CPFR. Much less attention is given to improving forecasts for "C" items for which there is some history and fairly steady demand.

Finally, Fiskars instituted a Web-based program that gives the entire company visibility to forecast information in whatever form it needs. For example, Finance wants monthly, quarterly, and yearly projections in dollars, whereas Operations wants projections in units as well as accuracy measures. Everybody can track updated forecast information by customer, brand, and SKU.

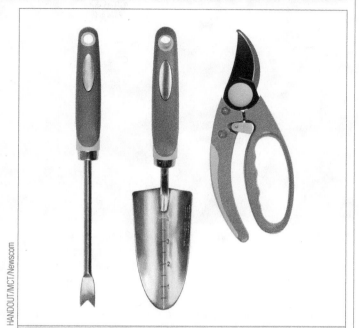

HANDOUT/MCT/Newscom

Fiskars Brands, Inc., totally overhauled its forecasting process. Its products include garden shears, pruners, hand tools, scissors, ratchet tools, and the like. It introduced time-series tools, with much emphasis placed on combination forecasts. Instead of asking members of the sales staff to provide their own forecasts, forecasts were sent to them, and they were asked for validation and refinement. Their judgmental inputs provide valuable information relative to additions, deletions, and promotions. Combining multiple forecasts (forecasts from several time-series techniques and judgment inputs) into one number creates more accurate forecasts by SKU.

Source: David Montgomery, "Flashpoints for Changing Your Forecasting Process," *The Journal of Business Forecasting*, (Winter 2006–2007), pp. 35–37; **http://www.fiskars.com**, May 21, 2011.

Another way to take advantage of multiple techniques is **focus forecasting**, which selects the best forecast (based on past error measures) from a group of forecasts generated by individual techniques. Every period, all techniques are used to make forecasts for each item. The forecasts are made with a computer because there can be 100,000 SKUs at a company, each needing to be forecast. Using the history file as the starting point for each method, the computer generates forecasts for the current period. The forecasts are compared to actual demand, and the method that produces the forecast with the least error is used to make the forecast for the next period. The method used for each item may change from period to period.

Putting It All Together: Forecasting as a Process

Often companies must prepare forecasts for hundreds or even thousands of services or products repeatedly. For example, a large network of health care facilities must calculate demand forecasts for each of its services for every department. This undertaking involves voluminous data that must be manipulated frequently. However, software such as Motorola Mobility's system can ease the burden of making these forecasts and coordinating the forecasts between customers

judgmental adjustment
An adjustment made to forecasts from one or more quantitative models that accounts for recognizing which models are performing particularly well in recent past, or take into account contextual information.

focus forecasting
A method of forecasting that selects the best forecast from a group of forecasts generated by individual techniques.

West Marine acquired its East Coast competitor, E&B Marine, in 1997. The consequences were quickly apparent. Peak-season out-of-stock levels rose more than 12 percent compared to the prior year. After six years of steady growth, net income dropped from $15 million in 1997 to not much more than $1 million the next year. Fast-forward six years. They had no supply problems in any of their warehouses or stores. What changed? Two words: supply chain. Managers recognized that they needed to make a significant shift in managing its supply chain. A crucial element was greater collaboration with their suppliers. It is not enough to coordinate the supply chain within the boundaries of a single organization.

and suppliers. Many forecasting software packages are available, including Manugistics, Forecast Pro, and SAS. The forecasting routines in OM Explorer and POM for Windows give some hint of their capabilities. Forecasting is not just a set of techniques, but instead a process that must be designed and managed. While there is no one process that works for everyone, here we describe two comprehensive processes that can be quite effective in managing operations and the supply chain.

A Typical Forecasting Process

Many *inputs* to the forecasting process are informational, beginning with the *history file* on past demand. The history file is kept up-to-date with the actual demands. Clarifying notes and adjustments are made to the database to explain unusual demand behavior, such as the impact of special promotions and closeouts. Often the database is separated into two parts: *base* data and *nonbase* data. The second category reflects irregular demands. Final forecasts just made at the end of the prior cycle are entered in the history file, so as to track forecast errors. Other information sources are from salesforce estimates, outstanding bids on new orders, booked orders, market research studies, competitor behavior, economic outlook, new product introductions, pricing, and promotions. If CPFR is used, as is done by Motorola Mobility in our opening vignette, then considerable information sharing will take place with customers and suppliers. For new products, a history database is fabricated based on the firm's experience with prior products and the judgment of personnel.

Outputs of the process are forecasts for multiple time periods into the future. Typically, they are on a monthly basis and are projected out from six months to two years. Most software packages have the ability to "roll up" or "aggregate" forecasts for individual stock-keeping units (SKUs) into forecasts for whole product families. Forecasts can also be "blown down" or "disaggregated" into smaller pieces. In a make-to-stock environment, forecasts tend to be more detailed and can get down to specific individual products. In a make-to-order environment, the forecasts tend to be for groups of products. Similarly, if the lead times to buy raw materials and manufacture a product or provide a service are long, the forecasts go farther out into the future.

The forecast process itself, typically done on a monthly basis, consists of structured steps. These steps often are facilitated by someone who might be called a demand manager, forecast analyst, or demand/supply planner. However, many other people are typically involved before the plan for the month is authorized.

Step 1. The cycle begins mid-month just after the forecasts have been finalized and communicated to the stakeholders. Now is the time to update the history file and review forecast accuracy. At the end of the month, enter actual demand and review forecast accuracy.

Step 2. Prepare initial forecasts using some forecasting software package and judgment. Adjust the parameters of the software to find models that fit the past demand well and yet reflect the demand manager's judgment on irregular events and information about future sales pulled from various sources and business units.

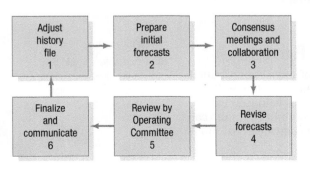

Step 3. Hold consensus meetings with the stakeholders, such as marketing, sales, supply chain planners, and finance. Make it easy for business unit and field sales personnel to make inputs. Use the Internet to get collaborative information from key customers and suppliers. The goal is to arrive at consensus forecasts from all of the important players.

Step 4. Revise the forecasts using judgment, considering the inputs from the consensus meetings and collaborative sources.

Step 5. Present the forecasts to the operating committee for review and to reach a final set of forecasts. It is important to have a set of forecasts that everybody agrees upon and will work to support.

Step 6. Finalize the forecasts based on the decisions of the operating committee and communicate them to the important stakeholders. Supply chain planners are usually the biggest users.

As with all work activity, forecasting is a process and should be continually reviewed for improvements. A better process will foster better relationships between departments such as marketing, sales, and operations. It will also produce better forecasts. This principle is the first one in Table 3.2 to guide process improvements.

Adding Collaboration to the System

This process is similar to the first one, except that it adds considerable collaboration with the company's customers and suppliers, particularly in step 3. **Collaborative planning, forecasting, and replenishment (CPFR)** is a specific nine-step process for supply chain integration that allows a supplier and its customers to collaborate on making the forecast by using the Internet. Many other firms, including Motorola as described in the opening vignette, are turning to CPFR to coordinate up and down the supply chain.

Forecasting as a Nested Process

Forecasting is not a stand-alone activity, but instead part of a larger process that encompasses the remaining chapters. After all, demand is only half of the equation—the other half is supply. Future plans must be developed to supply the resources needed to meet the forecasted demand. Resources include the workforce, materials, inventories, dollars, and equipment capacity. Making sure that demand and supply plans are in balance begins in the next chapter, Chapter 4, "Operations Planning and Scheduling" and continues with Chapter 5, "Resource Planning."

Mark Peterson/CORBIS

Walmart has long been known for its careful analysis of cash register receipts and for working with suppliers to reduce inventories. In the past, like many other retailers, Walmart did not share its forecasts with its suppliers. The result was forecast errors as much as 60 percent of actual demand. Retailers ordered more than they needed, and suppliers produced more than they could sell. To combat the ill effects of forecast errors on inventories, Benchmarking Partners, Inc., was funded in the mid-1990s by Walmart, IBM, SAP, and Manugistics to develop a software package. Walmart initiated this new approach with Listerine, a primary product of Warner-Lambert (now produced and distributed by Johnson & Johnson). The system worked in the following way during this pilot period. Walmart and Warner-Lambert independently calculated the demand they expected for Listerine six months into the future, taking into consideration factors such as past sales trends and promotion plans. They then exchanged their forecasts over the Internet. If the forecasts differed by more than a predetermined percentage, the retailer and the manufacturer used the Internet to exchange written comments and supporting data. The parties went through as many cycles as needed to converge on an acceptable forecast. They passed the pilot period in flying colors. Benefits to Walmart included a reduction in stockouts from 15 percent to 2 percent as well as significant increases in sales and reductions in inventory costs. Likewise, Warner-Lambert benefited by having a smoother production plan and lower average costs. This system was later generalized and dubbed CPFR, which stands for collaborative planning, forecasting, and replenishment.

TABLE 3.2 | SOME PRINCIPLES FOR THE FORECASTING PROCESS

- Better processes yield better forecasts.
- Demand forecasting is being done in virtually every company, either formally or informally. The challenge is to do it well—better than the competition.
- Better forecasts result in better customer service and lower costs, as well as better relationships with suppliers and customers.
- The forecast can and must make sense based on the big picture, economic outlook, market share, and so on.
- The best way to improve forecast accuracy is to focus on reducing forecast error.
- Bias is the worst kind of forecast error; strive for zero bias.
- Whenever possible, forecast at more aggregate levels. Forecast in detail only where necessary.
- Far more can be gained by people collaborating and communicating well than by using the most advanced forecasting technique or model.

collaborative planning, forecasting, and replenishment (CPFR)

A nine-step process for supply chain integration that allows a supplier and its customers to collaborate on making the forecast by using the Internet.

LEARNING GOALS IN REVIEW

1 **Identify the various forecasting methods available to forecasting systems.** The section "Choosing the Type of Forecasting Technique," on pp. 64–65, gives a quick introduction to the four groups of forecasting techniques. Each is described fully in subsequent sections.

2 **Identify the various measures of forecast errors.** Review the "Forecast Error," pp. 65–67, and "Choosing a Quantitative Forecasting Method," pp. 79–80, to understand CFE, MSE, σ, MAD, MAPE, and the tracking signals.

3 **Use regression to make forecasts with one or more independent variables.** The "Causal Methods: Linear Regression" section and Example 3.2, pp. 68–70, describe how linear regression, when historical data is available, can express demand as a linear function of one or more independent variables. Example 3.2 on pp. 69–70 and Solved Problem 1 illustrate the computer output, including the various statistics on how well the regression equation fits the data.

4 **Make forecasts using the most common approaches for time-series analysis.** The "Time-Series Methods" on pp. 70–79

explain the naïve method, simple moving average, weighted moving average, and exponential smoothing techniques that are used. Examples 3.3 and 3.4 demonstrate some of the methods, as do Solved Problems 2 and 3.

5 **Make forecasts using Trend Projection with Regression.** We cover this technique on pp. 74–76, with four figures illustrating the computer output and how varying number of periods included in the regression analysis can impact the results.

6 **Describe a typical forecasting process used by businesses.** See the section "A Typical Forecasting Process," pp. 82–83, and the six steps involved. There is much more complexity when you realize the number of SKUs involved and the need to update the history file.

7 **Explain collaborative planning, forecasting, and replenishment (CPFR).** The "Adding Collaboration to the System" section, p. 83, is a big step in increasing the coordination up and down the supply chain. In the chapter opener, we see what Motorola Mobility has done with its customers to improve its demand forecasts.

MyOMLab helps you develop analytical skills and assesses your progress with multiple problems on moving average, mean absolute deviation, mean absolute percent error, mean squared error (MSE), exponential smoothing, MAD, MAPE, multiplicative seasonal method, least squares regression model, and trend projection with regression.

MyOMLab Resources	Titles	Link to the Book
Video	*Forecasting and Supply Chain Management at Deckers Outdoor Corporation*	Using Multiple Techniques; Putting It All Together; Forecasting as a Process
Active Model Exercises	3.1 Linear Regression	Casual Methods: Linear Regression; Example 3.2 (pp. 69–70); Solved Problem 1
	3.2 Simple Moving Averages	Estimating the Average; Example 3.3 (pp. 71–72); Solved Problem 2
	3.3 Exponential Smoothing	Exponential Smoothing; Example 3.4 (p. 73); Solved Problem 3
OM Explorer Solvers	Regression Analysis	Casual Methods: Linear Regression; Example 3.2 (pp. 69–70); Solved Problem 1
	Seasonal Forecasting	Seasonal Patterns; Example 3.6 (pp. 77–78); Solved Problem 4
	Time Series Forecasting	Time Series Methods Examples 3.3 – 3.5
	Trend Projection with Regression	Trend Projection with Regression; Example 3.5 (pp. 74–76)
OM Explorer Tutors	3.1 Moving Average Method	Estimating the Average; Example 3.3 (pp. 71–72); Solved Problem 2
	3.2 Weighted Moving Average Method	Weighted Moving Average and Solved Problem 2
	3.3 Exponential Smoothing	Exponential Smoothing; Example 3.4 (p. 73); Solved Problem 3
Virtual Tours	Ferrara Pan	Key Decisions on Making Forecasts
	Cape Cod Chips	Demand Patterns; Judgment Methods
POM for Windows	Time Series Analysis	Time Series Methods; Examples 3.3 – 3.5; Seasonal Patterns; Example 3.6 (pp. 77–78); Solved Problem 4
	Regression Projector	Casual Methods: Linear Regression; Example 3.2 (pp. 69–70); Solved Problem 1
	Least Squares – Simple and Multiple Regression	Casual Methods: Linear Regression; Example 3.2 (pp. 69–70); Solved Problem 1
	Error Analysis	Judgment Methods; Forecast Error, Example 3.1 (p. 67), Choosing a Quantitative Forecasting Method; Solved Problem 3

MyOMLab Resources	Titles	Link to the Book
Student Data File	Experiential Exercise Two	Time-Series Methods; Choosing a Time-Series Method; Using Multiple Techniques
Tutorial	Trend-Adjusted Exponential Smoothing	Trend Projection with Regression (pp. 74–76)
Internet Exercise	National Climate Data Center	Casual Methods: Linear Regression; Example 3.2 (pp. 69–70); Trend Projection with Regression; Example 3.5 (pp. 74–76)
Key Equations		
Image Library		

Key Equations

1. Forecast error:

$$E_t = D_t - F_t$$

$$\text{CFE} = \Sigma E_t$$

$$\bar{E} = \frac{\text{CFE}}{n}$$

$$\text{MSE} = \frac{\Sigma E_t^2}{n}$$

$$\sigma = \sqrt{\frac{\Sigma (E_t - \bar{E})^2}{n - 1}}$$

$$\text{MAD} = \frac{\Sigma |E_t|}{n}$$

$$\text{MAPE} = \frac{(\Sigma |E_t|/D_t)(100\%)}{n}$$

2. Linear regression:

$$Y = a + bX$$

3. Naïve forecasting:

$$\text{Forecast} = D_t$$

4. Simple moving average:

$$F_{t+1} = \frac{D_t + D_{t-1} + D_{t-2} + \cdots + D_{t-n+1}}{n}$$

5. Weighted moving average:

$$F_{t+1} = \text{Weight}_1(D_t) + \text{Weight}_2(D_{t-1}) + \text{Weight}_3(D_{t-2}) + \cdots + \text{Weight}_n(D_{t-n+1})$$

6. Exponential smoothing:

$$F_{t+1} = \alpha D_t + (1 - \alpha)F_t$$

7. Trend Projection using Regression

$$F_t = a + bt$$

8. Tracking signal:

$$\frac{\text{CFE}}{\text{MAD}} \text{ or } \frac{\text{CFE}}{\text{MAD}_t}$$

9. Exponentially smoothed error:

$$\text{MAD}_t = \alpha |E_t| + (1 - \alpha)\text{MAD}_{t-1}$$

Key Terms

Solved Problem 1

Chicken Palace periodically offers carryout five-piece chicken dinners at special prices. Let Y be the number of dinners sold and X be the price. Based on the historical observations and calculations in the following table, determine the regression equation, correlation coefficient, and coefficient of determination. How many dinners can Chicken Palace expect to sell at $3.00 each?

Observation	Price (X)	Dinners Sold (Y)
1	$ 2.70	760
2	$ 3.50	510
3	$ 2.00	980
4	$ 4.20	250
5	$ 3.10	320
6	$ 4.05	480
Total	$19.55	3,300
Average	$ 3.258	550

SOLUTION

We use the computer (*Regression Analysis* Solver of OM Explorer or *Regression Projector* module of POM for Windows) to calculate the best values of a, b, the correlation coefficient, and the coefficient of determination.

$$a = 1,454.60$$
$$b = -277.63$$
$$r = -0.84$$
$$r^2 = 0.71$$

The regression line is

$$Y = a + bX = 1,454.60 - 277.63X$$

The correlation coefficient ($r = -0.84$) shows a negative correlation between the variables. The coefficient of determination ($r^2 = 0.71$) is not too large, which suggests that other variables (in addition to price) might appreciably affect sales.

If the regression equation is satisfactory to the manager, estimated sales at a price of $3.00 per dinner may be calculated as follows:

$$Y = a + bX = 1,454.60 - 277.63(3.00)$$
$$= 621.71 \text{ or } 622 \text{ dinners}$$

Solved Problem 2

The Polish General's Pizza Parlor is a small restaurant catering to patrons with a taste for European pizza. One of its specialties is Polish Prize pizza. The manager must forecast weekly demand for these special pizzas so that he can order pizza shells weekly. Recently, demand has been as follows:

Week	Pizzas	Week	Pizzas
June 2	50	June 23	56
June 9	65	June 30	55
June 16	52	July 7	60

a. Forecast the demand for pizza for June 23 to July 14 by using the simple moving average method with $n = 3$. Then, repeat the forecast by using the weighted moving average method with $n = 3$ and weights of 0.50, 0.30, and 0.20, with 0.50 applying to the most recent demand.

b. Calculate the MAD for each method.

SOLUTION

a. The simple moving average method and the weighted moving average method give the following results:

Current Week	Simple Moving Average Forecast for Next Week	Weighted Moving Average Forecast for Next Week
June 16	$\dfrac{52 + 65 + 50}{3} = 55.7$ or 56	$[(0.5 \times 52) + (0.3 \times 65) + (0.2 \times 50)] = 55.5$ or 56
June 23	$\dfrac{56 + 52 + 65}{3} = 55.7$ or 58	$[(0.5 \times 56) + (0.3 \times 52) + (0.2 \times 65)] = 56.6$ or 57
June 30	$\dfrac{55 + 56 + 52}{3} = 54.3$ or 54	$[(0.5 \times 55) + (0.3 \times 56) + (0.2 \times 52)] = 54.7$ or 55
July 7	$\dfrac{60 + 55 + 56}{3} = 57.0$ or 57	$[(0.5 \times 60) + (0.3 \times 55) + (0.2 \times 56)] = 57.7$ or 58

Forecasts in each row are for the next week's demand. For example, the simple moving average and weighted moving average forecasts (both are 56 units) calculated after learning the demand on June 16 apply to June 23's demand forecast.

b. The mean absolute deviation is calculated as follows:

Week	Actual Demand	SIMPLE MOVING AVERAGE Forecast for This Week	Absolute Errors $\lvert E_t \rvert$	WEIGHTED MOVING AVERAGE Forecast for This Week	Absolute Errors $\lvert E_t \rvert$
June 23	56	56	$\lvert 56 - 56 \rvert = 0$	56	$\lvert 56 - 56 \rvert = 0$
June 30	55	58	$\lvert 55 - 58 \rvert = 3$	57	$\lvert 55 - 57 \rvert = 2$
July 7	60	54	$\lvert 60 - 54 \rvert = 6$	55	$\lvert 60 - 55 \rvert = 5$
			$\text{MAD} = \dfrac{0 + 3 + 6}{3} = 3.0$		$\text{MAD} = \dfrac{0 + 2 + 5}{3} = 2.3$

For this limited set of data, the weighted moving average method resulted in a slightly lower mean absolute deviation. However, final conclusions can be made only after analyzing much more data.

Solved Problem 3

The monthly demand for units manufactured by the Acme Rocket Company has been as follows:

Month	Units	Month	Units
May	100	September	105
June	80	October	110
July	110	November	125
August	115	December	120

a. Use the exponential smoothing method to forecast the number of units for June to January. The initial forecast for May was 105 units; $\alpha = 0.2$.

b. Calculate the absolute percentage error for each month from June through December and the MAD and MAPE of forecast error as of the end of December.

c. Calculate the tracking signal as of the end of December. What can you say about the performance of your forecasting method?

SOLUTION

a.

Current Month, t	Calculating Forecast for Next Month $F_{t+1} = \alpha D_t + (1 - \alpha)F_t$	Forecast for Month $t + 1$
May	$0.2(100) + 0.8(105) = 104.0$ or 104	June
June	$0.2(80) + 0.8(104.0) = 99.2$ or 99	July
July	$0.2(110) + 0.8(99.2) = 101.4$ or 101	August
August	$0.2(115) + 0.8(101.4) = 104.1$ or 104	September
September	$0.2(105) + 0.8(104.1) = 104.3$ or 104	October
October	$0.2(110) + 0.8(104.3) = 105.4$ or 105	November
November	$0.2(125) + 0.8(105.4) = 109.3$ or 109	December
December	$0.2(120) + 0.8(109.3) = 111.4$ or 111	January

b.

Month, t	Actual Demand, D_t	Forecast, F_t	Error, $E_t = D_t - F_t$	Absolute Error, $|E_t|$	Absolute Percentage Error, $(|E_t|/D_t)(100\%)$
June	80	104	−24	24	30.0%
July	110	99	11	11	10.0
August	115	101	14	14	12.0
September	105	104	1	1	1.0
October	110	104	6	6	5.5
November	125	105	20	0	16.0
December	120	109	11	11	9.2
Total	765		39	87	83.7%

$$\text{MAD} = \frac{\Sigma|E_t|}{n} = \frac{87}{7} = 12.4 \text{ and MAPE} = \frac{(\Sigma|E_t|/D_t)(100)}{n} = \frac{83.7\%}{7} = 11.96\%$$

c. As of the end of December, the cumulative sum of forecast errors (CFE) is 39. Using the mean absolute deviation calculated in part (b), we calculate the tracking signal:

$$\text{Tracking signal} = \frac{\text{CFE}}{\text{MAD}} = \frac{39}{12.4} = 3.14$$

The probability that a tracking signal value of 3.14 could be generated completely by chance is small. Consequently, we should revise our approach. The long string of forecasts lower than actual demand suggests use of a trend method.

Solved Problem 4

The Northville Post Office experiences a seasonal pattern of daily mail volume every week. The following data for two representative weeks are expressed in thousands of pieces of mail:

Day	Week 1	Week 2
Sunday	5	8
Monday	20	15
Tuesday	30	32
Wednesday	35	30
Thursday	49	45
Friday	70	70
Saturday	15	10
Total	224	210

a. Calculate a seasonal factor for each day of the week.

b. If the postmaster estimates 230,000 pieces of mail to be sorted next week, forecast the volume for each day of the week.

SOLUTION

a. Calculate the average daily mail volume for each week. Then, for each day of the week, divide the mail volume by the week's average to get the seasonal factor. Finally, for each day, add the two seasonal factors and divide by 2 to obtain the average seasonal factor to use in the forecast (see part [b]).

Day	WEEK 1		WEEK 2		Average Seasonal Factor [(1) + (2)]/2
	Mail Volume	Seasonal Factor (1)	Mail Volume	Seasonal Factor (2)	
Sunday	5	5/32 = 0.15625	8	8/30 = 0.26667	0.21146
Monday	20	20/32 = 0.62500	15	15/30 = 0.50000	0.56250
Tuesday	30	30/32 = 0.93750	32	32/30 = 1.06667	1.00209
Wednesday	35	35/32 = 1.09375	30	30/30 = 1.00000	1.04688
Thursday	49	49/32 = 1.53125	45	45/30 = 1.50000	1.51563
Friday	70	70/32 = 2.18750	70	70/30 = 2.33333	2.26042
Saturday	15	15/32 = 0.46875	10	10/30 = 0.33333	0.40104
Total	224		210		
Average	224/7 = 32		210/7 = 30		

b. The average daily mail volume is expected to be 230,000/7 = 32,857 pieces of mail. Using the average seasonal factors calculated in part (a), we obtain the following forecasts:

Day	Calculation		Forecast
Sunday	0.21146(32,857) =		6,948
Monday	0.56250(32,857) =		18,482
Tuesday	1.00209(32,857) =		32,926
Wednesday	1.04688(32,857) =		34,397
Thursday	1.51563(32,857) =		49,799
Friday	2.26042(32,857) =		74,271
Saturday	0.40104(32,857) =		13,177
		Total	230,000

Discussion Questions

1. Figure 3.9 shows summer air visibility measurements for Denver, Colorado. The acceptable visibility standard is 100, with readings above 100 indicating clean air and good visibility, and readings below 100 indicating temperature inversions caused by forest fires, volcanic eruptions, or collisions with comets.

   a. Is a trend evident in the data? Which time-series techniques might be appropriate for estimating the average of these data?

   b. A medical center for asthma and respiratory diseases located in Denver has great demand for its services when air quality is poor. If you were in charge of developing a short-term (say, 3-day) forecast of visibility, which causal factor(s) would you analyze? In other words, which external factors hold the potential to significantly affect visibility in the *short term*?

   c. Tourism, an important factor in Denver's economy, is affected by the city's image. Air quality, as measured by visibility, affects the city's image. If you were responsible for development of tourism, which causal factor(s) would you analyze to forecast visibility for the *medium term* (say, the next two summers)?

   d. The federal government threatens to withhold several hundred million dollars in Department of Transportation funds unless Denver meets visibility standards within 8 years. How would you proceed to generate a *long-term* judgment forecast of technologies that will be available to improve visibility in the next 10 years?

2. Kay and Michael Passe publish *What's Happening?*—a biweekly newspaper to publicize local events. *What's Happening?* has few subscribers; it typically is sold at checkout stands. Much of the revenue comes from advertisers of garage sales and supermarket specials. In an effort to reduce costs associated with printing too many papers or delivering them to the wrong location, Michael implemented a computerized system to collect sales data. Sales-counter scanners accurately record sales data for each location. Since the system was implemented, total sales volume has steadily declined. Selling advertising space and maintaining shelf space at supermarkets are getting more difficult.

   Reduced revenue makes controlling costs all the more important. For each issue, Michael carefully makes a forecast based on sales data collected at each location. Then, he orders papers to be printed and distributed in quantities matching the forecast. Michael's forecast reflects a downward trend, which *is* present in the sales data. Now only a few papers are left over at only a few locations. Although the sales forecast accurately predicts the actual sales at most locations, *What's Happening?* is spiraling toward oblivion. Kay suspects that Michael is doing something wrong in preparing the forecast but can find no mathematical errors. Tell her what is happening.

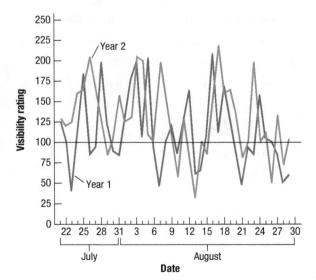

▲ **FIGURE 3.9**
Summer Air Visibility Measurements

Problems

The OM Explorer and POM for Windows software is available to all students using the 10th edition of this textbook. Go to **www.pearsonhighered.com/krajewski** to download these computer packages. If you purchased MyOMLab, you also have access to Active Models software and significant help in doing the following problems. Check with your instructor on how best to use these resources. In many cases, the instructor wants you to understand how to do the calculations by hand. At the least, the software provides a check on your calculations. When calculations are particularly complex and the goal is interpreting the results in making decisions, the software entirely replaces the manual calculations.

1. The owner of a computer store rents printers to some of her preferred customers. She is interested in arriving at a forecast of rentals so that she can order the correct quantities of supplies that go with the printers. Data for the last 10 weeks are shown here.

Week	Rentals	Week	Rentals
1	23	6	28
2	24	7	32
3	32	8	35
4	26	9	26
5	31	10	24

   a. Prepare a forecast for weeks 6 through 10 by using a 5-week moving average. What is the forecast for week 11?

   b. Calculate the mean absolute deviation as of the end of week 10.

2. Sales for the past 12 months at Dalworth Company are given here.

Month	Sales ($ millions)	Month	Sales ($ millions)
January	20	July	53
February	24	August	62
March	27	September	54
April	31	October	36
May	37	November	32
June	47	December	29

   a. Use a three-month moving average to forecast the sales for the months May through December.

   b. Use a four-month moving average to forecast the sales for the months May through December.

   c. Compare the performance of the two methods by using the mean absolute deviation as the performance criterion. Which method would you recommend?

   d. Compare the performance of the two methods by using the mean absolute percent error as the performance criterion. Which method would you recommend?

   e. Compare the performance of the two methods by using the mean squared error as the performance criterion. Which method would you recommend?

3. Karl's Copiers sells and repairs photocopy machines. The manager needs weekly forecasts of service calls so that he can schedule service personnel. Use the actual demand in the first period for the forecast for the first week so error measurement begins in the second week. The manager uses exponential smoothing with $\alpha = 0.20$. Forecast the number of calls for week 6, which is next week.

Week	Actual Service Calls
1	24
2	32
3	36
4	23
5	25

4. Consider the sales data for Dalworth Company given in Problem 2.

   a. Use a 3-month weighted moving average to forecast the sales for the months April through December. Use weights of (3/6), (2/6), and (1/6), giving more weight to more recent data.

   b. Use exponential smoothing with $\alpha = 0.6$ to forecast the sales for the months April through December. Assume that the initial forecast for January was $22 million. Start error measurement in April.

   c. Compare the performance of the two methods by using the mean absolute deviation as the performance criterion, with error measurement beginning in April. Which method would you recommend?

   d. Compare the performance of the two methods by using the mean absolute percent error as the performance criterion, with error measurement beginning in April. Which method would you recommend?

   e. Compare the performance of the two methods by using the mean squared error as the performance criterion, with error measurement beginning in April. Which method would you recommend?

5. A convenience store recently started to carry a new brand of soft drink. Management is interested in estimating future sales volume to determine whether it should continue to carry the new brand or replace it with another brand. The table at the top of the next page provides the number of cans sold per week. Use both the trend projection with regression and the exponential smoothing (let $\alpha = 0.4$ with an initial forecast for week 1 of 617) methods to forecast demand for week 13. Compare these methods by using the mean absolute deviation and mean absolute percent error performance criteria. Does your analysis suggest that sales are trending and if so, by how much?

Week	1	2	3	4	5	6	7	8	9	10	11	12
Sales	617	617	648	739	659	623	742	704	724	715	668	740

6. Community Federal Bank in Dothan, Alabama, recently increased its fees to customers who use employees as tellers. Management is interested in whether its new fee policy has increased the number of customers now using its automatic teller machines to that point that more machines are required. The following table provides the number of automatic teller transactions by week. Use trend projection with regression to forecast usage for weeks 13–16.

Week	1	2	3	4	5	6	7	8	9	10	11	12
Transactions	716	721	833	639	689	736	779	711	723	835	829	667

7. The number of heart surgeries performed at Heartville General Hospital has increased steadily over the past several years. The hospital's administration is seeking the best method to forecast the demand for such surgeries in year 6. The data for the past 5 years are shown.

Year	Demand
1	45
2	50
3	52
4	56
5	58

The hospital's administration is considering the following forecasting methods. Begin error measurement in year 3, so all methods are compared for the same years.

i. Exponential smoothing, with $\alpha = 0.6$. Let the initial forecast for year 1 be 45, the same as the actual demand.

ii. Exponential smoothing, with $\alpha = 0.9$. Let the initial forecast for year 1 be 45, the same as the actual demand.

iii. Trend projection with regression.

iv. Two-year moving average.

v. Two-year weighted moving average, using weights 0.6 and 0.4, with more recent data given more weight.

vi. If MAD is the performance criterion chosen by the administration, which forecasting method should it choose?

vii. If MSE is the performance criterion chosen by the administration, which forecasting method should it choose?

viii. If MAPE is the performance criterion chosen by the administration, which forecasting method should it choose?

8. The following data are for calculator sales in units at an electronics store over the past 9 weeks:

Week	Sales	Week	Sales
1	46	6	58
2	49	7	62
3	43	8	56
4	50	9	63
5	53		

Use trend projection with regression to forecast sales for weeks 10–13. What are the error measures (CFE, MSE, σ, MAD, and MAPE) for this forecasting procedure? How about r^2?

9. The demand for Krispee Crunchies, a favorite breakfast cereal of people born in the 1940s, is experiencing a decline. The company wants to monitor demand for this product closely as it nears the end of its life cycle. The following table shows the actual sales history for January–October. Generate forecasts for November–December, using the trend projection by regression method. Looking at the accuracy of its forecasts over the history file, as well as the other statistics provided, how confident are you in these forecasts for November–December?

Month	Sales	Month	Sales
January	890,000	July	710,000
February	800,000	August	730,000
March	825,000	September	680,000
April	840,000	October	670,000
May	730,000	November	
June	780,000	December	

10. Forrest and Dan make boxes of chocolates for which the demand is uncertain. Forrest says, "That's life." On the other hand, Dan believes that some demand patterns exist that could be useful for planning the purchase of sugar, chocolate, and shrimp. Forrest insists on placing a surprise chocolate-covered shrimp in some boxes so that "You never know what you'll get." Quarterly demand (in boxes of chocolates) for the last 3 years follows:

Quarter	Year 1	Year 2	Year 3
1	3,000	3,300	3,502
2	1,700	2,100	2,448
3	900	1,500	1,768
4	4,400	5,100	5,882
Total	10,000	12,000	13,600

a. Use intuition and judgment to estimate quarterly demand for the fourth year.

b. If the expected sales for chocolates are 14,800 cases for year 4, use the multiplicative seasonal method to prepare a forecast for each quarter of the year. Are any of the quarterly forecasts different from what you thought you would get in part (a)?

11. The manager of Snyder's Garden Center must make the annual purchasing plans for rakes, gloves, and other gardening items. One of the items the company stocks is Fast-Grow, a liquid fertilizer. The sales of this item are seasonal, with peaks in the spring, summer, and fall months. Quarterly demand (in cases) for the past 2 years follows:

Quarter	Year 1	Year 2
1	40	60
2	350	440
3	290	320
4	210	280
Total	890	1,100

If the expected sales for Fast-Grow are 1,150 cases for year 3, use the multiplicative seasonal method to prepare a forecast for each quarter of the year.

12. The manager of a utility company in the Texas panhandle wants to develop quarterly forecasts of power loads for the next year. The power loads are seasonal, and the data on the quarterly loads in megawatts (MW) for the last 4 years are as follows:

Quarter	Year 1	Year 2	Year 3	Year 4
1	103.5	94.7	118.6	109.3
2	126.1	116.0	141.2	131.6
3	144.5	137.1	159.0	149.5
4	166.1	152.5	178.2	169.0

The manager estimates the total demand for the next year at 600 MW. Use the multiplicative seasonal method to develop the forecast for each quarter.

13. Demand for oil changes at Garcia's Garage has been as follows:

Month	Number of Oil Changes
January	41
February	46
March	57
April	52
May	59
June	51
July	60
August	62

a. Use simple linear regression analysis to develop a forecasting model for monthly demand. In this application, the dependent variable, Y, is monthly demand and the independent variable, X, is the month. For January, let $X = 1$; for February, let $X = 2$; and so on.

b. Use the model to forecast demand for September, October, and November. Here, $X = 9$, 10, and 11, respectively.

14. At a hydrocarbon processing factory, process control involves periodic analysis of samples for a certain process quality parameter. The analytic procedure currently used is costly and time consuming. A faster and more economical alternative procedure has been proposed. However, the numbers for the quality parameter given by the alternative procedure are somewhat different from those given by the current procedure, not because of any inherent errors but because of changes in the nature of the chemical analysis.

Management believes that if the numbers from the new procedure can be used to forecast reliably the corresponding numbers from the current procedure, switching to the new procedure would be reasonable and cost effective. The following data were obtained for the quality parameter by analyzing samples using both procedures:

Current (Y)	Proposed (X)	Current (Y)	Proposed (X)
3.0	3.1	3.1	3.1
3.1	3.9	2.7	2.9
3.0	3.4	3.3	3.6
3.6	4.0	3.2	4.1
3.8	3.6	2.1	2.6
2.7	3.6	3.0	3.1
2.7	3.6	2.6	2.8

a. Use linear regression to find a relation to forecast Y, which is the quality parameter from the current procedure, using the values from the proposed procedure, X.

b. Is there a strong relationship between Y and X? Explain.

15. Ohio Swiss Milk Products manufactures and distributes ice cream in Ohio, Kentucky, and West Virginia. The company wants to expand operations by locating another plant in northern Ohio. The size of the new plant will be a function of the expected demand for ice cream within the area served by the plant. A market survey is currently under way to determine that demand.

Ohio Swiss wants to estimate the relationship between the manufacturing cost per gallon and the number of gallons sold in a year to determine the demand for ice cream and, thus, the size of the new plant. The following data have been collected:

a. Develop a regression equation to forecast the cost per gallon as a function of the number of gallons produced.

Plant	Cost per Thousand Gallons (Y)	Thousands of Gallons Sold (X)
1	$ 1,015	416.9
2	973	472.5
3	1,046	250.0
4	1,006	372.1
5	1,058	238.1
6	1,068	258.6
7	967	597.0
8	997	414.0
9	1,044	263.2
10	1,008	372.0
Total	$10,182	3,654.4

b. What are the correlation coefficient and the coefficient of determination? Comment on your regression equation in light of these measures.

c. Suppose that the market survey indicates a demand of 325,000 gallons in the Bucyrus, Ohio, area. Estimate the manufacturing cost per gallon for a plant producing 325,000 gallons per year.

Advanced Problems

16. Franklin Tooling, Inc., manufactures specialty tooling for firms in the paper-making industry. All of their products are engineer-to-order and so the company never knows exactly what components to purchase for a tool until a customer places an order. However, the company believes that weekly demand for a few components is fairly stable. Component 135.AG is one such item. The last 26 weeks of historical use of component 135.AG is recorded below.

Week	Demand	Week	Demand
1	137	14	131
2	136	15	132
3	143	16	124
4	136	17	121
5	141	18	127
6	128	19	118
7	149	20	120
8	136	21	115
9	134	22	106
10	142	23	120
11	125	24	113
12	134	25	121
13	118	26	119

Use OM Explorer's *Time Series Forecasting* Solver to evaluate the following forecasting methods. Start error measurement in the fifth week, so all methods are evaluated over the same time interval. Use the default settings for initial forecasts.

i. Naïve (1-Period Moving Average)

ii. 3-Period Moving Average

iii. Exponential Smoothing, with $\alpha = .28$

iv. Trend Projection with Regression

v. Which forecasting method should management use, if the performance criterion it chooses is:
- CFE?
- MSE?
- MAD?
- MAPE?

17. Create an Excel spreadsheet on your own that can create combination forecasts for Problem 16. Create a combination forecast using all four techniques from problem 16. Give each technique an equal weight. Create a second combination forecast by using the three techniques that seem best based on MAD. Give equal weight to each technique. Finally, create a third forecast by equally weighting the two best techniques. Calculate CFE, MAD, MSE, and MAPE for the combination forecast. Are these forecasts better or worse than the forecasting techniques identified in Problem 16?

18. The director of a large public library must schedule employees to reshelf books and periodicals checked out of the library. The number of items checked out will determine the labor requirements. The following data reflect the number of items checked out of the library for the past 3 years:

Month	Year 1	Year 2	Year 3
January	1,847	2,045	1,986
February	2,669	2,321	2,564
March	2,467	2,419	2,635
April	2,432	2,088	2,150
May	2,464	2,667	2,201
June	2,378	2,122	2,663
July	2,217	2,206	2,055
August	2,445	1,869	1,678
September	1,894	2,441	1,845
October	1,922	2,291	2,065
November	2,431	2,364	2,147
December	2,274	2,189	2,451

The director needs a time-series method for forecasting the number of items to be checked out during the next month. Find the best simple moving average forecast you can. Decide what is meant by "best" and justify your decision.

19. Using the data in Problem 18, find the best exponential smoothing solution you can. Justify your choice.

20. Using the data in Problem 18, find the best trend projection with regression solution you can. Compare the performance of this method with those of the best moving average method (from Problem 18) and the exponential smoothing method (from Problem 19). Which of these three methods would you choose?

21. Cannister, Inc., specializes in the manufacture of plastic containers. The data on the monthly sales of 10-ounce shampoo bottles for the past 5 years are as follows:

Year	1	2	3	4	5
January	742	741	896	951	1,030
February	697	700	793	861	1,032
March	776	774	885	938	1,126
April	898	932	1,055	1,109	1,285
May	1,030	1,099	1,204	1,274	1,468
June	1,107	1,223	1,326	1,422	1,637
July	1,165	1,290	1,303	1,486	1,611
August	1,216	1,349	1,436	1,555	1,608
September	1,208	1,341	1,473	1,604	1,528
October	1,131	1,296	1,453	1,600	1,420
November	971	1,066	1,170	1,403	1,119
December	783	901	1,023	1,209	1,013

a. Using the multiplicative seasonal method, calculate the monthly seasonal indices.

b. Develop a simple linear regression equation to forecast annual sales. For this regression, the dependent variable, Y, is the demand in each year and the independent variable, X, is the index for the year (i.e., $X = 1$ for year 1, $X = 2$ for year 2, and so on until $X = 5$ for year 5).

c. Forecast the annual sales for year 6 by using the regression model you developed in part (b).

d. Prepare the seasonal forecast for each month by using the monthly seasonal indices calculated in part (a).

22. The Midwest Computer Company serves a large number of businesses in the Great Lakes region. The company sells supplies and replacements and performs service on all computers sold through seven sales offices. Many items are stocked, so close inventory control is necessary to assure customers of efficient service. Recently, business has been increasing, and management is concerned about stockouts. A forecasting method is needed to estimate requirements several months in advance so that adequate replenishment quantities can be purchased. An example of the sales growth experienced during the last 50 months is the growth in demand for item EP-37, a laser printer cartridge, shown in Table 3.3.

a. Develop a trend projection with regression solution using OM Explorer. Forecast demand for month 51.

b. A consultant to Midwest's management suggested that new office building leases would be a good leading indicator for company sales. The consultant quoted a recent university study finding that new office building leases precede office equipment and supply sales by 3 months. According to the study findings, leases in month 1 would affect sales in month 4, leases in month 2 would affect sales in month 5, and so on. Use POM for Windows' linear regression module to develop a forecasting model for sales, with leases as the independent variable. Forecast sales for month 51.

c. Which of the two models provides better forecasts? Explain.

23. A certain food item at P&Q Supermarkets has the demand pattern shown in the table at the bottom of the next page. There are 5 periods per cycle. Find the "best" forecast you can for month 25 and justify your methodology. If you wish to explore the Seasonal Forecasting method as one of the techniques tested, you will find that OM Explorer's *Seasonal Forecasting* Solver does not cover the case where there are 5 periods in a cycle (or seasons in a year). You must do some manual calculations or write an Excel spreadsheet on your own.

TABLE 3.3 | EP-37 SALES AND LEASE DATA

Month	EP-37 Sales	Leases	Month	EP-37 Sales	Leases
1	80	32	26	1,296	281
2	132	29	27	1,199	298
3	143	32	28	1,267	314
4	180	54	29	1,300	323
5	200	53	30	1,370	309
6	168	89	31	1,489	343
7	212	74	32	1,499	357
8	254	93	33	1,669	353
9	397	120	34	1,716	360
10	385	113	35	1,603	370
11	472	147	36	1,812	386
12	397	126	37	1,817	389
13	476	138	38	1,798	399
14	699	145	39	1,873	409
15	545	160	40	1,923	410
16	837	196	41	2,028	413
17	743	180	42	2,049	439
18	722	197	43	2,084	454
19	735	203	44	2,083	441
20	838	223	45	2,121	470
21	1,057	247	46	2,072	469
22	930	242	47	2,262	490
23	1,085	234	48	2,371	496
24	1,090	254	49	2,309	509
25	1,218	271	50	2,422	522

Period	Demand	Period	Demand
1	33	13	37
2	37	14	43
3	31	15	56
4	39	16	41
5	54	17	36
6	38	18	39
7	42	19	41
8	40	20	58
9	41	21	42
10	54	22	45
11	43	23	41
12	39	24	38

24. The data for the visibility chart in Discussion Question 1 are shown in Table 3.4. The visibility standard is set at 100. Readings below 100 indicate that air pollution has reduced visibility, and readings above 100 indicate that the air is clearer.

   a. Use several methods to generate a visibility forecast for August 31 of the second year. Which method seems to produce the best forecast?

   b. Use several methods to forecast the visibility index for the summer of the third year. Which method seems to produce the best forecast? Support your choice.

25. Tom Glass forecasts electrical demand for the Flatlands Public Power District (FPPD). The FPPD wants to take its Comstock power plant out of service for maintenance when demand is expected to be low. After shutdown, performing maintenance and getting the plant back on line takes two weeks. The utility has enough other generating capacity to satisfy 1,550 megawatts (MW) of demand while Comstock is out of service. Table 3.5 at the end of

TABLE 3.4 | VISIBILITY DATA

Date	Year 1	Year 2	Date	Year 1	Year 2	Date	Year 1	Year 2
July 22	125	130	Aug 5	105	200	Aug 19	170	160
23	100	120	6	205	110	20	125	165
24	40	125	7	90	100	21	85	135
25	100	160	8	45	200	22	45	80
26	185	165	9	100	160	23	95	100
27	85	205	10	120	100	24	85	200
28	95	165	11	85	55	25	160	100
29	200	125	12	125	130	26	105	110
30	125	85	13	165	75	27	100	50
31	90	105	14	60	30	28	95	135
Aug 1	85	160	15	65	100	29	50	70
2	135	125	16	110	85	30	60	105
3	175	130	17	210	150			
4	200	205	18	110	220			

the Advanced Problems shows weekly peak demands (in MW) for the past several autumns. When next fall should the Comstock plant be scheduled for maintenance?

26. A manufacturing firm seeks to develop a better forecast for an important product, and believes that there is a trend to the data. OM Explorer's *Trend Projection with Regression* Solver has been set up with the 47 demands in the history file. Note the "Load Problem 26 Data" button in the *Trend Projection with Regression* Solver that when clicked will automatically input the demand data. Otherwise, you can enter the demand data directly into the Inputs sheet.

Yr	1	2	3	4
Jan	4507	4589	4084	4535
Feb	4400	4688	4158	4477
Mar	4099	4566	4174	4601
Apr	4064	4485	4225	4648
May	4002	4385	4324	4860
Jun	3963	4377	4220	4998
Jul	4037	4309	4267	5003
Aug	4162	4276	4187	4960
Sep	4312	4280	4239	4943
Oct	4395	4144	4352	5052
Nov	4540	4219	4331	5107
Dec	4471	4052	4371	

a. What is your forecast for December of Year 4, making period 1 as the starting period for the regression?

b. The actual demand for period 48 was just learned to be 5,100. Add this demand to the Inputs file and change the starting period for the regression to period 2 so that the number of periods in the regression remains unchanged. How much or little does the forecast for period 49 change from the one for period 48? The error measures? Are you surprised?

c. Now change the time when the regression starts to period 25 and repeat the process. What differences do you note now? What forecast will you make for period 49?

27. A manufacturing firm has developed a skills test, the scores from which can be used to predict workers' production rating factors. Data on the test scores of various workers and their subsequent production ratings are shown.

Worker	Test Score	Production Rating	Worker	Test Score	Production Rating
A	53	45	K	54	59
B	36	43	L	73	77
C	88	89	M	65	56
D	84	79	N	29	28
E	86	84	O	52	51
F	64	66	P	22	27
G	45	49	Q	76	76
H	48	48	R	32	34
I	39	43	S	51	60
J	67	76	T	37	32

a. Using POM for Windows' least squares-linear regression module, develop a relationship to forecast production ratings from test scores.

b. If a worker's test score was 80, what would be your forecast of the worker's production rating?

c. Comment on the strength of the relationship between the test scores and production ratings.

28. The materials handling manager of a manufacturing company is trying to forecast the cost of maintenance for the company's fleet of over-the-road tractors. The manager believes that the cost of maintaining the tractors increases with their age. The following data was collected:

Age (years)	Yearly Maintenance Cost ($)	Age (years)	Yearly Maintenance Cost ($)
4.5	619	5.0	1,194
4.5	1,049	0.5	163
4.5	1,033	0.5	182
4.0	495	6.0	764
4.0	723	6.0	1,373
4.0	681	1.0	978
5.0	890	1.0	466
5.0	1,522	1.0	549
5.5	987		

a. Use POM for Windows' least squares-linear regression module to develop a relationship to forecast the yearly maintenance cost based on the age of a tractor.

b. If a section has 20 three-year-old tractors, what is the forecast for the annual maintenance cost?

TABLE 3.5 | WEEKLY PEAK POWER DEMANDS

Year	AUGUST			SEPTEMBER				OCTOBER				NOVEMBER	
	1	2	3	4	5	6	7	8	9	10	11	12	13
1	2,050	1,925	1,825	1,525	1,050	1,300	1,200	1,175	1,350	1,525	1,725	1,575	1,925
2	2,000	2,075	2,225	1,800	1,175	1,050	1,250	1,025	1,300	1,425	1,625	1,950	1,950
3	1,950	1,800	2,150	1,725	1,575	1,275	1,325	1,100	1,500	1,550	1,375	1,825	2,000
4	2,100	2,400	1,975	1,675	1,350	1,525	1,500	1,150	1,350	1,225	1,225	1,475	1,850
5	2,275	2,300	2,150	1,525	1,350	1,475	1,475	1,175	1,375	1,400	1,425	1,550	1,900

VIDEO CASE | Forecasting and Supply Chain Management at Deckers Outdoor Corporation

Deckers Outdoor Corporation's footwear products are among some of the most well-known brands in the world. From UGG sheepskin boots and Teva sport sandals to Simple shoes, Deckers flip-flops, and Tsubo footwear, Deckers is committed to building niche footwear brands into global brands with market leadership positions. Net sales for fiscal year 2007 were close to $449 million. In addition to traditional retail store outlets for Deckers' footwear styles, the company maintains an active and growing "direct to consumer" e-commerce business. Since most retail stores cannot carry every style in every color and size, the company offers the full line for each of its brands directly to consumers through the brands' individual Web sites. Online sales at its virtual store are handled by its e-commerce group. Customers who want a pair of shoes not available at the retail store can always buy from the virtual store.

Founded in 1973, the company manufactured a single line of sandals in a small factory in Southern California. The challenges of managing the raw materials and finished goods inventories were small compared to today's global sourcing and sales challenges for the company's various brands. Today, each brand has its own development team and brand managers who generate, develop, and test-market the seasonal styles that appear on the shelves of retailers such as Nordstrom, Lord & Taylor, REI, the Walking Company, and the company's own UGG brand retail stores in the United States and Japan.

At Deckers, forecasting is the starting point for inventory management, sales and operations planning, resource planning, and scheduling—in short, managing its supply chain. It carries a considerable amount of seasonal stock. Shoes with seasonal demand that are left over at the end of their season must be sold at heavily discounted prices. Its products fall into three categories: (1) carry-over items that were sold in prior years, (2) new items that look similar to past models, and (3) completely new designs that are fashionable with no past history.

Pearson

Twice a year, the brand development teams work on the fall and spring product lines. They come up with new designs about one year in advance of each season. Each brand (UGG, Teva, Simple, Tsubo, and Deckers) contains numerous products, called stock keeping units (SKUs). The materials for new designs are selected and tested in prototypes. Approved designs are put into the seasonal line-up. Forecasts must be made at both the SKU and aggregate levels months before the season begins. "Bottoms-up" forecasts for each SKU begin by analyzing any available history files of past demand. Judgment forecasts are also important inputs, particularly for the second and third categories of shoes that are not carry-overs. For example, Char Nicanor-Kimball is an expert in spotting trends in shoe sales and makes forecasts for the virtual store. For new designs, historical sales on similar items are used to make a best guess on demand for those items. This process is facilitated by a forecasting and inventory system on the company's Intranet. At the same time, the sales teams for each brand call on their retail accounts and secure customer orders of approved designs for the coming season. Then, the virtual store forecasts are merged with orders from the retail store orders to get the total seasonal demand forecasted by SKU. Next, the SKU forecasts are "rolled up" by category and "top down" forecasts are also made.

These forecasts then go to top management where some adjustments may be made to account for financial market conditions, consumer credit, weather, demographic factors, and customer confidence. The impact of public relations and advertising must also be considered.

Actually, forecasting continues on throughout the year on a daily and weekly basis to "get a handle" on demand. Comparing actual demand with what was forecasted for different parts of the season also helps the forecasters make better forecasts for the future and better control inventories.

Based on initial demand forecasts, the company must begin sourcing the materials needed to produce the footwear. The company makes most of its products in China and sources many of the raw materials there as well. For UGG products sheepskin sourcing occurs in Australia with top grade producers, but the rawhide tanning still takes places in China. With potential suppliers identified and assurance from internal engineering that the footwear can be successfully made, the engineering and material data are handed over to the manufacturing department to determine how best to make the footwear in mass quantities. At this point, Deckers places a seasonal "buy" with its suppliers.

The orders for each SKU are fed into the manufacturing schedules at the Chinese factories. All the SKUs for a given brand are manufactured at the same factory. While Deckers agents negotiate the raw materials contracts early in the development process, the factories only place the orders for the raw materials when the company sends in the actual orders for the finished goods. No footwear is made by the factories until orders are received.

At the factories, finished goods footwear is inspected and packaged for the month-long ocean voyage from Hong Kong to ports in the United States. Deckers ships fifty containers a week from its Chinese manufacturing sources, each holding approximately 5,000 pairs of shoes. Ownership of the finished goods transfers from the factories to Deckers in Hong Kong.

When the shipping containers arrive in the United States, the footwear is transferred to Deckers' distribution centers in Southern California. Teva products are warehoused in Ventura, California; all other products are handled by the company's state-of-the-art facility in Camarillo, California. Typically, Deckers brings product into the distribution centers two to three months in advance of expected needs so that the production at the suppliers' factories and the labor activities at the distribution centers are leveled. There are definitive spikes in the demand for footwear, with Teva spiking in Quarter 1 and UGG spiking in Quarter 4. The leveling approach works to keep costs low in the supply chain. However, it also means that Deckers must maintain sizeable inventories. Most shipments from suppliers come in to the distribution centers and are stored in inventory for one to two months awaiting a customer order. By the time the footwear is stocked in the distribution center, the company knows which retail customers will be getting the various products, based on the orders booked months earlier. Then, according to delivery schedules negotiated with the customers, the company begins filling orders and shipping products to retail locations. The warehouse tracks incoming shipments, goods placed on the shelves for customers, and outgoing orders. The inventory system helps manage the customer order filling process.

Because the booked orders are a relatively large proportion of the total orders from retailers, and the number of unanticipated orders is very small, only small safety stocks are needed to service the retailers. Occasionally, the purchase order from Deckers to one of its suppliers matches the sales order from the customer. In such a case, Deckers uses a "cross-dock" system. When the shipment is received at the distribution center, it is immediately checked in and loaded on another truck for delivery to customers. Cross docking reduces the need to store vast quantities of product for long periods of time and cuts down on warehousing expenses for Deckers. The company has been successful in turning its inventory over about four times a year, which is in line with footwear industry standards.

The online sales traffic is all managed centrally. In fact, for ordering and inventory management purposes, the online side of the business is treated just like another major retail store account. As forecasted seasonal orders are generated by each brand's sales team, a manufacturing order for the online business is placed by the e-commerce sales team at the same time. However, unlike the retail outlets that take delivery of products on a regular schedule, the inventory pledged to the online business is held in the distribution center until a Web site order is received. Only then is it shipped directly to the consumer who placed the online order. If actual demand exceeds expected demand, Char Nicanor-Kimball checks if more inventory can be secured from other customer orders that have scaled back.

The forecasting and supply chain management challenges now facing Deckers are two-fold. First, the company plans to grow the brands that have enjoyed seasonal sales activity into year-round footwear options for consumers by expanding the number of SKUs for those brands. For example, most sales for UGG footwear occur in the fall/winter season. Sales for Teva historically have been in the spring and summer. Product managers are now working to develop styles that will allow the brands to cross over the seasons. Second, the company plans to expand internationally, and will have retail outlets in Europe, China, and other Asian locations in the very near future. Company managers are well aware of the challenges and opportunities such global growth will bring, and are taking steps now to assure that the entire supply chain is prepared to forecast and handle the demand when the time comes.

QUESTIONS

1. How much does the forecasting process at Deckers correspond with the "typical forecasting process" described at the end of this chapter?

2. Based on what you see in the video, what kinds of information technology are used to make forecasts, maintain accurate inventory records, and project future inventory levels?

3. What factors make forecasting at Deckers particularly challenging? How can forecasts be made for seasonal, fashionable products for which there is no history file? What are the costs of over-forecasting demand for such items? Under-forecasting?

4. How does the concept of *postponement* get implemented at Deckers by having online sales and positioning inventory at the DCs for every model, color, and size?

5. Where in the supply chain are cycle, pipeline, safety stock, and anticipation inventories being created?

6. What are the benefits of leveling aggregate demand by having a portfolio of SKUs that create 365-day demand?

7. Deckers plans to expand internationally, thereby increasing the volume of shoes it must manage in the supply chain and the pattern of material flows. What implications does this strategy have on forecasting, order quantities, logistics, and relationships with its suppliers and customers?

CASE   Yankee Fork and Hoe Company

The Yankee Fork and Hoe Company is a leading producer of garden tools ranging from wheelbarrows, mortar pans, and hand trucks to shovels, rakes, and trowels. The tools are sold in four different product lines ranging from the top-of-the-line Hercules products, which are rugged tools for the toughest jobs, to the Garden Helper products, which are economy tools for the occasional user. The market for garden tools is extremely competitive because of the simple design of the products and the large number of competing producers. In addition, more people are using power tools, such as lawn edgers, hedge trimmers, and thatchers, reducing demand for their manual counterparts. These factors compel Yankee to maintain low prices while retaining high quality and dependable delivery.

Garden tools represent a mature industry. Unless new manual products can be developed or a sudden resurgence occurs in home gardening, the prospects for large increases in sales are not bright. Keeping ahead of the competition is a constant battle. No one knows this better than Alan Roberts, president of Yankee.

The types of tools sold today are, by and large, the same ones sold 30 years ago. The only way to generate new sales and retain old customers is to provide superior customer service and produce a product with high customer value. This approach puts pressure on the manufacturing system, which has been having difficulties lately. Recently, Roberts has been receiving calls from long-time customers, such as Sears and True Value Hardware Stores, complaining about late shipments. These customers advertise promotions for garden tools and require on-time delivery.

Roberts knows that losing customers like Sears and True Value would be disastrous. He decides to ask consultant Sharon Place to look into the matter and report to him in one week. Roberts suggests that she focus on the bow rake as a case in point because it is a high-volume product and has been a major source of customer complaints of late.

Planning Bow Rake Production

A bow rake consists of a head with 12 teeth spaced 1 inch apart, a hardwood handle, a bow that attaches the head to the handle, and a metal ferrule that reinforces the area where the bow inserts into the handle. The bow is a metal strip that is welded to the ends of the rake head and bent in the middle to form a flat tab for insertion into the handle. The rake is about 64 inches long.

Place decides to find out how Yankee plans bow rake production. She goes straight to Phil Stanton, who gives the following account:

Planning is informal around here. To begin, marketing determines the forecast for bow rakes by month for the next year. Then they pass it along to me. Quite frankly, the forecasts are usually inflated—must be their big egos over there. I have to be careful because we enter into long-term purchasing agreements for steel, and having it just sitting around is expensive. So I usually reduce the forecast by 10 percent or so. I use the modified forecast to generate a monthly final-assembly schedule, which determines what I need to have from the forging and woodworking areas. The system works well if the forecasts are good. But when marketing comes to me and says they are behind on customer orders, as they often do near the end of the year, it wreaks havoc with the schedules. Forging gets hit the hardest. For example, the presses that stamp the rake heads from blanks of steel can handle only 7,000 heads per day, and the bow rolling machine can do only 5,000 per day. Both operations are also required for many other products.

Because the marketing department provides crucial information to Stanton, Place decides to see the marketing manager, Ron Adams. Adams explains how he arrives at the bow rake forecasts.

Things do not change much from year to year. Sure, sometimes we put on a sales promotion of some kind, but we try to give Phil enough warning before the demand kicks in—usually a month or so. I meet with several managers from the various sales regions to go over shipping data from last year and discuss anticipated promotions, changes in the economy, and shortages we experienced last year. Based on these meetings, I generate a monthly forecast for the next year. Even though we take a lot of time getting the forecast, it never seems to help us avoid customer problems.

The Problem

Place ponders the comments from Stanton and Adams. She understands Stanton's concerns about costs and keeping inventory low and Adams's concern about having enough rakes on hand to make timely shipments. Both are also somewhat concerned about capacity. Yet she decides to check actual customer demand for the bow rake over the past 4 years (in Table 3.6) before making her final report to Roberts.

QUESTIONS

1. Comment on the forecasting system being used by Yankee. Suggest changes or improvements that you believe are justified.

2. Develop your own forecast for bow rakes for each month of the next year (year 5). Justify your forecast and the method you used.

TABLE 3.6 | FOUR-YEAR DEMAND HISTORY FOR THE BOW RAKE

Month	DEMAND			
	Year 1	Year 2	Year 3	Year 4
1	55,220	39,875	32,180	62,377
2	57,350	64,128	38,600	66,501
3	15,445	47,653	25,020	31,404
4	27,776	43,050	51,300	36,504
5	21,408	39,359	31,790	16,888
6	17,118	10,317	32,100	18,909
7	18,028	45,194	59,832	35,500
8	19,883	46,530	30,740	51,250
9	15,796	22,105	47,800	34,443
10	53,665	41,350	73,890	68,088
11	83,269	46,024	60,202	68,175
12	72,991	41,856	55,200	61,100

Note: The demand figures shown in the table are the number of units promised for delivery each month. Actual delivery quantities differed because of capacity or shortages of materials.

EXPERIENTIAL LEARNING 3.1 | Forecasting with Holdout Sample

A company's history file, as shown in the following table, gives monthly sales in thousands of dollars "rolled up" into aggregated totals for one of its major product lines.

Your team should use the *Time Series Forecasting* Solver to make forecasts into the future. Note the "Load EL1 Data" button in this solver when clicked will automatically input the demand data. Otherwise, you can enter the demand data directly into the Inputs sheet. Seek out which models you wish to use in making in-class forecasts of monthly sales for the last two months of year 8 and several months into year 9. Perhaps you might want to know the forecasts of all of them, or alternately focus on just two or three of them. If one of the models is the combination forecast, you must decide on the weights to give the models going into its forecast. The weights should add up to 1.0.

Bring to class a one-page document that

- characterizes the monthly sales of the product line in terms of its forecastability.
- identifies the relative importance of four demand patterns: horizontal, trend, seasonal, and cyclical.
- identifies the forecasting models that you will use to make the forecasts for the last of year 8, and future months into year 9, and the extent that judgmental adjustments might be used during the holdout sample exercise. Explain why you made this selection, given that MAD will be used as your error measure.
- makes the November forecast for year 8.

At the start of the in-class portion of the experiential exercise, hand in your one-page document and open the final *Time Series Forecasting* Solver file that you used in modeling the history file. Do not change any of the final parameters chosen for your various forecasting models using the history file

(*n* for moving average, weights for weighted moving average, α for exponential smoothing, and weights for combination).

To start the Holdout Sample session, click on the Worksheet tab and set the time when error analysis begins to be period 95 (November, Year 8). In doing so, error analysis will be tracked only for the holdout periods. Now click on the "Holdout Sample" tab to begin the session. You will initially be presented with the November forecasts for all of the techniques used during your analysis of the history file (including the combination model if you used it). Your next step is to input your team's forecast for November. It can be the forecast from any of the techniques shown, or one of your own if you believe that judgmental adjustment is appropriate. You have no contextual information, but may observe that one model has been performing particularly well in the last few months. You team might have different opinions, but you must reach a consensus. Your instructor will then provide November's actual sales from the holdout sample. After you input that additional information, forecast errors are computed for each model and for your team's November forecast. In addition, computer forecasts (naïve, moving average, weighted moving average, exponential smoothing, trend projection, and combination) are posted for December.

Begin December by inputting your team's forecast. The instructor then provides December's actual sales, and so forth. Continue this process until all errors are calculated for the last period in the holdout sample, which will be announced by your instructor. At the end of this exercise, create a second one-page document that reports your forecasts for the holdout sample, the corresponding average MAD, and CFE whether (and how) you modified your forecasting process as the exercise progressed, and what you learned from this exercise. You will need to write an Excel spreadsheet to calculate the MAD and CFE statistics for the holdout sample. Its output can be attached to your second one-page document. Submit your report to your instructor at the end of the class session.

Your grade on this exercise will be based on (1) the insights provided in the two documents (50 percent of grade) (2) the average MAD for the history file (25 percent of grade), and (3) the average MAD for the holdout sample (25 percent of grade).

Yr	Jan	Feb	Mar	Apr	May	Jun	Jul	Aug	Sep	Oct	Nov	Dec
1	3,255	3,420	3,482	3,740	3,713	3,785	3,817	3,900	3,878	3,949	4,004	4,035
2	3,892	3,730	4,115	4,054	4,184	4,321	4,307	4,481	4,411	4,443	4,395	4,403
3	4,507	4,400	4,099	4,064	4,002	3,963	4,037	4,162	4,312	4,395	4,540	4,471
4	4,589	4,688	4,566	4,485	4,385	4,377	4,309	4,276	4,280	4,144	4,219	4,052
5	4,084	4,158	4,174	4,225	4,324	4,220	4,267	4,187	4,239	4,352	4,331	4,371
6	4,535	4,477	4,601	4,648	4,860	4,998	5,003	4,960	4,943	5,052	5,107	5,100
7	5,303	5,550	5,348	5,391	5,519	5,602	5,557	5,608	5,663	5,497	5,719	5,679
8	5,688	5,604	5,703	5,899	5,816	5,745	5,921	5,900	5,911	5,987		

Sources: This experiential exercise was adapted from an in-class exercise prepared by Dr. Richard J. Penlesky, Carroll University, as a basis for classroom discussion. By permission of Richard J. Penlesky.

EXPERIENTIAL LEARNING 3.2 | Forecasting a Vital Energy Statistic

The following time series data captures the weekly average of East Coast crude oil imports in thousands of barrels per day.

QUARTER 2 2010		QUARTER 3 2010		QUARTER 4 2010		QUARTER 1 2011	
Time Period	Data	Time Period	Data	Time Period	Data	Time Period	Data
Apr 02, 2010	1,160	Jul 02, 2010	1,116	Oct 01, 2010	1,073	Dec 31, 2010	994
Apr 09, 2010	779	Jul 09, 2010	1,328	Oct 08, 2010	857	Jan 07, 2011	1,307
Apr 16, 2010	1,134	Jul 16, 2010	1,183	Oct 15, 2010	1,197	Jan 14, 2011	997
Apr 23, 2010	1,275	Jul 23, 2010	1,219	Oct 22, 2010	718	Jan 21, 2011	1,082
Apr 30, 2010	1,355	Jul 30, 2010	1,132	Oct 29, 2010	817	Jan 28, 2011	887
May 07, 2010	1,513	Aug 06, 2010	1,094	Nov 05, 2010	946	Feb 04, 2011	1,067
May 14, 2010	1,394	Aug 13, 2010	1,040	Nov 12, 2010	725	Feb 11, 2011	890
May 21, 2010	1,097	Aug 20, 2010	1,053	Nov 19, 2010	748	Feb 18, 2011	865
May 28, 2010	1,206	Aug 27, 2010	1,232	Nov 26, 2010	1,031	Feb 25, 2011	858
Jun 04, 2010	1,264	Sep 03, 2010	1,073	Dec 03, 2010	1,061	Mar 04, 2011	814
Jun 11, 2010	1,153	Sep 10, 2010	1,329	Dec 10, 2010	1,074	Mar 11, 2011	871
Jun 18, 2010	1,424	Sep 17, 2010	1,096	Dec 17, 2010	941	Mar 18, 2011	1,255
Jun 25, 2010	1,274	Sep 24, 2010	1,125	Dec 24, 2010	994	Mar 25, 2011	980

Your instructor has a "holdout" sample representing the values for April 1, 2011 and beyond. Your task is to use the POM for Windows *Time Series Forecasting* module and the history file to project this statistic into the future. If you have MyOMLab, the demand data is available in the *Exercise 2* Excel file. It can be pasted into the Data Table of the *Time Series Forecasting*

module. Otherwise, you can enter the demand data directly into the Data Table. Prior to your next class meeting:

a. Use the POM for Windows *Time Series Forecasting* module to locate the best naïve, moving average, weighted moving average, and trend projection with regression models that you think will most accurately forecast demand during the holdout sample. *Begin your error calculations with period 5 (April 30, 2010).*

b. Create an Excel spreadsheet that begins with inputs of the four forecasts from the *Time Series Forecasting* module. Its purpose is to develop a combination forecast that will serve as your team's forecasts for each period. Assign a weight to each forecast model (the sum of all four forecast weights for one period should equal 1.0) and develop a "combination forecast" by multiplying each forecast by its weight. Keep the weights constant for the whole history file as you search for the best set of weights. If you do not like a particular model, give it a weight of 0. Calculate appropriate forecast error measures for your combination forecast in your Excel spreadsheet.

c. Create a management report that shows your period-by-period forecasts and their overall historical CFE and MAPE performance for each model and your combination forecast.

In-Class Exercise—Part 1

a. Input into your Excel spreadsheet the forecasts from the POM for Windows *Time Series Forecasting* module to get the combination forecast for the first period (the week of April 1, 2011) in the holdout sample. The combination forecast is considered your team's forecast.

b. Enter the actual data announced by your instructor, and have Excel compute appropriate forecast error measures for your four models and the combination forecast. Decide on any revisions of weights for the combination forecast.

c. Update the POM for Windows *Time Series Forecasting* module with the actual demand for the new period and get the new forecasts.

In-Class Exercise—Part 2

a. Input the forecasts from the POM for Windows *Time Series Forecasting* module into your Excel spreadsheet to get the final combination forecast for the next period (the week of April 8, 2011). At this point, you may change this period's weights on each forecasting technique going into the combination forecast. You have no contextual information, but may observe that one model has been performing particularly well in the last few periods. Your team might have different opinions, but you must reach a consensus.

b. Enter the actual data announced by your instructor, with Excel computing appropriate forecast error measures for your four models and the combination forecast.

c. Update the POM for Windows *Time Series Forecasting* module with the actual demand for the new period and get the new forecasts.

In-Class Exercise—Parts 3 and beyond

Continue in the fashion of Parts 1 and 2 to produce forecasts as directed by your instructor. At the end of the exercise, create a second management report that shows for the holdout sample your period-by-period forecasts, their individual forecast errors and percent deviations for each model and your combination forecast. Explain your logic regarding any changes made to your combination forecast weights over the holdout period.

Source: This experiential exercise was prepared as an in-class exercise prepared by Dr. John Jensen, University of South Carolina, as a basis for classroom discussion. By permission of John B. Jensen.

Selected References

Armstrong, J. Scott. "Findings from Evidence-based Forecasting: Methods for Reducing Forecast Error." *International Journal of Forecasting*, vol. 22, no. 3 (2006), pp. 583–598.

Attaran, Mohsen, and Sharmin Attaran. "Collaborative Supply Chain Management." *Business Process Management Journal Management Journal*, vol. 13, no. 13 (June 2007), pp. 390–404.

Cederlund, Jerold P., Rajiv Kohli, Susan A. Sherer, and Yuliang Yao. "How Motorola Put CPFR into Action." *Supply Chain Management Review* (October 2007), pp. 28–35.

Daugherty, Patricia J., R. Glenn Richey, Anthony S. Roath, Soonhong Min, Haozhe Chen, Aaron D. Arndt, and Stefan E. Genchev. "Is Collaboration Paying Off for Firms?" *Business Horizons* (2006), pp. 61–70.

Fildes, Robert, Paul Goodwin, Michael Lawrence, and Konstantinos Nikolopoulos. "Effective Forecasting and Judgmental Adjustments: An Empirical Evaluation and Strategies for Improvement in Supply-Chain Planning." *International Journal of Forecasting*, vol. 25, no. 1 (2009), pp. 3–23.

Lawrence, Michael, Paul Goodwin, Marcus O'Connor, and Dilek Onkal. "Judgmental Forecasting: A Review of Progress over the Last 25 Years." *International Journal of Forecasting* (June 2006), pp. 493–518.

McCarthy, Teresa, Donna F. Davis, Susan L. Golicic, and John T. Mentzer. "The Evolution of Sales Forecasting Management: A 20-Year Longitudinal Study of Forecasting Practices." *Journal of Forecasting*, vol. 25 (2006), pp. 303–324.

Min, Hokey, and Wen-Bin Vincent Yu. "Collaborative Planning, Forecasting and Replenishment: Demand Planning in Supply Chain Management." *International Journal of Information Technology and Management*, vol. 7, no. 1 (2008), pp. 4–20.

Montgomery, David. "Flashpoints for Changing Your Forecasting Process." *The Journal of Business Forecasting* (Winter 2006–2007), pp. 35–42.

Principles of Forecasting: A Handbook for Researchers and Practitioners. J. Scott Armstrong (ed.). Norwell, MA: Kluwer Academic Publishers, 2001. Also visit **http://www.forecastingprinciples.com** for valuable information on forecasting, including frequently asked questions, a forecasting methodology tree, and a dictionary.

Saffo, Paul. "Six Rules for Effective Forecasting." *Harvard Business Review* (July–August 2007), pp. 1–30.

Smaros, Johanna. "Forecasting Collaboration in the European Grocery Sector: Observations from a Case Study." *Journal of Operations Management*, vol. 25, no. 3 (April 2007), pp. 702–716.

Smith, Larry. "West Marine: A CPFR Success Story." *Supply Chain Management Review* (March 2006), pp. 29–36.

Syntetos, Aris Konstantinos Nikolopoulos, John Boylan, Robert Fildes, and Paul Goodwin. "The Effects of Integrating Management Judgement into Intermittent Demand Forecasts." *International Journal of Production Economics*, vol. 118, no. 1 (March, 2009), pp. 72–81.

Wikipedia, "Collaborative Planning, Forecasting, and Replenishment," http:en.wikipedia.org/wiki/Collaborative Planning Forecasting and Replenishment, (April, 2011).

4

OPERATIONS PLANNING AND SCHEDULING

Operations planning and scheduling at an airline like Air New Zealand goes through several stages to match supply with demand, from aggregate plans to short-term schedules. Even after finalizing flights and crew roster schedules, severe weather conditions or mechanical failures can cause last-minute changes. Long-term competitive strength depends on how well it performs this process.

Air New Zealand

How important is scheduling to an airline company? Certainly, customer satisfaction regarding on-time schedule performance is critical in a highly competitive industry such as air transportation. In addition, airlines lose a lot of money when expensive equipment, such as an aircraft, is idle. Flight and crew scheduling, however, is a complex process. For example, Air New Zealand is a group of five airlines with a combined fleet of 96 aircraft, with another 22 more on order. The average utilization is 8:44 hours per day. It has undergone an $800 million upgrade to its long-haul service, refitting its Boeing 747 fleet and adding eight new Boeing 777-200 aircraft for flights to North America. It directly serves 50 ports—26 domestic and 24 international within 15 countries. It carries 11.7 million passengers annually, and its network incorporates flight times ranging from 15 minutes to 13 hours. Operations planning and scheduling at the aggregate level begins with a market plan that identifies the new and existing flight segments that are needed to remain competitive. This general plan is further refined to a three-year plan, and then is put into an annual budget in which flight segments have specific departure and arrival times.

Next, crew availability must be matched to the flight schedules. The two types of crews—pilots and attendants—each comes with its own set of constraints. Pilots, for example, cannot be scheduled for more than 35 hours in a 7-day week and no more than 100 hours in a 28-day cycle. They also must have a 36-hour break every 7 days and 30 days off in an 84-day cycle. Each pilot's tour of duty begins and ends at a crew base and consists of an alternating sequence of duty periods and rest periods, with duty periods including one or more flights. The schedule must ensure that each flight has a qualified crew and that each crew member has a feasible tour of duty over the roster period. From the crew's point of view, it is also important to satisfy as many crew requests and preferences as possible.

Source: "Service Scheduling at Air New Zealand," *Operations Management 10e Video Library* (Upper Saddle River, NJ: Prentice Hall, 2010); **www.airnewzealand.com** (August, 2011). See video in MyOMLab.

LEARNING GOALS *After reading this chapter, you should be able to:*

1. Describe the operations planning and scheduling process.

2. Explain why the process of matching supply with demand begins with aggregation.

3. Identify the different demand and supply options.

4. Explain how operations plans and schedules relate to other plans.

5. Use spreadsheets to create sales and operations plans.

6. Develop employee schedules.

7. Develop schedules for single workstations.

Creating Value through Operations Management

↓

Using Operations to Compete
Project Management

Managing Processes

↓

Process Strategy
Process Analysis
Quality and Performance
Capacity Planning
Constraint Management
Lean Systems

Managing Supply Chains

↓

Supply Chain Inventory Management
Supply Chain Design
Supply Chain Location Decisions
Supply Chain Integration
Supply Chain Sustainability and Humanitarian Logistics
Forecasting
Operations Planning and Scheduling
Resource Planning

Managing supply chains effectively requires more than just good demand forecasts. Demand is the first half of the equation, and the other half is supply. The firm must develop plans to supply the resources needed to meet the forecasted demand. These resources include the workforce, materials, inventories, dollars, and equipment capacity.

Operations planning and scheduling is the process of making sure that demand and supply plans are in balance, from the aggregate level down to the short-term scheduling level. As we saw with Air New Zealand, the process begins at the aggregate level and gets progressively more specific until all crew members know their tour of duty. Operations planning and scheduling lies at the core of supply chain integration, around which plans are made up and down the supply chain, from supplier deliveries to customer due dates and services. Table 4.1 defines several types of plans related to operations planning and scheduling.

In this chapter, we focus on two major parts of the overall process: (1) sales and operations planning and (2) scheduling. We begin with the purpose of aggregation in sales and operations planning. We examine how S&OP relates with other plans and functional areas within the firm. We describe a typical planning process, and various strategies to cope with uneven demand. We show how spreadsheets can help find good solutions. Then, we conclude with scheduling, including performance measures and some basic techniques for creating schedules. MyOMLab Supplement J, "Operations Scheduling", provides additional help with scheduling problems.

Operations Planning and Scheduling across the Organization

Operations planning and scheduling is meaningful for each organization along the supply chain. First, it requires managerial inputs from all of the firm's functions. Marketing provides inputs on demand and accounting provides important cost data and a firm's financial condition. Second, each function is affected by the plan. A plan that calls for expanding the workforce has a direct impact on the hiring and training requirements for the human resources function. As the plan is implemented, it creates revenue and cost streams that finance must deal with as it manages the firm's cash flows. Third, each department and group in a firm has its own workforce. Managers of these departments must make choices on hiring, overtime, and vacations.

Scheduling is important for both service and manufacturing processes. Whether the business is an airline, hotel, computer manufacturer, or university, schedules are a part of everyday life. Schedules involve an enormous amount of detail and affect every process in a firm. For example, service, product, and employee schedules determine specific cash flow requirements, trigger the firm's billing process, and initiate requirements for the employee training process. Firms use the scheduling process to lower their costs and improve their responsiveness, affecting operations up and down the supply chain worldwide.

TABLE 4.1 | TYPES OF PLANS WITH OPERATIONS PLANNING AND SCHEDULING

Key Term	Definition
Sales and operations plan (S&OP)	A plan of future aggregate resource levels so that supply is in balance with demand. It states a company's or department's production rates, workforce levels, and inventory holdings that are consistent with demand forecasts and capacity constraints. The S&OP is time-phased, meaning that it is projected for several time periods (such as months or quarters) into the future.
Aggregate plan	Another term for the sales and operations plan. ·
Production plan	A sales and operations plan for a *manufacturing firm* that centers on production rates and inventory holdings.
Staffing plan	A sales and operations plan for a *service firm*, which centers on staffing and on other human resource-related factors.
Resource plan	An intermediate step in the planning process that lies between S&OP and scheduling. It determines requirements for materials and other resources on a more detailed level than the S&OP. It is covered in the next chapter.
Schedule	A detailed plan that allocates resources over shorter time horizons to accomplish specific tasks.

Stages in Operations Planning and Scheduling

In this section, we explain why companies begin with plans that take a macro, or big picture, view of their business. We also describe how these plans relate to their other plans, and how the long-term plans ultimately are translated into detailed schedules ready for immediate action.

operations planning and scheduling

The process of balancing supply with demand, from the aggregate level down to the short-term scheduling level.

Aggregation

The sales and operations plan is useful because it focuses on a general course of action, consistent with the company's strategic goals and objectives, without getting bogged down in details. We must first aggregate, and then use the targets and resources from the plan to create effective, coordinated schedules. A company's managers must determine whether they can satisfy budgetary goals without having to schedule each of the company's thousands of products and employees individually. While schedules with such detail are the goal, the operations planning and scheduling process begins at the aggregate level.

In general, companies perform aggregation along three dimensions: (1) services or products, (2) workforce, and (3) time.

Product Families   A group of customers, services, or products that have similar demand requirements and common process, workforce, and materials requirements is called a **product family**. Sometimes, product families relate to market groupings or to specific processes. A firm can aggregate its services or products into a set of relatively broad families, avoiding too much detail at this stage of the planning process. For instance, a manufacturer of bicycles that produces 12 different models of bikes might divide them into two groups, mountain bikes and road bikes, for the purpose of preparing the sales and operations plan. Common and relevant measurements should be used.

product family

A group of services or products that have similar demand requirements and common process, labor, and materials requirements.

Workforce   A company can aggregate its workforce in various ways as well, depending on its flexibility. For example, if workers at the bicycle manufacturer are trained to work on either mountain bikes or road bikes, for planning purposes management can consider its workforce to be a single aggregate group, even though the skills of individual workers may differ.

Time   The planning horizon covered by a sales and operations plan typically is one year, although it can differ in various situations. To avoid the expense and disruptive effect of frequent changes in output rates and the workforce, adjustments usually are made monthly or quarterly. In other words, the company looks at time in the aggregate—months, quarters, or seasons—rather than in weeks, days, or hours.

The Relationship of Operations Plans and Schedules to Other Plans

A financial assessment of the organization's near future—that is, for 1 or 2 years ahead—is called either a business plan (in for-profit firms) or an annual plan (in nonprofit service organizations). A **business plan** is a projected statement of income, costs, and profits. It usually is accompanied by budgets, a projected (pro forma) balance sheet, and a projected cash flow statement, showing sources and allocations of funds. The business plan unifies the plans and expectations of

business plan

A projected statement of income, costs, and profits.

a firm's operations, finance, sales, and marketing managers. In particular, it reflects plans for market penetration, new product introduction, and capital investment. Manufacturing firms and for-profit service organizations, such as a retail store, a firm of attorneys, or a hospital, prepare such plans. A nonprofit service organization, such as the United Way or a municipal government, prepares a different type of plan for financial assessment, called an **annual plan or financial plan**.

Figure 4.1 illustrates the relationships among the business or annual plan, sales and operations plan, and detailed plans and schedules derived from it. For **service providers** in the supply chain, top management sets the organization's direction and objectives in the business plan (in a for-profit organization) or annual plan (in a not-for-profit organization). This plan then provides the framework for developing the sales and operations plan, which typically focuses on staffing and other human resource-related factors at a more aggregate level. It presents the number and types of employees needed to meet the objectives of the business or annual plan.

annual plan or financial plan

A plan for financial assessment used by a nonprofit service organization.

FIGURE 4.1 ▶
The Relationship of Sales and Operations Plans and Schedules to Other Plans

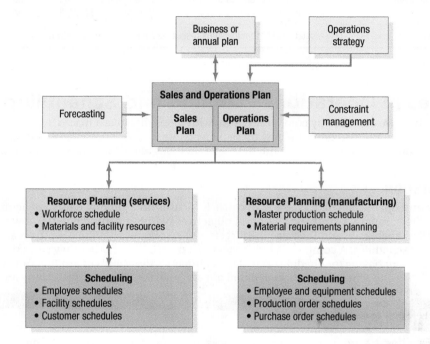

Based on the sales and operations plan for a service provider, the next planning level is *resource planning* to determine the firm's workforce schedules and other resource requirements, such as materials and facilities, on a more detailed level. The *workforce schedule* details the specific work schedule for each category of employee. For example, a sales and operations plan might allocate 10 police officers for the day shift in a particular district; the workforce schedule might assign 5 of them to work Monday through Friday and the other 5 to work Wednesday through Sunday to meet the varying daily needs for police protection in that district. The lowest planning level is *scheduling*, which puts together day-to-day schedules for individual employees and customers.

For **manufacturing firms** in the supply chain, top management sets the company's strategic objectives for at least the next year in the business plan. It provides the overall framework, along with inputs coming from operations strategy, forecasting, and capacity constraint management. The sales and operations plan specifies product family production rates, inventory levels, and workforce levels. The next planning level beneath the sales and operations plan is resource planning, which we cover in the next chapter. Resource planning gets specific as to individual products within each product family, purchased materials, and resources on a detailed level. The *master production schedule* specifies the timing and size of production quantities for each product in the product families. The *material requirements planning* process then derives plans for components, purchased materials, and workstations. As with service providers, the lowest and most detailed planning level is scheduling. It puts together day-to-day schedules or priorities for employees, equipment, and production or purchase orders. Thus, the sales and operations plan plays a key role in translating the strategies of the business plan into an operational plan for the manufacturing process.

As the arrows in Figure 4.1 indicate, information flows in two directions: from the top down (broad to detailed) and from the bottom up (detailed to broad). If a sales and operations plan cannot be developed to satisfy the objectives of the business or annual plan with the existing resources, the business or annual plan might need some adjustment. Similarly, if a feasible master production schedule or workforce schedule cannot be developed, the sales and operations plan might need some adjustment. The planning process is dynamic, with periodic plan revisions or adjustments based on two-way information flows, typically on a monthly basis.

Managing Demand

Matching supply with demand becomes a challenge when forecasts call for uneven demand patterns—and uneven demand is more the rule than the exception. Demand swings can be from one month to the next, one week to the next, or even one hour to the next. Peaks and valleys in demand are costly or can cause poor customer service. Air New Zealand can lose sales because capacity is exceeded for one of its flights, while another of its flights to the same destination at about the same time has many empty seats. If nothing is done to even out demand, sales are lost or greater capacity cushions might be needed. For other companies, the supply options for handing uneven demand could be overtime, hiring and curtailing the workforce, and anticipation inventories. All come at an extra cost. Here we deal with **demand management**, the process of changing demand patterns using one or more demand options.

demand management
The process of changing demand patterns using one or more demand options.

Demand Options

Various options are available in managing demand, including complementary products, promotional pricing, prescheduled appointments, reservations, revenue management, backlogs, backorders, and stockouts. The manager may select one or more of them, as we illustrate below.

Complementary Products   One demand option for a company to even out the load on resources is to produce **complementary products**, or services that have similar resource requirements but different demand cycles. For example, manufacturers of matzoh balls for the Jewish Passover holiday are in a seasonal business. The B. Manischewitz Company, a kosher foods manufacturer in Jersey City, New Jersey, previously experienced 40 percent of its annual sales for the 8-day Passover holiday alone. It expanded toward markets with year-round appeal such as low-carb, low-fat foods, including canned soups and crackers, borscht, cake mixes, dressing and spreads, juices, and condiments.

complementary products
Services or products that have similar resource requirements but different demand cycles.

For service providers, a city parks and recreation department can counterbalance seasonal staffing requirements for summer activities by offering ice skating, tobogganing, or indoor activities during the winter months. The key is to find services and products that can be produced with the existing resources and can level off the need for resources over the year.

Promotional Pricing   Promotional campaigns are designed to increase sales with creative pricing. Examples include automobile rebate programs, price reductions for winter clothing in the late summer months, reduced prices for hotel rooms during off-peak periods, and "two-for-the-price-of-one" automobile tire sales. Lower prices can increase demand for the product or service from new and existing customers, take sales from competitors, or encourage customers to move up future buying. The first two outcomes increase overall demand, while the third shifts demand to the current period.

Prescheduled Appointments   Service providers often can schedule customers for definite periods of order fulfillment. With this approach, demand is leveled to not exceed supply capacity. An appointment system assigns specific times for service to customers. The advantages of this method are timely customer service and the high utilization of service personnel.

Doctors, dentists, lawyers, and automobile repair shops are examples of service providers that use appointment systems. Doctors can use the system to schedule parts of their day to visit hospital patients, and lawyers can set aside time to prepare cases. Care must be taken to tailor the length of appointments to individual customer needs rather than merely scheduling customers at equal time intervals.

This doctor's office uses the appointment system to schedule patients for definite periods of order fulfillment. Times are selected that are agreeable with the patient and fit with the doctor's schedule. Demand is leveled and does not exceed capacity.

Thinkstock Images/Getty Images

Reservations   Reservation systems, although quite similar to appointment systems, are used when the customer actually occupies or uses facilities associated with the service. For example, customers reserve hotel rooms, automobiles, airline seats, and concert seats. The major advantage of reservation systems is the lead time they give service managers and the ability to level demand. Managers can deal with no-shows with a blend of overbooking, deposits, and cancellation penalties. Sometimes overbooking means that a customer with reservations cannot be served as promised. In such cases, bonuses can be offered for compensation. For example, an airline passenger might not only get on the next available flight, but also may be given a free ticket for a second flight sometime in the future.

Revenue Management   A specialized combination of the pricing and reservation options for service providers is revenue management. **Revenue management** (sometimes called *yield management*) is the process of varying price at the right time for different customer segments to maximize revenues generated from existing supply capacity. It works best if customers can be segmented, prices can be varied by segment, fixed costs are high, variable costs are low, service duration is predictable, and capacity is lost if not used (sometimes called *perishable capacity*). Airlines, hotels, cruise lines, restaurants (early-bird specials), and rental cars are good examples. Computerized reservation systems can make hour-by-hour updates, using decision rules for opening or closing price classes depending on the difference between supply and continually updated demand forecasts. In the airlines industry, prices are lowered if a particular airline flight is not selling as fast as expected, until more seats are booked. Alternately, if larger than expected demand is developing, prices for the remaining seats may be increased. Last-minute business travelers pay the higher prices, whereas leisure travelers making reservations well in advance and staying over the weekend get the bargain prices. Southwest Airlines now segments its customers by creating a "Business Select" ticket class that rewards more perks to frequent fliers willing to pay higher prices. Managerial Practice 4.1 describes an unusual way of segmenting customers and setting prices at casinos.

revenue management

Varying price at the right time for different customer segments to maximize revenues yielded by existing supply capacity.

MANAGERIAL PRACTICE 4.1   Harrah's Cherokee Casino & Hotel

Decision rules in revenue management systems are entirely different at casinos. The payoff from revenue management, when combined with its customer relationship process, is particularly pronounced at Harrah's Cherokee Casino & Hotel even though it serves no alcohol and has no traditional gaming tables. The difference with casinos is that their biggest source of revenue is from gambling, not their hotel rooms and restaurants. Customers are segmented not by when they make the reservation or whether their booking includes a weekend, but by how much they are likely to gamble. Top gamblers may lose thousands of dollars per day, whereas risk-adverse customers may lose only $25 per day. Information on the willingness to gamble comes from Cherokee's customer relationship management system that uses a "Total Rewards" card program. Customers present this card each time they make a bet, and in return receive perks and gifts based on the number of points accumulated. When a customer calls in to make reservations, the state-of-the-art revenue management system takes over. The customer is asked for his or her Total Rewards number, which the system uses to estimate how much the customer bets per night, based on past history. The number can be translated probabilistically into the casino's expected net profit per night from the customer. Considerable room capacity is reserved up to the last minute for the big betters. They not only get a room, but one at no cost. With Cherokee's revenue management system, everyone self-prices, depending on how much they want to gamble.

Harrah's Cherokee Casino & Hotel has a unique approach to revenue management. Using a state-of-the-art revenue management system, considerable room capacity is reserved for big betters, and their rooms are free. Everyone self prices, depending on their gambling history.

DAVID T. FOSTER III KRT/Newscom

Source: Richard Metters, C. Queenan, M. Ferguson, L. Harrison, J. Higbie, S. Ward, B. Barfield, T. Farley, A. Kuyumcu, and A. Duggasani, "The 'Killer Application' of Revenue Management: Harrah's Cherokee Casino & Hotel," *Interfaces*, vol. 38 (2008); **www.harrascherokee.com** (2011)

Backlogs   Much like the appointments or reservations of service providers, a **backlog** is an accumulation of customer orders that a manufacturer has promised for delivery at some future date. Manufacturers in the supply chain that maintain a backlog of orders as a normal business practice can allow the backlog to grow during periods of high demand and then reduce it during periods of low demand. Airplane manufacturers do not promise instantaneous delivery, as do wholesalers or retailers farther forward in the supply chain. Instead, they impose a lead time between when the order is placed and when it is delivered. For example, an automotive parts manufacturer may agree to deliver to the repair department of a car dealership a batch of 100 door latches for a particular car model next Tuesday. The parts manufacturer uses that due date to plan its production of door latches within its capacity limits. Firms that are most likely to use backlogs—and increase the size of them during periods of heavy demand—make customized products and tend to have a make-to-order strategy. Backlogs reduce the uncertainty of future production requirements and also can be used to level demand. However, they become a competitive disadvantage if they get too big.

backlog
An accumulation of customer orders that a manufacturer has promised for delivery at some future date.

Backorders and Stockouts   A last resort in demand management is to set lower standards for customer service, either in the form of backorders or stockouts. Not to be confused with a backlog, a *backorder* is a customer order that cannot be filled immediately but is filled as soon as possible. Demand may be too unpredictable or the item may be too costly to hold it in inventory. Although the customer is not pleased with the delay, the customer order is not lost and it is filled at a later date. In contrast, a *stockout* is much the same, except that the order is lost and the customer goes elsewhere. A backorder adds to the next period's demand requirement, whereas a stockout does not. Backorders and stockouts can lead dissatisfied customers to do their future business with another firm. Generally, backorders and stockouts are to be avoided.

Combinations of demand options can also be used. For example, a manufacturer of lighting equipment had several products characterized as "slow movers with spikes," where only 2 or 3 units were sold for several weeks, and then suddenly there was a huge order for 10,000 units the next week. The reason is that their product was purchased by commercial property managers who might be upgrading the lighting in a large office building. The result was a forecasting nightmare and having to resort to high cost supply options to meet the demand spikes. The breakthrough in solving this problem was to combine the pricing and backlog options. Contractors are now offered a 3 percent discount (the pricing option) on any order in excess of 10,000 units that are placed five or more weeks before they are needed (the backlog option). The advanced warning allows the manufacturer to smooth out its production processes, saving millions of dollars annually.

The left side of Table 4.2 summarizes the demand options for operations planning and scheduling, and the right side lists the supply options for balancing supply with demand. The following two sections on sales and operations planning and scheduling cover the supply options.

TABLE 4.2 | DEMAND AND SUPPLY OPTIONS FOR OPERATIONS PLANNING
AND SCHEDULING

Demand Options	Supply Options
Complementary products	Anticipation inventory
Promotional pricing	Workforce adjustment (hiring and layoffs)
Prescheduled appointments	Workforce utilization (overtime and undertime)
Reservations	Part-time workers and subcontractors
Revenue management	Vacation schedules
Backlogs	Workforce schedules
Backorders	Job and customer sequences
Stockouts	Expediting

Sales and Operations Plans

Developing sales and operations plans means making decisions. In this section, we concentrate on the information inputs, the supply options themselves, and strategies that go into the sales and operations planning (S&OP) decisions.

Information Inputs

Just as it is needed to manage the demand side, consensus is needed among the firm's departments when decisions for the supply side are made. Information inputs are sought to create a plan that works for all. Figure 4.2 lists inputs from each functional area. They must be accounted for to make sure that the plan is a good one and also doable. Such coordination helps synchronize the flow of services, materials, and information through the supply chain to best balance supply with customer demand.

FIGURE 4.2 ▶

Managerial Inputs from Functional Areas to Sales and Operations Plans

Supply Options

Given demand forecasts, as modified by demand management choices, operations managers must develop a plan to meet the demand, drawing from the supply options listed in Table 4.2.

An employee stocks a Whirlpool air conditioner at a Lowe's store in Westborough, Massachusetts. The demand for window units is highly seasonal and also depends on variations in the weather. Typically, Whirlpool begins production of room air conditioners in the fall and holds them as inventory until they are shipped in the spring. Building anticipation inventory in the slack season allows the company to even out production rates over much of the year and still satisfy demand in the peak periods (spring and summer) when retailers are placing most of their orders.

Anticipation Inventory   *Anticipation inventory* can be used to absorb uneven rates of demand or supply. For example, a plant facing seasonal demand can stock anticipation inventory during light demand periods and use it during heavy demand periods. Manufacturers of air conditioners, such as Whirlpool, can experience 90 percent of their annual demand during just three months of a year. Extra, or anticipation inventory, also can help when supply, rather than demand, is uneven. For example, a company can stock up on a certain purchased item if the company's suppliers expect severe capacity limitations. Despite its advantages, anticipation inventory can be costly to hold, particularly if stocked in its finished state. Moreover, when services or products are customized, anticipation inventory is not usually an option. Service providers in the supply chain generally cannot use anticipation inventory because services cannot be stocked.

Workforce Adjustment   Management can adjust workforce levels by hiring or laying off employees. The use of this alternative can be attractive if the workforce is largely unskilled or semiskilled and the labor pool is large. These conditions are more likely found in some countries than in others. However, for a particular company, the size of the qualified labor pool may limit the number of new employees that can be hired at any one time. Also, new employees must be trained, and the capacity of the training facilities themselves might limit the number of new hires at any one time. In some industries, laying off employees is difficult or unusual for contractual reasons (unions); in other industries, such as tourism and agriculture, seasonal layoffs and hirings are the norm.

overtime

The time that employees work that is longer than the regular workday or workweek for which they receive additional pay.

Workforce Utilization   An alternative to a workforce adjustment is a change in workforce utilization involving overtime and undertime. **Overtime** means that employees work longer than the regular workday or workweek and receive additional pay for the extra hours. It can be used to satisfy output requirements that cannot be completed on regular time. Overtime is expensive (typically 150 percent of the regular-time pay rate) and workers often do not want to work a lot of overtime for an extended period of time. Excessive overtime also can result in declining quality and productivity. On the other hand, it helps avoid the costly fringe benefits (such as health insurance, dental care, Social Security, retirement funds, paid vacations, and holidays) that come with hiring a new full-time employee,

Undertime means that employees do not have enough work for the regular-time workday or workweek. For example, they cannot be fully utilized for eight hours per day or for five days per week. Undertime occurs when labor capacity exceeds demand requirements (net of anticipation inventory), and this excess capacity cannot or should not be used productively to build up inventory or to satisfy customer orders earlier than the delivery dates already promised.

Undertime can either be paid or unpaid. An example of *paid undertime* is when employees are kept on the payroll rather than being laid off. In this scenario, employees work a full day and receive their full salary but are not as busy because of the light workload. Some companies use paid undertime (though they do not call it that) during slack periods, particularly with highly skilled, hard-to-replace employees or when there are obstacles to laying off workers. The disadvantages of paid undertime include the cost of paying for work not performed and lowered productivity.

Part-Time Workers   Another option apart from undertime is to hire part-time workers, who are paid only for the hours and days worked. Perhaps they only work during the peak times of the day or peak days of the week. Sometimes, part-time arrangements provide predictable work schedules, but in other cases workers are not called in if the workload is light. Such arrangements are more common in low-skill positions or when the supply of workers seeking such an arrangement is sufficient. Part-time workers typically do not receive fringe benefits.

Subcontractors   Subcontractors can be used to overcome short-term capacity shortages, such as during peaks of the season or business cycle. Subcontractors can supply services, make components and subassemblies, or even assemble an entire product.

Vacation Schedules   A manufacturer can shut down during an annual lull in sales, leaving a skeleton crew to cover operations and perform maintenance. Hospital employees might be encouraged to take all or part of their allowed vacation time during slack periods. The use of this alternative depends on whether the employer can mandate the vacation schedules of its employees. In any case, employees may be strongly discouraged from taking vacations during peak periods or encouraged to take vacations during slack periods.

Planning Strategies

Here we focus on supply options that define output rates and workforce levels. Two basic strategies are useful starting points in searching for the best plan.

1. *Chase Strategy.* The **chase strategy** involves hiring and laying off employees to match the demand forecast over the planning horizon. Varying the workforce's regular-time capacity to equate supply to demand requires no inventory investment, overtime, or undertime. The drawbacks are the expense of continually adjusting workforce levels, the potential alienation of the workforce, and the loss of productivity and quality because of constant changes in the workforce.

2. *Level Strategy.* The **level strategy** involves keeping the workforce constant (except possibly at the beginning of the planning horizon). It can vary its utilization to match the demand forecast via overtime, undertime (paid or unpaid), and vacation planning (i.e., paid vacations when demand is low). A constant workforce can be sized at many levels: Managers can choose to maintain a large workforce so as to minimize the planned use of overtime during peak periods (which, unfortunately, also maximizes the need for undertime during slack periods). Alternately, they can choose to maintain a smaller workforce and rely heavily on overtime during the peak periods (which places a strain on the workforce and endangers quality).

undertime
The situation that occurs when employees do not have enough work for the regular-time workday or workweek.

chase strategy
A strategy that involves hiring and laying off employees to match the demand forecast.

level strategy
A strategy that keeps the workforce constant, but varies its utilization via overtime, undertime, and vacation planning to match the demand forecast.

Even though Hallmark's business is seasonal, the company has never laid off employees. Instead the company's employees are trained to do different jobs at different times, and at different plants, if need be. Because they know they have greater job security, they work hard to keep setup times short and Hallmark's costs low.

mixed strategy

A strategy that considers the full range of supply options.

These two "pure" strategies used alone usually do not produce the best sales and operations plan. It might not be best to keep the workforce exactly level, or to vary it to exactly match forecasted demand on a period-by-period basis. The best strategy, therefore, usually is a **mixed strategy** that considers the full range of supply options. The chase strategy is limited to just hiring and laying off employees. The level strategy is limited to overtime, undertime, and vacation schedules. The mixed strategy opens things up to all options, including anticipation inventory, part-time workers, subcontractors, backorders, and stockouts.

Constraints and Costs

An acceptable sales and operations plan must recognize relevant constraints or costs. Constraints can be either physical limitations or related to managerial policies. Examples of physical constraints might be machine capacities that limit maximum output or inadequate inventory storage space. Policy constraints might include limitations on the number of backorders or the use of subcontractors or overtime, as well as the minimum inventory levels needed to achieve desired safety stocks. Ethical issues may also be involved, such as excessive layoffs or required overtime.

Typically, many plans can contain a number of constraints. Table 4.3 lists the costs that the planner considers when preparing sales and operations plans.

Sales and Operations Planning as a Process

Sales and operations planning is a decision-making process, involving both planners and management. It is dynamic and continuing, as aspects of the plan are updated periodically when new information becomes available and new opportunities emerge. It is a cross-functional process that seeks a set of plans that all of a firm's functions can support. For each product family, decisions are made based on cost trade-offs, recent history, recommendations by planners and middle management, and the executive team's judgment.

Figure 4.3 shows a typical plan for a manufacturer. The plan is for one of the manufacturer's make-to-stock product families expressed in aggregate units. This simple spreadsheet shows the interplay between demand and supply. The history on the left for January through March shows how forecasts are tracking actual sales, and how well actual production conforms to the plan. The inventory projections are of particular interest to finance because they significantly affect the manufacturer's cash requirements. The last two columns on the top right show how current fiscal year sales projections match up with the current business plan.

This particular plan is projected out for 18 months, beginning with April. The forecast, operations, and inventory sections for the first 6 months are shown on a month-by-month basis. They then are shown on a quarterly basis for the second 6 months. Finally, the totals for the last 6 months in the time horizon are given in just one column. This display gives more precision to the short term and yet gives coverage well into the future—all with a limited number of columns.

This particular make-to-stock family experiences highly seasonal demand. The operations plan is to build up seasonal inventory in the slack season, schedule vacations as much as

TABLE 4.3 | TYPES OF COSTS WITH SALES AND OPERATIONS PLANNING

Cost	Definition
Regular time	Regular-time wages paid to employees plus contributions to benefits, such as health insurance, dental care, Social Security, retirement funds, and pay for vacations, holidays, and certain other types of absences.
Overtime	Wages paid for work beyond the normal workweek, typically 150 percent of regular-time wages (sometimes up to 200 percent for Sundays and holidays), exclusive of fringe benefits. Overtime can help avoid the extra cost of fringe benefits that come with hiring another full-time employee.
Hiring and layoff	Costs of advertising jobs, interviews, training programs for new employees, scrap caused by the inexperience of new employees, loss of productivity, and initial paperwork. Layoff costs include the costs of exit interviews, severance pay, retaining and retraining remaining workers and managers, and lost productivity.
Inventory holding	Costs that vary with the level of inventory investment: the costs of capital tied up in inventory, variable storage and warehousing costs, pilferage and obsolescence costs, insurance costs, and taxes.
Backorder and stockout	Additional costs to expedite past-due orders, the costs of lost sales, and the potential cost of losing a customer to a competitor (sometimes called loss of goodwill).

Artic Air Company—April Sales and Operations Plan

Family: Medium window units (make-to-stock)   *Unit of measure:* 100 units

SALES	J	F	M	A*	M	J	J	A	S	3rd 3 Mos**	4th 3 Mos	Mos 13–18	Fiscal Year Projection ($000)	Business Plan ($000)
	HISTORY													
New forecast	45	55	60	70	85	95	130	110	70	150	176	275	$8,700	$8,560
Actual sales	52	40	63											
Diff for month	7	–15	3											
Cum		–8	–5											

OPERATIONS												
New Plan	75	75	75	75	75	85	85	85	75	177	225	
Actual	75	78	76									
Diff for month	0	3	1									
Cum		3	4									

INVENTORY												
Plan	85	105	120	125	115	105	60	35	40	198	321	
Actual	92	130	143									

DEMAND ISSUES AND ASSUMPTIONS
1. New product design to be launched in January of next year.

SUPPLY ISSUES
1. Vacations primarily in November and December.
2. Overtime in July–August.

* April is the first month of the planning horizon for this current plan. When next month's plan is developed, its first month in the planning horizon will be May, and the most recent month of the history will be April (with January no longer shown in the history).

** This column provides the sales, operations, and inventory totals for October through December. For example, the forecast of 150 units translates into an average of 50 units per month (or 150/3 = 50).

◄ **FIGURE 4.3**

Sales and Operations Plan for Make-to-Stock Product Family

possible in November and December, and use overtime in the peak season of June, July, and August. For example, the Operations plan increases monthly production from 75 to 85 for June through August, returns to 75 for September, and then drops to an average of only 59 (or 177/3) for October through December. Plan spreadsheets use different formats depending on production and inventory strategy. For an assemble-to-order strategy, the inventory does not consist of finished goods. Instead, it is inventory of standardized components and subassemblies built for the finishing and assembly operations. For the make-to-order strategy, the inventory section in the plan of Figure 4.3 is replaced by a section showing the planned and actual order backlog quantities.

Plans for service providers are quite different. For one thing, their plan does not contain an inventory section, but focuses instead on the demand and supply of human resources. Forecasts are typically expressed in terms of employees required, with separate rows for regular time, overtime, vacations, part-time workers, and so on. Different departments or worker classifications replace product families.

The process itself, typically done on a monthly basis, consists of six basic steps. They are much like the steps we discussed in Chapter 3, "Forecasting."

Step 1. Begin to "roll forward" the plan for the new planning horizon. Start preliminary work right after the month's end. Update files with actual sales, production, inventory, costs, and constraints.

Step 2. Participate in the forecasting and demand planning to create the authorized demand forecasts. For service providers, the forecasts are staff requirements for each workforce group. For example, a director of nursing in a hospital can develop a workload index for a nursing staff and translate a projection of the month-to-month patient load into an equivalent total amount of nursing care time—and thus the number of nurses—required for each month of the year.

Step 3. Update the sales and operations planning spreadsheet for each family, recognizing relevant constraints and costs including availability of materials from suppliers, training facilities capable of handling only so many new hires at a time, machine capacities, or limited storage space. Policy constraints might include limitations on the number of backorders, or the use of subcontractors or overtime, as well as the minimum inventory levels needed to achieve desired safety stocks. Typically, many plans can satisfy a specific set of constraints. The planner searches for a plan that best balances costs, customer service, workforce stability, and the like. This process may necessitate revising the plan several times.

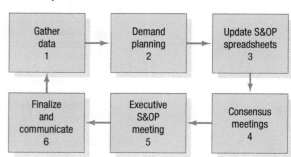

FUJIFILM Imaging Colorants makes inks and dyes, primarily for inkjet printer cartridges, and operates an effective S&OP process. It must coordinate between a U.S. finishing plant and a UK bulk manufacturing plant. Managers from all functions teleconference at the U.S. site with seven other UK managers. At this Partnership meeting (step 4 in the S&OP process), they review the demand, production, and inventory plans, as well as the projected working capital plan.

Step 4. Have one or more consensus meetings with the stakeholders on how best to balance supply with demand. Participants could include the supply chain manager, plant manager, controller, purchasing manager, production control manager, or logistics manager. The goal is one set of recommendations to present at the firm's executive sales and operations planning (S&OP) meeting. Where agreement cannot be reached, prepare scenarios of alternative plans. Also prepare an updated financial view of business by rolling up the plans for all product families into a spreadsheet expressed in total dollars.

Step 5. Present recommendations by product family at the executive S&OP meeting, which typically includes the firm's president and the vice presidents of functional areas. The plan is reviewed relative to the business plan, new product issues, special projects, and other relevant factors. The executives may ask for final changes to the plan, such as to balance conflicting objectives better. Acceptance of this authorized plan does not necessarily mean that everyone is in total agreement, but it does imply that everyone will work to achieve the plan.

Step 6. Update the spreadsheets to reflect the authorized plan, and communicate the plans to the important stakeholders for implementation. Important recipients include those who do resource planning, covered in the next chapter.

Using Spreadsheets

The sales and operations plan in Figure 4.3 does not show much on the supply options used in the operations plan or their cost implications. Here we discuss using spreadsheets that do just that. One could also use the transportation method for production planning. Both techniques could be used on the side as a planner develops prospective plans in step 3 of the planning process.

Various spreadsheets can be used, including ones that you develop on your own. Here we work with the *Sales and Operations Planning with Spreadsheets* Solver in OM Explorer. Figure 4.4 shows a plan for a manufacturer, which uses all supply options except overtime.

FIGURE 4.4 ▶

Manufacturer's Plan Using a Spreadsheet and Mixed Strategy

	1	2	3	4	5	6	Total
Inputs							
Forecasted demand	24	142	220	180	136	168	870
Workforce level	120	158	158	158	158	158	910
Undertime	6	0	0	0	0	0	6
Overtime	0	0	0	0	0	0	0
Vacation time	20	6	0	0	4	10	40
Subcontracting time	0	0	0	0	0	6	6
Backorders	0	0	0	4	0	0	4
Derived							
Utilized time	94	152	158	158	154	148	864
Inventory	70	80	18	0	14	0	182
Hires	0	38	0	0	0	0	38
Layoffs	0	0	0	0	0	0	0
Calculated							
Utilized time cost	$376,000	$608,000	$632,000	$632,000	$616,000	$592,000	$3,456,000
Undertime cost	$24,000	$0	$0	$0	$0	$0	$24,000
Overtime cost	$0	$0	$0	$0	$0	$0	$0
Vacation time cost	$80,000	$24,000	$0	$0	$16,000	$40,000	$160,000
Inventory cost	$2,800	$3,200	$720	$0	$560	$0	$7,280
Backorders cost	$0	$0	$0	$4,000	$0	$0	$4,000
Hiring cost	$0	$91,200	$0	$0	$0	$0	$91,200
Layoff cost	$0	$0	$0	$0	$0	$0	$0
Subcontracting cost	$0	$0	$0	$0	$0	$43,200	$43,200
Total cost	$482,800	726,400	632,720	636,000	632,560	675,200	$3,785,680

Cultura Creative/Alamy

Spreadsheets for a Manufacturer   The top part of the spreadsheet shows the *input values* that give the forecasted demand requirements and the supply option choices period by period. Vary these "levers" as you search for better plans.

The next part of the spreadsheet (in green) shows the *derived values* that must follow from the input values. The first row of derived values is called *utilized time*, which is that portion of the workforce's regular time that is paid for and productively used. In any period, the utilized time equals the workforce level minus undertime and vacation time. For example, in period 1 the utilized time is 94 (or 120 – 6 – 20). The hires and layoffs rows can be derived from the workforce levels. In this example, the workforce is increased for period 2 from its initial size of 120 employees to 158, which means that 38 employees are hired. Because the workforce size remains constant at 158 throughout the rest of the planning horizon, no other hirings or layoffs happen. When additional alternatives, such as vacations, inventory, and backorders are all possible, the overtime and undertime cannot be derived just from information on forecasted demand and workforce levels. Thus, undertime and overtime are shown as input values (rather than derived values) in the spreadsheet, and the user must be careful to specify consistent input values.

The final part of the spreadsheet, the *calculated values* of the plan, shows the plan's cost consequences. Along with qualitative considerations, the cost of each plan determines whether the plan is satisfactory or whether a revised plan should be considered. When seeking clues about how to improve a plan already evaluated, we identify its highest cost elements. Revisions that would reduce these specific costs might produce a new plan with lower overall costs. Spreadsheet programs make analyzing these plans easy, and they present a whole new set of possibilities for developing sound sales and operations plans.

The plan in Figure 4.4 definitely is for a manufacturer because it uses inventory to advantage, particularly in the first two periods. It is a mixed strategy, and not just because it uses anticipation inventory, backorders, and subcontracting. The workforce level changes in period 2, but it does not exactly match the forecasted demand as with a chase strategy. It has some elements of the level strategy, because undertime and vacation time are part of the plan, but it does not rely exclusively on these supply options.

Care must be taken to recognize differences in how inputs are measured. The workforce level might be expressed as the number of employees, but the forecasted demand and inventory are expressed as units of the product. The OM Explorer spreadsheets require a common unit of measure, so we must translate some of the data prior to entering the input values. Perhaps the easiest approach is to express the forecasted demand and supply options as *employee-period equivalents*. If demand forecasts are given as units of product, we can convert them to employee-period equivalents by dividing them by the productivity of a worker. For example, if the demand is for 1,500 units of product and the average employee produces 100 units in one period, the demand requirement is 15 employee-period equivalents.

Spreadsheets for a Service Provider   The same spreadsheets can be used by service providers, except anticipation inventory is not an option. You can unprotect the sheet and then hide the rows that are not relevant. It is useful not to hide the inventory row until the end, however, because positive or negative values signal an inconsistency in your plan. Whereas Figure 4.4 shows a good plan found after several revisions, here we illustrate with Example 4.1 how to find a good plan for a service provider beginning with the chase and level (ignoring vacations) strategies. These plans can provide insights that lead to even better mixed strategy plans.

EXAMPLE 4.1	Using the Chase and Level Strategies as Starting Points

The manager of a large distribution center must determine how many part-time stockpickers to maintain on the payroll. She wants to develop a staffing plan that minimizes total costs, and wants to begin with the chase strategy and level strategy. For the level strategy, she wants to first try the workforce level that meets demand with the minimum use of undertime and not consider vacation scheduling.

First, the manager divides the next year into six time periods, each one 2 months long. Each part-time employee can work a maximum of 20 hours per week on regular time, but the actual number can be less. Instead of paying undertime, each worker's day is shortened during slack periods. Once on the payroll, each worker is used each day, but they may work only a few hours. Overtime can be used during peak periods.

The distribution center's forecasted demand is shown as the number of part-time employees required for each time period at the maximum regular time of 20 hours per week. For example, in period 3, an estimated 18 part-time employees working 20 hours per week on regular time will be needed.

	1	2	3	4	5	6	Total
Forecasted demand*	6	12	18	15	13	14	78

*Number of part-time employees

Currently, 10 part-time clerks are employed. They have not been subtracted from the forecasted demand shown. Constraints and cost information are as follows:

a. The size of training facilities limits the number of new hires in any period to no more than 10.

b. No backorders are permitted; demand must be met each period.

c. Overtime cannot exceed 20 percent of the regular-time capacity (that is, 4 hours) in any period. Therefore, the most that any part-time employee can work is 1.20(20) = 24 hours per week.

d. The following costs can be assigned:

Regular-time wage rate	$2,000 per time period at 20 hours per week
Overtime wages	150 percent of the regular-time rate
Hires	$1,000 per person
Layoffs	$500 per person

Framed by thousands of ski poles, a part-time worker sorts and inventories new products in the receiving department of REI's distribution center in Sumner, Washington. REI employs a high percentage of part-time workers, many of whom are college students. They tend to be young people who participate in outdoor sports and are familiar with the equipment that REI sells.

MyOMLab

Tutor 4.1 in MyOMLab provides a new example for planning using the chase strategy with hiring and layoffs.

SOLUTION

a. Chase Strategy

This strategy simply involves adjusting the workforce as needed to meet demand, as shown in Figure 4.5. Rows in the spreadsheet that do not apply (such as inventory and vacations) are hidden. The workforce level row is identical to the forecasted demand row. A large number of hirings and layoffs begin with laying off four part-time employees immediately because the current staff is 10 and the staff level required in period 1 is only six. However, many employees, such as college students, prefer part-time work. The total cost is $173,500, and most of the cost increase comes from frequent hiring and layoffs, which add $17,500 to the cost of utilized regular-time costs.

FIGURE 4.5 ▶
Spreadsheet for Chase Strategy

	1	2	3	4	5	6	Total
Inputs							
Forecasted demand	6	12	18	15	13	14	78
Workforce level	6	12	18	15	13	14	78
Undertime	0	0	0	0	0	0	0
Overtime	0	0	0	0	0	0	0
Derived							
Utilized time	6	12	18	15	13	14	78
Hires	0	6	6	0	0	1	13
Layoffs	4	0	0	3	2	0	9
Calculated							
Utilized time cost	$12,000	$24,000	$36,000	$30,000	$26,000	$28,000	$156,000
Undertime cost	$0	$0	$0	$0	$0	$0	$0
Hiring cost	$0	$6,000	$6,000	$0	$0	$1,000	$13,000
Layoff cost	$2,000	$0	$0	$1,500	$1,000	$0	$4,500
Total cost	$14,000	30,000	42,000	31,500	27,000	29,000	$173,500

b. Level Strategy

In order to minimize undertime, the maximum use of overtime possible must occur in the peak period. For this particular level strategy (other workforce options are possible), the most overtime that the manager can use is 20 percent of the regular-time capacity, w, so

$$1.20w = 18 \text{ employees required in peak period (period 3)}$$

$$w = \frac{18}{1.20} = 15 \text{ employees}$$

A 15-employee staff size minimizes the amount of undertime for this level strategy. Because the staff already includes 10 part-time employees, the manager should immediately hire five more. The complete plan is shown in Figure 4.6. The total cost is $164,000, which seems reasonable because the minimum conceivable cost is only $156,000 (78 periods $\times$ $2,000/period). This cost could be achieved only if the manager found a way to cover the forecasted demand for all 78 periods with regular time. The plan seems reasonable primarily because it involves the use of large amounts of undertime (15 periods), which in this example are unpaid.

	1	2	3	4	5	6	Total
Inputs							
Forecasted demand	6	12	18	15	13	14	78
Workforce level	15	15	15	15	15	15	90
Undertime	9	3	0	0	2	1	15
Overtime	0	0	3	0	0	0	3
Derived							
Utilized time	6	12	15	15	13	14	75
Hires	5	0	0	0	0	0	5
Layoffs	0	0	0	0	0	0	0
Calculated							
Utilized time cost	$12,000	$24,000	$30,000	$30,000	$26,000	$28,000	$150,000
Undertime cost	$0	$0	$0	$0	$0	$0	$0
Overtime cost	$0	$0	$9,000	$0	$0	$0	$9,000
Hiring cost	$5,000	$0	$0	$0	$0	$0	$5,000
Layoff cost	$0	$0	$0	$0	$0	$0	$0
Total cost	$17,000	24,000	39,000	30,000	26,000	28,000	$164,000

◀ **FIGURE 4.6**
Spreadsheet for Level Strategy

MyOMLab
Tutor 4.2 in MyOMLab provides a new example for planning using the level strategy with overtime and undertime.

DECISION POINT

The manager, now having a point of reference with which to compare other plans, decided to evaluate some other plans before making a final choice, beginning with the chase strategy. The only way to reduce costs is somehow to reduce the premium for three overtime employee periods (3 periods $\times$ $3,000/period) or to reduce the hiring cost of five employees (5 hires $\times$ $1,000/person). Nonetheless, better solutions may be possible. For example, undertime can be reduced by delaying the hiring until period 2 because the current workforce is sufficient until then. This delay would decrease the amount of unpaid undertime, which is a qualitative improvement. See Active Model 4.1 for additional insights.

MyOMLab
Active Model 4.1 in MyOMLab shows the impact of changing the workforce level, the cost structure, and overtime capacity.

Scheduling

Scheduling is the last step in Figure 4.1. It takes the operations and scheduling process from planning to execution, and is where the "rubber meets the road." This important aspect of supply chain management is itself a process. It requires gathering data from sources such as demand forecasts or specific customer orders, resource availability from the sales and operations plan, and specific constraints to be reckoned with from employees and customers. It then involves generating a work schedule for employees or sequences of jobs or customers at workstations. The schedule has to be coordinated with the employees and suppliers to make sure that all constraints are satisfied. Here we cover Gantt charts, employee schedules, job sequencing at workstations, and software support.

Gantt Charts

Schedules can be displayed in various ways. For different jobs or activities they can simply list their due dates, show in a table their start and finish times, or show in a graph their start and finish times. The *Gantt chart* uses the third approach. As the saying goes, a "picture can be worth a thousand words" in managing projects. Associates not familiar with scheduling techniques can still grasp the essence of the plan. This tool can be used to monitor the progress of work and to view the load on workstations. The chart takes two basic forms: (1) the job or activity progress chart and (2) the workstation chart. The *Gantt progress chart* graphically displays the current status of each job or activity relative to its scheduled completion date. For example, suppose that an automobile parts manufacturer has three jobs under way, one each for Ford, Nissan, and Buick. The actual status of these orders is shown by the colored bars in Figure 4.7; the red lines indicate the desired schedule for the start and finish of each job. For the current date, April 21, this Gantt chart shows that the Ford order is behind schedule because operations has completed only the work scheduled through April 18. The Nissan order is exactly on schedule, and the Buick order is ahead of schedule.

FIGURE 4.7 ▶
Gantt Progress Chart for an
Auto Parts Company

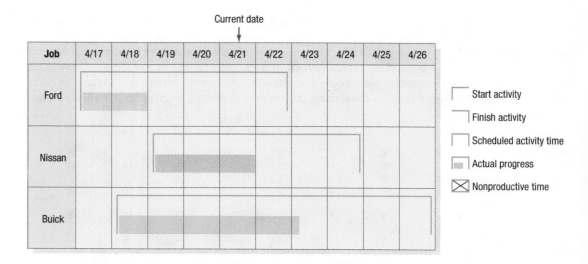

Figure 4.8 shows a *Gantt workstation chart* of the operating rooms at a hospital for a particular day. Using the same notation as in Figure 4.7, the chart shows the load on the operating rooms and the nonproductive time. The time slots assigned to each doctor include the time needed to clean the room prior to the next surgery. The chart can be used to identify time slots for unscheduled emergency surgeries. It can also be used to accommodate requests to change the time of surgeries. For example, Dr. Flowers may be able to change the start of her surgery to 2 P.M. by swapping time slots with Dr. Gillespie in operating room C or by asking Dr. Brothers to start her surgery one hour earlier in operating room A and asking Dr. Bright to schedule her surgery for the morning in operating room C. In any event, the hospital administrator would have to get involved in rescheduling the surgeries.

FIGURE 4.8 ▼
Gantt Workstation Chart
for Operating Rooms at a
Hospital

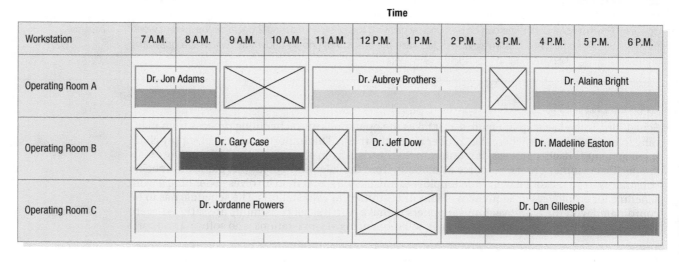

Scheduling Employees

workforce scheduling

A type of scheduling that determines when employees work.

Another way to manage capacity is **workforce scheduling**, which is a type of scheduling that determines when employees work. Of particular interest are situations when not all employees work the same five days a week, and same eight hours per day. The schedule specifies the on-duty and off-duty periods for each employee over a certain time period, as in assigning postal clerks, nurses, pilots, attendants, or police officers to specific workdays and shifts. This approach is used when customers demand quick response and total demand can be forecasted with reasonable accuracy. In these instances, capacity is adjusted to meet the expected loads on the service system.

Workforce schedules translate the staffing plan into specific schedules of work for each employee. Determining the workdays for each employee in itself does not make the staffing plan operational. Daily workforce requirements, stated in aggregate terms in the staffing plan, must be satisfied. The workforce capacity available each day must meet or exceed daily workforce requirements. If it does not, the scheduler must try to rearrange days off until the requirements are met. If no such schedule can be found, management might have to change the staffing plan and hire more employees, authorize overtime hours, or allow for larger backlogs.

Constraints   The technical constraints imposed on the workforce schedule are the resources provided by the staffing plan and the requirements placed on the operating system. However, other constraints, including legal and behavioral considerations, also can be imposed. For example, Air New Zealand is required to have at least a minimum number of flight attendants on duty at all times. Similarly, a minimum number of fire and safety personnel must be on duty at a fire station at all times. Such constraints limit management's flexibility in developing workforce schedules.

An air hostess serves coffee to the pilots in the cockpit. Airlines provide service for more than eight hours per day and five days per week, and there are many technical, behavioral, and legal constraints to be met. Such conditions make scheduling a challenging task.

The constraints imposed by the psychological needs of workers complicate scheduling even more. Some of these constraints are written into labor agreements. For example, an employer might agree to give employees a certain number of consecutive days off per week or to limit employees' consecutive workdays to a certain maximum. Other provisions might govern the allocation of vacations, days off for holidays, or rotating shift assignments. In addition, the preferences of the employees themselves need to be considered.

One way that managers deal with certain undesirable aspects of scheduling is to use a **rotating schedule**, which rotates employees through a series of workdays or hours. Thus, over a period of time, each person has the same opportunity to have weekends and holidays off and to work days, as well as evenings and nights. A rotating schedule gives each employee the next employee's schedule the following week. In contrast, a **fixed schedule** calls for each employee to work the same days and hours each week.

rotating schedule

A schedule that rotates employees through a series of workdays or hours.

fixed schedule

A schedule that calls for each employee to work the same days and hours each week.

Developing a Workforce Schedule   Suppose that we are interested in developing a workforce schedule for a company that operates seven days a week and provides each employee with two consecutive days off. In this section, we demonstrate a method that recognizes this constraint. The objective is to identify the two consecutive days off for each employee that will minimize the amount of total slack capacity, thereby maximizing the utilization of the workforce. The work schedule for each employee, then, is the five days that remain after the two days off have been determined. The procedure involves the following steps.

Step 1.   From the schedule of net requirements for the week, find all the pairs of consecutive days, excluding the day (or days) with the maximum daily requirement. Select the unique pair that has the lowest total requirements for the two days. In some unusual situations, all pairs may contain a day with the maximum requirements. If so, select the pair with the lowest total requirements. Suppose that the numbers of employees required are

Monday: 8	Thursday: 12	Saturday: 4
Tuesday: 9	Friday: 7	Sunday: 2
Wednesday: 2		

The maximum daily requirement is 12 employees, on Thursday. The consecutive pair with the lowest total requirements is Saturday and Sunday, with $4 + 2 = 6$.

Step 2.   If a tie occurs, choose one of the tied pairs, consistent with the provisions written into the labor agreement, if any. Alternatively, the tie could be broken by asking the employee being scheduled to make the choice. As a last resort, the tie could be broken arbitrarily. For example, preference could be given to Saturday–Sunday pairs.

Step 3. Assign the employee the selected pair of days off. Subtract the requirements satisfied by the employee from the net requirements for each day the employee is to work. In this example, the employee is assigned Saturday and Sunday off. After requirements are subtracted, Monday's requirement is 7, Tuesday's is 8, Wednesday's is 1, Thursday's is 11, and Friday's is 6. Saturday's and Sunday's requirements do not change because no employee is yet scheduled to work those days.

Step 4. Repeat steps 1 through 3 until all the requirements have been satisfied or a certain number of employees have been scheduled.

This method reduces the amount of slack capacity assigned to days with low requirements and forces the days with high requirements to be scheduled first. It also recognizes some of the behavioral and contractual aspects of workforce scheduling in the tie-breaking rules.

| EXAMPLE 4.2 | **Developing a Workforce Schedule** |

The Amalgamated Parcel Service is open seven days a week. The schedule of requirements is

Day	M	T	W	Th	F	S	Su
Required number of employees	6	4	8	9	10	3	2

The manager needs a workforce schedule that provides two consecutive days off and minimizes the amount of total slack capacity. To break ties in the selection of off days, the scheduler gives preference to Saturday and Sunday if it is one of the tied pairs. If not, she selects one of the tied pairs arbitrarily.

MyOMLab

Tutor 4.3 in MyOMLab provides a new example to practice workforce scheduling.

SOLUTION

Friday contains the maximum requirements, and the pair S–Su has the lowest total requirements. Therefore, Employee 1 is scheduled to work Monday through Friday.

Note that Friday still has the maximum requirements and that the requirements for the S–Su pair are carried forward because these are Employee 1's days off. These updated requirements are the ones the scheduler uses for the next employee.

The day-off assignments for the employees are shown in the following table.

SCHEDULING DAYS OFF

M	T	W	Th	F	S	Su	Employee	Comments
6	4	8	9	10	3	2	1	The S–Su pair has the lowest total requirements. Assign Employee **1** to a Monday through Friday schedule and update the requirements.
5	3	7	8	9	3	2	2	The S–Su pair has the lowest total requirements. Assign Employee **2** to a Monday through Friday schedule and update the requirements.
4	2	6	7	8	3	2	3	The S–Su pair has the lowest total requirements. Assign Employee **3** to a Monday through Friday schedule and update the requirements.
3	1	5	6	7	3	2	4	The M–T pair has the lowest total requirements. Assign Employee **4** to a Wednesday through Sunday schedule and update the requirements.
3	1	4	5	6	2	1	5	The S–Su pair has the lowest total requirements. Assign Employee **5** to a Monday through Friday schedule and update the requirements.
2	0	3	4	5	2	1	6	The M–T pair has the lowest total requirements. Assign Employee **6** to a Wednesday through Sunday schedule and update the requirements.
2	0	2	3	4	1	0	7	The S–Su pair has the lowest total requirements. Assign Employee **7** to a Monday through Friday schedule and update the requirements.
1	0	1	2	3	1	0	8	Four pairs have the minimum requirement and the lowest total: S–Su, Su–M, M–T, and T–W. Choose the S–Su pair according to the tie-breaking rule. Assign Employee **8** to a Monday through Friday schedule and update the requirements.
0	0	0	1	2	1	0	9	Arbitrarily choose the Su–M pair to break ties because the S–Su pair does not have the lowest total requirements. Assign Employee **9** to a Tuesday through Saturday schedule and update the requirements.
0	0	0	0	1	0	0	10	Choose the S–Su pair according to the tie-breaking rule. Assign Employee **10** to a Monday through Friday schedule.

In this example, Friday always has the maximum requirements and should be avoided as a day off. The final schedule for the employees is shown in the following table.

Employee	M	T	W	Th	F	S	Su	Total
				FINAL SCHEDULE				
1	X	X	X	X	X	off	off	
2	X	X	X	X	X	off	off	
3	X	X	X	X	X	off	off	
4	off	off	X	X	X	X	X	
5	X	X	X	X	X	off	off	
6	off	off	X	X	X	X	X	
7	X	X	X	X	X	off	off	
8	X	X	X	X	X	off	off	
9	off	X	X	X	X	X	off	
10	X	X	X	X	X	off	off	
Capacity, C	7	8	10	10	10	3	2	50
Requirements, R	6	4	8	9	10	3	2	42
Slack, C − R	1	4	2	1	0	0	0	8

DECISION POINT
With its substantial amount of slack capacity, the schedule is not unique. Employee 9, for example, could have Sunday and Monday, Monday and Tuesday, or Tuesday and Wednesday off without causing a capacity shortage. Indeed, the company might be able to get by with one fewer employee because of the total of eight slack days of capacity. However, all 10 employees are needed on Fridays. If the manager were willing to get by with only nine employees on Fridays or if someone could work one day of overtime on a rotating basis, he would not need Employee 10. As indicated in the table, the net requirement left for Employee 10 to satisfy amounts to only one day, Friday. Thus, Employee 10 can be used to fill in for vacationing or sick employees.

Managers try to staff their call centers to meet certain performance measures. One such measure is the percentage of calls answered (PCA) within a specified time interval, termed the service objective (SO). Typically in a call center, the PCA is in the range of 80 to 90 percent, and the SO is 15 to 30 seconds. The problem is that the requirements for agents change over time, depending on the time of day and day of the year. Also, the callers are likely to speak different languages. Determining how many of each group of agents to have on hand at all times is not easy. Fortunately, employee scheduling software is available to estimate call volumes, project skill requirements, and identify employee start and end times or preferred days off.

Sequencing Jobs at a Workstation

Another aspect of scheduling is sequencing work at workstations. **Sequencing** determines the order in which jobs or customers are processed in the waiting line at a workstation. When combined with the expected processing time, the sequence allows you to estimate the start and finish times of each job.

sequencing

Determining the order in which jobs or customers are processed in the waiting line at a workstation.

Priority Sequencing Rules   One way to determine what job or customer to process next is with the help of a **priority sequencing rule**. The following two priority sequencing rules are commonly used in practice.

- *First-Come, First-Served.* The job or customer arriving at the workstation first has the highest priority under a **first-come, first-served (FCFS)** rule. This rule is the most "democratic" in that each job is treated equally, with no one stepping ahead of others already in line. It is commonly used at service facilities, and will be used in Supplement B, "Waiting Lines."

- *Earliest Due Date.* The job or customer with the **earliest due date (EDD)** is the next one to be processed. The *due date* specifies when work on a job or customer should be finished. Due dates are commonly used by manufacturers and suppliers in the supply chain. For example, a product cannot be assembled until all of its purchased and produced components are available. If these components were not already in inventory, they must be ordered prior to when the product assembly can begin. Their due date is the start date for assembling the product to be assembled. This simple relationship is fundamental to coordinating with suppliers and with the manufacturer's own shops in the supply chain. It is also the key to **expediting**, which is the process of completing a job sooner than would otherwise be done. Expediting can be done by revising the due date, moving the job to the front of the waiting line, making a special appeal by phone or e-mail to the supplier, adding extra capacity, or even putting a red tag on the job that says the job is urgent.

Neither rule guarantees finding an optimal solution. Different sequences found by trial and error can produce better schedules. In fact, there are multiple performance measures for judging a schedule. A schedule that does well on one measure may do poorly on another.

Performance Measures   The quality of a schedule can be judged in various ways. Two commonly used performance measures are flow time and past due.

- *Flow Time.* The amount of time a job spends in the service or manufacturing system is called **flow time**. It is the sum of the waiting time for servers or machines; the process time, including setups; the time spent moving between operations; and delays resulting from machine breakdowns, unavailability of facilitating goods or components, and the like. Flow time is sometimes referred to as *throughput time* or *time spent in the system, including service.* For a set of jobs to be processed at a single workstation. a job's flow time is

$$\text{Flow time} = \text{Finish time} + \text{Time since job arrived at workstation}$$

When using this equation, we assume for convenience that the first job scheduled starts at time zero (0). At time 0, all the jobs were available for processing at the workstation.

- *Past Due.* The measure **past due** can be expressed as the amount of time by which a job missed its due date (also referred to as **tardiness**) or as the percentage of total jobs processed over some period of time that missed their due dates. Minimizing these past due measures supports the competitive priorities of cost (penalties for missing due dates), quality (perceptions of poor service), and time (on-time delivery).

| EXAMPLE 4.3 | **Using the Two Priority Sequencing Rules** |

Currently a consulting company has five jobs in its backlog. The time since the order was placed, processing time, and promised due dates are given in the following table. Determine the schedule by using the FCFS rule, and calculate the average days past due and flow time. How can the schedule be improved, if average flow time is the most critical?

Customer	Time Since Order Arrived (days ago)	Processing Time (days)	Due Date (days from now)
A	15	25	29
B	12	16	27
C	5	14	68
D	10	10	48
E	0	12	80

SOLUTION

a. The FCFS rule states that Customer A should be the first one in the sequence, because that order arrived earliest—15 days ago. Customer E's order arrived today, so it is processed last. The sequence is shown in the following table, along with the days past due and flow times.

Customer Sequence	Start Time (days)		Processing Time (days)		Finish Time (days)	Due Date	Days Past Due	Days Ago Since Order Arrived	Flow Time (days)
A	0	+	25	=	25	29	0	15	40
B	25	+	16	=	41	27	14	12	53
D	41	+	10	=	51	48	3	10	61
C	51	+	14	=	65	68	0	5	70
E	65	+	12	=	77	80	0	0	77

The *finish time* for a job is its start time plus the processing time. Its finish time becomes the start time for the next job in the sequence, assuming that the next job is available for immediate processing. The days past due for a job is zero (0) if its due date is equal to or exceeds the finish time. Otherwise it equals the shortfall. The flow time for each job equals its finish time plus the number of days ago since the order first arrived at the workstation. For example, Customer C's flow time is its scheduled finish time of 65 days plus the 5 days since the order arrived, or 70 days. The days past due and average flow time performance measures for the FCFS schedule are

$$\text{Average days past due} = \frac{0 + 14 + 3 + 0 + 0}{5} = 3.4 \text{ days}$$

$$\text{Average flow time} = \frac{40 + 53 + 61 + 70 + 77}{5} = 60.2 \text{ days}$$

b. The average flow time can be reduced. One possibility is the sequence shown in the following table, which uses the Shortest Processing Time (SPT) rule, which is one of several rules developed more fully in MyOMLab Supplement J, "Operations Scheduling." (For still another possibility, see Solved Problem 3, which applies the EDD rule.)

MyOMLab

Customer Sequence	Start Time (days)		Processing Time (days)		Finish Time (days)	Due Date	Days Past Due	Days Ago Since Order Arrived	Flow Time (days)
D	0	+	10	=	10	48	0	10	20
E	10	+	12	=	22	80	0	0	22
C	22	+	14	=	36	68	0	5	41
B	36	+	16	=	52	27	25	12	64
A	52	+	25	=	77	29	48	15	92

$$\text{Average days past due} = \frac{0 + 0 + 0 + 25 + 48}{5} = 14.6 \text{ days}$$

$$\text{Average flow time} = \frac{20 + 22 + 41 + 64 + 92}{5} = 47.8 \text{ days}$$

This schedule reduces the average flow time from 60.2 to 47.8 days—a 21 percent improvement. However, the past due times for jobs A and B have increased.

DECISION POINT

Management decided to use a modified version of the second schedule, adding overtime when Customer B is processed. Further, Customer A agreed to extend its due date to 77 days, because in this case the advanced warning allowed it to reschedule its own operations with little problem.

When Nissan introduced the Almera to the European market, it decided to produce it at the most efficient Sunderland plant in the United Kingdom. It already manufactured the Micra and Primera models there. Multi-vehicle scheduling is quite complex because of the many constraints involved. The painting portion of the job is particularly time consuming, but is only one of thousands of tasks the plant must efficiently schedule. A sophisticated software package, called ILOG Solver, assists the scheduling process for a coordinated flow.

Software Support

Computerized scheduling systems are available to cope with the complexity of workforce scheduling, such as the myriad constraints and concerns at Air New Zealand. In some types of firms, such as telephone companies, mail-order catalog houses, or emergency hotline agencies, employees must be on duty 24 hours a day, 7 days a week.

Sometimes a portion of the staff is part time, which allows management a great deal of flexibility but adds considerable complexity to the scheduling requirements. The flexibility comes from the opportunity to match anticipated loads closely through the use of overlapping shifts or odd shift lengths; the complexity comes from the need to evaluate the numerous possible alternatives. Management also must consider the timing of lunch breaks and rest periods, the number and starting times of shift schedules, and the days off for each employee. The programs select the schedule that minimizes the sum of expected costs of over- and understaffing.

Software is also available for sequencing jobs at workstations. They help firms design and manage the linkages between customers and suppliers in the supply chain. True integration requires the manipulation of large amounts of complex data in real time because the customer order work flow must be synchronized

advanced planning and scheduling (APS) systems

Computer software systems that seek to optimize resources across the supply chain and align daily operations with strategic goals.

with the required material, manufacturing, and distribution activity. Coupled with the Internet and improved data storage and manipulation methods, such computer software has given rise to **advanced planning and scheduling (APS) systems**, which seek to optimize resources across the supply chain and align daily operations with strategic goals. A firm's ability to change its schedules quickly and still keep the goods and services flowing smoothly through the supply chain provides a competitive edge.

LEARNING GOALS IN REVIEW

1 **Describe the operations planning and scheduling process.** The section "Stages in Operations Planning and Scheduling," pp. 107–109, shows its various stages and how it relates with other plans in the organization. Pay particular attention to Figure 4.1.

2 **Explain why the process of matching supply with demand begins with aggregation.** Aggregation allows the general course of action to be established, without being bogged down in details. The section on "Aggregation," p. 107, shows that aggregation is performed across three dimensions: product families, workforce, and time.

3 **Identify the different demand and supply options.** Sections "Managing Demand" and "Sales and Operations Plans," pp. 109–119, describe the various options, along with their positive and negative aspects. Focus on Table 4.2 for the complete list.

4 **Explain how operations plans and schedules relate to other plans.** Figure 4.2 shows how Sales and Operations Plans are related with other functional areas. Also, check out the section "The Relationship of Operations Plans and Schedules to Other Plans," pp. 107–109.

5 **Use spreadsheets to create sales and operations plans.** Turn to "Using Spreadsheets" on pp. 116–119 to better understand how to use this tool. Solved Problem 1 is also helpful.

6 **Develop employee schedules.** The section on "Scheduling Employees," pp. 120–123, describes how to create a workforce schedule. Also see Example 4.2, pp. 122–123, and Solved Problem 2, pp. 129–130.

7 **Develop schedules for single workstations.** The FCFS and EDD rules, and the flow time and past due performance measures, are described in the "Sequencing Jobs at a Workstation," pp. 123–125. Example 4.3 illustrates their use, along with Solved Problem 3.

MyOMLab helps you develop analytical skills and assesses your progress with multiple problems on level, chase, and mixed strategy plans, total costs, anticipation inventory, break-even analysis, FCFS and EDD scheduling rules, average flow time, and average days past due.

MyOMLab Resources	Titles	Link to the Book
Video	Air New Zealand: Service Scheduling	Operations Planning and Scheduling Across the Organization; Stages in Operations Planning and Scheduling;
	Sales and Operations Planning at Starwood	Stages in Operations Planning and Scheduling; Demand Options
Active Model Exercise	4.1 Level Strategy	Planning Strategies; Example 4.1 (pp. 117–119)
OM Explorer Solvers	Sales and Operations Planning with Spreadsheets	Using Spreadsheets; Figure 4.3 (p. 108); Figure 4.4 (p. 116); Solved Problem 1 (pp. 128–129)
	Workforce Scheduler	Scheduling Employees; Example 4.2 (pp. 122–123); Solved Problem 2
	Single Work-Station Scheduler	Sequencing Jobs at a Workstation; Example 4.3 (pp. 124–125); Solved Problem 3 (p. 131)
OM Explorer Tutors	4.1 Chase Strategy	Planning Strategies; Example 4.1 (pp. 117–119); Solved Problem 1
	4.2 Level Strategy	Planning Strategies; Example 4.1 (pp. 117–119); Solved Problem 1
	4.3 Developing a Workforce Schedule	Scheduling Employees; Example 4.2 (pp. 122–123); Solved Problem 2
	4.4 Staffing Strategies with Spreadsheets (4 pds)	Scheduling Employees; Example 4.2 (pp. 122–123); Solved Problem 2
Tutor Exercises	4.1 Results of Different Scenarios with a Level Strategy	Planning Strategies; Example 4.1 (pp. 117–119); Solved Problem 2
	4.2 Staffing for the Newest MBA Class	Scheduling Employees; Example 4.2 (pp. 122–123)
POM for Windows	Scheduling	Sequencing Jobs at a Workstation; Example 4.3 (pp. 124–125); Solved Problem 3 (p. 131)
Virtual Tours	Stratton Furniture Company	Stages in Operations Planning and Scheduling; Demand Options; Supply Options; Planning Strategies
	Stihl Chain Saws	
	Stihl Factory Tour	
MyOMLab Supplements	H. Measuring Output Rates	MyOMLab Supplement H
	I. Learning Curve Analysis	MyOMLab Supplement I
Internet Exercise	United Parcel Service	Managing Demand; Supply Options; Planning Strategies
	United Parcel Service Centers	
	Internal Revenue Service	Managing Demand; Supply Options; Planning Strategies
	H&R Block	
	Hoovers	
Additional Case	Food King	Scheduling Employees; Example 4.2 (pp. 122–123)
Key Equations		
Image Library		

Key Terms

advanced planning and scheduling (APS) systems 126
aggregate plan 107
annual plan or financial plan 108
backlog 111
backorder and stockout 114
business plan 107
chase strategy 113
complementary products 109
demand management 109
earliest due date (EDD) 124
expediting 124
first-come, first-served (FCFS) 124

fixed schedule 121
flow time 124
hiring and layoff 114
inventory holding 114
level strategy 113
mixed strategy 114
operations planning and scheduling 106
overtime 112
past due 124
priority sequencing rule 124
product family 107
production plan 107

regular time 114
resource plan 107
revenue management 110
rotating schedule 121
sales and operations planning (S&OP) 107
schedule 107
sequencing 123
staffing plan 107
tardiness 124
undertime 113
workforce scheduling 120

Solved Problem 1

MyOMLab

Tutor 4.4 in MyOMLab provides another example for practicing sales and operations planning using a variety of strategies.

The Cranston Telephone Company employs workers who lay telephone cables and perform various other construction tasks. The company prides itself on good service and strives to complete all service orders within the planning period in which they are received.

Each worker puts in 600 hours of regular time per planning period and can work as many as an additional 100 hours of overtime. The operations department has estimated the following workforce requirements for such services over the next four planning periods:

Planning Period	1	2	3	4
Demand (hours)	21,000	18,000	30,000	12,000

Cranston pays regular-time wages of $6,000 per employee per period for any time worked up to 600 hours (including undertime). The overtime pay rate is $15 per hour over 600 hours. Hiring, training, and outfitting a new employee costs $8,000. Layoff costs are $2,000 per employee. Currently, 40 employees work for Cranston in this capacity. No delays in service, or backorders, are allowed. Use the spreadsheet approach to answer the following questions:

a. Prepare a chase strategy using only hiring and layoffs. What are the total numbers of employees hired and laid off?

b. Develop a workforce plan that uses the level strategy, relaying only on overtime and undertime. Maximize the use of overtime during the peak period so as to minimize the workforce level and amount of undertime.

c. Propose an effective mixed-strategy plan.

d. Compare the total costs of the three plans.

SOLUTION

a. The chase strategy workforce is calculated by dividing the demand for each period by 600 hours, or the amount or regular-time work for one employee during one period. This strategy calls for a total of 20 workers to be hired and 40 to be laid off during the four-period plan. Figure 4.9 shows the "chase strategy" solution that OM Explorer's *Sales and Operations Planning with Spreadsheets* Solver produces. We simply hide any unneeded columns and rows in this general-purpose solver.

FIGURE 4.9 ▶
Spreadsheet for Chase Strategy

	1	2	3	4	Total
Inputs					
Forecasted demand	35	30	50	20	135
Workforce level	35	30	50	20	135
Undertime	0	0	0	0	0
Overtime	0	0	0	0	0
Derived					
Utilized time	35	30	50	20	135
Hires	0	0	20	0	20
Layoffs	5	5	0	30	40
Calculated					
Utilized time cost	$210,000	$180,000	$300,000	$120,000	$810,000
Undertime cost	$0	$0	$0	$0	$0
Overtime cost	$0	$0	$0	$0	$0
Hiring cost	$0	$0	$160,000	$0	$160,000
Layoff cost	$10,000	$10,000	$0	$60,000	$80,000
Total cost	$220,000	190,000	460,000	180,000	$1,050,000

b. The peak demand is 30,000 hours in period 3. As each employee can work 700 hours per period (600 on regular time and 100 on overtime), the workforce level of the level strategy that minimizes undertime is 30,000/700 = 42.86, or 43 employees. This strategy calls for three employees to be hired in the first quarter and for none to be laid off. To convert the demand requirements into employee-period equivalents, divide the demand in hours by 600. For example, the demand of 21,000 hours in period 1 translates into 35 employee-period equivalents (21,000/600) and demand in period 3 translates into 50 employee-period equivalents (30,000/600). Figure 4.10 shows OM Explorer's spreadsheet for this level strategy that minimizes undertime.

	1	2	3	4	Total
Inputs					
Forecasted demand	35	30	50	20	135
Workforce level	43	43	43	43	172
Undertime	8	13	0	23	44
Overtime	0	0	7	0	7
Derived					
Utilized time	35	30	43	20	128
Hires	3	0	0	0	3
Layoffs	0	0	0	0	0
Calculated					
Utilized time cost	$210,000	$180,000	$258,000	$120,000	$768,000
Undertime cost	$48,000	$78,000	$0	$138,000	$264,000
Overtime cost	$0	$0	$63,000	$0	$63,000
Hiring cost	$24,000	$0	$0	$0	$24,000
Layoff cost	$0	$0	$0	$0	$0
Total cost	$282,000	258,000	321,000	258,000	$1,119,000

◀ **FIGURE 4.10**
Spreadsheet for Level Strategy

c. The mixed-strategy plan that we propose uses a combination of hires, layoffs, and overtime to reduce total costs. The workforce is reduced by 5 at the beginning of the first period, increased by 8 in the third period, and reduced by 13 in the fourth period. Figure 4.11 shows the results.

	1	2	3	4	Total
Inputs					
Forecasted demand	35	30	50	20	135
Workforce level	35	35	43	30	143
Undertime	0	5	0	10	15
Overtime	0	0	7	0	7
Derived					
Utilized time	35	30	43	20	128
Hires	0	0	8	0	8
Layoffs	5	0	0	13	18
Calculated					
Utilized time cost	$210,000	$180,000	$258,000	$120,000	$768,000
Undertime cost	$0	$30,000	$0	$60,000	$90,000
Overtime cost	$0	$0	$63,000	$0	$63,000
Hiring cost	$0	$0	$64,000	$0	$64,000
Layoff cost	$10,000	$0	$0	$26,000	$36,000
Total cost	$220.000	210,000	385,000	206,000	$1,021,000

◀ **FIGURE 4.11**
Spreadsheet for Mixed Strategy

d. The total cost of the chase strategy is $1,050,000. The level strategy results in a total cost of $1,119,000. The mixed-strategy plan was developed by trial and error and results in a total cost of $1,021,000. Further improvements are possible.

Solved Problem 2

The Food Bin grocery store operates 24 hours per day, 7 days per week. Fred Bulger, the store manager, has been analyzing the efficiency and productivity of store operations recently. Bulger decided to observe the need for checkout clerks on the first shift for a one-month period. At the end of the month, he calculated the average number of checkout registers that should be open during the first shift each day. His results showed peak needs on Saturdays and Sundays.

Day	M	T	W	Th	F	S	Su
Number of Clerks Required	3	4	5	5	4	7	8

Bulger now has to come up with a workforce schedule that guarantees each checkout clerk two consecutive days off, but still covers all requirements.

a. Develop a workforce schedule that covers all requirements while giving two consecutive days off to each clerk. How many clerks are needed? Assume that the clerks have no preference regarding which days they have off.

b. Plans can be made to use the clerks for other duties if slack or idle time resulting from this schedule can be determined. How much idle time will result from this schedule, and on what days?

SOLUTION

a. We use the method demonstrated in Example 4.2 to determine the number of clerks needed. The minimum number of clerks is eight.

	DAY						
	M	**T**	**W**	**Th**	**F**	**S**	**Su**
Requirements	3	4	5	5	4	7	8*
Clerk 1	off	off	X	X	X	X	X
Requirements	3	4	4	4	3	6	7*
Clerk 2	off	off	X	X	X	X	X
Requirements	3	4	3	3	2	5	6*
Clerk 3	X	X	X	off	off	X	X
Requirements	2	3	2	3	2	4	5*
Clerk 4	X	X	X	off	off	X	X
Requirements	1	2	1	3	2	3	4*
Clerk 5	X	off	off	X	X	X	X
Requirements	0	2	1	2	1	2	3*
Clerk 6	off	off	X	X	X	X	X
Requirements	0	2*	0	1	0	1	2*
Clerk 7	X	X	off	off	X	X	X
Requirements	0	1*	0	1*	0	0	1*
Clerk 8	X	X	X	X	off	off	X
Requirements	0	0	0	0	0	0	0

*Maximum requirements

b. Based on the results in part (a), the number of clerks on duty minus the requirements is the number of idle clerks available for other duties:

	M	T	W	Th	F	S	Su
Number on duty	5	4	6	5	5	7	8
Requirements	3	4	5	5	4	7	8
Idle clerks	2	0	1	0	1	0	0

The slack in this schedule would indicate to Bulger the number of employees he might ask to work part time (fewer than 5 days per week). For example, Clerk 7 might work Tuesday, Saturday, and Sunday and Clerk 8 might work Tuesday, Thursday, and Sunday. That would eliminate slack from the schedule.

Solved Problem 3

Revisit Example 4.3, where the consulting company has five jobs in its backlog. Create a schedule using the EDD rule, calculating the average days past due and flow time. In this case, does EDD outperform the FCFS rule?

SOLUTION

Customer Sequence	Start Time (days)		Processing Time (days)		Finish Time (days)	Due Date	Days Past Due	Days Ago Since Order Arrived	Flow Time (days)
B	0	+	16	=	16	27	**0**	12	**28**
A	16	+	25	=	41	29	**12**	15	**56**
D	41	+	10	=	51	48	**3**	10	**61**
C	51	+	14	=	65	68	**0**	5	**70**
E	65	+	12	=	77	80	**0**	0	**77**

The days past due and average flow time performance measures for the EDD schedule are

$$\text{Average days past due} = \frac{0 + 12 + 3 + 0 + 0}{5} = 3.0 \text{ days}$$

$$\text{Average flow time} = \frac{28 + 56 + 61 + 70 + 77}{5} = 58.4 \text{ days}$$

By both measures, EDD outperforms the FCFS (3.0 versus 3.4 past due and 58.4 versus 60.2 flow time). However, the solution found in part (b) of Example 4.3 still has the best average flow time of only 47.8 days.

Discussion Questions

1. Quantitative methods can help managers evaluate alternative sales and operations plans on the basis of cost. These methods require cost estimates for each of the controllable variables, such as overtime, subcontracting, hiring, firing, and inventory investment. Say that the existing workforce is made up of 10,000 workers, each having skills valued at $40,000 per year. The plan calls for "creating alternative career opportunities"—in other words, laying off 500 employees. List the types of costs incurred when employees are laid off, and make a rough estimate of the length of time required for payroll savings to recover restructuring costs. If business is expected to improve in one year, are layoffs financially justified? What costs are incurred in a layoff that are difficult to estimate in monetary terms?

2. In your community, some employers maintain stable workforces at all costs, and others furlough and recall workers seemingly at the drop of a hat. What are the differences in markets, management, products, financial position, skills, costs, and competition that could explain these two extremes in personnel policy?

3. Consider the revenue management policies used by Harrah's Cherokee Casino & Hotel, as described in Managerial Practice 4.1. From a business ethics perspective, argue for the policies. Now argue against them.

4. Explain why management should be concerned about priority systems in service and manufacturing organizations.

Problems

The OM Explorer and POM for Windows software is available to all students using the 10th edition of this textbook. Go to **www.pearsonhighered.com/krajewski** to download these computer packages. If you purchased MyOMLab, you also have access to Active Models software and significant help in doing the following problems. Check with your instructor on how best to use these resources. In many cases, the instructor wants you to understand how to do the calculations by hand. At the least, the software provides a check on your calculations. When calculations are particularly complex and the goal is interpreting the results in making decision, the software entirely replaces the manual calculations.

1. The Barberton Municipal Division of Road Maintenance is charged with road repair in the city of Barberton and the surrounding area. Cindy Kramer, road maintenance director, must submit a staffing plan for the next year based on a set schedule for repairs and on the city budget. Kramer estimates that the labor hours required for the next four quarters are 6,000, 12,000, 19,000, and 9,000, respectively. Each of the 11 workers on the workforce can contribute 500 hours per quarter. Payroll costs are $6,000 in wages per worker for regular time worked up to 500 hours, with an overtime pay rate of $18 for each overtime hour. Overtime is limited to 20 percent of the

regular-time capacity in any quarter. Although unused overtime capacity has no cost, unused regular time is paid at $12 per hour. The cost of hiring a worker is $3,000, and the cost of laying off a worker is $2,000. Subcontracting is not permitted.

a. Find a level workforce plan that relies just on overtime and the minimum amount of undertime possible. Overtime can be used to its limits in any quarter. What is the total cost of the plan and how many undertime hours does it call for?

b. Use a chase strategy that varies the workforce level without using overtime or undertime. What is the total cost of this plan?

c. Propose a plan of your own. Compare your plan with those in part (a) and part (b) and discuss its comparative merits.

2. Bob Carlton's golf camp estimates the following workforce requirements for its services over the next 2 years.

Quarter	1	2	3	4
Demand (hours)	4,200	6,400	3,000	4,800
Quarter	5	6	7	8
Demand (hours)	4,400	6,240	3,600	4,800

Each certified instructor puts in 480 hours per quarter regular time and can work an additional 120 hours overtime. Regular-time wages and benefits cost Carlton $7,200 per employee per quarter for regular time worked up to 480 hours, with an overtime cost of $20 per hour. Unused regular time for certified instructors is paid at $15 per hour. There is no cost for unused overtime capacity. The cost of hiring, training, and certifying a new employee is $10,000. Layoff costs are $4,000 per employee. Currently, eight employees work in this capacity.

a. Find a workforce plan using the level strategy that allows for no delay in service. It should rely only on overtime and the minimum amount of undertime necessary. What is the total cost of this plan?

b. Use a chase strategy that varies the workforce level without using overtime or undertime. What is the total cost of this plan?

c. Propose a better plan and calculate its total cost.

3. Continuing Problem 2, now assume that Carlton is permitted to employ some uncertified, part-time instructors, provided they represent no more than 15 percent of the total workforce hours in any quarter. Each part-time instructor can work up to 240 hours per quarter, with no overtime or undertime cost. Labor costs for part-time instructors are $12 per hour. Hiring and training costs are $2,000 per uncertified instructor, and there are no layoff costs.

a. Propose a low-cost, mixed-strategy plan and calculate its total cost.

b. What are the primary advantages and disadvantages of having a workforce consisting of both regular and temporary employees?

4. The Donald Fertilizer Company produces industrial chemical fertilizers. The projected manufacturing requirements (in thousands of gallons) for the next four quarters are 80, 50, 80, and 130, respectively. A level workforce is desired, relying only on anticipation inventory as a supply option. Stockouts and backorders are to be avoided, as are overtime and undertime.

a. Determine the quarterly production rate required to meet total demand for the year, and minimize the anticipation inventory that would be left over at the end of the year. Beginning inventory is zero.

b. Specify the anticipation inventory that will be produced.

c. Suppose that the requirements for the next four quarters are revised to 80, 130, 50, and 80, respectively. If total demand is the same, what level of production rate is needed now, using the same strategy as part (a)?

5. Management at the Kerby Corporation has determined the following aggregated demand schedule (in units):

Month	1	2	3	4
Demand	500	800	1,000	1,400
Month	5	6	7	8
Demand	2,000	3,000	2,700	1,500
Month	9	10	11	12
Demand	1,400	1,500	2,000	1,200

An employee can produce an average of 10 units per month. Each worker on the payroll costs $2,000 in regular-time wages per month. Undertime is paid at the same rate as regular time. In accordance with the labor contract in force, Kerby Corporation does not work overtime or use subcontracting. Kerby can hire and train a new employee for $2,000 and lay off one for $500. Inventory costs $32 per unit on hand at the end of each month. At present, 140 employees are on the payroll and anticipation inventory is zero.

a. Prepare a production plan that only uses a level workforce and anticipation inventory as its supply options. Minimize the inventory left over at the end of the year. Layoffs, undertime, vacations, subcontracting, backorders, and stockouts are not options. The plan may call for a one-time adjustment of the workforce before month 1 begins.

b. Prepare a production plan using a chase strategy, relying only on hiring and layoffs.

c. Prepare a mixed-strategy production plan that uses only a level workforce and anticipation inventory through month 7 (an adjustment of the workforce may be made before month 1 begins) then switches to a chase strategy for months 8–12.

d. Contrast these three plans on the basis of annual costs.

6. Tax Prep Advisers, Inc., has forecasted the following staffing requirements for tax preparation associates over the next 12 months. Management would like three alternative staffing plans to be developed.

Month	1	2	3	4
Demand	5	8	10	13
Month	5	6	7	8
Demand	18	20	20	14
Month	9	10	11	12
Demand	12	8	2	1

The company currently has 10 associates. No more than 10 new hires can be accommodated in any month because of limited training facilities. No backorders are allowed, and overtime cannot exceed 25 percent of regular time capacity on any month. There is no cost for unused overtime capacity. Regular-time wages are $1,500 per month, and overtime wages are 150 percent of regular time wages. Undertime is paid at the same rate as regular time. The hiring cost is $2,500 per person, and the layoff cost is $2.000 per person.

a. Prepare a staffing plan utilizing a level workforce strategy, minimizing undertime. The plan may call for a one-time adjustment of the workforce before month 1.

b. Using a chase strategy, prepare a plan that is consistent with the constraint on hiring and minimizes use of overtime.

c. Prepare a mixed strategy in which the workforce level is slowly increased by two employees per month through month 5 and is then decreased by two employees per month starting in month 6 and continuing through month 12. Does this plan violate the hiring or overtime constraints set the company?

d. Contrast these three plans on the basis of annual costs.

7. Climate Control, Inc., makes expedition-quality rain gear for outdoor enthusiasts. Management prepared a forecast of sales (in suits) for next year and now must prepare a production plan. The company has traditionally maintained a level workforce strategy. All nine workers are treated like family and have been employed by the company for a number of years. Each employee can produce 2,000 suits per month. At present, finished goods inventory holds 24,000 suits. The demand forecast follows:

Month	1	2	3	4
Demand	25,000	16,000	15,000	19,000
Month	5	6	7	8
Demand	32,000	29,000	27,000	22,000
Month	9	10	11	12
Demand	14,000	15,000	20,000	6,000

a. Management is willing to authorize overtime in periods for which regular production and current levels of anticipation inventory do not satisfy demand. However, overtime must be strictly limited to no more than 20 percent of regular time capacity. Management wants to avoid stockouts and backorders and is not willing to accept a plan that calls for shortages. Is it feasible to hold the workforce constant, assuming that overtime is only used in periods for which shortages would occur?

b. Assume that management is not willing to authorize any overtime. Instead, management is willing to negotiate with customers so that backorders may be used as a supply option. However, management is not willing to carry more than 5,000 suits from one month to the next in backorder. Is it feasible to hold the workforce constant, assuming that a maximum backorder of 5,000 suits may be maintained from month to month?

c. Assume management is willing to authorize the use of overtime over the next four months to build additional anticipation inventory. However, overtime must be strictly limited to no more than 20 percent of regular time capacity. Management wants to avoid stockouts and backorders and is not willing to accept a plan that calls for shortages. Is it feasible to hold the workforce constant, assuming that overtime is only used in months 1–4? If not, in which months would additional overtime be required?

8. Gretchen's Kitchen is a fast-food restaurant located in an ideal spot near the local high school. Gretchen Lowe must prepare an annual staffing plan. The only menu items are hamburgers, chili, soft drinks, shakes, and French fries. A sample of 1,000 customers taken at random revealed that they purchased 2,100 hamburgers, 200 pints of chili, 1,000 soft drinks and shakes, and 1,000 bags of French fries. Thus, for purposes of estimating staffing requirements, Lowe assumes that each customer purchases 2.1 hamburgers, 0.2 pint of chili, 1 soft drink or shake, and 1 bag of French fries. Each hamburger requires 4 minutes of labor, a pint of chili requires 3 minutes, and a soft drink or shake and a bag of fries each take 2 minutes of labor.

The restaurant currently has 10 part-time employees who work 80 hours a month on staggered shifts. Wages are $400 per month for regular time and $7.50 per hour for overtime. Hiring and training costs are $250 per new employee, and layoff costs are $50 per employee.

Lowe realizes that building up seasonal inventories of hamburgers (or any of the products) would not be wise because of shelf-life considerations. Also, any demand not satisfied is a lost sale and must be avoided. Three strategies come to mind.

- Use a level strategy relying on overtime and undertime, with up to 20 percent of regular-time capacity on overtime.

- Maintain a base of 10 employees, hiring and laying off as needed to avoid any overtime.

- Utilize a chase strategy, hiring and laying off employees as demand changes to avoid overtime.

When performing her calculations, Lowe always rounds to the next highest integer for the number of employees. She also follows a policy of not using an employee more than 80 hours per month, except when overtime is needed. The projected demand by month (number of customers) for next year is as follows:

Jan.	3,200	July	4,800
Feb.	2,600	Aug.	4,200
Mar.	3,300	Sept.	3,800
Apr.	3,900	Oct.	3,600
May	3,600	Nov.	3,500
June	4,200	Dec.	3,000

a. Develop the schedule of service requirements (hours per month) for the next year.

b. Which strategy is most effective?

c. Suppose that an arrangement with the high school enables the manager to identify good prospective employees without having to advertise in the local newspaper. This source reduces the hiring cost to $50, which is mainly the cost of charred hamburgers during training. If cost is her only concern, will this method of hiring change Gretchen Lowe's strategy? Considering other objectives that may be appropriate, do you think she should change strategies?

9. The Kool King Company has followed a policy of no layoffs for most of the manufacturer's life, even though the demand for its air conditioners is highly seasonal. Management wants to evaluate the cost-effectiveness of this policy. Competitive pressures are increasing, and ways need to be found to reduce costs. The following demand (expressed in employee–month equivalents) has been forecast for next year:

Jan.	70	May	130	Sept.	110
Feb.	90	June	170	Oct.	60
Mar.	100	July	170	Nov.	20
Apr.	100	Aug.	150	Dec.	40

Additional planning data follow, with costs, inventory, and backorders expressed in employee–month equivalents:

Regular-time production cost	$1,500	Hire cost	$500/ person
Overtime production cost	150% of regular-time production cost	Layoff cost	$2,000/ person
Subcontracting cost	$2,500	Current backorders	10
Inventory holding cost	$100	Current inventory	0
Backorder cost	$1,000	Desired ending inventory	0
Maximum overtime	20% of regular-time capacity	Current employment	130 employees

Hiring costs are lower than layoff costs because the facility is located near a Technical Training School. Undertime is paid at the rate equivalent to regular-time production. Each employee who has been with the company at least one year also received 0.5 months of paid vacation. All 130 employees currently employed qualify for vacations next year, assuming that they remain on the workforce. Answer the following questions using *Sales and Operations Planning with Spreadsheets* Solver in OM Explorer, or an Excel spreadsheet that you developed on your own.

a. Develop an S&OP with the level strategy using overtime, undertime, and vacations as the only supply options. Use the maximum amount of overtime so as to minimize undertime. What is the total cost of this plan, and what are its advantages and disadvantages?

b. Develop an S&OP with the chase strategy. Part of your decision will be when and how many vacation periods to grant. What is the total cost of this plan, and what are its advantages and disadvantages?

c. Develop an S&OP with a lower cost than found with either the level or chase strategy, being open to the full range of supply options (including anticipation inventory). Subcontractors can supply up to 50 employee–month equivalents. What is the total cost of this plan, and what are its advantages and disadvantages?

10. A manager faces peak (weekly) demand for one of her operations, but is not sure how long the peak will last. She can either use overtime from the current workforce, or hire/lay off and just pay regular-time wages. Regular-time pay is $500 per week, overtime is $750 per week, the hiring cost is $2,000, and the layoff cost is $3,000. Assuming that people are available seeking such a short-term arrangement, how many weeks must the surge in demand last to justify a temporary hire? *Hint:* Use break-even analysis (see Supplement A, "Decision Making"). Let w be the number of weeks of the high demand (rather than using Q for the break-even quantity). What is the fixed cost for the regular-time option? Overtime option?

11. Gerald Glynn manages the Michaels Distribution Center. After careful examination of his database information, he has determined the daily requirements for part-time loading dock personnel. The distribution center operates 7 days a week, and the daily part-time staffing requirements are

Day	M	T	W	Th	F	S	Su
Requirements	6	3	5	3	7	2	3

Find the minimum number of workers Glynn must hire. Prepare a workforce schedule for these individuals so that each will have two consecutive days off per week and all staffing requirements will be satisfied. Give preference to the S–Su pair in case of a tie.

12. Cara Ryder manages a ski school in a large resort and is trying to develop a schedule for instructors. The instructors receive little salary and work just enough to earn room and board. They receive free skiing and spend most of their free time tackling the resort's notorious double black-diamond slopes. Hence, the instructors work only 4 days a week. One of the lesson packages offered at the resort is a 4-day beginner package. Ryder likes to keep the same instructor with a group over the 4-day period, so she schedules the instructors for 4 consecutive days and then 3 days off. Ryder uses years of experience with demand forecasts provided by management to formulate her instructor requirements for the upcoming month.

Day	M	T	W	Th	F	S	Su
Requirements	7	5	4	5	6	9	8

a. Determine how many instructors Ryder needs to employ. Give preference to Saturday and Sunday off. (*Hint:* Look for the group of *3* days with the lowest requirements.)

b. Specify the work schedule for each employee. How much slack does your schedule generate for each day?

13. The mayor of Cambridge, Colorado, wanting to be environmentally progressive, decides to implement a recycling plan. All residents of the city will receive a special three-part bin to separate their glass, plastic, and aluminum, and the city will be responsible for picking up the materials. A young city and regional planning graduate, Michael Duffy, has been hired to manage the recycling program. After carefully studying the city's population density, Duffy decides that the following numbers of recycling collectors will be needed:

Day	M	T	W	Th	F	S	Su
Requirements	12	7	9	9	5	3	6

The requirements are based on the populations of the various housing developments and subdivisions in the city and surrounding communities. To motivate residents of some areas to have their pickups scheduled on weekends, a special tax break will be given.

a. Find the minimum number of recycling collectors required if each employee works 5 days a week and has two consecutive days off. Give preference to the S–Su pair when that pair is involved in a tie.

b. Specify the work schedule for each employee. How much slack does your schedule generate for each day?

c. Suppose that Duffy can smooth the requirements further through greater tax incentives. The requirements then will be eight collectors on Monday and seven on the other days of the week. How many collectors will be needed now? Does smoothing of requirements have capital investment implications? If so, what are they?

14. Little 6, Inc., an accounting firm, forecasts the following weekly workload during the tax season:

	DAY						
	M	T	W	Th	F	S	Su
Personal Tax Returns	24	14	18	18	10	28	16
Corporate Tax Returns	16	10	12	15	24	12	4

Corporate tax returns each require 4 hours of an accountant's time, and personal returns each require 90 minutes. During tax season, each accountant can work up to 10 hours per day. However, error rates increase to unacceptable levels when accountants work more than five consecutive days per week.

Let x_i = number for each working schedule, e.g., x_1 = number for Tuesday through Saturday.

a. Create an effective and efficient work schedule by formulating the problem as a Linear Program and solve using POM for Windows.

b. Assume that management has decided to offer a pay differential to those accountants who are scheduled to work on a weekend day. Normally, accountants earn $1,200 per week, but management will pay a bonus of $100 for Saturday work and $150 for Sunday work. What schedule will cover all demand as well as minimize payroll cost?

c. Assume that Little 6 has three part-time employees available to work Friday, Saturday, and Sunday at a rate of $800. Could these employees be cost effectively utilized?

15. Return to Problem 11 and the workforce schedule for part-time loading dock workers. Suppose that each part-time worker can work only 3 days, but the days must be consecutive. Formulate and solve this workforce scheduling problem as a Linear Program and solve it using POM for Windows. Your objective is to minimize total slack capacity. What is the minimum number of loaders needed now and what are their schedules?

Let x_i = number for each 3-day schedule, e.g., x_1 = number for Tuesday through Thursday.

16. The Hickory Company manufactures wooden desks. Management schedules overtime every weekend to reduce the backlog on the most popular models. The automatic routing machine is used to cut certain types of edges on the desktops. The following orders need to be scheduled for the routing machine:

Order	Time Since Order Arrived (hours ago)	Estimated Machine Time (hours)	Due Date (hours from now)
1	6	10	12
2	5	3	8
3	3	15	18
4	1	9	20
5	0	7	21

The due dates reflect the need for the order to be at its next operation.

a. Develop separate schedules by using the FCFS and EDD rules. Compare the schedules on the basis of average flow time and average past due hours.

b. Comment on the performance of the two rules relative to these measures.

17. Currently a company that designs Web sites has five customers in its backlog. The day when the order arrived, processing time, and promised due dates are given in the following table. The customers are listed in the order of when they arrived. They are ready to be scheduled today, which is the start of day 190.

Customer	Time Since Order Arrived (days ago)	Processing Time (days)	Due Date (days from now)
A	10	20	26
B	8	12	50
C	6	28	66
D	3	24	58
E	2	32	100

a. Develop separate schedules by using the FCFS and EDD rules. Compare the schedules on the basis of average flow time and average days past due.

b. Comment on the performance of the two rules relative to these measures. Which one gives the best schedule? Why?

18. The Mowry Machine Shop still has five jobs to be processed as of 8 A.M. today (day 23) at its bottleneck operation. The day when the order arrived, processing time, and promised due dates are given in the following table. The jobs are listed in the order of arrival.

Job	Time Since Order Arrived (days ago)	Processing Time (days)	Due Date (days from now)
A	11	10	22
B	10	8	13
C	8	4	19
D	6	4	16
E	1	3	30

a. Develop separate schedules by using the FCFS and EDD rules. Compare the schedules on the basis of average flow time and average days past due.

b. Which rule gives the best schedule, in your judgment? Why?

Active Model Exercise

This Active Model appears in MyOMLab. It allows you to evaluate the effects of modifying the size of a constant workforce.

QUESTIONS

1. If we use the same number of workers in each period, what happens as the number of workers increases from 15?

2. If we use the same number of workers in each period, what happens as the number of workers decreases from 15?

3. Suppose the hiring cost is $1,100. What happens as the number of workers increases?

4. Suppose the overtime cost is $3,300. What happens as the number of workers increases?

5. Suppose the undertime cost is the same as the regular-time cost (i.e., paid undertime). What is the best number of workers to have in each month and still meet the demand?

6. If the overtime capacity increases to 30 percent, what is the minimum number of workers that meets the demand in every month?

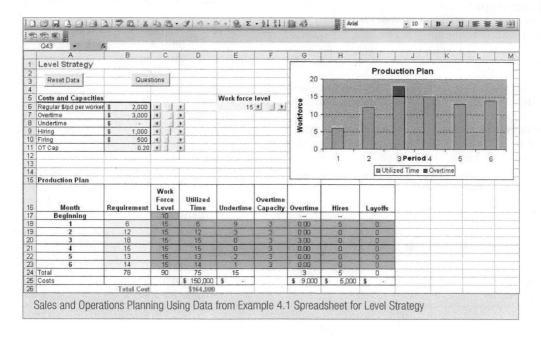

Sales and Operations Planning Using Data from Example 4.1 Spreadsheet for Level Strategy

VIDEO CASE | Sales and Operations Planning at Starwood

Business travel often means staying overnight in a hotel. Upon arrival, you may be greeted by a doorman or valet to assist you with your luggage. Front desk staff awaits your check-in. Behind the scenes, housekeeping, maintenance, and culinary staff prepare for your stay. Making a reservation gives the hotel notice of your plan to stay, but even before your trip is ever conceived, the hotel is staffed and ready. How? Through a process called *sales and operations planning.*

Sales and operations planning is a process every organization performs to some degree. Called a staffing plan (or service resource plan if more detailed) in service organizations, the plan must strike the right level of customer service while maintaining workforce stability and cost control so as to achieve the organization's profit expectations. So where do companies begin? Let us take a look at Starwood Hotels and Resorts to see how it is done.

Starwood operates in more than 750 locations around the globe. At the highest levels, Starwood engages in sales and operations planning on an annual basis, with adjustments made as needed each month by region and by property. Budgeted revenues and other projections come from headquarters; the regions and individual properties then break down the forecasts to meet their expected occupancies. Typically, the director of human resources determines the staffing mix needed across divisions such as food and beverage service, rooms (including housekeeping, spa, and guest services), engineering, Six Sigma (see Chapter 7, "Quality and Performance"), revenue management, and accounting.

At the property level, general managers and their staff must provide input into next year's plan while implementing and monitoring activity in the current year. For most properties, payroll is close to 40 percent of budgeted revenues and represents the largest single expense the hotel incurs. It is also the most controllable expense. Many of Starwood's hotels and most resorts experience patterns of seasonality that affect demand for rooms and services. This seasonality, in turn, significantly affects the organization's staffing plan.

To determine the staffing levels, the company uses a proprietary software program that models occupancy demand based on historical data. The key drivers of staffing are occupied rooms and restaurant meals, called "covers." Starwood knows on a *per room* and *per cover* basis how many staff are required to function properly. When occupancy and covers are entered into the software program, the output models a recommended staffing level for each division. This recommendation is then reviewed by division managers and adjusted, as needed, to be sure staffing is in line with budgeted financial plans. Job fairs to recruit nonmanagement staff are held several times a year so a qualified candidate pool of both part-time and full-time staff is ready when needed. Most hotels maintain a pool of part-time workers who can contract or expand the hours worked if required by property guest levels. Vacations for management are scheduled for the low season. Overtime will be worked as needed, but is less desirable than scheduling the appropriate level of staff in each division.

The program also takes into account both the complexity and positioning of the property within Starwood. For example, a 400-room city hotel that is essentially a high-rise building is not as complex as a 400-room sprawling resort with golf, spa, convention, and other services not offered by the city hotel. Positioning also is important. A five-star resort hotel's customer service

Pearson

A software program that forecasts occupancy based on historical data helps Starwood maintain proper staffing levels at its hotels. Managers know on a per-room, and "per-cover," basis how many hotel employees should be scheduled so that customers get good service.

expectations are much greater than a three-star airport hotel location and requires much higher ratios of staff to guests. Finally, if the hotel is a brand new property, historical data from similar properties is used to model staffing for the first year or two of operation.

Starwood attempts to modify demand and smooth out the peaks and valleys of its demand patterns. Many of the company's hotels experience three seasons: high, mid (called "shoulder"), and low season. Starwood, like its competitors, offers special rates, family packages, and weekend specials to attract different segments of the market during slower business periods. Staff is cross-trained to work in multiple areas, such as front reception and the concierge desk, so additional staff does not have to be added across seasons. Employees may also be temporarily redeployed among Starwood's properties to help out during peak periods. For example, when occupancy is forecast to be high in one region of the country, staff from areas entering their low season will be assigned to cover the demand.

QUESTIONS

1. At what points in the planning process would you expect accounting/finance, marketing, information systems, and operations to play a role? What inputs should these areas provide, and why?

2. Does Starwood employ a chase, level, or mixed strategy? Why is this approach the best choice for the company?

3. How would staffing for the opening of a new hotel or resort differ from that of an existing property? What data might Starwood rely upon to make sure the new property is not over- or understaffed in its first year of operation?

CASE | Memorial Hospital

Memorial Hospital is a 265-bed regional health care facility located in the mountains of western North Carolina. The mission of the hospital is to provide quality health care to the people of Ashe County and the six surrounding counties. To accomplish this mission, Memorial Hospital's CEO has outlined three objectives: (1) maximize customer service to increase customer satisfaction, (2) minimize costs to remain competitive, and (3) minimize fluctuations in workforce levels to help stabilize area employment.

The hospital's operations are segmented into eight major wards for the purposes of planning and scheduling the nursing staff. These wards are listed in Table 4.4, along with the number of beds, targeted patient-to-nurse ratios, and average patient census for each ward. The overall demand for hospital services remained relatively constant over the past few years even though the population of the seven counties served increased. This stable demand can be attributed to increased competition from other hospitals in the area and the rise in alternative health care delivery systems, such as health maintenance organizations (HMOs). However, demand for Memorial Hospital's services does vary considerably by type of ward and time of year. Table 4.5 provides a historical monthly breakdown of the average daily patient census per ward.

The director of nursing for Memorial Hospital is Darlene Fry. Each fall she confronts one of the most challenging aspects of her job: planning the nurse-staffing levels for the next calendar year. Although the average demand for nurses has remained relatively stable over the past couple of years, the staffing plan usually changes because of changing work policies, changing pay structures, and temporary nurse availability and cost. With fall quickly approaching, Fry is collecting information to plan next year's staffing levels.

The nurses at Memorial Hospital work a regular schedule of four 10-hour days per week. The average regular-time pay across all nursing grades is $12.00 per hour. Overtime may be scheduled when necessary. However, because of the intensity of the demands placed on nurses, only a limited amount of overtime is permitted per week. Nurses may be scheduled for as many as 12 hours per day, for a maximum of 5 days per week. Overtime is compensated at a rate of $18.00 per hour. In periods of extremely high demand, temporary part-time nurses may be hired for a limited period of time. Temporary nurses are paid $15.00 per hour. Memorial Hospital's policy limits the proportion of temporary nurses to 15 percent of the total nursing staff.

Finding, hiring, and retaining qualified nurses is an ongoing problem for hospitals. One reason is that various forms of private practice lure many nurses away from hospitals with higher pay and greater flexibility. This situation has caused Memorial to guarantee its full-time staff nurses pay for a minimum of 30 hours per week, regardless of the demand placed on nursing services. In addition, each nurse receives 4 weeks of paid vacation each year. However, vacation scheduling may be somewhat restricted by the projected demand for nurses during particular times of the year.

TABLE 4.4 | WARD CAPACITY DATA

Ward	Number of Beds	Patients per Nurse	Patient Census*
Intensive Care	20	2	10
Cardiac	25	4	15
Maternity	30	4	10
Pediatric	40	4	22
Surgery	5	†	†
Post-Op	15	5	8 (T–F daily equivalent)‡
Emergency	10	3	5 (daily equivalent)‡
General	120	8	98

*Yearly average per day

†The hospital employs 20 surgical nurses. Routine surgery is scheduled on Tuesdays and Fridays; five surgeries can be scheduled per day per operating room (bed) on these days. Emergency surgery is scheduled as needed.

‡Daily equivalents are used to schedule nurses because patients flow through these wards in relatively short periods of time. A daily equivalent of 5 indicates that throughout a typical day, an average of five patients are treated in the ward.

At present, the hospital employs 130 nurses, including 20 surgical nurses. The other 110 nurses are assigned to the remaining seven major areas of the hospital. The personnel department informed Fry that the average cost to the hospital for hiring a new full-time nurse is $400 and for laying off or firing a nurse is $150. Although layoffs are an option, Fry is aware of the hospital's objective of maintaining a level workforce.

After looking over the information that she collected, Darlene Fry wants to consider staffing changes in all areas except the surgery ward, which is already correctly staffed.

QUESTIONS

1. Explain the alternatives available to Darlene Fry as she develops a nurse staffing plan for Memorial Hospital. How does each alternative plan meet the objective stated by the CEO?

2. Based on the data presented, develop a nurse staffing plan for Memorial Hospital. Explain your rationale for this plan.

TABLE 4.5 | AVERAGE DAILY PATIENT CENSUS PER MONTH

	MONTH											
Ward	**J**	**F**	**M**	**A**	**M**	**J**	**J**	**A**	**S**	**O**	**N**	**D**
Intensive Care	13	10	8	7	7	6	11	13	9	10	12	14
Cardiac	18	16	15	13	14	12	13	12	13	15	18	20
Maternity	8	8	12	13	10	8	13	13	14	10	8	7
Pediatric	22	23	24	24	25	21	22	20	18	20	21	19
Surgery*	20	18	18	17	16	16	22	21	17	18	20	22
Post-Op†	10	8	7	7	6	6	10	10	7	8	9	10
Emergency†	6	4	4	7	8	5	5	4	4	3	4	6
General	110	108	100	98	95	90	88	92	98	102	107	94

Source: This case was prepared by Dr. Brooke Saladin, Wake Forest University, North Carolina, as a basis for classroom discussion. Copyright © Brooke Saladin. Used with permission.

*Average surgeries per day on Tuesday and Thursday.

†Daily equivalents

Selected References

Chiang, Wen-Chyuan, Jason C.H. Chen, and Xiaojing Xu. "An Overview of Research on Revenue Management: Current Issues and Future Research." *International Journal of Revenue Management*, vol. 1, no. 1 (2007), pp. 97–128.

Dougherty, John R. "Lessons from the Pros." *APICS Magazine* (November/December, 2007), pp. 31–33.

Dougherty, John R., and Christopher Gray. *Sales & Operations Planning—Best Practices.* Victoria, Canada: Trafford Publishing, 2006.

Esper, Terry L., Alexander E. Ellinger, Theodore P. Stank, Daniel J. Flint, and Mark Moon. "Demand and Supply Integration: A Conceptual Framework of Value Creation through Knowledge Management." *Journal of the Academy of Marketing Science*, vol. 38 (2010), pp. 5–18.

Gray, Christopher. *Sales & Operations Planning—Standard System.* Victoria, Canada: Trafford Publishing, 2007.

Gupta, Jatinder N.D., and Edward Stafford Jr. "Flowshop Scheduling Research after Five Decades." *European Journal of Operational Research*, vol. 169 (2006), pp. 699–711.

Jacobs, F. Robert, William Berry, and D. Clay Whybark. *Manufacturing Planning and Control Systems for Supply Chain Management*, 6th ed. New York: McGraw-Hill/Irwin, 2010.

Kelly, Erin L., and Phyllis Moen. "Rethinking the ClockWork of Work: Why Schedule Control May Pay Off at Work and at Home." *Advances in Developing Human Resources*, vol. 9, no. 4 (Nov 2007), pp. 487–605.

Maher, Kris. "Wal-Mart Seeks New Flexibility in Worker Shifts." *The Wall Street Journal* (January 3, 2007), p. A1.

Muzumdar, Maha, and John Fontanella. "The Secrets to S&OP Success." *Supply Chain Management* (April 2006), pp. 34–41.

Nakano, Mikihisa. "Collaborative Forecasting and Planning in Supply Chains: The Impact on Performance in Japanese Manufacturers." *International Journal of Physical Distribution & Logistics Management*, vol. 39, no. 2, pp. 84–105.

Olhager, Jan, and Erik Selldin. "Manufacturing Planning and Control Approaches: Market Alignment and Performance." *International Journal of Production Research*, vol 45, no. 6 (2007), pp. 1469–1484.

Pinedo, Michael. "Planning and Scheduling in Manufacturing and Services." New York: Springer 2006.

Quadt, Daniel, and Heinrich Kuhn. "A Taxonomy of Flexible Flow Line Scheduling Procedures." *European Journal of Operational Research*, vol. 178 (2007), pp. 686–698.

Rennie, Elizabeth. "All Fired UP: Why Food and Beverage Professionals Must Put S&OP on the Menu." *APICS Magazine* (July/August 2006), pp. 32–35.

Rennie, Elizabeth. "Remote Possibilities: Improved Logistics Management Leads to Promising New Distribution Activities." *APICS Magazine* (July/August 2006), pp. 36–37.

Singhal, Jaya, and Kalyan Singhal. "Holt, Modigliani, Muth, and Simon's Work and Its Role in the Renaissance and Evolution of Operations Management." *Journal of Operations Management*, vol. 25, no. 2 (March 2007), pp. 300–309.

Slone, Reuben, John T. Mentzer, and J. Paul Dittmann. "Are You the Weakest Link in Your Company's Supply Chain?" *Harvard Business Review* (October, 2007), pp.1–11.

Smith, Larry, Joseph C. Andraski, and E. Fawcett. "Integrated Business Planning: A Roadmap to Linking S&OP and CPFR." *Business Forecasting*, vol. 29, no. 4 (Winter 2011), pp. 1–17.

Takey, Flavia, and Marco A. Mesquita. "Aggregate Planning for a Large Food Manufacturer with High Seasonal Demand," *Brazilian Journal of Operations & Production Management*, vol. 3, no. 1 (2006), pp. 5–20.

Trottman, Melanie. "Choices in Stormy Weather: How Airline Employees Make Hundreds of Decisions to Cancel or Reroute Flights." *Wall Street Journal* (February 14, 2006), pp. B1–B3.

Wallace, Thomas F., and Robert A. Stahl. "Sales Forecasting: Improving Cooperation Between the Demand People and the Supply People," *Foresight*. Issue 12 (Winter, 2009), pp. 14–20.

Wallace, Thomas F. *Sales & Operations Planning: The How-To Handbook*, 3rd ed. Cincinnati, OH: T. E. Wallace & Company, 2008.

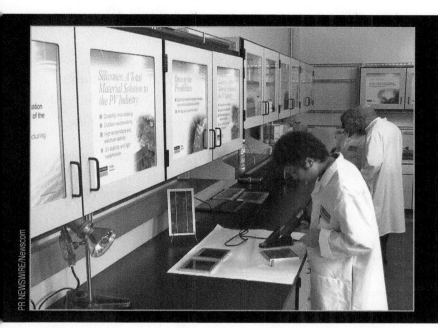

PR NEWSWIRE/Newscom

Dow Corning scientists research next generation solar technologies at the company's Solar
Application Center

RESOURCE PLANNING

Dow Corning

Dow Corning, created as a joint venture between Corning Incorporated and the Dow Chemical Company in 1943, is a global leader that offers over 7,000 innovative products and services using silicon-based technology in diverse industries such as electronics, aviation and aerospace, textile, automotive, and health care, among others. As an example, Dow Corning's Electrical Insulating Compounds are used for creating moisture proof seals for aircraft, automotive, and marine ignition systems. With 11,500 employees, over 25,000 customers, and 45 manufacturing and warehouse locations worldwide, its annual revenues of $6 billion generated a net income of $866 million in 2010. More than half its sales are outside the United States. In order to integrate different business functions and enhance resource planning across the entire firm and its supply chain, Dow Corning turned to SAP, a leading provider of enterprise resource planning (ERP) software solutions. SAP delivers role based access to crucial data, applications, and analytical tools, and has a suite of applications for Business Processes (like Financial Management, Customer Relationship Management, Human Capital Management, and Supply Chain Management), Business Analytics, and Technology. Dow installed the SAP R/3 and mySAP Supply Chain Management solution, with SAP Advanced Planner and Optimizer (APO) at its core.

Prior to the ERP implementation, limited transparency and redundancy within the existing legacy systems made it difficult to access and analyze data needed for effective resource planning, and also hampered decision making and responsiveness. A sequenced implementation of the SAP modules facilitated the linking of key processes from order generation to production planning to warehousing to delivery and final billing. The SAP APO solution enabled the SCOR model of plan, source, make, and deliver, which allowed the linkage of shop floor processes and manufacturing operations with the rest of the business. With a transparent view of orders, materials, equipment, product quality, and cost information, Dow Corning can now coordinate plants and processes with greater ease and better match production to market requirements on a global scale. Employee productivity and satisfaction are also up, due mostly to faster response times and accurate on-time deliveries.

Source: End to End Supply Chain Management at Dow Corning, **http://www.sap.com/usa/solutions/business-suite/ erp/operations/pdf/CS_Dow_Corning.pdf**; Dow Corning, Optimizing Operational Performance to Sharpen Competitive Advantage, **www.sap.com**; **http://www.dowcorning.com/content/about/aboutmedia/fastfacts.asp**; May 29, 2011; **http://www12.sap.com/index.epx#/solutions/index.epx**; May 29, 2011.

LEARNING GOALS   *After reading this chapter, you should be able to:*

1. Explain how enterprise resource planning (ERP) systems can foster better resource planning.

2. Explain how the concept of dependent demand is fundamental to resource planning.

3. Describe a master production schedule (MPS) and compute available-to-promise quantities.

4. Apply the logic of a material requirements planning (MRP) system to identify production and purchase orders needed for dependent demand items.

5. Apply MRP principles to the provision of services and distribution inventories.

Dow Corning demonstrates that companies can gain a competitive edge by using an effective information system to help with their resource planning. Companies must ensure that all of the resources they need to produce finished services or products are available at the right time. If they are not, a firm risks losing business. For a manufacturer, this task can mean keeping track of thousands of subassemblies, components, and raw materials as well as key equipment capacities. For a service provider, this task can mean keeping track of numerous supplies and carefully scheduling the time and capacity requirements of different employees and types of equipment.

We begin this chapter by describing enterprise resource planning (ERP) systems, which have become a valuable tool for, among other things, resource planning. We then examine a specific approach to resource planning, called material requirements planning (MRP). The concluding section of the chapter illustrates how service providers manage their supplies, human resources, equipment, and financial resources.

resource planning

A process that takes sales and operations plans; processes information in the way of time standards, routings, and other information on how services or products are produced; and then plans the input requirements.

enterprise process

A companywide process that cuts across functional areas, business units, geographical regions, and product lines.

enterprise resource planning (ERP) systems

Large, integrated information systems that support many enterprise processes and data storage needs.

Resource Planning across the Organization

Resource planning lies at the heart of any organization, cutting across all of its different functional areas. It takes sales and operations plans; processes information in the way of time standards, routings, and other information on how services or products are produced; and then plans the input requirements. It also can create reports for managers of the firm's major functional areas, such as human resources, purchasing, sales and marketing, and finance and accounting. In essence, resource planning is a process in and of itself that can be analyzed relative to the firm's competitive priorities.

Enterprise Resource Planning

An **enterprise process** is a companywide process that cuts across functional areas, business units, geographic regions, product lines, suppliers, and customers. **Enterprise resource planning (ERP) systems** are large, integrated information systems that support many enterprise processes and data storage needs. By integrating the firm's functional areas, ERP systems allow an organization to view its operations as a whole rather than having to try to put together the different information pieces produced by its various functions and divisions. Today, ERP systems are being used by traditional brick-and-mortar organizations such as manufacturers, restaurants, hospitals, and hotels, as well as by Internet companies that rely extensively on Web connectivity to link their customers and suppliers.

How ERP Systems Are Designed

ERP revolves around a single comprehensive database that can be made available across the entire organization (or enterprise). Passwords are generally issued to allow certain personnel to access certain areas of the system. Having a single database for all of the firm's information makes it much easier for managers to monitor all of the company's products at all locations and at all times. The database collects data and feeds them into the various modular applications (or suites) of the software system. As new information is entered as a *transaction* in one application, related information is automatically updated in the other applications, including the firm's financial and accounting databases, its human resource and payroll databases, sales, supplier and customer databases, and so forth. In this way, the ERP system streamlines the data flows throughout the organization and supply chain and provides employees with direct access to a wealth of real-time operating information scattered across different functions in the organization. Figure 5.1 shows some of the typical applications with a few subprocesses nested within each one. Some of the applications are for back-office operations such as manufacturing and payroll, while others are for front-office operations such as customer service.

Amazon.com is one company that uses an ERP system. The supply chain application of Amazon's system is particularly important because it allows Amazon.com to link customer orders to warehouse shipments and, ultimately, to supplier replenishment orders. Other applications are more important in other businesses. For example, universities put particular emphasis on the human resources and accounting and finance applications, and manufacturers have an interest in almost every application suite. Not all applications in Figure 5.1 need to be integrated into an ERP system, but those left out will not share their information with the ERP system. Sometimes, however, ERP systems are designed to interface with a firm's existing, older information systems (called "legacy systems").

Designing an ERP system requires that a company carefully analyze its major processes so that appropriate decisions about the coordination of legacy systems and new software can be made. Sometimes, a company's processes that involve redundancies and convoluted information flows must be completely reengineered before the firm can enjoy the benefits of an integrated

◄ **FIGURE 5.1**
ERP Application Modules
Source: Based on *Enterprise Resource Planning (ERP)* by Scalle and Cotteleer, Harvard Business School Press. Boston, MA, 1999, No. 9-699-020.

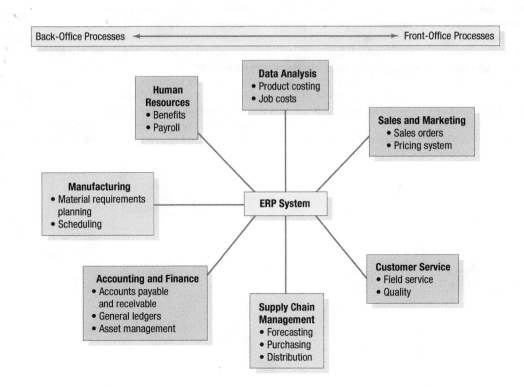

Headquarters of the software company SAP AG in Walldorf, Baden-Wuerttemberg, Germany, Europe

information system. However, a recent study showed that companies reap the greatest rewards when they keep their ERP implementations simple, work with a small number of software vendors, and use standardized systems rather than customizing them extensively. Firms can otherwise end up spending excessive amounts of money on ERP systems that are complex to use and costly to manage. UK confectionary giant Cadbury had to take a 12-million pound hit to their profits due to a build-up of excess inventory of chocolate bars caused by information technology problems arising from the roll out of a new SAP-based ERP system.

Most ERP systems today use a graphical user interface, although the older, keyboard-driven, text-based systems are still popular because of their dependability and technical simplicity. Users navigate through various screens and menus. Training, such as during ERP implementation, focuses on these screens and how users can utilize them to get their jobs done. The biggest suppliers of these off-the-shelf commercial ERP packages are SAP AG, a German company that was also used by Dow Corning in the opening vignette, followed by Oracle Corporation.

Material Requirements Planning

material requirements planning (MRP)

A computerized information system developed specifically to help manufacturers manage dependent demand inventory and schedule replenishment orders.

MRP explosion

A process that converts the requirements of various final products into a material requirements plan that specifies the replenishment schedules of all the subassemblies, components, and raw materials needed to produce final products.

The Manufacturing and Supply Chain Management modules in Figure 5.1 deal with resource planning. Understanding resource planning begins with the concept of *dependent demand*, which sets it apart from the techniques that will be covered in Chapter 6, "Supply Chain Inventory Management." **Material requirements planning (MRP)** is a computerized information system developed specifically to help manufacturers manage dependent demand inventory and schedule replenishment orders. The key inputs of an MRP system are a bill of materials database, a master production schedule, and an inventory record database, as shown in Figure 5.2. Using this information, the MRP system identifies the actions planners must take to stay on schedule, such as releasing new production orders, adjusting order quantities, and expediting late orders.

An MRP system translates the master production schedule and other sources of demand, such as independent demand for replacement parts and maintenance items, into the requirements for all subassemblies, components, and raw materials needed to produce the required parent items. This process is called an **MRP explosion** because it converts the requirements of various final products into a material requirements plan that specifies the replenishment schedules of all the subassemblies, components, and raw materials needed to produce final products.

We first explore the nature of dependent demand and how it differs from independent demand, followed by a discussion of each of the key inputs to the MRP system shown in Figure 5.2.

FIGURE 5.2 ▶
Material Requirements Plan Inputs

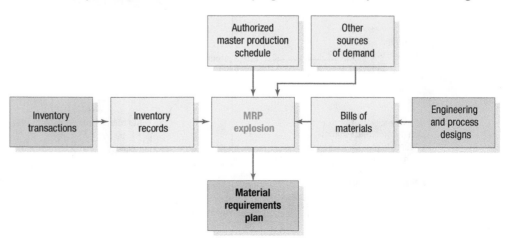

Dependent Demand

For years, many companies tried to manage production and their dependent demand inventories using independent demand systems similar to those that will be discussed in Chapter 6, "Supply Chain Inventory Management," but the outcome was seldom satisfactory because dependent demand is fundamentally different from independent demand. To illustrate the concept of dependent demand, let us consider a Huffy bicycle produced for retail outlets. Demand for a final product, such as a bicycle, is called *independent demand* because it is influenced only by market conditions. In contrast, the demand for spokes going into the bicycle "depends" on the production planned for its wheels. Huffy must forecast this demand using techniques such as those discussed in Chapter 3, "Forecasting." However, Huffy also keeps many other items in inventory—handlebars, pedals, frames, and wheel rims—used to make completed bicycles. Each of these items has a **dependent demand** because the quantity required varies with the production plans for other items held in the firm's inventory—finished bikes, in this case. For example, the demand for frames, pedals, and wheel rims is *dependent* on the production of completed bicycles. Operations can calculate the demand for dependent demand items once the bicycle production levels are laid out in the sales and operations plan. For example, every bicycle needs two wheel rims, so 1,000 completed bicycles need 1,000(2) = 2,000 rims. Forecasting techniques are not needed for the rims.

The bicycle, or any other product that is manufactured from one or more components, is called a **parent**. The wheel rim is an example of a **component**—an item that goes through one or more operations to be transformed into or become part of one or more parents. A wheel rim, for example, will have several different parents if the rim is used to make more than one style of bicycle. This parent–component relationship can cause erratic dependent demand patterns for components. Suppose that every time inventory falls to 500 units (a reorder point), an order for 1,000 more bicycles is placed, as shown in Figure 5.3(a). The assembly supervisor then authorizes the withdrawal of 2,000 rims from inventory, along with other components for the finished product. The demand for the rim is shown in Figure 5.3(b). So, even though customer demand for the finished bicycle is continuous and reasonably uniform, the production demand for wheel rims is "lumpy"; that is, it occurs sporadically, usually in relatively large quantities. Thus, the production decisions for the assembly of bicycles, which account for the costs of assembling the bicycles and the projected assembly capacities at the time the decisions are made, determine the demand for wheel rims.

Managing dependent demand inventories is complicated because some components may be subject to both dependent and independent demand. For example, the shop floor needs 2,000 wheel rims for the new bicycles, but the company also sells replacement rims for old bicycles directly to retail outlets. This practice places an independent demand on the inventory of wheel rims. Materials requirements planning can be used in complex situations involving components that may have independent demand as well as dependent demand inventories.

Bill of Materials

The replenishment schedule for a component is determined from the production schedules of its parents. Hence, the system needs accurate information on parent–component relationships. A **bill of materials (BOM)** is a record of all the components of an item, the parent–component

dependent demand

The demand for an item that occurs because the quantity required varies with the production plans for other items held in the firm's inventory.

parent

Any product that is manufactured from one or more components.

component

An item that goes through one or more operations to be transformed into or become part of one or more parents.

bill of materials (BOM)

A record of all the components of an item, the parent–component relationships, and the usage quantities derived from engineering and process designs.

◀ **FIGURE 5.3**
Lumpy Dependent Demand Resulting from Continuous Independent Demand

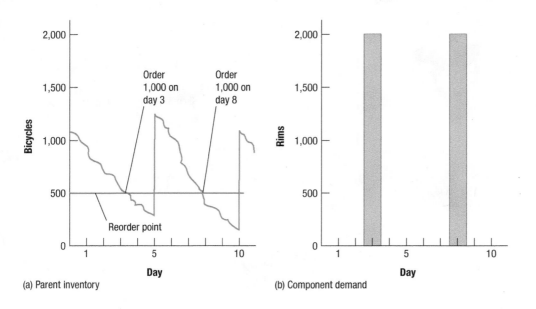

(a) Parent inventory

(b) Component demand

relationships, and the usage quantities derived from engineering and process designs. In Figure 5.4, the BOM of a simple ladder-back chair shows that the chair is made from a ladder-back subassembly, a seat subassembly, front legs, and leg supports. In turn, the ladder-back subassembly is made from back legs and back slats, and the seat subassembly is made from a seat frame and a seat cushion. Finally, the seat frame is made from seat-frame boards. For convenience, we refer to these items by the letters shown in Figure 5.4.

All items except item A are components because they are needed to make a parent. Items A, B, C, and H are parents because they all have at least one component. The BOM also specifies the **usage quantity**, or the number of units of a component that are needed to make one unit of its immediate parent. Figure 5.4 shows usage quantities for each parent–component relationship in parentheses. Note that one chair (item A) is made from one ladder-back subassembly (item B), one seat subassembly (item C), two front legs (item D), and four leg supports (item E). In addition, item B is made from two back legs (item F) and four back slats (item G). Item C needs one seat frame (item H) and one seat cushion (item I). Finally, item H needs four seat-frame boards (item J).

Four terms frequently used to describe inventory items are *end items*, *intermediate items*, *subassemblies*, and *purchased items*. An **end item** typically is the final product sold to the customer; it is a parent but not a component. Item A in Figure 5.4, the completed ladder-back chair, is an end item. Accounting statements classify inventory of end items as either work-in-process (WIP), if work remains to be done, or finished goods. An **intermediate item**, such as item B, C, or H, has at least one parent and at least one component. Some products have several levels of intermediate items; the parent of one intermediate item can also be an intermediate item. Inventory of intermediate items—whether completed or still on the shop floor—is classified as WIP. A **subassembly** is an intermediate item that is assembled (as opposed to being transformed by other means) from more than one component.

usage quantity

The number of units of a component that are needed to make one unit of its immediate parent.

end item

The final product sold to a customer.

intermediate item

An item that has at least one parent and at least one component.

subassembly

An intermediate item that is *assembled* (as opposed to being transformed by other means) from more than one component.

FIGURE 5.4 ▶
BOM for a Ladder-Back Chair

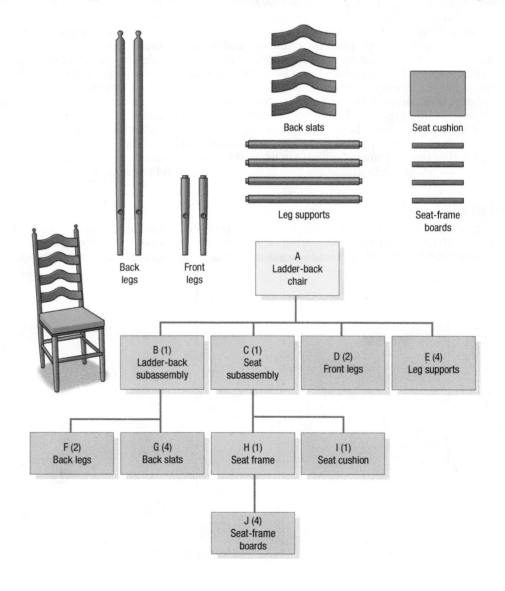

Items B and C are subassemblies. A **purchased item** has no components because it comes from a supplier, but it has one or more parents. Examples are items D, E, F, G, I, and J in Figure 5.4. Inventory of purchased items is treated as raw materials in accounting statements.

A component may have more than one parent. **Part commonality**, sometimes called *standardization of parts* or *modularity*, is the degree to which a component has more than one immediate parent. As a result of commonality, the same item may appear in several places in the bill of materials for a product, or it may appear in the bills of materials for several different products. For example, the seat subassembly in Figure 5.4 is a component of the ladder-back chair and of a kitchen chair that is part of the same family of products. The usage quantity specified in the bill of materials relates to a specific parent–component relationship. The usage quantity for any component can therefore change, depending on the parent item. Part commonality, or using the same part in many parents, increases its volume and repeatability, which provides several process advantages and helps minimize inventory costs.

A careful dissection of the popular iPAD and iPAD 2 products from Apple shows that their bill of materials differ in the enclosure and battery, but are otherwise remarkably similar in their components and design. Same suppliers are used for many components, and costs are very comparable for new revisions of chips found in the previous iPad and iPhones. Standardization of designs and components across different products and generations allows Apple to be very competitive and profitable.

Master Production Scheduling

The second input into a material requirements plan is the **master production schedule (MPS)**, which details how many end items will be produced within specified periods of time. It breaks the sales and operations plan into specific product schedules. Figure 5.5 shows how a sales and operations plan for a family of chairs breaks down into the weekly MPS for each specific chair type (the time period can be hours, days, weeks, or months). The chair example demonstrates the following aspects of master scheduling:

1. The sums of the quantities in the MPS must equal those in the sales and operations plan. This consistency between the plans is desirable because of the economic analysis done to arrive at the sales and operations plan.

2. The production quantities must be allocated efficiently over time. The specific mix of chair types—the number of each type as a percent of the total family's quantity—is based on historic demand and on marketing and promotional considerations. The planner must select lot sizes for each chair type, taking into consideration economic factors such as production setup costs and inventory carrying costs.

purchased item

An item that has one or more parents but no components because it comes from a supplier.

part commonality

The degree to which a component has more than one immediate parent.

master production schedule (MPS)

A part of the material requirements plan that details how many end items will be produced within specified periods of time.

iPad total product costs $270		iPad 2 total product costs $267
	LCD display – 9.7-inch multi-touch screen $59	LCD display – 9.7-inch multi-touch screen $50	
	Camera – None $0	Camera – Front & Rear $4.50	
	Memory – Samsung $47	Memory – Samsung/Toshiba $30	
	Apple Processor – Apple A4 $17	Apple Processor – Apple A5 $25	
	Radio Components Infineon/Broadcom $26	Radio Components Infineon/Broadcom or Qualcomm/Broadcom $25	
	Sensors – STMicroelectronics $1.00	Sensors – STMicroelectronics $2.50	
	Battery $23	Battery $20 – $25	

Bill of Materials for Apple's iPad and iPad2.

D. Hurst/Alamy and PSL Images/Alamy

FIGURE 5.5 ▶
MPS for a Family of Chairs

	April				May			
	1	2	3	4	5	6	7	8
Ladder-back chair	150					150		
Kitchen chair				120			120	
Desk chair		200	200		200			200
Sales and operations plan for chair family		670				670		

3. Capacity limitations and bottlenecks, such as machine or labor capacity, storage space, or working capital, may determine the timing and size of MPS quantities. The planner must acknowledge these limitations by recognizing that some chair styles require more resources than others and setting the timing and size of the production quantities accordingly.

Figure 5.6 shows the master production scheduling process. Operations must first create a prospective MPS to test whether it meets the schedule with the resources (e.g., machine capacities, workforce, overtime, and subcontractors) provided for in the sales and operations plan. Operations then revises the MPS until a schedule that satisfies all of the resource limitations is developed or until it is determined that no feasible schedule can be developed. In the latter event, the production plan must be revised to adjust production requirements or increase authorized resources. Once a feasible prospective MPS has been accepted by the firm's managers, operations uses the authorized MPS as input to material requirements planning. Operations can then determine specific schedules for component production and assembly. Actual performance data such as inventory levels and shortages are inputs to preparing the prospective MPS for the next period, and so the master production scheduling process is repeated from one period to the next.

FIGURE 5.6 ▶
Master Production Scheduling
Process

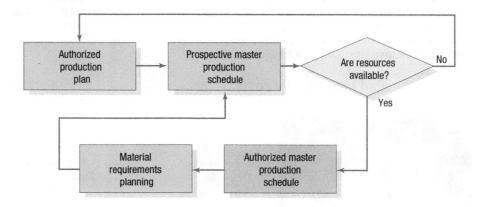

Developing a Master Production Schedule The process of developing a master production schedule includes (1) calculating the projected on-hand inventory and (2) determining the timing and size of the production quantities of specific products. We use the manufacturer of the ladder-back chair to illustrate the process. For simplicity, we assume that the firm does not utilize safety stocks for end items, even though many firms do. In addition, we use weeks as our planning periods, even though hours, days, or months could be used.

Step 1. *Calculate Projected On-Hand Inventories.* The first step is to calculate the projected on-hand inventory, which is an estimate of the amount of inventory available each week after demand has been satisfied:

$$\begin{pmatrix} \text{Projected on-hand} \\ \text{inventory at end} \\ \text{of this week} \end{pmatrix} = \begin{pmatrix} \text{On-hand} \\ \text{inventory at} \\ \text{end of last week} \end{pmatrix} + \begin{pmatrix} \text{MPS quantity} \\ \text{due at start} \\ \text{of this week} \end{pmatrix} - \begin{pmatrix} \text{Projected} \\ \text{requirements} \\ \text{this week} \end{pmatrix}$$

In some weeks, no MPS quantity for a product may be needed because sufficient inventory already exists. For the projected requirements for this week, the scheduler uses whichever is larger—the forecast or the customer orders booked—recognizing that the forecast is subject to error. If actual booked orders exceed the forecast, the projection will be more accurate if the scheduler uses the booked orders because booked orders are a known quantity. Conversely, if the forecast exceeds booked orders for a week, the forecast will provide a better estimate of the requirements needed for that week because some orders are yet to come in.

The manufacturer of the ladder-back chair produces the chair to stock and needs to develop an MPS for it. Marketing has forecasted a demand of 30 chairs for the first week of April, but actual customer orders booked are for 38 chairs. The current on-hand inventory is 55 chairs. No MPS quantity is due in week 1. Figure 5.7 shows an MPS record with these quantities listed. Because actual orders for week 1 are greater than the forecast, the scheduler uses that figure for actual orders to calculate the projected inventory balance at the end of week 1:

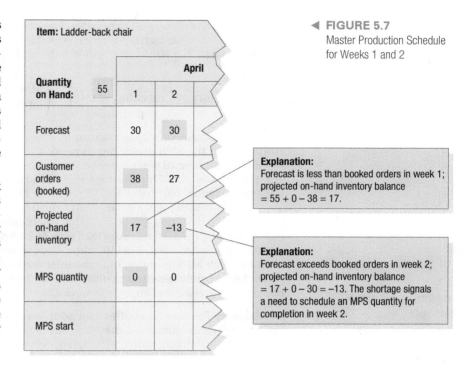

◀ **FIGURE 5.7**
Master Production Schedule for Weeks 1 and 2

Explanation:
Forecast is less than booked orders in week 1; projected on-hand inventory balance = 55 + 0 − 38 = 17.

Explanation:
Forecast exceeds booked orders in week 2; projected on-hand inventory balance = 17 + 0 − 30 = −13. The shortage signals a need to schedule an MPS quantity for completion in week 2.

$$\text{Inventory} = \begin{pmatrix} 55 \text{ chairs} \\ \text{currently} \\ \text{in stock} \end{pmatrix} + \begin{pmatrix} \text{MPS quantity} \\ (0 \text{ for week } 1) \end{pmatrix} - \begin{pmatrix} 38 \text{ chairs already} \\ \text{promised for} \\ \text{delivery in week } 1 \end{pmatrix} = 17 \text{ chairs}$$

▼ **FIGURE 5.8**
Master Production Schedule for Weeks 1–8

In week 2, the forecasted quantity exceeds actual orders booked, so the projected on-hand inventory for the end of week 2 is 17 + 0 − 30 = −13. The shortage signals the need for more chairs to be produced and available for week 2.

Step 2. *Determine the Timing and Size of MPS Quantities.* The goal of determining the timing and size of MPS quantities is to maintain a nonnegative projected on-hand inventory balance. As shortages in inventory are detected, MPS quantities should be scheduled to cover them. The first MPS quantity should be scheduled for the week when the projected on-hand inventory reflects a shortage, such as week 2 in Figure 5.7.[1] The scheduler adds the MPS quantity to the projected on-hand inventory and searches for the next period when a shortage occurs. This shortage signals a need for a second MPS quantity, and so on.

Figure 5.8 shows a master production schedule for the ladder-back chair for the next 8 weeks. The order policy requires production lot sizes of 150 units. A shortage of 13 chairs in week 2 will occur unless the scheduler provides for an MPS quantity for that period. Our convention is to show blanks instead of zeroes in all rows, which improves

Item: Ladder-back chair — **Order Policy:** 150 units — **Lead Time:** 1 week

		April				May			
Quantity on Hand: 55		1	2	3	4	5	6	7	8
Forecast		30	30	30	30	35	35	35	35
Customer orders (booked)		38	27	24	8	0	0	0	0
Projected on-hand inventory		17	137	107	77	42	7	122	87
MPS quantity			150					150	
MPS start		150					150		

Explanation:
The time needed to assemble 150 chairs is 1 week. The assembly department must start assembling chairs in week 1 to have them ready by week 2.

Explanation:
On-hand inventory balance = 17 + 150 − 30 = 137. The MPS quantity is needed to avoid a shortage of 30 − 17 = 13 chairs in week 2.

---

[1] In some cases, new orders will be planned before a shortage is encountered. Two such instances occur when safety stocks and anticipation inventories are built up.

readability and is often used in practice. The only exception is in the projected on-hand inventory row, where a number is always shown, even if it is a 0 or negative number.

Once the MPS quantity is scheduled, the updated projected inventory balance for week 2 is

$$\text{Inventory} = \begin{pmatrix} 17 \text{ chairs in} \\ \text{inventory at the} \\ \text{end of week 1} \end{pmatrix} + \begin{pmatrix} \text{MPS quantity} \\ \text{of 150 chairs} \end{pmatrix} - \begin{pmatrix} \text{Forecast of} \\ 30 \text{ chairs} \end{pmatrix} = 137 \text{ chairs}$$

The scheduler proceeds column by column through the MPS record until it reaches the end, filling in the MPS quantities as needed to avoid shortages. The 137 units will satisfy forecasted demands until week 7, when the inventory shortage in the absence of an MPS quantity is $7 + 0 - 35 = -28$. This shortage signals the need for another MPS quantity of 150 units. The updated inventory balance is $7 + 150 - 35 = 122$ chairs for week 7.

The last row in Figure 5.8 indicates the periods in which production of the MPS quantities must *begin* so that they will be available when indicated in the MPS quantity row. In the upper-right portion of the MPS record, a lead time of 1 week is indicated for the ladder-back chair; that is, 1 week is needed to assemble 150 ladder-back chairs, assuming that items B, C, D, and E are available. For each MPS quantity, the scheduler works backward through the lead time to determine when the assembly department must start producing chairs. Consequently, a lot of 150 units must be started in week 1 and another in week 6.

available-to-promise (ATP) inventory

The quantity of end items that marketing can promise to deliver on specified dates.

▼ **FIGURE 5.9**
MPS Record with an ATP Row

Available-to-Promise Quantities In addition to providing manufacturing with the timing and size of production quantities, the MPS provides marketing with information useful for negotiating delivery dates with customers. The quantity of end items that marketing can promise to deliver on specified dates is called **available-to-promise (ATP) inventory**. It is the difference between the customer orders already booked and the quantity that operations is planning to produce. As new customer orders are accepted, the ATP inventory is reduced to reflect the commitment of the firm to ship those quantities, but the actual inventory stays unchanged until the order is removed from inventory and shipped to the customer. An available-to-promise inventory is associated with each MPS quantity because the MPS quantity specifies the timing and size of new stock that can be earmarked to meet future bookings.

Figure 5.9 shows an MPS record with an additional row for the available-to-promise quantities. The ATP in week 2 is the MPS quantity minus booked customer orders until the next MPS quantity, or $150 - (27 + 24 + 8 + 0 + 0) = 91$ units. The ATP indicates to marketing that, of the 150 units scheduled for completion in week 2, 91 units are uncommitted, and total new orders up to that quantity can be promised for delivery as early as week 2. In week 7, the ATP is 150 units because there are no booked orders in week 7 and beyond.

The procedure for calculating available-to-promise information is slightly different for the first (current) week of the schedule than for other weeks because it accounts for the inventory currently in stock. The ATP inventory for the first week equals *current on-hand inventory* plus the MPS quantity for the first week, minus the cumulative total of booked orders up to (but not including) the week in which the next MPS quantity arrives. So, in Figure 5.9, the ATP for the first week is $55 + 0 - 38 = 17$. This information indicates to the sales department that it can promise as many as 17 units this week, 91 more units sometime in weeks 2

Item: Ladder-back chair					Order Policy: 150 units Lead Time: 1 week				
		April				May			
Quantity on Hand: 55		1	2	3	4	5	6	7	8
Forecast		30	30	30	30	35	35	35	35
Customer orders (booked)		38	27	24	8	0	0	0	0
Projected on-hand inventory		17	137	107	77	42	7	122	87
MPS quantity			150					150	
MPS start		150					150		
Available-to-promise (ATP) inventory		17	91					150	

Explanation:
The total of customer orders booked until the next MPS receipt is 38 units. The ATP = 55 (on-hand) + 0 (MPS quantity) − 38 = 17.

Explanation:
The total of customer orders booked until the next MPS receipt is 27 + 24 + 8 = 59 units. The ATP = 150 (MPS quantity) − 59 = 91 units.

through 6, and 150 more units in week 7 or 8. If customer order requests exceed ATP quantities in those time periods, the MPS must be changed before the customer orders can be booked or the customers must be given a later delivery date—when the next MPS quantity arrives. See Solved Problem 2 at the end of this chapter for an example of decision making using the ATP quantities.

Inventory planners do not create master production plans manually, although they thoroughly understand the logic built into them. Figure 5.10 is typical of the computer support available. It was created with the *Master Production Scheduling* Solver in OM Explorer, and confirms the output shown in Figure 5.9.

Freezing the MPS The master production schedule is the basis of all end item, subassembly, component, and materials schedules. For this reason, changes to the MPS can be costly, particularly if they are made to MPS quantities soon to be completed. Increases in an MPS quantity can result in material shortages, delayed shipments to customers, and excessive expediting costs. Decreases in MPS quantities can result in unused materials or components (at least until another need for them arises) and valuable capacity being used to create products not needed. Similar costs occur when forecasted need dates for MPS quantities are changed. For these reasons, many firms, particularly those with a make-to-stock strategy and a focus on low-cost operations, *freeze*, or disallow changes to, the near-term portion of the MPS.

Reconciling the MPS with Sales and Operations Plans Because the master production schedule is based on both forecasts as well as actual orders received, it can differ from the sales and operations plan when summed across different periods in a month. For instance, in Figure 5.5, if the sum total MPS quantities of the three models of chairs in the month of April was 725 instead of 670, then either the management must revise the sales and operations plan upwards by authorizing additional resources to match supply with demand, or reduce the quantities of MPS in the month of April to match the sales and operations plan. Master production schedules drive plant and supplier activity, so they must be synchronized with actual customer demands and the sales and operations plans to ensure that the firm's planning decisions are actually being implemented on an ongoing basis.

Inventory Record

Inventory records are a third major input to MRP, and inventory transactions are the basic building blocks of up-to-date records (see Figure 5.2). These transactions include releasing new orders, receiving scheduled receipts, adjusting due dates for scheduled receipts, withdrawing inventory, canceling orders, correcting inventory errors, rejecting shipments, and verifying scrap losses and stock returns. Recording the transactions accurately is essential if the firm's on-hand inventory balances are to be correct and its MRP system is to operate effectively.

The **inventory record** divides the future into time periods called *time buckets*. In our discussion, we use weekly time buckets for consistency with our MPS example, although other time periods could as easily be used. The inventory record shows an item's lot-size policy, lead time, and various time-phased data. The purpose of the inventory record is to keep track of inventory levels and component replenishment needs. The time-phased information contained in the inventory record consists of (1) *gross requirements*, (2) *scheduled receipts*, (3) *projected on-hand inventory*, (4) *planned receipts*, and (5) *planned order releases*.

We illustrate the discussion of inventory records with the seat subassembly, item C that was shown in Figure 5.4. Suppose that it is used in two products: a ladder-back chair and a kitchen chair.

Gross Requirements The **gross requirements** are the total demand derived from *all* parent production plans. They also include demand not otherwise accounted for, such as demand for replacement parts for units already sold. Figure 5.11 shows an inventory record for item C, the seat subassembly. Item C is produced in lots of 230 units and has a lead time of 2 weeks. The inventory

Lot Size	150								
Lead Time	1								
Quantity on Hand	55	1	2	3	4	5	6	7	8
Forecast		30	30	30	30	35	35	35	35
Customer Orders (Booked)		38	27	24	8				
Projected On-Hand Inventory		17	137	107	77	42	7	122	87
MPS Quantity			150					150	
MPS Start		150					150		
Available-to-Promise Inv (ATP)		17	91					150	

FIGURE 5.10 ▲

Master Production Scheduling Solver Output Using *OM Explorer*

inventory record

A record that shows an item's lot-size policy, lead time, and various time-phased data.

gross requirements

The total demand derived from *all* parent production plans.

Cypress Semiconductor, a California-based company that manufactures logic devices, USB controllers, general-purpose programmable clocks, memories, and wireless connectivity solutions for consumer and automotive markets, uses commercial software solutions to manage the complexity of its master production scheduling processes.

Item: C				Week						Lot Size: 230 units
Description: Seat subassembly										Lead Time: 2 weeks
		1	2	3	4	5	6	7	8	
Gross requirements		150	0	0	120	0	150	120	0	
Scheduled receipts		230	0	0	0	0	0	0	0	
Projected on-hand inventory	37	117	117	117	−3	−3	−153	−273	−273	
Planned receipts										
Planned order releases										

Explanation:
Gross requirements are the total demand for the two chairs. Projected on-hand inventory in week 1 is 37 + 230 − 150 = 117 units.

FIGURE 5.11 ▲
MRP Record for the Seat Subassembly

projected on-hand inventory

An estimate of the amount of inventory available each week after gross requirements have been satisfied.

planned receipts

Orders that are not yet released to the shop or the supplier.

record also shows item C's gross requirements for the next 8 weeks, which come from the master production schedule for the ladder-back and kitchen chairs (see Figure 5.5). The MPS start quantities for each parent are added to arrive at each week's gross requirements. The seat subassembly's gross requirements exhibit lumpy demand: Operations will withdraw seat subassemblies from inventory in only 4 of the 8 weeks.

The MRP system works with release dates to schedule production and delivery for components and subassemblies. Its program logic anticipates the removal of all materials required by a parent's production order from inventory at the beginning of the parent item's lead time—when the scheduler first releases the order to the shop.

Scheduled Receipts   Recall that *scheduled receipts* (sometimes called open orders) are orders that have been placed but not yet completed. For a purchased item, the scheduled receipt could be in one of several stages: being processed by a supplier, being transported to the purchaser, or being inspected by the purchaser's receiving department. If the firm is making the item in-house, the order could be on the shop floor being processed, waiting for components, waiting for a machine to become available, or waiting to be moved to its next operation. According to Figure 5.11, one 230-unit order of item C is due in week 1. Given the 2-week lead time, the inventory planner probably released the order 2 weeks ago. Scheduled receipts due in beyond the item's lead time are unusual, caused by events such as a last-minute change in the MPS.

Projected On-Hand Inventory   The **projected on-hand inventory** is an estimate of the amount of inventory available each week after gross requirements have been satisfied. The beginning inventory, shown as the first entry (37) in Figure 5.11, indicates the on-hand inventory available at the time the record was computed. As with scheduled receipts, entries are made for each actual withdrawal and receipt to update the MRP database. Then, when the MRP system produces the revised record, the correct inventory will appear.

Other entries in the row show inventory expected in future weeks. Projected on-hand inventory is calculated as

$$\begin{pmatrix} \text{Projected on-hand} \\ \text{inventory balance} \\ \text{at end of week } t \end{pmatrix} = \begin{pmatrix} \text{Inventory on} \\ \text{hand at end of} \\ \text{week } t-1 \end{pmatrix} + \begin{pmatrix} \text{Scheduled} \\ \text{or planned} \\ \text{reeipts in} \\ \text{week } t \end{pmatrix} - \begin{pmatrix} \text{Gross} \\ \text{requirements} \\ \text{in week } t \end{pmatrix}$$

The projected on-hand calculation includes the consideration of **planned receipts**, which are orders not yet released to the shop or the supplier. Planned receipts should not be confused with scheduled receipts. Planned receipts are still at the planning stage and can still change from one week to the next, whereas scheduled receipts are actual orders that are being acted upon by the shop or supplier. In Figure 5.11, the planned receipts are all zero. The on-hand inventory calculations for each week are as follows:

Week 1:	37 + 230 − 150 = 117
Weeks 2 and 3:	117 + 0 − 0 = 117
Week 4:	117 + 0 − 120 = −3
Week 5:	−3 + 0 − 0 = −3
Week 6:	−3 + 0 − 150 = −153
Week 7:	−153 + 0 − 120 = −273
Week 8:	−273 + 0 − 0 = −273

In week 4, the balance drops to −3 units, which indicates that a shortage of 3 units will occur unless more seat subassemblies are built. This condition signals the need for a planned receipt to arrive in week 4. In addition, unless more stock is received, the shortage will grow to 273 units in weeks 7 and 8.[2]

Planned Receipts Planning for the receipt of new orders will keep the projected on-hand balance from dropping below zero. The planned receipt row is developed as follows:

1. Weekly on-hand inventory is projected until a shortage appears. Completion of the initial planned receipt is scheduled for the week in which the shortage is projected. The addition of the newly planned receipt should increase the projected on-hand balance so that it equals or exceeds zero. It will exceed zero when the lot size exceeds requirements in the week it is planned to arrive.

2. The projection of on-hand inventory continues until the next shortage occurs. This shortage signals the need for the second planned receipt.

This process is repeated until the end of the planning horizon by proceeding column by column through the MRP record—filling in planned receipts as needed and completing the projected on-hand inventory row. Figure 5.12 shows the planned receipts for the seat subassem-

Item: C
Description: Seat subassembly
Lot Size: 230 units
Lead Time: 2 weeks

		Week							
		1	2	3	4	5	6	7	8
Gross requirements		150	0	0	120	0	150	120	0
Scheduled receipts		230	0	0	0	0	0	0	0
Projected on-hand inventory	37	117	117	117	227	227	77	187	187
Planned receipts					230			230	
Planned order releases			230			230			

Explanation:
Without a planned receipt in week 4, a shortage of 3 units will occur: 117 + 0 + 0 − 120 = −3 units. Adding the planned receipt brings the balance to 117 + 0 + 230 − 120 = 227 units. Offsetting for a 2-week lead time puts the corresponding planned order release back to week 2.

Explanation:
The first planned receipt lasts until week 7, when projected inventory would drop to 77 + 0 + 0 − 120 = −43 units. Adding the second planned receipt brings the balance to 77 + 0 + 230 − 120 = 187 units. The corresponding planned order release is for week 5 (or week 7 minus 2 weeks).

▲ **FIGURE 5.12**
Completed Inventory Record for the Seat Subassembly

bly. In week 4, the projected on-hand inventory will drop below zero, so a planned receipt of 230 units is scheduled for week 4. The updated inventory on-hand balance is 117 (inventory at end of week 3) + 230 (planned receipts) − 120 (gross requirements) = 227 units. The projected on-hand inventory remains at 227 for week 5 because no scheduled receipts or gross requirements are anticipated. In week 6, the projected on-hand inventory is 227 (inventory at end of week 5) − 150 (gross requirements) = 77 units. This quantity is greater than zero, so no new planned receipt is needed. In week 7, however, a shortage will occur unless more seat subassemblies are received. With a planned receipt in week 7, the updated inventory balance is 77 (inventory at end of week 6) + 230 (planned receipts) − 120 (gross requirements) = 187 units.

Planned Order Releases A **planned order release** indicates when an order for a specified quantity of an item is to be issued. We must place the planned order release quantity in the proper time bucket. To do so, we must assume that all inventory flows—scheduled receipts, planned receipts, and gross requirements—occur at the same point of time in a time period. Some firms assume that all flows occur at the beginning of a time period; other firms assume that they occur at the end of a time period or at the middle of the time period. Regardless of when the flows are assumed to occur, we find the release date by subtracting the lead time from the receipt date. For example, the release date for the first planned order release in Figure 5.12 is 4 (planned receipt date) −2 (lead time) = 2 (planned order release date). Figure 5.12 shows the planned order releases for the seat subassembly. If all goes according to the plan, we will release an order for 230 seat assemblies next week (in week 2). This order release sets off a series of updates to the inventory record. First, the planned order release for the order is removed. Next, the planned receipt for 230 units in week 4 is also removed. Finally, a new scheduled receipt for 230 units will appear in the scheduled receipt row for week 4.

planned order release

An indication of when an order for a specified quantity of an item is to be issued.

---

[2]There is an exception to the rule of scheduling a planned receipt whenever the projected inventory otherwise becomes negative. When a scheduled receipt is coming in *after* the inventory becomes negative, the first recourse is to expedite the scheduled receipt (giving it an earlier due date), rather than scheduling a new planned receipt.

Planning Factors

The planning factors in a MRP inventory record play an important role in the overall performance of the MRP system. By manipulating these factors, managers can fine-tune inventory operations. In this section, we discuss planning lead time, lot-sizing rules, and safety stock.

Planning Lead Time   Planning lead time is an estimate of the time between placing an order for an item and receiving the item in inventory. Accuracy is important in planning lead time. If an item arrives in inventory sooner than needed, inventory holding costs increase. If an item arrives too late, stockouts, excessive expediting costs, or both may occur.

For purchased items, the planning lead time is the time allowed for receiving a shipment from the supplier after the order has been sent, including the normal time to place the order. Often, the purchasing contract stipulates the delivery date. For items manufactured in-house, a rough-cut estimate of the planning lead time can be obtained by keeping track of the actual lead times for recent orders and computing an average. A more extensive estimating process consists of breaking down each of the following factors:

- Setup time
- Processing time
- Materials handling time between operations
- Waiting time

Each of these times must be estimated for every operation along the item's route. Estimating setup, processing, and materials handling times can be relatively easy, but estimating the waiting time for materials handling equipment or for a workstation to perform a particular operation can be more difficult. In a facility that uses a make-to-order strategy, such as a machine shop, the load on the shop varies considerably over time, causing actual waiting times for a particular order to fluctuate widely. Therefore, being able to accurately estimate the waiting time is especially important when it comes to estimating the planning lead time. However, in a facility that uses a make-to-stock strategy, such as an assembly plant, product routings are more standard and waiting time is more predictable; hence, waiting time generally is a less-troublesome part of planning lead times.

Lot-Sizing Rules   A lot-sizing rule determines the timing and size of order quantities. A lot-sizing rule must be assigned to each item before planned receipts and planned order releases can be computed. The choice of lot-sizing rules is important because they determine the number of setups required and the inventory holding costs for each item. We present three lot-sizing rules: (1) fixed order quantity, (2) periodic order quantity, and (3) lot-for-lot.

Fixed Order Quantity   The **fixed order quantity (FOQ)** rule maintains the same order quantity each time an order is issued.[3] For example, the lot size might be the size dictated by equipment capacity limits, such as when a full lot must be loaded into a furnace at one time. For purchased items, the FOQ could be determined by the quantity discount level, truckload capacity, or minimum purchase quantity. Alternatively, the lot size could be determined by the economic order quantity (EOQ) formula (see Chapter 6, "Supply Chain Inventory Management"). Figure 5.12 illustrated the FOQ rule. However, if an item's gross requirement within a week is particularly large, the FOQ might be insufficient to avoid a shortage. In such unusual cases, the inventory planner must increase the lot size beyond the FOQ, typically to a size large enough to avoid a shortage. Another option is to make the order quantity an integer multiple of the FOQ. This option is appropriate when capacity constraints limit production to FOQ sizes (at most).

Periodic Order Quantity   The **periodic order quantity (POQ)** rule allows a different order quantity for each order issued but issues the order for predetermined time intervals, such as every two weeks. The order quantity equals the amount of the item needed during the predetermined time between orders and must be large enough to prevent shortages. Specifically, the POQ is

$$\begin{pmatrix} \text{POQ lot size} \\ \text{to arrive in} \\ \text{week } t \end{pmatrix} = \begin{pmatrix} \text{Total gross requirements} \\ \text{for } P \text{ weeks, including} \\ \text{week } t \end{pmatrix} - \begin{pmatrix} \text{Projected on-hand} \\ \text{inventory balance at} \\ \text{end of week } t-1 \end{pmatrix}$$

This amount exactly covers P weeks' worth of gross requirements. That is, the projected on-hand inventory should equal zero at the end of the Pth week.

---

[3] The *kanban* system essentially uses a FOQ rule, except that the order quantity is very small.

Suppose that we want to switch from the FOQ rule used in Figure 5.12 to the POQ rule. Figure 5.13 was created with the *Single-Item MRP* Solver in OM Explorer. It shows the application of the POQ rule, with $P = 3$ weeks, to the seat subassembly inventory. The first order is required in week 4 because it is the first week that projected inventory balance will fall below zero. The first order using $P = 3$ weeks is

$$(\text{POQ lot size}) = \begin{pmatrix} \text{Gross requirements} \\ \text{for weeks} \\ 4, 5, \text{and } 6 \end{pmatrix} - \begin{pmatrix} \text{Inventory at} \\ \text{end of week 3} \end{pmatrix}$$

$$= (120 + 0 + 150) - 117 = 153 \text{ units}$$

The second order must arrive in week 7 with a lot size of $(120 + 0) - 0 = 120$ units. This second order reflects only two weeks' worth of gross requirements—to the end of the planning horizon.

Periods	8									
Item	Seat Assembly			Period (P) for POQ		3	Lot Size (FOQ)			
Description							Lead Time			2
POQ Rule ▼										
		1	2	3	4	5	6	7	8	
Gross requirements		150			120		150	120		
Scheduled receipts		230								
Projected on-hand inventory	37	117	117	117	150	150				
Planned receipts					153			120		
Planned order releases			153			120				

◀ **FIGURE 5.13**
The POQ ($P = 3$) Rule for the Seat Subassembly

The POQ rule does not mean that the planner must issue a new order every P weeks. Rather, when an order is planned, its lot size must be enough to cover P successive weeks. One way to select a P value is to divide the average lot size desired, such as the EOQ or some other applicable lot size, by the average weekly demand. That is, express the target lot size as the desired weeks of supply (P) and round to the nearest integer.

Lot for Lot   A special case of the POQ rule is the **lot-for-lot (L4L) rule**, under which the lot size ordered covers the gross requirements of a single week. Thus, $P = 1$, and the goal is to minimize inventory levels. This rule ensures that the planned order is just large enough to prevent a shortage in the single week it covers. The L4L lot size is

$$\begin{pmatrix} \text{L4L lot size} \\ \text{to arrive in} \\ \text{week } t \end{pmatrix} = \begin{pmatrix} \text{Gross requirements} \\ \text{for week } t \end{pmatrix} - \begin{pmatrix} \text{Projected on-hand} \\ \text{inventory balance at} \\ \text{end of week } t-1 \end{pmatrix}$$

The projected on-hand inventory combined with the new order will equal zero at the end of week t. Following the first planned order, an additional planned order will be used to match each subsequent gross requirement.

This time we want to switch from the FOQ rule to the L4L rule. Figure 5.14 shows the application of the L4L rule to the seat subassembly inventory. As before, the first order is needed in week 4:

$$(\text{L4L lot size}) = \begin{pmatrix} \text{Gross requirements} \\ \text{in week 4} \end{pmatrix} - \begin{pmatrix} \text{Inventory balance} \\ \text{at end of week 3} \end{pmatrix}$$

$$= 120 - 117 = 3$$

Periods	8									
Item	Seat Assembly			Period (P) for POQ			Lot Size (FOQ)			
Description							Lead Time			2
L4L Rule ▼										
		1	2	3	4	5	6	7	8	
Gross requirements		150			120		150	120		
Scheduled receipts		230								
Projected on-hand inventory	37	117	117	117						
Planned receipts					3		150	120		
Planned order releases			3		150	120				

◀ **FIGURE 5.14**
The L4L Rule for the Seat Subassembly

MyOMLab

Tutor 5.2 in MyOMLab provides a new example to practice lot-sizing decisions using FOQ, POQ, and L4L rules.

lot-for-lot (L4L) rule

A rule under which the lot size ordered covers the gross requirements of a single week.

The stockroom must receive additional orders in weeks 6 and 7 to satisfy each of the subsequent gross requirements. The planned receipt for week 6 is 150 and for week 7 is 120.

Comparing Lot-Sizing Rules Choosing a lot-sizing rule can have important implications for inventory management. Lot-sizing rules affect inventory costs and setup and ordering costs. The FOQ, POQ, and L4L rules differ from one another in one or both respects. In our example, each rule took effect in week 4, when the first order was placed. Let us compare the projected on-hand inventory averaged over weeks 4 through 8 of the planning horizon. The data are shown in Figures 5.12, 5.13, and 5.14, respectively.

$$\text{FOQ: } \frac{227 + 227 + 77 + 187 + 187}{5} = 181 \text{ units}$$

$$\text{POQ: } \frac{150 + 150 + 0 + 0 + 0}{5} = 60 \text{ units}$$

$$\text{L4L: } \frac{0 + 0 + 0 + 0 + 0}{5} = 0 \text{ units}$$

The performance of the L4L rule with respect to average inventory levels comes at the expense of an additional planned order and its accompanying setup time and cost. We can draw three conclusions from this comparison:

1. The FOQ rule generates a high level of average inventory because it creates inventory *remnants*. A remnant is inventory carried into a week, but it is too small to prevent a shortage. Remnants occur because the FOQ does not match requirements exactly. For example, according to Figure 5.12, the stockroom must receive a planned order in week 7, even though 77 units are on hand at the beginning of that week. The remnant is the 77 units that the stockroom will carry for 3 weeks, beginning with receipt of the first planned order in week 4. Although they increase average inventory levels, inventory remnants introduce stability into the production process by buffering unexpected scrap losses, capacity bottlenecks, inaccurate inventory records, or unstable gross requirements.

2. The POQ rule reduces the amount of average on-hand inventory because it does a better job of matching order quantity to requirements. It adjusts lot sizes as requirements increase or decrease. Figure 5.13 shows that in week 7, when the POQ rule has fully taken effect, the projected on-hand inventory is zero—no remnants.

3. The L4L rule minimizes inventory investment, but it also maximizes the number of orders placed. This rule is most applicable to expensive items or items with small ordering or setup costs. It is the only rule that can be used for a low-volume item made to order. It can also approximate the small-lot inventory levels of a lean system.

By avoiding remnants, both the POQ and the L4L rule may introduce instability by tying the lot-sizing decision so closely to requirements. If any requirement changes, so must the lot size, which can disrupt component schedules. Last-minute increases in parent orders may be hindered by missing components.

Safety Stock An important managerial decision is the quantity of safety stock to carry. It is more complex for dependent demand items than for independent demand items. Safety stock for dependent demand items with lumpy demand (gross requirements) is helpful only when future gross requirements, the timing or size of scheduled receipts, and the amount of scrap that will be produced are uncertain. As these uncertainties are resolved, safety stock should be reduced and ultimately eliminated. The usual policy is to use safety stock for end items and purchased items to protect against fluctuating customer orders and unreliable suppliers of components but to avoid using it as much as possible for intermediate items. Safety stocks can be incorporated in the MRP logic by using the following rule: Schedule a planned receipt whenever the projected on-hand inventory balance drops below the desired safety stock level (rather than zero, as before). The objective is to keep a minimum level of planned inventories equal to the safety stock quantity. Figure 5.15 shows what happens when the safety stock requirement has just been increased from 0 units to 80 units of safety stock for the seat assembly using an FOQ of 230 units. The beginning projected on-hand quantity is still 37 units when the safety stock policy is introduced, and cannot fall below 80 units in any future period thereafter. Compare the results in

▼ **FIGURE 5.15**

Inventory Record for the Seat Subassembly Showing the Application of a Safety Stock

FOQ Rule						Lot Size: 230 units Lead Time: 2 weeks Safety Stock: 80 units			
					Week				
		1	2	3	4	5	6	7	8
Gross requirements		150	0	0	120	0	150	120	0
Scheduled receipts		230	0	0	0	0	0	0	0
Projected on-hand inventory	37	117	117	117	227	227	307	187	187
Planned receipts		0	0	0	230	0	230	0	0
Planned order releases		0	230	0	230	0	0	0	0

Figure 5.15 to Figure 5.12. The net effect is to move the second planned order release from week 5 to week 4 to avoid dropping below 80 units in week 6.

Outputs from MRP

MRP systems provide many reports, schedules, and notices to help planners control dependent demand inventories, as indicated in Figure 5.16. In this section, we discuss the MRP explosion process, notices that alert planners to items needing attention, resource requirement reports, and performance reports.

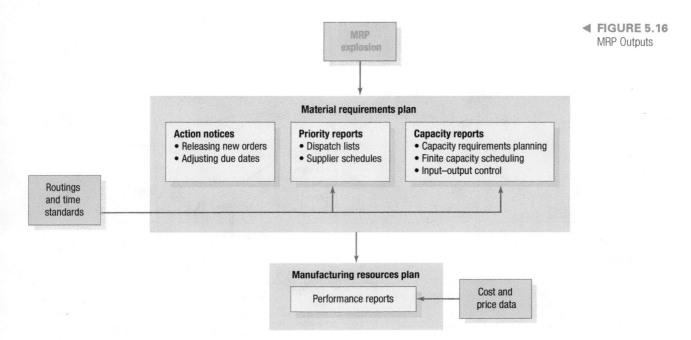

◀ **FIGURE 5.16**
MRP Outputs

MRP Explosion   MRP translates, or *explodes*, the MPS and other sources of demand into the requirements needed for all of the subassemblies, components, and raw materials the firm needs to produce parent items. This process generates the material requirements plan for each component item.

An item's gross requirements are derived from three sources:

1. The MPS for immediate parents that are end items

2. The planned order releases (*not* the gross requirements, scheduled receipts, or planned receipts) for immediate parents below the MPS level

3. Any other requirements not originating in the MPS, such as the demand for replacement parts

Consider the seat subassembly and its inventory record shown in Figure 5.12. The seat subassembly requires a seat cushion and a seat frame, which in turn needs four seat-frame boards. Its BOM is shown in Figure 5.17 (see also Figure 5.4, which shows how the seat subassembly BOM relates to the product as a whole). How many seat cushions should we order from the supplier? How many seat frames should we produce to support the seat subassembly schedule? How many seat-frame boards do we need to make? The answers to these questions depend on the existing inventories of these items and the replenishment orders already in progress. MRP can help answer these questions through the explosion process.

Figure 5.18 shows the MRP records for the seat subassembly and its components. We already showed how to develop the MRP record for the seat subassembly. We now concentrate on the MRP records of its components. The lot-size rules are an FOQ of 300 units for the seat frame, L4L for the seat cushion, and an FOQ of 1,500 for the seat-frame boards. All three components have a 1-week lead time. The key to the explosion process is to determine the proper timing and size of the gross requirements for each component. After we make those determinations, we can derive the planned order release schedule for each component by using the logic already demonstrated.

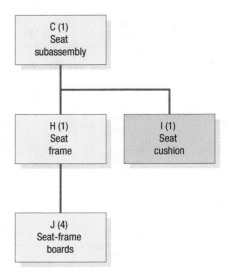

FIGURE 5.17 ▲
BOM for the Seat Subassembly

Item: Seat subassembly
Lot size: 230 units

Lead time: 2 weeks		Week							
		1	2	3	4	5	6	7	8
Gross requirements		150	0	0	120	0	150	120	0
Scheduled receipts		230	0	0	0	0	0	0	0
Projected inventory	37	117	117	117	227	227	77	187	187
Planned receipts					230			230	
Planned order releases			230			230			

Usage quantity: 1   Usage quantity: 1

Item: Seat frames
Lot size: 300 units

Lead time: 1 week		Week							
		1	2	3	4	5	6	7	8
Gross requirements		0	230	0	0	230	0	0	0
Scheduled receipts		0	300	0	0	0	0	0	0
Projected inventory	40	40	110	110	110	180	180	180	180
Planned receipts						300			
Planned order releases					300				

Item: Seat cushion
Lot size: L4L

Lead time: 1 week		Week							
		1	2	3	4	5	6	7	8
Gross requirements		0	230	0	0	230	0	0	0
Scheduled receipts		0	0	0	0	0	0	0	0
Projected inventory	0	0	0	0	0	0	0	0	0
Planned receipts			230			230			
Planned order releases		230			230				

Usage quantity: 4

Item: Seat-frame boards
Lot size: 1,500 units

Lead time: 1 week		Week							
		1	2	3	4	5	6	7	8
Gross requirements		0	0	0	1,200	0	0	0	0
Scheduled receipts		0	0	0	0	0	0	0	0
Projected inventory	200	200	200	200	500	500	500	500	500
Planned receipts					1,500				
Planned order releases				1,500					

FIGURE 5.18 ▲
MRP Explosion of Seat Assembly Components

In our example, the components have no independent demand for replacement parts. Consequently, in Figure 5.18 the gross requirements of a component come from the planned order releases of its parents. The seat frame and the seat cushion get their gross requirements from the planned order release schedule of the seat subassembly. Both components have gross requirements of 230 units in weeks 2 and 5, the same weeks in which we will be releasing orders to make more seat subassemblies. In week 2, for example, the materials handler for the assembly department will withdraw 230 seat frames and 230 seat cushions from inventory so that the assembly department can produce the seat subassemblies in time to avoid a stockout in week 4. The materials plans for the seat frame and the seat cushion must allow for that.

Using the gross requirements in weeks 2 and 5, we can develop the MRP records for the seat frame and the seat cushion, as shown in Figure 5.18. For a scheduled receipt of 300 seat frames in week 2, an on-hand quantity of 40 units, and a lead time of 1 week, we need to release an order of 300 seat frames in week 4 to cover the assembly schedule for the seat subassembly. The seat cushion has no scheduled receipts and no inventory on hand; consequently, we must place orders for 230 units in weeks 1 and 4, using the L4L logic with a lead time of 1 week.

After determining the replenishment schedule for the seat frame, we can calculate the gross requirements for the seat-frame boards. We plan to begin producing 300 seat frames in week 4. Each frame requires 4 boards, so we need to have $300(4) = 1{,}200$ boards available in week 4. Consequently, the gross requirement for seat-frame boards is 1,200 in week 4. Given no scheduled receipts, 200 boards in stock, a lead time of 1 week, and an FOQ of 1,500 units, we need a planned order release of 1,500 in week 3.

The questions posed earlier can now be answered. We should plan to release the following orders: 300 seat frames in week 4; 230 seat cushions in each of weeks 1 and 4; and 1,500 seat-frame boards in week 3. If MRP plans are updated weekly, only the planned order for week 1 should be released now. Releasing it creates a scheduled receipt of 230 seat cushions that will appear in the updated inventory record. The other orders remain in the planning stage, and even might be revised by the MRP explosion done next week.

Computer Support   In practice a company can have thousands of dependent demand items with an average of six bills of materials levels. Time horizons often stretch out for 30 or more time periods into the future. Doing a MRP explosion by hand (as shown in Figure 5.18) would be impractical. What is needed is massive data processing, the very thing that computers do best, leaving the decision making to the inventory analyst. The *Material Requirements Planning* Solver of OM Explorer in MyOMLab represents a small example of what is done on a much larger scale by commercial packages, can compute requirements for up to two end items. It has the ability to develop inventory records up to 18 items deep with little effort, and can easily re-compute these requirements if there is any change in planning parameters.

Figure 5.19 shows the output from the *Material Requirements Planning* Solver of OM Explorer. It confirms the same results as Figure 5.18. Based on this output, only one thing would be brought to the attention of the inventory planner—the planned order release of 230 units for seat cushions. Its planned order release is now "mature" for release this week. Unless the planner knows of a problem, the planner would place the order with the supplier. At the same time, the planner would input a transaction that automatically eliminates the planned order release in period 1, removes the planned receipt in period 2, and inserts a scheduled receipt for 230 units in period 2. The planner need not look at the records for seat frames or seat-frame boards, because no action is needed for them.

Other Important Reports   Once computed, inventory records for any item appearing in the BOM can be printed in hard copy or displayed on a computer video screen. Inventory planners use a computer-generated memo called an **action notice** to make decisions about releasing new orders and adjusting the due dates of scheduled receipts. These notices are generated every time the system is updated, typically once per week. The action notice alerts planners to only the items that need their attention, such as those items that have a planned order release in the current period or a scheduled receipt that needs its due date revised. Planners can then view the full records for those items and take the necessary actions. An action notice can simply be a list of part numbers for items that need attention; or it can be the full record for such items, with a note at the bottom identifying the action needed.

By itself, the MRP system does not recognize capacity limitations when computing planned orders; that is, it may call for a planned order release that exceeds the amount that can be physically produced. An essential role of planners is to monitor the capacity requirements of material requirements plans, adjusting a plan when it cannot be met. Particular attention is paid to bottlenecks. The planner can apply theory of constraints (TOC) principles to keep bottleneck operations fed by adjusting some lot sizing rules or occasionally overriding planned order releases. To facilitate this process, various types of capacity reports can be provided. For example, **capacity requirements planning (CRP)** reports project time-phased

MyOMLab

action notice

A computer-generated memo alerting planners about releasing new orders and adjusting the due dates of scheduled receipts.

capacity requirements planning (CRP)

A technique used for projecting time-phased capacity requirements for work stations; its purpose is to match the materials requirements plan with the capacity of key processes.

FIGURE 5.19 ▶
Material Requirements Planning Solver Output of OM Explorer for Seat Assembly Components

Master Production Schedule

	1	2	3	4	5	6	7	8	9	10
Item A MPS Start Descr: Seat		230			230					
Item B MPS Start Descr:										

☑ Use second finished item

Material Requirements Planning

Item C   Descr: Seat Frames   Period (P) for POQ   Lot Size (FOQ) 300
FOQ Rule ▼   Lead Time 1   Safety Stock

Usage Quantity for Item: A 1 B

	1	2	3	4	5	6	7	8	9	10
Gross Requirements		230			230					
Scheduled Receipts		300								
Projected On-Hand Inventory	40	40	110	110	110	180	180	180	180	180	180
Planned Receipts					300					
Planned Order Releases				300						

Item D   Descr: Seat Cushion   Period (P) for POQ   1   Lot Size (FOQ)
L4L Rule ▼   Lead Time 1   Safety Stock

Usage Quantity for Item: A 1 B   C

	1	2	3	4	5	6	7	8	9	10
Gross Requirements		230			230					
Scheduled Receipts										
Projected On-Hand Inventory	0	0	0	0	0	0	0	0	0	0	0
Planned Receipts		230			230					
Planned Order Releases	230			230						

Item E   Descr: Seat-frame boards   Period (P) for POQ   Lot Size (FOQ) 1500
FOQ Rule ▼   Lead Time 1   Safety Stock

Usage Quantity for Item: A   B   C 4 D

	1	2	3	4	5	6	7	8	9	10
Gross Requirements				1200						
Scheduled Receipts										
Projected On-Hand Inventory	200	200	200	200	500	500	500	500	500	500	500
Planned Receipts				1500						
Planned Order Releases			1500							

capacity requirements for workstations. They calculate workload according to the work required to complete the scheduled receipts already in the shop and to complete the planned order releases not yet released. Bottlenecks are those workstations at which the projected loads exceed station capacities.

Other types of outputs are also possible, such as priority reports on orders already placed to the shop or with suppliers. Priority reports begin with the due dates assigned to scheduled receipts, which planners keep up to date so that they continue to reflect when receipt is really needed. On a broader scale, the information in an MRP system is useful to functional areas other than operations. MRP evolved into **manufacturing resource planning (MRP II)**, a system that ties the basic MRP system to the company's financial system and to other core and supporting processes. For example, management can project the dollar value of shipments, product costs, overhead allocations, inventories, backlogs, and profits by using the MRP plan along with prices and product and activity costs from the accounting system. Also, information from the MPS, scheduled receipts, and planned orders can be converted into cash flow projections, which are broken down by product families. Similar computations are possible for other performance measures of interest to management. In fact, MRP II ultimately evolved into enterprise resource planning (ERP), which was introduced at the beginning of this chapter. Some firms may, however, forego the cost of vendor-delivered MRP and ERP systems because of the huge budgets and company resources involved in their deployment, and instead create their own MRP system implementations in-house. Managerial Practice 5.1 illustrates how Winnebago created and adapted its own homegrown software for the MRP system to achieve business self sufficiency.

manufacturing resource planning (MRP II)

A system that ties the basic MRP system to the company's financial system and to other core and supporting processes.

Winnebago Industries, based in Forest City, Iowa, is a leading manufacturer of motor homes and related products and services in the United States since 1958. In a challenging business environment, the firm improves the quality of its products at lowered production costs by emphasizing employee teamwork and involvement. So it is no surprise that Winnebago has for decades kept away from software packages, preferring instead to create and adapt its own applications. It can thereby achieve a closer fit to the company's business needs, an objective that is at times not met by the ERP vendors described at the beginning of this chapter. It can also be more responsive to users of its systems at lowered costs since it can reuse its code as needed.

An example of Winnebago's homegrown approach is its MRP system, which runs on an IBM zSeries mainframe and is used to plan material needs and schedule production orders. When the company added a new model to its fleet of motor homes, it took only a few hundred hours of development, including a new bill of materials, to make the required changes to the MRP system in order to support production of the new vehicle. Such agility in adapting the MRP system to manufacturing and supplier needs can be especially rewarding in an environment where the change in product variety is constant. In 2007 alone, Winnebago offered 20 different models in 86 different floor plans, each of which can be outfitted with a variety of options including colors, wood stains, and drawer pulls. For the 2011 model year, several new floorplans were added. When you are in the business of building customized homes-on-wheels ranging in prices from $60,000 to $285,000, combining cost consciousness with common sense and employee involvement in developing your own MRP, sales order management, and purchasing systems can prove valuable.

CRAIG BORCK KRT/Newscom

Workmen at the Winnebago factory in Forest City, Iowa, lift a completed side of a Winnebago, with interior and exterior surfaces, wiring, framework and foam insulation all in place, onto a cart so it can be hauled to the next step in the assembly process. Since 1995, Winnebago has spent approximately $5 million annually to automate some of its assembly-line processes, up from $2 million per year previously.

Source: "Road Rules: Creating and Adapting Homegrown Software is the Key to Winnebago's Drive for Business Self Sufficiency," October 15, 2006; **http://www** **.winnebagoind.com/** (May 28, 2011).

MRP, Core Processes, and Supply Chain Linkages

Among the four core processes of an organization that link activities within and across firms in a supply chain, the MRP system interacts with all of them either through its inputs or its outputs. It all begins with customer orders, which consist of orders for end items as well as replacement parts. MRP and resource planning typically reside inside the order fulfillment process. Master Production Scheduling is an integral part of MRP (see Figure 5.2). As shown schematically in Figure 5.20, the MPS drives the feedback between the order fulfillment process and the customer relationship process through confirmation of order receipts and promised due dates. MPS also provides guidance to the sales group within the customer relationship process with respect to when future orders can be promised, and whether the due dates for existing orders can be adjusted in the time frame requested. The new service and product development process provides an updated bill of materials to the MRP system, and makes sure that every component and assembly needed for manufacturing of end items is properly recognized.

FIGURE 5.20 ▶
MRP Related Information
Flows in the Supply Chain

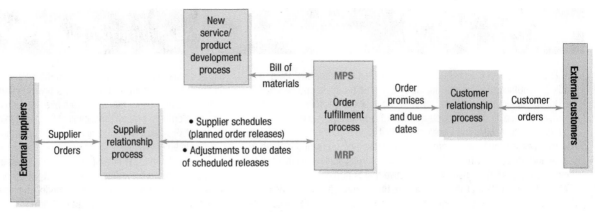

In a similar vein on the inbound side, orders to external suppliers are based on the planned order releases, which come directly from the output of MRP reports. The power of MRP, however, becomes evident when changes to an existing schedule are needed. These changes can be generated, for example, by changes to the MPS because a customer wants to change the timing or size of future orders, by some internal failure such as material shortages or unexpected machine downtime, or by supplier failure. In a supply chain, schedule changes have implications for customers as well as suppliers. Some firms, in partnership with their suppliers, have ERP/MRP systems that can actually "see" into their suppliers' inventory to determine if a particular item is in stock or, if not, when it can be expected. This is an advantage when contemplating a change to the original schedule of order releases. While systems such as this are powerful tools for making changes, care must be taken to avoid unnecessary fluctuations in the timing and size of PORs because of the choice of lot sizing policy. As we have seen, lot sizing rules such as POQ or L4L are susceptible to changes in requirements, and using them indiscriminately can cause instability in replenishment orders. In turn, this instability can be transmitted up the supply chain if the firm's MRP system is electronically linked to the production planning and control systems of its immediate suppliers.

Execution of MRP-based plans using the information flows between core processes as shown in Figure 5.20 properly link a firm with its upstream and downstream supply chain partners. Valid customer and supplier priorities would not be effectively recognized without such an MRP-based framework, which in many firms is actually implemented through an ERP system discussed earlier in the chapter.

MRP and the Environment

Consumer and governmental concern about the deterioration of the natural environment has driven manufacturers to reengineer their processes to become more environmentally friendly. The recycling of base materials is becoming more commonplace, and products are being designed in such a way that they can be remanufactured after their useful lives. Nonetheless, manufacturing processes often produce a number of waste materials that need to be properly disposed of. Wastes come in many forms:

- Effluents, such as carbon monoxide, sulfur dioxide, and hazardous chemicals associated with the processes used to manufacture the product
- Materials, such as metal shavings, oils, and chemicals associated with specific operations
- Packaging materials, such as unusable cardboard and plastics associated with certain products or purchased items
- Scrap associated with unusable products or component defects generated by the manufacturing process

Companies can modify their MRP systems to help them track these wastes and plan for their disposal. The type and amount of waste associated with each item can be entered into its BOM by treating the waste much like you would a component of the item. When the MPS is developed for a product, reports can be generated that project the amount of waste expected during the production process and when it will occur. Although this approach can require that a firm's BOM be modified substantially, the benefits are also substantial. Firms can identify their waste problems in advance to eliminate them in some cases (through process improvement efforts) or plan for their proper disposal in others. It also gives the firm a way to generate any formal documentation required by the government to verify that it has complied with environmental laws and policies.

Resource Planning for Service Providers

We have seen how manufacturing companies can disaggregate an MPS of finished products, which in turn must be translated into the needs for resources, such as staff, equipment, components, and financial assets. The driver for these resource requirements is a material requirements plan. Service providers, of course, must plan their resources just as manufacturers do. However, unlike finished goods, services cannot be inventoried. They must be provided on demand. In terms of resource planning then, service organizations must focus on maintaining the *capacity* to serve their customers. In this section, we will discuss how service providers use the concept of dependent demand and a bill of resources in managing capacity.

Dependent Demand for Services

When we discussed planning and control systems for manufacturers earlier in this chapter, we introduced the concept of *dependent demand*, which is demand for an item that is a function of the production plans for some other item the company produces. For service resource planning, it is useful to define the concept of dependent demand to include demands for resources that are driven by forecasts of customer requests for services or by plans for various activities in support of the services the company provides. Here are some other examples of dependent demands for service providers.

Restaurants   Every time you order from the menu at a restaurant, you initiate the restaurant's need for certain types of goods (uncooked food items, plates, and napkins), staff (chef, servers, and dishwashers), and equipment (stoves, ovens, and cooking utensils). Using a forecast of the demand for each type of meal, the manager of the restaurant can estimate the need for these resources. Many restaurants, for example, feature "specials" on certain days, say, fish on Fridays or prime rib on Saturdays. Specials improve the accuracy of the forecasts managers need to make for different types of meals (and the food products that are required to make them) and typically signal the need for above-average staffing levels. How much of these resources will be needed, however, depends on the number of meals the restaurant ultimately expects to serve. As such, these items—food products and staff members—are dependent demands.

Airlines   Whenever an airline schedules a flight, certain supporting goods are needed (beverages, snacks, and fuel), labor (pilots, flight attendants, and airport services), and equipment (a plane and airport gate). The number of flights and passengers the airline forecasts it will serve determines the amount of these resources needed. Just like a manufacturer, the airline can explode its master schedule of flights to make this determination.

Hospitals   With the exception of the emergency room services, hospitals can use their admission appointments to create a master schedule. The master schedule can be exploded to determine the resources the hospital will need during a certain period. For example, when you schedule a surgical procedure, you generate a need for facilitating goods such as medicines, surgical gowns, linens, staff (a surgeon, nurses, and anesthesiologist), and equipment (an operating room, surgical tools, and recovery bed). As they build their master schedules, hospitals must ensure that certain equipment and personnel do not become overcommitted—that capacity is maintained, in other words. For example, an appointment for a key operation might have to be scheduled in advance at a time a surgeon is available to do it, even though the hospital's other resources—operating room, nurses, and so forth—might be currently be available.

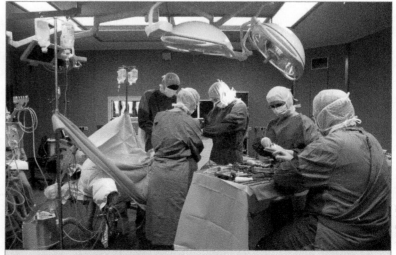

Doctors and nurses in operation room during surgery

ochen Tack/PhotoLibrary

Hotels   A traveler who makes a reservation at a hotel generates demand for facilitating goods (soap and towels), staff (front desk, housekeeping, and concierge), and equipment (fax, television, and exercise bicycle). To determine its dependent resource needs, a hotel adds the number of reservations already booked to the number of "walk-in" customers it forecasts it will have. This figure is used to create the hotel's master schedule. One resource a hotel cannot easily adjust, however, is the number of rooms it has. If the hotel is overbooked, for instance, it cannot simply add more rooms. If it has too few guests, it cannot "downsize" its number of rooms. Given the high capital costs needed for this resource, hotels try to maintain as high a utilization rate as possible by offering group rates or special promotions at certain times of the year. In other words, they try to drive up dependent demand for this particular resource.

Bill of Resources

bill of resources (BOR)

A record of a service firm's parent-component relationships and all of the materials, equipment time, staff, and other resources associated with them, including usage quantities.

The service analogy to the bill of materials in a manufacturing company is the **bill of resources (BOR)**, which is a record of a service firm's parent–component relationships and all of the materials, equipment time, staff, and other resources associated with them, including usage quantities. Once the service firm has completed its master schedule, the BOR can be used to determine what resources the firm will need, how much of them it will need, and when. A BOR for a service provider can be as complex as a BOM for a manufacturer. Consider a hospital that just scheduled treatment of a patient with an aneurysm. As shown in Figure 5.21 (a), the BOR for treatment of an aneurysm has seven levels, starting at the top (end item): (1) discharge, (2) intermediate care, (3) postoperative care (step down), (4) postoperative care (intensive), (5) surgery, (6) preoperative

FIGURE 5.21 ▶
BOR for Treating an Aneurysm

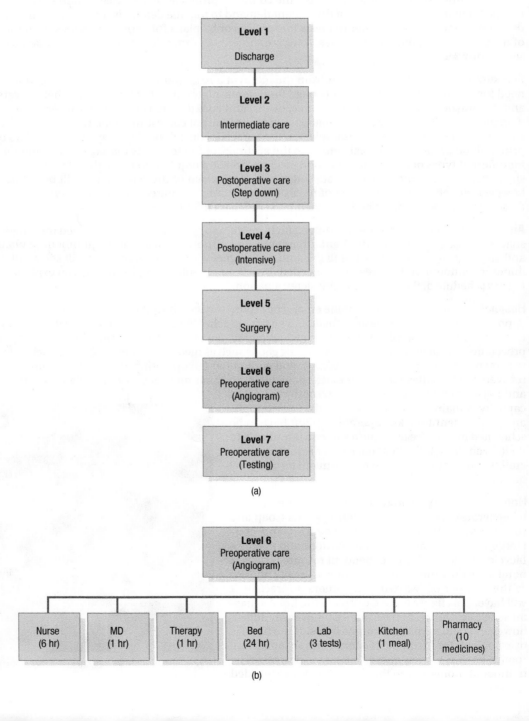

care (angiogram), and (7) preoperative care (testing). Each level of the BOR has a set of material and resource requirements and an associated lead time. For example, at level 6, shown in Figure 5.21(b), the patient needs 6 hours of nurses' time, 1 hour of the primary MD's time, 1 hour of the respiratory therapist's time, 24 hours of bed time, 3 different lab tests, 1 meal, and 10 different medicines from the pharmacy. The lead time for this level is 1 day. The lead time for the entire stay for treatment of the aneurysm is 12.2 days. A master schedule of patient admissions and the BORs for each illness enable the hospital to manage its critical resources. Reports analogous to the MRP II reports we discussed earlier in the chapter can be generated for the people who manage the various functional areas of the hospital.

One resource every service provider needs, however, is cash. Service organizations have to forecast the number of customers they expect to serve so that they have enough cash on hand to purchase materials that support the services—labor and other products. Purchasing these items increases the firm's accounts payable. As services are actually completed for customers, the firm's accounts receivable increases. The firm's master schedule and its accounts receivable and payable help a company predict the amount and timing of its cash flows.

LEARNING GOALS IN REVIEW

1 **Explain how enterprise resource planning (ERP) systems can foster better resource planning**. Review the opening vignette on Dow Corning, and the section on "Enterprise Resource Planning," pp. 142–144. Pay attention to Figure 5.1 to understand how different application modules come together to create functionality and value in the ERP systems.

2 **Explain how the concept of dependent demand is fundamental to resource planning**. See the section on "Dependent Demand," p. 145, which shows how continuous independent demand can lead to lumpy requirements for dependent demand. Then, a separate system, called material requirements planning, is needed to manage dependent demand situations.

3 **Describe a master production schedule (MPS) and compute available-to-promise quantities.** The section "Master Production Scheduling," pp. 147–151, shows you how firms break down a production plan into more detailed schedules. Understand the key relationships between Figures 5.5, 5.6, and 5.8.

4 **Apply the logic of a material requirements planning (MRP) system to identify production and purchase orders needed for dependent demand items**. Using Figure 5.12, page 153, understand how an inventory record is created for a given lot size rule. The section on "Planning Factors," pp. 154–157, shows you how choice of different managerial policies affect material plans. Finally, focus on understanding the MRP explosion process as illustrated in Figure 5.18 on page 158 and Solved Problem 3 on page 168.

5 **Apply MRP principles to the provision of services and distribution inventories.** The section, "Resource Planning for Service Providers," pp. 163–165, illustrates how the Bill of Resources can be used to plan dependent demand for services in settings such as the restaurants, airlines, hospitals, and hotels.

MyOMLab helps you develop analytical skills and assesses your progress with multiple problems on bills of material, parents, intermediate items, components, purchased items, lead times, master production schedules, MRP record, FOQ, L4L, POQ, scheduled receipts, and multi-level material requirements plans.

MyOMLab Resources	Titles	Link to the Book
Video	*Nantucket Nectars: ERP*	Enterprise Resource Planning
Active Model Exercise	5.1 Material Requirements Plan	Bill of Resources
OM Explorer Solvers	Master Production Scheduling Material Requirements Planning Single-Item MRP	Master Production Scheduling; Solved Problem 2 (p. 167) Material Requirements Planning; Solved Problem 3 (p. 168) Material Requirements Planning; Solved Problem 3 (p. 168)
OM Explorer Tutors	5.1 Master Production Scheduling 5.2 FOQ, POQ, and L4L Rules	Master Production Scheduling; Solved Problem 2 (p. 167) Planning Factors; Solved Problem 3 (p. 168)
Tutor Exercises	5.1 Applying Different MRP Lot Sizing Rules	Planning Factors; Solved Problem 3 (p. 168)
Virtual Tours	Vaughn Hockey Equipment Winslow Life Rafts	Bill of Materials Enterprise Resource Planning

MyOMLab Resources	Titles	Link to the Book
MyOMLab Supplements	H. Measuring Output Rates I. Learning Curve Analysis	MyOMLab Supplement H MyOMLab Supplement I
Internet Exercise	Schwinn Hewlett-Packard	Material Requirements Planning Material Requirements Planning
Blank MRP Records		
Key Equations		
Image Library		

Key Terms

Solved Problem 1

Refer to the bill of materials for product A shown in Figure 5.22.

FIGURE 5.22 ▶
BOM for Product A

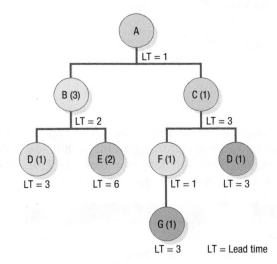

LT = Lead time

If there is no existing inventory and no scheduled receipts, how many units of items G, E, and D must be purchased to produce 5 units of end item A?

SOLUTION

Five units of item G, 30 units of item E, and 20 units of item D must be purchased to make 5 units of A. The usage quantities shown in Figure 5.22 indicate that 2 units of E are needed to make 1 unit of B and that 3 units of B are needed to make 1 unit of A; therefore, 5 units of A require 30 units of E ($2 \times 3 \times 5 = 30$). One unit of D is consumed to make 1 unit of B, and 3 units of B per unit of A result in 15 units of D ($1 \times 3 \times 5 = 15$); 1 unit of D in each unit of C and 1 unit of C per unit of A result in another 5 units of D ($1 \times 1 \times 5 = 5$). The total requirements to make 5 units of A are 20 units of D ($15 + 5$). The calculation of requirements for G is simply $1 \times 1 \times 1 \times 5 = 5$ units.

Solved Problem 2

The order policy is to produce end item A in lots of 50 units. Using the data shown in Figure 5.23 and the FOQ lot-sizing rule, complete the projected on-hand inventory and MPS quantity rows. Then, complete the MPS start row by offsetting the MPS quantities for the final assembly lead time. Compute the available-to-promise inventory for item A. Finally, assess the following customer requests for new orders. Assume that these orders arrive consecutively and their affect on ATP is cumulative. Which of these orders can be satisfied without altering the MPS Start quantities?

a. Customer A requests 30 units in week 1.

b. Customer B requests 30 units in week 4.

c. Customer C requests 10 units in week 3.

d. Customer D requests 50 units in week 5.

Item: A												Order Policy: 50 units Lead Time: 1 week
						Week						
Quantity on Hand:	5	1	2	3	4	5	6	7	8	9	10	
Forecast		20	10	40	10	0	0	30	20	40	20	
Customer orders (booked)		30	20	5	8	0	2	0	0	0	0	
Projected on-hand inventory		25										
MPS quantity		50										
MPS start												
Available-to-promise (ATP) inventory												

▲ FIGURE 5.23
MPS Record for End Item A

SOLUTION

The projected on-hand inventory for the second week is

$$\begin{pmatrix} \text{Projected on-hand} \\ \text{inventory at end} \\ \text{of week 2} \end{pmatrix} = \begin{pmatrix} \text{On-hand} \\ \text{inventory in} \\ \text{week 1} \end{pmatrix} + \begin{pmatrix} \text{MPS quantity} \\ \text{due in week 2} \end{pmatrix} - \begin{pmatrix} \text{Requirements} \\ \text{in week 2} \end{pmatrix}$$

$$= 25 + 0 - 20 = 5 \text{ units}$$

where requirements are the larger of the forecast or actual customer orders booked for shipment during this period. No MPS quantity is required.

Without an MPS quantity in the third period, a shortage of item A will occur: $5 + 0 - 40 = -35$. Therefore, an MPS quantity equal to the lot size of 50 must be scheduled for completion in the third period. Then, the projected on-hand inventory for the third week will be $5 + 50 - 40 = 15$.

Figure 5.24 shows the projected on-hand inventories and MPS quantities that would result from completing the MPS calculations. The MPS start row is completed by simply shifting a copy of the MPS quantity row to the left by one column to account for the 1-week final assembly lead time. Also shown are the available-to-promise quantities. In week 1, the ATP is

$$\begin{pmatrix} \text{Available-to-} \\ \text{Promise in} \\ \text{week 1} \end{pmatrix} = \begin{pmatrix} \text{On-hand} \\ \text{quantity in} \\ \text{week 1} \end{pmatrix} + \begin{pmatrix} \text{MPS quantity} \\ \text{in week 1} \end{pmatrix} - \begin{pmatrix} \text{Orderes booked up} \\ \text{to week 3 when the} \\ \text{next MPS arrives} \end{pmatrix}$$

$$= 5 + 50 - (30 + 20) = 5 \text{ units}$$

The ATP for the MPS quantity in week 3 is

$$\begin{pmatrix} \text{Available-to-} \\ \text{Promise in} \\ \text{week 3} \end{pmatrix} = \begin{pmatrix} \text{MPS quantity} \\ \text{in week 3} \end{pmatrix} - \begin{pmatrix} \text{Orderes booked up} \\ \text{to week 7 when the} \\ \text{next MPS arrives} \end{pmatrix}$$

$$= 50 - (5 + 8 + 0 + 2) = 35 \text{ units}$$

The other ATPs equal their respective MPS quantities because no orders are booked for those weeks. As for the new orders, Customer A's request for 30 units in week 1 cannot be accommodated; the earliest it can be shipped is week 3 because the ATP for week 1 is insufficient. Assuming that Customer A's order is rejected, Customer B's request may be satisfied. The ATP for week 1 will

										Lot Size: 50 units					
										Lead Time: 1 week					

		Week													
Quantity on Hand:	5	1	2	3	4	5	6	7	8	9	10	11	12	13	14	15
Forecast		20	10	40	10			30	20	40	20					
Customer orders (booked)		30	20	5	8		2									
Projected on-hand inventory		25	5	15	5	5	3	23	3	13	43					
MPS quantity		50		50				50		50	50					
MPS start			50				50		50	50						
Available-to-promise (ATP) inventory		5		35				50		50	50					

FIGURE 5.24 ▲
Completed MPS Record for
End Item A

stay at 5 units and the ATP for week 3 will be reduced to 5 units. This acceptance allows the firm the flexibility to immediately satisfy an order for 5 units or less, if one comes in. When the MPS is updated next, the customer orders booked for week 4 will be increased to 38 to reflect the new order's shipping date. Customer C's order for 10 units in week 3 is likewise accepted. The ATP for weeks 1 and 3 will be reduced to 0, and when the MPS is updated, the customer orders booked for week 3 will be increased to 15. Finally, Customer D's order for 50 units in week 5 cannot be satisfied without changing the MPS.

Solved Problem 3

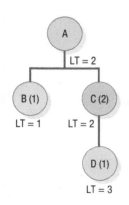

FIGURE 5.25 ▲
BOM for Product A

The MPS start quantities for product A calls for the assembly department to begin final assembly according to the following schedule: 100 units in week 2; 200 units in week 4; 120 units in week 6; 180 units in week 7; and 60 units in week 8. Develop a material requirements plan for the next 8 weeks for items B, C, and D. The BOM for A is shown in Figure 5.25, and data from the inventory records are shown in Table 5.1.

SOLUTION
We begin with items B and C and develop their inventory records, as shown in Figure 5.26. The MPS for product A must be multiplied by 2 to derive the gross requirements for item C because of the usage quantity. Once the planned order releases for item C are found, the gross requirements for item D can be calculated.

TABLE 5.1 | INVENTORY RECORD DATA

	ITEM		
Data Category	**B**	**C**	**D**
Lot-sizing rule	POQ ($P = 3$)	L4L	FOQ = 500 units
Lead time (LT)	1 week	2 weeks	3 weeks
Scheduled receipts	None	200 (week 1)	None
Beginning (on-hand) inventory	20	0	425

MyOMLab

Active Model 5.1 in MyOMLab provides additional insight on lotsizing decisions for this problem.

Item: B								Lot Size: POQ (P = 3)		
Description:								Lead Time: 1 week		

		Week									
		1	2	3	4	5	6	7	8	9	10
Gross requirements			100		200		120	180	60		
Scheduled receipts											
Projected on-hand inventory	20	20	200	200	0	0	240	60	0	0	0
Planned receipts			280				360				
Planned order releases		280				360					

Item: C								Lot Size: L4L		
Description:								Lead Time: 2 weeks		

		Week									
		1	2	3	4	5	6	7	8	9	10
Gross requirements			200		400		240	360	120		
Scheduled receipts		200									
Projected on-hand inventory	0	200	0	0	0	0	0	0	0	0	0
Planned receipts					400		240	360	120		
Planned order releases			400		240	360	120				

Item: D								Lot Size: FOQ = 500 units		
Description:								Lead Time: 3 weeks		

		Week									
		1	2	3	4	5	6	7	8	9	10
Gross requirements			400		240	360	120				
Scheduled receipts											
Projected on-hand inventory	425	425	25	25	285	425	305	305	305	305	305
Planned receipts					500	500					
Planned order releases		500	500								

◄ **FIGURE 5.26**
Inventory Records for Items B, C, and D

Discussion Questions

1. For an organization of your choice, such as where you previously worked, discuss how an ERP system could be used and whether it would increase effectiveness.

2. Form a group in which each member represents a different functional area of a firm. Provide a priority list of the information that could be generated from an MPS, from the most important to the least important, for each functional area. Rationalize the differences in the lists.

3. Consider the master flight schedule of a major airline, such as Air New Zealand. Discuss the ways in which it is analogous to a master production schedule for a manufacturer.

4. Consider a service provider that is in the delivery business, such as UPS or FedEx. How can the principles of MRP be useful to such a company?

Problems

The OM Explorer and POM for Windows software is available to all students using the 10th edition of this textbook. Go to **www.pearsonhighered.com/krajewski** website to download these computer packages. If you purchased MyOMLab, you also have access to Active Models software and significant help in doing the following problems. Check with your instructor on how best to use these resources. In many cases, the instructor wants you to understand how to do the calculations by hand. At the least, the software provides a check on your calculations. When calculations are particularly complex and the goal is interpreting the results in making decision, the software entirely replaces the manual calculations.

1. Consider the bill of materials (BOM) in Figure 5.27.

   a. How many immediate parents (one level above) does item I have? How many immediate parents does item E have?

   b. How many unique components does product A have at all levels?

   c. Which of the components are purchased items?

   d. How many intermediate items does product A have at all levels?

   e. Given the lead times (LT) in weeks noted on Figure 5.27, how far in advance of shipment must a purchase commitment be for any of the purchased items identified in part (c)?

2. Product A is made from components B, C, and D. Item B is a subassembly that requires 2 units of C and 1 unit of E. Item D also is an intermediate item, made from one unit of F. All other usage quantities are 2. Draw the BOM for product A.

3. What is the lead time (in weeks) to respond to a customer order for product A, based on the BOM shown in Figure 5.28, assuming no existing inventories or scheduled receipts?

4. Product A is made from components B and C. Item B, in turn, is made from D and E. Item C also is an intermediate item, made from F and H. Finally, intermediate item E is made from H and G. Note that item H has two parents. The following are item lead times:

Item	A	B	C	D	E	F	G	H
Lead Time (weeks)	1	2	2	6	5	6	4	3

   a. What lead time (in weeks) is needed to respond to a customer order for product A, assuming no existing inventories or scheduled receipts?

   b. What is the customer response time if all purchased items (i.e., D, F, G, and H) are in inventory?

   c. If you are allowed to keep just one purchased item in stock, which one would you choose?

5. Refer to Figure 5.22 and Solved Problem 1. If inventory consists of 2 units of B, 1 unit of F, and 3 units of G, how many units of G, E, and D must be purchased to produce 5 units of product A?

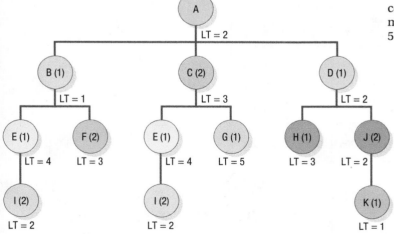

FIGURE 5.27 ▲
BOM for Product A

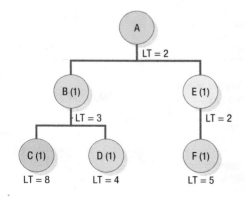

FIGURE 5.28 ▲
BOM for Product A

6. Complete the MPS record in Figure 5.29 for a single item.

◄ **FIGURE 5.29**
MPS Record for Single Item

Item: A						Order Policy: 60 units Lead Time: 1 week			
Quantity on Hand: 35		Week							
		1	2	3	4	5	6	7	8
Forecast		20	18	28	28	23	30	33	38
Customer orders (booked)		15	17	9	14	9	0	7	0
Projected on-hand inventory									
MPS quantity									
MPS start									

7. Complete the MPS record shown in Figure 5.30 for a single item.

◄ **FIGURE 5.30**
MPS Record for Single Item

Item: A						Order Policy: 100 units Lead Time: 1 week			
Quantity on Hand: 75		January				February			
		1	2	3	4	5	6	7	8
Forecast		65	65	65	45	50	50	50	50
Customer orders (booked)		40	10	85	0	35	70	0	0
Projected on-hand inventory									
MPS quantity									
MPS start									

8. An end item's demand forecasts for the next 10 weeks are 30, 20, 35, 50, 25, 25, 0, 40, 0, and 50 units. The current on-hand inventory is 80 units. The order policy is to produce in lots of 100. The booked customer orders for the item, starting with week 1, are 22, 30, 15, 9, 0, 0, 5, 3, 7, and 0 units. At present, no MPS quantities are on-hand for this item. The lead time is 2 weeks. Develop an MPS for this end item.

9. Figure 5.31 shows a partially completed MPS record for ball bearings.

    a. Develop the MPS for ball bearings.

    b. Four customer orders arrived in the following sequence:

Order	Quantity	Week Desired
1	500	4
2	400	5
3	300	1
4	300	7

    Assume that you must commit to the orders in the sequence of arrival and cannot change the desired shipping dates or your MPS. Which orders should you accept?

10. Tabard Industries forecasted the following demand for one of its most profitable products for the next 8 weeks: 120, 120, 120, 100, 100, 100, 80, and 80 units. The booked customer orders for this product, starting in week 1 are: 100, 80, 60, 40, 10, 10, 0, and 0 units. The current on-hand inventory is 150 units, the order quantity is 200 units, and the lead time is one week.

    a. Develop a MPS for this product.

    b. The marketing department revised its forecast. Starting with week 1, the new forecasts are: 120, 120, 120, 150, 150, 150, 100, and 100 units. Assuming that the prospective MPS you developed in part (a) does not change, prepare a revised MPS record. Comment on the situation that Tabard now faces.

    c. Returning to the original forecasted demand level and the MPS record you developed in part (a), assume

that marketing accepted a new customer order for 200 units in week 2 and thereby booked orders in week 2 is now 280 units. Assuming that the prospective MPS you developed in part (a) does not change, prepare a revised MPS record. Comment on the situation that Tabard now faces.

11. Figure 5.32 shows a partially completed MPS record for 2" pneumatic control valves. Suppose that you receive the following orders for the valves (shown in the order of their arrival). As they arrive, you must decide whether to accept or reject them. Which orders would you accept for shipment?

Order	Amount (Units)	Week Requested
1	15	2
2	30	5
3	25	3
4	75	7

12. The forecasted requirements for an electric hand drill for the next 6 weeks are 15, 40, 10, 20, 50, and 30 units. The marketing department has booked orders totaling 20, 25, 10, and 20 units for delivery in the first (current), second, third, and fourth weeks. Currently, 30 hand drills are in stock. The policy is to order in lots of 60 units. Lead time is one week.

    a. Develop the MPS record for the hand drills.

    b. A distributor of the hand drills places an order for 15 units. What is the appropriate shipping date for the entire order?

13. A forecast of 240 units in January, 320 units in February, and 240 units in March has been approved for the

FIGURE 5.31 ▶
MPS Record for Ball Bearings

Item: Ball bearings										Order Policy: 500 units Lead Time: 1 week		
						Week						
Quantity on Hand:	400	1	2	3	4	5	6	7	8	9	10
Forecast		550	300	400	450	300	350	200	300	450	400
Customer orders (booked)		300	350	250	250	200	150	100	100	100	100
Projected on-hand inventory											
MPS quantity	500										
MPS start											
Available-to-promise (ATP) inventory											

Item: 2" Pneumatic control valve

Order Policy: 75 units
Lead Time: 1 week

Quantity on Hand: 10	Week							
	1	2	3	4	5	6	7	8
Forecast	40	40	40	40	30	30	50	50
Customer orders (booked)	60	45	30	35	10	5	5	0
Projected on-hand inventory								
MPS quantity	75	75						
MPS start	75							
Available-to-promise (ATP) inventory								

◄ **FIGURE 5.32**
MPS Record for 2" Pneumatic Control Valve

seismic-sensory product family manufactured at the Rockport facility of Maryland Automated, Inc. Three products, A, B, and C, comprise this family. The product mix ratio for products A, B, and C for the past 2 years has been 35 percent, 40 percent, and 25 percent, respectively. Management believes that the monthly forecast requirements are evenly spread over the 4 weeks of each month. Currently, 10 units of product C are on hand. The company produces product C in lots of 40, and the lead time is 2 weeks. A production quantity of 40 units from the previous period is scheduled to arrive in week 1. The company has accepted orders of 25, 12, 8, 10, 2, and 3 units of product C in weeks 1 through 6, respectively.

Prepare a prospective MPS for product C and calculate the available-to-promise inventory quantities.

14. The partially completed inventory record for the tabletop subassembly in Figure 5.33 shows gross requirements, scheduled receipts, lead time, and current on-hand inventory.

   a. Complete the last three rows of the record for an FOQ of 110 units.

   b. Complete the last three rows of the record by using the L4L lot-sizing rule.

   c. Complete the last three rows of the record by using the POQ lot-sizing rule, with $P = 2$.

Item: M405—X
Description: Tabletop subassembly

Lot Size:
Lead Time: 2 weeks

	Week									
	1	2	3	4	5	6	7	8	9	10
Gross requirements	90		85		80		45	90		
Scheduled receipts	110									
Projected on-hand inventory 40										
Planned receipts										
Planned order releases										

◄ **FIGURE 5.33**
Inventory Record for the Tabletop Subassembly

15. The partially completed inventory record for the rotor subassembly in Figure 5.34 shows gross requirements, scheduled receipts, lead time, and current on-hand inventory.

    a. Complete the last three rows of the record for an FOQ of 150 units.

    b. Complete the last three rows of the record by using the L4L lot-sizing rule.

    c. Complete the last three rows of the record by using the POQ lot-sizing rule, with $P = 2$.

FIGURE 5.34 ▶
Inventory Record for the Rotor Subassembly

Item: Rotor subassembly								Lot Size: Lead Time: 2 weeks	
		Week							
		1	2	3	4	5	6	7	8
Gross requirements		65	15	45	40	80	80	80	80
Scheduled receipts		150							
Projected on-hand inventory	20								
Planned receipts									
Planned order releases									

16. The partially completed inventory record for the drive-shaft subassembly in Figure 5.35 shows gross requirements, scheduled receipts, lead time, and current on-hand inventory.

    a. Complete the last three rows of the record for an FOQ of 50 units.

    b. Complete the last three rows of the record by using the L4L lot-sizing rule.

    c. Complete the last three rows of the record by using the POQ lot-sizing rule, with $P = 4$.

17. Figure 5.36 shows a partially completed inventory record for the real wheel subassembly. Gross requirements, scheduled receipts, lead time, and current on-hand inventory are shown.

    a. Complete the last three rows of the record for an FOQ of 200 units.

    b. Complete the last three rows of the record by using an FOQ of 100 units.

    c. Complete the last three rows of the record by using the L4L rule.

FIGURE 5.35 ▶
Inventory Record for the Driveshaft Subassembly

Item: Driveshaft subassembly								Lot Size: Lead Time: 3 weeks	
		Week							
		1	2	3	4	5	6	7	8
Gross requirements		35	25	15	20	40	40	50	50
Scheduled receipts		80							
Projected on-hand inventory	10								
Planned receipts									
Planned order releases									

Item: MQ–09 Description: Rear wheel subassembly								Lot Size: Lead Time: 1 week		
	Week									
	1	2	3	4	5	6	7	8	9	10
Gross requirements	25	105	110	90		45	110	60		
Scheduled receipts										
Projected on-hand inventory 50										
Planned receipts										
Planned order releases										

◀ **FIGURE 5.36**
Inventory Record for the Rear Wheel Subassembly

18. A partially completed inventory record for the motor subassembly is shown in Figure 5.37.

    a. Complete the last three rows of the record by using the L4L rule.

    b. Complete the last three rows of the record by using the POQ rule with $P = 2$.

    c. Complete the last three rows of the record by using the POQ rule with $P = 4$.

    d. If it costs the company \$1 to hold a unit in inventory from one week to the next, and the cost to release an order is \$50, which of the lot sizing rules used above will provide the lowest inventory holding + order release cost?

Item: GF–4 Description: Motor subassembly								Lot Size: Lead Time: 2 weeks		
	Week									
	1	2	3	4	5	6	7	8	9	10
Gross requirements		80	50	35	20	55	15	30	25	10
Scheduled receipts	60									
Projected on-hand inventory 20										
Planned receipts										
Planned order releases										

▲ **FIGURE 5.37**
Inventory Record for the Motor Subassembly

Advanced Problems

Depending on the time available to cover this chapter, your instructor may not assign these problems. Perhaps, your assignment for the multi-level problems allows the use of the *Material Requirements Planning* Solver of OM Explorer, with main requirement of looking for situations that need the inventory planner's attention (i.e., an action notice).

19. The BOM for product A is shown in Figure 5.38, and data from the inventory records are shown in Table 5.2. In the master production schedule for product A, the MPS start row has 100 units in week 3 and 200 in week 6. Develop the material requirements plan for the next 6 weeks for items B, C, and D.

a. Develop the material requirements plan for the next 6 weeks for items B, C, and D.

b. What specific managerial actions are required in week 1?

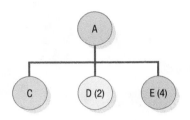

FIGURE 5.38 ▲
BOM for Product A

TABLE 5.2 | **INVENTORY RECORD DATA**

	ITEM		
Data Category	**C**	**D**	**E**
Lot-Sizing Rule	L4L	FOQ = 200	POQ (P = 3 weeks)
Lead time	2 weeks	1 week	1 week
Scheduled receipts	None	200 (in week 3)	200 (in week 3)
Beginning inventory	50	200	0

20. The BOMs for products A & B and data from the inventory records are shown in Figure 5.39. Data from the inventory records are shown in Table 5.3. In the master production schedule for product A, the MPS start row has 85 units in week 2 and 200 in week 4 and 50 in week 8. In the master production schedule for product B, the MPS start row has 65 units in week 3 and 50 in week 4 and 50 in week 5 and 75 in week 8.

a. Develop the material requirements plan for the next 8 weeks for items C, D, and E. Note any difficulties you observe in the inventory records.

b. Can the difficulties noted in part a be rectified by expediting any Scheduled Receipts?

FIGURE 5.39 ▶
BOMs for Product A and Product B

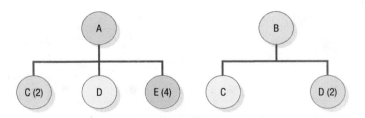

TABLE 5.3 | **INVENTORY RECORD DATA**

	ITEM		
Data Category	**C**	**D**	**E**
Lot-sizing rule	L4L	FOQ = 200	POQ (P = 2 weeks)
Lead time	2 weeks	1 week	1 week
Scheduled receipts	200 (in week 3)	0	0
Beginning inventory	0	0	200

21. Figure 5.40 illustrates the BOM for product A. The MPS start row in the master production schedule for product A calls for 50 units in week 2, 65 units in week 5, and 80 units in week 8. Item C is produced to make A and to meet the forecasted demand for replacement parts. Past replacement part demand has been 20 units per week (add 20 units to C's gross requirements). The lead times for items F and C are 1 week, and for the other items the lead time is 2 weeks. No safety stock is required for items B, C, D, E, and F. The L4L lot-sizing rule is used for items B and F; the POQ lot-sizing rule (P = 3) is used for C. Item E has an FOQ of 600 units, and D has an FOQ of 250 units. On-hand inventories are 50 units of B, 50 units of C, 120 units of D, 70 units of E, and 250 units of F. Item B has a scheduled receipt of 50 units in week 2. Develop a material requirements plan for the next 8 weeks for items B, C, D, E, and F.

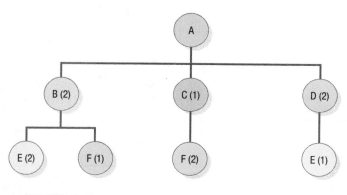

▲ **FIGURE 5.40**
BOM for Product A

22. The following information is available for three MPS items:

Product A	An 80-unit order is to be started in week 3.	
	A 55-unit order is to be started in week 6.	
Product B	A 125-unit order is to be started in week 5.	
Product C	A 60-unit order is to be started in week 4.	

Develop the material requirements plan for the next 6 weeks for items D, E, and F. The BOMs are shown in Figure 5.41, and data from the inventory records are shown in Table 5.4. (*Warning:* A safety stock requirement applies to item F. Be sure to plan a receipt for any week in which the projected on-hand inventory becomes less than the safety stock.)

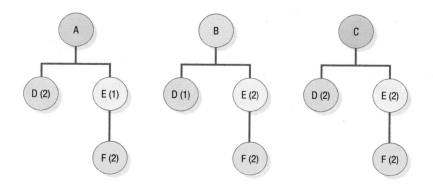

◄ **FIGURE 5.41**
BOMs for Products A, B, and C

TABLE 5.4 | INVENTORY RECORD DATA

	ITEM		
Data Category	**D**	**E**	**F**
Lot-sizing rule	FOQ = 150	L4L	POQ ($P = 2$)
Lead time	3 weeks	1 week	2 weeks
Safety stock	0	0	30
Scheduled receipts	150 (week 3)	120 (week 2)	None
Beginning inventory	150	0	100

▼ **FIGURE 5.42**
BOMs for Products A and B

23. Figure 5.42 shows the BOMs for two products, A and B. Table 5.5 shows the MPS quantity start date for each one. Table 5.6 contains data from inventory records for items C, D, and E. There are no safety stock requirements for any of the items.

   a. Determine the material requirements plan for items C, D, and E for the next 8 weeks.

   b. What specific managerial actions are required in week 1?

   c. Suppose that a very important customer places an emergency order for a quantity of product A. In order to satisfy this order, a new MPS of 200 units of product A is now required in week 5. Determine the changes to the material requirements plan if this order is accepted and note any problems that you detect.

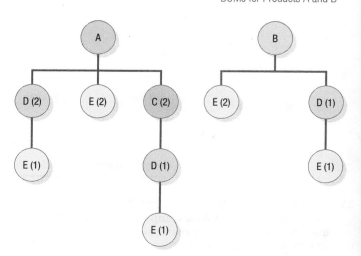

TABLE 5.5 | MPS QUANTITY START DATES

Product	DATE							
	1	2	3	4	5	6	7	8
A		125		95		150		130
B			80			70		

TABLE 5.6 | INVENTORY RECORD DATA

Data Category	ITEM		
	C	D	E
Lot-sizing rule	L4L	POQ (P = 3)	FOQ = 800
Lead time	3 weeks	2 weeks	1 week
Scheduled receipts	200 (week 2)	None	800 (week 1)
Beginning inventory	85	625	350

24. The BOM for product A is shown in Figure 5.43. The MPS for product A calls for 120 units to be started in weeks 2, 4, 5, and 8. Table 5.7 shows data from the inventory records.

   a. Develop the material requirements plan for the next 8 weeks for each item.

   b. What specific managerial actions are required in week 1? Make sure you address any specific difficulties you encounter in the inventory records.

FIGURE 5.43 ▶
BOM for Product A

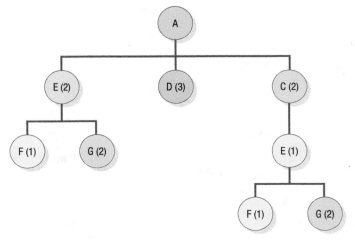

TABLE 5.7 | INVENTORY RECORD DATA

Data Category	ITEM				
	C	D	E	F	G
Lot-sizing rule	L4L	FOQ = 700	FOQ = 700	L4L	L4L
Lead time	3 weeks	3 weeks	4 weeks	2 weeks	1 week
Safety stock	0	0	0	50	0
Scheduled receipts	150 (week 2)	450 (week 2)	700 (week 1)	None	1,400 (week 1)
Beginning inventory	125	0	235	750	0

25. Refer to Solved Problem 1 (Figure 5.22) for the bill of materials and Table 5.8 for component inventory record information. Develop the material requirements plan for all components and intermediate items associated with product A for the next 10 weeks. The MPS for product A calls for 50 units to be started in weeks 2, 6, 8, and 9. (*Warning:* Safety stock requirements apply to items B and C.)

TABLE 5.8 | INVENTORY RECORD DATA

Data Category	ITEM					
	B	**C**	**D**	**E**	**F**	**G**
Lot-sizing rule	L4L	L4L	POQ (P = 2)	L4L	L4L	FOQ = 100
Lead time	2 weeks	3 weeks	3 weeks	6 weeks	1 week	3 weeks
Safety stock	30	10	0	0	0	0
Scheduled receipts	150 (week 2)	50 (week 2)	None	400 (week 6)	40 (week 3)	None
Beginning inventory	30	20	60	400	0	0

26. An end item's demand forecasts for the next 6 weeks are 30 units, followed by forecasts of 25 units for weeks 7 though 10. The current on-hand inventory is 60 units. The order policy is to produce in lots of 100. The booked customer orders for the item, starting with week 1, are 22, 30, 15, 11, 0, 0, 9, 0, 0, and 0 units. The lead time is 2 weeks.

    a. Develop an MPS for this end item.

    b. The marketing department has received six orders for this item in the following sequence:

    Order 1 is for 40 units to be delivered in period 3

    Order 2 is for 60 units to be delivered in period 4

    Order 3 is for 70 units to be delivered in period 6

    Order 4 is for 40 units to be delivered in period 3

    Order 5 is for 20 units to be delivered in period 5

    Order 6 is for 115 units to be delivered in period 9

    Assuming that the prospective MPS you developed in part (a) does not change, which orders would you be able to accept based on the available to promise (ATP)?

27. An end item's demand forecasts for the next 10 weeks are 30, 30, 30, 30, 20, 20, 30, 30, 30, and 30 units. The current on-hand inventory is 100 units. The order policy is to produce in lots of 75. The booked customer orders for the item, starting with week 1, are 15, 38, 7, 5, 0, 3, 10, 0, 0, and 0 units. The lead time is 2 weeks.

    a. Develop an MPS for this end item.

    b. The marketing department has received five orders for this item in the following sequence:

    Order 1 is for 20 units to be delivered in period 1

    Order 2 is for 75 units to be delivered in period 4

    Order 3 is for 90 units to be delivered in period 6

    Order 4 is for 75 units to be delivered in period 7

    Order 5 is for 90 units to be delivered in period 10

    Assuming that the prospective MPS you developed in part (a) does not change, which orders would you be able to accept based on the available to promise (ATP)?

28. The bill of materials and the data from the inventory records for product A are shown in Figure 5.44. Assume that the MPS start quantities for A are 100 units in weeks 1, 2, 3, 4, 7, 8, 9, and 10.

    Derive an MRP plan for the components going into product A using the data in Table 5.9.

    What specific managerial actions are required in week 1? Make sure you address any specific difficulties you encounter in the inventory records.

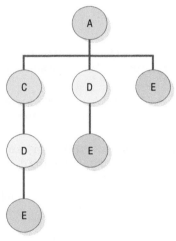

▲ **FIGURE 5.44**
BOM for product A

TABLE 5.9 | INVENTORY RECORD DATA

Data Category	ITEM		
	C	**D**	**E**
Lot-sizing rule	L4L	L4L	FOQ = 300
Lead time	1 week	2 weeks	2 weeks
Scheduled receipts		100 (in week 2)	300 (in week 2)
Beginning Inventory	225	350	100

29. The bill of materials and the data from the inventory records for product A are shown in Figure 5.45. Assume that the MPS start quantities for A are 50 units in weeks 1, 2 and 3, and 150 units in weeks 6 and 8. Derive an MRP plan for the components going into product A using the data in Table 5.10.

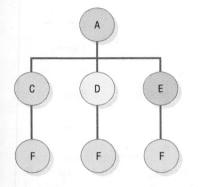

▲ FIGURE 5.45
BOM for Product A

TABLE 5.10 │ INVENTORY RECORD DATA

Data Category	ITEM			
	C	**D**	**E**	**F**
Lot-sizing rule	POQ ($P = 2$)	L4L	FOQ $= 300$	FOQ $= 400$
Lead time	1 week	1 week	2 weeks	4 weeks
Scheduled receipts		100 (week 2)		400 (week 1)
Beginning inventory	100	0	110	40

Active Model Exercise

This Active Model appears in MyOMLab. It allows you to evaluate the relationship between the inventory record data and the planned order releases.

QUESTIONS

1. Suppose that the POQ for item B is changed from 3 weeks to 2 weeks. How does this change affect the order releases for items B, C, and D?

2. As the on-hand inventory for item C increases from 0 to 200, what happens to the order releases for items B, C, and D?

3. As the fixed order quantity (FOQ) for item D increases from 500 to 750, what happens to the order releases for items B, C, and D?

4. As the lead time for item C changes, what happens to the order releases for items B, C, and D?

Material Requirements Plan

Reset Data   Questions

Master Produc

Finished Item A		1	2	3	4	5	6	7	8	9	10
Finished Item A MPS Start			100		200		120	180	60		

Scheduled rec

		1	2	3	4	5	6	7	8	9	10
Item B											
Item C		200									
Item D											

Inventory Rec

	B		C		D	
Lead time	1		2		3	
Beginning (on-hand) Inventory	20		0		425	
Fixed order quantity					500	
POQ	3					

Planned Order Releases

		Week							
	1	2	3	4	5	6	7	8	
B	280				360				
C		400		240	360	120			
D	500	500							

ACTIVE MODEL 5.1 ▲
Material Requirements Planning Using Data from Solved Problem 3 and Table 5.1

CASE   Flashy Flashers, Inc.

Flashy Flashers is a medium-sized firm employing 900 persons and 125 managerial and administrative personnel. The firm produces a line of automotive electrical components. It supplies about 95 auto parts stores and Moonbird Silverstreak car dealers in its region. Johnny Bennett, who serves as the president, founded the company by producing cable assemblies in his garage. By working hard, delivering consistent product quality, and by providing good customer service, he expanded his business to produce a variety of electrical components. Bennett's commitment to customer service is so strong that his company motto, "Love Thy Customers as Thyself," is etched on a big cast-iron plaque under his giant oil portrait in the building's front lobby.

The company's two most profitable products are the automotive front sidelamp and the headlamp. With the rising popularity of Eurosport sedans, such as the Moonbird Silverstreak, Flashy Flashers has enjoyed substantial demand for these two lamp items.

Last year, Kathryn Marley, the vice president of operations and supply chain management, approved the installation of a new MRP system. It is a

first important step toward the eventual goal of a full-fledged ERP system. Marley worked closely with the task force that was created to bring MRP online. She frequently attended the training sessions for selected employees, emphasizing how MRP should help Flashy Flashers secure a better competitive edge.

A year later, the MRP system is working fairly well. However, Marley believes that there is always a better way and seeks to continually improve the company's processes. To get a better sense for potential improvements, she met with the production and inventory control manager, the shop supervisor, and the purchasing manager. Here are some of their observations.

Production and Inventory Control Manager

Inventory records and BOM files are accurate and well maintained. Inventory transactions are faithfully made when inventory is replenished or removed from the stockroom so that current on-hand balances are credible. There is a MRP explosion each week, which gives the company the new material requirements plan. It provides information that helps identify when new orders need to be launched. Information can also be searched to help identify which scheduled receipts need to be expedited and which ones can be delayed by assigning them a later due date, thereby making room for more urgent jobs.

One planner suggested that the MRP outputs should be extended to provide priority and capacity reports, with pointers as to which items need their attention. The original plan was to get the order-launching capability implemented first. However, there is no formal system of priority planning, other than the initial due date assigned to each scheduled receipt when it is released, transforming it from a planned order release into a scheduled receipt. The due dates do not get updated later even when there are unexpected scrap losses, capacity shortages, short shipments, or last-minute changes in the MPS (responding to requests from favorite customers). Jobs are scheduled on the shop floor and by suppliers according to the EDD rule, based on their due dates. If due dates assigned to scheduled receipts were updated, it might help get open orders done when they are really needed. Furthermore, planned order releases in the action bucket are translated into scheduled receipts (using inventory transactions), after checking that its components are available. The current system does not consider possible capacity problems when releasing new orders.

Shop Supervisor

His primary complaint is that the shop workloads are anything but level. One week, they hardly have any work, and the supervisor overproduces (more than called for by the scheduled receipts) just to keep everyone busy. The next week can be just the opposite—so many new orders with short fuses that almost everyone needed to work overtime or else the scheduled receipt quantities are reduced to cover immediate needs. It is feast or famine,

unless they make things work on the shop floor! They do make inventory transactions to report deviations from plan for the scheduled receipts, but these "overrides" make the scheduled receipt information in the MRP records more uncertain for the planners. A particular concern is to make sure that the bottleneck workstations are kept busy.

Purchasing

Buyers are putting out too many fires, leaving little time for creative buying. In such cases, their time is spent following up on orders that are required in the very near future or that are even late. Sometimes, the MRP plan shows planned order releases for purchased items that that are needed almost immediately, not allowing for the planned lead time. In checking the MRP records, the planned lead times are realistic and what the suppliers expect. Last week, things were fine for an item, and this week a rush order needs to be placed. What is the problem?

Marley tried to assimilate all this information. She decided to collect all the required information about the sidelamps and headlamps (shown in Table 5.11 through Table 5.14 and in Figure 5.46) to gain further insight into possible problems and identify areas for improvement.

Your Assignment

Put yourself in Marley's place and prepare a report on your findings. Specifically, you are required to do a manual MRP explosion for the sidelamps and headlamps for the next 6 weeks (beginning with the current week). Assume that it is now the start of week 1. Fill in the planned order releases form provided in Table 5.15. It should show the planned order releases for all items for the next 6 weeks. Include it in your report.

TABLE 5.11 | PART NUMBERS AND DESCRIPTIONS

Part Number	Description
C206P	Screws
C310P	Back rubber gasket
HL200E	Headlamp
HL211A	Head frame subassembly
HL212P	Head lens
HL222P	Headlamp module
HL223F	Head frame
SL100E	Sidelamp
SL111P	Side lens
SL112A	Side frame subassembly
SL113P	Side lens rubber gasket
SL121F	Side frame
SL122A	Side bulb subassembly
SL123A	Flasher bulb subassembly
SL131F	Side cable grommet and receptacle
SL132P	Side bulb
SL133F	Flasher cable grommet and receptacle
SL134P	Flasher bulb

TABLE 5.12 | MASTER PRODUCTION SCHEDULE

Item Description and Part Number	Quantity	MPS Start Date
Headlamp (HL200E)	120	Week 4
	90	Week 5
	75	Week 6
Sidelamp (SL100E)	100	Week 3
	80	Week 5
	110	Week 6

TABLE 5.13 | REPLACEMENT PART DEMAND

Item Description and Part Number	Quantity	Date
Side lens (SL111P)	40	Week 3
	35	Week 6

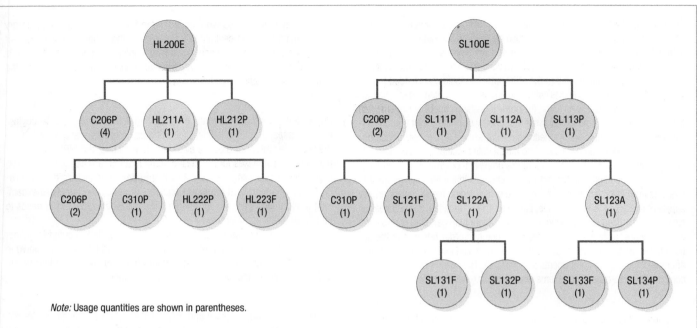

Note: Usage quantities are shown in parentheses.

▲ **FIGURE 5.46**
BOMs for Headlamps and Sidelamps

Supplement your report with worksheets on the manual MRP explosion, and list the actions that planners should consider this week to (1) release new orders, (2) expedite scheduled receipts, and (3) delay a scheduled receipt's due date.

Finally, identify the good and bad points of MRP implementation at Flashy Flashers. Conclude by making suggestions on ways to improve its resource planning process.

TABLE 5.14 | SELECTED DATA FROM INVENTORY RECORDS

Part Number	Lead Time (Weeks)	Safety Stock (Units)	Lot-Sizing Rule	On-Hand (Units)	Scheduled Receipt (Units and Due Dates)
C206P	1	30	FOQ = 2,500	270	—
C310P	1	20	FOQ = 180	40	180 (week 1)
HL211A	3	0	L4L	0	—
HL212P	2	15	FOQ = 350	15	—
HL222P	3	10	POQ (P = 4 weeks)	10	285 (week 1)
HL223F	1	0	POQ (P = 4 weeks)	0	120 (week 1)
SL111P	2	0	FOQ = 350	15	—
SL112A	3	0	L4L	20	80 (week 2)
SL113P	1	20	FOQ = 100	20	—
SL121F	2	0	L4L	0	80 (week 2)
SL122A	2	0	L4L	0	80 (week 2)
SL123A	2	0	FOQ = 200	0	—
SL131F	2	0	POQ (P = 2 weeks)	0	110 (week 1)
SL132P	1	25	FOQ = 100	35	100 (week 1)
SL133F	2	0	FOQ = 250		—
SL134P	1	0	FOQ = 400	100	—

TABLE 5.15 | PLANNED ORDER RELEASE FORM

FILL IN THE PLANNED ORDER RELEASES FOR ALL COMPONENTS.

Item Description and Part Number	Week					
	1	2	3	4	5	6
Side lens (SL111P)						
Side lens rubber gasket (SL113P)						
Side frame subassembly (SL112A)						
Side frame (SL121F)						
Side bulb subassembly (SL122A)						
Flasher bulb subassembly (SL123A)						
Side cable grommet and receptacle (SL131F)						
Flasher cable grommet and receptacle (SL133F)						
Side bulb (SL132P)						
Flasher bulb (SL134P)						
Head frame subassembly (HL211A)						
Head lens (HL212P)						
Headlamp module (HL222P)						
Head frame (HL223F)						
Back rubber gasket (C310P)						
Screws (C206P)						

Selected References

Becker, Nathan. "iPad's Bill of Materials Close to first iPad." *Wall Street Journal*, March 14, 2011.

Bendoly, E., and M. Cotteleer. "Understanding Behaviroral Sources of Process Variation following Enterprise System Deployment." *Journal of Operations Management*, vol. 26, no. 1 (2008).

Davenport, Thomas H. "Putting the Enterprise into the Enterprise System." *Harvard Business Review* (July–August 1998), pp. 121–131.

Hendricks, Kevin B., Vinod R. Singhal, and Jeff K. Stratman. "The Impact of Enterprise Systems on Corporate Performance: A Study of ERP, SCM and CRM System Implementations." *Journal of Operations Management*, vol. 25, no. 1 (2007), pp. 65–82.

Jacobs, F. Robert, William Berry, and D. Clay Whybark. *Manufacturing Planning and Control Systems for Supply Chain Management*, 6th ed. New York: McGraw-Hill/Irwin, 2010.

Jacobs, F. Robert, and Weston, F.C. (Ted) Jr. "Enterprise Resource Planning (ERP)—A Brief History." *Journal of Operations Management*, vol. 25, no. 2 (2007), pp. 357–363.

Mabert, Vincent A. "The Early Road to Materials Requirements Planning." *Journal of Operations Management*, vol. 25, no. 2 (2007), pp. 346–356.

McAfee, A., and E. Brynjolfsson. "Investing in the IT That Makes a Competitive Advantage." *Harvard Business Review*, vol. 86 (July–August 2008), pp. 98–107.

McCue, Andy. "Too Much Candy: IT Glitch Costs Cadbury." *Business Week*, June 8, 2006.

Scalle, Cedric X., and Mark J. Cotteleer. *Enterprise Resource Planning (ERP)*. Boston, MA: Harvard Business School Publishing, 1999, No. 9-699-020.

Wallace, Thomas F. *Sales & Operations Planning: The How-To Handbook*, 3rd ed. Cincinnati, OH: T. E. Wallace & Company, 2008.

Wallace, Thomas F., and Robert A. Stahl. *Master Scheduling in the 21st Century*. Cincinnati, OH: T. E. Wallace & Company, 2003.

An employee stacks a shipment of pet supplies at a new Walmart distribution center in Fort Pierce, Florida. The 1.2 million square foot facility will serve 45 Walmart stores on the east coast of Florida.

SUPPLY CHAIN INVENTORY MANAGEMENT

Inventory Management at Walmart

In the market for shaver blade replacements? A printer? First-aid supplies? Dog food? Hair spray? If so, you expect that the store you shop at will have what you want. However, making sure that the shelves are stocked with tens of thousands of products is no simple matter for inventory managers at Walmart, which has 8,800 Walmart stores and Sam's Club locations in 15 markets, employs more than 2 million associates, serves 200 million customers per week worldwide, and uses 100,000 suppliers. You can imagine in an operation this large that some things can get lost. Linda Dillman, then CIO at Walmart, recounts the story of the missing hair spray at one of the stores. The shelf needed to be restocked with a specific hair spray; however, it took three days to find the case in the backroom. Most customers will not swap hair sprays, so Walmart lost three days of sales on that product.

Knowing what is in stock, in what quantity, and where it is being held is critical to effective inventory management. Without accurate inventory information, companies can make major mistakes by ordering too much, not enough, or shipping products to the wrong location. Companies can have large inventories and still have stockouts of product because they have too much inventory of some products and not enough of others. Walmart, a $405 billion company with inventories in excess of $33 billion, is certainly aware of the potential benefits from improved inventory management and is constantly experimenting with ways to reduce inventory investment. Knowing when to replenish inventory stocks and

inventory management

The planning and controlling of inventories in order to meet the competitive priorities of the organization.

lot size

The quantity of an inventory item management either buys from a supplier or manufactures using internal processes.

how much to order each time is critical when dealing with so much inventory investment. The application of technology is also important, such as using radio frequency identification (RFID) to track inventory shipments and stock levels at stores and warehouses throughout the supply chain. One handheld RFID reader could have found the missing case of hair spray in a few minutes.

Source: Laurie Sullivan, "Walmart's Way," Informationweek.com (September 27, 2004), pp. 36–50; Gus Whitcomb and Christi Gallagher, "Walmart Begins Roll-Out of Electronic Product Codes in Dallas/Fort Worth Area," **www.walmartstores .com** (February 2011), and Walmart 2010 Annual Report.

LEARNING GOALS *After reading this chapter, you should be able to:*

1 Identify the advantages, disadvantages, and costs of holding inventory.

2 Define the different types of inventory and the roles they play in supply chains.

3 Explain the basic tactics for reducing inventories in supply chains.

4 Determine the items deserving most attention and tightest inventory control.

5 Calculate the economic order quantity and apply it to various situations.

6 Determine the order quantity and reorder point for a continuous review inventory control system.

7 Determine the review interval and target inventory level for a periodic review inventory control system.

8 Define the key factors that determine the appropriate choice of an inventory system.

Inventory management, the planning and controlling of inventories in order to meet the competitive priorities of the organization, is an important concern for managers in all types of businesses. Effective inventory management is essential for realizing the full potential of any supply chain. The challenge is not to pare inventories to the bone to reduce costs or to have plenty around to satisfy all demands, but to have the right amount to achieve the competitive priorities of the business most efficiently. This type of efficiency can only happen if the right amount of inventory is flowing through the supply chain—through suppliers, the firm, warehouses or distribution centers, and customers. These decisions were so important for Walmart that it decided to use RFID to improve the information flows in the supply chain. Much of inventory management involves *lot sizing*, which is the determination of how frequently and in what quantity to order inventory. We make ample reference to the term **lot size**, which is the quantity of an inventory item management either buys from a supplier or manufactures using internal processes. In this chapter, we focus on the decision-making aspects of inventory management. We begin with an overview of the importance of inventory management to the organization and how to choose the items most deserving of management attention. We then introduce the basics of inventory decision making by exploring the economic order quantity and how it can be used to balance inventory holding costs with ordering costs. A major segment of the chapter is devoted to retail and distribution inventory control systems and how to use them.

[handwritten]: Planning + controlling of inventories in order to meet the competitive priorities of the organization.

Inventory Management across the Organization

Inventories are important to all types of organizations, their employees, and their supply chains. Inventories profoundly affect everyday operations because they must be counted, paid for, used in operations, used to satisfy customers, and managed. Inventories require an investment of funds, as does the purchase of a new machine. Monies invested in inventory are not available for investment in other things; thus, they represent a drain on the cash flows of an organization. Nonetheless, companies realize that the availability of products is a key selling point in many markets and downright critical in many more.

So, is inventory a boon or a bane? Certainly, too much inventory on hand reduces profitability, and too little inventory on hand creates shortages in the supply chain and ultimately damages customer confidence. Inventory management, therefore, involves trade-offs. Let us discover how companies can effectively manage inventories across the organization.

Inventory and Supply Chains

The value of inventory management becomes apparent when the complexity of the supply chain is recognized. The performance of numerous suppliers determines the inward flow of materials and services to a firm. The performance of the firm determines the outward flow of services or products to the next stage of the supply chain. The flow of materials, however, determines inventory levels. **Inventory** is a stock of materials used to satisfy customer demand or to support the production of services or goods. Figure 6.1 shows how inventories are created at one node in a supply chain through the analogy of a water tank. The flow of water into the tank raises the water level. The inward flow of water represents input materials, such as steel, component parts, office supplies, or a finished product. The water level represents the amount of inventory held at a plant, service facility, warehouse, or retail outlet. The flow of water from the tank lowers the water level in the tank. The outward flow of water represents the demand for materials in inventory, such as customer orders for a Huffy bicycle or service requirements for supplies such as soap, food, or furnishings. The rate of the outward flow also reflects the ability of the firm to match the demand for services or products. Another possible outward flow is that of scrap, which also lowers the level of useable inventory. Together, the difference between input flow rate and the output flow rate determines the level of inventory. Inventories rise when more material flows into the tank than flows out; they fall when more material flows out than flows in. Figure 6.1 also shows clearly why firms utilize Six Sigma and total quality management (TQM) to reduce defective materials: The larger the scrap flows, the larger the input flow of materials required for a given level of output.

A fundamental question in supply chain management is how much inventory to have. The answer to this question involves a tradeoff between the advantages and disadvantages of holding inventory. Depending on the situation, the pressures for having small inventories may or may not exceed the pressures for having large inventories.

inventory

A stock of materials used to satisfy customer demand or to support the production of services or goods.

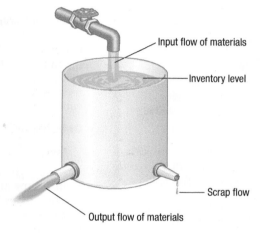

▲ **FIGURE 6.1**
Creation of Inventory

Pressures for Small Inventories

An inventory manager's job is to balance the advantages and disadvantages of both small and large inventories and find a happy medium between the two levels. The primary reason for keeping inventories small is that inventory represents a temporary monetary investment. As such, the firm incurs an opportunity cost, which we call the cost of capital, arising from the money tied up in inventory that could be used for other purposes. The **inventory holding cost** (or *carrying cost*) is the sum of the cost of capital plus the variable costs of keeping items on hand, such as storage and handling costs and taxes, insurance, and shrinkage costs. When these components change with inventory levels, so does the holding cost.

Companies usually state an item's holding cost per period of time as a percent of its value. The annual cost to maintain one unit in inventory typically ranges from 15 to 35 percent of its value. Suppose that a firm's holding cost is 20 percent. If the average value of total inventory is 20 percent of sales, the average annual cost to hold inventory is 4 percent [0.20(0.20)] of total sales. This cost is sizable in terms of gross profit margins, which often are less than 10 percent. Thus, the components of holding cost create pressures for small inventories.

inventory holding cost

The sum of the cost of capital and the variable costs of keeping items on hand, such as storage and handling, taxes, insurance, and shrinkage.

Cost of Capital   The cost of capital is the opportunity cost of investing in an asset relative to the expected return on assets of similar risk. Inventory is an asset; consequently, we should use a cost measure that adequately reflects the firm's approach to financing assets. Most firms use the *weighted average cost of capital (WACC)*, which is the average of the required return on a firm's stock equity and the interest rate on its debt, weighted by the proportion of equity and debt in its portfolio. The cost of capital usually is the largest component of holding cost, as high as 15 percent of inventory value, depending on the particular capitalization portfolio of the firm. Firms typically update the WACC on an annual basis because it is used to make many financial decisions.

Storage and Handling Costs   Inventory takes up space and must be moved into and out of storage. Storage and handling costs may be incurred when a firm rents space on either a long- or short-term basis. An inventory holding cost is incurred when a firm could use storage space productively in some other way.

Taxes, Insurance, and Shrinkage   More taxes are paid if end-of-year inventories are high, and the cost of insuring the inventories increases, too. Shrinkage takes three forms. The first, *pilferage*, or theft of inventory by customers or employees, is a significant percentage of sales for some businesses. The second form of shrinkage, called *obsolescence*, occurs when inventory cannot be used or sold at full value, owing to model changes, engineering modifications, or unexpectedly low demand. Obsolescence is a big expense in the retail clothing industry. Drastic discounts on seasonal clothing frequently must be offered on many of these products at the end of a season. Finally, *deterioration* through physical spoilage or damage due to rough or excessive material handling results in lost value. Food and beverages, for example, lose value and might even have to be discarded when their shelf life is reached. When the rate of deterioration is high, building large inventories may be unwise.

Pressures for Large Inventories

Given the costs of holding inventory, why not eliminate it altogether? Let us look briefly at the pressures related to maintaining large inventories.

Customer Service   Creating inventory can speed delivery and improve the firm's on-time delivery of goods. High inventory levels reduce the potential for stockouts and backorders, which are key concerns of wholesalers and retailers. A **stockout** is an order that cannot be satisfied, resulting in loss of the sale. A **backorder** is a customer order that cannot be filled when promised or demanded but is filled later. Customers do not like waiting for backorders to be filled. Many of them will take their business elsewhere. Sometimes, customers are given discounts for the inconvenience of waiting.

Ordering Cost   Each time a firm places a new order, it incurs an **ordering cost**, or the cost of preparing a purchase order for a supplier or a production order for manufacturing. For the same item, the ordering cost is the same, regardless of the order size. The purchasing agent must take the time to decide how much to order and, perhaps, select a supplier and negotiate terms. Time also is spent on paperwork, follow-up, and receiving the item(s). In the case of a production order for a manufactured item, a blueprint and routing instructions often must accompany the order. However, the Internet streamlines the order process and reduces the costs of placing orders.

Setup Cost   The cost involved in changing over a machine or workspace to produce a different item is the **setup cost**. It includes labor and time to make the changeover, cleaning, and sometimes new tools or equipment. Scrap or rework costs are also higher at the start of the production run. Setup cost also is independent of order size, which creates pressure to make or order a large supply of the items and hold them in inventory rather than order smaller batches.

Labor and Equipment Utilization   By creating more inventory, management can increase workforce productivity and facility utilization in three ways. First, placing larger, less frequent production orders reduces the number of unproductive setups, which add no value to a service or product. Second, holding inventory reduces the chance of the costly rescheduling of production orders because the components needed to make the product are not in inventory. Third, building inventories improves resource utilization by stabilizing the output rate when demand is cyclical or seasonal. The firm uses inventory built during slack periods to handle extra demand in peak seasons. This approach minimizes the need for extra shifts, hiring, layoffs, overtime, and additional equipment.

Transportation Cost   Sometimes, outbound transportation cost can be reduced by increasing inventory levels. Having inventory on hand allows more full-carload shipments to be made and minimizes the need to expedite shipments by more expensive modes of transportation. Inbound transportation costs can also be reduced by creating more inventory. Sometimes, several items are ordered from the same supplier. Placing these orders at the same time will increase inventories because some items will be ordered before they are actually needed; nonetheless, it may lead to rate discounts, thereby decreasing the costs of transportation and raw materials.

---

stockout

An order that cannot be satisfied, resulting in a loss of the sale.

backorder

A customer order that cannot be filled when promised or demanded but is filled later.

ordering cost

The cost of preparing a purchase order for a supplier or a production order for manufacturing.

setup cost

The cost involved in changing over a machine or workspace to produce a different item.

quantity discount

A drop in the price per unit when an order is sufficiently large.

raw materials (RM)

The inventories needed for the production of services or goods.

Metal saws, such as this one, require time to changeover from one product to the next. The depth and length of the cut must be adjusted and the blade itself may have to be changed.

GlowImages/Alamy

Payments to Suppliers   A firm often can reduce total payments to suppliers if it can tolerate higher inventory levels. Suppose that a firm learns that a key supplier is about to increase its prices. In this case, it might be cheaper for the firm to order a larger quantity than usual—in effect delaying the price increase—even though inventory will increase temporarily. A firm can also take advantage of quantity discounts this way. A **quantity discount**, whereby the price per unit drops when the order is sufficiently large, is an incentive to order larger quantities. Supplement A, "Special Inventory Models," shows how to determine order quantities in such a situation.

Types of Inventory

Inventory exists in three aggregate categories that are useful for accounting purposes. **Raw materials (RM)** are the inventories needed for the production of services or goods. They are considered to be inputs to the transformation processes of the firm. **Work-in-process (WIP)** consists of items, such as components or assemblies, needed to produce a final product in manufacturing. WIP is also present in some service operations, such as repair shops, restaurants, check-processing centers, and package delivery services. **Finished goods (FG)** in manufacturing plants, warehouses, and retail outlets are the items sold to the firm's customers. The finished goods of one firm may actually be the raw materials for another.

Raw materials, work-in-process, and finished goods inventories can all be stocked in the same facility. Modern warehouses allow for efficient inventory access.

Marcin Balcerzak/Shutterstock.com

Figure 6.2 shows how inventory can be held in different forms and at various stocking points. In this example, raw materials—the finished goods of the supplier—are held both by the supplier and the manufacturer. Raw materials at the plant pass through one or more processes, which transform them into various levels of WIP inventory. Final processing of this inventory yields finished goods inventory. Finished goods can be held at the plant, the distribution center (which may be a warehouse owned by the manufacturer or the retailer), and retail locations.

Another perspective on inventory is to classify it by how it is created. In this context, inventory takes four forms: (1) cycle, (2) safety stock, (3) anticipation, and (4) pipeline. They cannot be identified physically; that is, an inventory manager cannot look at a pile of widgets and identify which ones are cycle inventory and which ones are safety stock inventory. However, conceptually, each of the four types comes into being in an entirely different way. Once you understand these differences, you can prescribe different ways to reduce inventory, which we discuss in the next section.

> **work-in-process (WIP)**
>
> Items, such as components or assemblies, needed to produce a final product in manufacturing or service operations.

> ▼ **FIGURE 6.2**
> Inventory of Successive Stocking Points

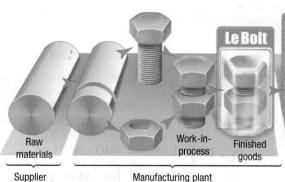
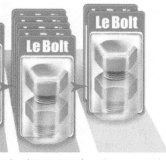

| Raw materials | Work-in-process | Finished goods | | |
| Supplier | Manufacturing plant | | Distribution center | Retailer |

Cycle Inventory   The portion of total inventory that varies directly with lot size is called **cycle inventory**. Determining how frequently to order, and in what quantity, is called **lot sizing**. Two principles apply.

1. The lot size, Q, varies directly with the elapsed time (or cycle) between orders. If a lot is ordered every 5 weeks, the average lot size must equal 5 weeks' demand.

2. The longer the time between orders for a given item, the greater the cycle inventory must be.

At the beginning of the interval, the cycle inventory is at its maximum, or Q. At the end of the interval, just before a new lot arrives, cycle inventory drops to its minimum, or 0. The average cycle inventory is the average of these two extremes:

$$\text{Average cycle inventory} = \frac{Q + 0}{2} = \frac{Q}{2}$$

> **finished goods (FG)**
>
> The items in manufacturing plants, warehouses, and retail outlets that are sold to the firm's customers.

> **cycle inventory**
>
> The portion of total inventory that varies directly with lot size.

> **lot sizing**
>
> The determination of how frequently and in what quantity to order inventory.

Pipeline inventories result from moving items and materials from one location to another. Because trains offer an economical way to transport large quantities of goods, they are a favorite choice to reduce the costs of pipeline inventories.

Susan E. Benson/Stock Connection

This formula is exact only when the demand rate is constant and uniform. However, it does provide a reasonably good estimate even when demand rates are not constant. Factors other than the demand rate (e.g., scrap losses) also may cause estimating errors when this simple formula is used.

Safety Stock Inventory To avoid customer service problems and the hidden costs of unavailable components, companies hold safety stock. **Safety stock inventory** is surplus inventory that protects against uncertainties in demand, lead time, and supply changes. Safety stocks are desirable when suppliers fail to deliver either the desired quantity on the specified date or items of acceptable quality, or when manufactured items require significant amounts of scrap or rework. Safety stock inventory ensures that operations are not disrupted when such problems occur, allowing subsequent operations to continue.

To create safety stock, a firm places an order for delivery earlier than when the item is typically needed.[1] The replenishment order therefore arrives ahead of time, giving a cushion against uncertainty. For example, suppose that the average lead time from a supplier is 3 weeks, but a firm orders 5 weeks in advance just to be safe. This policy creates a safety stock equal to a 2 weeks' supply (5 − 3).

Anticipation Inventory Inventory used to absorb uneven rates of demand or supply, which businesses often face, is referred to as **anticipation inventory**. Predictable, seasonal demand patterns lend themselves to the use of anticipation inventory. Uneven demand can motivate a manufacturer to stockpile anticipation inventory during periods of low demand so that output levels do not have to be increased much when demand peaks. Anticipation inventory also can help when suppliers are threatened with a strike or have severe capacity limitations.

Pipeline Inventory Inventory that is created when an order for an item is issued but not yet received is called **pipeline inventory**. This form of inventory exists because the firm must commit to enough inventory (on-hand plus in-transit) to cover the lead time for the order. Longer lead times or higher demands per week create more pipeline inventory. As such, the average pipeline inventory between two stocking points can be measured as the average demand during lead time, $\bar{D}_L$, which is the average demand for the item per period ($\bar{d}$) multiplied by the number of periods in the item's lead time (L) to move between the two points, or

$$\text{Pipeline inventory} = \bar{D}_L = \bar{d}L$$

The equation assumes that both $\bar{d}$ and L are constants and that L is not affected by the order or lot size, Q. Changing an item's lot size does not directly affect the average level of the pipeline inventory. Nonetheless, the lot size can *indirectly* affect pipeline inventory if it is related to the lead time. In such a case, pipeline inventory will change depending on the relationship of L to Q. Example 6.1 shows how this can happen.

$\bar{D}_L$ = avg. Demand during lead time
$\bar{d}$ = avg. demand for item per period $\times$ L = # of periods in items lead time

safety stock inventory

Surplus inventory that a company holds to protect against uncertainties in demand, lead time, and supply changes.

anticipation inventory

Inventory used to absorb uneven rates of demand or supply.

pipeline inventory

Inventory that is created when an order for an item is issued but not yet received.

EXAMPLE 6.1	**Estimating Inventory Levels**
MyOMLab Tutor 6.1 in MyOMLab provides a new example to practice the estimation of inventory levels.	A plant makes monthly shipments of electric drills to a wholesaler in average lot sizes of 280 drills. The wholesaler's average demand is 70 drills a week, and the lead time from the plant is 3 weeks. The wholesaler must pay for the inventory from the moment the plant makes a shipment. If the wholesaler is willing to increase its purchase quantity to 350 units, the plant will give priority to the wholesaler and guarantee a lead time of only 2 weeks. What is the effect on the wholesaler's cycle and pipeline inventories?

---

[1] When orders are placed at fixed intervals, a second way to create safety stock is used. Each new order placed is larger than the quantity typically needed through the next delivery date.

SOLUTION

The wholesaler's current cycle and pipeline inventories are

$$\text{Cycle inventory} = \frac{Q}{2} = \frac{280}{2} = 140 \text{ drills}$$

$$\text{Pipeline inventory} = \overline{D}_L = \overline{d}L = (70 \text{ drills/week})(3 \text{ weeks}) = 210 \text{ drills}$$

Figure 6.3 shows the cycle and pipeline inventories if the wholesaler accepts the new proposal.

1. Enter the average lot size, average demand during a period, and the number of periods of lead time:

Average lot size	350
Average demand	70
Lead time	2

2. To compute cycle inventory, simply divide average lot size by 2. To compute pipeline inventory, multiply average demand by lead time:

Cycle inventory	175
Pipeline inventory	140

◀ **FIGURE 6.3**
Estimating Inventory Levels Using Tutor 6.1

DECISION POINT

The effect of the new proposal on cycle inventories is to increase them by 35 units, or 25 percent. The reduction in pipeline inventories, however, is 70 units, or 33 percent. The proposal would reduce the total investment in cycle and pipeline inventories. Also, it is advantageous to have shorter lead times because the wholesaler only has to commit to purchases 2 weeks in advance, rather than 3 weeks.

Inventory Reduction Tactics

Managers always are eager to find cost-effective ways to reduce inventory in supply chains. Later in this chapter we examine various ways for finding optimal lot sizes. Here, we discuss something more fundamental—the basic tactics (which we call *levers*) for reducing inventory in supply chains. A primary lever is one that must be activated if inventory is to be reduced. A secondary lever reduces the penalty cost of applying the primary lever and the need for having inventory in the first place.

Cycle Inventory   The primary lever to reduce cycle inventory is simply to reduce the lot sizes of items moving in the supply chain. However, making such reductions in Q without making any other changes can be devastating. For example, setup costs or ordering costs can skyrocket. If these changes occur, two secondary levers can be used:

1. Streamline the methods for placing orders and making setups in order to reduce ordering and setup costs and allow Q to be reduced. This may involve redesigning the infrastructure for information flows or improving manufacturing processes.

2. Increase repeatability to eliminate the need for changeovers. **Repeatability** is the degree to which the same work can be done again. Repeatability can be increased through high product demand; the use of specialization; the devotion of resources exclusively to a product; the use of the same part in many different products; the use of *flexible automation*; the use of the *one-worker, multiple-machines* concept; or through *group technology*. Increased repeatability may justify new setup methods, reduce transportation costs, and allow quantity discounts from suppliers.

repeatability
The degree to which the same work can be done again.

Safety Stock Inventory   The primary lever to reduce safety stock inventory is to place orders closer to the time when they must be received. However, this approach can lead to unacceptable customer service unless demand, supply, and delivery uncertainties can be minimized. Four secondary levers can be used in this case:

1. Improve demand forecasts so that fewer surprises come from customers. Design the mechanisms to increase collaboration with customers to get advanced warnings for changes in demand levels.

2. Cut the lead times of purchased or produced items to reduce demand uncertainty. For example, local suppliers with short lead times could be selected whenever possible.

3. Reduce supply uncertainties. Suppliers are likely to be more reliable if production plans are shared with them. Put in place the mechanisms to increase collaboration with suppliers.

Surprises from unexpected scrap or rework can be reduced by improving manufacturing processes. Preventive maintenance can minimize unexpected downtime caused by equipment failure.

4. Rely more on equipment and labor buffers, such as capacity cushions and cross-trained workers. These buffers are important to businesses in the service sector because they generally cannot inventory their services.

Anticipation Inventory   The primary lever to reduce anticipation inventory is simply to match demand rate with production rate. Secondary levers can be used to even out customer demand in one of the following ways:

1. Add new products with different demand cycles so that a peak in the demand for one product compensates for the seasonal low for another.

2. Provide off-season promotional campaigns.

3. Offer seasonal pricing plans.

Pipeline Inventory   An operations manager has direct control over lead times but not demand rates. Because pipeline inventory is a function of demand during the lead time, the primary lever is to reduce the lead time. Two secondary levers can help managers cut lead times:

1. Find more responsive suppliers and select new carriers for shipments between stocking locations or improve materials handling within the plant. Improving the information system could overcome information delays between a distribution center and retailer.

2. Change Q in those cases where the lead time depends on the lot size.

ABC Analysis

stock-keeping unit (SKU)

An individual item or product that has an identifying code and is held in inventory somewhere along the supply chain.

ABC analysis

The process of dividing SKUs into three classes, according to their dollar usage, so that managers can focus on items that have the highest dollar value.

Thousands of items, often referred to as stock-keeping units, are held in inventory by a typical organization, but only a small percentage of them deserve management's closest attention and tightest control. A **stock-keeping unit (SKU)** is an individual item or product that has an identifying code and is held in inventory somewhere along the supply chain. **ABC analysis** is the process of dividing SKUs into three classes according to their dollar usage so that managers can focus on items that have the highest dollar value. This method is the equivalent of creating a *Pareto chart* except that it is applied to inventory rather than to process errors. As Figure 6.4 shows, class A items typically represent only about 20 percent of the SKUs but account for 80 percent of the dollar usage. Class B items account for another 30 percent of the SKUs but only 15 percent of the dollar usage. Finally, 50 percent of the SKUs fall in class C, representing a mere 5 percent of the dollar usage. The goal of ABC analysis is to identify the class A SKUs so management can control their inventory levels.

The analysis begins by multiplying the annual demand rate for an SKU by the dollar value (cost) of one unit of that SKU to determine its dollar usage. After ranking the SKUs on the basis of dollar usage and creating the Pareto chart, the analyst looks for "natural" changes in slope. The dividing lines in Figure 6.4 between classes are inexact. Class A SKUs could be somewhat higher or lower than 20 percent of all SKUs but normally account for the bulk of the dollar usage.

Class A SKUs are reviewed frequently to reduce the average lot size and to ensure timely deliveries from suppliers. It is important to maintain high inventory turnover for these items. By contrast, class B SKUs require an intermediate level of control. Here, less frequent monitoring of suppliers coupled with adequate safety stocks can provide cost-effective coverage of demands. For class C SKUs, much looser control is appropriate. While a stockout of a class C SKU can be as crucial as for a class A SKU, the inventory holding cost of class C SKUs tends to be low. These features suggest that higher inventory levels can be tolerated and that more safety stock and larger lot sizes may suffice for class C SKUs. See Solved Problem 2 for a detailed example of ABC analysis.

Creating ABC inventory classifications is useless unless inventory records are accurate. Technology can help; many companies are tracking inventory wherever it exists in the supply chain. Chips imbedded in product packaging contain information on the product and send signals that can be accessed by sensitive receivers and transmitted to a central location for processing. There are other, less sophisticated approaches of achieving accuracy that can be used. One way is to assign responsibility to specific employees for issuing and receiving materials and accurately reporting each transaction. Another method is to secure inventory behind locked doors or gates to prevent unauthorized

▼ **FIGURE 6.4**
Typical Chart Using ABC Analysis

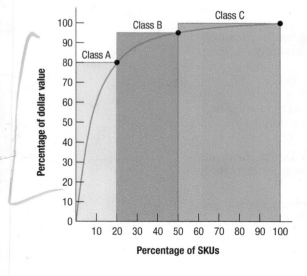

or unreported withdrawals. This method also guards against accidentally storing newly received inventory in the wrong locations, where it can be lost for months. **Cycle counting** can also be used, whereby storeroom personnel physically count a small percentage of the total number of SKUs each day, correcting errors that they find. Class A SKUs are counted most frequently. A final method, for computerized systems, is to make logic error checks on each transaction reported and fully investigate any discrepancies. The discrepancies can include (1) actual receipts when no receipts are scheduled, (2) disbursements that exceed the current on-hand inventory balance, and (3) receipts with an inaccurate (nonexistent) SKU number.

Now that we have identified the inventory items deserving of most attention, we devote the remainder of the chapter to the decisions of how much to order and when.

cycle counting

An inventory control method, whereby storeroom personnel physically count a small percentage of the total number of items each day, correcting errors that they find.

Economic Order Quantity

Supply chain managers face conflicting pressures to keep inventories low enough to avoid excess inventory holding costs but high enough to reduce ordering and setup costs. *Inventory holding cost* is the sum of the cost of capital and the variable costs of keeping items on hand, such as storage and handling, taxes, insurance, and shrinkage. *Ordering cost* is the cost of preparing a purchase order for a supplier or a production order for the shop, while *setup cost* is the cost of changing over a machine to produce a different item. In this section, we will address the *cycle inventory*, which is that portion of total inventory that varies directly with lot size. A good starting point for balancing these conflicting pressures and determining the best cycle-inventory level for an item is finding the **economic order quantity (EOQ)**, which is the lot size that minimizes total annual cycle-inventory holding and ordering costs. The approach to determining the EOQ is based on the following assumptions:

economic order quantity (EOQ)

The lot size that minimizes total annual inventory holding and ordering costs.

1. The demand rate for the item is constant (for example, always 10 units per day) and known with certainty.

2. No constraints are placed (such as truck capacity or materials handling limitations) on the size of each lot.

3. The only two relevant costs are the inventory holding cost and the fixed cost per lot for ordering or setup.

4. Decisions for one item can be made independently of decisions for other items. In other words, no advantage is gained in combining several orders going to the same supplier.

5. The lead time is constant (e.g., always 14 days) and known with certainty. The amount received is exactly what was ordered and it arrives all at once rather than piecemeal.

The economic order quantity will be optimal when all five assumptions are satisfied. In reality, few situations are so simple. Nonetheless, the EOQ is often a reasonable approximation of the appropriate lot size, even when several of the assumptions do not quite apply. Here are some guidelines on when to use or modify the EOQ.

- **Do not use the EOQ**
  - If you use the "make-to-order" strategy and your customer specifies that the entire order be delivered in one shipment
  - If the order size is constrained by capacity limitations such as the size of the firm's ovens, amount of testing equipment, or number of delivery trucks
- **Modify the EOQ**
  - If significant quantity discounts are given for ordering larger lots
  - If replenishment of the inventory is not instantaneous, which can happen if the items must be used or sold as soon as they are finished without waiting until the entire lot has been completed (see Supplement C, "Special Inventory Models," for several useful modifications to the EOQ)
- **Use the EOQ**
  - If you follow a "make-to-stock" strategy and the item has relatively stable demand
  - If your carrying costs per unit and setup or ordering costs are known and relatively stable

The EOQ was never intended to be an optimizing tool. Nonetheless, if you need to determine a reasonable lot size, it can be helpful in many situations.

Calculating the EOQ

We begin by formulating the total cost for any lot size Q for a given SKU. Next, we derive the EOQ, which is the Q that minimizes total annual cycle-inventory cost. Finally, we describe how to convert the EOQ into a companion measure, the elapsed time between orders.

When the EOQ assumptions are satisfied, cycle inventory behaves as shown in Figure 6.5. A cycle begins with Q units held in inventory, which happens when a new order is received. During the cycle, on-hand inventory is used at a constant rate and, because demand is known with certainty and the lead time is a constant, a new lot can be ordered so that inventory falls to 0 precisely when the new lot is received. Because inventory varies uniformly between Q and 0, the average cycle inventory equals half the lot size, Q.

FIGURE 6.5 ▶
Cycle-Inventory Levels

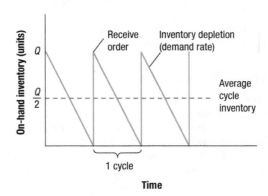

The annual holding cost for this amount of inventory, which increases linearly with Q, as Figure 6.6(a) shows, is

$$\text{Annual holding cost} = (\text{Average cycle inventory})(\text{Unit holding cost})$$

The annual ordering cost is

$$\text{Annual ordering cost} = (\text{Number of orders/Year})(\text{Ordering or setup cost})$$

The average number of orders per year equals annual demand divided by Q. For example, if 1,200 units must be ordered each year and the average lot size is 100 units, then 12 orders will be placed during the year. The annual ordering or setup cost decreases nonlinearly as Q increases, as shown in Figure 6.6(b), because fewer orders are placed.

FIGURE 6.6 ▶
Graphs of Annual
Holding, Ordering,
and Total Costs

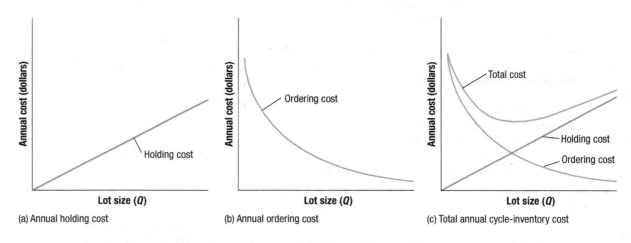

(a) Annual holding cost   (b) Annual ordering cost   (c) Total annual cycle-inventory cost

The total annual cycle-inventory cost,[2] as graphed in Figure 6.6(c), is the sum of the two cost components:

$$\text{Total cost} = \text{Annual holding cost} + \text{Annual ordering or setup cost}[3]$$

$$C = \frac{Q}{2}(H) + \frac{D}{Q}(S)$$

---

[2] Expressing the total cost on an annual basis usually is convenient (although not necessary). Any time horizon can be selected as long as D and H cover the same time period. If the total cost is calculated on a monthly basis, D must be monthly demand and H must be the cost of holding a unit for 1 month.

[3] The number of orders actually placed in any year is always a whole number, although the formula allows the use of fractional values. However, rounding is not needed because what is being calculated is an average for multiple years. Such averages often are nonintegers.

where

C = total annual cycle-inventory cost

Q = lot size, in units

H = cost of holding one unit in inventory for a year, often expressed as a percentage of the item's value

D = annual demand, in units per year

S = cost of ordering or setting up one lot, in dollars per lot

EXAMPLE 6.2	The Cost of a Lot-Sizing Policy

A museum of natural history opened a gift shop two years ago. Managing inventories has become a problem. Low inventory turnover is squeezing profit margins and causing cash-flow problems.

One of the top-selling SKUs in the container group at the museum's gift shop is a bird feeder. Sales are 18 units per week, and the supplier charges $60 per unit. The cost of placing an order with the supplier is $45. Annual holding cost is 25 percent of a feeder's value, and the museum operates 52 weeks per year. Management chose a 390-unit lot size so that new orders could be placed less frequently. What is the annual cycle-inventory cost of the current policy of using a 390-unit lot size? Would a lot size of 468 be better?

SOLUTION

We begin by computing the annual demand and holding cost as

$$D = (18 \text{ units/week})(52 \text{ weeks/year}) = 936 \text{ units}$$

$$H = 0.25(\$60/\text{unit}) = \$15$$

The total annual cycle-inventory cost for the current policy is

$$C = \frac{Q}{2}(H) + \frac{D}{Q}(S)$$

$$= \frac{390}{2}(\$15) + \frac{936}{390}(\$45) = \$2{,}925 + \$108 = \$3{,}033$$

The total annual cycle-inventory cost for the alternative lot size is

$$C = \frac{468}{2}(\$15) + \frac{936}{468}(\$45) = \$3{,}510 + \$90 = \$3{,}600$$

DECISION POINT

The lot size of 468 units, which is a half-year supply, would be a more expensive option than the current policy. The savings in ordering costs are more than offset by the increase in holding costs. Management should use the total annual cycle-inventory cost function to explore other lot-size alternatives.

Figure 6.7 displays the impact of using several Q values for the bird feeder in Example 6.2. Eight different lot sizes were evaluated in addition to the current one. Both holding and ordering costs were plotted, but their sum—the total annual cycle-inventory cost curve—is the important feature. The graph shows that the best lot size, or EOQ, is the lowest point on the total annual cost curve, or between 50 and 100 units. Obviously, reducing the current lot-size policy ($Q = 390$) can result in significant savings.

A more efficient approach is to use the EOQ formula:

$$EOQ = \sqrt{\frac{2DS}{H}}$$

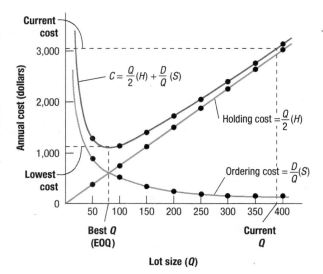

◀ **FIGURE 6.7**
Total Annual Cycle-Inventory Cost Function for the Bird Feeder

We use calculus to obtain the EOQ formula from the total annual cycle-inventory cost function. We take the first derivative of the total annual cycle-inventory cost function with respect to Q, set it equal to 0, and solve for Q. As Figure 6.7 indicates, the EOQ is the order quantity for which annual holding cost equals annual ordering cost. Using this insight, we can also obtain the EOQ formula by equating the formulas for annual ordering cost and annual holding cost and solving for Q. The graph in Figure 6.7 also reveals that when the annual holding cost for any Q exceeds the annual ordering cost, as with the 390-unit order, we can immediately conclude that Q is too high. A lower Q reduces holding cost and increases ordering cost, bringing them into balance. Similarly, if the annual ordering cost exceeds the annual holding cost, Q should be increased.

Sometimes, inventory policies are based on the time between replenishment orders, rather than on the number of units in the lot size. The **time between orders (TBO)** for a particular lot size is the average elapsed time between receiving (or placing) replenishment orders of Q units. Expressed as a fraction of a year, the TBO is simply Q divided by annual demand. When we use the EOQ and express time in terms of months, the TBO is

time between orders (TBO)

The average elapsed time between receiving (or placing) replenishment orders of Q units for a particular lot size.

$$\text{TBO}_{\text{EOQ}} = \frac{\text{EOQ}}{D}\ (12 \text{ months/year})$$

In Example 6.3, we show how to calculate TBO for years, months, weeks, and days.

EXAMPLE 6.3	**Finding the EOQ, Total Cost, and TBO**

MyOMLab

Tutor 6.2 in MyOMLab provides a new example to practice the application of the EOQ model.

MyOMLab

Active Model 6.1 in MyOMLab provides additional insight on the EOQ model and its uses.

FIGURE 6.8 ▶

Total Annual Cycle-Inventory Costs Based on EOQ Using Tutor 6.3

For the bird feeder in Example 6.2, calculate the EOQ and its total annual cycle-inventory cost. How frequently will orders be placed if the EOQ is used?

SOLUTION

Using the formulas for EOQ and annual cost, we get

$$\text{EOQ} = \sqrt{\frac{2DS}{H}} = \sqrt{\frac{2(936)(45)}{15}} = 74.94, \text{ or } 75 \text{ units}$$

Figure 6.8 shows that the total annual cost is much less than the $3,033 cost of the current policy of placing 390-unit orders.

Parameters				
Current Lot Size (Q)	390		Economic Order Quantity	75
Demand (D)	936			
Order Cost (S)	$45			
Unit Holding Cost (H)	$15			

Annual Costs		Annual Costs based on EOQ	
Orders per Year	2.4	Orders per Year	12.48
Annual Ordering Cost	$108.00	Annual Ordering Cost	$561.60
Annual Holding Cost	$2,925.00	Annual Holding Cost	$562.50
Annual Inventory Cost	$3,033.00	Annual Inventory Cost	$1,124.10

When the EOQ is used, the TBO can be expressed in various ways for the same time period.

$$\text{TBO}_{\text{EOQ}} = \frac{\text{EOQ}}{D} = \frac{75}{936} = 0.080 \text{ year}$$

$$\text{TBO}_{\text{EOQ}} = \frac{\text{EOQ}}{D}(12 \text{ months/year}) = \frac{75}{936}(12) = 0.96 \text{ month}$$

$$\text{TBO}_{\text{EOQ}} = \frac{\text{EOQ}}{D}(52 \text{ weeks/year}) = \frac{75}{936}(52) = 4.17 \text{ weeks}$$

$$\text{TBO}_{\text{EOQ}} = \frac{\text{EOQ}}{D}(365 \text{ days/year}) = \frac{75}{936}(365) = 29.25 \text{ days}$$

DECISION POINT

Using the EOQ, about 12 orders per year will be required. Using the current policy of 390 units per order, an average of 2.4 orders will be needed each year (every 5 months). The current policy saves on ordering costs but incurs a much higher cost for carrying the cycle inventory. Although it is easy to see which option is best on the basis of total ordering and holding costs, other factors may affect the final decision. For example, if the supplier would reduce the price per unit for large orders, it may be better to order the larger quantity.

Managerial Insights from the EOQ

Subjecting the EOQ formula to *sensitivity analysis* can yield valuable insights into the management of inventories. Sensitivity analysis is a technique for systematically changing crucial parameters to determine the effects of a change. Table 6.1 shows the effects on the EOQ when we substitute different values into the numerator or denominator of the formula.

TABLE 6.1 | SENSITIVITY ANALYSIS OF THE EOQ

Parameter	EOQ	Parameter Change	EOQ Change	Comments
Demand	$\sqrt{\dfrac{2DS}{H}}$	↑	↑	Increase in lot size is in proportion to the square root of D.
Order/Setup Costs	$\sqrt{\dfrac{2DS}{H}}$	↓	↓	Weeks of supply decreases and inventory turnover increases because the lot size decreases.
Holding Costs	$\sqrt{\dfrac{2DS}{H}}$	↓	↑	Larger lots are justified when holding costs decrease.

As Table 6.1 shows, the EOQ provides support for some of the intuition you may have about inventory management. However, the effect of ordering or setup cost changes on inventories is especially important for *lean systems*. This relationship explains why manufacturers are so concerned about reducing setup time and costs; it makes small lot production economic. Actually, lean systems provide an environment conducive to the use of the EOQ. For example, yearly, monthly, daily, or hourly demand rates are known with reasonable certainty in lean systems, and the rate of demand is relatively uniform. Lean systems may have few process constraints if the firm practices *constraint management*. In addition, lean systems strive for constant delivery lead times and dependable delivery quantities from suppliers, both of which are assumptions of the EOQ. Consequently, the EOQ as a lot sizing tool is quite compatible with the principles of lean systems.

Inventory Control Systems

The EOQ and other lot-sizing methods answer the important question: *How much* should we order? Another important question that needs an answer is: *When* should we place the order? An inventory control system responds to both questions. In selecting an inventory control system for a particular application, the nature of the demands imposed on the inventory items is crucial. An important distinction between types of inventory is whether an item is subject to dependent or independent demand. Retailers, such as JCPenney, and distributors must manage **independent demand items**—that is, items for which demand is influenced by market conditions and is not related to the inventory decisions for any other item held in stock or produced. Independent demand inventory includes

- Wholesale and retail merchandise
- Service support inventory, such as stamps and mailing labels for post offices, office supplies for law firms, and laboratory supplies for research universities
- Product and replacement-part distribution inventories
- Maintenance, repair, and operating (MRO) supplies—that is, items that do not become part of the final service or product, such as employee uniforms, fuel, paint, and machine repair parts

Managing independent demand inventory can be tricky because demand is influenced by external factors. For example, the owner of a bookstore may not be sure how many copies of the latest best-seller novel customers will purchase during the coming month. As a result, the manager may decide to stock extra copies as a safeguard. Independent demand, such as the demand for various book titles, must be *forecasted*.

In this chapter, we focus on inventory control systems for independent demand items, which is the type of demand the bookstore owner, other retailers, service providers, and distributors face. Even though demand from any one customer is difficult to predict, low demand from some customers for a particular item often is offset by high demand from others. Thus, total demand for any independent demand item may follow a relatively smooth pattern, with some random fluctuations. *Dependent demand items* are those required as components or inputs to a service or

independent demand items
Items for which demand is influenced by market conditions and is not related to the inventory decisions for any other item held in stock or produced.

Aurelia Ventura/La Opinion/Newscom

Retailers typically face independent demands for their products. Here shoppers look for bargains at a JCPenney store in the Glendale Galleria in California.

product. Dependent demand exhibits a pattern very different from that of independent demand and must be managed with different techniques (see Chapter 5, "Resource Planning").

In this section, we discuss and compare two inventory control systems: (1) the continuous review system, called a *Q* system, and (2) the periodic review system, called a *P* system. We close with a look at hybrid systems, which incorporate features of both the *P* and *Q* systems.

Continuous Review System

A **continuous review (*Q*) system**, sometimes called a **reorder point (ROP) system** or *fixed order-quantity system*, tracks the remaining inventory of a SKU each time a withdrawal is made to determine whether it is time to reorder. In practice, these reviews are done frequently (e.g., daily) and often continuously (after each withdrawal). The advent of computers and electronic cash registers linked to inventory records has made continuous reviews easy. At each review, a decision is made about a SKU's inventory

continuous review (*Q*) system

A system designed to track the remaining inventory of a SKU each time a withdrawal is made to determine whether it is time to reorder.

reorder point (ROP) system

See continuous review (*Q*) system.

inventory position (IP)

The measurement of a SKU's ability to satisfy future demand.

scheduled receipts (SR)

Orders that have been placed but have not yet been received.

open orders

See scheduled receipts (SR).

reorder point (*R*)

The predetermined minimum level that an inventory position must reach before a fixed quantity *Q* of the SKU is ordered.

position. If it is judged to be too low, the system triggers a new order. The **inventory position (IP)** measures the SKU's ability to satisfy future demand. It includes **scheduled receipts (SR)**, which are orders that have been placed but have not yet been received, plus on-hand inventory (OH) minus backorders (BO). Sometimes. scheduled receipts are called **open orders**. More specifically,

$$\text{Inventory position} = \text{On-hand inventory} + \text{Scheduled receipts} - \text{Backorders}$$

$$\text{IP} = \text{OH} + \text{SR} - \text{BO}$$

When the inventory position reaches a predetermined minimum level, called the **reorder point (*R*)**, a fixed quantity *Q* of the SKU is ordered. In a continuous review system, although the order quantity *Q* is fixed, the time between orders can vary. Hence, *Q* can be based on the EOQ, a price break quantity (the minimum lot size that qualifies for a quantity discount), a container size (such as a truckload), or some other quantity selected by management.

Selecting the Reorder Point When Demand and Lead Time Are Constant   To demonstrate the concept of a reorder point, suppose that the demand for feeders at the museum gift shop in Example 6.3 is always 18 per week, the lead time is a constant 2 weeks, and the supplier always ships the exact number ordered on time. With both demand and lead time constant, the museum's buyer can wait until the inventory position drops to 36 units, or (18 units/week) (2 weeks), to place a new order. Thus, in this case, the reorder point, *R*, equals the *total demand during lead time*, with no added allowance for safety stock.

Figure 6.9 shows how the system operates when demand and lead time are constant. The downward-sloping line represents the on-hand inventory, which is being depleted at a constant rate. When it reaches reorder point *R* (the horizontal line), a new order for *Q* units is placed. The on-hand inventory continues to drop throughout lead time *L* until the order is received. At that time, which marks the end of the lead time, on-hand inventory jumps by *Q* units. A new order arrives just when inventory drops to 0. The TBO is the same for each cycle.

The inventory position, IP, shown in Figure 6.9 corresponds to the on-hand inventory, except during the lead time. Just after a new order is placed, at the start of the lead time, IP increases by *Q*, as shown by the dashed line. The IP exceeds OH by this same margin

FIGURE 6.9 ▶

Q System When Demand and Lead Time Are Constant and Certain

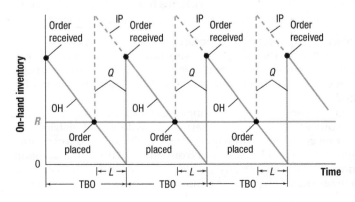

throughout the lead time.[4] At the end of the lead time, when the scheduled receipts convert to on-hand inventory, IP = OH once again. The key point here is to compare IP, not OH, with R in deciding whether to reorder. A common error is to ignore scheduled receipts or backorders.

EXAMPLE 6.4	**Placing a New Order When Demand and Lead Time Are Constant**

Demand for chicken soup at a supermarket is always 25 cases a day and the lead time is always 4 days. The shelves were just restocked with chicken soup, leaving an on-hand inventory of only 10 cases. No backorders currently exist, but there is one open order in the pipeline for 200 cases. What is the inventory position? Should a new order be placed?

SOLUTION

$$R = \text{Total demand during lead time} = (25)(4) = 100 \text{ cases}$$
$$IP = OH + SR - BO$$
$$= 10 + 200 - 0 = 210 \text{ cases}$$

DECISION POINT

Because IP exceeds R (210 versus 100), do not reorder. Inventory is almost depleted, but a new order need not be placed because the scheduled receipt is in the pipeline.

Selecting the Reorder Point When Demand Is Variable and Lead Time Is Constant   In reality demand is not always predictable. For instance, the museum's buyer knows that *average* demand is 18 feeders per week. That is, a variable number of feeders may be purchased during the lead time, with an average demand during lead time of 36 feeders (assuming that each week's demand is identically distributed and lead time is a constant 2 weeks). This situation gives rise to the need for safety stocks. Suppose that the museum's buyer sets R at 46 units, thereby placing orders before they typically are needed. This approach will create a safety stock, or stock held in excess of expected demand, of 10 units (46 − 36) to buffer against uncertain demand. In general

$$\text{Reorder point} = \text{Average demand during lead time} + \text{Safety stock}$$

$$= \overline{d}L + \text{safety stock}$$

where

$$\overline{d} = \text{average demand per week (or day or month)}$$

$$L = \text{constant lead tome in weeks (or days or months)}$$

Figure 6.10 shows how the Q system operates when demand is variable and lead time is constant. The wavy downward-sloping line indicates that demand varies from day to day. Its slope is steeper in the second cycle, which means that the demand rate is higher during this time period. The changing demand rate means that the time between orders changes, so $TBO_1 \neq TBO_2 \neq TBO_3$. Because of uncertain demand, sales during the lead time are unpredictable, and safety stock is added to hedge against lost sales. This addition is why R is higher in Figure 6.10 than in Figure 6.9. It also explains why the on-hand inventory usually does not drop to 0 by the time a replenishment order arrives. The greater the safety stock and thus the higher reorder point R, the less likely a stockout.

Because the average demand during lead time is variable, the real decision to be made when selecting R concerns the safety stock level. Deciding on a small or large safety stock is a trade-off between customer service and inventory holding costs. Cost minimization models can be used to find the best safety stock, but they require estimates of stockout and back-order costs, which are usually difficult to make with any precision because it is hard to estimate the effect of lost sales, lost customer confidence, future loyalty of customers, and market share because the customer went to a competitor. The usual approach for determining R is for management—based on

▼ **FIGURE 6.10**
Q System When Demand Is Uncertain

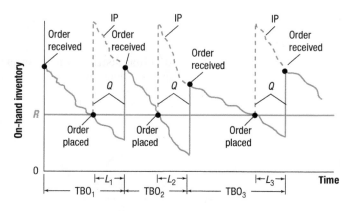

---

[4]A possible exception is the unlikely situation when more than one scheduled receipt is open at the same time because of long lead times.

judgment—to set a reasonable service-level policy for the inventory and then determine the safety stock level that satisfies this policy. There are three steps to arrive at a reorder point:

1. Choose an appropriate service-level policy.

2. Determine the distribution of demand during lead time.

3. Determine the safety stock and reorder point levels.

Step 1: Service level policy Select a **service level**, or **cycle-service level** (the desired probability of not running out of stock in any one ordering cycle), which begins at the time an order is placed and ends when it arrives in stock. The intent is to provide coverage over the **protection interval**, or the period over which safety stock must protect the user from running out of stock. For the Q system, the lead time is the protection interval. For example, in a bookstore the manager may select a 90 percent cycle-service level for a book. In other words, the probability is 90 percent that demand will not exceed the supply during the lead time. The probability of running short *during the protection interval*, creating a stockout or backorder, is only 10 percent $(100 - 90)$ in our example. This stockout risk, which occurs only during the lead time in the Q system, is greater than the overall risk of a stockout because the risk is nonexistent outside the ordering cycle.

Step 2: Distribution of demand during lead time Determine the distribution of demand during lead time, which requires the specification of its mean and standard deviation. To translate a cycle-service level policy into a specific safety stock level, we must know how demand during the lead time is distributed. If demand and lead times vary little around their averages, the safety stock can be small. Conversely, if they vary greatly from one order cycle to the next, the safety stock must be large. Variability is measured by the distribution of demand during lead time. Sometimes, average demand during the lead time and the standard deviation of demand during the lead time are not directly available and must be calculated by combining information on the demand rate with information on the lead time. Suppose that lead time is constant and demand is variable, but records on demand are not collected for a time interval that is exactly the same as the lead time. The same inventory control system may be used to manage thousands of different SKUs, each with a different lead time. For example, if demand is reported *weekly*, these records can be used directly to compute the average and the standard deviation of demand during the lead time if the lead time is exactly 1 week. However, if the lead time is 3 weeks, the computation is more difficult.

We can determine the demand during the lead time distribution by making some reasonable assumptions. Suppose that the average demand, $\overline{d}$, is known along with the standard deviation of demand, σ_d, over some time interval such as days or weeks. Also, suppose that the probability distributions of demand for each time interval are identical and independent of each other. For example, if the time interval is a week, the probability distributions of demand are assumed to be the same each week (identical $\overline{d}$ and σ_d), and the total demand in 1 week does not affect the total demand in another week. Let L be the constant lead time, expressed in the same time units as the demand. Under these assumptions, average demand during the lead time will be the sum of the averages for each of the L identical and independent distributions of demand, or $\overline{d} + \overline{d} + \overline{d} + \ldots = \overline{d}L$. In addition, the variance of the distribution of demand during lead time will be the sum of the variances of the L identical and independent distributions of demand, or

$$\sigma_d^2 + \sigma_d^2 + \sigma_d^2 + \ldots = \sigma_d^2 L$$

Finally, the standard deviation of the distribution of demand during lead time is

$$\sigma_{dLT} = \sqrt{\sigma_d^2 L} = \sigma_d \sqrt{L}$$

Figure 6.11 shows how the demand distribution of the lead time is developed from the individual distributions of weekly demands, where $\overline{d} = 75$, $\sigma_d = 15$, and $L = 3$. In this example, average demand during the lead time is $(75)(3) = 225$ units and $\sigma_{dLT} = 15\sqrt{3} = 25.98$.

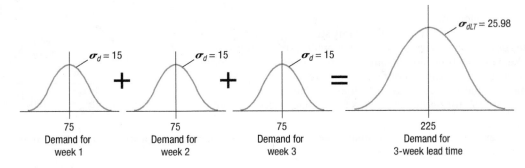

service level

The desired probability of not running out of stock in any one ordering cycle, which begins at the time an order is placed and ends when it arrives in stock.

cycle-service level

See service level.

protection interval

The period over which safety stock must protect the user from running out of stock.

FIGURE 6.11 ▶
Development of Distribution of Demand During Lead Time

Step 3: Safety stock and reorder point   When selecting the safety stock, the inventory planner often assumes that demand during the lead time is normally distributed, as shown in Figure 6.12.

The average demand during the lead time is the centerline of the graph, with 50 percent of the area under the curve to the left and 50 percent to the right. Thus, if a cycle-service level of 50 percent were chosen, the reorder point R would be the quantity represented by this centerline. Because R equals the average demand during the lead time plus the safety stock, the safety stock is 0 when R equals this average demand. Demand is less than average 50 percent of the time and, thus, having no safety stock will be sufficient only 50 percent of the time.

To provide a service level above 50 percent, the reorder point must be higher than the average demand during the lead time. As Figure 6.12 shows, that requires moving the reorder point to the right of the centerline so that more than 50 percent of the area under the curve is to the left of R. An 85 percent cycle-service level is achieved in Figure 6.12 with 85 percent of the area under the curve to the left of R (in **blue**) and only 15 percent to the right (in pink). We compute the safety stock as follows:

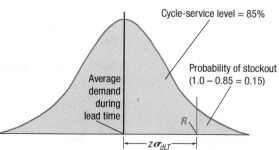

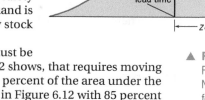

▲ **FIGURE 6.12**
Finding Safety Stock with Normal Probability Distribution for an 85 Percent Cycle-Service Level

$$\text{Safety stock} = z\,\sigma_{dLT}$$

where

  $z =$ the number of standard deviations needed to achieve the cycle-service level

  $\sigma_{dLT} =$ standard deviation of demand during the lead time

The reorder point becomes

$$R = \bar{d}L + \text{safety stock}$$

The higher the value of z, the higher the safety stock and the cycle-service level should be. If $z = 0$, there is no safety stock, and stockouts will occur during 50 percent of the order cycles. For a cycle-service level of 85 percent, $z = 1.04$. Example 6.5 shows how to use the Normal Distribution appendix to find the appropriate z value, safety stock, and reorder point.

EXAMPLE 6.5	**Reorder Point for Variable Demand and Constant Lead Time**

Let us return to the bird feeder in Example 6.3. The EOQ is 75 units. Suppose that the average demand is 18 units per week with a standard deviation of 5 units. The lead time is constant at 2 weeks. Determine the safety stock and reorder point if management wants a 90 percent cycle-service level.

MyOMLab
Tutor 6.3 in MyOMLab provides a new example to determine the safety stock and the reorder point for a Q system.

SOLUTION
In this case, $\sigma_d = 5$, $\bar{d} = 18$ units, and $L = 2$ weeks, so $\sigma_{dLT} = \sigma_d\sqrt{L} = 5\sqrt{2} = 7.07$. Consult the body of the table in the Normal Distribution appendix for 0.9000, which corresponds to a 90 percent cycle-service level. The closest number is 0.8997, which corresponds to 1.2 in the row heading and 0.08 in the column heading. Adding these values gives a z value of 1.28. With this information, we calculate the safety stock and reorder point as follows:

$$\text{Safety stock} = z\sigma_{dLT} = 1.28(7.07) = 9.05, \text{ or } 9 \text{ units}$$
$$\text{Reorder point} = \bar{d}L + \text{Safety stock}$$
$$= 2(18) + 9 = 45 \text{ units}$$

DECISION POINT
The Q system for the bird feeder operates as follows: Whenever the inventory position reaches 45 units, order the EOQ of 75 units. Various order quantities and safety stock levels can be used in a Q system. For example, management could specify a different order quantity (because of shipping constraints) or a different safety stock (because of storage limitations).

Selecting the Reorder Point When Both Demand and Lead Time Are Variable   In practice, it is often the case that both the demand and the lead time are variable. Unfortunately, the equations for the safety stock and reorder point become more complicated. In the model below we make two simplifying assumptions. First, the demand distribution and the lead time distribution are measured in the same time units. For example, both demand and lead time are measured in weeks. Second, demand and lead time are *independent*. That is, demand per week is not affected by the length of the lead time.

$$\text{Safety stock} = z\sigma_{dLT}$$

$$R = (\text{Average weekly demand} \times \text{Average lead time in weeks}) + \text{Safety stock}$$

$$= \overline{d}\,\overline{L} + \text{Safety stock}$$

where

$$\overline{d} = \text{Average weekly (or daily or monthly) demand}$$

$$\overline{L} = \text{Average weekly (or daily or monthly) lead time}$$

$$\sigma_d = \text{Standard deviation of weekly (or daily or monthly) demand}$$

$$\sigma_{LT} = \text{Standard deviation of the lead time, and}$$

$$\sigma_{dLT} = \sqrt{\overline{L}\sigma_d^2 + \overline{d}^2\sigma_{LT}^2}$$

Now that we have determined the mean and standard deviation of the distribution of demand during lead time under these more complicated conditions, we can select the reorder point as we did before for the case where the lead time was constant.

EXAMPLE 6.6	**Reorder Point for Variable Demand and Variable Lead Time**

The Office Supply Shop estimates that the average demand for a popular ball-point pen is 12,000 pens per week with a standard deviation of 3,000 pens. The current inventory policy calls for replenishment orders of 156,000 pens. The average lead time from the distributor is 5 weeks, with a standard deviation of 2 weeks. If management wants a 95 percent cycle-service level, what should the reorder point be?

SOLUTION
We have $\overline{d} = 12{,}000$ pens, $\sigma_d = 3{,}000$ pens, $\overline{L} = 5$ weeks, and $\sigma_{LT} = 2$ weeks.

$$\sigma_{dLT} = \sqrt{\overline{L}\sigma_d^2 + \overline{d}^2\sigma_{LT}^2} = \sqrt{(5)(3{,}000)^2 + (12{,}000)^2(2)^2} = 24{,}919.87 \text{ pens}$$

Consult the body of the Normal Distribution appendix for 0.9500, which corresponds to a 95 percent cycle-service level. That value falls exactly in the middle of the tabular values of 0.9495 (for a z value of 1.64) and 0.9505 (for a z value of 1.65). Consequently, we will use the more conservative value of 1.65. We calculate the safety stock and reorder point as follows:

$$\text{Safety stock} = z\sigma_{dLT} = (1.65)(24{,}919.87) = 41{,}117.79, \text{ or } 41{,}118 \text{ pens}$$

$$\text{Reorder point} = \overline{d}\,\overline{L} + \text{Safety stock} = (12{,}000)(5) + 41{,}118 = 101{,}118 \text{ pens}$$

DECISION POINT
Whenever the stock of ball-point pens drops to 101,118, management should place another replenishment order of 156,000 pens to the distributor.

Sometimes, the theoretical distributions for demand and lead time are not known. In those cases, we can use simulation to find the distribution of demand during lead time using discrete distributions for demand and lead times. Simulation can also be used to estimate the performance of an inventory system. More discussion, and an example, can be found in MyOMLab.

MyOMLab

visual system

A system that allows employees to place orders when inventory visibly reaches a certain marker.

Two-Bin System   The concept of a Q system can be incorporated in a **visual system**, that is, a system that allows employees to place orders when inventory visibly reaches a certain marker. Visual systems are easy to administer because records are not kept on the current inventory position. The historical usage rate can simply be reconstructed from past purchase orders. Visual systems are intended for use with low-value SKUs that have a steady demand, such as nuts and bolts or office supplies. Overstocking is common, but the extra inventory holding cost is minimal because the items have relatively little value.

A visual system version of the Q system is the **two-bin system** in which a SKU's inventory is stored at two different locations. Inventory is first withdrawn from one bin. If the first bin is empty, the second bin provides backup to cover demand until a replenishment order arrives. An empty first bin signals the need to place a new order. Premade order forms placed near the bins let workers send one to purchasing or even directly to the supplier. When the new order arrives, the second bin is restored to its normal level and the rest is put in the first bin. The two-bin system operates like a Q system, with the normal level in the second bin being the reorder point R. The system also may be implemented with just one bin by marking the bin at the reorder point level.

two-bin system

A visual system version of the Q system in which a SKU's inventory is stored at two different locations.

Calculating Total Q System Costs   Total costs for the continuous review (Q) system is the sum of three cost components:

Total cost = Annual cycle inventory holding cost + annual ordering cost

+ annual safety stock holding cost

$$C = \frac{Q}{2}(H) + \frac{D}{Q}(S) + (H)(\text{Safety stock})$$

The annual cycle-inventory holding cost and annual ordering cost are the same equations we used for computing the total annual cycle-inventory cost in Example 6.2. The annual cost of holding the safety stock is computed under the assumption that the safety stock is on hand at all times. Referring to Figure 6.10 in each order cycle, we will sometimes experience a demand greater than the average demand during lead time, and sometimes we will experience less. On average over the year, we can assume the safety stock will be on hand. See Solved Problems 4 and 6 at the end of this chapter for an example of calculating the total costs for a Q system.

Periodic Review System

An alternative inventory control system is the **periodic review (P) system**, sometimes called a *fixed interval reorder system* or *periodic reorder system*, in which an item's inventory position is reviewed periodically rather than continuously. Such a system can simplify delivery scheduling because it establishes a routine. A new order is always placed at the end of each review, and the time between orders (TBO) is fixed at P. Demand is a random variable, so total demand between reviews varies. In a P system, the lot size, Q, may change from one order to the next, but the time between orders is fixed. An example of a periodic review system is that of a soft-drink supplier making weekly rounds of grocery stores. Each week, the supplier reviews the store's inventory of soft drinks and restocks the store with enough items to meet demand and safety stock requirements until the next week.

periodic review (P) sytem

A system in which an item's inventory position is reviewed periodically rather than continuously.

Under a P system, four of the original EOQ assumptions are maintained: (1) no constraints are placed on the size of the lot, (2) the relevant costs are holding and ordering costs, (3) decisions for one SKU are independent of decisions for other SKUs, and (4) lead times are certain and supply is known. However, demand uncertainty is again allowed for. Figure 6.13 shows the peri-

odic review system under these assumptions. The downward-sloping line again represents on-hand inventory. When the predetermined time, P, has elapsed since the last review, an order is placed to bring the inventory position, represented by the dashed line, up to the target inventory level, T. The lot size for the first review is Q_1, or the difference between inventory position IP_1 and T. As with the continuous review system, IP and OH differ only during the lead time. When the order arrives at the end of the lead time, OH and IP again are identical. Figure 6.13 shows that lot sizes vary from one order cycle to the next. Because the inventory position is lower at the second review, a greater quantity is needed to achieve an inventory level of T.

▼ **FIGURE 6.13**
P System When Demand Is Uncertain

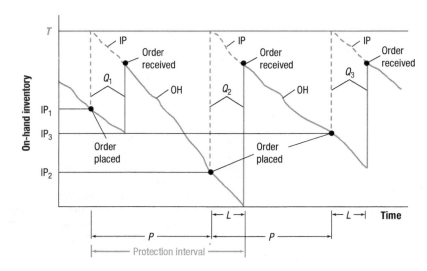

Managerial Practice 6.1 shows how the use of periodic inventory review systems is important in supply chains in the chemical industry.

MANAGERIAL PRACTICE 6.1 | The Supply Chain Implications of Periodic Review Inventory Systems at Celanese

What do products such as paints, adhesives, coatings, plastics, medicines, cosmetics, detergents, textiles, or fragrances have in common? All of these products use acetic acid as a major component. Celanese, a $6.5 billion chemical company with $640 million in total inventories, is a major supplier of acetic acid in the world. The large investment in inventory forces Celanese to take a hard look at inventory policies for all products, including acetic acid. The key to successful management of the inventories was to acknowledge the interaction between the inventory policies at each stage of the supply chain with the realities of material flows and logistics in the chemical industry.

The supply chain for acetic acid is complex, involving 90 stages. For example, the supply chain is comprised of stages such as vendors supplying a liner to transport the acid, manufacturing sites producing the acid, transportation modes moving acid, warehouses storing it, and customer demand locations to which the acid is finally shipped. There are four manufacturing facilities, three in the United States and one in Singapore, each of which supplies several storage locations worldwide. Transportation stages correspond to rail, barges, trucks, and ocean vessels. Material typically moves in large quantities because of economies of scale and transportation schedules. Storage facilities may be supplied by multiple upstream facilities as well as the manufacturing plant itself.

The use of periodic review inventory systems at the storage and demand locations in this supply chain scenario makes sense for several reasons. First, the transportation modes have defined schedules of operation. Review periods at storage facilities reflect the schedule of the supplying transportation mode. Second, customer orders are typically batched and timed with weekly, bi-weekly, or monthly frequencies. Celanese often assigns customers and storage facilities specific days to place orders so that their own production

Large, fixed capacity modes of transportation require defined schedules of operation. Such a situation supports the use of periodic inventory systems. Here ocean vessels await loads of petro-chemicals at the Vopak terminal in the Port of Rotterdam.

schedules can be coordinated. Finally, the cyclic ordering is often a function of the capital intensity of the industry. Long production runs are scheduled to gain production efficiency; it is costly to set up the equipment for another product.

Specifying the best review period and target inventory levels for the various stages of the supply chain takes sophisticated mathematical models. Regardless of the effort required, it is important to recognize the implications of the supply chain when determining inventory policies.

Source: John M. Bossert and Sean P. Williams, "A Periodic-Review Modeling Approach for Guaranteed Service Supply Chains," *Interfaces*, Vol. 37, No. 5 (September/October 2007), pp. 420–435; **http://finance.yahoo.com; www.Celanese.com**, 2008.

EXAMPLE 6.7 | Determining How Much to Order in a P System

A distribution center has a backorder for five 46-inch LCD TV sets. No inventory is currently on hand, and now is the time to review. How many should be reordered if $T = 400$ and no receipts are scheduled?

SOLUTION

$$IP = OH + SR - BO$$

$$= 0 + 0 - 5 = -5 \text{ sets}$$

$$T - IP = 400 - (-5) = 405 \text{ sets}$$

That is, 405 sets must be ordered to bring the inventory position up to T sets.

Selecting the Time between Reviews   To run a P system, managers must make two decisions: the length of time between reviews, P, and the target inventory level, T. Let us first consider the time between reviews, P. It can be any convenient interval, such as each Friday or every other Friday. Another option is to base P on the cost trade-offs of the EOQ. In other words, P can be set equal to the average time between orders for the economic order quantity, or TBO_{EOQ}. Because demand is variable, some orders will be larger than the EOQ and some will be smaller. However, over an extended period of time, the average lot size should be close to the EOQ. If other models are used to determine the lot size (e.g., those described in Supplement C, "Special Inventory Models"), we divide the lot size chosen by the annual demand, D, and use this ratio as P. It will be expressed as the fraction of a year between orders, which can be converted into months, weeks, or days as needed.

Selecting the Target Inventory Level When Demand Is Variable and Lead Time Is Constant

Now, let us calculate the target inventory level, T, when demand is variable but the lead time is constant. Figure 6.13 reveals that an order must be large enough to make the inventory position, IP, last beyond the next review, which is P time periods away. The checker must wait P periods to revise, correct, and reestablish the inventory position. Then, a new order is placed, but it does not arrive until after the lead time, L. Therefore, as Figure 6.13 shows, a protection interval of $P + L$ periods is needed. A fundamental difference between the Q and P systems is the length of time needed for stockout protection. A Q system needs stockout protection only during the lead time because orders can be placed as soon as they are needed and will be received L periods later. A P system, however, needs stockout protection for the longer $P + L$ protection interval because orders are placed only at fixed intervals, and the inventory is not checked until the next designated review time.

As with the Q system, we need to develop the appropriate distribution of demand during the protection interval to specify the system fully. In a P system, we must develop the distribution of demand for $P + L$ time periods. The target inventory level T must equal the expected demand during the protection interval of $P + L$ periods, plus enough safety stock to protect against demand uncertainty over this same protection interval. We assume that lead time is constant and that demand in one period is independent of demand in the next period. Thus, the average demand during the protection interval is $\overline{d}(P + L)$, or

$$T = \overline{d}(P + L) + \text{Safety stock for the protection interval}$$

We compute safety stock for a P system much as we did for the Q system. However, the safety stock must cover demand uncertainty for a longer period of time. When using a normal probability distribution, we multiply the desired standard deviations to implement the cycle-service level, z, by the standard deviation of demand during the protection interval, σ_{P+L}. The value of z is the same as for a Q system with the same cycle-service level. Thus,

$$\text{Safety stock} = z\sigma_{P+L}$$

Based on our earlier logic for calculating σ_{dLT}, we know that the standard deviation of the distribution of demand during the protection interval is

$$\sigma_{P+L} = \sigma_d\sqrt{P + L}$$

Because a P system requires safety stock to cover demand uncertainty over a longer time period than a Q system, a P system requires more safety stock; that is, σ_{P+L} exceeds σ_{dLT}. Hence, to gain the convenience of a P system requires that overall inventory levels be somewhat higher than those for a Q system.

EXAMPLE 6.8	**Calculating P and T**

Again, let us return to the bird feeder example. Recall that demand for the bird feeder is normally distributed with a mean of 18 units per week and a standard deviation in weekly demand of 5 units. The lead time is 2 weeks, and the business operates 52 weeks per year. The Q system developed in Example 6.5 called for an EOQ of 75 units and a safety stock of 9 units for a cycle-service level of 90 percent. What is the equivalent P system? Answers are to be rounded to the nearest integer.

MyOMLab

Tutor 6.4 in MyOMLab provides a new example to determine the review interval and the target inventory for a P system.

SOLUTION

We first define D and then P. Here, P is the time between reviews, expressed in weeks because the data are expressed as demand *per week*:

$$D = (18 \text{ units/week})(52 \text{ weeks/year}) = 936 \text{ units}$$

$$P = \frac{\text{EOQ}}{D}(52) = \frac{75}{936}(52) = 4.2, \text{ or } 4 \text{ weeks}$$

With $\overline{d} = 18$ units per week, an alternative approach is to calculate P by dividing the EOQ by $\overline{d}$ to get $75/18 = 4.2$, or 4 weeks. Either way, we would review the bird feeder inventory every 4 weeks. We now find the standard deviation of demand over the protection interval $(P + L = 6)$:

$$\sigma_{P+L} = \sigma_d\sqrt{P + L} = 52\sqrt{6} = 12.25 \text{ units}$$

Before calculating T, we also need a z value. For a 90 percent cycle-service level, $z = 1.28$ (see the Normal Distribution appendix). The safety stock becomes

$$\text{Safety stock} = z\sigma_{P+L} = 1.28(12.25) = 15.68, \text{ or } 16 \text{ units}$$

We now solve for T:

$$T = \text{Average demand during the protection interval} + \text{Safety stock}$$

$$= \overline{d}(P + L) + \text{Safety stock}$$

$$= (18 \text{ units/week})(6 \text{ weeks}) + 16 \text{ units} = 124 \text{ units}$$

DECISION POINT

Every 4 weeks we would order the number of units needed to bring inventory position IP (counting the new order) up to the target inventory level of 124 units. The P system requires 16 units in safety stock, while the Q system only needs 9 units. If cost were the only criterion, the Q system would be the choice for the bird feeder. As we discuss later, other factors may sway the decision in favor of the P system.

Selecting the Target Inventory Level When Both Demand and Lead Time Are Variable   A useful approach for finding P and T in practice is simulation. Given discrete probability distributions for demand and lead time, simulation can be used to estimate the demand during the protection interval distribution. The *Demand During the Protection Interval Simulator* in OM Explorer can be used to determine the distribution. Once determined, the distribution can be used to select a value for T, given a desired cycle-service level. More discussion, and an example, can be found in MyOMLab.

Single-Bin System   The concept of a P system can be translated into a simple visual system of inventory control. In the **single-bin system**, a maximum level is marked on the storage shelf or bin, and the inventory is brought up to the mark periodically—say, once a week. The single bin may be, for example, a gasoline storage tank at a service station or a storage bin for small parts at a manufacturing plant.

Calculating Total P System Costs   The total costs for the P system are the sum of the same three cost elements for the Q system. The differences are in the calculation of the order quantity and the safety stock. As shown in Figure 6.13, the average order quantity will be the average consumption of inventory during the P periods between orders. Consequently, $Q = \overline{d}P$. Total costs for the P system are

$$C = \frac{\overline{d}P}{2}(H) + \frac{D}{\overline{d}P}(S) + (H)(\text{Safety stock})$$

See Solved Problem 5 at the end of this chapter for an example of calculating total P system costs.

Comparative Advantages of the Q and P Systems

Neither the Q nor the P system is best for all situations. Three P-system advantages must be balanced against three Q-system advantages. The advantages of one system are implicitly disadvantages of the other system.

The primary advantages of P systems are the following:

1. The system is convenient because replenishments are made at fixed intervals. Fixed replenishment intervals allow for standardized pickup and delivery times.

2. Orders for multiple items from the same supplier can be combined into a single purchase order. This approach reduces ordering and transportation costs and can result in a price break from the supplier.

3. The inventory position, IP, needs to be known only when a review is made (not continuously, as in a Q system). However, this advantage is moot for firms using computerized record-keeping systems, in which a transaction is reported upon each receipt or withdrawal. When inventory records are always current, the system is called a **perpetual inventory system**.

The primary advantages of Q systems are the following:

1. The review frequency of each SKU may be individualized. Tailoring the review frequency to the SKU can reduce total ordering and holding costs.

MyOMLab

single-bin system

A system of inventory control in which a maximum level is marked on the storage shelf or bin, and the inventor is brought up to the mark periodically.

perpetual inventory system

A system of inventory control in which the inventory records are always current.

2. Fixed lot sizes, if large enough, can result in quantity discounts. The firm's physical limitations, such as its truckload capacities, materials handling methods, and shelf space might also necessitate a fixed lot size.

3. Lower safety stocks result in savings.

In conclusion, the choice between Q and P systems is not clear cut. Which system is better depends on the relative importance of its advantages in various situations.

Hybrid Systems

Various hybrid inventory control systems merge some but not all the features of the P and Q systems. We briefly examine two such systems: (1) optional replenishment and (2) base stock.

Optional Replenishment System   Sometimes called the optional review, min–max, or (s, S) system, the **optional replenishment system** is much like the P system. It is used to review the inventory position at fixed time intervals and, if the position has dropped to (or below) a predetermined level, to place a variable-sized order to cover expected needs. The new order is large enough to bring the inventory position up to a target inventory, similar to T for the P system. However, orders are not placed after a review unless the inventory position has dropped to the predetermined minimum level. The minimum level acts as the reorder point R does in a Q system. If the target is 100 and the minimum level is 60, the minimum order size is 40 (or $100 - 60$). Because continuous reviews need not be made, this system is particularly attractive when both review and ordering costs are high.

Base-Stock System   In its simplest form, the **base-stock system** issues a replenishment order, Q, each time a withdrawal is made, for the same amount as the withdrawal. This one-for-one replacement policy maintains the inventory position at a base-stock level equal to expected demand during the lead time plus safety stock. The base-stock level, therefore, is equivalent to the reorder point in a Q system. However, order quantities now vary to keep the inventory position at R at all times. Because this position is the lowest IP possible that will maintain a specified service level, the base-stock system may be used to minimize cycle inventory. More orders are placed, but each order is smaller. This system is appropriate for expensive items, such as replacement engines for jet airplanes. No more inventory is held than the maximum demand expected until a replacement order can be received.

optional replenishment system

A system used to review the inventory position at fixed time intervals and, if the position has dropped to (or below) a predetermined level, to place a variable-sized order to cover expected needs.

base-stock system

An inventory control system that issues a replenishment order, Q, each time a withdrawal is made, for the same amount of the withdrawal.

LEARNING GOALS IN REVIEW

① Identify the advantages, disadvantages, and costs of holding inventory. We cover these important aspects of inventories in the section "Inventory and Supply Chains," pp. 187–192. Focus on the pressures for small or large inventories and Figure 6.1.

② Define the different types of inventory and the roles they play in supply chains. The section "Types of Inventory," p. 189–191, explains each type of inventory and provides an example in Figure 6.2. Example 6.1 and Solved Problem 1 show how to estimate inventory levels.

③ Explain the basic tactics for reducing inventories in supply chains. See the section "Inventory Reduction Tactics," pp. 191–192, for important approaches to managing inventory levels.

④ Determine the inventory items deserving most attention and tightest inventory control. The section "ABC Analysis," pp. 192–193, shows a simple approach to categorizing inventory items for ease of management oversight. Figure 6.4 has an example. Solved Problem 2 demonstrates the calculations.

⑤ Calculate the economic order quantity and apply it to various situations. See the section "Economic Order Quantity," pp. 193–197, for a complete discussion of EOQ model. Focus

on Figures 6.5 through 6.7 to see how the EOQ model affects inventory levels under the standard assumptions and how the EOQ provides the lowest cost solution. Review Examples 6.2 and 6.3 and Solved Problem 3 for help in calculating the total costs of various lot-size choices. Table 6.1 reveals important managerial insights from the EOQ.

⑥ Determine the order quantity and reorder point for a continuous review inventory system. The section "Continuous Review System," pp. 198–203, builds the essence of the Q system from basic principles to more-realistic assumptions. Be sure to understand Figures 6.10 and 6.12. Examples 6.4 through 6.6 and Solved Problems 4 and 6 show how to determine the parameters Q and R under various assumptions.

⑦ Determine the review interval and target inventory level for a periodic review inventory control system. We summarize the key concepts in the section "Periodic Review System," pp. 203–206. Figure 6.13 shows how a P system operates while Examples 6.7 and 6.8 and Solved Problem 5 demonstrate how to calculate the parameters P and T.

⑧ Define the key factors that determine the appropriate choice of an inventory system. See the section "Comparative Advantages of the Q and P Systems," pp. 206–207.

MyOMLab helps you develop analytical skills and assesses your progress with multiple problems on cycle inventory, pipeline inventory, safety stock, inventory turns, weeks of supply, aggregate inventory value, time between orders, optimal order quantity, EOQ, optimal interval between orders, reorder point, demand during lead time, cycle-service level, target inventory *T*, and *P*.

MyOMLab Resources	Titles	Link to the Book
Video	*Inventory and Textbooks*	Entire chapter
Active Model Exercise	6.1 Economic Order Quantity	Economic Order Quantity; Example 6.3 (p. 196); Active Model Exercise (p. 219)
OM Explorer Solvers	ABC Analysis	ABC Analysis (p. 192–193); Solved Problem 2 (p. 210–211)
	Inventory Systems Designer	Inventory Control Systems; Example 6.3 (p. 196); Example 6.8 (p. 205–206); Solved Problem 3 (p. 212); Solved Problem 4 (p. 212–213); Solved Problem 5 (p. 213); Figure 6.15 (p. 213)
	Demand During Protection Interval Simulator	Selecting the Reorder Point When Both Demand and Lead Time Are Variable; Selecting the Target Inventory Level When Both Demand and Lead Time Are Variable
	Q System Simulator	Continuous Review System
OM Explorer Tutors	6.1 Estimating Inventory Levels	Inventory and Supply Chains; Example 6.1 (p. 190–191); Figure 6.3 (p. 191); Solved Problem 1 (p. 210)
	6.2 ABC Analysis	ABC Analysis; Solved Problem 2 (p. 210–211); Figure 6.14 (p. 211)
	6.3 Finding EOQ and Total Cost	Economic Order Quantity; Example 6.3 (p. 196); Figure 6.8 (p. 196); Solved Problem 3 (p. 212)
	6.4 Finding the Safety Stock and R	Continuous Review System; Example 6.5 (p. 201); Solved Problem 4 (p. 212–213)
	6.5 Calculating *P* and *T*	Periodic Review System; Example 6.8 (p. 205–206); Solved Problem 5 (p. 213)
POM for Windows	Economic Order Quantity (EOQ) Model	Economic Order Quantity; Example 6.3 (p. 196); Solved Problem 3 (p. 212)
	ABC Analysis	ABC Analysis; Solved Problem 2 (p. 210–211)
Tutor Exercises	6.1 Finding EOQ, Safety Stock, *R*, *P*, *T* at Bison College Bookstore	Economic Order Quantity; Inventory Control Systems
Tutorial on Inventory Management Systems	Using Simulation to Develop Inventory Management Systems	Selecting the Reorder Point When Demand and Lead Time Are Variable; Selecting the Target Inventory Level When Both Demand and Lead Time Are Variable
Advanced Problems	1. Office Supply Shop Simulation	Continuous Review System; Selecting the Reorder Point When Both Demand and Lead Time Are Variable
	2. Grocery Store Simulation	Periodic Review System; Selecting the Target Inventory Level when Both Demand and Lead Time Are Variable
	3. Floral Shop Simulation	Continuous Review System; Selecting the Reorder Point When Demand and Lead Time Are Variable
Virtual Tours	Stickley	Inventory and Supply Chains
	United Wood Treating	Entire chapter
Internet Exercise	6.1 Round House	Inventory and Supply Chains
SimQuick Simulation Exercise	Inventory Control Systems	Continuous Review System; Periodic Review System
Key Equations		
Image Library		

Key Equations

1. Average cycle inventory: $\dfrac{Q}{2}$

2. Pipeline inventory: $\overline{D}_L = \overline{d}L$

3. Total annual cycle-inventory cost = Annual holding cost + Annual ordering or setup cost:

$$C = \frac{Q}{2}(H) + \frac{D}{Q}(S)$$

4. Economic order quantity:

$$\text{EOQ} = \sqrt{\frac{2DS}{H}}$$

5. Time between orders, expressed in weeks:

$$\text{TBO}_{\text{EOQ}} = \frac{\text{EOQ}}{D}(52 \text{ weeks/year})$$

6. Inventory position = On-hand inventory + Scheduled receipts − Backorders:

$$\text{IP} = \text{OH} + \text{SR} - \text{BO}$$

7. Continuous review system:

Protection interval = Lead time (L)

Standard deviation of demand during the lead time (constant L) = $\sigma_{dLT} = \sigma_d\sqrt{L}$

Standard deviation of demand during the lead time (variable L) =

$\sigma_{dLT} = \sqrt{\overline{L}\sigma_d^2 + \overline{d}^2\sigma_{LT}^2}$

Safety stock = $z\sigma_{dLT}$

Reorder point (R) for constant lead time = $\overline{d}L$ + Safety stock

Reorder point (R) for variable lead time = $\overline{d}\overline{L}$ + Safety stock

Order quantity = EOQ

Replenishment rule: Order EOQ units when IP $\leq R$

Total Q system cost: $C = \dfrac{Q}{2}(H) + \dfrac{D}{Q}(S) + (H)(\text{Safety stock})$

8. Periodic review system:

Review interval = Time between orders = P

Protection interval = Time between orders + Lead time = $P + L$

Standard deviation of demand during the protection interval $\sigma_{P+L} = \sigma_d\sqrt{P + L}$

Safety stock = $z\sigma_{P+L}$

Target inventory level (T) = Average demand during the protection interval + Safety stock

$$= \overline{d}(P + L) + \text{Safety stock}$$

Order quantity = Target inventory level − Inventory position = $T - \text{IP}$

Replenishment rule: Every P time periods, order $T - \text{IP}$ units

Total P system cost: $C = \dfrac{\overline{d}P}{2}(H) + \dfrac{D}{\overline{d}P}(S) + (H)(\text{Safety stock})$

Key Terms

Solved Problem 1

A distribution center experiences an average weekly demand of 50 units for one of its items. The product is valued at $650 per unit. Inbound shipments from the factory warehouse average 350 units. Average lead time (including ordering delays and transit time) is 2 weeks. The distribution center operates 52 weeks per year; it carries a 1-week supply of inventory as safety stock and no anticipation inventory. What is the value of the average aggregate inventory being held by the distribution center?

SOLUTION

Type of Inventory	Calculation of Aggregate Average Inventory	
Cycle	$\dfrac{Q}{2} = \dfrac{350}{2}$	= 175 units
Safety stock	1-week supply	= 50 units
Anticipation	None	
Pipeline	$\bar{d}L$ = (50 units/week)(2 weeks)	= 100 units
	Average aggregate inventory	= 325 units
	Value of aggregate inventory	= $650(325)
		= $211,250

Solved Problem 2

Booker's Book Bindery divides SKUs into three classes, according to their dollar usage. Calculate the usage values of the following SKUs and determine which is most likely to be classified as class A.

SOLUTION

The annual dollar usage for each SKU is determined by multiplying the annual usage quantity by the value per unit. As shown in Figure 6.14, the SKUs are then sorted by annual dollar usage, in declining order. Finally, A–B and B–C class lines are drawn roughly, according to the guidelines presented in the text. Here, class A includes only one SKU (signatures), which represents only 1/7, or 14 percent, of the SKUs but accounts for 83 percent of annual dollar usage. Class B includes the next two SKUs, which taken together represent 28 percent of the SKUs and account for 13 percent of annual dollar usage. The final four SKUs, class C, represent over half the number of SKUs but only 4 percent of total annual dollar usage.

SKU Number	Description	Quantity Used per Year	Unit Value ($)
1	Boxes	500	3.00
2	Cardboard (square feet)	18,000	0.02
3	Cover stock	10,000	0.75
4	Glue (gallons)	75	40.00
5	Inside covers	20,000	0.05
6	Reinforcing tape (meters)	3,000	0.15
7	Signatures	150,000	0.45

SKU Number	Description	Quantity Used per Year		Unit Value ($)		Annual Dollar Usage ($)
1	Boxes	500	×	3.00	=	1,500
2	Cardboard (square feet)	18,000	×	0.02	=	360
3	Cover stock	10,000	×	0.75	=	7,500
4	Glue (gallons)	75	×	40.00	=	3,000
5	Inside covers	20,000	×	0.05	=	1,000
6	Reinforcing tape (meters)	3,000	×	0.15	=	450
7	Signatures	150,000	×	0.45	=	67,500
					Total	81,310

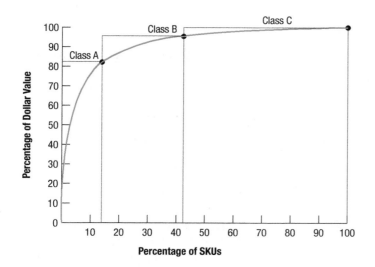

SKU #	Description	Qty Used/Year	Value	Dollar Usage	Pct of Total	Cumulative % of Dollar Value	Cumulative % of SKU	Class
7	Signatures	150,000	$0.45	$67,500	83.0%	83.0%	14.3%	A
3	Cover stock	10,000	$0.75	$7,500	9.2%	92.2%	28.6%	B
4	Glue	75	$40.00	$3,000	3.7%	95.9%	42.9%	B
1	Boxes	500	$3.00	$1,500	1.8%	97.8%	57.1%	C
5	Inside covers	20,000	$0.05	$1,000	1.2%	99.0%	71.4%	C
6	Reinforcing tape	3,000	$0.15	$450	0.6%	99.6%	85.7%	C
2	Cardboard	18,000	$0.02	$360	0.4%	100.0%	100.0%	C
Total				$81,310				

◀ **FIGURE 6.14**
Annual Dollar Usage for
Class A, B, and C SKUs Using
Tutor 6.2

Solved Problem 3

Nelson's Hardware Store stocks a 19.2 volt cordless drill that is a popular seller. Annual demand is 5,000 units, the ordering cost is $15, and the inventory holding cost is $4/unit/year.

a. What is the economic order quantity?

b. What is the total annual cost for this inventory item?

SOLUTION

a. The order quantity is

$$EOQ = \sqrt{\frac{2DS}{H}} = \sqrt{\frac{2(5,000)(\$15)}{\$4}} = \sqrt{37,500}$$

$$= 193.65, \text{ or } 194 \text{ drills}$$

b. The total annual cost is

$$C = \frac{Q}{2}(H) + \frac{D}{Q}(S) = \frac{194}{2}(\$4) + \frac{5,000}{194}(\$15) = \$774.60$$

Solved Problem 4

A regional distributor purchases discontinued appliances from various suppliers and then sells them on demand to retailers in the region. The distributor operates 5 days per week, 52 weeks per year. Only when it is open for business can orders be received. Management wants to reevaluate its current inventory policy, which calls for order quantities of 440 counter-top mixers. The following data are estimated for the mixer:

Average daily demand $(\bar{d}) = 100$ mixers
Standard deviation of daily demand $(\sigma_d) = 30$ mixers
Lead time $(L) = 3$ days
Holding cost $(H) = \$9.40/\text{unit/year}$
Ordering cost $(S) = \$35/\text{order}$
Cycle-service level $= 92$ percent
The distributor uses a continuous review (Q) system.

a. What order quantity Q, and reorder point, R, should be used?

b. What is the total annual cost of the system?

c. If on-hand inventory is 40 units, one open order for 440 mixers is pending, and no backorders exist, should a new order be placed?

SOLUTION

a. Annual demand is

$$D = (5 \text{ days/week}) (52 \text{ weeks/year}) (100 \text{ mixers/day}) = 26,000 \text{ mixers/year}$$

The order quantity is

$$EOQ = \sqrt{\frac{2DS}{H}} = \sqrt{\frac{2(26,000)(\$35)}{\$9.40}} = \sqrt{193,167} = 440.02, \text{ or } 440 \text{ mixers}$$

The standard deviation of the distribution of demand during lead time is

$$\sigma_{dLT} = \sigma_d\sqrt{L} = 30\sqrt{3} = 51.96$$

A 92 percent cycle-service level corresponds to $z = 1.41$ (see the Normal Distribution appendix). Therefore,

$$\text{Safety stock} = z\sigma_{dLT} = 1.41(51.96 \text{ mixers}) = 73.26, \text{ or } 73 \text{ mixers}$$
$$\text{Average demand during the lead time} = \bar{d}L = 100(3) = 300 \text{ mixers}$$
$$\text{Reorder point } (R) = \text{Average demand during the lead time } + \text{ Safety stock}$$
$$= 300 \text{ mixers} + 73 \text{ mixers} = 373 \text{ mixers}$$

With a continuous review system, $Q = 440$ and $R = 373$.

b. The total annual cost for the Q systems is

$$C = \frac{Q}{2}(H) + \frac{D}{Q}(S) + (H) \text{ (Safety stock)}$$

$$C = \frac{440}{2}(\$9.40) + \frac{26{,}000}{440}(35) + (\$9.40)(73) = \$4{,}822.38$$

c. Inventory position $=$ On-hand inventory $+$ Scheduled receipts $-$ Backorders

$$\text{IP} = \text{OH} + \text{SR} - \text{BO} = 40 + 440 - 0 = 480 \text{ mixers}$$

Because IP (480) exceeds R (373), do not place a new order.

Solved Problem 5

Suppose that a periodic review (P) system is used at the distributor in Solved Problem 4, but otherwise the data are the same.

a. Calculate the P (in workdays, rounded to the nearest day) that gives approximately the same number of orders per year as the EOQ.

b. What is the target inventory level, T? Compare the P system to the Q system in Solved Problem 4.

c. What is the total annual cost of the P system?

d. It is time to review the item. On-hand inventory is 40 mixers; receipt of 440 mixers is scheduled, and no backorders exist. How much should be reordered?

SOLUTION

a. The time between orders is

$$P = \frac{\text{EOQ}}{D}(260 \text{ days/year}) = \frac{440}{26{,}000}(260) = 4.4, \text{ or 4 days}$$

b. Figure 6.15 shows that $T = 812$ and safety stock $= (1.41)(79.37) = 111.91$, or about 112 mixers. The corresponding Q system for the counter-top mixer requires less safety stock.

c. The total annual cost of the P system is

$$C = \frac{\overline{dP}}{2}(H) + \frac{D}{\overline{dP}}(S) + (H)(\text{Safety stock})$$

$$C = \frac{(100)(4)}{2}(\$9.40) + \frac{26{,}000}{(100)(4)}(\$35) + (\$9.40)(1.41)(79.37)$$

$$= \$5{,}207.80$$

d. Inventory position is the amount on hand plus scheduled receipts minus backorders, or

$$\text{IP} = \text{OH} + \text{SR} - \text{BO} = 40 + 440 - 0 = 480 \text{ mixers}$$

The order quantity is the target inventory level minus the inventory position, or

$$Q = T - \text{IP} = 812 \text{ mixers} - 480 \text{ mixers} = 332 \text{ mixers}$$

An order for 332 mixers should be placed.

Continuous Review (Q) System		Periodic Review (P) System		
z	1.41	Time Between Reviews (P)	4.00	Days
Safety Stock	73	☑ Enter manually		
Reorder Point	373	Standard Deviation of Demand During Protection Interval	79.37	
Annual Cost	$4,822.38	Safety Stock	112	
		Average Demand During Protection Interval	700	
		Target Inventory Level (T)	812	
		Annual Cost	$5,207.80	

◀ **FIGURE 6.15**
OM Explorer Solver for Inventory Systems

Solved Problem 6

Grey Wolf Lodge is a popular 500-room hotel in the North Woods. Managers need to keep close tabs on all room service items, including a special pine-scented bar soap. The daily demand for the soap is 275 bars, with a standard deviation of 30 bars. Ordering cost is $10 and the inventory holding cost is $0.30/bar/year. The lead time from the supplier is 5 days, with a standard deviation of 1 day. The lodge is open 365 days a year.

   a. What is the economic order quantity for the bar of soap?

   b. What should the reorder point be for the bar of soap if management wants to have a 99 percent cycle-service level?

   c. What is the total annual cost for the bar of soap, assuming a Q system will be used?

SOLUTION

   a. We have $D = (275)(365) = 100{,}375$ bars of soap; $S = \$10$; and $H = \$0.30$. The EOQ for the bar of soap is

$$\text{EOQ} = \sqrt{\frac{2DS}{H}} = \sqrt{\frac{2(100{,}375)(\$10)}{\$0.30}} = \sqrt{6{,}691{,}666.7}$$

$$= 2{,}586.83, \text{ or } 2{,}587 \text{ bars}$$

   b. We have $\bar{d} = 275$ bars/day, $\sigma_d = 30$ bars, $\bar{L} = 5$ days, and $\sigma_{LT} = 1$ day.

$$\sigma_{dLT} = \sqrt{\bar{L}\sigma_d^2 + \bar{d}^2\sigma_{LT}^2} = \sqrt{(5)(30)^2 + (275)^2(1)^2} = 283.06 \text{ bars}$$

Consult the body of the Normal Distribution appendix for 0.9900, which corresponds to a 99 percent cycle-service level. The closest value is 0.9901, which corresponds to a z value of 2.33. We calculate the safety stock and reorder point as follows:

$$\text{Safety stock } = z\sigma_{dLT} = (2.33)(283.06) = 659.53, \text{ or } 660 \text{ bars}$$

$$\text{Reorder point } = \bar{d}\bar{L} + \text{Safety stock} = (275)(5) + 600 = 2{,}035 \text{ bars}$$

   c. The total annual cost for the Q system is

$$C = \frac{Q}{2}(H) + \frac{D}{Q}(S) + (H)(\text{Safety stock})$$

$$= \frac{2{,}587}{2}(\$0.30) + \frac{100{,}375}{2{,}587}(\$10) + (\$0.30)(660) = \$974.05$$

Discussion Questions

1. What is the relationship between inventory and the nine competitive priorities we discussed in Chapter 1, "Using Operations to Compete"? Suppose that two competing manufacturers, Company H and Company L, are similar except that Company H has much higher investments in raw materials, work-in-process, and finished goods inventory than Company L. In which of the nine competitive priorities will Company H have an advantage?

2. Suppose that a large discount retailer with a lot of purchasing power in a supply chain requires that all suppliers incorporate a new information system that will reduce the cost of placing orders between the retailer and its suppliers as well as between the suppliers and their suppliers. Suppose also that order quantities and lead times are related; the smaller the order quantity the shorter the lead time from suppliers. Assume that all members of the supply chain use a continuous review system and EOQ order quantities. Explain the implications of the new information system for the supply chain in general and the inventory systems of the supply chain members in particular.

3. Will organizations ever get to the point where they will no longer need inventories? Why or why not?

Problems

The OM Explorer and POM for Windows software is available to all students using the 10th edition of this textbook. Go to **www.pearsonhighered.com/krajewski** to download these computer packages. If you purchased MyOMLab, you also have access to Active Models software and significant help in doing the following problems. Check with your instructor on how best to use these resources. In many cases, the instructor wants you to understand how to do the calculations by hand. At the least, the software provides a check on your calculations. When calculations are particularly complex and the goal is interpreting the results in making decisions, the software replaces entirely the manual calculations.

1. A part is produced in lots of 1,000 units. It is assembled from 2 components worth $50 total. The value added in production (for labor and variable overhead) is $60 per unit, bringing total costs per completed unit to $110. The average lead time for the part is 6 weeks and annual demand is 3,800 units, based on 50 business weeks per year.

   a. How many units of the part are held, on average, in cycle inventory? What is the dollar value of this inventory?

   b. How many units of the part are held, on average, in pipeline inventory? What is the dollar value of this inventory? (*Hint:* Assume that the typical part in pipeline inventory is 50 percent completed. Thus, half the labor and variable overhead cost has been added, bringing the unit cost to $80, or $50 + $60/2.)

2. Prince Electronics, a manufacturer of consumer electronic goods, has five distribution centers in different regions of the country. For one of its products, a high-speed modem priced at $350 per unit, the average weekly demand at *each* distribution center is 75 units. Average shipment size to each distribution center is 400 units, and average lead time for delivery is 2 weeks. Each distribution center carries 2 weeks' supply as safety stock but holds no anticipation inventory.

   a. On average, how many dollars of pipeline inventory will be in transit to each distribution center?

   b. How much total inventory (cycle, safety, and pipeline) does Prince hold for all five distribution centers?

3. Terminator, Inc., manufactures a motorcycle part in lots of 250 units. The raw materials cost for the part is $150, and the value added in manufacturing 1 unit from its components is $300, for a total cost per completed unit of $450. The lead time to make the part is 3 weeks, and the annual demand is 4,000 units. Assume 50 working weeks per year.

   a. How many units of the part are held, on average, as cycle inventory? What is its value?

   b. How many units of the part are held, on average, as pipeline inventory? What is its value?

4. Oakwood Hospital is considering using ABC analysis to classify laboratory SKUs into three categories: those that will be delivered daily from their supplier (Class A items), those that will be controlled using a continuous review system (B items), and those that will be held in a two bin system (C items). The following table shows the annual dollar usage for a sample of eight SKUs. Rank the SKUs, and assign them to their appropriate category.

SKU	Dollar Value	Annual Usage
1	$0.01	1,200
2	$0.03	120,000
3	$0.45	100
4	$1.00	44,000
5	$4.50	900
6	$0.90	350
7	$0.30	70,000
8	$1.50	200

5. Southern Markets, Inc., is considering the use of ABC analysis to focus on the most critical SKUs in its inventory. Currently, there are approximately 20,000 different SKUs with a total dollar usage of $10,000,000 per year.

   a. What would you expect to be the number of SKUs and the total annual dollar usage for A items, B items and C items at Southern Markets, Inc.?

   b. The following table provides a random sample of the unit values and annual demands of eight SKUs. Categorize these SKUs as A, B, and C items.

SKU Code	Unit Value	Demand (Units)
A104	$2.10	2,500
D205	$2.50	30
X104	$0.85	350
U404	$0.25	250
L205	$4.75	20
S104	$0.02	4,000
X205	$0.35	1,020
L104	$4.25	50

6. Yellow Press, Inc., buys paper in 1,500-pound rolls for printing. Annual demand is 2,500 rolls. The cost per roll is $800, and the annual holding cost is 15 percent of the cost. Each order costs $50 to process.

   a. How many rolls should Yellow Press, Inc., order at a time?

   b. What is the time between orders?

7. Babble, Inc., buys 400 blank cassette tapes per month for use in producing foreign language courseware. The ordering cost is $12.50. Holding cost is $0.12 per cassette per year.

   a. How many tapes should Babble, Inc., order at a time?

   b. What is the time between orders?

8. At Dot Com, a large retailer of popular books, demand is constant at 32,000 books per year. The cost of placing an order to replenish stock is $10, and the annual cost of holding is $4 per book. Stock is received 5 working days after an order has been placed. No backordering is allowed. Assume 300 working days a year.

   a. What is Dot Com's optimal order quantity?

   b. What is the optimal number of orders per year?

   c. What is the optimal interval (in working days) between orders?

   d. What is demand during the lead time?

   e. What is the reorder point?

   f. What is the inventory position immediately after an order has been placed?

9. Leaky Pipe, a local retailer of plumbing supplies, faces demand for one of its SKUs at a constant rate of 30,000 units per year. It costs Leaky Pipe $10 to process an order to replenish stock and $1 per unit per year to carry the item in stock. Stock is received 4 working days after an order is placed. No backordering is allowed. Assume 300 working days a year.

a. What is Leaky Pipe's optimal order quantity?

b. What is the optimal number of orders per year?

c. What is the optimal interval (in working days) between orders?

d. What is the demand during the lead time?

e. What is the reorder point?

f. What is the inventory position immediately after an order has been placed?

10. Sam's Cat Hotel operates 52 weeks per year, 6 days per week, and uses a continuous review inventory system. It purchases kitty litter for $11.70 per bag. The following information is available about these bags.

Demand = 90 bags/week

Order cost = $54/order

Annual holding cost = 27 percent of cost

Desired cycle-service level = 80 percent

Lead time = 3 weeks (18 working days)

Standard deviation of *weekly* demand = 15 bags

Current on-hand inventory is 320 bags, with no open orders or backorders.

a. What is the EOQ? What would be the average time between orders (in weeks)?

b. What should R be?

c. An inventory withdrawal of 10 bags was just made. Is it time to reorder?

d. The store currently uses a lot size of 500 bags (i.e., $Q = 500$). What is the annual holding cost of this policy? Annual ordering cost? Without calculating the EOQ, how can you conclude from these two calculations that the current lot size is too large?

e. What would be the annual cost saved by shifting from the 500-bag lot size to the EOQ?

11. Consider again the kitty litter ordering policy for Sam's Cat Hotel in Problem 10.

a. Suppose that the weekly demand forecast of 90 bags is incorrect and actual demand averages only 60 bags per week. How much higher will total costs be, owing to the distorted EOQ caused by this forecast error?

b. Suppose that actual demand is 60 bags but that ordering costs are cut to only $6 by using the Internet to automate order placing. However, the buyer does not tell anyone, and the EOQ is not adjusted to reflect this reduction in S. How much higher will total costs be, compared to what they could be if the EOQ were adjusted?

12. In a Q system, the demand rate for strawberry ice cream is normally distributed, with an average of 300 pints *per week*. The lead time is 9 weeks. The standard deviation of *weekly* demand is 15 pints.

a. What is the standard deviation of demand during the 9-week lead time?

b. What is the average demand during the 9-week lead time?

c. What reorder point results in a cycle-service level of 99 percent?

13. Petromax Enterprises uses a continuous review inventory control system for one of its SKUs. The following information is available on the item. The firm operates 50 weeks in a year.

Demand = 50,000 units/year

Ordering cost = $35/order

Holding cost = $2/unit/year

Average lead time = 3 weeks

Standard deviation of weekly demand = 125 units

a. What is the economic order quantity for this item?

b. If Petromax wants to provide a 90 percent cycle-service level, what should be the safety stock and the reorder point?

14. In a continuous review inventory system, the lead time for door knobs is 5 weeks. The standard deviation of demand during the lead time is 85 units. The desired cycle-service level is 99 percent. The supplier of door knobs streamlined its operations and now quotes a one-week lead time. How much can safety stock be reduced without reducing the 99 percent cycle-service level?

15. In a two-bin inventory system, the demand for three-inch lag bolts during the 2-week lead time is normally distributed, with an average of 53 units per week. The standard deviation of weekly demand is 5 units.

a. What is the probability of demand exceeding the reorder point when the normal level in the second bin is set at 130 units?

b. What is the probability of demand exceeding the 130 units in the second bin if it takes 3 weeks to receive a replenishment order?

16. Nationwide Auto Parts uses a periodic review inventory control system for one of its stock items. The review interval is 6 weeks, and the lead time for receiving the materials ordered from its wholesaler is 3 weeks. Weekly demand is normally distributed, with a mean of 100 units and a standard deviation of 20 units.

a. What is the average and the standard deviation of demand during the protection interval?

b. What should be the target inventory level if the firm desires 97.5 percent stockout protection?

c. If 350 units were in stock at the time of a periodic review, how many units should be ordered?

17. In a P system, the lead time for a box of weed-killer is 2 weeks and the review period is 1 week. Demand during the protection interval averages 218 boxes, with a standard deviation of 40 boxes.

a. What is the cycle-service level when the target inventory is set at 300 boxes?

b. In the fall season, demand for weed-killer decreases but also becomes more highly variable. Assume that during the fall season, demand during the protection interval is expected to decrease to 180 boxes, but with a standard deviation of 50 boxes. What would be the cycle-service level if management keeps the target inventory level set at 300 boxes?

18. You are in charge of inventory control of a highly successful product retailed by your firm. Weekly demand for this item varies, with an average of 200 units and a standard deviation of 16 units. It is purchased from a wholesaler at a cost of $12.50 per unit. The supply lead time is 4 weeks. Placing an order costs $50, and the inventory carrying

rate per year is 20 percent of the item's cost. Your firm operates 5 days per week, 50 weeks per year.

    a. What is the optimal ordering quantity for this item?

    b. How many units of the item should be maintained as safety stock for 99 percent protection against stockouts during an order cycle?

    c. If supply lead time can be reduced to 2 weeks, what is the percent reduction in the number of units maintained as safety stock for the same 99 percent stockout protection?

    d. If through appropriate sales promotions, the demand variability is reduced so that the standard deviation of weekly demand is 8 units instead of 16, what is the percent reduction (compared to that in part [b]) in the number of units maintained as safety stock for the same 99 percent stockout protection?

19. Suppose that Sam's Cat Hotel in Problem 10 uses a P system instead of a Q system. The average daily demand is $\overline{d} = 90/6 = 15$ bags. and the standard deviation of *daily* demand is $\sigma_d = \dfrac{\sigma_{week}}{\sqrt{6}} = (15/\sqrt{6}) = 6.124$ bags.

    a. What P (in working days) and T should be used to approximate the cost trade-offs of the EOQ?

    b. How much more safety stock is needed than with a Q system?

    c. It is time for the periodic review. How much kitty litter should be ordered?

20. Your firm uses a continuous review system and operates 52 weeks per year. One of the SKUs has the following characteristics.

    Demand $(D) = 20,000$ units/year

    Ordering cost $(S) = \$40/$order

    Holding cost $(H) = \$2/$unit/year

    Lead time $(L) = 2$ weeks

    Cycle-service level $= 95$ percent

Demand is normally distributed, with a standard deviation of *weekly* demand of 100 units.

Current on-hand inventory is 1,040 units, with no scheduled receipts and no backorders.

    a. Calculate the item's EOQ. What is the average time, in weeks, between orders?

    b. Find the safety stock and reorder point that provide a 95 percent cycle-service level.

    c. For these policies, what are the annual costs of (i) holding the cycle inventory and (ii) placing orders?

    d. A withdrawal of 15 units just occurred. Is it time to reorder? If so, how much should be ordered?

21. Your firm uses a periodic review system for all SKUs classified, using ABC analysis, as B or C items. Further, it uses a continuous review system for all SKUs classified as A items. The demand for a specific SKU, currently classified as an A item, has been dropping. You have been asked to evaluate the impact of moving the item from continuous review to periodic review. Assume your firm operates 52 weeks per year; the item's current characteristics are:

    Demand $(D) = 15,080$ units/year

    Ordering cost $(S) = \$125.00/$order

    Holding cost $(H) = \$3.00/$unit/year

    Lead time $(L) = 5$ weeks

    Cycle-service level $= 95$ percent

Demand is normally distributed, with a standard deviation of weekly demand of 64 units.

    a. Calculate the item's EOQ.

    b. Use the EOQ to define the parameters of an appropriate continuous review and periodic review system for this item.

    c. Which system requires more safety stock and by how much?

22. A company begins a review of ordering policies for its continuous review system by checking the current policies for a sample of SKUs. Following are the characteristics of one item.

    Demand $(D) = 64$ units/week (Assume 52 weeks per year)

    Ordering and setup cost $(S) = \$50/$order

    Holding cost $(H) = \$13/$unit/year

    Lead time $(L) = 2$ weeks

    Standard deviation of *weekly* demand $= 12$ units

    Cycle-service level $= 88$ percent

    a. What is the EOQ for this item?

    b. What is the desired safety stock?

    c. What is the reorder point?

    d. What are the cost implications if the current policy for this item is $Q = 200$ and $R = 180$?

23. Using the same information as in Problem 22, develop the best policies for a periodic review system.

    a. What value of P gives the same approximate number of orders per year as the EOQ? Round to the nearest week.

    b. What safety stock and target inventory level provide an 88 percent cycle-service level?

24. Wood County Hospital consumes 1,000 boxes of bandages per week. The price of bandages is $35 per box, and the hospital operates 52 weeks per year. The cost of processing an order is $15, and the cost of holding one box for a year is 15 percent of the value of the material.

    a. The hospital orders bandages in lot sizes of 900 boxes. What *extra* cost does the hospital incur, which it could save by using the EOQ method?

    b. Demand is normally distributed, with a standard deviation of weekly demand of 100 boxes. The lead time is 2 weeks. What safety stock is necessary if the hospital uses a continuous review system and a 97 percent cycle-service level is desired? What should be the reorder point?

    c. If the hospital uses a periodic review system, with $P = 2$ weeks, what should be the target inventory level, T?

25. A golf specialty wholesaler operates 50 weeks per year. Management is trying to determine an inventory policy for its 1-irons, which have the following characteristics:

    Demand $(D) = 2,000$ units/year

    Demand is normally distributed

    Standard deviation of *weekly* demand $= 3$ units

Ordering cost = $40/order

Annual holding cost $(H) = \$5$/units

Desired cycle-service level = 90 percent

Lead time $(L) = 4$ weeks

a. If the company uses a periodic review system, what should P and T be? Round P to the nearest week.

b. If the company uses a continuous review system, what should R be?

26. Osprey Sports stocks everything that a musky fisherman could want in the Great North Woods. A particular musky lure has been very popular with local fishermen as well as those who buy lures on the Internet from Osprey Sports. The cost to place orders with the supplier is $30/order; the demand averages 4 lures per day, with a standard deviation of 1 lure; and the inventory holding cost is $1.00/lure/year. The lead time form the supplier is 10 days, with a standard deviation of 3 days. It is important to maintain a 97 percent cycle-service level to properly balance service with inventory holding costs. Osprey Sports is open 350 days a year to allow the owners the opportunity to fish for muskies during the prime season. The owners want to use a continuous review inventory system for this item.

a. What order quantity should be used?

b. What reorder point should be used?

c. What is the total annual cost for this inventory system?

27. The Farmer's Wife is a country store specializing in knickknacks suitable for a farm-house décor. One item experiencing a considerable buying frenzy is a miniature Holstein cow. Average weekly demand is 30 cows, with a standard deviation of 5 cows. The cost to place a replenishment order is $15 and the holding cost is $0.75/cow/year. The supplier, however, is in China. The lead time for new orders is 8 weeks, with a standard deviation of 2 weeks. The Farmer's Wife, which is open only 50 weeks a year, wants to develop a continuous review inventory system for this item with a cycle-service level of 90 percent.

a. Specify the continuous review system for the cows. Explain how it would work in practice.

b. What is the total annual cost for the system you developed?

Advanced Problems

It may be helpful to review MyOMLab Supplement E, "Simulation," before working Problem 29.

28. Muscle Bound is a chain of fitness stores located in many large shopping centers. Recently, an internal memo from the CEO to all operations personnel complained about the budget overruns at Muscle Bound's central warehouse. In particular, she said that inventories were too high and that the budget will be cut dramatically and proportionately equal for all items in stock. Consequently, warehouse management set up a pilot study to see what effect the budget cuts would have on customer service. They chose 5-pound barbells, which are a high volume SKU and consume considerable warehouse space. Daily demand for the barbells is 1,000 units, with a standard deviation of 150 units. Ordering costs are $40 per order. Holding costs are $2/unit/year. The supplier is located in the Philippines; consequently, the lead time is 35 days with a standard deviation of 5 days. Muscle Bound stores operate 313 days a year (no Sundays).

Suppose that the barbells are allocated a budget of $16,000 for total annual costs. If Muscle Bound uses a continuous review system for the barbells and cannot change the ordering costs and holding costs or the distributions of demand or lead time, what is the best cycle-service level management can expect from their system?

29. The Georgia Lighting Center stocks more than 3,000 lighting fixtures, including chandeliers, swags, wall lamps, and track lights. The store sells at retail, operates six days per week, and advertises itself as the "brightest spot in town." One expensive fixture is selling at an average rate of 5 units per day. The reorder policy is $Q = 40$ and $R = 15$. A new order is placed on the day the reorder point is reached. The lead time is 3 business days. For example, an order placed on Monday will be delivered on Thursday. Simulate the performance of this Q system for the next 3 weeks (18 workdays). Any stockouts result in lost sales (rather than backorders). The beginning inventory is 19 units, and no receipts are scheduled. Table 6.2 simulates the first week of operation. Extend Table 6.2 to simulate operations for the next 2 weeks if demand for the next 12 business days is 7, 4, 2, 7, 3, 6, 10, 0, 5, 10, 4, and 7.

a. What is the average daily ending inventory over the 18 days? How many stockouts occurred?

b. Simulate the inventory performance of the same item assuming a $Q = 30$, $R = 20$ system is used. Calculate the average inventory level and number of stockouts and compare with part (a).

TABLE 6.2 | FIRST WEEK OF OPERATION

Workday	Beginning Inventory	Orders Received	Daily Demand	Ending Inventory	Inventory Position	Order Quantity
1. Monday	19	—	5	14	14	40
2. Tuesday	14	—	3	11	51	—
3. Wednesday	11	—	4	7	47	—
4. Thursday	7	40	1	46	46	—
5. Friday	46	—	10	36	36	—
6. Saturday	36	—	9	27	27	—

Active Model Exercise

This Active Model appears in MyOMLab. It allows you to evaluate the sensitivity of the EOQ and associated costs to changes in the demand and cost parameters.

QUESTIONS

1. What is the EOQ and what is the lowest total cost?

2. What is the annual cost of holding inventory at the EOQ and the annual cost of ordering inventory at the EOQ?

3. From the graph, what can you conclude about the relationship between the lowest total cost and the costs of ordering and holding inventory?

4. How much does the total cost increase if the store manager orders twice as many bird feeders as the EOQ? How much does the total cost increase if the store manager orders half as many bird feeders as the EOQ?

5. What happens to the EOQ and the total cost when demand is doubled? What happens to the EOQ and the total cost when unit price is doubled?

6. Scroll through the lower order cost values and describe the changes to the graph. What happens to the EOQ?

7. Comment on the sensitivity of the EOQ model to errors in demand or cost estimates.

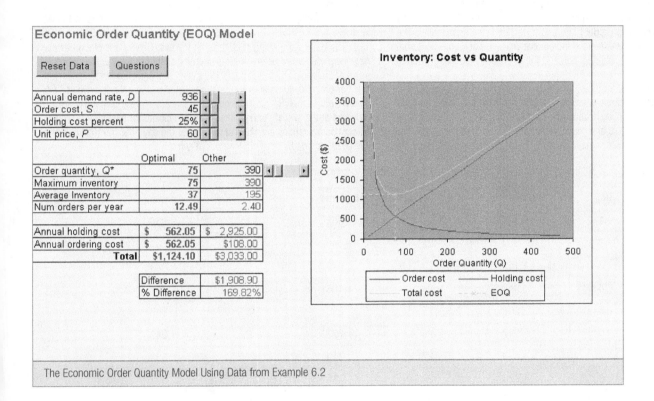

The Economic Order Quantity Model Using Data from Example 6.2

EXPERIENTIAL LEARNING | Swift Electronic Supply, Inc.

It was a typical fall afternoon in Southern California, with thousands of tourists headed to the beaches to have fun. About 40 miles away, however, Steven Holland, the CEO of the Swift Electronic Supply, Inc., faced a severe problem with Swift's inventory management.

An Intel veteran, Steven Holland worked in the electronic components distribution industry for more than 20 years. Seven years ago, he founded the Swift Electronic Supply, Inc., an electronic distributor. After several successful years, the company is now troubled with eroding profit margins. Recent economic downturns further worsened the situation. Factors such as the growth of B2B e-commerce, the globalization of markets, the increased popularity of value-added services, and ongoing consolidations among electronic distributors affect the future of Swift.

To reverse these influences, Holland talked to a prestigious local university. After consultation, Holland found the most effective way to increase profitability is to cut inventory costs. As a starting point, he studied in detail a representative product, dynamic random access memory (DRAM), as the basis for his plan.

Industry and Company Preview

Owing to a boom in the telecommunications industry and the information technology revolution, electronics distributors experienced double-digit annual growth over the last decade. To cut the cost of direct purchasing forces, large component manufacturers such as Intel, Cisco, and Texas Instruments decided to outsource their procurement so that they could focus on product development and manufacturing. Therefore, independent electronic distributors like Swift started offering procurement services to these companies.

Swift serves component manufacturers in California and Arizona. Working as the intermediary between its customers and overseas original equipment manufacturers (OEMs), Swift's business model is quite simple. Forecasting customer demand, Swift places orders to a number of OEMs, stocks those products, breaks the quantities down, and delivers the products to its end customers.

Recently, due to more intense competition and declines in demand, Swift offered more flexible delivery schedules and was willing to accommodate small order quantities. However, customers can always shift to Swift's competitors should Swift not fulfill their orders. Steven Holland was in a dilemma: The intangible costs of losing customers can be enormous; however, maintaining high levels of inventory can also be costly.

Dram

Holland turned his attention to DRAM as a representative product. Previously, the company ordered a large amount every time it felt it was necessary. Holland's assistant developed a table (Table 6.3) that has 2 months of demand history. From Holland's experience, the demand for DRAM is relatively stable in the company's product line and it had no sales seasonality. The sales staff agrees that conditions in the current year will not be different from those of past years, and historical demand will be a good indicator of what to expect in the future.

The primary manufacturers of DRAM are those in Southeast Asia. Currently, Swift can purchase one unit of 128M DRAM for $10. After negotiation with a reputable supplier, Holland managed to sign a long-term agreement, which kept the price at $10 and allowed Swift to place orders at any time. The supplier also supplies other items in Swift's inventory. In addition, it takes the supplier of the DRAM 2 days to deliver the goods to Swift's warehouse using air carriers.

When Swift does not have enough inventory to fill a customer's order, the sales are lost; that is, Swift is not able to backorder the shortage because its customers fill their requirements through competitors. The customers will accept partial shipments, however.

It costs Swift $200 to place an order with the suppliers. This amount covers the corresponding internal ordering costs and the costs of delivering the products to the company. Holland estimates that the cost of lost sales amounts to $2 per unit of DRAM. This rough estimate includes the loss of profits, as well as the intangible damage to customer goodwill.

To simplify its inventory management system, Swift has a policy of maintaining a cycle-service level of 95 percent. The holding cost per day per unit is estimated to be 0.5 percent of the cost of goods, regardless of the product. Inventory holding costs are calculated on the basis of the ending inventory each day. The current balance is 1,700 units of DRAM in stock.

The daily purchasing routine is as follows. Orders are placed at the *beginning* of the day, before Swift is open for customer business. The orders arrive at the beginning of the day, 2 days later, and can be used for sales that day. For example, an order placed at the beginning of day 1 will arrive at Swift before Swift is open for business on day 3. The actual daily demand is always recorded at the *end* of the day, after Swift has closed for customer business. All cost computations are done at the end of the day after the total demand has been recorded.

TABLE 6.3 | HISTORICAL DEMAND DATA FOR THE DRAM (UNITS)

Day	Demand	Day	Demand	Day	Demand
1	869	21	663	41	959
2	902	22	1,146	42	703
3	1,109	23	1,016	43	823
4	947	24	1,166	44	862
5	968	25	829	45	966
6	917	26	723	46	1,042
7	1,069	27	749	47	889
8	1,086	28	766	48	1,002
9	1,066	29	996	49	763
10	929	30	1,122	50	932
11	1,022	31	962	51	1,052
12	959	32	829	52	1,062
13	756	33	862	53	989
14	882	34	793	54	1,029
15	829	35	1,039	55	823
16	726	36	1,009	56	942
17	666	37	979	57	986
18	879	38	976	58	736
19	1,086	39	856	59	1,009
20	992	40	1,036	60	852

Simulation

Holland believes that simulation is a useful approach to assess various inventory control alternatives. The historical data from Table 6.3 could be used to develop attractive inventory policies. The table was developed to record various costs and evaluate different alternatives. An example showing some recent DRAM inventory decisions is shown in Table 6.4.

1. Design a new inventory system for Swift Electronic Supply, Inc., using the data provided.

2. Provide the rationale for your system, which should include the decision rules you would follow to determine how much to order and when.

3. Simulate the use of your inventory system and record the costs. Develop a table such as Table 6.4 to record your results. Your instructor will provide actual demands on a day-to-day basis during the simulation.

TABLE 6.4 | EXAMPLE SIMULATION

Day	1	2	3	4	5	6	7	8	9	10
Beginning inventory position	1,700	831	1,500	391	3,000	3,232	2,315			
Number ordered	1,500		3,000	1,200			1,900			
Daily demand	869	902	1,109	947	968	917	1,069			
Day-ending inventory	831	−71	391	−556	2,032	2,315	1,246			
Ordering costs ($200 per order)	200		200	200			200			
Holding costs ($0.05 per piece per day)	41.55	0.00	19.55	0.00	101.60	115.75	62.30			
Shortage costs ($2 per piece)	0	142	0	1,112	0	0	0			
Total cost for day	241.55	142.00	219.55	1,312.00	101.60	115.75	262.30			
Cumulative cost from last day	0.00	241.55	383.55	603.10	1,915.10	2,016.70	2,132.45			
Cumulative costs to date	241.55	383.55	603.10	1,915.10	2,016.70	2,132.45	2,394.75			

CASE   Parts Emporium

Parts Emporium, Inc., is a wholesale distributor of automobile parts formed by two disenchanted auto mechanics, Dan Block and Ed Spriggs. Originally located in Block's garage, the firm showed slow but steady growth for 7 years before it relocated to an old, abandoned meat-packing warehouse on Chicago's South Side. With increased space for inventory storage, the company was able to begin offering an expanded line of auto parts. This increased selection, combined with the trend toward longer car ownership, led to an explosive growth of the business. Fifteen years later, Parts Emporium was the largest independent distributor of auto parts in the north central region.

Recently, Parts Emporium relocated to a sparkling new office and warehouse complex off Interstate 55 in suburban Chicago. The warehouse space alone occupied more than 100,000 square feet. Although only a handful of new products have been added since the warehouse was constructed, its utilization increased from 65 percent to more than 90 percent of capacity. During this same period, however, sales growth stagnated. These conditions motivated Block and Spriggs to hire the first manager from outside the company in the firm's history.

It is June 6, Sue McCaskey's first day in the newly created position of materials manager for Parts Emporium. A recent graduate of a prominent business school, McCaskey is eagerly awaiting her first real-world problem. At approximately 8:30 A.M., it arrives in the form of status reports on inventory and orders shipped. At the top of an extensive computer printout is a handwritten note from Joe Donnell, the purchasing manager: "Attached you will find the inventory and customer service performance data. Rest assured

that the individual inventory levels are accurate because we took a complete physical inventory count at the end of last week. Unfortunately, we do not keep compiled records in some of the areas as you requested. However, you are welcome to do so yourself. Welcome aboard!"

A little upset that aggregate information is not available, McCaskey decides to randomly select a small sample of approximately 100 items and compile inventory and customer service characteristics to get a feel for the "total picture." The results of this experiment reveal to her why Parts Emporium decided to create the position she now fills. It seems that the inventory is in all the wrong places. Although an *average* of approximately 60 days of inventory is on hand, the firm's customer service is inadequate. Parts Emporium tries to backorder the customer orders not immediately filled from stock, but some 10 percent of demand is being lost to competing distributorships. Because stockouts are costly, relative to inventory holding costs, McCaskey believes that a cycle-service level of at least 95 percent should be achieved.

McCaskey knows that although her influence to initiate changes will be limited, she must produce positive results immediately. Thus, she decides to concentrate on two products from the extensive product line: the EG151 exhaust gasket and the DB032 drive belt. If she can demonstrate significant gains from proper inventory management for just two products, perhaps Block and Spriggs will give her the backing needed to change the total inventory management system.

The EG151 exhaust gasket is purchased from an overseas supplier, Haipei, Inc. Actual demand for the first 21 weeks of this year is shown in the following table:

Week	Actual Demand	Week	Actual Demand
1	104	12	97
2	103	13	99
3	107	14	102
4	105	15	99
5	102	16	103
6	102	17	101
7	101	18	101
8	104	19	104
9	100	20	108
10	100	21	97
11	103		

A quick review of past orders, shown in another document, indicates that a lot size of 150 units is being used and that the lead time from Haipei is fairly constant at 2 weeks. Currently, at the end of week 21, no inventory is on hand, 11 units are backordered, and the company is awaiting a scheduled receipt of 150 units.

The DB032 drive belt is purchased from the Bendox Corporation of Grand Rapids, Michigan. Actual demand so far this year is shown in the following table:

Week	Actual Demand	Week	Actual Demand
11	18	17	50
12	33	18	53
13	53	19	54
14	54	20	49
15	51	21	52
16	53		

Because this product is new, data are available only since its introduction in week 11. Currently, 324 units are on hand, with no backorders and no scheduled receipts. A lot size of 1,000 units is being used, with the lead time fairly constant at 3 weeks.

The wholesale prices that Parts Emporium charges its customers are $12.99 for the EG151 exhaust gasket and $8.89 for the DB032 drive belt. Because no quantity discounts are offered on these two highly profitable items, gross margins based on current purchasing practices are 32 percent of the wholesale price for the exhaust gasket and 48 percent of the wholesale price for the drive belt.

Parts Emporium estimates its cost to hold inventory at 21 percent of its inventory investment. This percentage recognizes the opportunity cost of tying money up in inventory and the variable costs of taxes, insurance, and shrinkage. The annual report notes other warehousing expenditures for utilities and maintenance and debt service on the 100,000-square-foot warehouse, which was built for $1.5 million. However, McCaskey reasons that these warehousing costs can be ignored because they will not change for the range of inventory policies that she is considering.

Out-of-pocket costs for Parts Emporium to place an order with suppliers are estimated to be $20 per order for exhaust gaskets and $10 per order for drive belts. On the outbound side, the company can charge a delivery fee. Although most customers pick up their parts at Parts Emporium, some orders are delivered to customers. To provide this service, Parts Emporium contracts with a local company for a flat fee of $21.40 per order, which is added to the customer's bill. McCaskey is unsure whether to increase the ordering costs for Parts Emporium to include delivery charges.

QUESTIONS

1. Put yourself in Sue McCaskey's position and prepare a detailed report to Dan Block and Ed Spriggs on managing the inventory of the EG151 exhaust gasket and the DB032 drive belt. Be sure to present a proper inventory system and recognize all relevant costs.

2. By how much do your recommendations for these two items reduce annual cycle inventory, stockout, and ordering costs?

Selected References

Arnold, Tony J.R., Stephen Chapman, and Lloyd M. Clive. *Introduction to Materials Management*, 7th ed. Upper Saddle River, NJ: Prentice Hall, 2012.

Axsäter, Sven. *Inventory Control*, 2nd ed. New York: Springer Science + Business Media, LLC, 2006.

Bastow, B. J. "Metrics in the Material World." *APICS—The Performance Advantage* (May 2005), pp. 49–52.

Benton, W.C. *Purchasing and Supply Chain Management*, 2nd ed. New York: McGraw-Hill, 2010.

Callioni, Gianpaolo, Xavier de Montgros, Regine Slagmulder, Luk N. Van Wassenhove, and Linda Wright. "Inventory-Driven Costs." *Harvard Business Review* (March 2005), pp. 135–141.

Cannon, Alan R., and Richard E. Crandall. "The Way Things Never Were." *APICS—The Performance Advantage* (January 2004), pp. 32–35.

Hartvigsen, David. *SimQuick: Process Simulation with Excel*, 2nd ed. Upper Saddle River, NJ: Prentice Hall, 2004.

Operations Management Body of Knowledge. Falls Church, VA: American Production and Inventory Control Society, 2009.

Timme, Stephen G., and Christine Williams-Timme. "The Real Cost of Holding." *Supply Chain Management Review* (July/August 2003), pp. 30–37.

Walters, Donald. *Inventory Control and Management*, 2nd ed. West Sussex, England: John Wiley and Sons, Ltd, 2003.

SPECIAL INVENTORY MODELS

Many real world problems require relaxation of certain assumptions on which the economic order quantity (EOQ) model is based. This supplement addresses three realistic situations that require going beyond the simple EOQ formulation.

1. **Noninstantaneous Replenishment.** Particularly in situations in which manufacturers use a continuous process to make a primary material, such as a liquid, gas, or powder, production is not instantaneous. Thus, inventory is replenished gradually, rather than in lots.

2. **Quantity Discounts.** Three annual costs are (1) the inventory holding cost, (2) the fixed cost for ordering and setup, and (3) the cost of materials. For service providers and for manufacturers alike, the unit cost of purchased materials sometimes depends on the order quantity.

3. **One-Period Decisions.** Retailers and manufacturers of fashion goods often face a situation in which demand is uncertain and occurs during just one period or season.

This supplement assumes you have read Chapter 6, "Supply Chain Inventory Management,"

Noninstantaneous Replenishment

If an item is being produced internally rather than purchased, finished units may be used or sold as soon as they are completed, without waiting until a full lot is completed. For example, a restaurant that bakes its own dinner rolls begins to use some of the rolls from the first pan even before the baker finishes a five-pan batch. The inventory of rolls never reaches the full five-pan level, the way it would if the rolls all arrived at once on a truck sent by a supplier.

Figure A.1 depicts the usual case, in which the production rate, p, *exceeds* the demand rate, d. If demand and production were equal, manufacturing would be continuous with no buildup of cycle inventory. If the production rate is lower than the demand rate, sales opportunities are being missed on an ongoing basis. We assume that $p > d$ in this supplement.

LEARNING GOALS *After reading this supplement, you should be able to:*

1. Identify the situations where the economic lot size should be used rather than the economic order quantity.

2. Calculate the optimal lot size when replenishment is not instantaneous.

3. Define the relevant costs that should be considered to determine the order quantity when discounts are available.

4. Determine the optimal order quantity when materials are subject to quantity discounts.

5. Calculate the order quantity that maximizes the expected profits for a one-period inventory decision.

FIGURE A.1 ▶

Lot Sizing with Noninstantaneous
Replenishment

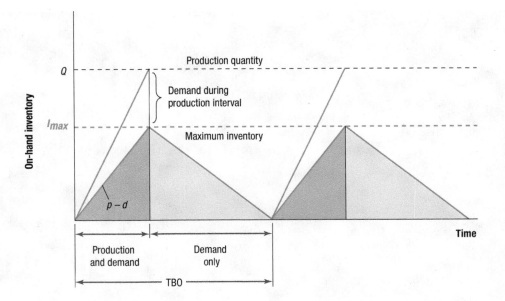

Ulrich Mueller/Shutterstock.com

This chemical plant stores its products in stainless steel silos. The production of each product is scheduled to start when its silo is nearly empty.

Cycle inventory accumulates faster than demand occurs; that is, a buildup of $p - d$ units occurs per time period. For example, if the production rate is 100 units per day and the demand is 5 units per day, the buildup is 95 (or 100 − 5) units each day. This buildup continues until the lot size, Q, has been produced, after which the inventory depletes at a rate of 5 units per day. Just as the inventory reaches 0, the next production interval begins. To be consistent, both p and d must be expressed in units of the same time period, such as units per day or units per week. Here, we assume that they are expressed in units per day.

The $p - d$ buildup continues for Q/p days because Q is the lot size and p units are produced each day. In our example, if the lot size is 300 units, the production interval is 3 days (300/100). For the given rate of buildup over the production interval, the maximum cycle inventory, I_{max}, is

$$I_{max} = \frac{Q}{p}(p - d) = Q\left(\frac{p - d}{p}\right)$$

Cycle inventory is no longer $Q/2$, as it was with the basic EOQ method; instead, it is $I_{max}/2$. Setting up the total annual cost equation for this production situation, where D is annual demand, as before, and d is daily demand, we get

Total annual cost = Annual holding cost + Annual ordering or setup cost

$$C = \frac{I_{max}}{2}(H) + \frac{D}{Q}(S) = \frac{Q}{2}\left(\frac{p - d}{p}\right)(H) + \frac{D}{Q}(S)$$

economic production lot size (ELS)

The optimal lot size in a situation in which replenishment is not instantaneous.

Based on this cost function, the optimal lot size, often called the **economic production lot size (ELS)**, is

$$ELS = \sqrt{\frac{2DS}{H}}\sqrt{\frac{p}{p - d}}$$

Because the second term is a ratio greater than 1, the ELS results in a larger lot size than the EOQ.

| EXAMPLE A.1 | **Finding the Economic Production Lot Size** |

A plant manager of a chemical plant must determine the lot size for a particular chemical that has a steady demand of 30 barrels per day. The production rate is 190 barrels per day, annual demand is 10,500 barrels, setup cost is $200, annual holding cost is $0.21 per barrel, and the plant operates 350 days per year.

a. Determine the economic production lot size (ELS).

b. Determine the total annual setup and inventory holding cost for this item.

c. Determine the time between orders (TBO), or cycle length, for the ELS.

d. Determine the production time per lot.

What are the advantages of reducing the setup time by 10 percent?

MyOMLab

Tutor A.1 in MyOMLab provides a new example to determine the ELS.

MyOMLab

Active Model A.1 in MyOMLab provides additional insight on the ELS model and its uses.

SOLUTION

a. Solving first for the ELS, we get

$$ELS = \sqrt{\frac{2DS}{H}}\sqrt{\frac{p}{p-d}} = \sqrt{\frac{2(10,500)(\$200)}{\$0.21}}\sqrt{\frac{190}{190-30}}$$

$$= 4,873.4 \text{ barrels}$$

b. The total annual cost with the ELS is

$$C = \frac{Q}{2}\left(\frac{p-d}{p}\right)(H) + \frac{D}{Q}(S)$$

$$= \frac{4,873.4}{2}\left(\frac{190-30}{190}\right)(\$0.21) + \frac{10,500}{4,873.4}(\$200)$$

$$= \$430.91 + \$430.91 = \$861.82$$

c. Applying the TBO formula to the ELS, we get

$$TBO_{ELS} = \frac{ELS}{D}(350 \text{ days/year}) = \frac{4,873.4}{10,500}(350)$$

$$= 162.4, \text{ or } 162 \text{ days}$$

d. The production time during each cycle is the lot size divided by the production rate:

$$\frac{ELS}{p} = \frac{4,873.4}{190} = 25.6, \text{ or } 26 \text{ days}$$

DECISION POINT

As OM Explorer shows in Figure A.2, the net effect of reducing the setup cost by 10 percent is to reduce the lot size, the time between orders, and the production cycle time. Consequently, total annual costs are also reduced. This adds flexibility to the manufacturing process because items can be made more quickly with less expense. Management must decide whether the added cost of improving the setup process is worth the added flexibility and inventory cost reductions.

Period Used in Calculations	Day ▼	
Demand per Day	30	
Production Rate/Day	190	
Annual Demand	10,500	
Setup Cost	$180	
Annual Holding Cost ($)	$0.21	● Enter Holding Cost Manually ○ Holding Cost As % of Value
Operating Days per Year	350	
Economic Lot Size (ELS)	4,623	
Annual Total Cost	$817.60	
Time Between Orders (days)	154.1	
Production Time	24.3	

◀ **FIGURE A.2**

OM Explorer Solver for the Economic Production Lot Size Showing the Effect of a 10 Percent Reduction in Setup Cost

Many hospitals join cooperatives (or co-ops) to gain the clout needed to garner price discounts from suppliers. Here a hospital pharmacist checks inventory records of supplies.

Quantity Discounts

Quantity discounts, which are price incentives to purchase large quantities, create pressure to maintain a large inventory. For example, a supplier may offer a price of $4.00 per unit for orders between 1 and 99 units, a price of $3.50 per unit for orders between 100 and 199 units, and a price of $3.00 per unit for orders of 200 or more units. The item's price is no longer fixed, as assumed in the EOQ derivation; instead, if the order quantity is increased enough, the price is discounted. Hence, a new approach is needed to find the best lot size—one that balances the advantages of lower prices for purchased materials and fewer orders (which are benefits of large order quantities) against the disadvantage of the increased cost of holding more inventory.

The total annual cost now includes not only the holding cost, $(Q/2)(H)$, and the ordering cost, $(D/Q)(S)$, but also the cost of purchased materials. For any per-unit price level, P, the total cost is

Total annual cost = Annual holding cost + Annual ordering or setup cost + Annual cost of materials

$$C = \frac{Q}{2}(H) + \frac{D}{Q}(S) + PD$$

The unit holding cost, H, usually is expressed as a percent of the unit price because the more valuable the item held in inventory, the higher the holding cost is. Thus, the lower the unit price, P, the lower H is. Conversely, the higher P is, the higher H is.

The total cost equation yields U-shaped total cost curves. Adding the annual cost of materials to the total cost equation raises each total cost curve by a fixed amount, as shown in Figure A.3 (a). The three cost curves illustrate each of the price levels. The top curve applies when no discounts are received; the lower curves reflect the discounted price levels. No single curve is relevant to all purchase quantities. The relevant, or feasible, total cost begins with the top curve, then drops down, curve by curve, at the price breaks. A price break is the minimum quantity needed to get a discount. In Figure A.3, two price breaks occur at $Q = 100$ and $Q = 200$. The result is a total cost curve, with steps at the price breaks.

▼ **FIGURE A.3**

Total Cost Curves with Quantity Discounts

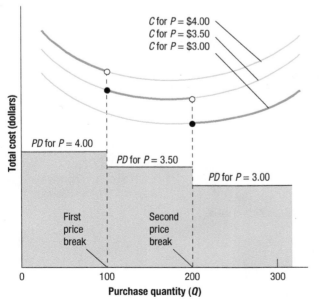

(a) Total cost curves with purchased materials added

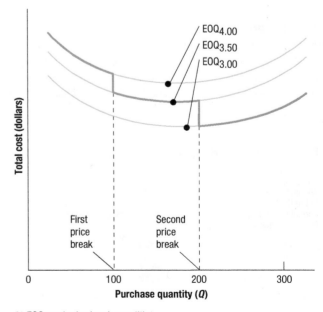

(b) EOQs and price break quantities

Figure A.3 (b) also shows three additional points—the minimum point on each curve—obtained with the EOQ formula at each price level. These EOQs do not necessarily produce the best lot size for two reasons.

1. The EOQ at a particular price level may not be feasible. The lot size may not lie in the range corresponding to its per-unit price. Figure A.3 (b) illustrates two instances of an infeasible EOQ. First, the minimum point for the $3.00 curve appears to be fewer than 200 units. However, the supplier's quantity discount schedule does not allow purchases of that small a quantity at the $3.00 unit price. Similarly, the EOQ for the $4.00 price level is greater than the first price break, so the price charged would be only $3.50.

2. The EOQ at a particular price level may be feasible but may not be the best lot size. The feasible EOQ may have a higher cost than is achieved by the EOQ or price break quantity on a lower price curve. In Figure A.3 (b), for example, the 200-unit price break quantity for the $3.00 price level has a lower total cost than the feasible EOQ for the $3.50 price level. A feasible EOQ always is better than any feasible point on cost curves with higher price levels, but not necessarily those with lower levels. Thus, the only time we can immediately conclude, without comparing total costs, that a feasible EOQ is the best order quantity is when it is on the curve for the lowest price level. This conclusion is not possible in Figure A.3 (b) because the only feasible EOQ is at the middle price level, $P = \$3.50$.

We must, therefore, pay attention only to feasible price–quantity combinations, shown as solid lines in Figure A.3 (b), as we search for the best lot size. The following two-step procedure may be used to find the best lot size.

Step 1. Beginning with the lowest price, calculate the EOQ for each price level until a feasible EOQ is found. It is feasible if it lies in the range corresponding to its price. Each subsequent EOQ is smaller than the previous one because P, and thus H, gets larger and because the larger H is in the denominator of the EOQ formula.

Step 2. If the first feasible EOQ found is for the lowest price level, this quantity is the best lot size. Otherwise, calculate the total cost for the first feasible EOQ and for the larger price break quantity at each lower price level. The quantity with the lowest total cost is optimal.

EXAMPLE A.2	**Finding Q with Quantity Discounts at St. LeRoy Hospital**

A supplier for St. LeRoy Hospital has introduced quantity discounts to encourage larger order quantities of a special catheter. The price schedule is

Order Quantity	Price per Unit
0 to 299	$60.00
300 to 499	$58.80
500 or more	$57.00

The hospital estimates that its annual demand for this item is 936 units, its ordering cost is $45.00 per order, and its annual holding cost is 25 percent of the catheter's unit price. What quantity of this catheter should the hospital order to minimize total costs? Suppose the price for quantities between 300 and 499 is reduced to $58.00. Should the order quantity change?

SOLUTION

Step 1. Find the first feasible EOQ, starting with the lowest price level:

$$EOQ_{57.00} = \sqrt{\frac{2DS}{H}} = \sqrt{\frac{2(936)(\$45.00)}{0.25(\$57.00)}} = 77 \text{ units}$$

A 77-unit order actually costs $60.00 per unit, instead of the $57.00 per unit used in the EOQ calculation, so this EOQ is infeasible. Now, try the $58.80 level:

$$EOQ_{58.80} = \sqrt{\frac{2DS}{H}} = \sqrt{\frac{2(936)(\$45.00)}{0.25(\$58.80)}} = 76 \text{ units}$$

MyOMLab

Tutor A.2 in MyOMLab provides a new example for choosing the best order quantity when discounts are available.

MyOMLab

Active Model A.2 in MyOMLab provides additional insight on the quantity discount model and its uses.

This quantity also is infeasible because a 76-unit order is too small to qualify for the $58.80 price. Try the highest price level:

$$EOQ_{60.00} = \sqrt{\frac{2DS}{H}} = \sqrt{\frac{2(936)(\$45.00)}{0.25(\$60.00)}} = 75 \text{ units}$$

This quantity is feasible because it lies in the range corresponding to its price, $P = \$60.00$.

Step 2. The first feasible EOQ of 75 does not correspond to the lowest price level. Hence, we must compare its total cost with the price break quantities (300 and 500 units) at the lower price levels ($58.80 and $57.00):

$$C = \frac{Q}{2}(H) + \frac{D}{Q}(S) + PD$$

$$C_{75} = \frac{75}{2}[(0.25)(\$60.00)] + \frac{936}{75}(\$45.00) + \$60.00(936) = \$57,284$$

$$C_{300} = \frac{300}{2}[(0.25)(\$58.80)] + \frac{936}{300}(\$45.00) + \$58.80(936) = \$57,382$$

$$C_{500} = \frac{500}{2}[(0.25)(\$57.00)] + \frac{936}{500}(\$45.00) + \$57.00(936) = \$56,999$$

The best purchase quantity is 500 units, which qualifies for the deepest discount.

DECISION POINT

If the price per unit for the range of 300 to 499 units is reduced to $58.00, the best decision is to order 300 catheters, as shown by OM Explorer in Figure A.4. This result shows that the decision is sensitive to the price schedule. A reduction of slightly more than 1 percent is enough to make the difference in this example. In general, however, it is not always the case that you should order more than the economic order quantity when given price discounts. When discounts are small, holding cost H is large, and demand D is small, small lot sizes are better even though price discounts are forgone.

FIGURE A.4 ▶

OM Explorer Solver for Quantity Discounts Showing the Best Order Quantity

Min. Amount Req'd for Price Point	Lot Sizes	Price/Unit
...	0–299	$60.00
300	300–499	$58.00
500	500 or more	$57.00

Annual Demand	936
Order Cost	$45
Holding Cost (% or price)	25%

Best Order Quantity   300

Price Point	EOQ or Req'd Order for Price Point	Inventory Cost	Order Cost	Purchase Cost	Total Cost
$60.00	75	$562.50	$561.60	$56,160	$57,284
$58.00	300	$2,175	$140.40	$54,288	$56,603
$57.00	500	$3,563	$84.24	$53,352	$56,999

One-Period Decisions

One of the dilemmas facing many retailers is how to handle seasonal goods, such as winter coats. Often, they cannot be sold at full markup the next year because of changes in styles. Furthermore, the lead time can be longer than the selling season, allowing no second chance to rush through another order to cover unexpectedly high demand. A similar problem exists for manufacturers of other fashion goods.

This type of situation is often called the *newsboy problem*. If the newspaper seller does not buy enough newspapers to resell on the street corner, sales opportunities are lost. If the seller buys too many newspapers, the overage cannot be sold because nobody wants yesterday's newspaper.

The following process is a straightforward way to analyze such problems and decide on the best order quantity.

1. List the different levels of demand that are possible, along with the estimated probability of each.

2. Develop a *payoff* table that shows the profit for each purchase quantity, Q, at each assumed demand level, D. Each row in the table represents a different order quantity, and each column represents a different demand level. The payoff for a given quantity–demand combination depends on whether all units are sold at the regular profit margin during the regular season, which results in two possible cases.

    a. If demand is high enough ($Q \leq D$), then all units are sold at the full profit margin, p, during the regular season,

$$\text{Payoff} = (\text{Profit per unit})\,(\text{Purchase quantity}) = pQ$$

    b. If the purchase quantity exceeds the eventual demand ($Q > D$), only D units are sold at the full profit margin, and the remaining units purchased must be disposed of at a loss, l, after the season. In this case,

$$\text{Payoff} = \left(\begin{array}{c}\text{Profit per unit sold}\\\text{during season}\end{array}\right)(\text{Demand}) - \left(\begin{array}{c}\text{Loss per}\\\text{unit}\end{array}\right)\left(\begin{array}{c}\text{Amount disposed of}\\\text{after season}\end{array}\right)$$

$$= pD - l(Q - D)$$

3. Calculate the expected payoff for each Q (or row in the payoff table) by using the *expected value* decision rule. For a specific Q, first multiply each payoff in the row by the demand probability associated with the payoff, and then add these products.

4. Choose the order quantity Q with the highest expected payoff.

Using this decision process for all such items over many selling seasons will maximize profits. However, it is not foolproof, and it can result in an occasional bad outcome.

EXAMPLE A.3	**Finding *Q* for One-Period Inventory Decisions**

One of many items sold at a museum of natural history is a Christmas ornament carved from wood. The gift shop makes a $10 profit per unit sold during the season, but it takes a $5 loss per unit after the season is over. The following discrete probability distribution for the season's demand has been identified:

Demand	10	20	30	40	50
Demand Probability	0.2	0.3	0.3	0.1	0.1

How many ornaments should the museum's buyer order?

SOLUTION

Each demand level is a candidate for best order quantity, so the payoff table should have five rows. For the first row, where $Q = 10$, demand is at least as great as the purchase quantity. Thus, all five payoffs in this row are

$$\text{Payoff} = pQ = (\$10)(10) = \$100$$

This formula can be used in other rows but only for those quantity–demand combinations where all units are sold during the season. These combinations lie in the upper-right portion of the payoff table, where $Q \leq D$. For example, the payoff when $Q = 40$ and $D = 50$ is

$$\text{Payoff} = pQ = (\$10)(40) = \$400$$

The payoffs in the lower-left portion of the table represent quantity–demand combinations where some units must be disposed of after the season ($Q > D$). For this case, the payoff must be calculated with the second formula. For example, when $Q = 40$ and $D = 30$,

$$\begin{aligned}\text{Payoff} = pD = l(Q - D) &= (\$10)(30) -\\ (\$5)(40 - 30) &= \$250\end{aligned}$$

OM Explorer or POM for Windows can be used to analyze this problem. Using OM Explorer, we obtain the payoff table in Figure A.5.

MyOMLab
Tutor A.3 in MyOMLab provides a new example to practice the one-period inventory decision.

MyOMLab
Active Model A.3 in MyOMLab provides additional insight on the one-period inventory decision model and its uses.

▼ **FIGURE A.5**
OM Explorer Solver for One-Period Inventory Decisions Showing the Payoff Table

Profit	$10.00	(if sold during preferred period)
Loss	$5.00	(if sold after preferred period)

Enter the possible demands along with the probability of each occuring. Use the buttons to increase or decrease the number of allowable demand forecasts. NOTE: Be sure to enter demand forecasts and probablities in all tinted cells, and be sure probabilities add up to 1.

	<	>			
Demand	10	20	30	40	50
Profitability	0.2	0.3	0.3	0.1	0.1

Payoff Table

		Demand			
	10	20	30	40	50
Quantity					
10	100	100	100	100	100
20	50	200	200	200	200
30	0	150	300	300	300
40	−50	100	250	400	400
50	−100	50	200	350	500

Now we calculate the expected payoff for each Q by multiplying the payoff for each demand quantity by the probability of that demand and then adding the results. For example, for $Q = 30$,

$$\text{Payoff} = 0.2(\$0) + 0.3(\$150) + 0.3(\$300) + 0.1(\$300) + 0.1(\$300) = \$195$$

Using OM Explorer, Figure A.6 shows the expected payoffs.

DECISION POINT

Because $Q = 30$ has the highest payoff at $195, it is the best order quantity. Management can use OM Explorer or POM for Windows to do sensitivity analysis on the demands and their probabilities to see how confident they are with that decision.

FIGURE A.6 ▶

OM Explorer Solver Showing the Expected Payoffs

Weighted Payoffs

Order Quantity	Expected Payoff
10	100
20	170
30	195
40	175
50	140

Greatest Expected Payoff	195
Associated with Order Quantity	30

The need for one-time inventory decisions also can arise in manufacturing plants when (1) customized items are made (or purchased) to a single order, and (2) scrap quantities are high. A customized item produced for a single order is never intentionally held in stock because the demand for it is too unpredictable. In fact, it may never be ordered again so the manufacturer would like to make just the amount requested by the customer—no more, no less. The manufacturer also would like to satisfy an order in just one run to avoid an extra setup and a delay in delivering goods ordered. These two goals may conflict if the likelihood of some units being scrapped is high. Suppose that a customer places an order for 20 units. If the manager orders 20 units from the shop or from the supplier, one or two units may have to be scrapped. This shortage will force the manager to place a second (or even third) order to replace the defective units. Replacement can be costly if setup time is high and can also delay shipment to the customer. To avoid such problems, the manager could order more than 20 units the first time. If some units are left over, the customer might be willing to buy the extras or the manager might find an internal use for them. For example, some manufacturing companies set up a special account for obsolete materials. These materials can be "bought" by departments within the company at less than their normal cost, as an incentive to use them.

LEARNING GOALS IN REVIEW

① **Identify the situations where the economic lot size should be used rather than the economic order quantity**. See the section "Noninstantaneous Replenishment," pp. 223–225. Figure A.1 shows the behavior of inventories when the ELS is appropriate.

② **Calculate the optimal lot size when replenishment is not instantaneous**. Study Example A.1 and Solved Problem 1 for help on determining the ELS.

③ **Define the relevant costs that should be considered to determine the order quantity when discounts are available**. See the section "Quantity Discounts," pp. 226–228. Figure A.3 shows how the relevant costs affect the best lot size decision.

④ **Determine the optimal order quantity when materials are subject to quantity discounts**. Study Example A.2 and Solved Problem 2 for a step-by-step approach to determine the best order quantity.

⑤ **Calculate the order quantity that maximizes the expected profits for a one-period inventory decision**. See the section "One-Period Decisions," pp. 228–230. Be sure to understand Example A.3 and Solved Problem 3.

MyOMLab helps you develop analytical skills and assesses your progress with multiple problems on economic production lot sizes, TBO, production time per lot, total annual costs, quantity discounts, one-period inventory decisions, and the payoff matrix.

MyOMLab Resources	Titles	Link to the Book
Active Models Exercises	A.1 Economic Production Lot Size	Noninstantaneous Replenishment; Example A.1 (p. 225); Solved Problem 1 (p. 232)
	A.2 Quantity Discounts	Quantity Discounts; Example A.2 (pp. 227–228)
	A.3 One-Time Inventory Decision	One-Period Decisions; Example A.3 (pp. 229–230)
OM Explorer Solvers	Economic Production Lot Size	Noninstantaneous Replenishment; Example A.1 (p. 225); Figure A.2 (p. 225); Solved Problem 1 (p. 232)
	Quantity Discounts	Quantity Discounts; Example A.2 (pp. 227–228); Figure A.4 (p. 228); Solved Problem 2 (pp. 232–233)
	One-Period Inventory	One-Period Decisions; Example A.3 (pp. 229–230); Figure A.5 (p. 229); Figure A.6 (p. 230); Solved Problem 3 (p. 233)
OM Explorer Tutors	A.1 Economic Production Lot Size	Noninstantaneous Replenishment; Example A.1 (p. 225); Solved Problem 1 (p. 232)
	A.2 Finding Q with Quantity Discounts	Quantity Discounts; Example A.2 (pp. 227–228); Solved Problem 2 (pp. 232–233)
	A.3 One-Period Inventory Decisions	One-Period Decisions; Example A.3 (pp. 229–230); Solved Problem 3 (p. 233)
POM for Windows	Decision Tables	One-Period Decisions; Example A.3 (pp. 229–230); Solved Problem 3 (p. 233)
	Economic Production Lot Size Model	Noninstantaneous Replenishment; Example A.1 (p. 225); Solved Problem 1 (p. 232)
	Quantity Discount Model	Quantity Discounts; Example A.2 (pp. 227–228); Solved Problem 2 (pp. 232–233)
Virtual Tours	Sierra Nevada	Entire supplement
	United Wood Treating	Entire supplement
	Woot	Entire supplement
Internet Exercise	Continental Cement	Noninstantaneous Replenishment
Key Equations		
Image Library		

Key Equations

1. Noninstantaneous replenishment:

   Maximum inventory: $I_{\max} = Q\left(\dfrac{p-d}{p}\right)$

   Total annual cost = Annual holding cost + Annual ordering or setup cost

   $$C = \frac{Q}{2}\left(\frac{p-d}{p}\right)(H) + \frac{D}{Q}(S)$$

   Economic production lot size: $\text{ELS} = \sqrt{\dfrac{2DS}{H}}\sqrt{\dfrac{p}{p-d}}$

   Time between orders, expressed in years: $\text{TBO}_{\text{ELS}} = \dfrac{\text{ELS}}{D}$

2. Quantity discounts:

   Total annual cost = Annual holding cost + Annual ordering
   or setup cost + Annual cost of material

   $$C = \frac{Q}{2}(H) + \frac{D}{Q}(S) + PD$$

3. One-period decisions:

   Payoff matrix: Payoff $= \begin{cases} pQ & \text{if } Q \le D \\ pD - l(Q - D) & \text{if } Q > D \end{cases}$

Key Term

economic production lot size (ELS) 224

Solved Problem 1

Peachy Keen, Inc., makes mohair sweaters, blouses with Peter Pan collars, pedal pushers, poodle skirts, and other popular clothing styles of the 1950s. The average demand for mohair sweaters is 100 per week. Peachy's production facility has the capacity to sew 400 sweaters per week. Setup cost is $351. The value of finished goods inventory is $40 per sweater. The annual per-unit inventory holding cost is 20 percent of the item's value.

a. What is the economic production lot size (ELS)?
b. What is the average time between orders (TBO)?
c. What is the total of the annual holding cost and setup cost?

SOLUTION

a. The production lot size that minimizes total cost is

$$\text{ELS} = \sqrt{\frac{2DS}{H}}\sqrt{\frac{p}{p-d}} = \sqrt{\frac{2(100 \times 52)(\$351)}{0.20(\$40)}}\sqrt{\frac{400}{(400-100)}}$$

$$= \sqrt{456,300}\sqrt{\frac{4}{3}} = 780 \text{ sweaters}$$

b. The average time between orders is

$$\text{TBO}_{\text{ELS}} = \frac{\text{ELS}}{D} = \frac{780}{5,200} = 0.15 \text{ year}$$

Converting to weeks, we get

$$\text{TBO}_{\text{ELS}} = (0.15 \text{ year})(52 \text{ weeks/year}) = 7.8 \text{ weeks}$$

c. The minimum total of setup and holding costs is

$$C = \frac{Q}{2}\left(\frac{p-d}{p}\right)(H) + \frac{D}{Q}(S) = \frac{780}{2}\left(\frac{400-100}{400}\right)(0.20 \times \$40) + \frac{5,200}{780}(\$351)$$

$$= \$2,340/\text{year} + \$2,340/\text{year} = \$4,680/\text{year}$$

Solved Problem 2

A hospital buys disposable surgical packages from Pfisher, Inc. Pfisher's price schedule is $50.25 per package on orders of 1 to 199 packages and $49.00 per package on orders of 200 or more packages. Ordering cost is $64 per order, and annual holding cost is 20 percent of the per-unit purchase price. Annual demand is 490 packages. What is the best purchase quantity?

SOLUTION

We first calculate the EOQ at the *lowest* price:

$$\text{EOQ}_{49.00} = \sqrt{\frac{2DS}{H}} = \sqrt{\frac{2(490)(\$64.00)}{0.20(\$49.00)}} = \sqrt{6,400} = 80 \text{ packages}$$

This solution is infeasible because, according to the price schedule, we cannot purchase 80 packages at a price of $49.00 each. Therefore, we calculate the EOQ at the next lowest price ($50.25):

$$\text{EOQ}_{50.25} = \sqrt{\frac{2DS}{H}} = \sqrt{\frac{2(490)(\$64.00)}{0.20(\$50.25)}} = \sqrt{6,241} = 79 \text{ packages}$$

This EOQ is feasible, but $50.25 per package is not the lowest price. Hence, we have to determine whether total costs can be reduced by purchasing 200 units and thereby obtaining a quantity discount.

$$C = \frac{Q}{2}(H) + \frac{D}{Q}(S) + PD$$

$$C_{79} = \frac{79}{2}(0.20 \times \$50.25) + \frac{490}{79}(\$64.00) + \$50.25(490)$$

$$= \$396.98/\text{year} + \$396.68/\text{year} + \$24,622.50/\text{year} = \$25,416.44/\text{year}$$

$$C_{200} = \frac{200}{2}(0.20 \times \$49.00) + \frac{490}{200}(\$64.00) + \$49.00(490)$$

$$= \$980.00/\text{year} + \$156.80/\text{year} + \$24,010.00/\text{year} = \$25,146.80/\text{year}$$

Purchasing 200 units per order will save $269.64/year, compared to buying 79 units at a time.

Solved Problem 3

Swell Productions is sponsoring an outdoor conclave for owners of collectible and classic Fords. The concession stand in the T-Bird area will sell clothing such as T-shirts and official Thunderbird racing jerseys. Jerseys are purchased from Columbia Products for $40 each and are sold during the event for $75 each. If any jerseys are left over, they can be returned to Columbia for a refund of $30 each. Jersey sales depend on the weather, attendance, and other variables. The following table shows the probability of various sales quantities. How many jerseys should Swell Productions order from Columbia for this one-time event?

Sales Quantity	Probability	Quantity Sales	Probability
100	0.05	400	0.34
200	0.11	500	0.11
300	0.34	600	0.05

SOLUTION

Table A.1 is the payoff table that describes this one-period inventory decision. The upper-right portion of the table shows the payoffs when the demand, D, is greater than or equal to the order quantity, Q. The payoff is equal to the per-unit profit (the difference between price and

TABLE A.1 PAYOFFS

	DEMAND, D						
Q	100	200	300	400	500	600	Expected Payoff
100	$3,500	$3,500	$ 3,500	$ 3,500	$ 3,500	$ 3,500	$ 3,500
200	$2,500	$7,000	$ 7,000	$ 7,000	$ 7,000	$ 7,000	$ 6,775
300	$1,500	$6,000	$10,500	$10,500	$10,500	$10,500	$ 9,555
400	$ 500	$5,000	$ 9,500	$14,000	$14,000	$14,000	$10,805
500	($ 500)	$4,000	$ 8,500	$13,000	$17,500	$17,500	$10,525
600	($1,500)	$3,000	$ 7,500	$12,000	$16,500	$21,000	$ 9,750

cost) multiplied by the order quantity. For example, when the order quantity is 100 and the demand is 200,

$$\text{Payoff} = (p - c)Q = (\$75 - \$40)100 = \$3,500$$

The lower-left portion of Table A.1 shows the payoffs when the order quantity exceeds the demand. Here the payoff is the profit from sales, pD, minus the loss associated with returning overstock, $l(Q - D)$, where l is the difference between the cost and the amount refunded for each jersey returned and $Q - D$ is the number of jerseys returned. For example, when the order quantity is 500 and the demand is 200,

$$\text{Payoff} = pD - l(Q - D) = (\$75 - \$40)200 - (\$40 - \$30)(500 - 200) = \$4,000$$

The highest expected payoff occurs when 400 jerseys are ordered:

$$\text{Expected payoff}_{400} = (\$500 \times 0.05) + (\$5,000 \times 0.11) + (\$9,500 \times 0.34)$$

$$+ (\$14,000 \times 0.34) + (\$14,000 \times 0.11) + (\$14,000 \times 0.05)$$

$$= \$10,805$$

Problems

The OM Explorer and POM for Windows software is available to all students using the 10th edition of this textbook. Go to **www.pearsonhighered.com/krajewski** to download these computer packages. If you purchased MyOMLab, you also have access to Active Models software and significant help in doing the following problems. Check with your instructor on how best to use these resources. In many cases, the instructor wants you to understand how to do the calculations by hand. At the least, the software provides a check on your calculations. When calculations are particularly complex and the goal is interpreting the results in making decisions, the software entirely replaces the manual calculations. The software also can be a valuable resource well after your course is completed.

1. Bold Vision, Inc., makes laser printer and photocopier toner cartridges. The demand rate is 625 EP cartridges per week. The production rate is 1,736 EP cartridges per week, and the setup cost is $100. The value of inventory is $130 per unit, and the holding cost is 20 percent of the inventory value. Bold Vision operates 52 weeks a year. What is the economic production lot size?

2. Sharpe Cutter is a small company that produces specialty knives for paper cutting machinery. The annual demand for a particular type of knife is 100,000 units. The demand is uniform over the 250 working days in a year. Sharpe Cutter produces this type of knife in lots and, on average, can produce 450 knives a day. The cost to set up a production lot is $300, and the annual holding cost is $1.20 per knife.

   a. Determine the economic production lot size (ELS).

   b. Determine the total annual setup and inventory holding cost for this item.

   c. Determine the TBO, or cycle length, for the ELS.

   d. Determine the production time per lot.

3. Suds's Bottling Company does bottling, labeling, and distribution work for several local microbreweries. The demand rate for Wortman's beer is 600 cases (24 bottles each) per week. Suds's bottling production rate is 2,400 cases per week, and the setup cost is $800. The value of inventory is $12.50 per case, and the annual holding cost is 30 percent of the inventory value. Suds's facilities operate 52 weeks each year. What is the economic production lot size?

4. The Bucks Grande exhibition baseball team plays 50 weeks each year and uses an average of 350 baseballs per week. The team orders baseballs from Coopers-Town, Inc., a ball manufacturer noted for six-sigma–level consistency and high product quality. The cost to order baseballs is $100 per order and the annual holding cost per ball is 38 percent of the purchase price. Coopers-Town's price structure is:

Order Quantity	Price per Unit
1–999	$7.50
1,000–4999	$7.25
5,000 or more	$6.50

   a. How many baseballs should the team buy per order?

   b. What is the total annual cost associated with the best order quantity?

   c. Coopers-Town, Inc., discovers that, owing to special manufacturing processes required for the Buck's baseballs, it has underestimated the setup time required on a capacity-constrained piece of machinery. Coopers-Town adds another category to the price structure to provide an incentive for larger orders and thereby hopes to reduce the number of setups required. If the Bucks buy 15,000 baseballs or more, the price will drop to $6.25 each. Should the Bucks revise their order quantity?

5. To boost sales, Pfisher (refer to Solved Problem 2) announces a new price structure for disposable surgical packages. Although the price break no longer is available at 200 units, Pfisher now offers an even greater discount if larger quantities are purchased. On orders of 1 to 499 packages, the price is $50.25 per package. For orders of 500 or more, the price per unit is $47.80. Ordering costs, annual holding costs, and annual demand remain at $64 per order, 20 percent of the per-unit cost, and 490 packages per year, respectively. What is the new lot size?

6. The University Bookstore at a prestigious private university buys mechanical pencils from a wholesaler. The wholesaler offers discounts for large orders according to the following price schedule:

Order Quantity	Price per Unit
0 to 200	$4.00
201 to 2,000	$3.50
2,001 or more	$3.25

The bookstore expects an annual demand of 2,500 units. It costs $10 to place an order, and the annual cost of holding a unit in stock is 30 percent of the unit's price. Determine the best order quantity.

7. Mac-in-the-Box, Inc., sells computer equipment by mail and telephone order. Mac sells 1,200 flat-bed scanners per year. Ordering cost is $300, and annual holding cost is 16 percent of the item's price. The scanner manufacturer offers the following price structure to Mac-in-the-Box:

Order Quantity	Price per Unit
0 to 11	$520
12 to 143	$500
144 or more	$400

What order quantity minimizes total annual costs?

8. As inventory manager, you must decide on the order quantity for an item that has an annual demand of 2,000 units. Placing an order costs you $20 each time. Your annual holding cost, expressed as a percentage of

average inventory value, is 20 percent. Your supplier has provided the following price schedule:

Minimum Order Quantity	Price per Unit
1	$2.50
200	$2.40
300	$2.25
1,000	$2.00

What ordering policy do you recommend?

9. Downtown Health Clinic needs to order influenza vaccines for the next flu season. The Clinic charges its patients $15.00 per vaccination and each dose of vaccine costs the clinic $4.00 to purchase. The Center for Disease Control has a long standing policy of buying back unused vaccines for $1.00 per dose. The Clinic estimates the following probability distribution for the season's demand:

Demand	Probability
2,000	0.05
3,000	0.20
4,000	0.25
5,000	0.40
6,000	0.10

a. How many vaccines should the Clinic order to maximize its expected profit?

b. The Clinic is trying to determine if they should participate in a new Federal program in which the cost of each dose is reduced to $2.00. However, to participate in the program, they can charge no more than $10.00 per vaccine. On strictly a profit maximizing basis, should the Clinic agree to participate?

10. Dorothy's pastries are freshly baked and sold at several specialty shops throughout Perth. When they are a day old, they must be sold at reduced prices. Daily demand is distributed as follows:

Demand	Probability
50	0.25
150	0.50
200	0.25

Each pastry sells for $1.00 and costs $0.60 to make. Each one not sold at the end of the day can be sold the next day for $0.30 as day-old merchandise. How many pastries should be baked each day?

11. The Aggies will host Tech in this year's homecoming football game. Based on advance ticket sales, the athletic department has forecast hot dog sales as shown in the following table. The school buys premium hot dogs for $1.50 and sells them during the game at $3.00 each. Hot dogs left over after the game will be sold for $0.50 each to the Aggie student cafeteria, where they will be used in making hotdog casserole.

Sales Quantity	Probability
2,000	0.10
3,000	0.30
4,000	0.30
5,000	0.20
6,000	0.10

Use a payoff matrix to determine the number of hot dogs to buy for the game.

12. Bold Vision, Inc. (from Problem 1), must purchase toner from a local supplier. The company does not wish to carry raw material inventory and therefore only purchases enough toner to satisfy the demand of each individual batch of cartridges. Each toner cartridge requires one pound of toner. The raw material supplier offers Bold Vision a purchase discount of $2.00 per pound if the company orders at least 2,000 pounds at a time. Should Bold Vision accept this offer and alter its toner purchase quantity?

Selected References

Arnold, Tony J.R., Stephen Chapman, and Lloyd M. Clive. *Introduction to Materials Management*, 7th ed. Upper Saddle River, NJ: Prentice Hall, 2012.

Axsäter, Sven. *Inventory Control*, 2nd ed. New York: Springer Science + Business Media, LLC, 2006.

Bastow, B.J. "Metrics in the Material World." *APICS—The Performance Advantage* (May 2005), pp. 49–52.

Benton, W.C. *Purchasing and Supply Chain Management*, 2nd ed. New York: McGraw-Hill, 2010.

Callioni, Gianpaolo, Xavier de Montgros, Regine Slagmulder, Luk N. Van Wassenhove, and Linda Wright. "Inventory-Driven Costs." *Harvard Business Review* (March 2005), pp. 135–141.

Cannon, Alan R., and Richard E. Crandall. "The Way Things Never Were." *APICS—The Performance Advantage* (January 2004), pp. 32–35.

Hartvigsen, David. *SimQuick: Process Simulation with Excel*, 2nd ed. Upper Saddle River, NJ: Prentice Hall, 2004.

Manikas, Andrew. "Fighting Pests with the EOQ," *APICS Magazine* (April 2007), pp. 34–37.

Operations Management Body of Knowledge. Falls Church, VA: American Production and Inventory Control Society, 2009.

Timme, Stephen G., and Christine Williams-Timme. "The Real Cost of Holding." *Supply Chain Management Review* (July/August 2003), pp. 30–37.

Walters, Donald. *Inventory Control and Management*, 2nd ed. West Sussex, England: John Wiley and Sons, Ltd, 2003.

A Baseline Engineer for Verizon readies his computer that will control a bank of cell phones making and receiving calls on different networks. He travels through northern Virginia, Washington, DC, and Maryland with a truck outfitted to test the services of Verizon and its competitors to see where faults lie in Verizon's system.

Verizon Wireless

Anyone who owns a cell phone knows the agony of a dropped call. Did you know that the reason for the dropped call may be the phone itself, and not the strength of the signal? Verizon Wireless serves more than 62 million customers in the United States and, along with the other major carriers, it knows that if the phone does not work, the company, and not the manufacturer, will likely take the blame from the customer. Verizon touts the reliability of its services and can ill afford the failure of cell phones due to the quality of manufacture. Verizon expects manufacturers such as Motorola, Samsung, and LG Electronics to provide defect-free phones; however, experience has indicated that extensive testing by Verizon employees is also needed.

In addition to a tear-down analysis that looks for weaknesses in a phone's hardware and components, the device is tested for its ability to withstand temperature extremes, vibration, and stress. Beyond these physical tests, Verizon uses two approaches to assess a phone's capability to receive cellular signals and clearly communicate to the caller. First, Verizon hires 98 test personnel who drive $300,000 specially equipped vans more than 1 million miles a year to measure network performance using prospective new cell phones. They make more than 3 million voice call attempts and 16 million data tests annually. The tests check the coverage of the network as well as the capability of the cell phones to pick up the signals and clearly communicate to the caller. Second, Verizon uses Mr. Head, a robotic mannequin, who has a recorded voice and is electronically equipped with a rubber ear that evaluates how well the phone's mouthpiece transmits certain phonetics. Mr. Head utters what sounds like gibberish; however, it actually covers the range of sounds in normal speech patterns. Other systems monitor the tests and summarize results.

Some phones spend so much time in the test phase that ultimately they never make it to the market. Clearly, in those cases, the cost of poor quality to the manufacturer is very high.

Source: Amol Sharma, "Testing, Testing," *Wall Street Journal* (October 23, 2007); Janet Hefler, "Verizon Tester Checks Vineyard Networks," *The Martha's Vineyard Times* (August 30, 2007); Jon Gales, "Ride Along With a Verizon Wireless Test Man," *Mobile Tracker* (April 4, 2005) **http:// investor.verizon.com** (2007).

LEARNING GOALS *After reading this chapter, you should be able to:*

1 Define the four major costs of quality.

2 Describe the role of ethics in the quality of services and products.

3 Explain the basic principles of TQM programs.

4 Explain the basic principles of Six Sigma programs.

5 Describe how to construct control charts and use them to determine whether a process is out of statistical control.

6 Describe how to determine whether a process is capable of producing a service or product to specifications.

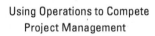

Creating Value through Operation Management

Using Operations to Compete
Project Management

Managing Processes

Process Strategy
Process Analysis
Quality and Performance
Capacity Planning
Constraint Management
Lean Systems

Managing Supply Chains

Supply Chain Inventory Management
Supply Chain Design
Supply Chain Location Decisions
Supply Chain Integration
Supply Chain Sustainability and Humanitarian Logistics
Forecasting
Operations Planning and Scheduling
Resource Planning

The challenge for businesses today is to satisfy their customers through the exceptional performance of their processes. Verizon Wireless is one example of a company that met the challenge by designing and managing processes that provide customers with total satisfaction. Evaluating process performance is important if this is to happen.

Evaluating process performance is also necessary for managing supply chains. For example, at Verizon Wireless, the process of delivering cell phone communications to the customer might be measured on the consistency of service and the sound quality of the voice transmissions. The procurement process, which involves selecting the suppliers for the cell phones and evaluating how they deliver their products, might be measured in terms of the quality of the cell phones delivered to Verizon, the on-time delivery performance of the suppliers, and the cost of the cell phones. Ultimately, the evaluation of the supply chain consisting of these two processes and many others will depend on how well it satisfies the customers of Verizon, who consider the value of the service to be how well it meets or exceeds expectations. The performance of these individual processes must be consistent with the performance measures for the supply chain.

Quality and Performance across the Organization

Quality and performance should be everybody's concern. Take for example QVC, a $7.4 billion televised shopping service. QVC airs 24 hours a day, all year round. QVC sells some 60,000 items ranging from jewelry, tools, cookware, clothing, and gourmet food to computers and annually ships more than 166 million packages worldwide.

QVC's processes, which span all the functional areas, spring into action with a customer order: Order taking and delivery date promising, billing, and order delivery all ensue once an order is placed. QVC operates four call centers that handle 179 million calls annually from customers who want to order something, complain about a problem, or just get product information. The call center representative's demeanor and skill are critical to achieving a successful customer encounter. QVC management keeps track of productivity, quality, and customer satisfaction measures for all processes. When the measures slip, problems are addressed aggressively. Knowing how to assess whether the process is performing well and when to take action are key skills QVC managers must have. In this chapter, we first address the costs of quality and then focus on Total Quality Management and Six Sigma, two philosophies and supporting tools that many companies embrace to evaluate and improve quality and performance.

Costs of Quality

When a process fails to satisfy a customer, the failure is considered a **defect**. For example, according to the California Academy of Family Physicians, defects for the processes in a doctor's practice are defined as "anything that happened in my office that should not have happened, and that I absolutely do not want to happen again." Obviously, this definition covers process failures that the patient sees, such as poor communication and errors in prescription dosages. It also includes failures the patient does not see, such as incorrect charting.

Many companies spend significant time, effort, and expense on systems, training, and organizational changes to improve the quality and performance of their processes. They believe that it is important to be able to gauge current levels of performance so that any process gaps can be determined. Gaps reflect potential dissatisfied customers and additional costs for the firm. Most experts estimate that the costs of quality range from 20 to 30 percent of gross sales. These costs can be broken down into four major categories: (1) prevention, (2) appraisal, (3) internal failure, and (4) external failure.

defect
Any instance when a process fails to satisfy its customer.

Prevention Costs

Prevention costs are associated with preventing defects before they happen. They include the costs of redesigning the process to remove the causes of poor performance, redesigning the service or product to make it simpler to produce, training employees in the methods of continuous improvement, and working with suppliers to increase the quality of purchased items or contracted services. In order to prevent problems from happening, firms must invest additional time, effort, and money.

prevention costs
Costs associated with preventing defects before they happen.

Appraisal Costs

Appraisal costs are incurred when the firm assesses the level of performance of its processes. As the costs of prevention increase and performance improves, appraisal costs decrease because fewer resources are needed for quality inspections and the subsequent search for causes of any problems that are detected.

appraisal costs
Costs incurred when the firm assess the performance level of its processes.

Internal Failure Costs

Internal failure costs result from defects that are discovered during the production of a service or product. Defects fall into two main categories: (1) *rework*, which is incurred if some aspect of a service must be performed again or if a defective item must be rerouted to some previous operation(s) to correct the defect; and (2) *scrap*, which is incurred if a defective item is unfit for further processing. For example, an analysis of the viability of acquiring a company might be sent back to the mergers and acquisitions department if an assessment of the company's history of environmental compliance is missing. The proposal for the purchase of the company may be delayed, which may result in the loss of the purchase opportunity.

internal failure costs
Costs resulting from defects that are discovered during the production of a service or product.

External Failure Costs

External failure costs arise when a defect is discovered after the customer receives the service or product. Dissatisfied customers talk about bad service or products to their friends, who in turn tell others. If the problem is bad enough, consumer protection groups may even alert the media. The potential impact on future profits is difficult to assess, but without doubt external failure costs erode market share and profits. Encountering defects and correcting them after the product is in the customer's hands is costly.

External failure costs also include warranty service and litigation costs. A **warranty** is a written guarantee that the producer will replace or repair defective parts or perform the service to the customer's satisfaction. Usually, a warranty is given for some specified period. For example, television repairs are usually guaranteed for 90 days and new automobiles for 5 years or 50,000 miles, whichever comes first. Warranty costs must be considered in the design of new services or products.

external failure costs
Costs that arise when a defect is discovered after the customer receives the service or product.

warranty
A written guarantee that the producer will replace or repair defective parts or perform the service to the customer's satisfaction.

Ethics and Quality

The costs of quality go beyond the out-of-pocket costs associated with training, appraisal, scrap, rework, warranties, litigation, or the lost sales from dissatisfied customers. There is a greater societal effect that must be factored into decision making involving the production of services or products, which often requires balancing the traditional measures of quality performance and the overall benefits to society. For example, in the health care industry, aiming for zero complications in cardiac surgery might sound good; however, if it comes at the cost of turning down high-risk patients, is society being served in the best way? Or, how much time, energy, and money should go into delivering vaccines or preventing complications? These are questions that often do not have clear answers.

Deceptive business practices are another source of concern for service or product quality. Deceptive business practice involves three elements: (1) the conduct of the provider is intentional and motivated by a desire to exploit the customer; (2) the provider conceals the truth based upon what is actually known to the provider; and (3) the transaction is intended to generate a disproportionate economic benefit to the provider at the expense of the customer. This behavior is unethical, diminishes the quality of the customers' experience, and may impose a substantial cost on society. Quality is all about increasing the satisfaction of customers. When a firm engages in unethical behavior and the customer finds out about it, the customer is unlikely to favorably assess the quality of his or her experience with that firm or to return as a customer.

Firms that produce better quality services or products can expect to earn a premium for that higher quality. They can also expect to grow and prosper over time because of their ability to create true value for customers. Firms that engage in deception, however, undermine the ability and competence of their employees and demean their relationship with external customers. The unfortunate message these firms send to their employees, who are also their internal customers, is that management views them as being less capable of producing quality services or products than their counterparts in ethical firms. Under these conditions employees are also less likely to be motivated to put forth their best effort. The message unethical firms send to their external customers is that their product or service cannot effectively compete with that of others and so they must engage in deception in order to be profitable. Employees of firms that attempt to profit by deceiving customers are less likely to create true value for customers through product or service improvements that can enhance the customers' experience. That erodes a firm's ability to compete now and in the future.

Ethical behavior falls on the shoulders of all employees of an organization. It is not ethical to knowingly deceive customers and pass defective services or products to internal or external customers. The well-being of all stakeholders, such as stockholders, customers, employees, partners, and creditors, should be considered.

The quality costs of prevention, assessment, internal failure, and external failure must be balanced with ethical considerations to arrive at the appropriate processes and approaches to manage them. Nonetheless, developing the cultural environment for ethical behavior is not cost-free. Employees must be educated in how ethics interfaces with their jobs. The firm may organize an ethics task force or an ethics public relations group to provide an interface between the firm and society. Documentation may be required. We now turn to a discussion of Total Quality Management and Six Sigma, two philosophies companies use to evaluate and improve quality and process performance along technical, service, and ethical dimensions.

total quality management (TQM)

A philosophy that stresses three principles for achieving high levels of process performance and quality: (1) customer satisfaction, (2) employee involvement, and (3) continuous improvement in performance.

quality

A term used by customers to describe their general satisfaction with a service or product.

Total Quality Management

Total quality management (TQM) is a philosophy that stresses three principles for achieving high levels of process performance and quality. These principles are related to (1) customer satisfaction, (2) employee involvement, and (3) continuous improvement in performance. As Figure 7.1 indicates, TQM also involves a number of other important elements. We will cover tools and process analysis techniques useful for process problem solving, redesign, and improvement in Chapter 8. Service/product design and purchasing are covered later in this text. Here, we just focus on the three main principles of TQM.

Customer Satisfaction

Customers, internal or external, are satisfied when their expectations regarding a service or product have been met or exceeded. Often, customers use the general term **quality** to describe their level of satisfaction with a service or product. Quality has multiple dimensions in the mind of the customer, which cut across the nine competitive priorities we introduced in Chapter 1, "Using Operations to Compete." One or more of the following five definitions apply at any one time.

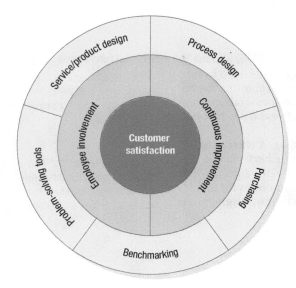

▲ FIGURE 7.1
TQM Wheel

Conformance to Specifications   Although customers evaluate the service or product they receive, it is the processes that produced the service or product that are really being judged. In this case, a process failure would be the process's inability to meet certain advertised or implied performance standards. Conformance to specifications may relate to consistent quality, on-time delivery, or delivery speed.

Value   Another way customers define quality is through value, or how well the service or product serves its intended purpose at a price customers are willing to pay. The service/product development process plays a role here, as do the firm's competitive priorities relating to top quality versus low-cost operations. The two factors must be balanced to produce value for the customer. How much value a service or product has in the mind of the customer depends on the customer's expectations before purchasing it.

Fitness for Use   When assessing how well a service or product performs its intended purpose, the customer may consider the convenience of a service, the mechanical features of a product, or other aspects such as appearance, style, durability, reliability, craftsmanship, and serviceability. For example, you may define the quality of the entertainment center you purchased on the basis of how easy it was to assemble and its appearance and styling.

Support   Often the service or product support provided by the company is as important to customers as the quality of the service or product itself. Customers get upset with a company if its financial statements are incorrect, responses to its warranty claims are delayed, its advertising is misleading, or its employees are not helpful when problems are incurred. Good support once the sale has been made can reduce the consequences of quality failures.

Psychological Impressions   People often evaluate the quality of a service or product on the basis of psychological impressions: atmosphere, image, or aesthetics. In the provision of services where the customer is in close contact with the provider, the appearance and actions of the provider are especially important. Nicely dressed, courteous, friendly, and sympathetic employees can affect the customer's perception of service quality.

Call centers provide support for a firm's products or services as well as contribute to the psychological impression of the customer regarding the experience. Calls to the center are often monitored to ensure that the customer is satisfied.

Attaining quality in all areas of a business is a difficult task. To make things even more difficult, consumers change their perceptions of quality. In general, a business's success depends on the accuracy of its perceptions of consumer expectations and its ability to bridge the gap between those expectations and operating capabilities. Good quality pays off in higher profits. High-quality services and products can be priced higher and yield a greater return. Poor quality erodes the firm's ability to compete in the marketplace and increases the costs of producing its service or product. Managerial Practice 7.1 shows how Steinway & Sons balanced consumer expectations for high-end pianos with its capability to meet those expectations.

Employee Involvement

One of the important elements of TQM is employee involvement, as shown in Figure 7.1. A program in employee involvement includes changing organizational culture and encouraging teamwork.

Cultural Change   One of the main challenges in developing the proper culture for TQM is to define *customer* for each employee. In general, customers are internal or external. *External customers* are the people or firms who buy the service or product. Some employees, especially those having little contact with external customers, may have difficulty seeing how their jobs contribute to the whole effort.

It is helpful to point out to employees that each employee also has one or more *internal customers*—employees in the firm who rely on the output of other employees. All employees must do a good job of serving their internal customers if external customers ultimately are to be satisfied. They will be satisfied only if each internal customer demands value be added that the external customer will recognize and pay for. The notion of internal customers applies to all parts of a firm and enhances cross-functional coordination. For example, accounting must prepare accurate and timely reports for management, and purchasing must provide high-quality materials on time for operations.

MANAGERIAL PRACTICE 7.1   Quality and Performance at Steinway & Sons

A specialist adjusts the levers and dampers of a grand concert piano at the Steinway & Sons factory in Hamburg.

Christian Charisius/Reuters/Corbis

The first contestant in the Van Cliburn International Piano Competition is about to play Tchaikovsky Piano Concerto No. 1 before a packed audience in Fort Worth, Texas. The tension mounts as his fingers approach the keyboard of the Steinway & Sons grand concert piano; both the contestant and piano perform admirably much to the relief of the contestant and the operations manager of the concert. Why was the Steinway piano chosen for such a visible event? It is one of the highest-quality grand pianos you can buy. In addition, Steinway has a market share of over 95 percent in concert halls and it is the piano of choice for professional musicians from Van Cliburn to Billy Joel.

Steinway began operations in the 1880s. Today, the company blends the art of hand crafting, which uses methods essentially the same as when the company started, with twenty-first-century manufacturing technology to produce about 3,100 grand pianos a year. Some 12,000 parts are fashioned, mostly in-house, and assembled for each piano; it takes 9 months to a year compared to 20 days for a mass-produced piano. Eight different species of wood go into every grand piano, each selected for its physical properties and aesthetic characteristics. The craft-oriented production process is painstaking to ensure quality at each step. For example, each board for a piano is hand

selected for a given part. In a time-consuming process, craftsmen bend 17 laminations of the piano's hard maple rim into place with clamps. The Alaska Sitka spruce soundboard is hand-planed so it is arched, thicker at its center than its tapered edges, to withstand the 1,000 pounds of pressure from the more than 200 strings. The piano's "action," which contains keys (88 of them), whippens, shanks, and hammers, uses 100 parts, manufactured on numerical control machines, to sound each note and is pieced together at 30 different desks. Quality is checked at each operation to avoid passing defective parts downstream.

There are six characteristics of quality in Steinway pianos:

- **Sound** Tone and pitch contribute to the fullness and roundness of the sound from the piano. In a process called "voicing," minute adjustments are made to the felt pad of each hammer in the piano's action to either mellow the tone or increase its brilliance. Then a tone regulator listens to the piano's pitch and turns the tuning pins to adjust string tension. Steinways are world renowned for their sound; however, because of the natural characteristics of the wood, each piano will have its own personality.

- **Finish** Wood veneers are selected for their beauty. Boards not meeting standards are discarded, creating a large amount of scrap.

- **Feel** Each of the 88 keys must require the same amount of pressure to activate. In a process called "action weigh-off," lead is added to each key so that there is a consistent feel. Action parts are held to tolerances within +/−0.0005 inch.

- **Durability** The piano must have a long life and perform up to expectations throughout.

- **Image** There is a certain mystique associated with the Steinway brand. Some people attribute a cult-like experience to owning a Steinway.

- **Service** Steinway will go out of its way to service a piano that is inoperative, even to the extent of providing a loaner for a major concert.

The six characteristics link to four of our definitions of quality: (1) conformance to specifications (*feel*), (2) fitness for use (*sound, finish, durability*); (3) support (*service*); and (4) psychological impressions (*image*). As for value, our fifth definition of quality, Steinway grand pianos cost anywhere from $47,000 to $165,000 unless you want a nine-foot recreation of the famous Alma-Tadema piano built in 1887, in which case it will cost $675,000. Want to buy one?

Sources: Andy Serwer, "Happy Birthday, Steinway," *Fortune*, vol. 147, no. 5 (March 17, 2003), pp. 94–97; Leo O'Connor, "Engineering on a Grand scale," *Mechanical Engineering*, vol. 116, no. 10 (October, 1994), pp. 52–58; Steinway Musical Instruments, Inc. Annual Report 2006, **www.steinwaymusical.com**; **www.steinway.com/factory/tour.shtml**, 2007.

quality at the source

A philosophy whereby defects are caught and corrected where they were created.

teams

Small groups of people who have a common purpose, set their own performance goals and approaches, and hold themselves accountable for success.

In TQM, everyone in the organization must share the view that quality control is an end in itself. Errors or defects should be caught and corrected at the source, not passed along to an internal or external customer. For example, a consulting team should make sure its billable hours are correct before submitting them to the accounting department. This philosophy is called **quality at the source**. In addition, firms should avoid trying to "inspect quality into the product" by using inspectors to weed out unsatisfactory services or defective products after all operations have been performed. By contrast, in some manufacturing firms, workers have the authority to stop a production line if they spot quality problems.

Teams   Employee involvement is a key tactic for improving processes and quality. One way to achieve employee involvement is by the use of **teams**, which are small groups of people who have a common purpose, set their own performance goals and approaches, and hold themselves accountable for success.

The three approaches to teamwork most often used are (1) problem-solving teams, (2) special-purpose teams, and (3) self-managed teams. All three use some amount of **employee empowerment**, which moves responsibility for decisions further down the organizational chart—to the level of the employee actually doing the job.

First introduced in the 1920s, *problem-solving teams*, also called **quality circles**, became popular in the late 1970s after the Japanese used them successfully. Problem-solving teams are small groups of supervisors and employees who meet to identify, analyze, and solve process and quality problems. Employees take more pride and interest in their work if they are allowed to help shape it. Although problem-solving teams can successfully reduce costs and improve quality, they die if management fails to implement many of the suggestions they generate.

An outgrowth of the problem-solving teams, **special-purpose teams** address issues of paramount concern to management, labor, or both. For example, management may form a special-purpose team to design and introduce new work policies or new technologies or to address customer service problems. Essentially, this approach gives workers a voice in high-level decisions. Special-purpose teams first appeared in the United States in the early 1980s.

The **self-managed team** approach takes worker participation to its highest level: A small group of employees work together to produce a major portion, or sometimes all, of a service or product. Members learn all the tasks involved in the operation, rotate from job to job, and take over managerial duties such as work and vacation scheduling, ordering supplies, and hiring. In some cases, team members design the process and have a high degree of latitude as to how it takes shape. Self-managed teams essentially change the way work is organized because employees have control over their jobs. Some self-managed teams have increased productivity by 30 percent or more in their firms.

Process measurement is the key to quality improvement. Here a quality inspector measures the diameter of holes in a machined part.

Continuous Improvement

Continuous improvement, based on a Japanese concept called *kaizen*, is the philosophy of continually seeking ways to improve processes. Continuous improvement involves identifying benchmarks of excellent practice and instilling a sense of employee ownership in the process. The focus of continuous improvement projects is to reduce waste, such as reducing the length of time required to process requests for loans at a bank, the amount of scrap generated at a milling machine, or the number of employee injuries at a construction site. The basis of the continuous improvement philosophy are the beliefs that virtually any aspect of a process can be improved and that the people most closely associated with a process are in the best position to identify the changes that should be made. The idea is not to wait until a massive problem occurs before acting.

Employees should be given problem-solving tools, such as the statistical process control (SPC) methods we discuss later in this chapter, and a sense of ownership of the process to be improved. A sense of operator ownership emerges when employees feel a responsibility for the processes and methods they use and take pride in the quality of the service or product they produce. It comes from participation on work teams and in problem-solving activities, which instill in employees a feeling that they have some control over their workplace and tasks.

Most firms actively engaged in continuous improvement train their work teams to use the **plan-do-study-act cycle** for problem solving. Another name for this approach is the Deming Wheel, named after the renowned statistician W. Edwards Deming who taught quality improvement techniques to the Japanese after World War II. Figure 7.2 shows this cycle, which lies at the heart of the continuous improvement philosophy. The cycle comprises the following steps:

1. *Plan.* The team selects a process (an activity, method, machine, or policy) that needs improvement. The team then documents the selected process, usually by analyzing related data; sets qualitative goals for improvement; and discusses various ways to achieve the goals. After assessing the benefits and costs of the alternatives, the team develops a plan with quantifiable measures for improvement.

2. *Do.* The team implements the plan and monitors progress. Data are collected continuously to measure the improvements in the process. Any changes in the process are documented, and further revisions are made as needed.

employee empowerment

An approach to teamwork that moves responsibility for decisions further down the organizational chart—to the level of the employee actually doing the job.

quality circles

Another name for problem-solving teams; small groups of supervisors and employees who meet to identify, analyze, and solve process and quality problems.

special-purpose teams

Groups that address issues of paramount concern to management, labor, or both.

self-managed team

A small group of employees who work together to produce a major portion, or sometimes all, of a service or product.

continuous improvement

The philosophy of continually seeking ways to improve processes based on a Japanese concept called *kaizen*.

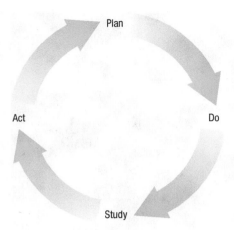

plan-do-study-act cycle

A cycle, also called the Deming Wheel, used by firms actively engaged in continuous improvement to train their work teams in problem solving.

Six Sigma

A comprehensive and flexible system for achieving, sustaining, and maximizing business success by minimizing defects and variability in processes.

▼ FIGURE 7.3
Six Sigma Approach Focuses on Reducing Spread and Centering the Process

3. *Study*. The team analyzes the data collected during the *do* step to find out how closely the results correspond to the goals set in the *plan* step. If major shortcomings exist, the team reevaluates the plan or stops the project.

4. *Act*. If the results are successful, the team documents the revised process so that it becomes the standard procedure for all who may use it. The team may then instruct other employees in the use of the revised process.

Problem-solving projects often focus on those aspects of processes that do not add value to the service or product. Value is added in processes such as machining a part or serving a customer through a Web page. No value is added in activities such as inspecting parts for defects or routing requests for loan approvals to several different departments. The idea of continuous improvement is to reduce or eliminate activities that do not add value and, thus, are wasteful.

Six Sigma

Six Sigma, which relies heavily on the principles of TQM, is a comprehensive and flexible system for achieving, sustaining, and maximizing business success by minimizing defects and variability in processes. Six Sigma has a different focus than TQM: It is driven by a close understanding of customer needs; the disciplined use of facts, data, and statistical analysis; and diligent attention to managing, improving, and reinventing business processes. Figure 7.3 shows how Six Sigma focuses on reducing variation in processes as well as centering processes on their target measures of performance. Either flaw—too much variation or an off-target process—degrades performance of the process. For example, a mortgage loan department of a bank might advertise loan approval decisions in 2 days. If the actual performance ranges from 1 day to 5 days, with an average of 2 days, those customers who had to wait longer than 2 days would be upset. Process variability causes customer dissatisfaction. Similarly, if actual performance consistently produced loan decisions in 3 days, all customers would be dissatisfied. In this case, the process is consistent, but off the target. Six Sigma is a rigorous approach to align processes with their target performance measures with low variability.

The name Six Sigma, originally developed by Motorola for its manufacturing operations, relates to the goal of achieving low rates of defective output by developing processes whose mean output for a performance measure is +/− six standard deviations (sigma) from the limits of the design specifications for the service or product. We will discuss variability and its implications on the capability of a process to perform at acceptable levels when we present the tools of statistical process control.

Although Six Sigma was rooted in an effort to improve manufacturing processes, credit General Electric with popularizing the application of the approach to non-manufacturing processes such as sales, human resources, customer service, and financial services. The concept of eliminating defects is the same, although the definition of "defect" depends on the process involved. For example, a human resource department's failure to meet a hiring target counts as a defect. Six Sigma has been successfully applied to a host of service processes, including financial services, human resource processes, marketing processes, and health care administrative processes.

Six Sigma Improvement Model

Figure 7.4 shows the Six Sigma Improvement Model, a five-step procedure that leads to improvements in process performance. The model bears a lot of similarity to Figure 4.1, the Blueprint for Process Analysis, for good reason: Both models strive for process improvement. Either model can be applied to projects involving incremental improvements to processes or to projects requiring major changes, including a redesign of an existing process or the development of a new process. The Six Sigma Improvement Model, however, is heavily reliant on statistical process control. The following steps comprise the model:

- *Define*. Determine the characteristics of the process's output that are critical to customer satisfaction and identify any gaps between these characteristics and the

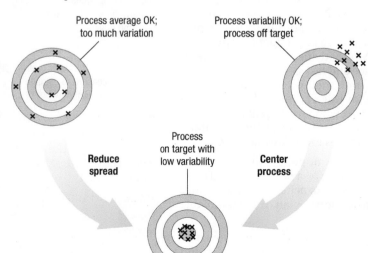

process's capabilities. Get a picture of the current process by documenting it using *flowcharts* and *process charts*.

- *Measure.* Quantify the work the process does that affects the gap. Select what to measure, identify data sources, and prepare a data collection plan.

- *Analyze.* Use the data on measures to perform process analysis, applying tools such as Pareto charts, scatter diagrams, and cause-and-effect diagrams and the statistical process control (SPC) tools in this chapter to determine where improvements are necessary. Whether or not major redesign is necessary, establish procedures to make the desired outcome routine.

- *Improve.* Modify or redesign existing methods to meet the new performance objectives. Implement the changes.

- *Control.* Monitor the process to make sure that high performance levels are maintained. Once again, data analysis tools such as Pareto charts, bar charts, scatter diagrams, as well as the statistical process control tools can be used to control the process.

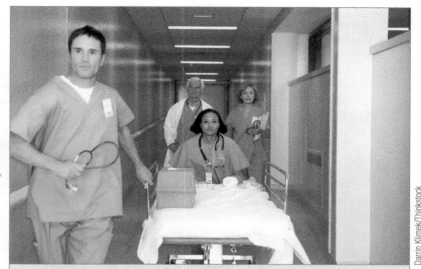

Hospital personnel rush to help a patient in an emergency. Six Sigma can be used to improve service processes in a hospital.

Darrin Klimek/Thinkstock

Successful users of Six Sigma have found that it is essential to rigorously follow the steps in the Six Sigma Improvement Model, which is sometimes referred to as the *DMAIC process* (whose name comes from using the first letter of each step in the model). To accomplish the goals of Six Sigma, employees must be trained in the "whys" and the "how-tos" of quality and what it means to customers, both internal and external. Successful firms using Six Sigma develop a cadre of internal teachers who then are responsible for teaching and assisting teams involved in a process improvement project. These teachers have different titles depending on their experience and level of achievement. **Green Belts** devote part of their time to teaching and helping teams with their projects and the rest of their time to their normally assigned duties. **Black Belts** are full-time teachers and leaders of teams involved in Six Sigma projects. Finally, **Master Black Belts** are full-time teachers who review and mentor Black Belts.

Acceptance Sampling

Before any internal process can be evaluated for performance, the inputs to that process must be of good quality. **Acceptance sampling**, which is the application of statistical techniques to determine if a quantity of material from a supplier should be accepted or rejected based on the inspection or test of one or more samples, limits the buyer's risk of rejecting good-quality materials (and unnecessarily delaying the production of goods or services) or accepting bad-quality materials (and incurring downtime due to defective materials or passing bad products to customers). Relative to the specifications for the material the buyer is purchasing, the buyer specifies an **acceptable quality level (AQL)**, which is a statement of the proportion of defective items (outside of specifications) that the buyer will accept in a shipment. These days, that proportion is getting very small, often measured in parts per ten-thousand. The idea of acceptance sampling is to take a sample, rather than testing the entire quantity of material, because that is often less expensive. Therein lies the risk—the sample may not be representative of the entire lot of goods from the supplier. The basic procedure is straightforward.

1. A random sample is taken from a large quantity of items and tested or measured relative to the specifications or quality measures of interest.

2. If the sample passes the test (low number of defects), the entire quantity of items is accepted.

3. If the sample fails the test, either (a) the entire quantity of items is subjected to 100 percent inspection and all defective items repaired or replaced or (b) the entire quantity is returned to the supplier.

In a supply chain, any company can be both a producer of goods purchased by another company and a consumer of goods or raw materials supplied by another company. Figure 7.5 shows

Define

↓

Measure

↓

Analyze

↓

Improve

↓

Control

▲ **FIGURE 7.4**
Six Sigma Improvement Model

Green Belt

An employee who achieved the first level of training in a Six Sigma program and spends part of his or her time teaching and helping teams with their projects.

Black Belt

An employee who reached the highest level of training in a Six Sigma program and spends all of his or her time teaching and leading teams involved in Six Sigma projects.

Master Black Belt

Full-time teachers and mentors to several Black Belts.

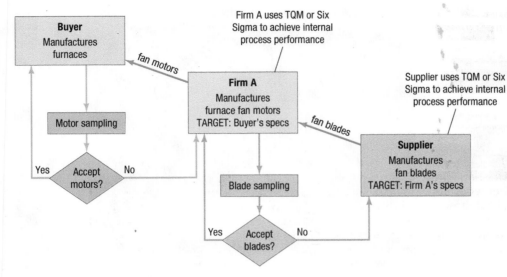

▲ FIGURE 7.5
Interface of Acceptance
Sampling and Process
Performance Approaches
in a Supply Chain

acceptable quality level (AQL)

The quality level desired by the
consumer.

acceptance sampling

The application of statistical
techniques to determine whether
a quantity of material should be
accepted or rejected based on
the inspection or test of a sample.

**statistical process control
(SPC)**

The application of statistical
techniques to determine whether
a process is delivering what the
customer wants.

a flowchart of how acceptance sampling and internal process performance (TQM or Six Sigma) interface in a supply chain. From the perspective of the supply chain, the buyer's specifications for various dimensions of quality become the targets the supplier shoots for in a supply contract. The supplier's internal processes must be up to the task; TQM or Six Sigma can help achieve the desired performance. The buyer's sampling plan will provide a high probability of accepting AQL (or better). MyOMLab Supplement G, "Acceptance Sampling Plans," shows how to design an acceptance sampling plan that meets the level of risk desired.

Statistical Process Control

Regardless of whether a firm is producing a service or a product, it is important to ensure that the firm's processes are providing the quality that customers want. A key element of TQM or Six Sigma is building the capability to monitor the performance of processes so that corrective action can be initiated in a timely fashion. Evaluating the performance of processes requires a variety of data gathering approaches. We already discussed checklists, histograms and bar charts, Pareto charts, scatter diagrams, cause-and-effect diagrams, and graphs (see Chapter 4, "Process Analysis"). All of these tools can be used with TQM or Six Sigma. Here. we focus on the powerful statistical tools that can be used to monitor and manage repetitive processes.

Statistical process control (SPC) is the application of statistical techniques to determine whether a process is delivering what customers want. In SPC, tools called control charts are used primarily to detect defective services or products or to indicate that the process has changed and that services or products will deviate from their design specifications, unless something is done to correct the situation. SPC can also be used to inform management of improved process changes. Examples of process changes that can be detected by SPC include the following:

- A decrease in the average number of complaints per day at a hotel
- A sudden increase in the proportion of defective gear boxes
- An increase in the time to process a mortgage application
- A decline in the number of scrapped units at a milling machine
- An increase in the number of claimants receiving late payment from an insurance company

Let us consider the last situation. Suppose that the manager of the accounts payable department of an insurance company notices that the proportion of claimants receiving late payments rose from an average of 0.01 to 0.03. The first question is whether the rise is a cause for alarm or just a random occurrence. Statistical process control can help the manager decide whether further action should be taken. If the rise in the proportion is not just a random occurrence, the manager should seek explanations of the poor performance. Perhaps the number of claims significantly increased, causing an overload on the employees in the department. The decision might be to hire more personnel. Or perhaps the procedures being used are ineffective or the training of employees is inadequate. SPC is an integral part of TQM and Six Sigma.

Variation of Outputs

No two services or products are exactly alike because the processes used to produce them contain many sources of variation, even if the processes are working as intended. Nonetheless, it is important to minimize the variation in outputs because frequently variation is what the customer sees and feels. Suppose a physicians' clinic submits claims on behalf of its patients to a particular insurance company. In this situation, the physicians' clinic is the customer of the insurance company's bill payment process. In some cases, the clinic receives payment in 4 weeks, and in other cases 20 weeks. The time to process a request for payment varies because of the load on the insurance company's processes, the medical history of the patient, and the skills and attitudes of the employees. Meanwhile, the clinic must cover its expenses while it waits for payment. Regardless of whether the process is producing services or products, nothing can be done to eliminate variation in output completely; however, management should investigate the *causes* of the variation in order to minimize it.

Performance Measurements   Performance can be evaluated in two ways. One way is to measure **variables**—that is, service or product characteristics, such as weight, length, volume, or time, that can be *measured*. The advantage of using performance variables is that if a service or product misses its performance specifications, the inspector knows by how much. The disadvantage is that such measurements typically involve special equipment, employee skills, exacting procedures, and time and effort.

Another way to evaluate performance is to measure **attributes**; service or product characteristics that can be quickly *counted* for acceptable performance. This method allows inspectors to make a simple "yes/no" decision about whether a service or product meets the specifications. Attributes often are used when performance specifications are complex and measurement of variables is difficult or costly. Some examples of attributes that can be counted are the number of insurance forms containing errors that cause underpayments or overpayments, the proportion of airline flights arriving within 15 minutes of scheduled times, and the number of stove-top assemblies with spotted paint.

The advantage of counting attributes is that less effort and fewer resources are needed than for measuring variables. The disadvantage is that, even though attribute counts can reveal that process performance has changed, they do not indicate by how much. For example, a count may determine that the proportion of airline flights arriving within 15 minutes of their scheduled times declined, but the result does not show how much beyond the 15-minute allowance the flights are arriving. For that, the actual deviation from the scheduled arrival, a variable, would have to be measured.

Sampling   The most thorough approach to inspection is to inspect each service or product at each stage of the process for quality. This method, called *complete inspection*, is used when the costs of passing defects to an internal or external customer outweigh the inspection costs. Firms often use automated inspection equipment that can record, summarize, and display data. Many companies find that automated inspection equipment can pay for itself in a reasonably short time.

A well-conceived **sampling plan** can approach the same degree of protection as complete inspection. A sampling plan specifies a **sample size**, which is a quantity of randomly selected observations of process outputs, the time between successive samples, and decision rules that determine when action should be taken. Sampling is appropriate when inspection costs are high because of the special knowledge, skills, procedures, and expensive equipment that are required to perform the inspections, or because the tests are destructive.

Sampling Distributions   Relative to a performance measure, a process will produce output that can be described by a *process distribution*, with a mean and variance that will be known only with a complete inspection with 100 percent accuracy. The purpose of sampling, however, is to estimate a variable or attribute measure for the output of the process without doing a complete inspection. That measure is then used to assess the performance of the process itself. For example, the time required to process specimens at an intensive care unit lab in a hospital (a variable measure) will vary. If you measured the time to complete an analysis of a large number of patients and plotted the results, the data would tend to form a pattern that can be described as a process distribution. With sampling, we try to estimate the parameters of the process distribution using statistics such as the sample mean and the sample range or standard deviation.

1. The *sample mean* is the sum of the observations divided by the total number of observations:

$$\bar{x} = \frac{\sum_{i=1}^{n} x_i}{n}$$

variables

Service or product characteristics, such as weight, length, volume, or time, that can be measured.

attributes

Service or product characteristics that can be quickly counted for acceptable performance.

sampling plan

A plan that specifies a sample size, the time between successive samples, and decision rules that determine when action should be taken.

sample size

A quantity of randomly selected observations of process outputs.

Wine production is an example of a situation where complete inspection is not an option. Here a quality inspector draws a sample of white wine from a stainless steel maturation tank.

Ian Shaw/Alamy

where

$$x_i = \text{observation of a quality characteristic (such as time)}$$

$$n = \text{total number of observations}$$

$$\bar{x} = \text{mean}$$

2. The *range* is the difference between the largest observation in a sample and the smallest. The *standard deviation* is the square root of the variance of a distribution. An estimate of the process standard deviation based on a sample is given by

$$\sigma = \sqrt{\frac{\sum_{i=1}^{n}(x_i - \bar{x})^2}{n - 1}} \quad \text{or} \quad \sigma = \sqrt{\frac{\sum_{i=1}^{n}x^2 - \frac{\left(\sum_{i=1}^{n}x_i\right)^2}{n}}{n - 1}}$$

where

$$\sigma = \text{standard deviation of a sample}$$

$$n = \text{total number of observations in the sample}$$

$$\bar{x} = \text{mean}$$

$$x_i = \text{observation of a quality characteristic}$$

Relatively small values for the range or the standard deviation imply that the observations are clustered near the mean.

These sample statistics have their own distribution, which we call a *sampling distribution*. For example, in the lab analysis process, an important performance variable is the time it takes to get results to the critical care unit. Suppose that management wants results available in an average of 25 minutes. That is, it wants the process distribution to have a mean of 25 minutes. An inspector periodically taking a sample of five analyses and calculating the sample mean could use it to determine how well the process is doing. Suppose that the process is actually producing the analyses with a mean of 25 minutes. Plotting a large number of these sample means would show that they have their own sampling distribution with a mean centered on 25 minutes, as does the process distribution mean, but with much less variability. The reason is that the sample means offset the highs and lows of the individual times in each sample. Figure 7.6 shows the relationship between the sampling distribution of sample means and the process distribution for the analysis times.

Some sampling distributions (e.g., for means with sample sizes of four or more and proportions with sample sizes of 20 or more) can be approximated by the normal distribution, allowing the use of the normal tables (see Appendix 1, "Normal Distribution"). For example, suppose you wanted to determine the probability that a sample mean will be more than 2.0 standard deviations higher than the process mean. Go to Appendix 1 and note that the entry in the table for $z = 2.0$ standard deviations is 0.9772. Consequently, the probability is $1.0000 - 0.9772 = 0.0228$, or 2.28 percent. The probability that the sample mean will be more than 2.0 standard deviations lower than the process mean is also 2.28 percent because the normal distribution is symmetric to the mean. The ability to assign probabilities to sample results is important for the construction and use of control charts.

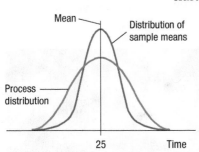

▲ **FIGURE 7.6**
Relationship Between the Distribution of Sample Means and the Process Distribution

common causes of variation

The purely random, unidentifiable sources of variation that are unavoidable with the current process.

Common Causes   The two basic categories of variation in output include common causes and assignable causes. **Common causes of variation** are the purely random, unidentifiable sources of variation that are unavoidable with the current process. A process distribution can be characterized by its *location*, *spread*, and *shape*. Location is measured by the *mean* of the distribution, while spread is measured by the *range* or *standard deviation*. The shape of process distributions can be characterized as either symmetric or skewed. A *symmetric* distribution has the same number of observations above and below the mean. A *skewed* distribution has a greater number of observations either above or below the mean. If process variability results solely from common causes of variation, a typical assumption is that the distribution is symmetric, with most observations near the center.

assignable causes of variation

Any variation-causing factors that can be identified and eliminated.

Assignable Causes   The second category of variation, **assignable causes of variation**, also known as *special causes*, includes any variation-causing factors that can be identified and eliminated. Assignable causes of variation include an employee needing training or a machine needing repair. Let us return to the example of the lab analysis process. Figure 7.7 shows how assignable causes can change the distribution of output for the analysis process. The green curve

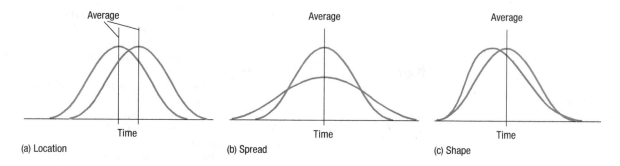

(a) Location   (b) Spread   (c) Shape

is the process distribution when only common causes of variation are present. The **purple** curves depict a change in the distribution because of assignable causes. In Figure 7.7(a), the **purple** curve indicates that the process took more time than planned in many of the cases, thereby increasing the average time of each analysis. In Figure 7.7(b), an increase in the variability of the time for each case affected the spread of the distribution. Finally, in Figure 7.7(c), the **purple** curve indicates that the process produced a preponderance of the tests in less than average time. Such a distribution is skewed, or no longer symmetric to the average value. A process is said to be in statistical control when the location, spread, or shape of its distribution does not change over time. After the process is in statistical control, managers use SPC procedures to detect the onset of assignable causes so that they can be addressed.

▲ **FIGURE 7.7**
Effects of Assignable Causes on the Process Distribution for the Lab Analysis Process

control chart

A time-ordered diagram that is used to determine whether observed variations are abnormal.

Control Charts

To determine whether observed variations are abnormal, we can measure and plot the performance measure taken from the sample on a time-ordered diagram called a **control chart**. A control chart has a nominal value, or central line, which can be the process's historic average or a target that managers would like the process to achieve, and two control limits based on the sampling distribution of the quality measure. The control limits are used to judge whether action is required. The larger value represents the *upper control limit* (UCL), and the smaller value represents the *lower control limit* (LCL). Figure 7.8 shows how the control limits relate to the sampling distribution. A sample statistic that falls between the UCL and the LCL indicates that the process is exhibiting common causes of variation. A statistic that falls outside the control limits indicates that the process is exhibiting assignable causes of variation.

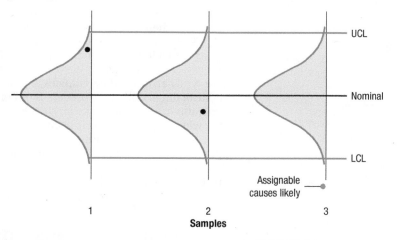

▲ **FIGURE 7.8**
How Control Limits Relate to the Sampling Distribution: Observations from Three Samples

Observations falling outside the control limits do not always mean poor quality. For example, in Figure 7.8 the assignable cause may be a new billing process introduced to reduce the number of incorrect bills sent to customers. If the proportion of incorrect bills, that is, the performance measure from a sample of bills, falls *below* the LCL of the control chart, the new procedure likely changed the billing process for the better, and a new control chart should be constructed.

Managers or employees responsible for evaluating a process can use control charts in the following way:

1. Take a random sample from the process and calculate a variable or attribute performance measure.

2. If the statistic falls outside the chart's control limits or exhibits unusual behavior, look for an assignable cause.

3. Eliminate the cause if it degrades performance; incorporate the cause if it improves performance. Reconstruct the control chart with new data.

4. Repeat the procedure periodically.

Sometimes, problems with a process can be detected even though the control limits have not been exceeded. Figure 7.9 contains four examples of control charts. Chart (a) shows a process that is in statistical control. No action is needed. However, chart (b) shows a pattern called a *run* or a sequence of observations with a certain characteristic. A typical rule is to take remedial action

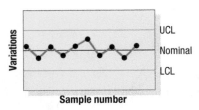

(a) Normal—No action

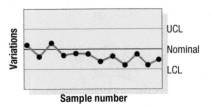

(b) Run—Take action

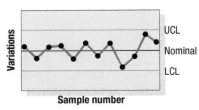

(c) Sudden change—Monitor

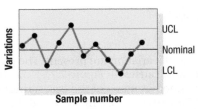

(d) Exceeds control limits—Take action

▲ **FIGURE 7.9**
Control Chart Examples

type I error

An error that occurs when the employee concludes that the process is out of control based on a sample result that falls outside the control limits, when in fact it was due to pure randomness.

type II error

An error that occurs when the employee concludes that the process is in control and only randomness is present, when actually the process is out of statistical control.

when five or more observations show a downward or upward trend, even if the points have not yet exceeded the control limits. Here, nine sequential observations are below the mean and show a downward trend. The probability is low that such a result could take place by chance.

Chart (c) shows that the process takes a sudden change from its normal pattern. The last four observations are unusual: The first drops close to the LCL, the next two rise toward the UCL, and the fourth remains above the nominal value. Managers or employees should monitor processes with such sudden changes even though the control limits have not been exceeded. Finally, chart (d) indicates that the process went out of control twice because two sample results fell outside the control limits. The probability that the process distribution has changed is high. We discuss more implications of being out of statistical control when we discuss process capability later in this chapter.

Control charts are not perfect tools for detecting shifts in the process distribution because they are based on sampling distributions. Two types of error are possible with the use of control charts. A **type I error** occurs when the conclusion is made that the process is out of control based on a sample result that falls outside the control limits, when in fact it was due to pure randomness. A **type II error** occurs when the conclusion is that the process is in control and only randomness is present, when actually the process is out of statistical control.

These errors can be controlled by the choice of control limits. The choice would depend on the costs of looking for assignable causes when none exist versus the cost of not detecting a shift in the process. For example, setting control limits at +/− three standard deviations from the mean reduces the type I error because chances are only 0.26 percent that a sample result will fall outside of the control limits unless the process is out of statistical control. However, the type II error may be significant; more subtle shifts in the nature of the process distribution will go undetected because of the wide spread in the control limits. Alternatively, the spread in the control limits can be reduced to +/− two standard deviations, thereby increasing the likelihood of sample results from a non-faulty process falling outside of the control limits to 4.56 percent. Now, the type II error is smaller, but the type I error is larger because employees are likely to search for assignable causes when the sample result occurred solely by chance. As a general rule, use wider limits when the cost for searching for assignable causes is large relative to the cost of not detecting a shift in the process distribution.

Statistical Process Control Methods

Statistical process control (SPC) methods are useful for both measuring the current process performance and detecting whether the process has changed in a way that will affect future performance. In this section, we first discuss mean and range charts for variable measures of performance and then consider control charts for attributes measures.

Control Charts for Variables

Control charts for variables are used to monitor the mean and the variability of the process distribution.

R-chart

A chart used to monitor process variability.

R-Chart A range chart, or **R-chart**, is used to monitor process variability. To calculate the range of a set of sample data, the analyst subtracts the smallest from the largest measurement in each sample. If any of the ranges fall outside the control limits, the process variability is not in control.

The control limits for the *R*-chart are

$$\text{UCL}_R = D_4\overline{R} \quad \text{and} \quad \text{LCL}_R = D_3\overline{R}$$

where

$\overline{R}$ = average of several past *R* values and the central line of the control chart

D_3, D_4 = constants that provide three standard deviation (three-sigma) limits for a given sample size

Notice that the values for D_3 and D_4 shown in Table 7.1 change as a function of the sample size. Notice, too, that the spread between the control limits narrows as the sample size increases. This change is a consequence of having more information on which to base an estimate for the process range.

TABLE 7.1 | FACTORS FOR CALCULATING THREE-SIGMA LIMITS FOR THE $\bar{x}$-CHART AND R-CHART

Size of Sample (n)	Factor for UCL and LCL for $\bar{x}$-Chart (A_2)	Factor for LCL for R-Chart (D_3)	Factor for UCL for R-Chart (D_4)
2	1.880	0	3.267
3	1.023	0	2.575
4	0.729	0	2.282
5	0.577	0	2.115
6	0.483	0	2.004
7	0.419	0.076	1.924
8	0.373	0.136	1.864
9	0.337	0.184	1.816
10	0.308	0.223	1.777

Source: Reprinted with permission from *ASTM Manual on Quality Control of Materials*, copyright © ASTM International, 100 Barr Harbor Drive, West Conshohocken, PA 19428.

$\bar{x}$-Chart   An $\bar{x}$-**Chart** (read "x-bar chart") is used to see whether the process is generating output, on average, consistent with a target value set by management for the process or whether its current performance, with respect to the average of the performance measure, is consistent with its past performance. A target value is useful when a process is completely redesigned and past performance is no longer relevant. When the assignable causes of process variability have been identified and the process variability is in statistical control, the analyst can then construct an $\bar{x}$-chart. The control limits for the $\bar{x}$-chart are

$$\text{UCL}_{\bar{x}} = \bar{\bar{x}} + A_2\bar{R} \quad \text{and} \quad \text{LCL}_{\bar{x}} = \bar{\bar{x}} - A_2\bar{R}$$

where

$\bar{\bar{x}}$ = central line of the chart, which can be either the average of past sample means or a target value set for the process

A_2 = constant to provide three-sigma limits for the sample mean

The values for A_2 are contained in Table 7.1. Note that the control limits use the value of $\bar{R}$; therefore, the $\bar{x}$-chart must be constructed *after* the process variability is in control.

To develop and use $\bar{x}$- and R-charts, do the following:

Step 1. Collect data on the variable quality measurement (such as time, weight, or diameter) and organize the data by sample number. Preferably, at least 20 samples of size n should be taken for use in constructing a control chart.

Step 2. Compute the range for each sample and the average range, $\bar{R}$, for the set of samples.

Step 3. Use Table 7.1 to determine the upper and lower control limits of the R-chart.

Step 4. Plot the sample ranges. If all are in control, proceed to step 5. Otherwise, find the assignable causes, correct them, and return to step 1.

Step 5. Calculate $\bar{x}$ for each sample and determine the central line of the chart, $\bar{\bar{x}}$.

Step 6. Use Table 7.1 to determine the parameters for $\text{UCL}_{\bar{x}}$ and $\text{LCL}_{\bar{x}}$ and construct the $\bar{x}$-chart.

Step 7. Plot the sample means. If all are in control, the process is in statistical control in terms of the process average and process variability. Continue

$\bar{x}$-chart

A chart used to see whether the process is generating output, on average, consistent with a target value set by management for the process or whether its current performance, with respect to the average of the performance measure, is consistent with past performance.

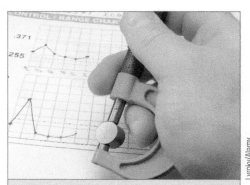

An analyst measures the diameter of a part with a micrometer. After he measures the sample, he plots the range on the control chart.

Lyroky/Alamy

to take samples and monitor the process. If any are out of control, find the assignable causes, address them, and return to step 1. If no assignable causes are found after a diligent search, assume that the out-of-control points represent common causes of variation and continue to monitor the process.

| EXAMPLE 7.1 | Using x̄- and *R*-Charts to Monitor a Process |

MyOMLab

Active Model 7.1 in MyOMLab provides additional insight on the x-bar and *R*-charts and their uses for the metal screw problem.

MyOMLab

Tutor 7.1 in MyOMLab provides a new example to practice the use of x-bar and R-charts.

The management of West Allis Industries is concerned about the production of a special metal screw used by several of the company's largest customers. The diameter of the screw is critical to the customers. Data from five samples appear in the accompanying table. The sample size is 4. Is the process in statistical control?

SOLUTION

Step 1: For simplicity, we use only 5 samples. In practice, more than 20 samples would be desirable. The data are shown in the following table.

DATA FOR THE x̄- AND *R*-CHARTS: OBSERVATIONS OF SCREW DIAMETER (IN.)

Sample Number	Observations				*R*	x̄
	1	2	3	4		
1	0.5014	0.5022	0.5009	0.5027	0.0018	0.5018
2	0.5021	0.5041	0.5024	0.5020	0.0021	0.5027
3	0.5018	0.5026	0.5035	0.5023	0.0017	0.5026
4	0.5008	0.5034	0.5024	0.5015	0.0026	0.5020
5	0.5041	0.5056	0.5034	0.5047	0.0022	0.5045
				Average	0.0021	0.5027

Step 2: Compute the range for each sample by subtracting the lowest value from the highest value. For example, in sample 1 the range is $0.5027 - 0.5009 = 0.0018$ in. Similarly, the ranges for samples 2, 3, 4, and 5 are 0.0021, 0.0017, 0.0026, and 0.0022 in., respectively. As shown in the table, $\bar{R} = 0.0021$.

Step 3: To construct the *R*-chart, select the appropriate constants from Table 7.1 for a sample size of 4. The control limits are

$$UCL_R = D_4\bar{R} = 2.282(0.0021) = 0.00479 \text{ in.}$$

$$LCL_R = D_3\bar{R} = 0(0.0021) = 0 \text{ in.}$$

Step 4: Plot the ranges on the *R*-chart, as shown in Figure 7.10. None of the sample ranges falls outside the control limits. Consequently, the process variability is in statistical control. If any of the sample ranges fall outside of the limits, or an unusual pattern appears (see Figure 7.9), we would search for the causes of the excessive variability, address them, and repeat step 1.

FIGURE 7.10 ▶
Range Chart from the *OM Explorer* x̄- and *R-Chart* Solver, Showing that the Process Variability Is In Control

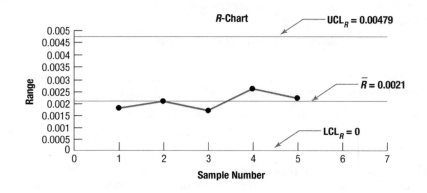

Step 5: Compute the mean for each sample. For example, the mean for sample 1 is

$$\frac{0.5014 + 0.5022 + 0.5009 + 0.5027}{4} = 0.5018 \text{ in.}$$

Similarly, the means of samples 2, 3, 4, and 5 are 0.5027, 0.5026, 0.5020, and 0.5045 in., respectively. As shown in the table, $\bar{\bar{x}} = 0.5027$.

Step 6: Now, construct the $\bar{x}$-chart for the process average. The average screw diameter is 0.5027 in., and the average range is 0.0021 in., so use $\bar{\bar{x}} = 0.5027$, $\bar{R} = 0.0021$, and A_2 from Table 7.1 for a sample size of 4 to construct the control limits:

$$\text{UCL}_{\bar{x}} = \bar{\bar{x}} + A_2\bar{R} = 0.5027 + 0.729(0.0021) = 0.5042 \text{ in.}$$

$$\text{LCL}_{\bar{x}} = \bar{\bar{x}} - A_2\bar{R} = 0.5027 - 0.729(0.0021) = 0.5012 \text{ in.}$$

Step 7: Plot the sample means on the control chart, as shown in Figure 7.11.

The mean of sample 5 falls above the UCL, indicating that the process average is out of statistical control and that assignable causes must be explored, perhaps using a cause-and-effect diagram.

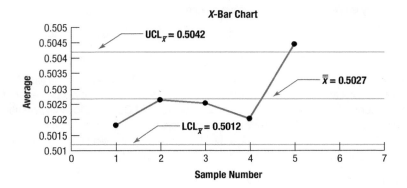

◀ **FIGURE 7.11**
The x-bar Chart from the *OM Explore $\bar{x}$-* and *R-Chart* Solver for the Metal Screw, Showing that Sample 5 Is Out of Control

DECISION POINT
A new employee operated the lathe machine that makes the screw on the day sample 5 was taken. To solve the problem, management initiated a training session for the employee. Subsequent samples showed that the process was back in statistical control.

If the standard deviation of the process distribution is known, another form of the $\bar{x}$-chart may be used:

$$\text{UCL}_{\bar{x}} = \bar{\bar{x}} + z\sigma_{\bar{x}} \quad \text{and} \quad \text{LCL}_{\bar{x}} = \bar{\bar{x}} - z\sigma_{\bar{x}}$$

where

$\sigma_{\bar{x}} = \sigma/\sqrt{n} = $ standard deviation of sample means

$\sigma = $ standard deviation of the process distribution

$n = $ sample size

$\bar{\bar{x}} = $ central line of the chart, which can be either the average of past sample means or a target value set for the process

$z = $ normal deviate (number of standard deviations from the average)

The analyst can use an *R*-chart to be sure that the process variability is in control before constructing the $\bar{x}$-chart. The advantage of using this form of the $\bar{x}$-chart is that the analyst can adjust the spread of the control limits by changing the value of z. This approach can be useful for balancing the effects of type I and type II errors.

EXAMPLE 7.2	Designing an $\bar{x}$-Chart Using the Process Standard Deviation

The Sunny Dale Bank monitors the time required to serve customers at the drive-by window because it is an important quality factor in competing with other banks in the city. After analyzing the data gathered in an extensive study of the window operation, bank management determined that the mean time to process a customer at the peak demand period is 5 minutes, with a standard deviation of 1.5 minutes. Management wants to monitor the mean time to process a customer by periodically using a sample size of six customers. Assume that the process variability is in statistical control. Design an $\bar{x}$-chart that has a type I error of 5 percent. That is, set the control limits so that there is a 2.5 percent chance a sample result will fall below the LCL and a 2.5 percent chance that a sample result will fall above the UCL. After several weeks of sampling, two successive samples came in at 3.70 and 3.68 minutes, respectively. Is the customer service process in statistical control?

SOLUTION

$$\bar{\bar{x}} = 5.0 \text{ minutes}$$

$$\sigma = 1.5 \text{ minutes}$$

$$n = 6 \text{ customers}$$

$$z = 1.96$$

The process variability is in statistical control, so we proceed directly to the $\bar{x}$-chart. The control limits are

$$UCL_{\bar{x}} = \bar{\bar{x}} + z\sigma/\sqrt{n} = 5.0 + 1.96(1.5)/\sqrt{6} = 6.20 \text{ minutes}$$

$$LCL_{\bar{x}} = \bar{\bar{x}} - z\sigma/\sqrt{n} = 5.0 - 1.96(1.5)/\sqrt{6} = 3.80 \text{ minutes}$$

The value for z can be obtained in the following way. The normal distribution table (see Appendix 1) gives the proportion of the total area under the normal curve from $-\infty$ to z. We want a type I error of 5 percent, or 2.5 percent of the curve above the UCL and 2.5 percent below the LCL. Consequently, we need to find the z value in the table that leaves only 2.5 percent in the upper portion of the normal curve (or 0.9750 in the table). The value is 1.96. The two new samples are below the LCL of the chart, implying that the average time to serve a customer has dropped. Assignable causes should be explored to see what caused the improvement.

DECISION POINT

Management studied the time period over which the samples were taken and found that the supervisor of the process was experimenting with some new procedures. Management decided to make the new procedures a permanent part of the customer service process. After all employees were trained in the new procedures, new samples were taken and the control chart reconstructed.

Control Charts for Attributes

Two charts commonly used for performance measures based on attributes measures are the p- and c-chart. The p-chart is used for controlling the proportion of defects generated by the process. The c-chart is used for controlling the number of defects when more than one defect can be present in a service or product.

p-Charts   The **p-chart** is a commonly used control chart for attributes. The performance characteristic is counted rather than measured, and the entire service or item can be declared good or defective. For example, in the banking industry, the attributes counted might be the number of nonendorsed deposits or the number of incorrect financial statements sent to customers. The method involves selecting a random sample, inspecting each item in it, and calculating the sample proportion defective, p, which is the number of defective units divided by the sample size.

Sampling for a p-chart involves a "yes/no" decision: The process output either is or is not defective. The underlying statistical distribution is based on the binomial distribution. However, for large sample sizes, the normal distribution provides a good approximation to it. The standard deviation of the distribution of proportion defectives, σ_p, is

$$\sigma_p = \sqrt{\bar{p}(1 - \bar{p})/n}$$

p-chart

A chart used for controlling the proportion of defective services or products generated by the process.

where

n = sample size

$\bar{p}$ = central line on the chart, which can be either the historical average population proportion defective or a target value

We can use σ_p to arrive at the upper and lower control limits for a p-chart:

$$\text{UCL}_p = \bar{p} + z\sigma_p \quad \text{and} \quad \text{LCL}_p = \bar{p} - z\sigma_p$$

where

z = normal deviate (number of standard deviations from the average)

The chart is used in the following way. Periodically, a random sample of size n is taken, and the number of defective services or products is counted. The number of defectives is divided by the sample size to get a sample proportion defective, p, which is plotted on the chart. When a sample proportion defective falls outside the control limits, the analyst assumes that the proportion defective generated by the process has changed and searches for the assignable cause. Observations falling below the LCL_p indicate that the process may actually have improved. The analyst may find no assignable cause because it is always possible that an out-of-control proportion occurred randomly. However, if the analyst discovers assignable causes, those sample data should not be used to calculate the control limits for the chart.

EXAMPLE 7.3	Using a p-Chart to Monitor a Process

The operations manager of the booking services department of Hometown Bank is concerned about the number of wrong customer account numbers recorded by Hometown personnel. Each week a random sample of 2,500 deposits is taken, and the number of incorrect account numbers is recorded. The results for the past 12 weeks are shown in the following table. Is the booking process out of statistical control? Use three-sigma control limits, which will provide a Type I error of 0.26 percent.

MyOMLab

Active Model 7.2 in MyOMLab provides additional insight on the p-chart and its uses for the booking services department.

MyOMLab

Tutor 7.2 in MyOMLab provides a new example to practice the use of the p-chart.

Sample Number	Wrong Account Numbers	Sample Number	Wrong Account Numbers
1	15	7	24
2	12	8	7
3	19	9	10
4	2	10	17
5	19	11	15
6	4	12	3
			Total 147

SOLUTION

Step 1: Using this sample data to calculate $\bar{p}$

$$\bar{p} = \frac{\text{Total defectives}}{\text{Total number of observations}} = \frac{147}{12(2,500)} = 0.0049$$

$$\sigma_p = \sqrt{\bar{p}(1 - \bar{p})/n} = \sqrt{0.0049(1 - 0.0049)/2,500} = 0.0014$$

$$\text{UCL}_p = \bar{p} + z\sigma_p = 0.0049 + 3(0.0014) = 0.0091$$

$$\text{LCL}_p = \bar{p} - z\sigma_p = 0.0049 - 3(0.0014) = 0.0007$$

Step 2: Calculate each sample proportion defective. For sample 1, the proportion of defectives is 15/2,500 = 0.0060.

Step 3: Plot each sample proportion defective on the chart, as shown in Figure 5.12.

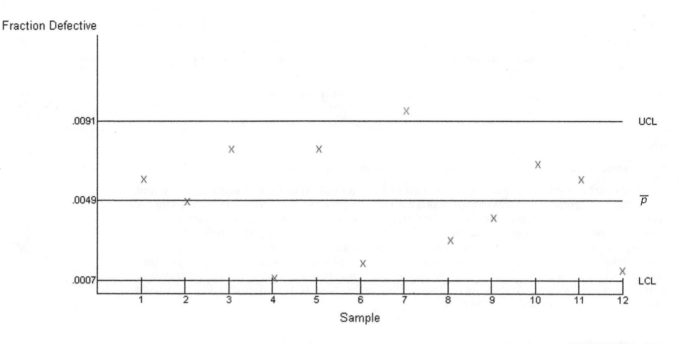

▲ **FIGURE 7.12**
The *p*-Chart from POM for Windows for Wrong Account Numbers, Showing that Sample 7 Is Out of Control

Sample 7 exceeds the UCL; thus, the process is out of control and the reasons for the poor performance that week should be determined.

DECISION POINT

Management explored the circumstances when sample 7 was taken. The encoding machine used to print the account numbers on the checks was defective that week. The following week the machine was repaired; however, the recommended preventive maintenance on the machine was not performed for months prior to the failure. Management reviewed the performance of the maintenance department and instituted changes to the maintenance procedures for the encoding machine. After the problem was corrected, an analyst recalculated the control limits using the data without sample 7. Subsequent weeks were sampled, and the booking process was determined to be in statistical control. Consequently, the *p*-chart provides a tool to indicate when a process needs adjustment.

c-Charts   Sometimes services or products have more than one defect. For example, a roll of carpeting may have several defects, such as tufted or discolored fibers or stains from the production process. Other situations in which more than one defect may occur include accidents at a particular intersection, bubbles in a television picture face panel, and complaints from a patron at a hotel. When management is interested in reducing the number of defects per unit or service encounter, another type of control chart, the ***c*-chart**, is useful.

c-chart

A chart used for controlling the number of defects when more than one defect can be present in a service or product.

The underlying sampling distribution for a *c*-chart is the Poisson distribution. The Poisson distribution is based on the assumption that defects occur over a continuous region on the surface of a product or a continuous time interval during the provision of a service. It further assumes that the probability of two or more defects at any one location on the surface or at any instant of time is negligible. The mean of the distribution is $\bar{c}$ and the standard deviation is $\sqrt{\bar{c}}$. A useful tactic is to use the normal approximation to the Poisson so that the central line of the chart is $\bar{c}$ and the control limits are

$$\text{UCL}_c = \bar{c} + z\sqrt{\bar{c}} \quad \text{and} \quad \text{LCL}_c = \bar{c} - z\sqrt{\bar{c}}$$

EXAMPLE 7.4	Using a *c*-Chart to Monitor Defects per Unit

The Woodland Paper Company produces paper for the newspaper industry. As a final step in the process, the paper passes through a machine that measures various product quality characteristics. When the paper production process is in control, it averages 20 defects per roll.

a. Set up a control chart for the number of defects per roll. For this example, use two-sigma control limits.

b. Five rolls had the following number of defects: 16, 21, 17, 22, and 24, respectively. The sixth roll, using pulp from a different supplier, had 5 defects. Is the paper production process in control?

MyOMLab

Tutor 7.3 in MyOMLab provides a new example to practice the use of the *c*-chart.

SOLUTION

a. The average number of defects per roll is 20. Therefore

$$UCL_c = \bar{c} + z\sqrt{\bar{c}} = 20 + 2(\sqrt{20}) = 28.94$$

$$LCL_c = \bar{c} - z\sqrt{\bar{c}} = 20 - 2(\sqrt{20}) = 11.06$$

The control chart is shown in Figure 7.13.

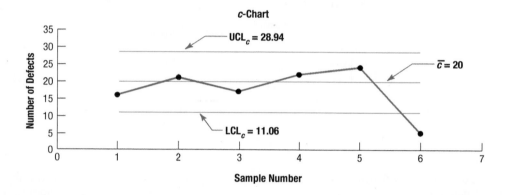

◀ **FIGURE 7.13**
The *c*-Chart from the *OM Explorer c-Chart* Solver for Defects per Roll of Paper

b. Because the first five rolls had defects that fell within the control limits, the process is still in control. The sixth roll's five defects, however, is below than the LCL, and therefore, the process is technically "out of control." The control chart indicates that something good has happened.

DECISION POINT

The supplier for the first five samples has been used by Woodland Paper for many years. The supplier for the sixth sample is new to the company. Management decided to continue using the new supplier for a while, monitoring the number of defects to see whether it stays low. If the number remains below the LCL for 20 consecutive samples, management will make the switch permanent and recalculate the control chart parameters.

Process Capability

Statistical process control techniques help managers achieve and maintain a process distribution that does not change in terms of its mean and variance. The control limits on the control charts signal when the mean or variability of the process changes. However, a process that is in statistical control may not be producing services or products according to their design specifications because the control limits are based on the mean and variability of the *sampling distribution*, not the design specifications. **Process capability** refers to the ability of the process to meet the design specifications for a service or product. Design specifications often are expressed as a **nominal value**, or target, and a **tolerance**, or allowance above or below the nominal value.

For example, the administrator of an intensive care unit lab might have a nominal value for the turnaround time of results to the attending physicians of 25 minutes and a tolerance of ±5 minutes because of the need for speed under life-threatening conditions. The tolerance gives an *upper specification* of 30 minutes and a *lower specification* of 20 minutes. The lab process must be capable of providing the results of analyses within these specifications; otherwise, it will produce a certain proportion of "defects." The administrator is also interested in detecting occurrences of turnaround times of less than 20 minutes because something might be learned that can be built into the lab process in the future. For the present, the physicians are pleased with results that arrive within 20 to 30 minutes.

nominal value
A target for design specifications.

process capability
The ability of the process to meet the design specifications for a service or product.

tolerance
An allowance above or below the nominal value.

Defining Process Capability

Figure 7.14 shows the relationship between a process distribution and the upper and lower specifications for the lab process turnaround time under two conditions. In Figure 7.14(a), the process is capable because the extremes of the process distribution fall within the upper and lower specifications. In Figure 7.14(b), the process is not capable because the lab process produces too many reports with long turnaround times.

FIGURE 7.14 ▶
The Relationship Between a Process Distribution and Upper and Lower Specifications

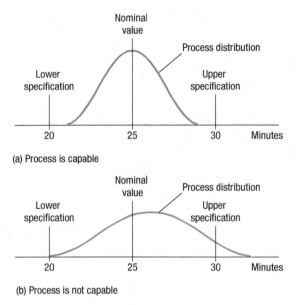

(a) Process is capable

(b) Process is not capable

Figure 7.14 shows clearly why managers are so concerned with reducing process variability. The less variability—represented by lower standard deviations—the less frequently bad output is produced. Figure 7.15 shows what reducing variability implies for a process distribution that is a normal probability distribution. The firm with two-sigma performance (the specification limits equal the process distribution mean ± 2 standard deviations) produces 4.56 percent defects, or 45,600 defects per million. The firm with four-sigma performance produces only 0.0063 percent defects, or 63 defects per million. Finally, the firm with six-sigma performance produces only 0.0000002 percent defects, or 0.002 defects per million.[1]

FIGURE 7.15 ▼
Effects of Reducing Variability on Process Capability

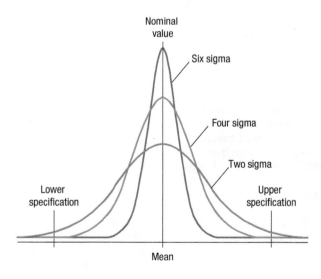

How can a manager determine quantitatively whether a process is capable? Two measures commonly are used in practice to assess the capability of a process: the process capability index and the process capability ratio.

Process Capability Index The **process capability index**, C_{pk}, is defined as

$$C_{pk} = \text{Minimum of} \left[\frac{\overline{\overline{x}} - \text{Lower specification}}{3\sigma}, \frac{\text{Upper specification} - \overline{\overline{x}}}{3\sigma} \right]$$

where

σ = standard deviation of the process distribution

The process capability index measures how well the process is centered as well as whether the variability is acceptable. As a general rule, most values of any process distribution fall within ± 3 standard deviations of the mean. Consequently, ± 3 standard deviations is used as the benchmark. Because the process capability index is concerned with how well the process distribution is centered relative to the specifications, it checks to see if the process average is at least three standard deviations

---

[1]Our discussion assumes that the process distribution has no assignable causes. Six Sigma programs, however, define defect performance with the assumption that the process average has moved 1.5 standard deviations. In such a case, there would be 3.4 defects per million. See **www.isixsigma.com** for the rationale behind that assumption.

from the upper and lower specifications. We take the minimum of the two ratios because it gives the *worst-case* situation.

The process capability index must be compared to a critical value to judge whether a process is capable. Firms striving to achieve three-sigma performance use a critical value for the ratio of 1.0. A firm targeting four-sigma performance will use 1.33 (or 4/3), a firm targeting five-sigma performance will use 1.67 (or 5/3), and a firm striving for six-sigma performance will use 2.00 (or 6/3). Processes producing services or products with less than three-sigma performance will have C_{pk} values less than 1.0.

If a process passes the process capability index test, we can declare the process is capable. Suppose a firm desires its processes to produce at the level of four-sigma performance. If C_{pk} is greater than or equal to the critical value of 1.33, we can say the process is capable. If C_{pk} is less than the critical value, either the process average is too close to one of the tolerance limits and is generating defective output, or the process variability is too large. To find out whether the variability is the culprit, we need another test.

Process Capability Ratio   If a process fails the process capability *index* test, we need a quick test to see if the process variability is causing the problem. If a process is *capable*, it has a process distribution whose extreme values fall within the upper and lower specifications for a service or product. For example, if the process distribution is normal, 99.74 percent of the values fall within ± 3 standard deviations. In other words, the range of values of the quality measure generated by a process is approximately 6 standard deviations of the process distribution. Hence, if a process is capable at the three-sigma level, the difference between the upper and lower specification, called the *tolerance width*, must be greater than 6 standard deviations. The **process capability ratio**, C_p, is defined as

$$C_p = \frac{\text{Upper specification} - \text{Lower specification}}{6\sigma}$$

Suppose management wants four-sigma capability in their processes, and a process just failed the process capability index test at that level. A C_p value of 1.33, say, implies that the variability of the process is at the level of four-sigma quality and that the process is capable of consistently producing outputs within specifications, assuming that the process is centered. Because C_p passed the test, but C_{pk} did not, we can assume that the problem is that the process is not centered adequately.

Using Continuous Improvement to Determine the Capability of a Process

To determine the capability of a process to produce outputs within the tolerances, use the following steps.

Step 1.   Collect data on the process output, and calculate the mean and the standard deviation of the process output distribution.

Step 2.   Use the data from the process distribution to compute process control charts, such as an $\overline{x}$- and an R-chart.

Step 3.   Take a series of at least 20 consecutive random samples of size n from the process and plot the results on the control charts. If the sample statistics are within the control limits of the charts, the process is in statistical control. If the process is not in statistical control, look for assignable causes and eliminate them. Recalculate the mean and standard deviation of the process distribution and the control limits for the charts. Continue until the process is in statistical control.

Step 4.   Calculate the process capability *index*. If the results are acceptable, the process is capable and document any changes made to the process; continue to monitor the output by using the control charts. If the results are unacceptable, calculate the process capability *ratio*. If the results are acceptable, the process variability is fine and management should focus on centering the process. If the results of the process capability ratio are unacceptable, management should focus on reducing the variability in the process until it passes the test. As changes are made, recalculate the mean and standard deviation of the process distribution and the control limits for the charts and return to step 3.

Quality Engineering

Successful quality performance is often more than process improvement; it also involves service/product design. Originated by Genichi Taguchi, **quality engineering** is an approach that involves

process capability index, C_{pk}

An index that measures the potential for a process to generate defective outputs relative to either upper or lower specifications.

process capability ratio, C_p

The tolerance width divided by six standard deviations.

quality engineering

An approach originated by Genichi Taguchi that involves combining engineering and statistical methods to reduce costs and improve quality by optimizing product design and manufacturing processes.

| EXAMPLE 7.5 | Assessing the Process Capability of the Intensive Care Unit Lab |

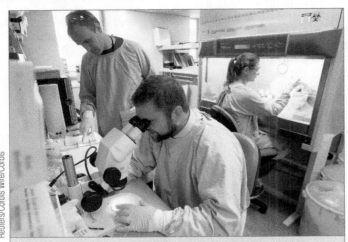

A doctor examines a specimen through his microscope in a lab at St. Vincent's Hospital.

The intensive care unit lab process has an average turnaround time of 26.2 minutes and a standard deviation of 1.35 minutes. The nominal value for this service is 25 minutes with an upper specification limit of 30 minutes and a lower specification limit of 20 minutes. The administrator of the lab wants to have four-sigma performance for her lab. Is the lab process capable of this level of performance?

SOLUTION

The administrator began by taking a quick check to see if the process is capable by applying the process capability index:

$$\text{Lower specification calculation} = \frac{26.2 - 20.0}{3(1.35)} = 1.53$$

$$\text{Upper specification calculation} = \frac{30.0 - 26.2}{3(1.35)} = 0.94$$

$$C_{pk} = \text{Minimum of } [1.53, 0.94] = 0.94$$

Since the target value for four-sigma performance is 1.33, the process capability index told her that the process was not capable. However, she did not know whether the problem was the variability of the process, the centering of the process, or both. The options available to improve the process depended on what is wrong.

She next checked the process variability with the process capability ratio:

$$C_p = \frac{30.0 - 20.0}{6(1.35)} = 1.23$$

The process variability did not meet the four-sigma target of 1.33. Consequently, she initiated a study to see where variability was introduced into the process. Two activities, report preparation and specimen slide preparation, were identified as having inconsistent procedures. These procedures were modified to provide consistent performance. New data were collected and the average turnaround was now 26.1 minutes with a standard deviation of 1.20 minutes. She now had the process variability at the four-sigma level of performance, as indicated by the process capability ratio:

$$C_p = \frac{30.0 - 20.0}{6(1.20)} = 1.39$$

However, the process capability index indicated additional problems to resolve:

$$C_{pk} = \text{Minimum of } \left[\frac{(26.1 - 20.0)}{3(1.20)}, \frac{(30.0 - 26.1)}{3(1.20)}\right] = 1.08$$

DECISION POINT

The lab process was still not at the level of four-sigma performance on turnaround time. The lab administrator searched for the causes of the off-center turnaround time distribution. She discovered periodic backlogs at a key piece of testing equipment. Acquiring a second machine provided the capacity to reduce the turnaround times to four-sigma capability.

MyOMLab

Active Model 7.3 in MyOMLab provides additional insight on the process capability problem at the intensive care unit lab.

MyOMLab

Tutor 7.4 in MyOMLab provides a new example to practice the process capability measures.

quality loss function

The rationale that a service or product that barely conforms to the specifications is more like a defective service or product than a perfect one.

combining engineering and statistical methods to reduce costs and improve quality by optimizing product design and manufacturing processes. Taguchi believes that unwelcome costs are associated with *any* deviation from a quality characteristic's target value. Taguchi's view is that the **quality loss function** is zero when the quality characteristic of the service or product is exactly on the target value, and that the quality loss function value rises exponentially as the quality characteristic gets closer to the specification limits. The rationale is that a service or product that barely conforms to the specifications is more like a defective service or product than a perfect one. Figure 7.16 shows Taguchi's quality loss function schematically. Taguchi concluded that managers should continually search for ways to reduce *all* variability from the target value in the production process and not be content with merely adhering to specification limits. See **http://elsmar.com/Taguchi.html** for a detailed discussion and animation of the Taguchi Loss Function.

International Quality Documentation Standards

Once a company has gone through the effort of making its processes capable, it must document its level of quality so as to better market its services or products. This documentation of quality is especially important in international trade. However, if each country had its own set of standards, companies selling in international markets would have difficulty complying with quality documentation standards in each country where they did business. To overcome this problem, the International Organization for Standardization devised a family of standards called ISO 9000 for companies doing business in the European Union. Subsequently, ISO 14000 was devised for environmental management systems and ISO 26000 for guidance on social responsibility.

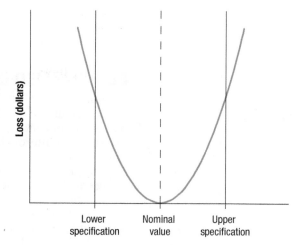

▲ **FIGURE 7.16**
Taguchi's Quality Loss Function

The ISO 9001:2008 Documentation Standards

ISO 9001:2008 is the latest update of the ISO 9000 standards governing documentation of a quality program. According to the International Organization for Standardization, the ISO 9001:2008 standards address *quality management* by specifying what the firm does to fulfill the customer's quality requirements and applicable regulatory requirements, while aiming to enhance customer satisfaction and achieve continual improvement of its performance in pursuit of these objectives. Companies become certified by proving to a qualified external examiner that they comply with all the requirements. Once certified, companies are listed in a directory so that potential customers can see which companies are certified and to what level. Compliance with ISO 9001:2008 standards says *nothing* about the actual quality of a product. Rather, it indicates to customers that companies can provide documentation to support whatever claims they make about quality. As of 2009, more than 1 million organizations worldwide have been certified in the ISO 9000 family of documentation standards.

ISO 9001:2008

A set of standards governing documentation of a quality program.

ISO 14000:2004 Environmental Management System

The **ISO 14000:2004** standards require documentation of a firm's environmental program. According to the International Organization for Standardization, the ISO 14000:2004 family addresses *environmental management* by specifying what the firm does to minimize harmful effects on the environment caused by its activities, and to achieve continual improvement of its environmental performance. The documentation standards require participating companies to keep track of their raw materials use and their generation, treatment, and disposal of hazardous wastes. Although not specifying what each company is allowed to emit, the standards require companies to prepare a plan for ongoing improvement in their environmental performance. ISO 14000:2004 covers a number of areas, including the following:

ISO 14000:2004

Documentation standards that require participating companies to keep track of their raw materials use and their generation, treatment, and disposal of hazardous wastes.

- *Environmental Management System.* Requires a plan to improve performance in resource use and pollutant output.
- *Environmental Performance Evaluation.* Specifies guidelines for the certification of companies.
- *Environmental Labeling.* Defines terms such as *recyclable, energy efficient*, and *safe for the ozone layer*.
- *Life-Cycle Assessment.* Evaluates the lifetime environmental impact from the manufacture, use, and disposal of a product.

To maintain their certification, companies must be inspected by outside, private auditors on a regular basis. As of 2010, more than 200,000 organizations in 155 countries have been certified for ISO 14000.

ISO 26000:2010 Social Responsibility Guidelines

The **ISO 26000:2010** guidelines, according to the International Organization for Standards, provide harmonized, globally relevant guidance on social responsibility for private and public sector organizations based on international consensus among experts. A firm does not get certified in ISO 26000; the guidelines are voluntary and are intended to promote best practice in ethical behavior in business. The seven core subjects of social responsibility covered in the guidelines are (1) human rights, (2) labor practices, (3) the environment, (4) fair operating practices,

ISO 26000:2010

International guidelines for organizational social responsibility.

(5) consumer issues, (6) community involvement and development, and (7) the organization. In this way the international community is encouraging ethical business behavior between businesses and consumers.

Benefits of ISO Certification

Completing the certification process can take as long as 18 months and involve many hours of management and employee time. The cost of certification can exceed $1 million for large companies. Despite the expense and commitment involved in ISO certification, it bestows significant external and internal benefits. The external benefits come from the potential sales advantage that companies in compliance have. Companies looking for a supplier will more likely select a company that has demonstrated compliance with ISO documentation standards, all other factors being equal. Consequently, more and more firms are seeking certification to gain a competitive advantage.

Internal benefits can be substantial. Registered companies report an average of 48 percent increased profitability and 76 percent improvement in marketing. The British Standards Institute, a leading third-party auditor, estimates that most ISO 9000-registered companies experience a 10 percent reduction in the cost of producing a product because of the quality improvements they make while striving to meet the documentation requirements. Certification in ISO 9001:2008 requires a company to analyze and document its procedures, which is necessary in any event for implementing continuous improvement, employee involvement, and similar programs. The guidelines and requirements of the ISO documentation standards provide companies with a jump-start in pursuing TQM programs.

Baldrige Performance Excellence Program

Regardless of where a company does business, it is clear that all organizations have to produce high-quality products and services if they are to be competitive. To emphasize that point, in August 1987 the U.S. Congress signed into law the Malcolm Baldrige National Quality Improvement Act, creating the Malcolm Baldrige National Quality Award, which is now entitled the **Baldrige Performance Excellence Program** (**www.quality.nist.gov**). Named for the late secretary of commerce, who was a strong proponent of enhancing quality as a means of reducing the trade deficit, the award promotes, recognizes, and publicizes quality strategies and achievements.

The application and review process for the Baldrige award is rigorous. However, the act of preparing the application itself is often a major benefit to organizations because it helps firms define what *quality* means for them. According to the U.S. Commerce Department's National Institute of Standards and Technology (NIST), investing in quality principles and performance excellence pays off in increased productivity, satisfied employees and customers, and improved profitability, both for customers and investors. The seven major criteria for the award are the following:

1. *Leadership.* Describes how senior leaders' actions guide and sustain the organization and how they communicate with the workforce and encourage high performance.

2. *Strategic Planning.* Describes how the organization establishes its strategy to address its strategic challenges, leverage its strategic advantages, and summarizes the organization's key strategic objectives and their related goals.

3. *Customer Focus.* Describes how the organization determines its service or product offerings and the mechanisms to support the customers' use of them.

4. *Measurement, Analysis, and Knowledge Management.* Describes how the organization measures, analyzes, reviews, and improves its performance through the use of data and information at all levels of the organization.

5. *Workforce Focus.* Describes how the organization engages, compensates, and rewards its workers and how they are developed to achieve high performance.

6. *Operations Focus.* Describes how the organization designs its work systems and determines its key processes to deliver customer value, prepare for potential emergencies, and achieve organizational success and sustainability.

7. *Results.* Describe the organization's performance and improvement in five categories: products and processes, customer focus, workforce focus, leadership and governance, and financial and market.

Customer satisfaction underpins these seven criteria. Criterion 7, Results, is given the most weight in selecting winners.

Baldrige Performance Excellence Program

A program named for the late secretary of commerce, Malcolm Baldrige, who was a strong proponent of enhancing quality as a means of reducing the trade deficit; organizations vie for an award that promotes, recognizes, and publicizes quality strategies and achievements.

LEARNING GOALS IN REVIEW

① **Define the four major costs of quality.** See the section "Costs of Quality," pp. 239.

② **Describe the role of ethics in the quality of services and products.** We explain how deceptive business practices can affect a customer's experiences and why the costs of quality should be balanced with ethical considerations in the section "Ethics and Quality," pp. 239–240.

③ **Explain the basic principles of TQM programs.** See the section "Total Quality Management," pp. 240–244. Focus on the five customer definitions of quality, Managerial Practice 7.1, which shows how one company matched processes to the five definitions, the importance of employee involvement, and how continuous improvement works. The key figures are Figures 7.1 and 7.2.

④ **Explain the basic principles of Six Sigma Programs.** We have summarized the essence of these important programs in the section "Six Sigma," pp. 244–245. Be sure to understand

Figure 7.3, which shows the goals of Six Sigma, and Figure 7.4, which provides the improvement model. Figure 7.5 shows how TQM or Six Sigma works in a supply chain through the tactic of acceptance sampling.

⑤ **Describe how to construct control charts and use them to determine whether a process is out of statistical control.** See the section "Statistical Process Control," pp. 246–250. Understanding Figures 7.6 and 7.7 is key to understanding the methods to follow. The section "Statistical Process Control Methods," pp. 250–257, shows you how to determine if a process is in statistical control. Study Examples 7.1 to 7.5 as well as Solved Problems 1 to 3.

⑥ **Describe how to determine whether a process is capable of producing a service or product to specifications.** The major take-away in the chapter is found in the section "Process Capability," pp. 257–260. Be sure you understand Figures 7.4 and 7.5; study Example 7.5 and Solved Problem 4.

MyOMLab helps and assesses students with 16 problems on *x*-bar and *R*-bar Charts, *p*-charts, *c*-Charts, and Process Capability.

MyOMLab Resources	Titles	Link to the Book
Video	*Starwood: Process Performance and Quality*	Costs of Quality; Total Quality Management; Six Sigma
	Christchurch Parkroyal TQM	Costs of Quality; Total Quality Management
Active Model Exercises	7.1 *x*-bar and *R*-Charts	Control Charts for Variables; Example 7.1 (pp. 252–253)
	7.2 *p*-Chart	Control Charts for Attributes; Example 7.3 (pp. 255–256)
	7.3 Process Capability	Process Capability; Example 7.5 (p. 260)
OM Explorer Solvers	*c*-Charts	Control Charts for Attributes; Example 7.4 (p. 257); Figure 7.13 (p. 257); Solved Problem 3 (p. 267)
	p-Charts	Control Charts for Attributes; Example 7.3 (pp. 255–256); Solved Problem 2 (pp. 266–267)
	Process Capability	Process Capability; Example 7.5 (p. 260); Solved Problem 4 (p. 268)
	R- and *x*-bar Charts	Control Charts for Variables; Example 7.1 (p. 252); Figure 7.10 and Figure 7.11 (pp. 252–253); Solved Problem 1 (pp. 265–266)
OM Explorer Tutors	7.1 *R*- and *x*-bar Charts	Control Charts for Variables; Example 7.1 (pp. 252–253)
	7.2 *p*-Charts	Control Charts for Attributes; Example 7.3 (pp. 255–256)
	7.3 *c*-Charts	Control Charts for Attributes; Example 7.4 (p. 257)
	7.4 Process Capability	Process Capability; Example 7.5 (p. 260)
POM for Windows	*p*-Charts	Control Charts for Attributes; Example 7.3 (pp. 255–256); Figure 7.12 (p. 256); Solved Problem 2 (pp. 266–267)
	x-bar Charts	Control Charts for Variables; Example 7.1 (pp. 252–253); Example 7.2 (p. 254); Solved Problem 1 (pp. 265–266)
	c-Charts	Control Charts for Attributes; Example 7.4 (p. 257); Solved Problem 3 (p. 267)
	Process Capability	Process Capability; Example 7.5 (p. 260); Solved Problem 4 (p. 268)
	Acceptance Sampling	Acceptance Sampling
SimQuick Simulation Exercises	Circuit Board Process	Six-Sigma Improvement Model

MyOMLab Resources	Titles	Link to the Book
Tutor Exercises	7.1 *x*-bar and *R*-Chart with Target Weight of 7.04 oz.	Control Charts for Variables
	7.2 *p*-Chart When Changes in Sample Values	Control Charts for Attributes
	7.3 Process Capability with a Change in Process Average and Variability	Process Capability
Virtual Tours	1. Steinway Factory, Verne O. Powell Flutes	Total Quality Management; Six Sigma
	2. Beach Beat Surfboards	Total Quality Management
MyOMLab Supplements	G. Acceptance Sampling Plans	Acceptance Sampling
Internet Exercise	1. National Institute of Standards and Technology, and International Organization for Standardization	Baldrige Performance Excellence Award International Quality Documentation Standards
	2. SAS Scandinavian Airline	Total Quality Management
	3. Jack in the Box	Customer Satisfaction
	4. Maybach	Customer Satisfaction
	5. Bureau of Transportation Statistics	Statistical Process Control
Key Equations		
Image Library		

Key Equations

1. Sample mean: $\bar{x} = \dfrac{\sum\limits_{i=1}^{n} x_i}{n}$

2. Standard deviation of a sample:

$$\sigma = \sqrt{\frac{\sum\limits_{i=1}^{n}(x_i - \bar{x})^2}{n-1}} \text{ or } \sigma = \sqrt{\frac{\sum\limits_{i=1}^{n} x_i^2 - \dfrac{(\sum x_i)^2}{n}}{n-1}}$$

3. Control limits for variable process control charts

    a. *R*-chart, range of sample:

    $$\text{Upper control limit} = \text{UCL}_R = D_4\overline{R}$$
    $$\text{Lower control limit} = \text{LCL}_R = D_3\overline{R}$$

    b. $\bar{x}$-chart, sample mean:

    $$\text{Upper control limit} = \text{UCL}_{\bar{x}} = \bar{\bar{x}} + A_2\overline{R}$$
    $$\text{Lower control limit} = \text{LCL}_{\bar{x}} = \bar{\bar{x}} - A_2\overline{R}$$

    c. When the standard deviation of the process distribution, σ, is known:

    $$\text{Upper control limit} = \text{UCL}_{\bar{x}} = \bar{\bar{x}} + z\sigma_{\bar{x}}$$
    $$\text{Lower control limit} = \text{LCL}_{\bar{x}} = \bar{\bar{x}} - z\sigma_{\bar{x}}$$

    where

    $$\sigma_{\bar{x}} = \frac{\sigma}{\sqrt{n}}$$

4. Control limits for attribute process control charts

   a. *p*-chart, proportion defective:

   $$\text{Upper control limit} = \text{UCL}_p = \bar{p} + z\sigma_p$$
   $$\text{Lower control limit} = \text{LCL}_p = \bar{p} - z\sigma_p$$

   where

   $$\sigma_p = \sqrt{\bar{p}(1 - \bar{p})/n}$$

   b. *c*-chart, number of defects:

   $$\text{Upper control limit} = \text{UCL}_c = \bar{c} + z\sqrt{\bar{c}}$$
   $$\text{Lower control limit} = \text{LCL}_c = \bar{c} - z\sqrt{\bar{c}}$$

5. Process capability index:

   $$C_{pk} = \text{Minimum of} \left[\frac{\bar{\bar{x}} - \text{Lower specification}}{3\sigma}, \frac{\text{Upper specification} - \bar{\bar{x}}}{3\sigma} \right]$$

6. Process capability ratio:

   $$C_p = \frac{\text{Upper specification} - \text{Lower specification}}{6\sigma}$$

Key Terms

Solved Problem 1

The Watson Electric Company produces incandescent lightbulbs. The following data on the number of lumens for 40-watt lightbulbs were collected when the process was in control.

	OBSERVATION			
Sample	1	2	3	4
1	604	612	588	600
2	597	601	607	603
3	581	570	585	592
4	620	605	595	588
5	590	614	608	604

a. Calculate control limits for an *R*-chart and an $\bar{x}$-chart.

b. Since these data were collected, some new employees were hired. A new sample obtained the following readings: 570, 603, 623, and 583. Is the process still in control?

SOLUTION

a. To calculate $\bar{x}$, compute the mean for each sample. To calculate R, subtract the lowest value in the sample from the highest value in the sample. For example, for sample 1,

$$\bar{x} = \frac{604 + 612 + 588 + 600}{4} = 601$$

$$R = 612 - 588 = 24$$

Sample	$\bar{X}$	R
1	601	24
2	602	10
3	582	22
4	602	32
5	604	24
Total	2,991	112
Average	$\bar{\bar{x}} = 598.2$	$\bar{R} = 22.4$

The R-chart control limits are

$$\text{UCL}_R = D_4\bar{R} = 2.282(22.4) = 51.12$$
$$\text{LCL}_R = D_3\bar{R} = 0(22.4) = 0$$

The $\bar{x}$-chart control limits are

$$\text{UCL}_{\bar{x}} = \bar{\bar{x}} + A_2\bar{R} = 598.2 + 0.729(22.4) = 614.53$$
$$\text{LCL}_{\bar{x}} = \bar{\bar{x}} - A_2\bar{R} = 598.2 - 0.729(22.4) = 581.87$$

b. First check to see whether the variability is still in control based on the new data. The range is 53 (or 623 − 570), which is outside the UCL for the R-chart. Since the process variability is out of control, it is meaningless to test for the process average using the current estimate for $\bar{R}$. A search for assignable causes inducing excessive variability must be conducted.

Solved Problem 2

The data processing department of the Arizona Bank has five data entry clerks. Each working day their supervisor verifies the accuracy of a random sample of 250 records. A record containing one or more errors is considered defective and must be redone. The results of the last 30 samples are shown in the table. All were checked to make sure that none was out of control.

Sample	Number of Defective Records	Sample	Number of Defective Records	Sample	Number of Defective Records	Sample	Number of Defective Records
1	7	9	6	17	12	24	7
2	5	10	13	18	4	25	13
3	19	11	18	19	6	26	10
4	10	12	5	20	11	27	14
5	11	13	16	21	17	28	6
6	8	14	4	22	12	29	11
7	12	15	11	23	6	30	9
8	9	16	8			Total	300

a. Based on these historical data, set up a *p*-chart using $z = 3$.

b. Samples for the next 4 days showed the following:

Sample	Number of Defective Records
Tues	17
Wed	15
Thurs	22
Fri	21

What is the supervisor's assessment of the data-entry process likely to be?

SOLUTION

a. From the table, the supervisor knows that the total number of defective records is 300 out of a total sample of 7,500 [or 30(250)]. Therefore, the central line of the chart is

$$\bar{p} = \frac{300}{7,500} = 0.04$$

The control limits are

$$\text{UCL}_p = \bar{p} + z\sqrt{\frac{\bar{p}(1 - \bar{p})}{n}} = 0.04 + 3\sqrt{\frac{0.04(0.96)}{250}} = 0.077$$

$$\text{LCL}_p = \bar{p} - z\sqrt{\frac{\bar{p}(1 - \bar{p})}{n}} = 0.04 - 3\sqrt{\frac{0.04(0.96)}{250}} = 0.003$$

b. Samples for the next 4 days showed the following:

Sample	Number of Defective Records	Proportion
Tues	17	0.068
Wed	15	0.060
Thurs	22	0.088
Fri	21	0.084

Samples for Thursday and Friday are out of control. The supervisor should look for the problem and, upon identifying it, take corrective action.

Solved Problem 3

The Minnow County Highway Safety Department monitors accidents at the intersection of Routes 123 and 14. Accidents at the intersection have averaged three per month.

a. Which type of control chart should be used? Construct a control chart with three-sigma control limits.

b. Last month, seven accidents occurred at the intersection. Is this sufficient evidence to justify a claim that something has changed at the intersection?

SOLUTION

a. The safety department cannot determine the number of accidents that did *not* occur, so it has no way to compute a proportion defective at the intersection. Therefore, the administrators must use a *c*-chart for which

$$\text{UCL}_c = \bar{c} + z\sqrt{\bar{c}} = 3 + 3\sqrt{3} = 8.20$$

$$\text{LCL}_c = \bar{c} - z\sqrt{\bar{c}} = 3 - 3\sqrt{3} = -2.196, \text{ adjusted to 0}$$

There cannot be a negative number of accidents, so the LCL in this case is adjusted to zero.

b. The number of accidents last month falls within the UCL and LCL of the chart. We conclude that no assignable causes are present and that the increase in accidents was due to chance.

Solved Problem 4

Pioneer Chicken advertises "lite" chicken with 30 percent fewer calories. (The pieces are 33 percent smaller.) The process average distribution for "lite" chicken breasts is 420 calories, with a standard deviation of the population of 25 calories. Pioneer randomly takes samples of six chicken breasts to measure calorie content.

a. Design an $\bar{x}$-chart using the process standard deviation. Use three-sigma limits.

b. The product design calls for the average chicken breast to contain 400 ± 100 calories. Calculate the process capability index (target = 1.33) and the process capability ratio. Interpret the results.

SOLUTION

a. For the process standard deviation of 25 calories, the standard deviation of the sample mean is

$$\sigma_{\bar{x}} = \frac{\sigma}{\sqrt{n}} = \frac{25}{\sqrt{6}} = 10.2 \text{ calories}$$

$$\text{UCL}_{\bar{x}} = \bar{\bar{x}} + z\sigma_{\bar{x}} = 420 + 3(10.2) = 450.6 \text{ calories}$$

$$\text{LCL}_{\bar{x}} = \bar{\bar{x}} - z\sigma_{\bar{x}} = 420 - 3(10.2) = 389.4 \text{ calories}$$

b. The process capability index is

$$C_{pk} = \text{Minimum of} \left[\frac{\bar{\bar{x}} - \text{Lower specification}}{3\sigma}, \frac{\text{Upper specification} - \bar{\bar{x}}}{3\sigma} \right]$$

$$= \text{Minimum of} \left[\frac{420 - 300}{3(25)} = 1.60, \frac{500 - 420}{3(25)} = 1.07 \right] = 1.07$$

The process capability ratio is

$$C_p = \frac{\text{Upper specification} - \text{Lower specification}}{6\sigma} = \frac{500 \text{ calories} - 300 \text{ calories}}{6(25)} = 1.33$$

Because the process capability ratio is 1.33, the process should be able to produce the product reliably within specifications. However, the process capability index is 1.07, so the current process is not centered properly for four-sigma performance. The mean of the process distribution is too close to the upper specification.

Discussion Questions

1. Consider Managerial Practice 7.1 and the discussion of Steinway's approach to achieving top quality. To get a better idea of the craft-oriented production process, visit **www.steinway.com/factory/tour.shtml**. However, Steinway also uses automation to produce the action mechanisms, a critical assembly in the grand pianos. Given the overall image of a Steinway piano, a very pricey hand-crafted object of beauty, what do you think of the use of automated equipment? Do you think it is a mistake to use automation in this way?

2. Recently, the Polish General Corporation, well-known for manufacturing appliances and automobile parts, initiated a $13 billion project to produce automobiles. A great deal of learning on the part of management and employees was required. Even though pressure was mounting to get a new product to market in early 2012, the production manager of the newly formed automobile division insisted on almost a year of trial runs before sales started because workers have to do their jobs 60 to 100 times before they can memorize the right sequence. The launch date was set for early 2013. What are the consequences of using this approach to enter the market with a new product?

3. Explain how unethical business practices degrade the quality of the experience a customer has with a service or product. How is the International Organization for Standardization trying to encourage ethical business behavior?

Problems

The OM Explorer and POM for Windows software is available to all students using the 10th edition of this textbook. Go to **www.pearsonhighered.com/krajewski** to download these computer packages. If you purchased MyOMLab, you also have access to Active Models software and significant help in doing the following problems. Check with your instructor on how best to use these resources. In many cases, the instructor wants you to understand how to do the calculations by hand. At the least, the software provides a check on your calculations. When calculations are particularly complex and the goal is interpreting the results in making decisions, the software replaces entirely the manual calculations. The software also can be a valuable resource well after your course is completed.

1. At Quickie Car Wash, the wash process is advertised to take less than 7 minutes. Consequently, management has set a target average of 390 seconds for the wash process. Suppose the average range for a sample of 9 cars is 10 seconds. Use Table 7.1 to establish control limits for sample means and ranges for the car wash process.

2. At Isogen Pharmaceuticals, the filling process for its asthma inhaler is set to dispense 150 milliliters (ml) of steroid solution per container. The average range for a sample of 4 containers is 3 ml. Use Table 7.1 to establish control limits for sample means and ranges for the filling process.

3. Garcia's Garage desires to create some colorful charts and graphs to illustrate how reliably its mechanics "get under the hood and fix the problem." The historic average for the proportion of customers that return for the same repair within the 30-day warranty period is 0.10. Each month, Garcia tracks 100 customers to see whether they return for warranty repairs. The results are plotted as a proportion to report progress toward the goal. If the control limits are to be set at two standard deviations on either side of the goal, determine the control limits for this chart. In March, 8 of the 100 customers in the sample group returned for warranty repairs. Is the repair process in control?

4. The Canine Gourmet Company produces delicious dog treats for canines with discriminating tastes. Management wants the box-filling line to be set so that the process average weight per packet is 45 grams. To make sure that the process is in control, an inspector at the end of the filling line periodically selects a random box of 10 packets and weighs each packet. When the process is in control, the range in the weight of each sample has averaged 6 grams.

   a. Design an R- and an $\bar{x}$-chart for this process.

   b. The results from the last 5 samples of 10 packets are

Sample	$\bar{x}$	R
1	44	9
2	40	2
3	46	5
4	39	8
5	48	3

   Is the process in control? Explain.

5. Aspen Plastics produces plastic bottles to customer order. The quality inspector randomly selects four bottles from the bottle machine and measures the outside diameter of the bottle neck, a critical quality dimension that determines whether the bottle cap will fit properly. The dimensions (in.) from the last six samples are

Sample	BOTTLE			
	1	2	3	4
1	0.594	0.622	0.598	0.590
2	0.587	0.611	0.597	0.613
3	0.571	0.580	0.595	0.602
4	0.610	0.615	0.585	0.578
5	0.580	0.624	0.618	0.614
6	0.585	0.593	0.607	0.569

   a. Assume that only these six samples are sufficient, and use the data to determine control limits for an R- and an $\bar{x}$-chart.

   b. Suppose that the specification for the bottle neck diameter is 0.600 ± 0.050 and the population standard deviation is 0.013 in. What is the Process Capability Index? The Process Capability Ratio?

   c. If the firm is seeking four-sigma performance, is the process capable of producing the bottle?

6. In an attempt to judge and monitor the quality of instruction, the administration of Mega-Byte Academy devised an examination to test students on the basic concepts that all should have learned. Each year, a random sample of 10 graduating students is selected for the test. The average score is used to track the quality of the educational process. Test results for the past 10 years are shown in Table 7.2.

   Use these data to estimate the center and standard deviation for this distribution. Then, calculate the two-sigma control limits for the process average. What comments would you make to the administration of the Mega-Byte Academy?

7. As a hospital administrator of a large hospital, you are concerned with the absenteeism among nurses' aides. The issue has been raised by registered nurses, who feel they often have to perform work normally done by their aides. To get the facts, absenteeism data were gathered for the last 3 weeks, which is considered a representative period for future conditions. After taking random samples of 64 personnel files each day, the following data were produced:

TABLE 7.2 | TEST SCORES ON EXIT EXAM

| Year | STUDENT | | | | | | | | | | Average |
	1	2	3	4	5	6	7	8	9	10	
1	63	57	92	87	70	61	75	58	63	71	69.7
2	90	77	59	88	48	83	63	94	72	70	74.4
3	67	81	93	55	71	71	86	98	60	90	77.2
4	62	67	78	61	89	93	71	59	93	84	75.7
5	85	88	77	69	58	90	97	72	64	60	76.0
6	60	57	79	83	64	94	86	64	92	74	75.3
7	94	85	56	77	89	72	71	61	92	97	79.4
8	97	86	83	88	65	87	76	84	81	71	81.8
9	94	90	76	88	65	93	86	87	94	63	83.6
10	88	91	71	89	97	79	93	87	69	85	84.9

Day	Aides Absent	Day	Aides Absent
1	4	9	7
2	3	10	2
3	2	11	3
4	4	12	2
5	2	13	1
6	5	14	3
7	3	15	4
8	4		

Because your assessment of absenteeism is likely to come under careful scrutiny, you would like a type I error of only 1 percent. You want to be sure to identify any instances of unusual absences. If some are present, you will have to explore them on behalf of the registered nurses.

a. Design a p-chart.

b. Based on your p-chart and the data from the last 3 weeks, what can you conclude about the absenteeism of nurses' aides?

8. A textile manufacturer wants to set up a control chart for irregularities (e.g., oil stains, shop soil, loose threads, and tears) per 100 square yards of carpet. The following data were collected from a sample of twenty 100-square-yard pieces of carpet:

Sample	1	2	3	4	5	6	7	8	9	10
Irregularities	11	8	9	12	4	16	5	8	17	10
Sample	11	12	13	14	15	16	17	18	19	20
Irregularities	11	5	7	12	13	8	19	11	9	10

a. Using these data, set up a c-chart with $z = 3$.

b. Suppose that the next five samples had 15, 18, 12, 22, and 21 irregularities. What do you conclude?

9. The IRS is concerned with improving the accuracy of tax information given by its representatives over the telephone. Previous studies involved asking a set of 25 questions of a large number of IRS telephone representatives to determine the proportion of correct responses. Historically, the average proportion of correct responses has been 72 percent. Recently, IRS representatives have been receiving more training. On April 26, the set of 25 tax questions were again asked of 20 randomly selected IRS telephone representatives. The numbers of correct answers were 18, 16, 19, 21, 20, 16, 21, 16, 17, 10, 25, 18, 25, 16, 20, 15, 23, 19, 21, and 19.

a. What are the upper and lower control limits for the appropriate p-chart for the IRS? Use $z = 3$.

b. Is the tax information process in statistical control?

10. A travel agency is concerned with the accuracy and appearance of itineraries prepared for its clients. Defects can include errors in times, airlines, flight numbers, prices, car rental information, lodging, charge card numbers, and reservation numbers, as well as typographical errors. As the possible number of errors is nearly infinite, the agency measures the number of errors that do occur. The current process results in an average of three errors per itinerary.

a. What are the two-sigma control limits for these defects?

b. A client scheduled a trip to Dallas. Her itinerary contained six errors. Interpret this information.

11. Jim's Outfitters, Inc., makes custom fancy shirts for cowboys. The shirts could be flawed in various ways, including flaws in the weave or color of the fabric, loose buttons or decorations, wrong dimensions, and uneven stitches. Jim randomly examined 10 shirts, with the following results:

Shirt	Defects
1	8
2	0
3	7
4	12
5	5
6	10
7	2
8	4
9	6
10	6

a. Assuming that 10 observations are adequate for these purposes, determine the three-sigma control limits for defects per shirt.

b. Suppose that the next shirt has 13 flaws. What can you say about the process now?

12. The Big Black Bird Company produces fiberglass camper tops. The process for producing the tops must be controlled so as to keep the number of dimples low. When the process was in control, the following defects were found in 10 randomly selected camper tops over an extended period of time:

Top	Dimples
1	7
2	9
3	14
4	11
5	3
6	12
7	8
8	4
9	7
10	6

a. Assuming 10 observations are adequate for this purpose, determine the three-sigma control limits for dimples per camper top.

b. Suppose that the next camper top has 15 dimples. What can you say about the process now?

13. The production manager at Sunny Soda, Inc., is interested in tracking the quality of the company's 12-ounce bottle filling line. The bottles must be filled within the tolerances set for this product because the dietary information on the label shows 12 ounces as the serving size.

The design standard for the product calls for a fill level of 12.00 ± 0.10 ounces. The manager collected the following sample data (in fluid ounces per bottle) on the production process:

Sample	OBSERVATION 1	2	3	4
1	12.00	11.97	12.10	12.08
2	11.91	11.94	12.10	11.96
3	11.89	12.02	11.97	11.99
4	12.10	12.09	12.05	11.95
5	12.08	11.92	12.12	12.05
6	11.94	11.98	12.06	12.08
7	12.09	12.00	12.00	12.03
8	12.01	12.04	11.99	11.95
9	12.00	11.96	11.97	12.03
10	11.92	11.94	12.09	12.00
11	11.91	11.99	12.05	12.10
12	12.01	12.00	12.06	11.97
13	11.98	11.99	12.06	12.03
14	12.02	12.00	12.05	11.95
15	12.00	12.05	12.01	11.97

a. Are the process average and range in statistical control?

b. Is the process capable of meeting the design standard at four-sigma quality? Explain.

14. The Money Pit Mortgage Company is interested in monitoring the performance of the mortgage process. Fifteen samples of 5 completed mortgage transactions each were taken during a period when the process was believed to be in control. The times to complete the transactions were measured. The means and ranges of the mortgage process transaction times, measured in days, are as follows:

Sample	1	2	3	4	5	6	7	8	9	10	11	12	13	14	15
Mean	17	14	8	17	12	13	15	16	13	14	16	9	11	9	12
Range	6	11	4	8	9	14	12	15	10	10	11	6	9	11	13

Subsequently, samples of size 5 were taken from the process every week for the next 10 weeks. The times were measured and the following results obtained:

Sample	16	17	18	19	20	21	22	23	24	25
Mean	11	14	9	15	17	19	13	22	20	18
Range	7	11	6	4	12	14	11	10	8	6

a. Construct the control charts for the mean and the range, using the original 15 samples.

b. On the control charts developed in part (a), plot the values from samples 16 through 25 and comment on whether the process is in control.

c. In part (b), if you concluded that the process was out of control, would you attribute it to a drift in the mean, or an increase in the variability, or both? Explain your answer.

15. The Money Pit Mortgage Company of Problem 14 made some changes to the process and undertook a process capability study. The following data were obtained for 15 samples of size 5. Based on the individual observations, management estimated the process standard deviation to be 4.21 (days) for use in the process capability analysis. The lower and upper specification limits (in days) for the mortgage process times were 5 and 25.

Sample	1	2	3	4	5	6	7	8	9	10	11	12	13	14	15
Mean	11	12	8	16	13	12	17	16	13	14	17	9	15	14	9
Range	9	13	4	11	10	9	8	15	14	11	6	6	12	10	11

a. Calculate the process capability index and the process capability ratio values.

b. Suppose management would be happy with three-sigma performance. What conclusions is management likely to draw from the capability analysis? Can valid conclusions about the process be drawn from the analysis?

c. What remedial actions, if any, do you suggest that management take?

16. Webster Chemical Company produces mastics and caulking for the construction industry. The product is blended in large mixers and then pumped into tubes and capped. Management is concerned about whether the filling process for tubes of caulking is in statistical control. The process should be centered on 8 ounces per tube. Several samples of eight tubes were taken, each tube was weighed, and the weights in Table 7.3 were obtained.

a. Assume that only six samples are sufficient and develop the control charts for the mean and the range.

b. Plot the observations on the control chart and comment on your findings.

17. Management at Webster, in Problem 16, is now concerned as to whether caulking tubes are being properly capped. If a significant proportion of the tubes are not being sealed, Webster is placing its customers in a messy situation. Tubes are packaged in large boxes of 144. Several boxes are inspected, and the following numbers of leaking tubes are found:

Sample	Tubes	Sample	Tubes	Sample	Tubes
1	3	8	6	15	5
2	5	9	4	16	0
3	3	10	9	17	2
4	4	11	2	18	6
5	2	12	6	19	2
6	4	13	5	20	1
7	2	14	1	Total	72

Calculate p-chart three-sigma control limits to assess whether the capping process is in statistical control.

18. At Webster Chemical Company, lumps in the caulking compound could cause difficulties in dispensing a smooth bead from the tube. Even when the process is in control, an average of four lumps per tube of caulk will remain. Testing for the presence of lumps destroys the product, so an analyst takes random samples. The following results are obtained:

Tube No.	Lumps	Tube No.	Lumps	Tube No.	Lumps
1	6	5	6	9	5
2	5	6	4	10	0
3	0	7	1	11	9
4	4	8	6	12	2

Determine the c-chart two-sigma upper and lower control limits for this process. Is the process in statistical control?

TABLE 7.3 | OUNCES OF CAULKING PER TUBE

Sample	TUBE NUMBER							
	1	2	3	4	5	6	7	8
1	7.98	8.34	8.02	7.94	8.44	7.68	7.81	8.11
2	8.33	8.22	8.08	8.51	8.41	8.28	8.09	8.16
3	7.89	7.77	7.91	8.04	8.00	7.89	7.93	8.09
4	8.24	8.18	7.83	8.05	7.90	8.16	7.97	8.07
5	7.87	8.13	7.92	7.99	8.10	7.81	8.14	7.88
6	8.13	8.14	8.11	8.13	8.14	8.12	8.13	8.14

19. Janice Sanders, CEO of Pine Crest Medical Clinic, is concerned over the number of times patients must wait more than 30 minutes beyond their scheduled appointments. She asked her assistant to take random samples of 64 patients to see how many in each sample had to wait more than 30 minutes. Each instance is considered a defect in the clinic process. The table below contains the data for 15 samples.

Sample	Number of Defects
1	5
2	2
3	1
4	3
5	1
6	5
7	2
8	3
9	6
10	3
11	9
12	9
13	5
14	2
15	3

a. Assuming Janice Sanders is willing to use three-sigma control limits, construct a p-chart.

b. Based on your p-chart and the data in the table, what can you conclude about the waiting time of the patients?

20. Representatives of the Patriot Insurance Company take medical information over the telephone from prospective policy applicants prior to a visit to the applicant's place of residence by a registered nurse who takes vital sign measurements. When the telephone interview has incorrect or incomplete information, the entire process of approving the application is unnecessarily delayed and has the potential of causing loss of business. The following data were collected to see how many applications contain errors. Each sample has 200 randomly selected applications.

Sample	Defects	Sample	Defects
1	20	16	15
2	18	17	40
3	29	18	35
4	12	19	21
5	14	20	24
6	11	21	9
7	30	22	20
8	25	23	17
9	27	24	28
10	16	25	10
11	25	26	17
12	18	27	22
13	25	28	14
14	16	29	19
15	20	30	20

a. What are the upper and lower control limits of a p-chart for the number of defective applications? Use $z = 3$.

b. Is the process in statistical control?

21. The Digital Guardian Company issues policies that protect clients from downtime costs due to computer system failures. It is very important to process the policies quickly because long cycle times not only put the client at risk, they could also lose business for Digital Guardian. Management is concerned that customer service is degrading because of long cycle times, measured in days. The following table contains the data from five samples, each sample consisting of eight random observations.

Sample	OBSERVATION (DAYS)							
	1	2	3	4	5	6	7	8
1	13	9	4	8	8	15	8	6
2	7	15	8	10	10	14	10	15
3	8	11	4	11	8	12	9	15
4	12	7	12	9	11	8	12	8
5	8	12	6	12	11	5	12	8

a. What is your estimate of the process average?

b. What is your estimate of the average range?

c. Construct an R- and an $\bar{x}$-chart for this process. Are assignable causes present?

22. The Farley Manufacturing Company prides itself on the quality of its products. The company is engaged in competition for a very important project. A key element is a part that ultimately goes into precision testing equipment. The specifications are 8.000 $\pm$ 3.000 millimeters.

Management is concerned about the capability of the process to produce that part. The following data (shown below) were randomly collected during test runs of the process:

	OBSERVATION (MILLIMETERS)							
Sample	1	2	3	4	5	6	7	8
1	9.100	8.900	8.800	9.200	8.100	6.900	9.300	9.100
2	7.600	8.000	9.000	10.100	7.900	9.000	8.000	8.800
3	8.200	9.100	8.200	8.700	9.000	7.000	8.800	10.800
4	8.200	8.300	7.900	7.500	8.900	7.800	10.100	7.700
5	10.000	8.100	8.900	9.000	9.300	9.000	8.700	10.000

Assume that the process is in statistical control. Is the process capable of producing the part at the three-sigma level? Explain.

23. A critical dimension of the service quality of a call center is the wait time of a caller to get to a sales representative. Periodically, random samples of three customer calls are measured for time. The results of the last four samples are in the following table:

Sample	Time (Sec)		
1	495	501	498
2	512	508	504
3	505	497	501
4	496	503	492

a. Assuming that management is willing to use three-sigma control limits, and using only the historical information contained in the four samples, show that the call center access time is in statistical control.

b. Suppose that the standard deviation of the process distribution is 5.77. If the specifications for the access time are 500 $\pm$ 18 sec., is the process capable? Why or why not? Assume three-sigma performance is desired.

24. An automatic lathe produces rollers for roller bearings, and the process is monitored by statistical process control charts. The central line of the chart for the sample means is set at 8.50 and for the range at 0.31 mm. The process is in control, as established by samples of size 5. The upper and lower specifications for the diameter of the rollers are (8.50 + 0.25) and (8.50 − 0.25) mm, respectively.

a. Calculate the control limits for the mean and range charts.

b. If the standard deviation of the process distribution is estimated to be 0.13 mm, is the process capable of meeting specifications? Assume four-sigma performance is desired.

c. If the process is not capable, what percent of the output will fall outside the specification limits? (*Hint:* Use the normal distribution.)

Advanced Problems

25. Canine Gourmet Super Breath dog treats are sold in boxes labeled with a net weight of 12 ounces (340 grams) per box. Each box contains 8 individual 1.5-ounce packets. To reduce the chances of shorting the customer, product design specifications call for the packet-filling process average to be set at 43.5 grams so that the average net weight per box of 8 packets will be 348 grams. Tolerances are set for the box to weigh 348 $\pm$ 12 grams. The standard deviation for the *packet-filling* process is 1.01 grams. The target process capability ratio is 1.33. One day, the packet-filling process average weight drifts down to 43.0 grams. Is the packaging process capable? Is an adjustment needed?

26. The Precision Machining Company makes hand-held tools on an assembly line that produces one product every minute. On one of the products, the critical quality dimension is the diameter (measured in thousandths of an inch) of a hole bored in one of the assemblies. Management wants to detect any shift in the process average diameter from 0.015 in. Management considers the variance in the process to be in control. Historically, the average range has been 0.002 in., regardless of the process average. Design an $\bar{x}$-chart to control this process, with a center line at 0.015 in. and the control limits set at three sigmas from the center line.

Management provided the results of 80 minutes of output from the production line, as shown in Table 7.4. During these 80 minutes, the process average changed once. All measurements are in thousandths of an inch.

a. Set up an $\bar{x}$-chart with $n = 4$. The frequency should be sample four and then skip four. Thus, your first sample would be for minutes 1 − 4, the second would be for minutes 9 − 12, and so on. When would you stop the process to check for a change in the process average?

b. Set up an $\bar{x}$-chart with $n = 8$. The frequency should be sample eight and then skip four. When would you stop the process now? What can you say about the desirability of large samples on a frequent sampling interval?

27. Using the data from Problem 26, continue your analysis of sample size and frequency by trying the following plans.

a. Using the $\bar{x}$-chart for $n = 4$, try the frequency sample four, then skip eight. When would you stop the process in this case?

b. Using the $\bar{x}$-chart for $n = 8$, try the frequency sample eight, then skip eight. When would you consider the process to be out of control?

TABLE 7.4 | SAMPLE DATA FOR PRECISION MACHINING COMPANY

Minutes	Diameter (thousandths of an inch)											
1–12	15	16	18	14	16	17	15	14	14	13	16	17
13–24	15	16	17	16	14	14	13	14	15	16	15	17
25–36	14	13	15	17	18	15	16	15	14	15	16	17
37–48	18	16	15	16	16	14	17	18	19	15	16	15
49–60	12	17	16	14	15	17	14	16	15	17	18	14
61–72	15	16	17	18	13	15	14	14	16	15	17	18
73–80	16	16	17	18	16	15	14	17				

TABLE 7.5 | SAMPLE DATA FOR DATA TECH CREDIT CARD SERVICE

Samples	Number of Errors in Sample of 250									
1–10	3	8	5	11	7	1	12	9	0	8
11–20	3	5	7	9	11	3	2	9	13	4
21–30	12	10	6	2	1	7	10	5	8	4

c. Using your results from parts (a) and (b), determine what trade-offs you would consider in choosing between them.

28. The manager of the customer service department of Data Tech Credit Card Service Company is concerned about the number of defects produced by the billing process. Every day a random sample of 250 statements was inspected for errors regarding incorrect entries involving account numbers, transactions on the customer's account, interest charges, and penalty charges. Any statement with one or more of these errors was considered a defect. The study lasted 30 days and yielded the data in Table 7.5.

   a. Construct a p-chart for the billing process.

   b. Is there any nonrandom behavior in the billing process that would require management attention?

29. Red Baron Airlines serves hundreds of cities each day, but competition is increasing from smaller companies affiliated with major carriers. One of the key competitive priorities is on-time arrivals and departures. Red Baron defines *on time* as any arrival or departure that takes place within 15 minutes of the scheduled time. To stay on top of the market, management set the high standard of 98 percent on-time performance. The operations department was put in charge of monitoring the performance of the airline. Each week, a random sample of 300 flight arrivals and departures was checked for schedule performance. Table 7.6 contains the numbers of arrivals and departures over the last 30 weeks that did not meet Red Baron's definition of on-time service. What can you tell management about the quality of service? Can you identify any nonrandom behavior in the process? If so, what might cause the behavior?

30. Beaver Brothers, Inc., is conducting a study to assess the capability of its 150-gram bar soap production line. A critical quality measure is the weight of the soap bars after stamping. The lower and upper specification limits are 162 and 170 grams, respectively. As a part of an initial capability study, 25 samples of size 5 were collected by the quality assurance group and the observations in Table 7.7 were recorded.

After analyzing the data by using statistical control charts, the quality assurance group calculated the process capability ratio, C_p, and the process capability index, C_{pk}. It then decided to improve the stamping process, especially the feeder mechanism. After making all the changes that were deemed necessary, 18 additional samples were collected. The summary data for these samples are

$$\bar{\bar{x}} = 163 \text{ grams}$$

$$\bar{R} = 2.326 \text{ grams}$$

$$\sigma = 1 \text{ gram}$$

All sample observations were within the control chart limits. With the new data, the quality assurance group recalculated the process capability measures. It was pleased with the improved C_p but felt that the process should be centered at 166 grams to ensure that everything was in order. Its decision concluded the study.

   a. Draw the control charts for the data obtained in the initial study and verify that the process was in statistical control.

   b. What were the values obtained by the group for C_p and C_{pk} for the initial capability study? Comment on your findings and explain why further improvements were necessary.

   c. What are the C_p and C_{pk} after the improvements? Comment on your findings, indicating why the group decided to change the centering of the process.

   d. What are the C_p and C_{pk} if the process were centered at 166? Comment on your findings.

TABLE 7.6 | SAMPLE DATA FOR RED BARON AIRLINES

Samples	Number of Late Planes in Sample of 300 Arrivals and Departures									
1–10	3	8	5	11	7	2	12	9	1	8
11–20	3	5	7	9	12	5	4	9	13	4
21–30	12	10	6	2	1	8	4	5	8	2

TABLE 7.7 | SAMPLE DATA FOR BEAVER BROTHERS, INC.

Sample	OBS.1	OBS.2	OBS.3	OBS.4	OBS.5
1	167.0	159.6	161.6	164.0	165.3
2	156.2	159.5	161.7	164.0	165.3
3	167.0	162.9	162.9	164.0	165.4
4	167.0	159.6	163.7	164.1	165.4
5	156.3	160.0	162.9	164.1	165.5
6	164.0	164.2	163.0	164.2	163.9
7	161.3	163.0	164.2	157.0	160.6
8	163.1	164.2	156.9	160.1	163.1
9	164.3	157.0	161.2	163.2	164.4
10	156.9	161.0	163.2	164.3	157.3
11	161.0	163.3	164.4	157.6	160.6
12	163.3	164.5	158.4	160.1	163.3
13	158.2	161.3	163.5	164.6	158.7
14	161.5	163.5	164.7	158.6	162.5
15	163.6	164.8	158.0	162.4	163.6
16	164.5	158.5	160.3	163.4	164.6
17	164.9	157.9	162.3	163.7	165.1
18	155.0	162.2	163.7	164.8	159.6
19	162.1	163.9	165.1	159.3	162.0
20	165.2	159.1	161.6	163.9	165.2
21	164.9	165.1	159.9	162.0	163.7
22	167.6	165.6	165.6	156.7	165.7
23	167.7	165.8	165.9	156.9	165.9
24	166.0	166.0	165.6	165.6	165.5
25	163.7	163.7	165.6	165.6	166.2

Active Model Exercise

This Active Model appears in MyOMLab. It allows you to see the effects of sample size and z-values on control charts.

QUESTIONS

1. Has the booking process been in statistical control?

2. Suppose we use a 95 percent p-chart. How do the upper and lower control limits change? What are your conclusions about the booking process?

3. Suppose that the sample size is reduced to 2,000 instead of 2,500. How does this affect the chart?

4. What happens to the chart as we reduce the z-value?

5. What happens to the chart as we reduce the confidence level?

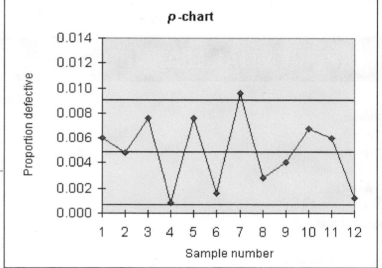

p-Chart

Reset Data	Questions

Number of samples	12
Sample size	2500 ◄ ☐ ►
z value	3.0000 ◄ ☐ ►
Confidence	99.73% ◄ ☐►

Total sample size	30000	Upper Control Limit	0.0091
Total defects	147	Center Line	0.0049
Percentage defects	0.0049	Lower Control Limit	0.0007
Std dev of p-bar	0.0014		

	# Defects	Fraction Defective
Sample 1	15	0.0060
Sample 2	12	0.0048
Sample 3	19	0.0076
Sample 4	2	0.0008
Sample 5	19	0.0076
Sample 6	4	0.0016
Sample 7	24	0.0096
Sample 8	7	0.0028
Sample 9	10	0.0040
Sample 10	17	0.0068
Sample 11	15	0.0060
Sample 12	3	0.0012

p-Chart Using Data from Example 7.3

VIDEO CASE   Process Performance and Quality at Starwood Hotels & Resorts

Starwood Hotels & Resorts is no stranger to quality measurement. In the most recent year, Starwood properties around the globe held 51 of approximately 700 spots on Condé Nast's Gold List of the world's best places to stay. Its spa and golf programs have consistently been ranked among the best in the world.

At Starwood, processes and programs are driven by the work of its team of Six Sigma experts, called Black Belts. Developed by Motorola more than 20 years ago, Six Sigma is a comprehensive and flexible system for achieving, sustaining, and maximizing business success by driving out defects and variability in a process. Starwood uses the five-step DMAIC process: (1) define, (2) measure, (3) analyze, (4) improve, and (5) control.

Clearly, understanding customer needs is paramount. To this end, Starwood collects data from customers on its Guest Satisfaction Index survey, called the "Voice of the Customer." The survey covers every department guests may have encountered during their stay, from the front desk and hotel room, to restaurants and concierge. Past surveys indicated that how well

problems were resolved during the guest stay was a key driver in high guest satisfaction scores. To increase its scores for problem resolution, the Sheraton brand of Starwood launched the Sheraton Service Promise program in the United States and Canada. The program was designed to give guests a single point of contact for reporting any problems. It was intended to focus associate (employee) attention on taking care of service issues during the guest's stay within 15 minutes of first receiving notice.

However, although scores did increase, they did not increase by enough. Consequently, Sheraton brought in its Six Sigma team to see what it could do. The team employed the basic Six Sigma model of define-measure-analyze-improve-control to guide its work. To define the problem, the Six Sigma team worked with data collected and analyzed by an independent survey organization, National Family Opinion. The study indicated that three key factors are needed in problem resolution: (1) speed, (2) empathy, and (3) efficiency. All three must be met in order for the guests to be satisfied and the Sheraton Service Promise fulfilled. Then, the team looked at the specific processes that affected performance: telephone operators' handling of requests, procedures for determining who to call, engineering workloads, and so on. The work identified in each area was measured. For example, call logs were established to track speed, empathy of associate handling the call, and efficiency of the staff charged with fixing the problem. The data collected were analyzed to determine why guests' problems were not resolved within the 15-minute standard. Pareto charts and other techniques were used for the analysis.

The final step involved control and monitoring to be sure that the improved processes developed by the Six Sigma team became part of the property's culture, and that they were not abandoned after the team's work was finished. Tracking continues for 12 to 18 months, with monthly feedback to the manager or department head responsible for the improvement of the Sheraton Service Promise program. The improvement effort also receives visibility through the company's intranet so the rest of the organization sees the benefits—including service levels and financial performance—and can use the experience to improve their own operations.

QUESTIONS

1. Implementing Six Sigma programs takes considerable time and commitment from an organization. In terms of top-down commitment, measurement systems to track progress, tough goal setting, education, communication, and customer priorities, evaluate the degree to which Starwood successfully addressed each with the redesign of the Sheraton Service Promise program.

2. How might the new Sheraton Service Promise process help Starwood avoid the four costs of poor process performance and quality (prevention, appraisal, internal failure, and external failure)?

3. Starwood is the first major hotel brand to commit to a dedicated Six Sigma program for improving quality. Why might an organization be reluctant to follow this type of formalized methodology? What other approaches could Starwood or its competitors use?

EXPERIENTIAL LEARNING   Statistical Process Control with a Coin Catapult

Exercise A: Control Charts for Variables

Materials

1 ruler

1 pen or pencil

1 coin (a quarter will do nicely)

1 yardstick

An exercise worksheet

Access to a calculator

Tasks

Divide into teams of two to four. If four people are on a team,

one person holds the yardstick and observes the action,

one person adjusts the catapult and launches the coin,

one person observes the maximum height for each trial, and

one person records the results.

If teams of fewer than four are formed, provide a support for the yardstick and combine the other tasks as appropriate.

Practice

To catapult the coin, put a pen or pencil under the 6-in. mark of the ruler. Put the coin over the 11-in. mark. Press both ends of the ruler down as far as they will go. Let the end that holds the coin snap up, catapulting the coin into the air. The person holding the yardstick should place the stick so that it is adjacent to, but does not interfere with, the trajectory of the coin. To observe the maximum height reached by the coin, the observer should stand back with his or her eye at about the same level as the top of the coin's trajectory. Practice until each person is comfortable with his or her role. The person operating the catapult should be sure that the pen or pencil fulcrum has not moved between shots and that the launch is done as consistently as possible.

Step 1: *Gather data.* Take four samples of five observations (launches) each. Record the maximum height reached by the coin in the first data table on the worksheet. When you have finished, determine the mean and range for each sample, and compute the mean of the means $\bar{x}$ and the mean of the ranges $\bar{R}$.

Step 2: *Develop an R-chart.* Using the data gathered and the appropriate D_3 and D_4 values, compute the upper and lower three-sigma control limits for the range. Enter these values and plot the range for each of the four samples on the range chart on the worksheet. Be sure to indicate an appropriate scale for range on the y-axis.

Step 3: *Develop an $\bar{x}$-chart.* Now, using the data gathered and the appropriate value for A_2, compute the upper and lower three-sigma control limits for the sample means. Enter these values and plot the mean for each of the four samples on the $\bar{x}$-chart on the worksheet. Again, indicate an appropriate scale for the y-axis.

Step 4: *Observe the process.* Once a control chart has been established for a process, it is used to monitor the process and to identify when it is not running "normally." Collect two more samples of five trials each, as you did to collect the first set of data. Plot the range and the sample mean on the charts you constructed on the worksheet each time you collect a sample. What have you observed that affects the process? Does the chart indicate that the process is operating the way it did when you first collected data?

Step 5: *Observe a changed process.* Now change something (for instance, move the pencil out to the 8-in. mark). Collect data for samples 7 and 8. Plot the range and the sample mean on the charts you constructed on the worksheet as you complete each sample. Can you detect a change in the process from your control chart? If the process has changed, how sure are you that this change is real and not just due to the particular sample you chose?

Exercise B: Control Charts for Attributes

Materials

1 ruler

1 pen or pencil

1 coin (a quarter will do nicely)

1 paper or plastic cup (with a 4-in. mouth)

An exercise worksheet

Access to a calculator

Tasks

Divide into teams of two or three. If three people are on a team,

one person adjusts the catapult and launches the coin,

one person observes the results and fetches the coin, and

one person records the results.

If teams of two are formed, combine the tasks as appropriate.

Practice

The object is to flip a coin into a cup using a ruler. To catapult the coin, put a pen or pencil under the 6-in. mark of the ruler.

Put a coin over the 11-in. mark and let its weight hold that end of the ruler on the tabletop. Strike the raised end of the ruler with your hand to flip the coin into the air. Position a cup at the place where the coin lands so that on the next flip, the coin will land inside. You will have to practice several times until you find out how hard to hit the ruler and the best position for the cup. Be sure that the pen or pencil fulcrum has not moved between shots and that the launch is done as consistently as possible.

Step 1: *Gather data.*   Try to catapult the coin into the cup 10 times for each sample. Record each trial in the data table on the worksheet as a hit (H) when the coin lands inside or a miss (M) when it does not. The proportion of misses will be the number of misses divided by the sample size, *n*, in this case 10. A miss is a "defect," so the proportion of misses is the proportion defective, *p*.

Step 2: *Develop a p-chart.*   Compute the upper and lower three-sigma control limits for the average fraction defective. Plot these values and the mean for each of the four samples on the *p*-chart on the worksheet.

Step 3: *Observe the process.*   Once a chart has been established for a process, it is used to monitor the process and to identify abnormal behavior. Exchange tasks so that someone else is catapulting the coin. After several practice launches, take four more samples of 10. Plot the proportion defective for this person's output. Is the process still in control? If it is not, how sure are you that it is out of control? Can you determine the control limits for a 95 percent confidence level? With these limits, was your revised process still in control?

Source: The basis for Exercise A was written by J. Christopher Sandvig, Western Washington University, as a variation of the "Catapulting Coins" exercise from *Games and Exercises for Operations Management* by Janelle Heinke and Larry Meile (Prentice Hall, 1995). Given these foundations, Larry Meile of Boston College wrote Exercise A. He also wrote Exercise B as a new extension.

Selected References

Babbar, Sunil. "Service Quality and Business Ethics," *International Journal of Service and Operations Management,* vol. 1, no. 3, 2005, pp. 203–219.

Babbar, Sunil. "Teaching Ethics for Quality as an Innovation in a Core Operations Management Course," *Decision Sciences Journal of Innovative Education,* vol. 8, no. 2, 2010, pp. 361–366.

Besterfield, Dale. *Quality Control,* 8th ed. Upper Saddle River, NJ: Prentice Hall, 2009.

Collier, David A. *The Service Quality Solution.* New York: Irwin Professional Publishing; Milwaukee: ASQC Quality Press, 1994.

Crosby, Philip B. *Quality Is Free: The Art of Making Quality Certain.* New York: McGraw-Hill, 1979.

Deming, W. Edwards. *Out of the Crisis.* Cambridge, MA: Massachusetts Institute of Technology Center for Advanced Engineering Study, 1986.

Duncan, Acheson J. *Quality Control and Industrial Statistics,* 5th ed. Homewood, IL: Irwin, 1986.

Feigenbaum, A.V. *Total Quality Control: Engineering and Management,* 3rd ed. New York: McGraw-Hill, 1983.

Hartvigsen, David. *SimQuick: Process Simulation with Excel,* 2nd ed. Upper Saddle River, NJ: Prentice Hall, 2004.

Hoyle, David. *ISO 9000,* 6th ed. Oxford: Butler-Heinemann, 2009.

Juran, J.M., and Frank Gryna, Jr. *Quality Planning and Analysis,* 2nd ed. New York: McGraw-Hill, 1980.

Kerwin, Kathleen. "When Flawless Isn't Enough." *Business Week* (December 8, 2003), pp. 80–82.

Lucier, Gregory T., and Sridhar Seshadri. "GE Takes Six Sigma Beyond the Bottom Line." *Strategic Finance* (May 2001), pp. 41–46.

Mitra, Amitava. *Fundamentals of Quality Control and Improvement,* 3rd ed. Hoboken, NJ: Wiley & Sons, 2008.

Pande, Peter S., Robert P. Neuman, and Roland R. Cavanagh. *The Six Sigma Way.* New York: McGraw-Hill, 2000.

Russell, J. P., and Dennis Arter. *ISO Lesson Guide to ISO 9001,* 3rd ed. Milwaukee: ASQC Quality Press, 2008.

Schwarz, Anne. "Listening to the Voice of the Customer Is the Key to QVC's Success." *Journal of Organizational Excellence* (Winter 2004), pp. 3–11.

Sester, Dennis. "Motorola: A Tradition of Quality." *Quality* (October 2001), pp. 30–34.

Yannick, Julliard. "Ethics Quality Management," *Techne' Journal,* vol. 8, no. 1 (Fall 2004), pp. 117–135.

PROCESS ANALYSIS

8

McDonald's continually seeks ways to improve its processes so as to provide better quality at a lower cost, with more sustainable resources. This effort combined with innovative menu options pays off. In September, 2011 it delivered its 100th consecutive month of positive global comparable sales. Sales were up by 3.9% in the US and 2.7% in Europe.

McDonald's Corporation

System revenues (company-operated and franchised restaurants) at McDonald's reached a record-high $24 billion in 2010. It has more than 32,000 restaurants around the world and 62 million customers visit them each day. It employs 1.7 million people across the globe. Its stock price in October 2011 was $89.94. Things were not so good in 2002, when customer complaints were growing more frequent and bitter. Its stock price was only $16.08 at the end of 2002. McDonald's is now listening to the customers again, and changing its processes to reflect it. The board brought on a new CEO who had spent 20 years on the operational side of the business. With a zeal for measuring customer satisfaction and sharing the data freely with operators, he pulled off a turnaround that stunned everyone in the business with its speed and scope.

Initiatives were launched to collect performance measures and revamp McDonald's processes to meet customer expectations. McDonald's sends mystery shoppers to restaurants to conduct anonymous reviews using a hard-number scoring system. Mystery diners from outside survey firms jot down on a paper checklist their grades for speed of service; food temperature; presentation and taste; cleanliness of the counter, tables and condiment islands; even whether the counter crewperson smiles at diners. Trailing six-month and year-to-date results are posted on an internal McDonald's Web site so owners can compare their scores with regional averages. Operators could now pinpoint lingering problems, and performance measures focus operators' attention on needed process changes. Customers now are encouraged to report their experience at a particular U.S. restaurant by e-mail, regular mail, or toll-free telephone call.

Another initiative was to send 900 operations missionaries into the field, each visiting stores multiple times to fine-tune processes while also conducting day-long seminars where store managers could share tips from corporate kitchen gurus—such as where to place staff—that would shave previous seconds off average service times. The process was changed back to toasting buns rather than microwaving them, giving them an even sweeter caramelized flavor. Other initiatives were taken on McDonald's fast lane. Every six seconds shaved off the wait time adds a percentage point to sales growth. Outdoor menu boards now have more pictures and fewer words. An LED display confirms what customers say, reducing confusion later on. Premium sandwiches are put in boxes rather than paper wrappers, saving a few seconds, and boxes are color coded by sandwich to improve speed and accuracy.

Processes are also being changed to be environment friendly, reaching back from the counters of its restaurants into its supply chain. The U.S. menu involves 330 unique consumer package designs, with 83 percent now made from paper or some other wood-fiber material. Its bulk cooking oil delivery system uses reusable containers, eliminating more than 1,500 pounds of packaging waste per restaurant per year. Its commitment to using sustainable resources has it working with its suppliers to improve coatings on its food packaging. It has shifted more than 18,000 metric tons of fish away from unsustainable sources over the past 5 years. It emphasizes reuse and recycling, managing electrical energy, and effective water management. It also seeks certified sustainable sources for its food. For example, it is piloting a three-year beef farm study to investigate the carbon emissions on 350 beef farms.

All in all, performance measurement and process analysis are increasing customer value and paying off on the bottom line.

Source: Daniel Kruger, "You Want Data with That?" *Forbes*, vol. 173, no. 6 (March 2004), pp. 58–60; **http://www.mcdonalds.com**, April 5, 2011.

LEARNING GOALS *After reading this chapter, you should be able to:*

1. Explain a systematic way to analyze processes.
2. Define flowcharts, swim lane flowcharts, service blueprints, and process charts.
3. Describe the various work measurement techniques.
4. Identify metrics for process evaluation.
5. Describe Pareto charts, cause-and-effect diagrams, and process simulation.
6. Create better processes using benchmarking.
7. Identify keys for effective process management.

Processes are perhaps the least understood and managed aspect of a business. No matter how talented and motivated people are, a firm cannot gain competitive advantage with faulty processes. Just as Mark Twain said of the Mississippi River, a process just keeps rolling on—with one big difference. Most processes can be improved if someone thinks of a way and implements it effectively. Indeed, companies will either adapt processes to the changing needs of customers or cease to exist. Long-term success comes from managers and employees who really understand their businesses. But all too often, highly publicized efforts that seem to offer quick-fix solutions fail to live up to expectations over the long haul, be they programs for conceptualizing a business vision, conducting culture transformation campaigns, or providing leadership training.

Within the field of operations management, many important innovations over the past several decades include work-simplification or better-methods programs, statistical process control, optimization techniques, statistical forecasting techniques, material requirements planning, flexible automation, lean manufacturing, total quality management, reengineering, Six Sigma programs, enterprise resource planning, and e-commerce. We cover these important approaches in the following chapters because they can add significant customer value to a process. However, they are best viewed as just part of a total system for the effective management of work processes, rather than cure-alls.

Of course, process analysis is needed for both reengineering and process improvement, but it is also part of monitoring performance over time. In this chapter, we begin with a systematic approach for analyzing a process that identifies opportunities for improvement, documents the current process, evaluates the process to spot performance gaps, redesigns the process to eliminate the gaps, and implements the desired changes. The goal is continual improvement.

Four supporting techniques—(1) flowcharts, (2) service blueprints, (3) work measurement techniques, and (4) process charts—can give good insights into the current process and the proposed changes. Data analysis tools, such as checklists, bar charts, Pareto charts, and cause-and-effect diagrams, allow the analyst to go from problem symptoms to root causes. Simulation is a more advanced technique to evaluate process performance. We conclude with some of the keys to managing processes effectively, to ensuring that changes are implemented and an infrastructure is set up for making continuous improvements. Process analysis, however, extends beyond the analysis of individual processes. It is also a tool for improving the operation of supply chains.

Creating Value through Operations Management

Using Operations to Compete
Project Management

Managing Processes

Process Strategy
Process Analysis
Quality and Performance
Capacity Planning
Constraint Management
Lean Systems

Managing Supply Chains

Supply Chain Inventory Management
Supply Chain Design
Supply Chain Location Decisions
Supply Chain Integration
Supply Chain Sustainability and Humanitarian Logistics
Forecasting
Operations Planning and Scheduling
Resource Planning

Process Analysis across the Organization

All parts of an organization need to be concerned about process analysis simply because they are doing work, and process analysis focuses on how work is actually done. Are they providing the most value to their customers (internal or external), or can they be improved? Operations and sales departments are often the first areas that come to mind because they are so closely connected with the core processes. However, support processes in accounting, finance, and human resources are crucial to an organization's success as well. Top management also gets involved, as do other departments. During these handoffs of the "baton," disconnects are often the worst and opportunities for improvement the greatest.

A Systematic Approach

Figure 8.1 shows a six-step blueprint for process analysis. **Process analysis** is the documentation and detailed understanding of how work is performed and how it can be redesigned. Process analysis begins with identifying a new opportunity for improvement and ends with implementing a revised process. The last step goes back to the first step, thus creating a cycle of continual improvement. We introduced a closely related model in Chapter 7, "Quality and Performance" as part of the Six Sigma Improvement (DMAIC) Model. Another approach to process improvement is reengineering in Chapter 2, "Process Strategy." We avoid overlap by covering each technique just once, while bringing out the essence of the approach covered in each chapter. The chapters do have a shared goal: better processes.

process analysis
The documentation and detailed understanding of how work is performed and how it can be redesigned.

▼ **FIGURE 8.1**
Blueprint for Process Analysis

Step 1: Identify Opportunities

In order to identify opportunities, managers must pay particular attention to the four core processes: (1) supplier relationship, (2) new service/product development, (3) order fulfillment, and (4) the customer relationship. Each of these processes, and the subprocesses nested within them, are involved in delivering value to external customers. Are customers currently satisfied with the services or products they receive, or is there room for improvement? How about internal customers? Customer satisfaction

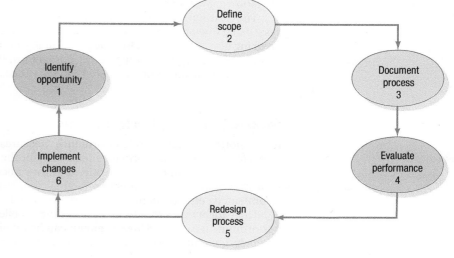

must be monitored periodically, either with a formal measurement system or with informal checks or studies. Managers sometimes develop an inventory of their core and support processes that provide a guide for what processes need scrutiny.

Another way to identify opportunities is by looking at the strategic issues. Do gaps exist between a process's competitive priorities and its current competitive capabilities, as was found for the assessment of operations strategy at a credit card division in Chapter 1, "Using Operations to Compete"? Do multiple measures of cost, top quality, quality consistency, delivery speed, and on-time delivery meet or exceed expectations? Is there a good *strategic fit* in the process? If the process provides a service, does its position on the customer-contact matrix (see Figure 2.2) seem appropriate? How does the degree of customer contact match up with process structure, customer involvement, resource flexibility, and capital intensity (see Figure 2.8)? Similar questions should be asked about manufacturing processes regarding the strategic fit between process choice, volume, and product customization (see Figure 2.10).

Employees who actually perform the process or internal suppliers or customers should be encouraged to bring their ideas to managers and staff specialists (such as industrial engineers), or perhaps pass on their ideas through a formal suggestion system. A **suggestion system** is a voluntary system by which employees submit their ideas on process improvements. Usually, a specialist evaluates the proposals, makes sure worthy suggestions are implemented, and provides feedback to those who make the suggestions. Sometimes, the person or team making a good suggestion is rewarded with money or special recognition.

suggestion system

A voluntary system by which employees submit their ideas on process improvements.

Step 2: Define the Scope

Step 2 establishes the boundaries of the process to be analyzed. Is it a broad process that stretches across the whole organization, involving many steps and many employees, or a more narrowly bracketed nested subprocess that is just part of one person's job? A process's scope can be too narrow or too broad. For example, a broadly defined process that outstrips the resources available, sometimes called "trying to boil the ocean," is doomed because it will increase employee frustration without producing any results.

The resources that management assigns to improving or reengineering a process should match the scope of the process. For a small nested process involving only one employee, perhaps he or she is asked to redesign the process. For a project that deals with a major core process, managers typically establish one or more teams. A **design team** consists of knowledgeable, team-oriented individuals who work at one or more steps in the process, conduct the process analysis, and make the necessary changes. Other resources may be full-time specialists called internal or external *facilitators*. Facilitators know process analysis methodology, and they can guide and train the design team. If the process cuts across several departmental lines, it may benefit from a *steering team* of several managers from various departments, headed by a project manager who oversees the process analysis.

design team

A group of knowledgeable, team-oriented individuals who work at one or more steps in the process, conduct the process analysis, and make the necessary changes.

Step 3: Document the Process

Once scope is established, the analyst should document the process. Documentation includes making a list of the process's inputs, suppliers (internal or external), outputs, and customers (internal or external). This information then can be shown as a diagram, with a more detailed breakdown given in a table.

The next part of documentation is understanding the different steps performed in the process, using one or more of the diagrams, tables, and charts described later in this chapter. When breaking down the process into steps, the analyst notes the degrees and types of customer contact and process divergence along the various steps in the process. The analyst also notes what steps are visible to the customer and where in the process work is handed off from one department to the next.

Step 4: Evaluate Performance

It is important to have good performance measures to evaluate a process for clues on how to improve it. **Metrics** are performance measures for the process and the steps within it. A good place to start is with competitive priorities, but they need to be specific. The analyst creates multiple measures of quality, customer satisfaction, time to perform each step or the whole process, cost, errors, safety, environmental measures, on-time delivery, flexibility, and the like.

Once the metrics are identified, it is time to collect information on how the process is currently performing on each one. Measurement can be rough-cut estimates or quite extensive. Techniques for analyzing wait times and delays can provide important information (see Supplement B, "Waiting

metrics

Performance measures that are established for a process and the steps within it.

Lines" and MyOMLab Supplement E, "Simulation"). Work measurement techniques are also more extensive and are previewed in a later section of this chapter.

Step 5: Redesign the Process

A careful analysis of the process and its performance on the selected metrics should uncover *disconnects*, or gaps, between actual and desired performance. Performance gaps can be caused by illogical, missing, or extraneous steps. They can be caused by metrics that reinforce the silo mentality of individual departments when the process spans across several departments. The analyst or design team should dig deep to find the root causes of performance gaps.

Using analytical and creative thinking, the design team generates a long list of ideas for improvements. These ideas are then sifted and analyzed. Ideas that are justifiable, where benefits outweigh costs, are reflected in a new process design. The new design should be documented "as proposed." Combining the new process design with the documentation of the current process gives the analysts clear before and after pictures. The new documentation should make clear how the revised process will work and the performance expected for the various metrics used.

McDonald's uses mystery shoppers to evaluate its stores. It also sends operations "emissaries" to its stores to help managers fine-tune their processes, while revising processes and its supply chain to be more environmentally friendly.

Step 6: Implement Changes

Implementation is more than developing a plan and carrying it out. Many processes have been redesigned effectively, but never get implemented. People resist change: "We have always done it that way" or "we tried that before." Widespread participation in process analysis is essential, not only because of the work involved but also because it builds commitment. It is much easier to implement something that is partly your own idea. In addition, special expertise may be needed, such as for developing software. New jobs and skills may be needed, involving training and investments in new technology. Implementation brings to life the steps needed to bring the redesigned process online. Management or the steering committee must make sure that the implementation project goes according to schedule.

In the remainder of this chapter, we examine steps in process analysis in detail.

Documenting the Process

Five techniques are effective for documenting and evaluating processes: (1) flowcharts, (2) swim lane flowcharts, (3) service blueprints, (4) work measurement techniques, and (5) process charts. They allow you to "lift the lid and peer inside" to see how an organization does its work. You can see how a process operates, at any level of detail, and how well it is performing. Trying to create one of these charts might even reveal a lack of any established process. It may not be a pretty picture, but it is how work actually gets done. Techniques for documenting the process lend themselves to finding performance gaps, generating ideas for process improvements, and documenting the look of a redesigned process.

flowchart

A diagram that traces the flow of information, customers, equipment, or materials through the various steps of a process.

Flowcharts

A **flowchart** traces the flow of information, customers, equipment, or materials through the various steps of a process. Flowcharts are also known as flow diagrams, process maps, relationship maps, or blueprints. Flowcharts have no precise format and typically are drawn with boxes (with a brief description of the step inside), and with lines and arrows to show sequencing. The rectangle (□) shape is the usual choice for a box, although other shapes (○, ⬭, ⬦, ▽, or ▱) can differentiate between different types of steps (e.g., operation, delay, storage, inspection, and so on). Colors and shading can also call attention to different types of steps, such as those particularly high on process divergence. Divergence is also communicated when an outgoing arrow from a step splits into two or more arrows that lead to different boxes. Although many representations are

A consultant discusses the proposal for a new organizational development program with clients during a follow-up meeting. The use of flowcharts can help in understanding this step as just one part of the overall sales process for a consulting company.

acceptable, there must be agreement on the conventions used. They can be given as a key somewhere in the flowchart, and/or described in accompanying text. It is also important to communicate *what* (e.g., information, customer order, customer, materials, and so on) is being tracked.

You can create flowcharts with several programs. Microsoft PowerPoint offers many different formatting choices for flowcharts (see the Flowchart submenu under AutoShapes). The tutorials "Flowcharting in Excel" and "Flowcharting in PowerPoint" in MyOMLab offer other options, and its live demonstrations of flowcharting in Figures 8.2 and 8.3 are instructive. Other powerful software packages for flowcharting and drawing diagrams (such as organization charts and decision trees) are SmartDraw (**www.smartdraw.com**), Microsoft Visio (**www.microsoft.com/office/visio**), and Micrografx (**www.micrografx.com**). Often, free downloads are available at such sites on a trial basis.

Flowcharts can be created for several levels in the organization. For example, at the strategic level, they could show the core processes and their linkages, as in Figure 1.4. At this level, the flowcharts would not have much detail; however, they would give a bird's eye view of the overall business. Just identifying a core process is often helpful. Let us now turn to the process level, where we get into the details of the process being analyzed. Figure 8.2 shows such a process, which consists of many steps that have subprocesses nested within them. Rather than representing everything in

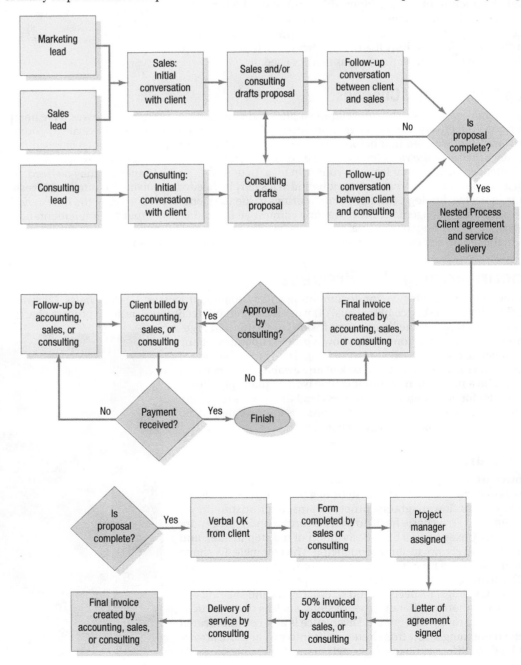

FIGURE 8.2 ▶
Flowchart of the Sales Process for a Consulting Company

FIGURE 8.3 ▶
Flowchart of the Nested Subprocess of Client Agreement and Service Delivery

MyOMLab

one flowchart, Figure 8.2 presents an overview of the whole process. It describes the sales process for a consulting firm that specializes in organizational development and corporate education programs. Four different departments (accounting, consulting, marketing, and sales) interact with the external customer (client). The process goes through three main phases: (1) generating business leads, (2) client agreement and service delivery, and (3) billing and collection.

Figure 8.2 illustrates one other feature. The diamond shape (◇) represents a yes/no decision or outcome, such as the results of an inspection or a recognition of different kinds of customer requirements. In Figure 8.2, the diamond represents three yes/no decision points: (1) whether the proposal is complete, (2) whether consulting approves the invoice, and (3) whether payment is received. These yes/no decision points are more likely to appear when a process is high in divergence.

Sometimes, it is impossible to get the whole flowchart on one page. Figures 8.2 and 8.3 show how to create nested processes for steps that can be more aggregated. For example, Figure 8.3 flowcharts a nested process within the client agreement and service delivery step in Figure 8.2. Figure 8.3 brings out more details, such as invoicing the customer for 50 percent of the total estimated cost of the service before the service is delivered, and then putting together a final invoice after the service is finished. This nesting approach often becomes a practical necessity because only so much detail can be shown in any single flowchart.

Swim Lane Flowcharts

The **swim lane flowchart** is a visual representation that groups functional areas responsible for different sub-processes into lanes. It is most appropriate when the business process spans several department boundaries, and where each department or a functional area is separated by parallel lines similar to lanes in a swimming pool. Swim lanes are labeled according to the functional groups they represent, and can be arranged either horizontally or vertically.

The swim lane flowchart in Figure 8.4 illustrates the order placement and acceptance process at a manufacturing company. The process starts when an order is generated by a customer and

swim lane flowchart

A visual representation that groups functional areas responsible for different sub-processes into lanes. It is most appropriate when the business process spans several department boundaries.

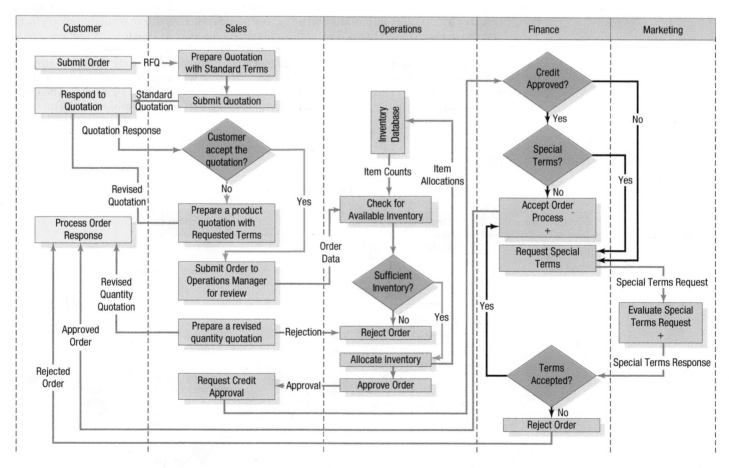

▲ **FIGURE 8.4**
Swim Lane Flowchart of the Order-Filling Process Showing Handoffs Between Departments
Source: D. Kroenke, *Using MIS*, 4th ed., 2012, p. 336. Reprinted by permission of Pearson, Upper Saddle River, NJ.

ends when the order is actually rejected, modified, or approved by the company in consultation with the customer. All functions contributing to this process are included in the flowchart. The columns represent different departments or functional areas, and the steps appear in the department column where they are performed. The customer is also shown as one of the column headings. This approach shows the *handoffs* from one department to another when the outgoing arrow from a step goes to another column. Special dotted-line arrows are one way to show handoffs. Handoffs are points where cross-functional coordination is at particular risk due to the silo mentality. Misunderstandings, backlogs, and errors are more likely at these points.

Flowcharts allow the process analyst and managers to look at the horizontal organization, rather than the vertical organization and departmental boundaries implied by a typical organizational chart. Flowcharts show how organizations produce their outputs through cross-functional work processes, and allow the design team to see all the critical interfaces between functions and departments.

Service Blueprints

service blueprint

A special flowchart of a service process that shows which steps have high customer contact.

A good design for service processes depends first and foremost on the type and amount of customer contact. A **service blueprint** is a special flowchart of a service process that shows which steps have high customer contact. It uses a line of visibility to identify which steps are visible to the customer (and thus. more of a front-office process) and those that are not (back office process).

Another approach to creating a service blueprint is to create three levels. The levels clarify how much control the customer has over each step. For example, consider a customer driving into a Fast Lube shop to have their car serviced. Level 1 would be when the customer is in control, such as driving in for service or paying the bill at the end. Level 2 could be when the customer interacts with the service provider, such as making the initial service request, or being notified on what needs to be done. Level 3 could be when the service is removed from the customer's control, such as when the work is performed and the invoice is prepared.

Figure 8.5 illustrates a fairly complex service blueprint. It not only shows steps with its customers, but also with its consumer's customers. It shows the steps taken by a consulting company that specializes in inventory appraisals and inventory liquidations. Its external customers are large banks that make asset-based loans. The bank's customers, in turn, are customers seeking a loan based on the value of their assets (including inventories). Figure 8.5 describes the consulting company's current evaluation and appraisal process. This service blueprint not only shows the steps in its current inventory evaluation and appraisal process, but also which steps are visible to its external customers (the banks) and its customers' customers (the company seeking a loan). The steps visible to the banks (salmon boxes) are partitioned with the vertical lines of visibility. The steps

▼ **FIGURE 8.5**
Service Blueprint of Consulting Company's Inventory Appraisal Process

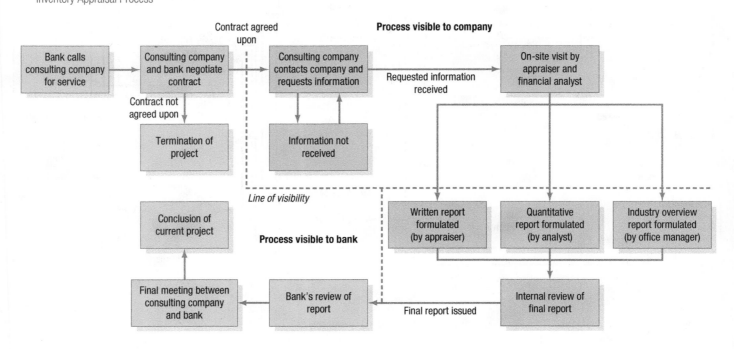

visible to the company seeking a loan (green boxes) are partitioned off by the top left vertical line of visibility and the horizontal line of visibility. The steps in purple are performed by the consulting company and not visible to external customers.

The process begins with a call from a bank seeking the service by the consulting company. There are three main steps in the overall process.

1. The bank contacts the consulting company and they agree on the contract.

2. The consulting company performs the inventory evaluation on the site of the company seeking a loan from the bank.

3. The consulting company prepares the final report and presents it to the bank.

Of course, visibility is just one aspect of customer contact, and it may not adequately capture how actively the customer is involved or how much personal attention is required. A service blueprint can use colors, shading, or box shapes, instead of the lines of visibility, to show the extent and type of customer contact. Another approach to service blueprinting is to tag each step with a number, and then have an accompanying table that describes in detail the customer contact for each numbered step. There is no one "right way" to create a flow chart or service blueprint.

Work Measurement Techniques

Process documentation would not be complete without estimates of the average time each step in the process would take. Time estimates are needed not just for process improvement efforts, but for capacity planning, constraint management, performance appraisal, and scheduling. Estimating task times can be as simple as making a reasoned guess, asking a knowledgeable person, or taking notes while observing the process. More extensive studies involve collecting data for several weeks, consulting cost accounting data, or checking data recorded in information systems.

Formal techniques are also available that rely on the judgment of skilled observers: (1) the time study method, (2) the elemental standard data approach, (3) the predetermined data approach, and (4) work sampling. A fifth method, (5) learning curve analysis, is particularly appropriate when a new product or process is introduced and the time per unit produced has not yet stabilized. The method chosen depends on the purpose of the data, process type (job or line), and degree of product customization. A more comprehensive treatment of these techniques is provided in MyOMLab Supplement H, "Measuring Output Rates" and MyOMLab Supplement I, "Learning Curve Analysis."

MyOMLab

time study

A work measurement method using a trained analyst to perform four basic steps in setting a time standard for a job or process: selecting the work elements (or nested processes) within the process to be studied, timing the elements, determining the sample size, and setting the final standard.

Time Study Method   **Time study** uses a trained analyst to perform four basic steps in setting a time standard for a job or process: (1) selecting the work elements (steps in a flowchart or process chart) within the process to be studied, (2) timing the elements, (3) determining the sample size, and (4) setting the final standard. It is essentially the average time observed, adjusted for normal effort and making an allowance for breaks, unavoidable delays, and the like. The analyst records time spent on each element of the process being studied using a stopwatch, and records the time spent on each element for several repetitions. The analyst assigns a performance rating for each element to adjust for normal effort. Some elements may be performed faster or slower than normal, in the analyst's judgment. The allowance is expressed as a proportion or percent of the total *normal* time.

Elemental Standard Data Approach   Another approach is needed when products or services are highly customized, job processes prevail, and process divergence is great. **Elemental standard data** is a database of standards compiled by a firm's analysts for basic elements that they can draw on later to estimate the time required for a particular job. This approach works well when work elements within certain jobs are similar to those in other jobs. Sometimes, the time required for a work element depends on variable characteristics of the jobs, such as the amount of metal to be deposited for a welding process. In such cases, an equation that relates these characteristics to the time required is also stored in the database. Another method, such as time study or past records, still must be used to compile the normal times (before the allowance is added) stored in the database.

elemental standard data

A database of standards compiled by a firm's analysts for basic elements that they can draw on later to estimate the time required for a particular job, which is most appropriate when products or services are highly customized, job processes prevail, and process divergence is great.

EXAMPLE 8.1	**Time Study of Watch Assembly Process**

A process at a watch assembly plant has been changed. The process is divided into three work elements. A time study has been performed with the following results. The time standard for the process previously was 14.5 minutes. Based on the new time study, should the time standard be revised?

SOLUTION

The new time study had an initial sample of four observations, with the results shown in the following table. The performance rating factor (RF) is shown for each element (to adjust for normal effort), and the allowance for the whole process is 18 percent of the total *normal* time.

	Obs 1	Obs 2	Obs 3	Obs 4	Average (min)	RF	Normal Time
Element 1	2.60	2.34	3.12	2.86	2.730	1.0	2.730
Element 2	4.94	4.78	5.10	4.68	4.875	1.1	5.363
Element 3	2.18	1.98	2.13	2.25	2.135	0.9	1.922
						Total Normal Time =	**10.015 minutes**

The normal time for an element in the table is its average time, multiplied by the RF. The total normal time for the whole process is the sum of the normal times for the three elements, or 10.015 minutes. To get the standard time (ST) for the process, just add in the allowance, or

$$ST = 10.015(1 + 0.18) = \mathbf{11.82} \text{ minutes/watch}$$

DECISION POINT

The time to assemble a watch appears to have decreased considerably. However, based on the precision that management wants, the analyst decided to increase the sample size before setting a new standard. MyOMLab Supplement H, "Measuring Output Rates," gives more information on determining the number of additional observations needed.

MyOMLab

---

predetermined data approach

A database approach that divides each work element into a series of micromotions that make up the element. The analyst then consults a published database that contains the normal times for the full array of possible micromotions.

work sampling

A process that estimates the proportion of time spent by people or machines on different activities, based on observations randomized over time.

FIGURE 8.6 ▼
Work Sampling Study of Admission Clerk at Health Clinic Using OM Explorer's *Time Study* Solver.

Predetermined Data Approach   The **predetermined data approach** divides each work element even more, into a series of micromotions that make up the element. The analyst then consults a published database that contains the normal times for the full array of possible micromotions. A process's normal time can then be calculated as the sum of the times given in the database for the elements performed in the process. This approach makes most sense for highly repetitive processes with little process divergence and line flows. The micromotions (such as reach, move, or apply pressure) are very detailed.

Work Sampling Method   **Work sampling** estimates the proportion of time spent by people or machines on different activities, based on observations randomized over time. Examples of these activities include working on a service or product, doing paperwork, waiting for instructions, waiting for maintenance, or being idle. Such data can then be used to assess a process's productivity, estimate the allowances needed to set standards for other work measurement methods, and spot areas for process improvement. It is best used when the processes are highly divergent with flexible flows. Figure 8.6 shows the input data and numerical results for one week of observations. Figure 8.6 shows an idle time of 23.81 percent for the week. It also reports that 237 more observations are needed to achieve the confidence and precision levels required with the input data. How these conclusions are reached is explained in MyOMLab Supplement H, "Measuring Output Rates".

(a) Input Data and Numerical Results

| Increase Observations | | Remove An Observation | |

Confidence *z*	1.96	Precision *p*	0.05

Observation Period	Times Busy	Times Idle	Observations
Monday	6	1	7
Tuesday	5	2	7
Wednesday	7	0	7
Thursday	9	2	11
Friday	5	5	10
Total	32	10	42

(b) Idle Time and Observations Required

Portion of idle times	0.2381
Total observations required	279
Additional observations required	237

Learning Curve Analysis   The time estimation techniques just covered assume that the process is stable. If the process is revised, then just repeat the method for the revised process after it stabilizes. Learning curve analysis, on the other hand, takes into account that learning takes place on an ongoing basis, such as when new products or services are introduced frequently. With instruction and repetition, workers learn to perform jobs more efficiently, process improvements are identified, and better administration methods are created. These learning effects can be anticipated with a **learning curve**, a line that displays the relationship between processing time and the cumulative quantity of a product or service produced. The time required to produce a unit or create a service decreases as more units or customers are processed. The learning curve for a process depends on the rate of learning and the actual or estimated time for the first unit processed. Figure 8.7 demonstrates the learning curve assuming an 80 percent learning rate, with the first unit taking 120,000 hours and the cumulative average time for the first 10 units produced. The learning rate deals with each *doubling* of the output total. The time for the second unit is 80 percent of the first (or $120,000 \times .80 = 96,000$ hours), the time for the fourth unit is 80 percent of the second unit (or $96,000 \times .80 = 76,800$ hours), and so on. Finding the time estimate for a unit that is not an exact doubling (such as the fifth unit), and also the cumulative average time for the first 10 units, is explained in MyOMLab Supplement I, "Learning Curve Analysis".

learning curve

A line that displays the relationship between processing time and the cumulative quantity of a product or service produced.

MyOMLab

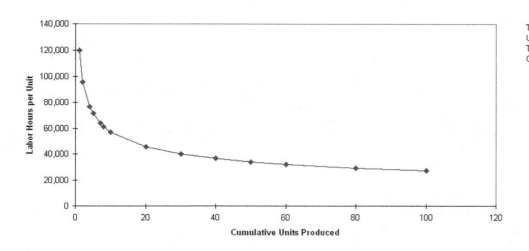

Time for first unit	120,000
Unit number	10
Time for unit 10	57,172
Cumulative average time per unit	75,784

◀ **FIGURE 8.7**
Learning Curve with 80% Learning Rate Using OM Explorer's *Learning Curves* Solver.

Process Charts

A **process chart** is an organized way of documenting all the activities performed by a person or group of people at a workstation, with a customer, or working with certain materials. It analyzes a process using a table, and provides information about each step in the process. In contrast to flowcharts, swim lane flowcharts, and service blueprints, it requires the time estimates (see work measurement techniques covered in the last section). Often it is used to drill down to the job level for an individual person, a team, or a focused nested process. It can have many formats. Here, we group the type of activities for a typical process into five categories:

process chart

An organized way of documenting all the activities performed by a person or group of people, at a workstation, with a customer, or on materials.

- *Operation.* Changes, creates, or adds something. Drilling a hole or serving a customer are examples of operations.

- *Transportation.* Moves the study's subject from one place to another (sometimes called *materials handling*). The subject can be a person, a material, a tool, or a piece of equipment. A customer walking from one end of a counter to the other, a crane hoisting a steel beam to a location, and a conveyor carrying a partially completed product from one workstation to the next are examples of transportation. It could also be the shipment of a finished product to the customer or a warehouse.

- *Inspection.* Checks or verifies something but does not change it. Getting customer feedback, checking for blemishes on a surface, weighing a product, and taking a temperature reading are examples of inspections.

- *Delay.* Occurs when the subject is held up awaiting further action. Time spent waiting for a server; time spent waiting for materials or equipment; cleanup time; and time that workers, machines, or workstations are idle because they have no work to complete are examples of delays.

■ *Storage.* Occurs when something is put away until a later time. Supplies unloaded and placed in a storeroom as inventory, equipment put away after use, and papers put in a file cabinet are examples of storage.

Depending on the situation, other categories can be used. For example, subcontracting for outside services might be a category, temporary storage and permanent storage, or environmental waste might be three separate categories. Choosing the right category for each activity requires taking the perspective of the subject charted. A delay for the equipment could be inspection or transportation for the operator.

To complete a chart for a new process, the analyst must identify each step performed. If the process is an existing one, the analyst can actually observe the steps and categorize each step according to the subject being studied. The analyst then records the distance traveled and the time taken to perform each step. After recording all the activities and steps, the analyst summarizes the steps, times, and distances data. Figure 8.8 shows a process chart prepared using OM Explorer's *Process Chart* Solver. It is for a patient with a twisted ankle being treated at a hospital. The process begins at the entrance and ends with the patient exiting after picking up the prescription.

After a process is charted, the analyst sometimes estimates the annual cost of the entire process. It becomes a benchmark against which other methods for performing the process can be evaluated. Annual labor cost can be estimated by finding the product of (1) time in hours to perform the process each time, (2) variable costs per hour, and (3) number of times the process is performed each year, or

$$\frac{\text{Annual}}{\text{labor cost}} = \left(\begin{array}{c}\text{Time to perfrom}\\\text{the process in hours}\end{array}\right)\left(\begin{array}{c}\text{Variable costs}\\\text{per hour}\end{array}\right)\left(\begin{array}{c}\text{Number of times process}\\\text{performed per year}\end{array}\right)$$

For example, if the average time to serve a customer is 4 hours, the variable cost is $25 per hour, and 40 customers are served per year, then the labor cost is $4,000 per year (or 4 hrs/customer × $25/hr × 40 customers/yr).

In the case of the patient in Figure 8.8, this conversion would not be necessary, with total patient time being sufficient. What is being tracked is the patient's time, not the time and costs of the service providers.

FIGURE 8.8 ▶
Process Chart for Emergency Room Admission

Process:	Emergency room admission
Subject:	Ankle injury patient
Beginning:	Enter emergency room
Ending:	Leave hospital

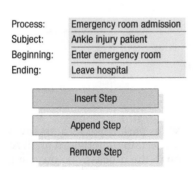

Summary

Activity	Number of Steps	Time (min)	Distance (ft)
Operation ●	5	23.00	
Transport ➡	9	11.00	815
Inspect ■	2	8.00	
Delay ◗	3	8.00	
Store ▼	—	—	

Step No.	Time (min)	Distance (ft)	●	➡	■	◗	▼	Step Description
1	0.50	15.0			X			Enter emergency room, approach patient window
2	10.00		X					Sit down and fill out patient history
3	0.75	40.0			X			Nurse escorts patient to ER triage room
4	3.00					X		Nurse inspects injury
5	0.75	40.0			X			Return to waiting room
6	1.00						X	Wait for available bed
7	1.00	60.0			X			Go to ER bed
8	4.00						X	Wait for doctor
9	5.00				X			Doctor inspects injury and questions patient
10	2.00	200.0			X			Nurse takes patient to radiology
11	3.00		X					Technician x-rays patient
12	2.00	200.0			X			Return to bed in ER
13	3.00						X	Wait for doctor to return
14	2.00		X					Doctor provides diagnosis and advice
15	1.00	60.0			X			Return to emergency entrance area
16	4.00		X					Check out
17	2.00	180.0			X			Walk to pharmacy
18	4.00		X					Pick up prescription
19	1.00	20.0			X			Leave the building

You can design your own process chart spreadsheets to bring out issues that are particularly important for the process you are analyzing, such as categories for customer contact, process divergence, and the like. You can also track performance measures other than time and distance traveled, such as error rates. In addition, you can also create a different version of the process chart spreadsheet that examines processes much as done with flowcharts, except now in the form of a table. The columns that categorize the activity type could be replaced by one or more columns reporting different metrics of interest, rather than trying to fit them into a flowchart. Although it might not look as elegant, it could be just as informative—and easier to create.

Evaluating Performance

Metrics and performance information complete the documentation of a process (see step 3 in Figure 8.1). Metrics can be displayed in various ways. Sometimes, they can be added directly on the flowchart or process chart. When the number of metrics gets unwieldy, another approach is to create a supporting table for the chart. Its rows are the steps in the flowchart, swim lane flowchart, service blueprint, or process chart. The columns are the current performance, goals, and performance gaps for various metrics.

The leader of a design team presents several charts that document a process in their office that they are analyzing. He is identifying several areas of substandard performance across a range of different metrics. The next step will be to redesign the process. The flipchart on the right will be quite useful in generating rapid fire ideas from the team on how the process might be improved.

The specific metrics analysts choose depends on the process being analyzed and on the competitive priorities. Good starting points are the per-unit processing time and cost at each step, and the time elapsed from beginning to end of the process. Capacity utilization, environmental issues, and customer (or job) waiting times reveal where in the process delays are most likely to occur. Customer satisfaction measures, error rates, and scrap rates identify possible quality problems. Figure 8.9 shows chapter 7 that relates to some basic metrics.

Chapter 7, Quality and Performance
• Customer satisfaction measures • Error rate • Rework or scrap rate • Internal failure cost

◄ **FIGURE 8.9**
Metrics for Flowcharts, Process Charts, and Accompanying Tables

Data Analysis Tools

Metrics may reveal a performance gap. Various tools are available to help you understand the causes of the problem[1]. Here we present six tools: (1) checklists, (2) histograms and bar charts, (3) Pareto charts, (4) scatter diagrams, (5) cause-and-effect diagrams, and (6) graphs. Many of them were developed initially to analyze quality issues, but they apply equally well to the full range of performance measures.

Checklists   Data collection through the use of a checklist is often the first step in the analysis of a metric. A **checklist** is a form used to record the frequency of occurrence of certain process failures. A **process failure** is any performance shortfall, such as error, delay, environmental waste, rework, and the like. The characteristics may be measurable on a continuous scale (e.g., weight, customer satisfaction on a 1-to-7 scale, unit cost, scrap loss percentage, time, or length) or on a yes-or-no basis (e.g., customer complaint, posting error, paint discoloration, or inattentive servers).

Histograms and Bar Charts   Data from a checklist often can be presented succinctly and clearly with histograms or bar charts. A **histogram** summarizes data measured on a continuous scale, showing the frequency distribution of some process failure (in statistical terms, the central tendency and dispersion of the data). Often the mean of the data is indicated on the histogram. A **bar chart** (see Figure 8.10) is a series of bars representing the frequency of occurrence of data characteristics measured on a yes-or-no basis. The bar height indicates the number of times a particular process failure was observed.

Pareto Charts   When managers discover several process problems that need to be addressed, they have to decide which should be attacked first. Vilfredo Pareto, a nineteenth-century Italian scientist whose statistical work focused on inequalities in data, proposed that most of an "activity" is caused by relatively few of its factors. In a restaurant quality problem, the activity could be customer complaints and the factor could be "discourteous server." For a manufacturer, the activity could be product defects and the factor could be "missing part." Pareto's concept, called the 80–20 rule, is that 80 percent of the activity is caused by 20 percent of the factors. By concentrating on the 20 percent of the factors (the "vital few"), managers can attack 80 percent of the process failure problems. Of course, the exact percentages vary with each situation, but inevitably relatively few factors cause most of the performance shortfalls.

The few vital factors can be identified with a **Pareto chart**, a bar chart on which the factors are plotted along the horizontal axis in decreasing order of frequency (see Figure 8.11). The chart has two vertical axes, the one on the left showing frequency (as in a histogram) and the one on the right showing the cumulative percentage of frequency. The cumulative frequency curve identifies the few vital factors that warrant immediate managerial attention.

checklist

A form used to record the frequency of occurrence of certain process failures.

process failure

Any performance shortfall, such as error, delay, environmental waste, rework, and the like.

histogram

A summarization of data measured on a continuous scale, showing the frequency distribution of some process failure (in statistical terms, the central tendency and dispersion of the data).

bar chart

A series of bars representing the frequency of occurrence of data characteristics measured on a yes-or-no basis.

Pareto chart

A bar chart on which factors are plotted along the horizontal axis in decreasing order of frequency.

EXAMPLE 8.2	**Pareto Chart for a Restaurant**

MyOMLab

Active Model 8.1 in MyOMLab provides additional insights on this Pareto chart example and its extensions.

MyOMLab

Tutor 8.2 in MyOMLab provides a new example on creating Pareto charts.

The manager of a neighborhood restaurant is concerned about the lower numbers of customers patronizing his eatery. Complaints have been rising, and he would like to find out what issues to address and present the findings in a way his employees can understand.

SOLUTION

The manager surveyed his customers over several weeks and collected the following data:

Complaint	Frequency
Discourteous server	12
Slow service	42
Cold dinner	5
Cramped tables	20
Atmosphere	10

---

[1]Several of these tools, particularly Pareto charts and cause-and-effect diagrams, are closely affiliated with Chapter 7, "Quality and Performance." We discuss them here because they apply to process failures in general, and not just to quality rejects.

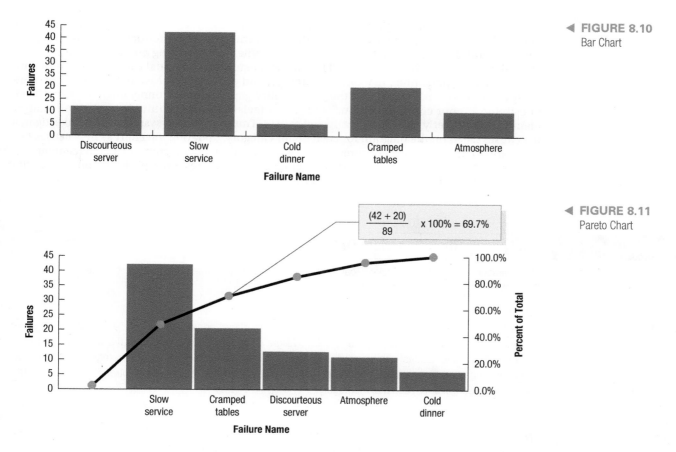

◀ **FIGURE 8.10**
Bar Chart

◀ **FIGURE 8.11**
Pareto Chart

$$\frac{(42 + 20)}{89} \times 100\% = 69.7\%$$

Figure 8.10 is a bar chart and Figure 8.11 is a Pareto chart, both created with OM Explorer's *Bar*, *Pareto*, *and Line Charts* Solver. They present the data in a way that shows which complaints are more prevalent (the vital few). You can reformat these charts for any "yes-or-no" metrics by unprotecting the spreadsheet and then making your revisions. For example, if you are using Microsoft Excel 2010, just click on Home/Format/Protection/Unprotect Sheet. Another approach is to create your own spreadsheets from scratch. More advanced software with point-and-click interfaces include Minitab (**www.minitab.com/index.htm**), SAS (**www.sas.com/rnd/app/qc.html**), and Microsoft Visio (**www.microsoft.com/office/visio**).

DECISION POINT

It was clear to the manager (and all employees) which complaints, if rectified, would cover most of the process failure problems in the restaurant. First, slow service will be addressed by training the existing staff, adding another server, and improving the food preparation process. Removing some decorative furniture from the dining area and spacing the tables better will solve the problem with cramped tables. The Pareto chart shows that these two problems, if rectified, will account for almost 70 percent of the complaints.

Scatter Diagrams   Sometimes managers suspect that a certain factor is causing a particular process failure. A **scatter diagram**, which is a plot of two variables showing whether they are related, can be used to verify or negate the suspicion. Each point on the scatter diagram represents one data observation. For example, the manager of a castings shop may suspect that casting defects are a function of the diameter of the casting. A scatter diagram could be constructed by plotting the number of defective castings found for each diameter of casting produced. After the diagram is completed, any relationship between diameter and number of process failures will be clear.

scatter diagram

A plot of two variables showing whether they are related.

Cause-and-Effect Diagrams   An important aspect of process analysis is linking each metric to the inputs, methods, and process steps that build a particular attribute into the service or product. One way to identify a design problem is to develop a **cause-and-effect diagram** that relates a key performance problem to its potential causes. First developed by Kaoru Ishikawa, the diagram helps management trace disconnects directly to the operations involved. Processes that have no bearing on a particular problem are not shown on the diagram.

cause-and-effect diagram

A diagram that relates a key performance problem to its potential causes.

The cause-and-effect diagram sometimes is called a *fishbone diagram*. The main performance gap is labeled as the fish's "head," the major categories of potential causes as structural "bones," and the likely specific causes as "ribs." When constructing and using a cause-and-effect diagram, an analyst identifies all the major categories of potential causes for the problem. These might be personnel, machines, materials, and processes. For each major category, the analyst lists all the likely causes of the performance gap. Under personnel might be listed "lack of training," "poor communication," and "absenteeism." Creative thinking helps the analyst identify and properly classify all suspected causes. The analyst then systematically investigates the causes listed on the diagram for each major category, updating the chart as new causes become apparent. The process of constructing a cause-and-effect diagram calls management and worker attention to the primary factors affecting process failures. Example 8.3 demonstrates the use of a cause-and-effect diagram by an airline.

| EXAMPLE 8.3 | **Analysis of Flight Departure Delays** |

The operations manager for Checker Board Airlines at Port Columbus International Airport noticed an increase in the number of delayed flight departures.

▼ **FIGURE 8.12**
Cause-and-Effect Diagram for Flight Departure Delays
Source: Adopted from D. Daryl Wyckoff, "New Tools for Achieving Service Quality," *The Cornell H.R.A. Quarterly.* Used by permission. All rights reserved.

SOLUTION
To analyze all the possible causes of that problem, the manager constructed a cause-and-effect diagram, shown in Figure 8.12. The main problem, delayed flight departures, is the "head" of the diagram. He brainstormed all possible causes with his staff, and together they identified several major categories: equipment, personnel, materials, procedures, and "other factors" that are beyond managerial control. Several suspected causes were identified for each major category.

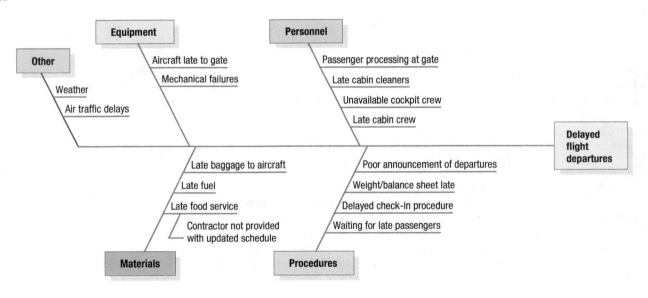

DECISION POINT
The operations manager, having a good understanding of the process, suspected that most of the flight delays were caused by problems with materials. Consequently, he had food service, fueling, and baggage-handling operations examined. He learned that the number of tow trucks for the baggage-transfer operations was insufficient and that planes were delayed waiting for baggage from connecting flights.

---

graphs

Representations of data in a variety of pictorial forms, such as line charts and pie charts.

Graphs   Graphs represent data in a variety of pictorial formats, such as line charts and pie charts. *Line charts* represent data sequentially with data points connected by line segments to highlight trends in the data. Line charts are used in control charts (see Chapter 7, "Quality and Performance") and forecasting (see Chapter 3, "Forecasting"). Pie charts represent process factors as slices of a pie; the size of each slice is in proportion to the number of occurrences of the factor.

Pie charts are useful for showing data from *a group of factors* that can be represented as percentages totaling 100 percent.

Each of the tools for improving quality may be used independently, but their power is greatest when they are used together. In solving a process-related problem, managers often must act as detectives, sifting data to clarify the issues involved and deducing the causes. We call this process *data snooping*. Example 8.4 demonstrates how the tools for improving quality can be used for data snooping.

A simulation model goes one step further than data analysis tools, because it can show how the process dynamically changes over time. **Process simulation** is the act of reproducing the behavior of a process, using a model that describes each step. Once the process is modeled, the analyst can make changes in the model to measure the impact on certain metrics, such as response time, waiting lines, resource utilization, and the like. To learn more about how simulation works, see MyOMLab Supplement E, "Simulation". A more advanced capability is possible using SimQuick, found in MyOMLab (**www.nd.edu/~dhartvig/simquick/top.html**). Other software packages include Extend (**http://www.extendsim.com//**), SIMPROCESS (**www.caciasl.com**), ProModel (**www.promodel.com**), and Witness (**www.lanner.com**).

> **process simulation**
>
> The act of reproducing the behavior of a process, using a model that describes each step.
>
> **MyOMLab**

Redesigning the Process

A doctor pinpoints an illness after a thorough examination of the patient, and then the doctor recommends treatments based on the diagnosis; so it is with processes. After a process is documented, metrics data collected, and disconnects identified, the process analyst or design team puts together a set of changes that will make the process better. At this step, people directly involved in the process are brought in to get their ideas and inputs.

Generating Ideas: Questioning and Brainstorming

Sometimes, ideas for reengineering or improving a process become apparent after documenting the process and carefully examining the areas of substandard performance, handoffs between departments, and steps where customer contact is high. Example 8.4 illustrates how such documentation pointed to a better way of handling the fiber boards through better training. In other cases, the better solution is less evident. Ideas can be uncovered (because there is always a better way) by asking six questions about each step in the process, and about the process as a whole:

1. *What* is being done?
2. *When* is it being done?
3. *Who* is doing it?
4. *Where* is it being done?
5. *How* is it being done?
6. *How* **well** does it do on the various metrics of importance?

Answers to these questions are challenged by asking still another series of questions. *Why* is the process even being done? *Why* is it being done where it is being done? *Why* is it being done when it is being done?

Creativity can also be stimulated by **brainstorming**, letting a group of people knowledgeable about the process propose ideas for change by saying whatever comes to mind. A facilitator records the ideas on a flipchart, so that all can see. Participants are discouraged from evaluating any of the ideas generated during the session. The purpose is to encourage creativity and to get as many ideas as possible, no matter how far-fetched the ideas may seem. The participants of a brainstorming session need not be limited to the design team as long as they have seen or heard the process documentation. A growing number of big companies, such as Sun Life Financial and Georgia-Pacific, are taking advantage of the Internet and specially designed software to run brainstorming sessions that allow people at far-flung locations to "meet" online and hash out solutions to particular problems. The technology lets employees see, and build on, one another's ideas, so that one person's seed of a notion can grow into a practical plan.

> **brainstorming**
>
> Letting a group of people, knowledgeable about the process, propose ideas for change by saying whatever comes to mind.

EXAMPLE 8.4	Identifying Causes of Poor Headliner Process Failures

The Wellington Fiber Board Company produces headliners, the fiberglass components that form the inner roof of passenger cars. Management wanted to identify which process failures were most prevalent and to find the cause.

Step 1. Checklist

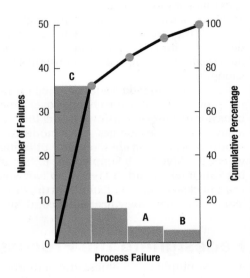

Headliner failures

Process failure	Tally	Total
A. Tears in fabric	IIII	4
B. Discolored fabric	III	3
C. Broken fiber board	IIII IIII IIII IIII IIII IIII IIII I	36
D. Ragged edges	IIII II	7
		Total 50

Step 2. Pareto Chart

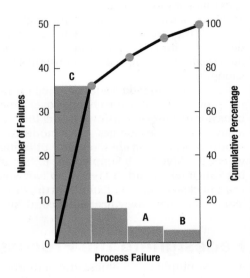

Step 3. Cause-and-Effect Diagram

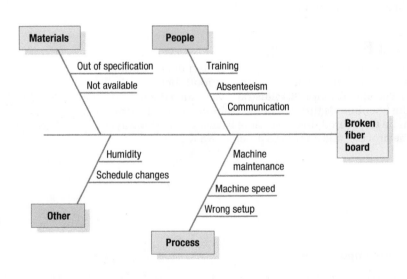

Step 4. Bar Chart

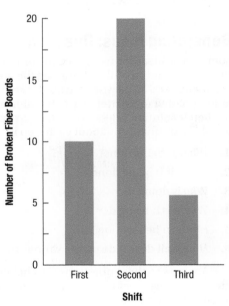

▲ **FIGURE 8.13**
Application of the Tools
for Improving Quality

SOLUTION

Figure 8.13 shows the sequential application of several tools for improving quality.

Step 1: A checklist of different types of process failures was constructed from last month's production records.

Step 2: A Pareto chart prepared from the checklist data indicated that broken fiber board accounted for 72 percent of the process failures.

Step 3: A cause-and-effect diagram for broken fiber board identified several potential causes for the problem. The one strongly suspected by the manager was employee training.

Step 4: The manager reorganized the production reports into a bar chart according to shift because the personnel on the three shifts had varied amounts of experience.

DECISION POINT

The bar chart indicated that the second shift, with the least experienced workforce, had most of the process failures. Further investigation revealed that workers were not using proper procedures for stacking the fiber boards after the press operation, which caused cracking and chipping. The manager set up additional training sessions focused on board handling. Although the second shift was not responsible for all the process failures, finding the source of many of the failures enabled the manager to improve the performance of her operations.

After the brainstorming session is over, the design team moves into the "get real" phase: They evaluate the different ideas. The team identifies the changes that give the best payoffs for process redesign. The redesign could involve issues of capacity, layout, technology, or even location, all of which are discussed in more detail in the following chapters.

The redesigned process is documented once again, this time as the "after" view of the process. Expected payoffs are carefully estimated, along with risks. For changes involving investments, the time value of money must be considered (see MyOMLab Supplement F, "Financial Analysis,"). The impact on people (skills, degree of change, training requirements, and resistance to change) must also be factored into the evaluation of the new design.

Managerial Practice 8.1 describes how Baptist Memorial Hospital analyzed its processes to solve its capacity problem and improve patient satisfaction at the same time without any addition of new resources.

MyOMLab

Benchmarking

Benchmarking can be another valuable source for process redesign. **Benchmarking** is a systematic procedure that measures a firm's processes, services, and products against those of industry leaders. Companies use benchmarking to better understand how outstanding companies do things so that they can improve their own processes.

benchmarking
A systematic procedure that measures a firm's processes, services, and products against those of industry leaders.

MANAGERIAL PRACTICE 8.1 | Baptist Memorial Hospital

Baptist Memorial Hospital—Memphis is a 760-bed tertiary care hospital. It had a capacity problem, or so it seemed, with occupancy routinely exceeding 90 percent. However, it solved the problem with process improvement, rather than adding staff or bed capacity. Administration, nurses, and physicians centralized bed assignments and added a new bed-tracking system to provide bed information in real time. They then focused on improving processes at the emergency department (ED). An express admission unit (EAU), a 21-bed dedicated area that processes direct and emergency department admissions, was opened to remove responsibility for a particularly time-intensive activity from busy unit nurses. The new processes were less divergent and had more of a line flow. They then began testing process improvement ideas for change on a small scale, altering processes to improve them, and spreading the processes to other areas when they are successful. They began to fax reports from the ED to the receiving unit, shifted more nurses to work during peak periods, began lab and X-ray diagnostic procedures at triage when the EU was at capacity, took patients directly to a room when one became available with bedside registration, and segmented the urgent care population within the ED.

Redesigned processes reduced patient delays. Turnaround time for the overall ED was reduced by 9 percent, even while the ED volume was increasing. Length of stay was reduced by 2 days, the equivalent of building 12 Intensive care unit (ICU) beds. The mortality rate decreased, volume increased by 20 percent, and patient satisfaction improved significantly. What first appeared to be a capacity problem was resolved without adding staff or the number of beds—it was solved with redesigned processes.

Baptist Memorial Hospital in Memphis, Tennessee, holds "huddle meetings" at least three times a day seeking out process improvements. The meetings bring together the hospital's house supervisor, housekeeping supervisor, and key nurses. Improvements have been dramatic. In 2011, the hospital was ranked in the top 5 percent nationally for emergency medicine.

Source: Suzanne S. Horton, "Increasing Capacity While Improving the Bottom Line," *Frontiers of Health Services Management,* vol. 20, no. 4 (Summer 2004), pp. 17–23; Richard S. Zimmerman, "Hospital Capacity, Productivity, and Patient Safety—It All Flows Together," *Frontiers of Health Services Management,* vol. 20, no. 4 (Summer 2004), pp. 33–38, *baptistonline.org,* April, 2011.

Omgeo is a behind-the-scenes company that settles trades between financial services firms. The process used to involve dozens of scribbled faxes, telexes, and telephone calls made for the typical trade costs from $10 to $12. Now, the process costs only 20 cents to $1 per trade—and investment managers essentially got the service free. A key change was using the Internet and new information technology solutions. Information goes into a central database that the broker, investment manager, and custodian banks all have access to in real time. The details of the trades are automatically compared to eliminate errors.

Benchmarking focuses on setting quantitative goals for improvement. *Competitive* benchmarking is based on comparisons with a direct industry competitor. *Functional* benchmarking compares areas such as administration, customer service, and sales operations with those of outstanding firms in any industry. For instance, Xerox benchmarked its distribution function against L.L. Bean's because L.L. Bean is renowned as a leading retailer in distribution efficiency and customer service.

Internal benchmarking involves using an organizational unit with superior performance as the benchmark for other units. This form of benchmarking can be advantageous for firms that have several business units or divisions. All forms of benchmarking are best applied in situations where you are looking for a long-term program of continuous improvement.

Typical measures used in benchmarking include cost per unit, service upsets (breakdowns) per customer, processing time per unit, customer retention rates, revenue per unit, return on investment, and customer satisfaction levels.

Benchmarking consists of four basic steps:

Step 1. Planning. Identify the process, service, or product to be benchmarked and the firm(s) to be used for comparison; determine the performance metrics for analysis; collect the data.

Step 2. Analysis. Determine the gap between the firm's current performance and that of the benchmark firm(s); identify the causes of significant performance gaps.

Step 3. Integration. Establish goals and obtain the support of managers who must provide the resources for accomplishing the goals.

Step 4. Action. Develop cross-functional teams of those most affected by the changes; develop action plans and team assignments; implement the plans; monitor progress; recalibrate benchmarks as improvements are made.

Collecting benchmarking data can sometimes be a challenge. Internal benchmarking data is surely the most accessible. One way of benchmarking is always available—tracking the performance of a process over time. Functional benchmarking data are often collected by professional associations or consulting firms. Several corporations and government organizations have agreed to share and standardize performance benchmarks. The American Productivity and Quality Center, a nonprofit organization, created thousands of measures, as Figure 8.14 illustrates. A full range of metrics can be explored at **www.apqc.org**. Another source is the Supply-Chain Council, which has defined key metrics in its Supply-Chain Operations Reference (SCOR) model.

Managing and Implementing Processes

Failure to manage processes is failure to manage the business. Implementing a beautifully redesigned process is only the beginning to continually monitoring and improving processes. Metrics goals must be continually evaluated and reset to fit changing requirements. Avoid the following seven mistakes when managing processes:[2]

1. *Not Connecting with Strategic Issues.* Is particular attention being paid to core processes, competitive priorities, impact of customer contact and volume, and strategic fit during process analysis?

---

[2]Geary A. Rummler and Alan P. Brache, *Improving Performance,* 2nd ed. (San Francisco: Jossey-Bass, 1995), pp. 126–133.

FIGURE 8.14
Illustrative Benchmarking Metrics by Type of Process

Customer Relationship Process

- Total cost of "enter, process, and track orders" per $1,000 revenue
- System costs of process per $100,000 revenue
- Value of sales order line item not fulfilled due to stockouts, as percentage of revenue
- Percentage of finished goods sales value that is returned
- Average time from sales order receipt until manufacturing or logistics is notified
- Average time in direct contact with customer per sales order line item
- Energy consumed in transporting product
- Total distance travelled for products
- Green house gas emissions

Order Fulfillment Process

- Value of plant shipments per employee
- Finished goods inventory turnover
- Reject rate as percentage of total orders processed
- Percentage of orders returned by customers due to quality problems
- Standard customer lead time from order entry to shipment
- Percentage of orders shipped on time
- Use of non-renewable energy sources
- Use of toxic ingredients
- Safe and healthy work environment

New Service/Product Development Process

- Percentage of sales due to services/products launched last year
- Cost of "generate new services/products" process per $1,000 revenue
- Ratio of projects entering the process to projects completing the process
- Time to market for existing service/product improvement project
- Time to market for new service/product project
- Time to profitability for existing service/product improvement project

Supplier Relationship Process

- Cost of "select suppliers and develop/maintain contracts" process per $1,000 revenue
- Number of employees per $1,000 of purchases
- Percentage of purchase orders approved electronically
- Average time to place a purchase order
- Total number of active vendors per $1,000 of purchases
- Percentage of value of purchased material that is supplier certified
- Amount of toxic chemicals used in supplies production process
- Energy consumed in transporting raw materials and parts
- Total distance travelled for raw materials and parts
- Green house gas emissions
- Supplier's use of toxic chemicals in production process
- Percentage of child labor used by supplier

Support Process

- Systems cost of finance function per $1,000 revenue
- Percentage of finance staff devoted to internal audit
- Total cost of payroll processes per $1,000 revenue
- Number of accepted jobs as percentage of job offers
- Total cost of "source, recruit, and select" process per $1,000 revenue
- Average employee turnover rate

2. *Not Involving the Right People in the Right Way.* Does process analysis closely involve the people performing the process, or those closely connected to it as internal customers and suppliers?
3. *Not Giving the Design Teams and Process Analysts a Clear Charter, and then Holding Them Accountable.* Does management set expectations for change and maintain pressure for results? Does it allow paralysis in process improvement efforts by requiring excessive analysis?
4. *Not Being Satisfied Unless Fundamental "Reengineering" Changes are Made.* Is the radical change from process reengineering the expectation? If so, the cumulative effect of many small improvements that could be made incrementally could be lost. Process management efforts should not be limited to downsizing or to reorganization only, even though jobs may be eliminated or the structure changed. It should not be limited to big technological innovation projects, even though technological change occurs often.

5. *Not Considering the Impact on People.* Are the changes aligned with the attitudes and skills of the people who must implement the redesigned process? It is crucial to understand and deal with the *people side* of process changes.

6. *Not Giving Attention to Implementation.* Are processes redesigned, but never implemented? A great job of flowcharting and benchmarking is of only academic interest if the proposed changes are not implemented. Sound project management practices are required.

7. *Not Creating an Infrastructure for Continuous Process Improvement.* Is a measurement system in place to monitor key metrics over time? Is anyone checking to see whether anticipated benefits of a redesigned process are actually being realized?

Managers must make sure that their organization spots new performance gaps in the continual search for process improvements. Process redesign efforts need to be part of periodic reviews and even annual plans. Measurement is the particular focus of the next chapter. It covers how a performance tracking system is the basis for feedback and improvement efforts. The essence of a learning organization is the intelligent use of such feedback.

LEARNING GOALS IN REVIEW

① **Explain a systematic way to analyze processes.** The section "A Systematic Approach" on pp. 283–285, gives six steps to analysis. Focus on Figure 8.1 for the sequence of these steps.

② **Define flowcharts, swim lane flowcharts, and service blueprints.** The "Documenting the Process" section, pp. 285–289, demonstrates these three techniques for documenting and evaluating processes. More than one flowchart can be used to handle nested processes. Service blueprints show the line of visibility where there is customer contact.

③ **Describe the various work measurement techniques.** The time study method, elemental standard data approach, predetermined data approach, work sampling method, and learning curve analysis are briefly described in the "Work Measurement Techniques" section, pp. 289–291. For a more complete description, see MyOMLab Supplement H, "Measuring Output Rates"

④ **Describe Pareto charts, cause-and-effect diagrams, and process simulation.** These techniques, described in the "Data

Analysis Tools" section on pp. 294–297, help you to understand the causes of performance gaps. Process simulation is a more advanced tool and described in more depth in MyOMLab Supplement E.

⑤ **Create better processes using benchmarking.** "Benchmarking," pp. 299–300, whether it is functional, internal, or competitive, is a systematic procedure that measures a firm's processes or products against those in other areas. Figure 4.14 provides an array of metrics that can be used, depending on the process being evaluated.

⑥ **Identify keys for effective process management.** The "Managing and Implementing Processes" section, pp. 300–301, gives seven mistakes that can be made. There must be a continual search for process improvements.

MyOMLab helps you develop analytical skills and assesses your progress with multiple problems on process charts, standard times, learning curves, bar charts, scatter diagrams, Pareto charts, and histograms.

MyOMLab Resources	Titles	Link to the Book
Videos	*Process Analysis at Starwood*	Entire chapter
Active Model Exercise	8.1 Pareto Chart	Active Model Exercise: 8.1 Pareto Chart; Evaluating Performance; Example 8.2 (pp. 294–295); Example 8.4 (p. 297–298)
OM Explorer Solvers	Process Charts Bar, Pareto, and Line Charts	Documenting the Process; Figure 8.8 (p. 292) Evaluating the Process; Example 8.2 (pp. 294–295); Example 8.4 (pp. 297–298)
OM Explorer Tutors	8.1 Process Charts 8.2 Pareto Charts	Process Charts; Figure 8.8 (p. 292); Solved Problem 2 (pp. 304–305) Evaluating Performance; Example 8.2 (pp. 294–295); Example 8.4 (pp. 297–298)
OM Explorer Tutor Exercises	8.1 Process Chart of your choosing 8.2 Pareto Chart	Documenting the Process; Figure 8.8 (p. 292) Evaluating Performance; Example 8.2 (pp. 294–295); Example 8.4 (pp. 297–298)

MyOMLab Resources	Titles	Link to the Book
Flowchart Tutorials	8.1 Flowcharting in Excel 8.2 Flowcharting in PowerPoint 8.3 Live Flowcharting for Figures 8.2–8.3	Documenting the Process Documenting the Process Documenting the Process
SmartDraw	Often used in practice to create flowcharts	Get free trial version online
Virtual Tours	1. Anrosia and Hershey Foods Corporation	Strategic Fit
MyOMLab Supplements	F. Financial Analysis H. Measuring Output Rates I. Learning Curve Analysis	Redesigning the Process Work Measurement Techniques Learning Curve Analysis
Internet Exercises	1. BIC Stationary, BIC Lighters, BIC Shavers 2. Fender Guild Guitars	Documenting the Process Benchmarking
Additional Case	The Facilities Maintenance Problem at Midwest University	Entire chapter
Key Equations		
Image Library		

Key Terms

bar chart 294
benchmarking 299
brainstorming 297
cause-and-effect diagram 295
checklist 294
design team 284
elemental standard data 289
flowchart 285

graphs 296
histogram 294
learning curve 291
metrics 284
Pareto chart 294
predetermined data approach 290
process analysis 283
process chart 291

process failure 294
process simulation 297
scatter diagram 295
service blueprint 288
suggestion system 284
swim lane flowchart 287
time study 289
work sampling 290

Solved Problem 1

Create a flowchart for the following telephone-ordering process at a retail chain that specializes in selling books and music CDs. It provides an ordering system via the telephone to its time-sensitive customers besides its regular store sales.

First, the automated system greets customers and identifies whether they have a tone or pulse phone. Customers choose 1 if they have a tone phone; otherwise, they wait for the first available service representative to process their request. If customers have a tone phone, they complete their request by choosing options on the phone. First, the system checks to see whether customers have an existing account. Customers choose 1 if they have an existing account or choose 2 if they want to open a new account. Customers wait for the service representative to open a new account if they choose 2.

Next, customers choose between the options of making an order, canceling an order, or talking to a customer representative for questions and/or complaints. If customers choose to make an order, then they specify the order type as a book or a music CD, and a specialized customer representative for books or music CDs picks up the phone to get the order details. If customers choose to cancel an order, then they wait for the automated response. By entering the order code via phone, customers can cancel the order. The automated system says the name of the ordered item and asks for the confirmation of the customer. If the customer validates the cancellation of the order, then the system cancels the order; otherwise, the system asks the customer to input the order code again. After responding to the request, the system asks whether the customer has additional requests; if not, the process terminates.

SOLUTION

Figure 8.15 shows the flowchart.

FIGURE 8.15 ▶
Flowchart of Telephone Ordering
Process

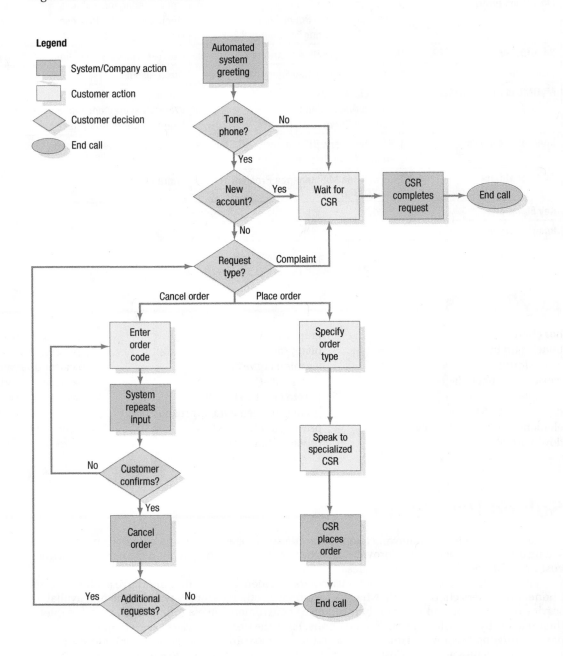

FIGURE 8.15 ▶
Flowchart of Telephone Ordering
Process

Solved Problem 2

An automobile service is having difficulty providing oil changes in the 29 minutes or less mentioned in its advertising. You are to analyze the process of changing automobile engine oil. The subject of the study is the service mechanic. The process begins when the mechanic directs the customer's arrival and ends when the customer pays for the services.

SOLUTION

Figure 8.16 shows the completed process chart. The process is broken into 21 steps. A summary of the times and distances traveled is shown in the upper right-hand corner of the process chart.

The times add up to 28 minutes, which does not allow much room for error if the 29-minute guarantee is to be met and the mechanic travels a total of 420 feet.

Process:	Changing engine oil
Subject:	Mechanic
Beginning:	Direct customer arrival
Ending:	Total charges, receive payment

◀ **FIGURE 8.16**
Process Chart for Changing Engine Oil

| Insert Step |
| Append Step |
| Remove Step |

Summary

Activity		Number of Steps	Time (min)	Distance (ft)
Operation	●	7	16.50	
Transport	➡	8	5.50	420
Inspect	■	4	5.00	
Delay	◗	1	0.70	
Store	▼	1	0.30	

Step No.	Time (min)	Distance (ft)	●	➡	■	◗	▼	Step Description
1	0.80	50.0		X				Direct customer into service bay
2	1.80		X					Record name and desired service
3	2.30				X			Open hood, verify engine type, inspect hoses, check fluids
4	0.80	30.0		X				Walk to customer in waiting area
5	0.60		X					Recommend additional services
6	0.70						X	Wait for customer decision
7	0.90	70.0		X				Walk to storeroom
8	1.90		X					Look up filter number(s), find filter(s)
9	0.40				X			Check filter number(s)
10	0.60	50.0		X				Carry filter(s) to service pit
11	4.20		X					Perform under-car services
12	0.70	40.0		X				Climb from pit, walk to automobile
13	2.70		X					Fill engine with oil, start engine
14	1.30				X			Inspect for leaks
15	0.50	40.0		X				Walk to pit
16	1.00				X			Inspect for leaks
17	3.00		X					Clean and organize work area
18	0.70	80.0		X				Return to auto, drive from bay
19	0.30					X		Park the car
20	0.50	60.0		X				Walk to customer waiting area
21	2.30		X					Total charges, receive payment

Solved Problem 3

What improvement can you make in the process shown in Figure 8.16?

SOLUTION

Your analysis should verify the following three ideas for improvement. You may also be able to come up with others.

a. **Move Step 17 to Step 21.** Customers should not have to wait while the mechanic cleans the work area.

b. **Store Small Inventories of Frequently Used Filters in the Pit.** Steps 7 and 10 involve travel to and from the storeroom. If the filters are moved to the pit, a copy of the reference material must also be placed in the pit. The pit will have to be organized and well lighted.

c. **Use Two Mechanics.** Steps 10, 12, 15, and 17 involve running up and down the steps to the pit. Much of this travel could be eliminated. The service time could be shortened by having one mechanic in the pit working simultaneously with another working under the hood.

Solved Problem 4

Vera Johnson and Merris Williams manufacture vanishing cream. Their packaging process has four steps: (1) mix, (2) fill, (3) cap, and (4) label. They have had the reported process failures analyzed, which shows the following:

Process failure		Frequency
Lumps of unmixed product		7
Over- or underfilled jars		18
Jar lids did not seal		6
Labels rumpled or missing		29
	Total	60

Draw a Pareto chart to identify the vital failures.

SOLUTION

Defective labels account for 48.33 percent of the total number of failures:

$$\frac{29}{60} \times 100\% = 48.33\%$$

Improperly filled jars account for 30 percent of the total number of failures:

$$\frac{18}{60} \times 100\% = 30.00\%$$

The cumulative percent for the two most frequent failures is

$$48.33\% + 30.00\% = 78.33\%$$

Lumps represent $\frac{7}{60} \times 100\% = 11.67\%$ of failures; the cumulative percentage is

$$78.33\% + 11.67\% = 90.00\%$$

Defective seals represent $\frac{6}{60} \times 100\% = 10\%$ of failures; the cumulative percentage is

$$10\% + 90\% = 100.00\%$$

The Pareto chart is shown in Figure 8.17.

FIGURE 8.17 ▶
Pareto Chart

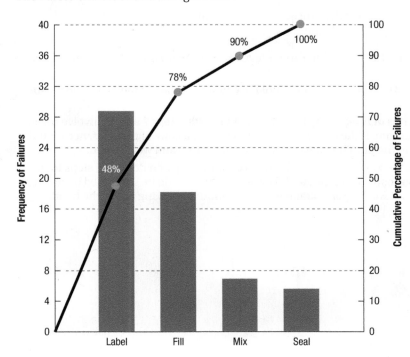

Discussion Questions

1. Continuous improvement recognizes that many small improvements add up to sizable benefits. Will continuous improvement take a company at the bottom of an industry to the top? Explain.

2. The Hydro-Electric Company (HEC) has three sources of power. A small amount of hydroelectric power is generated by damming wild and scenic rivers; a second source of power comes from burning coal, with emissions that create acid rain and contribute to global warming; the third source of power comes from nuclear fission. HEC's coal-fired plants use obsolete pollution-control technology, and an investment of several hundred million dollars would be required to update it. Environmentalists urge HEC to promote conservation and purchase power from suppliers that use the cleanest fuels and technology.

   However, HEC is already suffering from declining sales, which have resulted in billions of dollars invested in idle equipment. Its large customers are taking advantage of laws that permit them to buy power from low-cost suppliers. HEC must cover the fixed costs of idle capacity by raising rates charged to its remaining customers or face defaulting on bonds (bankruptcy). The increased rates motivate even more customers to seek low-cost suppliers, the start of a death spiral for HEC. To prevent additional rate increases, HEC implements a cost-cutting program and puts its plans to update pollution controls on hold.

   Form sides and discuss the ethical, environmental, and political issues and trade-offs associated with HEC's strategy.

3. Paul O'Neill, former U.S. Treasury Secretary, estimates that arguably half of the $2 trillion a year that Americans spend on health care is needlessly wasted. Brainstorm up to 10 blue-sky ideas to solve the following problems:

   a. A typical retail pharmacy spends 20 percent of its time playing telephone tag with doctors trying to find out what the intent was for a given prescription.

   b. After the person responsible for filling the prescription determines what they think they are supposed to do, errors can be made even in filling the prescription. For example, administering an adult dose (rather than the dose for a premature baby) of Heparin in a preemie ICU is fatal.

   c. Drugs get distributed at a hospital on a batch basis. For example, carts can be filled on Monday, Wednesday, and Friday. A huge volume of drugs can come back on Monday because they are not consumed on the wards between Friday and Monday, patient conditions changed, or the doctor decided on a different intervention. A technician spends the rest of the day restocking the shelves with the returns and 40 percent of the intravenous materials prepared on Friday morning are poured down the drain.

   d. Sometimes the administration of the drug was not done on the agreed schedule, because the nurses were busy doing something else.

   e. For every bed in an acute care hospital system, someone falls during the year. Most falls occur after 11 P.M. and before 6 A.M. Sometimes a bone is fractured, leading to immobilization and then pneumonia.

   f. One in every 14 people who goes to a U.S. hospital gets an infection they did not bring with them.

Problems

The OM Explorer and POM for Windows software is available to all students using the 10th edition of this textbook. Go to **www.pearsonhighered.com/krajewski** to download these computer packages. If you purchased MyOMLab, you also have access to Active Models software and significant help in doing the following problems. Check with your instructor on how best to use these resources. In many cases, the instructor wants you to understand how to do the calculations by hand. At the least, the software provides a check on your calculations. When calculations are particularly complex and the goal is interpreting the results in making decisions, the software replaces entirely the manual calculations.

1. Consider the Custom Molds, Inc. case at the end of Chapter 3, "Process Strategy." Prepare a flowchart of the mold fabrication process and the parts manufacturing process, showing how they are linked. For a good tutorial on how to create flowcharts, see **http://www.hci.com.au/hcisite5/library/materials/Flowcharting.htm.** Also check out the Flowcharting Tutor in Excel in MyOMLab.

2. Do Problem 1 using a process chart spreadsheet of your own design, one that differs from the *Process Chart* Solver in OM Explorer. It should have one or more columns to record information or metrics that you think are relevant, be it external customer contact, time delays, completion times, percent rework, costs, capacity, and/or demand rates. Your entries should show what information you would collect, even though only part of it is available in the case.

3. Founded in 1970, ABC is one of the world's largest insurance companies with locations in 28 countries. Given the following description, flowchart the new policy setup process as it existed in 1970:

   Individual customers who wanted to set up a new policy would visit one of ABC's 70 branch offices or make contact with an agent. They would then fill out an application and sometimes attach a check. The branch office then sent the application package through company mail to the XYZ division in London. In addition, a customer might also fill out the application at home and send it directly to any number of ABC locations, which would then transfer it to the London operation. Once received, XYZ separated the various parts of the application, then scanned and digitized it. The electronic image was then retrieved from a server and delivered to an associate's desktop client computer. The associate was responsible for entering the information on the form into the appropriate database. If the information supplied on the application was complete, a confirmation notice was automatically printed and sent to the customer. If the information was incomplete, then another associate, trained to deal with customers on the telephone, would call the customer to obtain the additional information. If the customer noticed something wrong on the confirmation notice received, she or he would either call a toll-free number or send in a letter describing the problem. The Customer Problem Resolution division dealt with problems arising at this point. An updated confirmation notice was sent to the customer. If the information was correct, the application transaction was complete.

4. Do Problem 3 using a process chart spreadsheet of your own design, one that differs from the *Process Chart* Solver in OM Explorer. It should have one or more columns to record information or metrics that you think should be collected to analyze the process (see Problem 2).

5. Prepare a flowchart of the field service division process at DEF, as described here. Start from the point where a call is received and end when a technician finishes the job.

DEF was a multibillion dollar company that manufactured and distributed a wide variety of electronic, photographic, and reprographic equipment used in many engineering and medical system applications. The Field Service Division employed 475 field service technicians, who performed maintenance and warranty repairs on the equipment sold by DEF. Customers would call DEF's National Service Center (NSC), which received about 3,000 calls per day. The NSC staffed its call center with about 40 call-takers. A typical incoming service call was received at the NSC and routed to one of the call-takers, who entered information about the machine, the caller's name, and the type of problem into DEF's mainframe computer. In some cases, the call-taker attempted to help the customer fix the problem. However, call-takers were currently only able to avoid about 10 percent of the incoming emergency maintenance service calls. If the service call could not be avoided, the call-taker usually stated the following script: "Depending upon the availability of our technicians, you should expect to see a technician sometime between now and (now 2 X)." ("X" was the target response time based on the model number and the zone.) This information was given to the customer because many customers wanted to know when a tech would arrive on site.

Call-takers entered service call information on DEF's computer system, which then sent the information electronically to the regional dispatch center assigned to that customer location. (DEF had four regional dispatch centers with a total of about 20 dispatchers.) Service call information was printed on a small card at the dispatch center. About every hour, cards were ripped off the printer and given to the dispatcher assigned to that customer location. The dispatcher placed each card on a magnetic board under the name of a tech that the dispatcher believed would be the most likely candidate for the service call, given the location of the machine, the current location of the tech, and the tech's training profile. After completing a service call, techs called the dispatcher in the regional dispatch center, cleared the call, and received a new call assigned by the dispatcher. After getting the service call from a dispatcher, a tech called the customer to give an expected time of arrival, drove to the customer site, diagnosed the problem, repaired the machine if parts were available in

the van, and then telephoned the dispatcher for the next call. If the tech did not have the right parts for a repair, the tech informed the NSC and the part was express mailed to the customer; the repair was done the next morning.

6. Big Bob's Burger Barn would like to graphically depict the interaction among its lunch-ordering customers and its three employees. Customers come into the restaurant and eat there, rather than drive through and eat in the car. Using the brief process descriptions below, develop a service blueprint.

Fry Employee: receive customer order from counter employee, retrieve uncooked food, drop food into fry vat, wrap cooked food into special packaging, place wrapped items on service counter.

Grill Employee: receive customer order from counter employee, retrieve uncooked food, place food onto grill, build sandwich with requested condiments, deliver sandwich to Counter Employee.

Counter Employee: take order from customer, transmit appropriate orders to Fry and Grill Employee, transact payment, retrieve drinks, wrap sandwich, package order, and deliver order to customer.

7. After viewing the *Process Choice at the King Soopers Bakery* video in MyOMLab, prepare a flowchart for the three processes at King Soopers. For additional information on the processes, see the *Big Picture* in MyOMLab.

8. Your class has volunteered to work for Referendum 13 on the November ballot, which calls for free tuition and books for all college courses except Operations Management. Support for the referendum includes assembling 10,000 yard signs (preprinted water-resistant paper signs to be glued and stapled to a wooden stake) on a fall Saturday. Construct a flowchart and a process chart for yard sign assembly. What inputs in terms of materials, human effort, and equipment are involved? Estimate the amount of volunteers, staples, glue, equipment, lawn and garage space, and pizza required.

9. Suppose you are in charge of a large mailing to the alumni of your college, inviting them to contribute to a scholarship fund. The letters and envelopes have been individually addressed (mailing labels were not used). The letters are to be processed (matched with correct envelope, time estimated to be 0.2 minutes each), folded (0.12 minutes each), and stuffed into the correct envelope (0.10 minutes each). The envelopes are to be sealed (0.05 minutes each), and a large commemorative stamp is to be placed in the upper right-hand corner of each envelope (0.10 minutes each).

   a. Make a process chart for this activity, assuming that it is a one-person operation.

   b. Estimate how long it will take to stuff, seal, and stamp 2,000 envelopes. Assume that the person doing this work is paid $8 per hour. How much will it cost to process 2,000 letters?

   c. Consider each of the following process changes. Which changes would reduce the time and cost of the current process?

   ■ Each letter has the same greeting "Dear Alumnus or Alumna," instead of the person's name.

   ■ Mailing labels are used and have to be put on the envelopes (0.10 minutes each).

- Prestamped envelopes are used.
- Envelopes are stamped by a postage meter which can stamp 200 letters per minute.
- Window envelopes are used.
- A preaddressed envelope is included with each letter for contributions (adds 0.05 minutes to stuffing step).

d. Would any of these changes be likely to reduce the effectiveness of the mailing? If so, which ones? Why?

e. Would the changes that increase time and cost be likely to increase the effectiveness of the mailing? Why or why not?

10. Diagrams of two self-service gasoline stations, both located on corners, are shown in Figure 8.18 (a) and (b). Both have two rows of four pumps and a booth at which an attendant receives payment for the gasoline. At neither station is it necessary for the customer to pay in advance. The exits and entrances are marked on the diagrams. Analyze the flows of cars and people through each station.

a. Which station has the more efficient flows from the standpoint of the customer?

b. Which station is likely to lose more potential customers who cannot gain access to the pumps because another car is headed in the other direction?

c. At which station can a customer pay without getting out of the car?

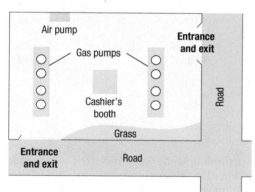

(a)

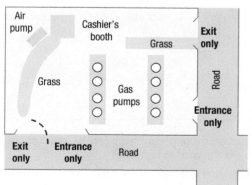

(b)

▲ **FIGURE 8.18**
Two Self-Service Gasoline Stations

11. The management of the Just Like Home Restaurant has asked you to analyze some of its processes. One of these processes is making a single-scoop ice cream cone. Cones can be ordered by a server (for table service) or by a customer (for takeout).

Figure 8.19 illustrates the process chart for this operation.

- The ice cream counter server earns $10 per hour (including variable fringe benefits).
- The process is performed 10 times per hour (on average).
- The restaurant is open 363 days a year, 10 hours a day.

a. Complete the Summary (top-right) portion of the chart.

b. What is the total labor cost associated with the process?

c. How can this operation be made more efficient? Make a process chart using OM Explorer's *Process Charts* Solver of the improved process. What are the annual labor savings if this new process is implemented?

12. As a graduate assistant, your duties include grading and keeping records for Operations Management course homework assignments. Five sections for 40 students each are offered each semester. A few graduate students attend sections 3 and 4. Graduate students must complete some extra work to higher standards for each assignment. Every student delivers (or is supposed to deliver) directly to (under) the door of your office one homework assignment every Tuesday. Your job is to correct the homework, record grades, sort the papers by class section, sort by student last name in alphabetical order, and return the homework papers to the appropriate instructors (not necessarily in that order). There are some complications. A fair majority of the students sign their names legibly, others identify work with their correct ID number, and a few do neither. Rarely do students identify their section number or graduate status. Prepare a list of process chart steps and place them in an efficient sequence.

13. At the Department of Motor Vehicles (DMV), the process of getting license plates for your car begins when you enter the facility and take a number. You walk 50 feet to the waiting area. During your wait, you count about 30 customers waiting for service. You notice that many customers become discouraged and leave. When a number is called, if a customer stands, the ticket is checked by a uniformed person, and the customer is directed to the available clerk. If no one stands, several minutes are lost while the same number is called repeatedly. Eventually, the next number is called, and more often than not, that customer has left too. The DMV clerk has now been idle for several minutes but does not seem to mind.

After 4 hours, your number is called and checked by the uniformed person. You walk 60 feet to the clerk, and the process of paying city sales taxes is completed in four minutes. The clerk then directs you to the waiting area for paying state personal property tax, 80 feet away. You take a different number and sit down with some different customers who are just renewing licenses. A 1-hour, 40-minute wait this time, and after a walk of 25 feet you pay property taxes in a process that takes two minutes. Now that you have paid taxes, you are eligible to pay registration and license fees. That department is 50 feet away, beyond the employees' cafeteria.

FIGURE 8.19 ▶
Process Chart for Making Ice Cream Cones

Process:	Making one ice cream cone
Subject:	Server at counter
Beginning:	Walk to cone storage area
Ending:	Give it to server or customer

Insert Step

Append Step

Remove Step

Summary

Activity	Number of Steps	Time (min)	Distance (ft)
Operation ●			
Transport ➡			
Inspect ■			
Delay ▶			
Store ▼			

Step No.	Time (min)	Distance (ft)	●	➡	■	▶	▼	Step Description
1	0.20	5.0		X				Walk to cone storage area
2	0.05		X					Remove empty cone
3	0.10	5.0		X				Walk to counter
4	0.05		X					Place cone in holder
5	0.20	8.0		X				Walk to sink area
6	0.50					X		Ask dishwasher to wash scoop
7	0.15	8.0		X				Walk to counter with clean scoop
8	0.05		X					Pick up empty cone
9	0.10	2.5		X				Walk to flavor ordered
10	0.75		X					Scoop ice cream from container
11	0.75		X					Place ice cream in cone
12	0.25				X			Check for stability
13	0.05	2.5		X				Walk to order placement area
14	0.05		X					Give server or customer the cone

The registration and license customers are called in the same order in which personal property taxes were paid. There is only a ten-minute wait and a three-minute process. You receive your license plates, take a minute to abuse the license clerk, and leave exactly six hours after arriving.

Make a process chart using OM Explorer's *Process Charts* Solver to depict this process, and suggest improvements.

14. Refer to the process chart for the automobile oil change in Solved Problem 2. Calculate the annual labor cost if:

   ■ The mechanic earns $40 per hour (including variable fringe benefits).

   ■ The process is performed twice per hour (on average).

   ■ The shop is open 300 days a year, 10 hours a day.

   a. What is the total labor cost associated with the process?

   b. If steps 7, 10, 12, and 15 were eliminated, estimate the annual labor savings associated with implementing this new process.

15. A time study of an employee assembling peanut valves resulted in the following set of observations. What is the standard time, given a performance rating of 95 percent and an allowance of 20 percent of the total normal time?

Average Time (seconds)	Observations
15	14
20	12
25	15

16. An initial time study was done on a process with the following results (in minutes). Based on the data obtained so far, assuming an allowance of 20 percent of the normal

time, what do you estimate for the time per customer served, based on this preliminary sample?

Element	Performance Rating	Obs 1	Obs 2	Obs 3	Obs 4	Obs 5
Element 1	70	4	3	5	4	3
Element 2	110	8	10	9	11	10
Element 3	90	6	8	7	7	6

17. A work sampling study was conducted to determine the proportion of the time a worker is idle. The following information was gathered on a random basis:

Day	Number of Times Worker Idle	Total Number of Observations
Monday	17	44
Tuesday	18	56
Wednesday	14	48
Thursday	16	60

   a. Based on these preliminary results, what percent of the time is the worker working?

   b. If idle time is judged to be excessive, what additional categories might you add to a follow-up work sampling study to identify the root causes?

18. A contractor is preparing a bid to install swimming pools at a new housing addition. The estimated time to build the first pool is 35 hours. The contractor estimates an 85 percent learning rate. Without using the computer:

a. How long do you estimate the time required to install the second pool?

b. How long do you estimate the time required to install the fourth pool?

19. Return to Problem 18. Using OM Explorer's *Learning Curves* Solver, how long do you estimate the time required to install the fifth pool? What is your estimate of the total time for all five pools?

20. The manager of Perrotti's Pizza collects data concerning customer complaints about pizza delivery. Either the pizza arrives late, or the wrong pizza is delivered.

Problem	Frequency
Topping is stuck to box lid	17
Pizza arrives late	35
Wrong topping or combination	9
Wrong style of crust	6
Wrong size	4
Pizza is partially eaten	3
Pizza never arrives	6

a. Use a Pareto chart to identify the "vital few" delivery problems. Comment on potential root causes of these problems and identify any especially egregious quality failures.

b. The manager of Perrotti's Pizza is attempting to understand the root causes of late pizza delivery and has asked each driver to keep a log of specific difficulties that create late deliveries. After one week, the logs included the following entries:

delivery vehicle broke down, couldn't make it across town to deliver second pizza in time, couldn't deliver four pizzas to four different customers in time, kitchen was late in producing order, got lost, order ticket was lost in production, couldn't read address on ticket and went to wrong house.

Organize these causes into a cause-and-effect diagram.

21. Smith, Schroeder, and Torn (SST) is a short-haul household furniture moving company. SST's labor force, selected from the local community college football team, is temporary and part-time. SST is concerned with recent complaints, as tabulated on the following tally sheet:

Complaint	Tally
Broken glass	⦀⦀ ⦀⦀ ⦀⦀⦀
Delivered to wrong address	⦀⦀ ⦀⦀⦀⦀
Furniture rubbed together while on truck	⦀⦀ ⦀⦀ ⦀⦀ ⦀⦀
Late delivery	⦀⦀
Late arrival for pickup	⦀⦀ ⦀⦀ ⦀⦀ ⦀⦀⦀
Missing items	⦀⦀ ⦀⦀ ⦀⦀ ⦀⦀ ⦀⦀⦀ ⦀
Nicks and scratches from rough handling	⦀⦀ ⦀⦀
Soiled upholstery	⦀⦀ ⦀⦀⦀

a. Draw a bar chart and a Pareto chart using OM Explorer to identify the most serious moving problems.

b. The manager of Smith, Schroeder, and Torn is attempting to understand the root causes of complaints. He has compiled the following list of issues that occurred during problem deliveries.

truck broke down, ran out of packing boxes, multiple deliveries in one day caused truck to be late, no furniture pads, employee dropped several items, drive got lost on route to address, ramp into truck was bent, no packing tape, new employee doesn't know how to pack, moving dolly has broken wheel, employee late to work

Organize these causes into a cause-and-effect diagram.

22. Rick DeNeefe, manager of the Golden Valley Bank credit authorization department, recently noticed that a major competitor was advertising that applications for equity loans could be approved within two working days. Because fast credit approval was a competitive priority, De-Neefe wanted to see how well his department was doing relative to the competitor's. Golden Valley stamps each application with the date and time it is received and again when a decision is made. A total of 104 applications were received in March. The time required for each decision, rounded to the nearest hour, is shown in the following table. Golden Valley's employees work 8 hours per day.

Decision Process Time (hours)	Frequency
8	8
11	19
14	28
17	10
20	25
23	4
26	10
Total	104

a. Draw a bar chart for these data.

b. Analyze the data. How is Golden Valley Bank doing with regard to this competitive priority?

23. Last year, the manager of the service department at East Woods Ford instituted a customer opinion program to find out how to improve service. One week after service on a vehicle was performed, an assistant would call the customer to find out whether the work had been done satisfactorily and how service could be improved. After one year of gathering data, the assistant discovered that the complaints could be grouped into the following five categories:

Complaint	Frequency
Unfriendly atmosphere	5
Long wait for service	17
Price too high	20
Incorrect bill	8
Needed to return to correct problem	50
Total	100

a. Use OM Explorer to draw a bar chart and a Pareto chart to identify the significant service problems.

b. Categorize the following causes of complaints into a cause-and-effect diagram: tools, scheduling, defective parts, training, billing system, performance measures, diagnostic equipment, and communications.

24. Oregon Fiber Board makes roof liners for the automotive industry. The manufacturing manager is concerned about product quality. She suspects that one particular failure, tears in the fabric, is related to production-run size. An assistant gathers the following data from production records:

Run	Size	Failures (%)	Run	Size	Failures (%)
1	1,000	3.5	11	6,500	1.5
2	4,100	3.8	12	1,000	5.5
3	2,000	5.5	13	7,000	1.0
4	6,000	1.9	14	3,000	4.5
5	6,800	2.0	15	2,200	4.2
6	3,000	3.2	16	1,800	6.0
7	2,000	3.8	17	5,400	2.0
8	1,200	4.2	18	5,800	2.0
9	5,000	3.8	19	1,000	6.2
10	3,800	3.0	20	1,500	7.0

a. Draw a scatter diagram for these data.

b. Does there appear to be a relationship between run size and percent failures? What implications does this data have for Oregon Fiber Board's business?

25. Grindwell, Inc., a manufacturer of grinding tools, is concerned about the durability of its products, which depends on the permeability of the sinter mixtures used in production. Suspecting that the carbon content might be the source of the problem, the plant manager collected the following data:

Carbon Content (%)	Permeability Index
5.5	16
3.0	31
4.5	21
4.8	19
4.2	16
4.7	23
5.1	20
4.4	11
3.6	20

a. Draw a scatter diagram for these data.

b. Is there a relationship between permeability and carbon content?

c. If low permeability is desirable, what does the scatter diagram suggest with regard to the carbon content?

26. The operations manager for Superfast Airlines at Chicago's O'Hare Airport noticed an increase in the number of delayed flight departures. She brainstormed possible causes with her staff:

■ Aircraft late to gate

■ Acceptance of late passengers

■ Passengers arriving late at gate

■ Passenger processing delays at gate

■ Late baggage to aircraft

■ Other late personnel or unavailable items

■ Mechanical failures

Draw a cause-and-effect diagram to organize the possible causes of delayed flight departures into the following major categories: equipment, personnel, material, procedures, and "other factors" beyond managerial control. Provide a detailed set of causes for each major cause identified by the operations manager, and incorporate them in your cause-and-effect diagram.

27. Plastomer, Inc. specializes in the manufacture of high-grade plastic film used to wrap food products. Film is rejected and scrapped for a variety of reasons (e.g., opacity, high carbon content, incorrect thickness or gauge, scratches, and so on). During the past month, management collected data on the types of rejects and the amount of scrap generated by each type. The following table presents the results:

Type of Failure	Amount of Scrap (lbs.)
Air bubbles	500
Bubble breaks	19,650
Carbon content	150
Unevenness	3,810
Thickness or gauge	27,600
Opacity	450
Scratches	3,840
Trim	500
Wrinkles	10,650

Draw a Pareto chart to identify which type of failure management should attempt to eliminate first.

28. Management of a shampoo bottling company introduced a new 13.5-ounce pack and used an existing machine, with some modifications, to fill it. To measure filling consistency by the modified machine (set to fill 13.85 ounces), an analyst collected the following data (volume in ounces) for a random sample of 100 bottles:

a. Draw a histogram for these data.

b. Bottles with less than 12.85 ounces or more than 14.85 ounces are considered to be out of specification. Based on the sample data, what percentage of the bottles filled by the machine will be out of specification?

Bottle Volume (ounces)									
13.0	13.3	13.6	13.2	14.0	12.9	14.2	12.9	14.5	13.5
14.1	14.0	13.7	13.4	14.4	14.3	14.8	13.9	13.5	14.3
14.2	14.1	14.0	13.9	13.9	14.0	14.5	13.6	13.3	12.9
12.8	13.1	13.6	14.5	14.6	12.9	13.1	14.4	14.0	14.4
13.1	14.1	14.2	12.9	13.3	14.0	14.1	13.1	13.6	13.7
14.0	13.6	13.2	13.4	13.9	14.5	14.0	14.4	13.9	14.6
12.9	14.3	14.0	12.9	14.2	14.8	14.5	13.1	12.7	13.9
13.6	14.4	13.1	14.5	13.5	13.3	14.0	13.6	13.5	14.3
13.2	13.8	13.7	12.8	13.4	13.8	13.3	13.7	14.1	13.7
13.7	13.8	13.4	13.7	14.1	12.8	13.7	13.8	14.1	14.3

Advanced Problems

29. This problem should be solved as a team exercise:

Shaving is a process that most men perform each morning. Assume that the process begins at the bathroom sink with the shaver walking (say, 5 feet) to the cabinet (where his shaving supplies are stored) to pick up bowl, soap, brush, and razor. He walks back to the sink, runs the water until it gets warm, lathers his face, shaves, and inspects the results. Then, he rinses the razor, dries his face, walks over to the cabinet to return the bowl, soap, brush, and razor, and comes back to the sink to clean it up and complete the process.

a. Develop a process chart for shaving. (Assume suitable values for the time required for the various activities involved in the process.)

b. Brainstorm to generate ideas for improving the shaving process. Having fewer than 20 ideas is unacceptable. (Do not try to evaluate the ideas until the group has compiled as complete a list as possible. Otherwise, judgment will block creativity.)

30. At Conner Company, a custom manufacturer of printed circuit boards, the finished boards are subjected to a final inspection prior to shipment to its customers. As Conner's quality assurance manager, you are responsible for making a presentation to management on quality problems at the beginning of each month. Your assistant has analyzed the reject memos for all the circuit boards that were rejected during the past month. He has given you a summary statement listing the reference number of the circuit board and the reason for rejection from one of the following categories:

A = Poor electrolyte coverage

B = Improper lamination

C = Low copper plating

D = Plating separation

E = Improper etching

For 50 circuit boards that had been rejected last month, the summary statement showed the following:

C B C C D E C C B A D A C C C B C A C D C A C C B

A C A C B C C A C A A C C D A C C C E C C A B A C

a. Prepare a tally sheet (or checklist) of the different reasons for rejection.

b. Develop a Pareto chart to identify the more significant types of rejection.

c. Examine the causes of the most significant type of defect, using a cause-and-effect diagram.

Active Model Exercise

This Active Model appears in MyOMLab. Continuing on with Example 8.2, it allows you to evaluate the structure of a Pareto chart.

QUESTIONS

1. What percentage of overall complaints does discourteous service account for?

2. What percentage of overall complaints do the three most common complaints account for?

3. How does it affect the chart if we eliminate discourteous service?

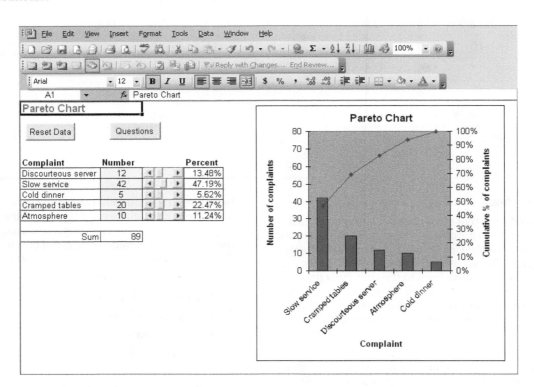

The features and layout of The Phoenician property of Starwood Hotels and Resorts at Scottsdale, Arizona, are shown in the following figure. Starwood Hotels and Resorts is no stranger to process improvement. In fact, the president's letter in a recent annual report stated that through "... benchmarking, Six Sigma, and recognition of excellence, [Starwood is] driving results in a virtual cycle of self-improvement at all levels of the Company." Recognizing that improved processes in one department of a single hotel, if rolled out across the organization, could lead to significant improvements, the company recently created a program called the "Power of Innovation," or POI.

The Power of Innovation program in Starwood seeks to capture best practices that exist throughout hotels across all brands in North America. An internal team with expertise in kitchen preparation and production, laundry, stewarding, front office, and housekeeping works with individual properties to build upon and maximize the existing knowledge of local property management teams. The team usually spends about a week on property entrenched in operations to really see day-to-day activity over an extended period. Of particular interest is scheduling the workforce to meet the demand of each hotel's individual operations while streamlining operations processes.

At the Westin Galleria-Oaks in Houston, Texas, for example, the POI team helped management achieve a 6 percent productivity improvement in the kitchen preparation and production job, with a reduction of 2,404 hours used and $23,320 in annual payroll savings alone. At the same time, other POI projects at the hotel generated an additional $14,400 in annual payroll savings.

The Phoenician in Scottsdale also had a visit from the POI team. One area the team focused on was stewarding. The typical stewarding process includes the following duties: dishwashing, kitchen trash removal, polishing silver, and assisting with banquet meal food prep lines. Stewards support eight kitchens and two bakeries, and work with housekeeping in keeping public areas, such as restrooms and pool cabanas, clean.

A flowchart that diagrams the existing stewarding process that the team documented is shown in the figure. In any given day, a particular steward may provide support to more than one kitchen, and be called upon to do a variety of tasks.

Before the POI team arrived, stewards were dedicated to a particular kitchen or area during their shift. Each kitchen required stewarding coverage as outlined by the executive chef, so more than one steward may be assigned to an area. A certain amount of stewarding work could be forecast

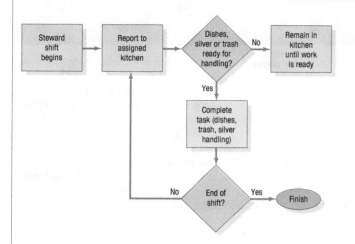

by the food and beverage manager, based on scheduled banquets, afternoon teas, conference buffets, and restaurant reservations. Considerable uncertainty also arose from traffic generated by leisure travelers and local clientele, meaning that stewards assigned to designated areas periodically did not have a steady flow of work.

On a weekly basis, activity levels for the dedicated stewarding staff were determined, based on executive chef input. Other factors considered in the weekly planning included prior year activity, special events and holidays, and number of children. With this information, the executive steward created a summary of all meals, called covers, by location, date, and time of day. Then, an Excel spreadsheet template was used to create the schedule for deployment of stewarding staff throughout the resort's kitchens and restaurants.

In performing its analysis, the POI team examined staff availability, banquet events, restaurants, occupied room counts, and other drivers of business to areas supported by stewards. Time studies were done to determine how far stewards were traveling throughout the property, and how long it

took to perform each stewarding task. Some restaurants and kitchens did not require full-time coverage by a steward, so the steward would be assigned multiple kitchens to fill a work shift. In the case of coverage between the 19th Hole restaurant on one side of the resort, and the Canyon Building on the other side, that steward would walk one-half mile, one way, to take care of duties in both locations because they lacked enough work for a dedicated steward in each location.

Often, stewards had downtime as they waited for banquet dishes to be cleared, or kitchen pots and utensils to be brought in for cleaning. Some restaurants had china with special cleaning requirements, meaning those dishes had to be handwashed instead of being placed in an automated sanitizing dishwasher. This situation required a dedicated steward to perform that task.

Time studies revealed how long it took stewards to move from one kitchen to the next. The studies also helped the POI team understand how long it took to wash dishes in the five-star restaurant versus the casual poolside dining area's kitchen. Additionally, the studies uncovered building design and landscaping limitations that prevented staff from moving between kitchens quickly. In some cases, a maze of corridors added miles to the distances covered each day, and thick privacy hedges barred entry to sidewalk shortcuts.

QUESTIONS

1. How can the management specifically improve the stewarding process at The Phoenician? Using the information provided, create a flowchart illustrating the new process.

2. What are the benefits that the POI program can bring to Starwood? Can these benefits be extended to other processes and properties within the Starwood system?

3. Of the seven mistakes organizations can make when managing processes (see last section of this chapter), which ones might Starwood be most at risk of making? Why?

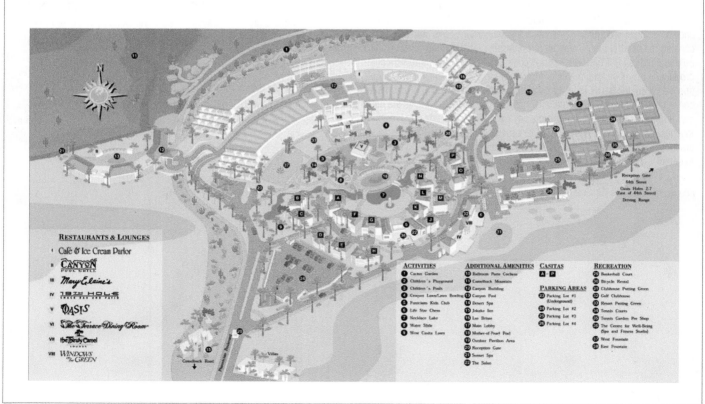

CASE   José's Authentic Mexican Restaurant

"Two bean tacos, a chicken burrito grande, and a side order of Spanish rice, please." Ivan Karetski called his table's order into the kitchen as he prepared the beverage orders. Business was brisk. Karetski liked it that way. Lots of customers meant lots of tips and, as a struggling graduate student, the extra income was greatly appreciated. Lately, however, his tips had been declining.

José's is a small, 58-seat restaurant that offers a reasonably broad range of Mexican food prepared and presented in a traditional Mexican style. It is located in New England in a mature business district on the edge of a large metropolitan area. The site is adjacent to a central artery and offers limited free off-street parking. The restaurant's interior decoration promotes the Mexican theme: The walls appear to be made of adobe and are draped with serapes, the furniture is Spanish–Mexican style, and flamenco guitar and mariachi alternate as background music.

Patrons enter the restaurant through a small vestibule that opens directly into the dining area; there is no separate waiting area. Upon arrival, patrons are greeted by a hostess and either seated directly or apprised of the expected wait. Seating at José's is usually immediate except for Friday and Saturday nights when waits of as long as 45 minutes can be encountered. Because space inside for waiting is very limited, patrons must remain outside until their party is called. José's does not take reservations.

After seating patrons, the hostess distributes menus and fills glasses with water. If standards are being met, the waiter assigned to the table greets the patrons within one minute of their being seated. (Being a traditional Mexican restaurant, its entire wait staff is male.) The waiter introduces himself, announces the daily specials, and takes the beverage orders. After delivering the beverages, the waiter takes the meal orders.

The menu consists of 23 main entrees assembled from eight basic stocks (chicken, beef, beans, rice, corn tortillas, flour tortillas, tomatoes, and lettuce) and a variety of other ingredients (fruits, vegetables, sauces, herbs, and spices). Before the dining hours begin, the cook prepares the basic stocks so that they can be quickly combined and finished off to complete the requested meals. The typical amount of time needed to complete a meal once it has been ordered is 12 minutes. A good portion of this time is for final cooking, so several meals may be in preparation at the same time. As can be imagined, one of the skills a good cook needs is to be able to schedule production of the various meals ordered at a table so that they are ready at approximately the same time. Once all the meals and any side dishes have been completed by the cook, the waiter checks to see that all meals are correct and pleasing to the eye, corrects any mistakes, and adds any finishing touches. When everything is in order, he assembles them on a tray and delivers them to the table. From this point on, the waiter keeps an eye on the table to detect when any additional service or assistance is needed.

When the diners at the table appear to be substantially finished with their main meal, the waiter approaches, asks if he can clear away any dishes, and takes any requests for dessert or coffee. When the entire meal has been completed, the waiter presents the bill and shortly thereafter collects payment. José's accepts cash or major credit card, but no checks.

Karetski feels that his relationship with the cook is important. As the cook largely controls the quality of the food, Karetski wants to stay on good terms with him. He treats the cook with respect, tries to place the items on his order slip in the sequence of longest preparation time, and makes sure to write clearly so that the orders are easy to read. Although it is not his job, he helps out by fetching food stocks from the refrigerator or the storage area when the cook is busy and by doing some of the food preparation himself. The cook has been irritable lately, complaining of the poor quality of some of the ingredients that have been delivered. Last week, for example, he received lettuce that appeared wilted and chicken that was tough and more bone than meat. During peak times, it can take more than 20 minutes to get good meals delivered to the table.

Karetski had been shown the results of a customer survey that management conducted last Friday and Saturday during the evening mealtime. The following table shows a summary of the responses:

Customer Survey Results		
Were you seated promptly?	Yes: 70	No: 13
Was your waiter satisfactory?	Yes: 73	No: 10
Were you served in a reasonable time?	Yes: 58	No: 25
Was your food enjoyable?	Yes: 72	No: 11
Was your dining experience worth the cost?	Yes: 67	No: 16

As Karetski carried the tray of drinks to the table, he wondered whether the recent falloff in tips was due to anything that he could control.

QUESTIONS

1. How should quality be defined at this restaurant?
2. What are the restaurant's costs of process failures?
3. Use some of the tools for process analysis to assess the situation at José's.

Source: This case was prepared by Larry Meile, Boston College, as a basis for classroom discussion. By permission of Larry Meile.

Selected References

Andersen, Bjørn. *Business Process Improvement Toolbox*. 2nd ed. Milwaukee, Wiscconsin: American Society for Quality, 2007.

Ahire, Sanjay L. and Manoj. K. Malhotra. "Scripting a Holistic Rx for Process Improvement at Palmetto Health Imaging Centers." *Journal of Global Business and Organizational Excellence*, vol. 30, no. 2 (January/February 2011), pp. 23–35.

Bhuiyan, Nadjia, Amit Baghel, Jim Wilson. "A Sustainable Continuous Improvement Methodology at an Aerospace Company," *International Journal of Productivity and Performance Management*, vol. 55, no. 8 (2006), pp. 671–687.

Carey, Susan. "Case of the Vanishing Airport Lines." *Wall Street Journal* (August 9, 2007).

Davenport, Thomas H. "The Coming Commoditization of Processes." *Harvard Business Review*, (June 2005), pp. 101–108.

Edmondson, Amy C. "The Competitive Imperative of Learning." *Harvard Business Review*, vol. 86 (July August, 2008), pp. 1–13.

Fisher, Anne. "Get Employees to Brainstorm Online." *Fortune*, vol. 150, no. 11 (November 2004), p. 72.

Fleming, John H., Curt Coffman, and James K. Harter. "Manage Your Human Sigma." *Harvard Business Review*, (July–August 2005), pp. 101–108.

Greasley, A. "Using Process Mapping and Business Process Simulation to Support a Process-Based Approach to Change in a Public Sector Organisation." *Technovation*, 26 (2006), pp. 95–103.

Grosskopf, Alexander, Gero Decker, and Mathias Weske. *The Process: Business Process Modelling Using BPMN*. Tampa, Florida: Meghan-Kiffer Press, 2009.

Hammer, Michael. "The Process Audit." *Harvard Business Review*, vol. 82, no. 4 (April 2007), pp. 111–123.

Hammer, Michael. "What is Business Process Management?" *Handbook on Business Process Management 1*, 2010, pp. 3–16.

Hartvigsen, David. *SimQuick: Process Simulation with Excel*, 2nd ed. Upper Saddle River, NJ: Prentice Hall, 2004.

Jain, Rashmi, Angappa Gunasekaran, and Anithashree Chandrasekaran. "Evolving Role of Process Reengineering: A Perspective of Employers." *Industrial and Commercial Training*, vol. 41, no. 7 (2009), pp. 382–390.

Jeston, John and Johan Nelis. *Management by Process: A Roadmap to Sustainable Business Process Management*, Oxford, UK: Elsevier, 2008.

Karmarkar, Uday. "Will You Survive the Services Revolution?" *Harvard Business Review*, vol. 82, no. 6 (June 2004), pp. 100–107.

Kulpa, Margaret, K. and Kent A. Johnson. *Interpeting the CMMI: A Process Improvement Approach*, 2nd ed. Boca Raton, FL: Auerbach Publications, 2008.

La Ferla, Beverly. "Mapping the Way to Process Improvement." *IEE Engineering Management* (December 2004–January 2005), pp. 16–17.

Lee, Hau L. "The Triple-A Supply Chain." *Harvard Business Review* (October 2004), pp. 102–112.

Rummler, Geary A., and Alan P. Brache. *Improving Performance*, 2nd ed. San Francisco: Jossey-Bass Inc., 1995.

Scott, Bradley, S., Anne E. Wilcock, and Vinay Kanetkar. "A Survey of Structured Continuous Improvement Programs in the Canadian Food Sector." *Food Control*, vol. 20 (2009), 209–217.

B

WAITING LINES

Anyone who has ever waited at a stoplight, at McDonald's, or at the registrar's office has experienced the dynamics of waiting lines. Perhaps one of the best examples of effective management of waiting lines is that of Walt Disney World. One day the park may have only 25,000 customers, but on another day the numbers may top 90,000. Careful analysis of process flows, technology for people-mover (materials handling) equipment, capacity, and layout keeps the waiting times for attractions to acceptable levels.

The analysis of waiting lines is of concern to managers because it affects process design, capacity planning, process performance, and ultimately, supply chain performance. In this supplement we discuss why waiting lines form, the uses of waiting-line models in operations management, and the structure of waiting-line models. We also discuss the decisions managers address with the models. Waiting lines can also be analyzed using computer simulation. Software such as SimQuick, a simulation package included in MyOMLab, or Excel spreadsheets can be used to analyze the problems in this supplement.

MyOMLab

Why Waiting Lines Form

A **waiting line** is one or more "customers" waiting for service. The customers can be people or inanimate objects, such as machines requiring maintenance, sales orders waiting for shipping, or inventory items waiting to be used. A waiting line forms because of a temporary imbalance between the demand for service and the capacity of the system to provide the service. In most real-life waiting-line problems, the demand rate varies; that is, customers arrive at unpredictable intervals. Most often, the rate of producing the service also varies, depending on customer needs. Suppose that bank customers arrive at an average rate of 15 per hour throughout the day and that

waiting line
One or more "customers" waiting for service.

LEARNING GOALS *After reading this supplement, you should be able to:*

1. Identify the elements of a waiting-line problem in a real situation.

2. Describe the single-server, multiple-server, and finite-source models.

3. Explain how to use waiting-line models to estimate the operating characteristics of a process.

4. Describe the situations where simulation should be used for waiting line analysis and the nature of the information that can be obtained.

5. Explain how waiting-line models can be used to make managerial decisions.

the bank can process an average of 20 customers per hour. Why would a waiting line ever develop? The answers are that the customer arrival rate varies throughout the day and the time required to process a customer can vary. During the noon hour, 30 customers may arrive at the bank. Some of them may have complicated transactions requiring above-average process times. The waiting line may grow to 15 customers for a period of time before it eventually disappears. Even though the bank manager provided for more than enough capacity on average, waiting lines can still develop.

Waiting lines can develop even if the time to process a customer is constant. For example, a subway train is computer controlled to arrive at stations along its route. Each train is programmed to arrive at a station, say, every 15 minutes. Even with the constant service time, waiting lines develop while riders wait for the next train or cannot get on a train because of the size of the crowd at a busy time of the day. Consequently, variability in the rate of demand determines the sizes of the waiting lines in this case. In general, if no variability in the demand or service rate occurs and enough capacity is provided, no waiting lines form.

Uses of Waiting-Line Theory

Waiting-line theory applies to service as well as manufacturing firms, relating customer arrival and service-system processing characteristics to service-system output characteristics. In our discussion, we use the term *service* broadly—the act of doing work for a customer. The service system might be hair cutting at a hair salon, satisfying customer complaints, or processing a production order of parts on a certain machine. Other examples of customers and services include lines of theatergoers waiting to purchase tickets, trucks waiting to be unloaded at a warehouse, machines waiting to be repaired by a maintenance crew, and patients waiting to be examined by a physician. Regardless of the situation, waiting-line problems have several common elements.

Structure of Waiting-Line Problems

Analyzing waiting-line problems begins with a description of the situation's basic elements. Each specific situation will have different characteristics, but four elements are common to all situations:

1. An input, or **customer population**, that generates potential customers
2. A waiting line of customers
3. The **service facility**, consisting of a person (or crew), a machine (or group of machines), or both necessary to perform the service for the customer
4. A **priority rule**, which selects the next customer to be served by the service facility

Figure B.1 shows these basic elements. The triangles, circles, and squares are intended to show a diversity of customers with different needs. The **service system** describes the number of lines and the arrangement of the facilities. After the service has been performed, the served customers leave the system.

Customer Population

A customer population is the source of input to the service system. If the potential number of new customers for the service system is appreciably affected by the number of customers already in the system, the input source is said to be *finite*. For example, suppose that a maintenance crew is assigned responsibility for the repair of 10 machines. The customer population for the

customer population

An input that generates potential customers.

service facility

A person (or crew), a machine (or group of machines), or both necessary to perform the service for the customer.

priority rule

A rule that selects the next customer to be served by the service facility.

service system

The number of lines and the arrangement of the facilities.

FIGURE B.1 ▶
Basic Elements of Waiting-Line Models

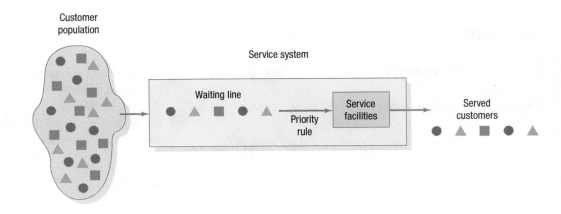

maintenance crew is 10 machines in working order. The population generates customers for the maintenance crew as a function of the failure rates for the machines. As more machines fail and enter the service system, either waiting for service or being repaired, the customer population becomes smaller and the rate at which it can generate another customer falls. Consequently, the customer population is said to be finite.

Alternatively, an *infinite* customer population is one in which the number of customers in the system does not affect the rate at which the population generates new customers. For example, consider a mail-order operation for which the customer population consists of shoppers who have received a catalog of products sold by the company. Because the customer population is so large and only a small fraction of the shoppers place orders at any one time, the number of new orders it generates is not appreciably affected by the number of orders waiting for service or being processed by the service system. In this case, the customer population is said to be infinite.

Customers in waiting lines may be *patient* or *impatient*, which has nothing to do with the colorful language a customer may use while waiting in line for a long time on a hot day. In the context of waiting-line problems, a patient customer is one who enters the system and remains there until being served; an impatient customer is one who either decides not to enter the system (balks) or leaves the system before being served (reneges). For the methods used in this supplement, we make the simplifying assumption that all customers are patient.

The Service System

The service system may be described by the number of lines and the arrangement of facilities.

Number of Lines   Waiting lines may be designed to be a *single line* or *multiple lines*. Figure B.2 shows an example of each arrangement. Generally, single lines are utilized at airline counters, inside banks, and at some fast-food restaurants; whereas multiple

Sometimes customers are not organized neatly into lines. Here ships wait to use the port facilities in Victoria Harbor, West Kowloon, Hong Kong.

Islemount Images/Alamy

lines are utilized in grocery stores, at drive-in bank operations, and in discount stores. When multiple servers are available and each one can handle general transactions, the single-line arrangement keeps servers uniformly busy and gives customers a sense of fairness. Customers believe that they are being served on the basis of when they arrived, and not on how well they guessed their waiting time when selecting a particular line. The multiple-line design is best when some of the servers provide a limited set of services. In this arrangement, customers select the services they need and wait in the line where that service is provided, such as at a grocery store that provides special lines for customers paying with cash or having fewer than 10 items.

Sometimes customers are not organized neatly into "lines." Machines that need repair on the production floor of a factory may be left in place, and the maintenance crew comes to them. Nonetheless, we can think of such machines as forming a single line or multiple lines, depending on the number of repair crews and their specialties. Likewise, passengers who telephone for a taxi also form a line even though they may wait at different locations.

Arrangement of Service Facilities   Service facilities consist of the personnel and equipment necessary to perform the service for the customer. Service facility arrangement is described by the number of channels and phases. A **channel** is one or more facilities required to perform a given service. A **phase** is a single step in providing the service. Some services require a single phase, while others require a sequence of phases. Consequently, a service facility uses some combination

channel

One or more facilities required to perform a given service.

phase

A single step in providing a service.

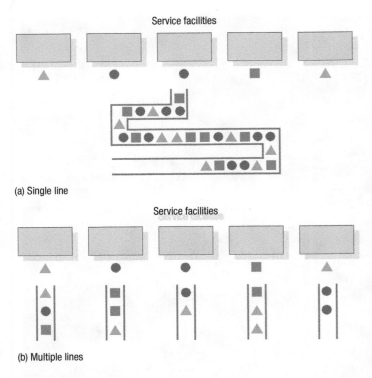

FIGURE B.2 ▲
Waiting-Line Arrangements

of channels and phases. Managers should choose an arrangement based on customer volume and the nature of services provided. Figure B.3 shows examples of the five basic types of service facility arrangements.

In the *single-channel, single-phase* system, all services demanded by a customer can be performed by a single-server facility. Customers form a single line and go through the service facility one at a time. Examples are a drive-through car wash and a machine that must process several batches of parts.

The *single-channel, multiple-phase* arrangement is used when the services are best performed in sequence by more than one facility, yet customer volume or other constraints limit the design to one channel. Customers form a single line and proceed sequentially from one service facility to the next. An example of this arrangement is a McDonald's drive-through, where the first facility takes the order, the second takes the money, and the third provides the food.

The *multiple-channel, single-phase* arrangement is used when demand is large enough to warrant providing the same service at more than one facility or when the services offered by the facilities are different. Customers form one or more lines, depending on the design. In the single-line design, customers are served by the first available server, as in the lobby of a bank. If each channel has its own waiting line, customers wait until the server for their line can serve them, as at a bank's drive-through facilities.

The *multiple-channel, multiple-phase* arrangement occurs when customers can be served by one of the first-phase facilities but then require service from a second-phase facility, and so on. In some cases, customers cannot switch channels after service has begun; in others they can. An example of this arrangement is a laundromat. Washing machines are the first-phase facilities, and dryers are the second-phase facilities. Some of the washing machines and dryers may be designed for extra-large loads, thereby providing the customer a choice of channels.

The most complex waiting-line problem involves customers who have unique sequences of required services; consequently, service cannot be described neatly in phases. A *mixed* arrangement is used in such a case. In the mixed arrangement, waiting lines can develop in front of each facility, as in a medical center, where a patient goes to an exam room for a nurse to take his or her blood pressure and weight, goes back to the waiting room until the doctor can see him or her, and

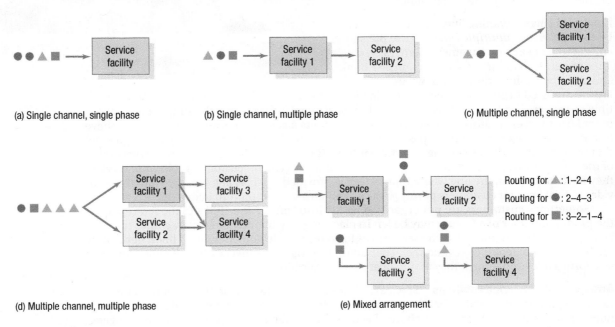

FIGURE B.3 ▲
Examples of Service Facility Arrangements

after consultation proceeds to the laboratory to give a blood sample, radiology to have an X–ray taken, or the pharmacy for prescribed drugs, depending on specific needs.

Priority Rule

The priority rule determines which customer to serve next. Most service systems that you encounter use the first-come, first-served (FCFS) rule. The customer at the head of the waiting line has the highest priority, and the customer who arrived last has the lowest priority. Other priority disciplines might take the customer with the earliest promised due date (EDD) or the customer with the shortest expected processing time (SPT).[1]

A **preemptive discipline** is a rule that allows a customer of higher priority to interrupt the service of another customer. For example, in a hospital emergency room, patients with the most life-threatening injuries receive treatment first, regardless of their order of arrival. Modeling of systems having complex priority disciplines is usually done using computer simulation.

preemptive discipline
A rule that allows a customer of higher priority to interrupt the service of another customer.

Probability Distributions

The sources of variation in waiting-line problems come from the random arrivals of customers and the variations in service times. Each of these sources can be described with a probability distribution.

Arrival Distribution

Customers arrive at service facilities randomly. The variability of customer arrivals often can be described by a Poisson distribution, which specifies the probability that n customers will arrive in T time periods:

$$P_n = \frac{(\lambda T)^n}{n!}e^{-\lambda T} \text{ for } n = 0,1,2,\dots$$

where

P_n = probability of n arrivals in T time periods

λ = average number of customer arrivals per period

e = 2.7183

The mean of the Poisson distribution is λT, and the variance also is λT. The Poisson distribution is a discrete distribution; that is, the probabilities are for a specific number of arrivals per unit of time.

EXAMPLE B.1	**Calculating the Probability of Customer Arrivals**

Management is redesigning the customer service process in a large department store. Accommodating four customers is important. Customers arrive at the desk at the rate of two customers per hour. What is the probability that four customers will arrive during any hour?

SOLUTION

In this case $\lambda = 2$ customers per hour, $T = 1$ hour, and $n = 4$ customers. The probability that four customers will arrive in any hour is

$$P_4 = \frac{[2(1)]^4}{4!}e^{-2(1)} = \frac{16}{24}e^{-2} = 0.090$$

DECISION POINT

The manager of the customer service desk can use this information to determine the space requirements for the desk and waiting area. There is a relatively small probability that four customers will arrive in any hour. Consequently, seating capacity for two or three customers should be more than adequate unless the time to service each customer is lengthy. Further analysis on service times is warranted.

---

[1]We focus on FCFS in this supplement. See Chapter 4, "Operations Planning and Scheduling," for additional discussion of FCFS and EDD. See also Supplement J, "Operations Scheduling," for SPT and additional rules.

interarrival times

The time between customer arrivals.

Another way to specify the arrival distribution is to do it in terms of customer **interarrival times**—that is, the time between customer arrivals. If the customer population generates customers according to a Poisson distribution, the *exponential distribution* describes the probability that the next customer will arrive in the next T time periods. As the exponential distribution also describes service times, we discuss the details of this distribution in the next section.

Service Time Distribution

The exponential distribution describes the probability that the service time of the customer at a particular facility will be no more than T time periods. The probability can be calculated by using the formula

$$P(t \leq T) = 1 - e^{-\mu T}$$

where

μ = average number of customers completing service per period

t = service time of the customer

T = target service time

The mean of the service time distribution is $1/\mu$, and the variance is $(1/\mu)^2$. As T increases, the probability that the customer's service time will be less than T approaches 1.0.

For simplicity, let us look at a single-channel, single-phase arrangement.

EXAMPLE B.2	Calculating the Service Time Probability

The management of the large department store in Example B.1 must determine whether more training is needed for the customer service clerk. The clerk at the customer service desk can serve an average of three customers per hour. What is the probability that a customer will require less than 10 minutes of service?

SOLUTION

We must have all the data in the same time units. Because $\mu = 3$ customers per hour, we convert minutes of time to hours, or $T = 10$ minutes $= 10/60$ hour $= 0.167$ hour. Then

$$P(t \leq T) = 1 - e^{-\mu T}$$
$$P(t \leq 0.167 \text{ hour}) = 1 - e^{-3(0.167)} = 1 - 0.61 = 0.39$$

DECISION POINT

The probability that the customer will require only 10 minutes or fewer is not high, which leaves the possibility that customers may experience lengthy delays. Management should consider additional training for the clerk so as to reduce the time it takes to process a customer request.

Some characteristics of the exponential distribution do not always conform to an actual situation. The exponential distribution model is based on the assumption that each service time is independent of those that preceded it. In real life, however, productivity may improve as human servers learn about the work. Another assumption underlying the model is that very small, as well as very large, service times are possible. However, real-life situations often require a fixed-length start-up time, some cutoff on total service time, or nearly constant service time.

Using Waiting-Line Models to Analyze Operations

Operations managers can use waiting-line models to balance the gains that might be made by increasing the efficiency of the service system against the costs of doing so. In addition, managers should consider the costs of *not* making improvements to the system: Long waiting lines or long waiting times may cause customers to balk or renege. Managers should therefore be concerned about the following operating characteristics of the system.

1. *Line Length.* The number of customers in the waiting line reflects one of two conditions. Short lines could mean either good customer service or too much capacity. Similarly, long lines could indicate either low server efficiency or the need to increase capacity.

2. *Number of Customers in System.* The number of customers in line and being served also relates to service efficiency and capacity. A large number of customers in the system causes congestion and may result in customer dissatisfaction, unless more capacity is added.

3. *Waiting Time in Line.* Long lines do not always mean long waiting times. If the service rate is fast, a long line can be served efficiently. However, when waiting time seems long, customers perceive the quality of service to be poor. Managers may try to change the arrival rate of customers or design the system to make long wait times seem shorter than they really are. For example, at Walt Disney World, customers in line for an attraction are entertained by videos and also are informed about expected waiting times, which seems to help them endure the wait.

4. *Total Time in System.* The total elapsed time from entry into the system until exit from the system may indicate problems with customers, server efficiency, or capacity. If some customers are spending too much time in the service system, it may be necessary to change the priority discipline, increase productivity, or adjust capacity in some way.

5. *Service Facility Utilization.* The collective utilization of service facilities reflects the percentage of time that they are busy. Management's goal is to maintain high utilization and profitability without adversely affecting the other operating characteristics.

The best method for analyzing a waiting-line problem is to relate the five operating characteristics and their alternatives to dollars. However, placing a dollar figure on certain characteristics (such as the waiting time of a shopper in a grocery store) is difficult. In such cases, an analyst must weigh the cost of implementing the alternative under consideration against a subjective assessment of the cost of *not* making the change.

We now present three models and some examples showing how waiting-line models can help operations managers make decisions. We analyze problems requiring the single-server, multiple-server, and finite-source models, all of which are single phase. References to more advanced models are cited at the end of this supplement.

Single-Server Model

The simplest waiting-line model involves a single server and a single line of customers. To further specify the model, we make the following assumptions:

1. The customer population is infinite and all customers are patient.

2. The customers arrive according to a Poisson distribution, with a mean arrival rate of λ.

3. The service distribution is exponential, with a mean service rate of μ.

4. The mean service rate exceeds the mean arrival rate.

5. Customers are served on a first-come, first-served basis.

6. The length of the waiting line is unlimited.

With these assumptions, we can apply various formulas to describe the operating characteristics of the system:

Visitors to Disney MGM Studios, Disney World, Orlando, Florida patiently wait in line for the Aerosmith Rock N Roller Coaster ride, which is an example of a single-channel, single-phase system.

Melvyn Longhurst/Alamy

ρ = Average utilization of the system

$$= \frac{\lambda}{\mu}$$

P_n = Probability that n customers are in the system

$$= (1 - \rho)\rho^n$$

L = Average number of customers in the service system

$$= \frac{\lambda}{\mu - \lambda}$$

L_q = Average number of customers in the waiting line

$$= \rho L$$

W = Average time spent in the system, including service

$$= \frac{1}{\mu - \lambda}$$

W_q = Average waiting time in line

$$= \rho W$$

EXAMPLE B.3 — Calculating the Operating Characteristics of a Single-Channel, Single-Phase System

MyOMLab

Active Model B.1 in MyOMLab provides additional insight on the single-server model and its uses for this problem.

The manager of a grocery store in the retirement community of Sunnyville is interested in providing good service to the senior citizens who shop in her store. Currently, the store has a separate checkout counter for senior citizens. On average, 30 senior citizens per hour arrive at the counter, according to a Poisson distribution, and are served at an average rate of 35 customers per hour, with exponential service times. Find the following operating characteristics:

a. Probability of zero customers in the system

b. Average utilization of the checkout clerk

c. Average number of customers in the system

d. Average number of customers in line

e. Average time spent in the system

f. Average waiting time in line

SOLUTION

The checkout counter can be modeled as a single-channel, single-phase system. Figure B.4 shows the results from the *Waiting-Lines* Solver from OM Explorer. Manual calculations of the equations for the *single-server model* are demonstrated in the Solved Problem at the end of the supplement.

FIGURE B.4 ▶
Waiting-Lines Solver for Single-Channel, Single-Phase System

		(Number of servers s assumed to be 1 in single-serve model)
Servers		
Arrival Rate (λ)	30	
Service Rate (μ)	35	

Probability of zero customers in the system (P_0)	0.1429
Probability of exactly ▼ 0 customers in the system	0.1429
Average utilization of the server (ρ)	0.8571
Average number of customers in the system (L)	6.0000
Average number of customers in line (L_q)	5.1429
Average waiting/service time in the system (W)	0.2000
Average waiting time in line (W_q)	0.1714

Both the average waiting time in the system (W) and the average time spent waiting in line (W_q) are expressed in hours. To convert the results to minutes, simply multiply by 60 minutes/hour. For example, $W = 0.20(60) = 12.00$ minutes, and $W_q = 0.1714(60) = 10.28$ minutes.

EXAMPLE B.4 — Analyzing Service Rates with the Single-Server Model

MyOMLab

Tutor B.1 in MyOMLab provides a new example to practice the single-server model.

The manager of the Sunnyville grocery in Example B.3 wants answers to the following questions:

a. What service rate would be required so that customers averaged only 8 minutes in the system?

b. For that service rate, what is the probability of having more than four customers in the system?

c. What service rate would be required to have only a 10 percent chance of exceeding four customers in the system?

SOLUTION

The *Waiting-Lines* Solver from OM Explorer could be used iteratively to answer the questions. Here we show how to solve the problem manually.

a. We use the equation for the average time in the system and solve for μ.

$$W = \frac{1}{\mu - \lambda}$$

$$8 \text{ minutes} = 0.133 \text{ hour} = \frac{1}{\mu - 30}$$

$$0.133\mu - 0.133(30) = 1$$

$$\mu = 37.52 \text{ customers/hour}$$

b. The probability of more than four customers in the system equals 1 minus the probability of four or fewer customers in the system.

$$P = 1 - \sum_{n=0}^{4} P_n$$

$$= 1 - \sum_{n=0}^{4} (1 - \rho)\rho^n$$

and

$$\rho = \frac{30}{37.52} = 0.80$$

Then,

$$P = 1 - 0.2(1 + 0.8 + 0.8^2 + 0.8^3 + 0.8^4)$$

$$= 1 - 0.672 = 0.328$$

Therefore, there is a nearly 33 percent chance that more than four customers will be in the system.

c. We use the same logic as in part (b), except that μ is now a decision variable. The easiest way to proceed is to find the correct average utilization first, and then solve for the service rate.

$$P = 1 - (1 - \rho)(1 + \rho + \rho^2 + \rho^3 + \rho^4)$$

$$= 1 - (1 + \rho + \rho^2 + \rho^3 + \rho^4) + \rho(1 + \rho + \rho^2 + \rho^3 + \rho^4)$$

$$= 1 - 1 - \rho - \rho^2 - \rho^3 - \rho^4 + \rho + \rho^2 + \rho^3 + \rho^4 + \rho^5$$

$$= \rho^5$$

or

$$\rho = P^{1/5}$$

If $P = 0.10$,

$$\rho = (0.10)^{1/5} = 0.63$$

Therefore, for a utilization rate of 63 percent, the probability of more than four customers in the system is 10 percent. For $\lambda = 30$, the mean service rate must be

$$\frac{30}{\mu} = 0.63$$

$$\mu = 47.62 \text{ customers/hour}$$

DECISION POINT
The service rate would only have to increase modestly to achieve the 8-minute target. However, the probability of having more than four customers in the system is too high. The manager must now find a way to increase the service rate from 35 per hour to approximately 48 per hour. She can increase the service rate in several different ways, ranging from employing a high school student to help bag the groceries to installing self checkout stations.

Multiple-Server Model

With the multiple-server model, customers form a single line and choose one of s servers when one is available. The service system has only one phase. We make the following assumptions in addition to those for the single-server model: There are s identical servers, and the service distribution for each server is exponential, with a mean service time of $1/\mu$. It should always be the case that $s\mu$ exceeds λ.

EXAMPLE B.5	Estimating Idle Time and Hourly Operating Costs with the Multiple-Server Model

The management of the American Parcel Service terminal in Verona, Wisconsin, is concerned about the amount of time the company's trucks are idle (not delivering on the road), which the company defines as waiting to be unloaded and being unloaded at the terminal. The terminal operates with four unloading bays. Each bay requires a crew of two employees, and each crew costs $30 per hour. The estimated cost of an idle truck is $50 per hour. Trucks arrive at an average rate of three per hour, according to a Poisson distribution. On average, a crew can unload a semitrailer rig in one hour, with exponential service times. What is the total hourly cost of operating the system?

MyOMLab

Tutor B.2 in MyOMLab provides a new example to practice the multiple-server model.

SOLUTION

The *multiple-server model* for $s = 4$, $\mu = 1$, and $\lambda = 3$ is appropriate. To find the total cost of labor and idle trucks, we must calculate the average number of trucks in the system at all times.

Figure B.5 shows the results for the American Parcel Service problem using the *Waiting-Lines* Solver from OM Explorer. The results show that the four-bay design will be utilized 75 percent of the time and that the average number of trucks either being serviced or waiting in line is 4.53 trucks. That is, on average at any point in time, we have 4.53 idle trucks. We can now calculate the hourly costs of labor and idle trucks:

Labor cost:	$\$30(s) = \$30(4) = \$120.00$
Idle truck cost:	$\$50(L) = \$50(4.53) = \$226.50$
	Total hourly cost $= \$346.50$

FIGURE B.5 ▶
Waiting-Lines Solver for Multiple-Server Model

Servers	4
Arrival Rate (λ)	3
Service Rate (μ)	1

Probability of zero customers in the system (P_0)	0.0377
Probability of ⌄ exactly ▼ 0 customers in the system	0.0377
Average utilization of the servers (p)	0.7500
Average number of customers in the system (L)	4.5283
Average number of customers in line (L_q)	1.5283
Average waiting/service time in the system (W)	1.5094
Average waiting time in line (W_q)	0.5094

DECISION POINT

Management must now assess whether $346.50 per day for this operation is acceptable. Attempting to reduce costs by eliminating crews will only increase the waiting time of the trucks, which is more expensive per hour than the crews. However, the service rate can be increased through better work methods; for example, L can be reduced and daily operating costs will be less.

Little's Law

Little's law

A fundamental law that relates the number of customers in a waiting-line system to the arrival rate and waiting time of customers.

One of the most practical and fundamental laws in waiting-line theory is **Little's law**, which relates the number of customers in a waiting-line system to the arrival rate and the waiting time of customers. Using the same notation we used for the single-server model, Little's law can be expressed as $L = \lambda W$ or $L_q = \lambda W_q$. However, this relationship holds for a wide variety of arrival processes, service-time distributions, and numbers of servers. The practical advantage of Little's law is that you only need to know two of the parameters to estimate the third. For example, consider the manager of a motor vehicle licensing facility who receives many complaints about the time people must spend either having their licenses renewed or getting new license plates. It would be difficult to obtain data on the times individual customers spend at the facility. However, the manager can have an assistant monitor the number of people who arrive at the facility each hour and compute the average (λ). The manager also could periodically count the number of people in the sitting area and at the stations being served and compute the average (L). Using Little's law, the manager can then estimate W, the average time each customer spent in the facility. For example, if 40 customers arrive per hour and the average number of customers being served or waiting is 30, the average time each customer spends in the facility can be computed as

$$\text{Average time in the facility} = W = \frac{L \text{ customers}}{\lambda \text{ customers/ hour}} = \frac{30}{40} = 0.75 \text{ hours, or 45 minutes}$$

If the time a customer spends at the facility is unreasonable, the manager can focus on either adding capacity or improving the work methods to reduce the time spent serving the customers.

Likewise, Little's law can be used for manufacturing processes. Suppose that a production manager knows the average time a unit of product spends at a manufacturing process (W) and the average number of units per hour that arrive at the process (λ). The production manager can then estimate the average work-in-process (L) using Little's law. *Work-in-process* (WIP) consists of items, such as components or assemblies, needed to produce a final product in manufacturing.

Cars line up at the Triborough Bridge toll, New York City. This is an example of a multiple-channel, single-phase system, where some channels are devoted to special services.

For example, if the average time a gear case used for an outboard marine motor spends at a machine center is 3 hours, and an average of five gear cases arrive at the machine center per hour, the average number of gear cases waiting and being processed (or work-in-process) at the machine center can be calculated as

$$\text{Work-in-process} = L = \lambda W = 5 \text{ gear cases/hour (3 hours)} = 15 \text{ gear cases}$$

Knowing the relationship between the arrival rate, the lead time, and the work-in-process, the manager has a basis for measuring the effects of process improvements on the work-in-process at the facility. For example, adding some capacity to a bottleneck in the process can reduce the average lead time of the product at the process, thereby reducing the work-in-process inventory.

Even though Little's law is applicable in many situations in both service and manufacturing environments, it is not applicable in situations where the customer population is finite, which we address next.

Finite-Source Model

We now consider a situation in which all but one of the assumptions of the single-server model are appropriate. In this case, the customer population is finite, having only N potential customers. If N is greater than 30 customers, the single-server model with the assumption of an infinite customer population is adequate. Otherwise, the finite-source model is the one to use.

EXAMPLE B.6	**Analyzing Maintenance Costs with the Finite-Source Model**

The Worthington Gear Company installed a bank of 10 robots about 3 years ago. The robots greatly increased the firm's labor productivity, but recently attention has focused on maintenance. The firm does no preventive maintenance on the robots because of the variability in the breakdown distribution. Each machine has an exponential breakdown (or interarrival) distribution with an average time between failures of 200 hours. Each machine hour lost to downtime costs $30, which means that the firm has to react quickly to machine failure. The firm employs one maintenance person, who needs 10 hours on average to fix a robot. Actual maintenance times are exponentially distributed. The wage rate is $10 per hour for the maintenance person, who can be put to work productively elsewhere when not fixing robots. Determine the daily cost of labor and robot downtime.

SOLUTION

The *finite-source model* is appropriate for this analysis because the customer population consists of only 10 machines and the other assumptions are satisfied. Here, $\lambda = 1/200$, or 0.005 break-down per hour, and $\mu = 1/10 = 0.10$ robot per hour. To calculate the cost of labor and robot downtime, we need to estimate the average utilization of the maintenance person and L, the average number of robots in the maintenance system at any time. Either OM Explorer or POM for Windows can be used to help with the calculations. Figure B.6

MyOMLab

Tutor B.3 in MyOMLab provides a new example to practice the finite-source model.

MyOMLab

Active Model B.3 in MyOMLab provides additional insight on the finite-source model and its uses for this problem.

shows the results for the Worthington Gear Problem using the *Waiting-Lines* Solver from OM Explorer. The results show that the maintenance person is utilized only 46.2 percent of the time, and the average number of robots waiting in line or being repaired is 0.76 robot. However, a failed robot will spend an average of 16.43 hours in the repair system, of which 6.43 hours of that time is spent waiting for service. While an individual robot may spend more than 2 days with the maintenance person, the maintenance person has a lot of idle time with a utilization rate of only 42.6 percent. That is why there is only an average of 0.76 robot being maintained at any point of time.

FIGURE B.6 ▶
Waiting-Lines Solver for
Finite-Source Model

Customers	10
Arrival Rate (λ)	0.005
Service Rate (μ)	0.1

Probability of zero customers in the system (P_0)	0.5380
Probability of [fewer than ▾] 0 customers in the system	#N/A
Average utilization of the server (p)	0.4620
Average number of customers in the system (L)	0.7593
Average number of customers in line (L_q)	0.2972
Average waiting/service time in the system (W)	16.4330
Average waiting time in line (W_q)	6.4330

The daily cost of labor and robot downtime is

Labor cost:	($10/hour)(8 hours/day)(0.462 utilization)	= $ 36.96
Idle robot cost:	(0.76 robot)($30/robot hour)(8 hours/day)	= 182.40
	Total daily cost	= $219.36

DECISION POINT

The labor cost for robot repair is only 20 percent of the idle cost of the robots. Management might consider having a second repair person on call in the event two or more robots are waiting for repair at the same time.

Waiting Lines and Simulation

For each of the problems we analyzed with the waiting-line models, the arrivals had a Poisson distribution (or exponential interarrival times), the service times had an exponential distribution, the service facilities had a simple arrangement, the waiting line was unlimited, and the priority discipline was first-come, first-served. Waiting-line theory has been used to develop other models in which these criteria are not met, but these models are complex. For example, POM for Windows includes a finite system-size model in which limits can be placed on the size of the system (waiting line and server capacity). It also has several models that relax assumptions on the service time distribution. Nonetheless, many times the nature of the customer population, the constraints on the line, the priority rule, the service-time distribution, and the arrangement of the facilities are such that waiting-line theory is no longer useful. In these cases, simulation often is used. MyOMLab Supplement E, "Simulation," discusses simulation programming languages and powerful PC-based packages. Here we illustrate process simulation with the SimQuick software (also provided in MyOMLab).

SimQuick   SimQuick is an easy-to-use package that is simply an Excel spreadsheet with some macros. Models can be created for a variety of simple processes, such as waiting lines, inventory control, and projects. Here, we consider the passenger security process at one terminal of a medium-sized airport between the hours of 8 A.M. and 10 A.M. The process works as follows. Passengers arriving at the security area immediately enter a single line. After waiting in line, each passenger goes through one of two inspection stations, which involves walking through a metal detector and running any carry-on baggage through a scanner. After completing this inspection, 10 percent of the passengers are randomly selected for an additional inspection, which involves a pat-down and a more thorough search of the person's

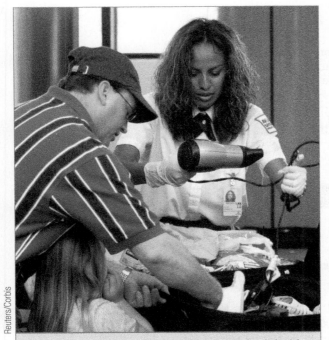

A passenger, randomly selected for additional screening, helps LA International Airport security personnel examine his luggage. The airport security process is a multiple-channel, multiple-phase system.

carry-on baggage. Two stations handle this additional inspection, and selected passengers go through only one of them. Management is interested in examining the effect of increasing the percentage of passengers who undergo the second inspection. In particular, they want to compare the waiting times for the second inspection when 10 percent, then 15 percent, and then 20 percent of the passengers are randomly selected for this inspection. Management also wants to know how opening a third station for the second inspection would affect these waiting times.

A first step in simulating this process with SimQuick is to draw a flowchart of the process using SimQuick's building blocks. SimQuick has five building blocks that can be combined in a wide variety of ways. Four of these types are used to model this process. An *entrance* is used to model the arrival of passengers at the security process. A *buffer* is used to model each of the two waiting lines, one before each type of inspection, as well as the passengers that have finished the process. Each of the four inspection stations is modeled with a *workstation*. Finally, the random selection of passengers for the second inspection is modeled with a *decision point*. Figure B.7 shows the flowchart.

Information describing each building block is entered into SimQuick tables. In this model, three key types of information are entered: (1) when people arrive at the entrance, (2) how long inspections take at the four stations, and (3) what percentage of passengers are randomly selected for the additional inspection. All of this information must be entered into SimQuick in the form of statistical distributions. The first two types of information are determined by observing the real process from 8 A.M. and 10 A.M. The third type of information is a policy decision (10 percent, 15 percent, or 20 percent).

The original model is run 30 times, simulating the arrival of passengers during the hours from 8 A.M. to 10 A.M. Statistics are collected by SimQuick and summarized. Figure B.8 provides some key results for the model of the present process as output by SimQuick (many other statistics are collected, but not displayed here).

The numbers shown are averages across the 30 simulations. The number 237.23 is the average number of passengers that enter line 1 during the simulated two hours. The two mean inventory statistics tell us, on average, 5.97 simulated passengers were standing in line 1 and 0.10 standing in line 2. The two statistics on *cycle time*, interpreted here as the time a passenger spends in one or more SimQuick building blocks, tell us that the simulated passengers in line 1 waited an average of 3.12 minutes, while those in line 2 waited 0.53 minutes. The final inventory statistic tells us that, on average, 224.57 simulated passengers passed through the security process in the simulated two hours. The next step is to change the percentage of simulated passengers selected for the second inspection to 15 percent, and then to 20 percent, and rerun the model. Of course, these process changes will increase the average waiting time for the second inspection, but by how much? The final step is to rerun these simulations with one more workstation and see its effect on the waiting time for the second inspection. All the details for this model (as well as many others) appear in the book *SimQuick: Process Simulation with Excel*, which is included, along with the SimQuick software, in MyOMLab.

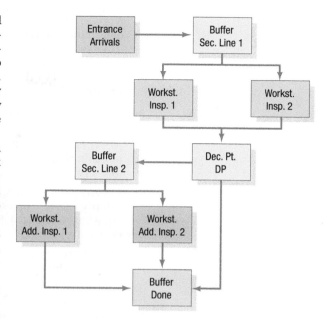

FIGURE B.7 ▲
Flowchart of Passenger Security Process

Element Types	Element Names	Statistics	Overall Means
Entrance(s)	Door	Objects entering process	237.23
Buffer(s)	Line 1	Mean inventory	5.97
		Mean cycle time	3.12
	Line 2	Mean inventory	0.10
		Mean cycle time	0.53
	Done	Final inventory	224.57

FIGURE B.8 ▲
Simulation Results of Passenger Security Process

MyOMLab

Decision Areas for Management

After analyzing a waiting-line problem, management can improve the service system by making changes in one or more of the following areas.

1. *Arrival Rates.*   Management often can affect the rate of customer arrivals, λ, through advertising, special promotions, or differential pricing. For example, hotels in the Caribbean will reduce their room rates during the hot, rainy season to attract more customers and increase their utilization.

2. *Number of Service Facilities.*   By increasing the number of service facilities, such as tool cribs, toll booths, or bank tellers, or by dedicating some facilities in a phase to a unique set of services, management can increase system capacity.

3. *Number of Phases.*   Managers can decide to allocate service tasks to sequential phases if they determine that two sequential service facilities may be more efficient than one. For instance, in assembly lines a decision concerns the number of phases or workers needed along the assembly line. Determining the number of workers needed on the line also involves assigning a certain set of work elements to each one. Changing the facility arrangement can increase the service rate, μ, of each facility and the capacity of the system.

4. *Number of Servers per Facility.*   Managers can influence the service rate by assigning more than one person to a service facility.

5. *Server Efficiency.*   By adjusting the capital-to-labor ratio, devising improved work methods, or instituting incentive programs, management can increase the efficiency of servers assigned to a service facility. Such changes are reflected in μ.

6. *Priority Rule.*   Managers set the priority rule to be used, decide whether to have a different priority rule for each service facility, and decide whether to allow preemption (and, if so, under what conditions). Such decisions affect the waiting times of the customers and the utilization of the servers.

7. *Line Arrangement.*   Managers can influence customer waiting times and server utilization by deciding whether to have a single line or a line for each facility in a given phase of service.

Obviously, these factors are interrelated. An adjustment in the customer arrival rate might have to be accompanied by an increase in the service rate, λ, in some way. Decisions about the number of facilities, the number of phases, and waiting-line arrangements also are related.

LEARNING GOALS IN REVIEW

1 **Identify the elements of a waiting-line problem in a real situation.** The section "Structure of Waiting-Line Problems," pp. 320–323, defines the four elements of every waiting-line problem. Figures B.1, B.2, and B.3 depict these elements and various service facility arrangements.

2 **Describe the single-server, multiple-server, and finite-source models.** See the section "Using Waiting-Line Models to Analyze Operations," pp. 324–330, for a description and demonstration of these three models. Examples B.3, B.4 and the Solved Problem at the end of the supplement apply the single-server model. Example B.5 shows the multiple-server model and Example B.6 applies the finite-source model.

3 **Explain how to use waiting-line models to estimate the operating characteristics of a process.** Examples B.3 through

B.6 show how to obtain estimates for the important operating characteristics of processes using waiting-line models.

4 **Describe the situations where simulation should be used for waiting line analysis and the nature of the information that can be obtained.** The section "Waiting Lines and Simulation," pp. 330–331, explains when simulation must be used and discusses an example that demonstrates the nature of the managerial information that can be obtained from that analysis.

5 **Explain how waiting-line models can be used to make managerial decisions.** The section "Decision Areas for Management," pp. 331–332, describes seven decision areas that can be analyzed with waiting-line models.

MyOMLab helps you develop analytical skills and assesses your progress with multiple problems on utilization rate, probability of more than *n* customers in the system, number of customers waiting, probability of no customers in the system, average number of customers in the system, and service rate to keep average number of customers to a certain level.

MyOMLab Resources	Titles	Link to the Book
Video	*1st Bank Villa Italia: Waiting Lines*	Entire supplement
Active Model Exercise	B.1 Single-Server Model	Single-Server Model; Example B.3 (p. 326)
	B.2 Multiple-Server Model with Costs	Multiple-Server Model; Example B.5 (p. 327)
	B.3 Finite-Source Model with Costs	Finite-Source Model; Example B.6 (p. 329)
OM Explorer Solvers	Single-Server Model	Single-Server Model; Example B.3 (p. 326); Figure B.4 (p. 326)
	Multiple-Server Model	Multiple-Server Model; Example B.5 (p. 327); Figure B.5 (p. 328)
	Finite-Source Model	Finite-Source Model; Example B.6 (p. 329); Figure B.6 (p. 330)

MyOMLab Resources	Titles	Link to the Book
OM Explorer Tutors	B.1 Single-Server Waiting-Line Model B.2 Multi-Server Model B.3 Finite Source	Single-Server Model; Example B.3 (p. 326) Multiple-Server Model; Example B.5 (p. 327) Finite-Source Model; Example B.6 (p. 329)
POM for Windows	B.1 Single-Server Model B.2 Multiple-Server Model with Costs B.3 Finite-Source Model with Costs B.4 Finite System-Size Model	Single-Server Model; Example B.3 (p. 326) Multiple-Server Model; Example B.5 (p. 327) Finite-Source Model; Example B.6 (p. 329) Using Waiting-Line Models to Analyze Operations
Virtual Tours	New York City Fire Department	Entire supplement
Internet Exercise	Surfing the net on Google	Structure of Waiting Lines
Online Text	SimQuick: Process Simulation with Excel, 2e	Waiting Lines and Simulation; Figure B.7 (p. 331); Figure B.8 (p. 331)
Key Equations		
Image Library		

Key Equations

1. Customer arrival Poisson distribution:

$$P_n = \frac{(\lambda T)^n}{n!} e^{-\lambda T}$$

2. Service time exponential distribution:

$$P(t \leq T) = 1 - e^{-\mu T}$$

3. Average utilization of the system:

$$\rho = \frac{\lambda}{\mu}$$

4. Probability that n customers are in the system:

$$P_n = (1 - \rho)\rho^n$$

5. Probability that zero customers are in the system:

$$P_0 = 1 - \rho$$

6. Average number of customers in the service system:

$$L = \frac{\lambda}{\mu - \lambda}$$

7. Average number of customers in the waiting line:

$$L_q = \rho L$$

8. Average time spent in the system, including service:

$$W = \frac{1}{\mu - \lambda}$$

9. Average waiting time in line:

$$W_q = \rho W$$

10. Little's Law

$$L = \lambda W$$

Key Terms

channel 321
customer population 320
interarrival times 324
Little's law 328

phase 321
preemptive discipline 323
priority rule 320
service facility 320

service system 320
waiting line 319

Solved Problem

A photographer takes passport pictures at an average rate of 20 pictures per hour. The photographer must wait until the customer smiles, so the time to take a picture is exponentially distributed. Customers arrive at a Poisson-distributed average rate of 19 customers per hour.

a. What is the utilization of the photographer?

b. How much time will the average customer spend with the photographer?

SOLUTION

a. The assumptions in the problem statement are consistent with a single-server model. Utilization is

$$\rho = \frac{\lambda}{\mu} = \frac{19}{20} = 0.95$$

b. The average customer time spent with the photographer is

$$W = \frac{1}{\mu - \lambda} = \frac{1}{20 - 19} = 1 \text{ hour}$$

Problems

The OM Explorer and POM for Windows software is available to all students using the 10th edition of this textbook. Go to **www.pearsonhighered.com/krajewski** to download these computer packages. If you purchased MyOMLab, you also have access to Active Models software and significant help in doing the following problems. Check with your instructor on how best to use these resources. In many cases, the instructor wants you to understand how to do the calculations by hand. At the least, the software provides a check on your calculations. When calculations are particularly complex and the goal is interpreting the results in making decisions, the software entirely replaces the manual calculations.

1. The Solomon, Smith, and Samson law firm produces many legal documents that must be word processed for clients and the firm. Requests average eight pages of documents per hour, and they arrive according to a Poisson distribution. The secretary can word process 10 pages per hour on average according to an exponential distribution.

   a. What is the average utilization rate of the secretary?

   b. What is the probability that more than four pages are waiting or being word processed?

   c. What is the average number of pages waiting to be word processed?

2. Benny's Arcade has six video game machines. The average time between machine failures is 50 hours. Jimmy, the maintenance engineer, can repair a machine in 15 hours on average. The machines have an exponential failure distribution, and Jimmy has an exponential service-time distribution.

   a. What is Jimmy's utilization?

   b. What is the average number of machines out of service, that is, waiting to be repaired or being repaired?

   c. What is the average time a machine is out of service?

3. Moore, Aiken, and Payne is a critical care dental clinic serving the emergency needs of the general public on a first-come, first-served basis. The clinic has five dental chairs, three of which are currently staffed by a dentist. Patients in distress arrive at the rate of five per hour, according to a Poisson distribution, and do not balk or renege. The average time required for an emergency treatment is 30 minutes, according to an exponential distribution. Use POM for Windows or OM Explorer to answer the following questions:

   a. If the clinic manager would like to ensure that patients do not spend more than 15 minutes on average waiting to see the dentist, are three dentists on staff adequate? If not, how many more dentists are required?

   b. From the current state of three dentists on staff, what is the change in each of the following operating characteristics when a fourth dentist is placed on staff:

   ■ Average utilization
   ■ Average number of customers in line
   ■ Average number of customers in the system

   c. From the current state of three dentists on staff, what is the change in each of the following operating characteristics when a fifth dentist is placed on staff:

- Average utilization
- Average number of customers in line
- Average number of customers in the system

4. Fantastic Styling Salon is run by three stylists, Jenny Perez, Jill Sloan, and Jerry Tiller, each capable of serving four customers per hour, on average. Use POM for Windows or OM Explorer to answer the following questions:

   During busy periods of the day, when nine customers on average arrive per hour, all three stylists are on staff.

   a. If all customers wait in a common line for the next available stylist, how long would a customer wait in line, on average, before being served?

   b. Suppose that each customer wants to be served by a specific stylist, 1/3 want Perez, 1/3 want Sloan, 1/3 want Tiller. How long would a customer wait in line, on average, before being served?

   During less busy periods of the day, when six customers on average arrive per hour, only Perez and Sloan are on staff.

   c. If all customers wait in a common line for the next available stylist, how long would a customer wait in line, on average, before being served?

   d. Suppose that each customer wants to be served by a specific stylist, 60 percent want Perez and 40 percent want Sloan. How long would a customer wait in line, on average, before being served by Perez? By Sloan? Overall?

5. You are the manager of a local bank where three tellers provide services to customers. On average, each teller takes 3 minutes to serve a customer. Customers arrive, on average, at a rate of 50 per hour. Having recently received complaints from some customers that they waited a long time before being served, your boss asks you to evaluate the service system. Specifically, you must provide answers to the following questions:

   a. What is the average utilization of the three-teller service system?

   b. What is the probability that no customers are being served by a teller or are waiting in line?

   c. What is the average number of customers waiting in line?

   d. On average, how long does a customer wait in line before being served?

   e. On average, how many customers would be at a teller's station and in line?

6. Pasquist Water Company (PWC) operates a 24-hour facility designed to efficiently fill water-hauling tanker trucks. Trucks arrive randomly to the facility and wait in line to access a wellhead pump. Since trucks vary in size and the filling operation is manually performed by the truck driver, the time to fill a truck is also random.

   a. If the manager of PWC uses the "multiple-server model" to calculate the operating characteristics of the facility's waiting line, list three assumptions she must make regarding the behavior of waiting trucks and the truck arrival process.

   b. Suppose an average of 336 trucks arrive each day, there are four wellhead pumps, and each pump can serve an average of four trucks per hour.

- What is the probability that exactly 10 trucks will arrive between 1:00 P.M. and 2:00 P.M. on any given day?
- How likely is it that once a truck is in position at a wellhead, the filling time will be less than 15 minutes?

   c. Contrast and comment on the performance differences between:

- One waiting line feeding all four stations.
- One waiting line feeding two wellhead pumps and a second waiting line feeding two other wellhead pumps. Assume that drivers cannot see each line and must choose randomly between them. Further, assume that once a choice is made, the driver cannot back out of the line.

7. The supervisor at the Precision Machine Shop wants to determine the staffing policy that minimizes total operating costs. The average arrival rate at the tool crib, where tools are dispensed to the workers, is eight machinists per hour. Each machinist's pay is $20 per hour. The supervisor can staff the crib either with a junior attendant who is paid $5 per hour and can process 10 arrivals per hour or with a senior attendant who is paid $12 per hour and can process 16 arrivals per hour. Which attendant should be selected, and what would be the total estimated hourly cost?

8. The daughter of the owner of a local hamburger restaurant is preparing to open a new fast-food restaurant called Hasty Burgers. Based on the arrival rates at her father's outlets, she expects customers to arrive at the drive-up window according to a Poisson distribution, with a mean of 20 customers per hour. The service rate is flexible; however, the service times are expected to follow an exponential distribution. The drive-in window is a single-server operation.

   a. What service rate is needed to keep the average number of customers in the service system (waiting line and being served) to four?

   b. For the service rate in part (a), what is the probability that more than four customers are in line and being served?

   c. For the service rate in part (a), what is the average waiting time in line for each customer? Does this average seem satisfactory for a fast-food business?

9. The manager of a branch office of Banco Mexicali observed that during peak hours an average of 20 customers arrives per hour and that there is an average of four customers in the branch office at any time. How long does the average customer spend waiting in line and being serviced?

10. Paula Caplin is manager of a major electronics repair facility owned by Fisher Electronics. Recently, top management expressed concern over the growth in the number of repair jobs in process at the facility. The average arrival rate is 120 jobs per day. The average job spends 4 days at the facility.

   a. What is the current work-in-process level at the facility?

   b. Suppose that top management has put a limit of one-half the current level of work-in-process. What goal must Paula establish and how might she accomplish it?

Advanced Problems

11. Failsafe Textiles employs three highly skilled maintenance workers who are responsible for repairing the numerous industrial robots used in its manufacturing process. A worker can fix one robot every 8 hours on average, with an exponential distribution. An average of one robot fails every 3 hours, according to a Poisson distribution. Each down robot costs the company $100.00 per hour in lost production. A new maintenance worker costs the company $80.00 per hour in salary, benefits, and equipment. Should the manager hire any new personnel? If so, how many people? What would you recommend to the manager, based on your analysis?

12. The College of Business and Public Administration at Benton University has a copy machine on each floor for faculty use. Heavy use of the five copy machines causes frequent failures. Maintenance records show that a machine fails every 2.5 days (or $\lambda = 0.40$ failure/day). The college has a maintenance contract with the authorized dealer of the copy machines. Because the copy machines fail so frequently, the dealer has assigned one person to the college to repair them. The person can repair an average of 2.5 machines per day. Using the finite-source model, answer the following questions:

    a. What is the average utilization of the maintenance person?

    b. On average, how many copy machines are being repaired or waiting to be repaired?

    c. What is the average time spent by a copy machine in the repair system (waiting and being repaired)?

13. You are in charge of a quarry that supplies sand and stone aggregates to your company's construction sites. Empty trucks from construction sites arrive at the quarry's huge piles of sand and stone aggregates and wait in line to enter the station, which can load either sand or aggregate. At the station, they are filled with material, weighed, checked out, and proceed to a construction site. Currently, nine empty trucks arrive per hour, on average. Once a truck has entered a loading station, it takes 6 minutes for it to be filled, weighed, and checked out. Concerned that trucks are spending too much time waiting and being filled, you are evaluating two alternatives to reduce the average time the trucks spend in the system. The first alternative is to add side boards to the trucks (so that more material could be loaded) and to add a helper at the loading station (so that filling time could be reduced) at a total cost of $50,000. The arrival rate of trucks would change to six per hour, and the filling time would be reduced to 4 minutes. The second alternative is to add another loading station identical to the current one at a cost of $80,000. The trucks would wait in a common line and the truck at the front of the line would move to the next available station.

    Which alternative would you recommend if you want to reduce the current average time the trucks spend in the system, including service?

Selected References

Cooper, Robert B. *Introduction to Queuing Theory*, 2nd ed. New York: Elsevier-North Holland, 1980.

Hartvigsen, David. *SimQuick: Process Simulation with Excel*, 2nd ed. Upper Saddle River, NJ: Prentice Hall, 2004.

Hillier, F.S., and G.S. Lieberman. *Introduction to Operations Research*, 2nd ed. San Francisco: Holden-Day, 1975.

Little, J.D.C. "A Proof for the Queuing Formula: $L = \lambda M$." *Operations Research*, vol. 9, (1961), pp. 383–387.

Moore, P.M. *Queues, Inventories and Maintenance*. New York: John Wiley & Sons, 1958.

Saaty, T.L. *Elements of Queuing Theory with Applications*. New York: McGraw-Hill, 1961.

NORMAL DISTRIBUTION

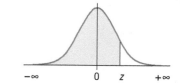

	.00	.01	.02	.03	.04	.05	.06	.07	.08	.09
.0	.5000	.5040	.5080	.5120	.5160	.5199	.5239	.5279	.5319	.5359
.1	.5398	.5438	.5478	.5517	.5557	.5596	.5636	.5675	.5714	.5753
.2	.5793	.5832	.5871	.5910	.5948	.5987	.6026	.6064	.6103	.6141
.3	.6179	.6217	.6255	.6293	.6331	.6368	.6406	.6443	.6480	.6517
.4	.6554	.6591	.6628	.6664	.6700	.6736	.6772	.6808	.6844	.6879
.5	.6915	.6950	.6985	.7019	.7054	.7088	.7123	.7157	.7190	.7224
.6	.7257	.7291	.7324	.7357	.7389	.7422	.7454	.7486	.7517	.7549
.7	.7580	.7611	.7642	.7673	.7704	.7734	.7764	.7794	.7823	.7852
.8	.7881	.7910	.7939	.7967	.7995	.8023	.8051	.8078	.8106	.8133
.9	.8159	.8186	.8212	.8238	.8264	.8289	.8315	.8340	.8365	.8389
1.0	.8413	.8438	.8461	.8485	.8508	.8531	.8554	.8577	.8599	.8621
1.1	.8643	.8665	.8686	.8708	.8729	.8749	.8770	.8790	.8810	.8830
1.2	.8849	.8869	.8888	.8907	.8925	.8944	.8962	.8980	.8997	.9015
1.3	.9032	.9049	.9066	.9082	.9099	.9115	.9131	.9147	.9162	.9177
1.4	.9192	.9207	.9222	.9236	.9251	.9265	.9279	.9292	.9306	.9319
1.5	.9332	.9345	.9357	.9370	.9382	.9394	.9406	.9418	.9429	.9441
1.6	.9452	.9463	.9474	.9484	.9495	.9505	.9515	.9525	.9535	.9545
1.7	.9554	.9564	.9573	.9582	.9591	.9599	.9608	.9616	.9625	.9633
1.8	.9641	.9649	.9656	.9664	.9671	.9678	.9686	.9693	.9699	.9706
1.9	.9713	.9719	.9726	.9732	.9738	.9744	.9750	.9756	.9761	.9767
2.0	.9772	.9778	.9783	.9788	.9793	.9798	.9803	.9808	.9812	.9817
2.1	.9821	.9826	.9830	.9834	.9838	.9842	.9846	.9850	.9854	.9857
2.2	.9861	.9864	.9868	.9871	.9875	.9878	.9881	.9884	.9887	.9890
2.3	.9893	.9896	.9898	.9901	.9904	.9906	.9909	.9911	.9913	.9916
2.4	.9918	.9920	.9922	.9925	.9927	.9929	.9931	.9932	.9934	.9936
2.5	.9938	.9940	.9941	.9943	.9945	.9946	.9948	.9949	.9951	.9952
2.6	.9953	.9955	.9956	.9957	.9959	.9960	.9961	.9962	.9963	.9964
2.7	.9965	.9966	.9967	.9968	.9969	.9970	.9971	.9972	.9973	.9974
2.8	.9974	.9975	.9976	.9977	.9977	.9978	.9979	.9979	.9980	.9981
2.9	.9981	.9982	.9982	.9983	.9984	.9984	.9985	.9985	.9986	.9986
3.0	.9987	.9987	.9987	.9988	.9988	.9989	.9989	.9989	.9990	.9990
3.1	.9990	.9991	.9991	.9991	.9992	.9992	.9992	.9992	.9993	.9993
3.2	.9993	.9993	.9994	.9994	.9994	.9994	.9994	.9995	.9995	.9995
3.3	.9995	.9995	.9995	.9996	.9996	.9996	.9996	.9996	.9996	.9997
3.4	.9997	.9997	.9997	.9997	.9997	.9997	.9997	.9997	.9997	.9998

Glossary

ABC analysis The process of dividing SKUs into three classes, according to their dollar usage, so that managers can focus on items that have the highest dollar value.

acceptable quality level (AQL) A statement of the proportion of defective items (outside of specifications) that the buyer will accept in a shipment.

acceptance sampling The application of statistical techniques to determine whether a quantity of material should be accepted or rejected based on the inspection or test of a sample.

action notice A computer-generated memo alerting planners about releasing new orders and adjusting the due dates of scheduled receipts.

activity The smallest unit of work effort consuming both time and resources that the project manager can schedule and control.

activity-on-node (AON) network An approach used to create a network diagram, in which nodes represent activities and arcs represent the precedence relationships between them.

activity slack The maximum length of time that an activity can be delayed without delaying the entire project, calculated as $S = LS - ES$ or $S = LF - EF$.

additive seasonal method A method in which seasonal forecasts are generated by adding a constant to the estimate of average demand per season.

advanced planning and scheduling (APS) systems Computer software systems that seek to optimize resources across the supply chain and align daily operations with strategic goals.

aggregate plan See sales and operations plan.

aggregation The act of clustering several similar services or products so that forecasts and plans can be made for whole families.

allowance time The time added to the normal time to adjust for certain factors.

annual plan or financial plan A plan for financial assessment used by a nonprofit service organization.

annuity A series of payments on a fixed amount for a specified number of years.

anticipation inventory Inventory used to absorb uneven rates of demand or supply.

appraisal costs Costs incurred when the firm assess the performance level of its processes.

assemble-to-order strategy A strategy for producing a wide variety of products from relatively few subassemblies and components after the customer orders are received.

assignable causes of variation Any variation-causing factors that can be identified and eliminated.

attributes Service or product characteristics that can be quickly counted for acceptable performance.

auction A marketplace where firms place competitive bids to buy something.

automation A system, process, or piece of equipment that is self-acting and self-regulating.

available-to-promise (ATP) inventory The quantity of end items that marketing can promise to deliver on specified dates.

average aggregate inventory value The total average value of all items held in inventory for a firm.

average outgoing quality (AOQ) The expressed proportion of defects that the plan will allow to pass.

average outgoing quality limit (AOQL) The maximum value of the average outgoing quality over all possible values of the proportion defective.

back office A process with low customer contact and little service customization.

backlog An accumulation of customer orders that a manufacturer has promised for delivery at some future date.

backorder A customer order that cannot be filled when promised or demanded but is filled later.

backorder and stockout Additional costs to expedite past-due orders, the costs of lost sales, and the potential cost of losing a customer to a competitor (sometimes called loss of goodwill).

backward integration A firm's movement upstream toward the sources of raw materials, parts, and services through acquisitions.

balance delay The amount by which efficiency falls short of 100 percent.

Baldrige Performance Excellence Program A program that promotes, recognizes, and publicizes quality strategies and achievements.

bar chart A series of bars representing the frequency of occurrence of data characteristics measured on a yes-or-no basis.

base case The act of doing nothing and losing orders from any demand that exceeds current capacity, or incur costs because capacity is too large.

base-stock system An inventory control system that issues a replenishment order, Q, each time a withdrawal is made, for the same amount of the withdrawal.

batch process A process that differs from the job process with respect to volume, variety, and quantity.

benchmarking A systematic procedure that measures a firm's processes, services, and products against those of industry leaders.

bill of materials (BOM)   A record of all the components of an item, the parent–component relationships, and the usage quantities derived from engineering and process designs.

bill of resources (BOR)   A record of a service firm's parent-component relationships and all of the materials, equipment time, staff, and other resources associated with them, including usage quantities.

binding constraint   A constraint that helps form the optimal corner point; it limits the ability to improve the objective function.

Black Belt   An employee who reached the highest level of training in a Six Sigma program and spends all of his or her time teaching and leading teams involved in Six Sigma projects.

block plan   A plan that allocates space and indicates placement of each operation.

bottleneck   A capacity constraint resource (CCR) whose available capacity limits the organization's ability to meet the product volume, product mix, or demand fluctuation required by the marketplace.

brainstorming   Letting a group of people, knowledgeable about the process, propose ideas for change by saying whatever comes to mind.

break-even analysis   The use of the break-even quantity; it can be used to compare processes by finding the volume at which two different processes have equal total costs.

break-even quantity   The volume at which total revenues equal total costs.

bullwhip effect   The phenomenon in supply chains whereby ordering patterns experience increasing variance as you proceed upstream in the chain.

business plan   A projected statement of income, costs, and profits.

c-**chart**   A chart used for controlling the number of defects when more than one defect can be present in a service or product.

capacity   The maximum rate of output of a process or a system.

capacity cushion   The amount of reserve capacity a process uses to handle sudden increases in demand or temporary losses of production capacity; it measures the amount by which the average utilization (in terms of total capacity) falls below 100 percent.

capacity gap   Positive or negative difference between projected demand and current capacity.

capacity requirement   What a process's capacity should be for some future time period to meet the demand of customers (external or internal), given the firm's desired capacity cushion.

capacity requirements planning (CRP)   A technique used for projecting time-phased capacity requirements for workstations; its purpose is to match the material requirements plan with the capacity of key processes.

capital intensity   The mix of equipment and human skills in a process.

carbon footprint   The total amount of greenhouse gasses produced to support operations, usually expressed in equivalent tons of carbon dioxide (CO_2).

cash flow   The difference between the flows of funds into and out of an organization over a period of time, including revenues, costs, and changes in assets and liabilities.

catalog hubs   A system whereby suppliers post their catalog of items on the Internet and buyers select what they need and purchase them electronically.

causal methods   A quantitative forecasting method that uses historical data on independent variables, such as promotional campaigns, economic conditions, and competitors' actions, to predict demand.

cause-and-effect diagram   A diagram that relates a key performance problem to its potential causes.

center of gravity   A good starting point to evaluate locations in the target area using the load–distance model.

centralized placement   Keeping all the inventory of a product at a single location such as a firm's manufacturing plant or a warehouse and shipping directly to each of its customers.

certainty   The word that is used to describe that a fact is known without doubt.

channel   One or more facilities required to perform a given service.

channel assembly   The process of using members of the distribution channel as if they were assembly stations in the factory.

chase strategy   A strategy that involves hiring and laying off employees to match the demand forecast.

checklist   A form used to record the frequency of occurrence of certain process failures.

close out   An activity that includes writing final reports, completing remaining deliverables, and compiling the team's recommendations for improving the project process.

closed-loop supply chain   A supply chain that integrates forward logistics with reverse logistics, thereby focusing on the complete chain of operations from the birth to the death of a product.

closeness matrix   A table that gives a measure of the relative importance of each pair of operations being located close together.

collaborative planning, forecasting, and replenishment (CPFR)   A nine-step process for supply chain integration that allows a supplier and its customers to collaborate on making the forecast by using the Internet.

combination forecasts   Forecasts that are produced by averaging independent forecasts based on different methods, different sources, or different data.

common causes of variation   The purely random, unidentifiable sources of variation that are unavoidable with the current process.

competitive capabilities The cost, quality, time, and flexibility dimensions that a process or supply chain actually possesses and is able to deliver.

competitive orientation A supplier relation that views negotiations between buyer and seller as a zero-sum game: Whatever one side loses, the other side gains, and short-term advantages are prized over long-term commitments.

competitive priorities The critical dimensions that a process or supply chain must possess to satisfy its internal or external customers, both now and in the future.

complementary products Services or products that have similar resource requirements but different demand cycles.

component An item that goes through one or more operations to be transformed into or become part of one or more parents.

compounding interest The process by which interest on an investment accumulates and then earns interest itself for the remainder of the investment period.

concurrent engineering A concept that brings product engineers, process engineers, marketers, buyers, information specialists, quality specialists, and suppliers together to design a product and the processes that will meet customer expectations.

consistent quality Producing services or products that meet design specifications on a consistent basis.

constraint Any factor that limits the performance of a system and restricts its output.

constraints In linear programming, the limitations that restrict the permissible choices for the decision variables.

consumer's risk (β) The probability of accepting a lot with LTPD quality (a type II error).

continuous flow process The extreme end of high-volume standardized production and rigid line flows, with production not starting and stopping for long time intervals.

continuous improvement The philosophy of continually seeking ways to improve processes based on a Japanese concept called *kaizen*.

continuous review (Q) system A system designed to track the remaining inventory of a SKU each time a withdrawal is made to determine whether it is time to reorder.

control chart A time-ordered diagram that is used to determine whether observed variations are abnormal.

cooperative orientation A supplier relation in which the buyer and seller are partners, each helping the other as much as possible.

core competencies The unique resources and strengths that an organization's management considers when formulating strategy.

core process A set of activities that delivers value to external customers.

corner point A point that lies at the intersection of two (or possibly more) constraint lines on the boundary of the feasible region.

crash cost (CC) The activity cost associated with the crash time.

crash time (CT) The shortest possible time to complete an activity.

critical mass A situation whereby several competing firms clustered in one location attract more customers than the total number who would shop at the same stores at scattered locations.

critical path The sequence of activities between a project's start and finish that takes the longest time to complete.

critical path method (CPM) A network planning method developed in the 1950s as a means of scheduling maintenance shutdowns at chemical-processing plants.

critical ratio (CR) A ratio that is calculated by dividing the time remaining until a job's due date by the total shop time remaining for the job, which is defined as the setup, processing, move, and expected waiting times of all remaining operations, including the operation being scheduled.

cross-docking The packing of products on incoming shipments so that they can be easily sorted at intermediate warehouses for outgoing shipments based on their final destinations; the items are carried from the incoming-vehicle docking point to the outgoing-vehicle docking point without being stored in inventory at the warehouse.

cumulative sum of forecast errors (CFE) A measurement of the total forecast error that assesses the bias in a forecast.

customer contact The extent to which the customer is present, is actively involved, and receives personal attention during the service process.

customer involvement The ways in which customers become part of the process and the extent of their participation.

customer population An input that generates potential customers.

customer relationship process A process that identifies, attracts, and builds relationships with external customers, and facilitates the placement of orders by customers; sometimes referred to as *customer relationship management*.

customization Satisfying the unique needs of each customer by changing service or product designs.

cycle counting An inventory control method, whereby storeroom personnel physically count a small percentage of the total number of items each day, correcting errors that they find.

cycle inventory The portion of total inventory that varies directly with lot size.

cycle-service level See service level.

cycle time The maximum time allowed for work on a unit at each station.

decision theory A general approach to decision making when the outcomes associated with alternatives are often in doubt.

decision tree A schematic model of alternatives available to the decision maker, along with their possible consequences.

decision variables Variables that represent the choices the decision maker can control.

defect Any instance when a process fails to satisfy its customer.

degeneracy A condition that occurs when the number of nonzero variables in the optimal solution is less than the number of constraints.

delivery speed Quickly filling a customer's order.

Delphi method A process of gaining consensus from a group of experts while maintaining their anonymity.

demand management The process of changing demand patterns using one or more demand options.

dependent demand The demand for an item that occurs because the quantity required varies with the production plans for other items held in the firm's inventory.

dependent variable The variable that one wants to forecast.

design team A group of knowledgeable, team-oriented individuals who work at one or more steps in the process, conduct the process analysis, and make the necessary changes.

development speed Quickly introducing a new service or a product.

discount rate The interest rate used in discounting the future value to its present value.

discounting The process of finding the present value of an investment when the future value and the interest rate are known.

diseconomies of scale Occurs when the average cost per unit increases as the facility's size increases.

distribution center A warehouse or stocking point where goods are stored for subsequent distribution to manufacturers, wholesalers, retailers, and customers.

double-sampling plan A plan in which management specifies two sample sizes and two acceptance numbers; if the quality of the lot is very good or very bad, the consumer can make a decision to accept or reject the lot on the basis of the first sample, which is smaller than in the single-sampling plan.

drum-buffer-rope (DBR) A planning and control system that regulates the flow of work-in-process materials at the bottleneck or the capacity constrained resource (CCR) in a productive system.

earliest due date (EDD) A priority sequencing rule that specifies that the job or customer with the earliest due date is the next job to be processed.

earliest finish time (EF) An activity's earliest start time plus its estimated duration, t, or $EF = ES + t$.

earliest start time (ES) The earliest finish time of the immediately preceding activity.

early supplier involvement A program that includes suppliers in the design phase of a service or product.

economic order quantity (EOQ) The lot size that minimizes total annual inventory holding and ordering costs.

economic production lot size (ELS) The optimal lot size in a situation in which replenishment is not instantaneous.

economies of scale A concept that states that the average unit cost of a service or good can be reduced by increasing its output rate.

economies of scope Economies that reflect the ability to produce multiple products more cheaply in combination than separately.

electronic commerce (e-commerce) The application of information and communication technology anywhere along the supply chain of business processes.

electronic data interchange (EDI) A technology that enables the transmission of routine business documents having a standard format from computer to computer over telephone or direct leased lines.

elemental standard data A database of standards compiled by a firm's analysts for basic elements that they can draw on later to estimate the time required for a particular job, which is most appropriate when products or services are highly customized, job processes prevail, and process divergence is great.

employee empowerment An approach to teamwork that moves responsibility for decisions further down the organizational chart—to the level of the employee actually doing the job.

end item The final product sold to a customer.

enterprise process A companywide process that cuts across functional areas, business units, geographical regions, and product lines.

enterprise resource planning (ERP) systems Large, integrated information systems that support many enterprise processes and data storage needs.

environmental responsibility An element of sustainability that addresses the ecological needs of the planet and the firm's stewardship of the natural resources used in the production of services and products.

Euclidean distance The straight-line distance, or shortest possible path, between two points.

exchange An electronic marketplace where buying firms and selling firms come together to do business.

executive opinion A forecasting method in which the opinions, experience, and technical knowledge of one or more managers are summarized to arrive at a single forecast.

expediting The process of completing a job or finishing with a customer sooner than would otherwise be done.

exponential smoothing method A weighted moving average method that calculates the average of a time series by implicitly giving recent demands more weight than earlier demands.

external customers A customer who is either an end user or an intermediary (e.g., manufacturers, financial institutions, or retailers) buying the firm's finished services or products.

external failure costs Costs that arise when a defect is discovered after the customer receives the service or product.

external suppliers The businesses or individuals who provide the resources, services, products, and materials for the firm's short-term and long-term needs.

facility location The process of determining geographic sites for a firm's operations.

feasible region A region that represents all permissible combinations of the decision variables in a linear programming model.

financial responsibility An element of sustainability that addresses the financial needs of the shareholders, employees, customers, business partners, financial institutions, and any other entity that supplies the capital for the production of services or products or relies on the firm for wages or reimbursements.

finished goods (FG) The items in manufacturing plants, warehouses, and retail outlets that are sold to the firm's customers.

first-come, first served (FCFS) A priority sequencing rule that specifies that the job or customer arriving at the workstation first has the highest priority.

five S (5S) A methodology consisting of five workplace practices—sorting, straightening, shining, standardizing, and sustaining—that are conducive to visual controls and lean production.

fixed automation A manufacturing process that produces one type of part or product in a fixed sequence of simple operations.

fixed cost The portion of the total cost that remains constant regardless of changes in levels of output.

fixed order quantity (FOQ) A rule that maintains the same order quantity each time an order is issued.

fixed schedule A schedule that calls for each employee to work the same days and hours each week.

flexible (or programmable) automation A manufacturing process that can be changed easily to handle various products.

flexible flow The customers, materials, or information move in diverse ways, with the path of one customer or job often crisscrossing the path that the next one takes.

flexible workforce A workforce whose members are capable of doing many tasks, either at their own workstations or as they move from one workstation to another.

flow shop A manufacturer's operation that specializes in medium- to high-volume production and utilizes line or continuous flow processes.

flow time The amount of time a job spends in the service or manufacturing system.

flowchart A diagram that traces the flow of information, customers, equipment, or materials through the various steps of a process.

focus forecasting A method of forecasting that selects the best forecast from a group of forecasts generated by individual techniques.

focused factories The result of a firm's splitting large plants that produced all the company's products into several specialized smaller plants.

forecast A prediction of future events used for planning purposes.

forecast error The difference found by subtracting the forecast from actual demand for a given period.

forward integration Acquiring more channels of distribution, such as distribution centers (warehouses) and retail stores, or even business customers.

forward placement Locating stock closer to customers at a warehouse, DC, wholesaler, or retailer.

front office A process with high customer contact where the service provider interacts directly with the internal or external customer.

future value of an investment The value of an investment at the end of the period over which interest is compounded.

Gantt chart A project schedule, usually created by the project manager using computer software, that superimposes project activities, with their precedence relationships and estimated duration times, on a time line.

geographical information system (GIS) A system of computer software, hardware, and data that the firm's personnel can use to manipulate, analyze, and present information relevant to a location decision.

graphic method of linear programming A type of graphic analysis that involves the following five steps: plotting the constraints, identifying the feasible region, plotting an objective function line, finding a visual solution, and finding the algebraic solution.

graphs Representations of data in a variety of pictorial forms, such as line charts and pie charts.

Green Belt An employee who achieved the first level of training in a Six Sigma program and spends part of his or her time teaching and helping teams with their projects.

green purchasing The process of identifying, assessing, and managing the flow of environmental waste and finding ways to reduce it and minimize its impact on the environment.

gross requirements The total demand derived from *all* parent production plans.

group technology (GT) An option for achieving line-flow layouts with low volume processes; this technique creates cells not limited to just one worker and has a unique way of selecting work to be done by the cell.

heijunka The leveling of production load by both volume and product mix.

hiring and layoff Costs of advertising jobs, interviews, training programs for new employees, scrap caused by the inexperience of new employees, loss of productivity, and initial paperwork. Layoff costs include the costs of exit interviews, severance pay, retaining and retraining remaining workers and managers, and lost productivity.

histogram A summarization of data measured on a continuous scale, showing the frequency distribution of some process failure (in statistical terms, the central tendency and dispersion of the data).

holdout sample Actual demands from the more recent time periods in the time series that are set aside to test different models developed from the earlier time periods.

humanitarian logistics The process of planning, implementing and controlling the efficient, cost-effective flow and storage of goods and materials, as well as related information, from the point of origin to the point of consumption for the purpose of alleviating the suffering of vulnerable people.

hurdle rate The interest rate that is the lowest desired return on an investment; the hurdle over which the investment must pass.

hybrid office A process with moderate levels of customer contact and standard services with some options available.

immediate predecessors Work elements that must be done before the next element can begin.

independent demand items Items for which demand is influenced by market conditions and is not related to the inventory decisions for any other item held in stock or produced.

independent variables Variables that are assumed to affect the dependent variable and thereby "cause" the results observed in the past.

industrial robot Versatile, computer-controlled machine programmed to perform various tasks.

interarrival times The time between customer arrivals.

intermediate item An item that has at least one parent and at least one component.

intermodal shipments Mixing the modes of transportation for a given shipment, such as moving shipping containers or truck trailers on rail cars.

internal customers One or more employees or processes that rely on inputs from other employees or processes in order to perform their work.

internal failure costs Costs resulting from defects that are discovered during the production of a service or product.

internal suppliers The employees or processes that supply important information or materials to a firm's processes.

inventory A stock of materials used to satisfy customer demand or to support the production of services or goods.

inventory holding cost The sum of the cost of capital and the variable costs of keeping items on hand, such as storage and handling, taxes, insurance, and shrinkage.

inventory management The planning and controlling of inventories in order to meet the competitive priorities of the organization.

inventory pooling A reduction in inventory and safety stock because of the merging of variable demands from customers.

inventory position (IP) The measurement of a SKU's ability to satisfy future demand.

inventory record A record that shows an item's lot-size policy, lead time, and various time-phased data.

inventory turnover An inventory measure obtained by dividing annual sales at cost by the average aggregate inventory value maintained during the year.

ISO 9001:2008 A set of standards governing documentation of a quality program.

ISO 14000:2004 Documentation standards that require participating companies to keep track of their raw materials use and their generation, treatment, and disposal of hazardous wastes.

ISO 26000:2010 International guidelines for organizational social responsibility.

jidoka Automatically stopping the process when something is wrong and then fixing the problems on the line itself as they occur.

JIT system A system that organizes the resources, information flows, and decision rules that enable a firm to realize the benefits of JIT principles.

job process A process with the flexibility needed to produce a wide variety of products in significant quantities, with considerable divergence in the steps performed.

job shop A manufacturer's operation that specializes in low- to medium-volume production and utilizes job or batch processes.

Johnson's rule A procedure that minimizes makespan when scheduling a group of jobs on two workstations.

judgment methods A forecasting method that translates the opinions of managers, expert opinions, consumer surveys, and salesforce estimates into quantitative estimates.

judgmental adjustment An adjustment made to forecasts from one or more quantitative models that accounts for recognizing which models are performing particularly well in recent past, or take into account contextual information.

just-in-time (JIT) philosophy The belief that waste can be eliminated by cutting unnecessary capacity or inventory and removing non-value-added activities in operations.

kanban A Japanese word meaning "card" or "visible record" that refers to cards used to control the flow of production through a factory.

labor-limited environment An environment in which the resource constraint is the amount of labor available, not the number of machines or workstations.

latest finish time (LF) The latest start time of the activity that immediately follows.

latest start time (LS) The latest finish time minus its estimated duration, t, or $LS = LF - t$.

layout The physical arrangement of operations created by the various processes.

lead time The elapsed time between the receipt of a customer order and filling it.

lean systems Operations systems that maximize the value added by each of a company's activities by removing waste and delays from them.

learning curve A line that displays the relationship between processing time and the cumulative quantity of a product or service produced.

learning curve analysis A time estimation technique that takes into account the learning that takes place on an ongoing basis, such as where new products or services are introduced.

level strategy A strategy that keeps the workforce constant, but varies its utilization with overtime, undertime, and vacation planning to match the demand forecast.

line balancing The assignment of work to stations in a line process so as to achieve the desired output rate with the smallest number of workstations.

line flow The customers, materials, or information move linearly from one operation to the next, according to a fixed sequence.

line process A process that lies between the batch and continuous processes on the continuum; volumes are high and products are standardized, which allows resources to be organized around particular products.

linear programming A technique that is useful for allocating scarce resources among competing demands.

linear regression A causal method in which one variable (the dependent variable) is related to one or more independent variables by a linear equation.

linearity A characteristic of linear programming models that implies proportionality and additivity—there can be no products or powers of decision variables.

Little's law A fundamental law that relates the number of customers in a waiting-line system to the arrival rate and waiting time of customers.

load–distance method A mathematical model used to evaluate locations based on proximity factors.

lot A quantity of items that are processed together.

lot-for-lot (L4L) rule A rule under which the lot size ordered covers the gross requirements of a single week.

lot size The quantity of an inventory item management either buys from a supplier or manufactures using internal processes.

lot sizing The determination of how frequently and in what quantity to order inventory.

lot tolerance proportion defective (LTPD) The worst level of quality that the consumer can tolerate.

low-cost operation Delivering a service or a product at the lowest possible cost to the satisfaction of external or internal customers of the process or supply chain.

make-or-buy decision A managerial choice between whether to outsource a process or do it in-house.

make-to-order strategy A strategy used by manufacturers that make products to customer specifications in low volumes.

make-to-stock strategy A strategy that involves holding items in stock for immediate delivery, thereby minimizing customer delivery times.

makespan The total amount of time required to complete a group of jobs.

manufacturing resource planning (MRP II) A system that ties the basic MRP system to the company's financial system and to other core and supporting processes.

market research A systematic approach to determine external consumer interest in a service or product by creating and testing hypotheses through data-gathering surveys.

mass customization The strategy that uses highly divergent processes to generate a wide variety of customized products at reasonably low costs.

mass production A term sometimes used in the popular press for a line process that uses the make-to-stock strategy.

Master Black Belt Full-time teachers and mentors to several Black Belts.

master production schedule (MPS) A part of the material requirements plan that details how many end items will be produced within specified periods of time.

material requirements planning (MRP) A computerized information system developed specifically to help manufacturers manage dependent demand inventory and schedule replenishment orders.

mean absolute deviation (MAD) A measurement of the dispersion of forecast errors.

mean absolute percent error (MAPE) A measurement that relates the forecast error to the level of demand and is useful for putting forecast performance in the proper perspective.

mean squared error (MSE) A measurement of the dispersion of forecast errors.

methods time measurement (MTM) A commonly used predetermined data system.

metrics Performance measures that are established for a process and the steps within it.

minimum-cost schedule A schedule determined by starting with the normal time schedule and crashing activities along the critical path, in such a way that the costs of crashing do not exceed the savings in indirect and penalty costs.

mixed-model assembly A type of assembly that produces a mix of models in smaller lots.

mixed-model line A production line that produces several items belonging to the same family.

mixed strategy A strategy that considers the full range of supply options.

Modified Accelerated Cost Recovery System (MACRS) The only acceptable depreciation method for tax purposes that shortens the lives of investments, giving firms larger early tax deductions.

Monte Carlo simulation A simulation process that uses random numbers to generate simulation events.

most likely time (m) The probable time required to perform an activity.

MRP explosion A process that converts the requirements of various final products into a material requirements plan that specifies the replenishment schedules of all the subassemblies, components, and raw materials needed to produce final products.

multiple-dimension rules A set of rules that apply to more than one aspect of a job.

multiplicative seasonal method A method whereby seasonal factors are multiplied by an estimate of average demand to arrive at a seasonal forecast.

nearest neighbor (NN) heuristic A technique that creates a route by deciding the next city to visit on the basis of its proximity.

naïve forecast A time-series method whereby the forecast for the next period equals the demand for the current period, or Forecast = D_t.

nested process The concept of a process within a process.

net present value (NPV) method The method that evaluates an investment by calculating the present values of all after-tax total cash flows and then subtracting the initial investment amount for their total.

network diagram A network planning method, designed to depict the relationships between activities, that consists of nodes (circles) and arcs (arrows).

new service/product development process A process that designs and develops new services or products from inputs received from external customer specifications or from the market in general through the customer relationship process.

nominal value A target for design specifications.

nonnegativity An assumption that the decision variables must be positive or zero.

normal cost (NC) The activity cost associated with the normal time.

normal time (NT) In the context of project management, the time necessary to complete an activity under normal conditions.

normal time (NT) In the context of time study, a measurement found by multiplying the select time (t), the frequency (F) of the work element per cycle, and the rating factor (RF).

normal time for the cycle (NTC) A measurement found by summing the normal time for each element.

objective function An expression in linear programming models that states mathematically what is being maximized or minimized.

offshoring A supply chain strategy that involves moving processes to another country.

one-worker, multiple-machines (OWMM) cell A one-person cell in which a worker operates several different machines simultaneously to achieve a line flow.

on-time delivery Meeting delivery-time promises.

open orders See scheduled receipts (SR).

operating characteristic (OC) curve A graph that describes how well a sampling plan discriminates between good and bad lots.

operations management The systematic design, direction, and control of processes that transform inputs into services and products for internal, as well as external, customers.

operations planning and scheduling The process of balancing supply with demand, from the aggregate level down to the short-term scheduling level.

operations scheduling A type of scheduling in which jobs are assigned to workstations or employees are assigned to jobs for specified time periods.

operations strategy The means by which operations implements the firm's corporate strategy and helps to build a customer-driven firm.

optimistic time (a) The shortest time in which an activity can be completed, if all goes exceptionally well.

optional replenishment system A system used to review the inventory position at fixed time intervals and, if the position has dropped to (or below) a predetermined level, to place a variable-sized order to cover expected needs.

order fulfillment process A process that includes the activities required to produce and deliver the service or product to the external customer.

order qualifier Minimal level required from a set of crteria for a firm to do business in a particular market segment.

order winner A criterion customers use to differentiate the services or products of one firm from those of another.

ordering cost The cost of preparing a purchase order for a supplier or a production order for manufacturing.

organizational learning The process of gaining experience with products and processes, achieving greater efficiency through automation and other capital investments, and making other improvements in administrative methods or personnel.

outsourcing Paying suppliers and distributors to perform processes and provide needed services and materials.

overtime The time that employees work that is longer than the regular workday or workweek for which they receive additional pay.

p-chart A chart used for controlling the proportion of defective services or products generated by the process.

pacing The movement of product from one station to the next as soon as the cycle time has elapsed.

parameter A value that the decision maker cannot control and that does not change when the solution is implemented.

parent Any product that is manufactured from one or more components.

Pareto chart A bar chart on which factors are plotted along the horizontal axis in decreasing order of frequency.

part commonality The degree to which a component has more than one immediate parent.

past due The amount of time by which a job missed its due date.

path The sequence of activities between a project's start and finish.

payback method A method for evaluating projects that determines how much time will elapse before the total of after-tax flows will equal, or pay back, the initial investment.

payoff table A table that shows the amount for each alternative if each possible event occurs.

performance rating factor (RF) An assessment that describes *how much* above or below average the worker's performance is on each work element.

periodic order quantity (POQ) A rule that allows a different order quantity for each order issued but issues the order for predetermined time intervals.

periodic review (P) sytem A system in which an item's inventory position is reviewed periodically rather than continuously.

perpetual inventory system A system of inventory control in which the inventory records are always current.

pessimistic time (b) The longest estimated time required to perform an activity.

phase A single step in providing a service.

pipeline inventory Inventory that is created when an order for an item is issued but not yet received.

plan-do-study-act cycle A cycle, also called the Deming Wheel, used by firms actively engaged in continuous improvement to train their work teams in problem solving.

planned order release An indication of when an order for a specified quantity of an item is to be issued.

planned receipts Orders that are not yet released to the shop or the supplier.

planning horizon The set of consecutive time periods considered for planning purposes.

plants within plants (PWPs) Different operations within a facility with individualized competitive priorities, processes, and workforces under the same roof.

poka-yoke Mistake-proofing methods aimed at designing fail-safe systems that minimize human error.

postponement The strategy of delaying final activities in the provision of a product until the orders are received.

precedence diagram A diagram that allows one to visualize immediate predecessors better; work elements are denoted by circles, with the time required to perform the work shown below each circle.

precedence relationship A relationship that determines a sequence for undertaking activities; it specifies that one activity cannot start until a preceding activity has been completed.

predetermined data approach A database approach that divides each work element into a series of micromotions that make up the element. The analyst then consults a published database that contains the normal times for the full array of possible micromotions.

preemptive discipline A rule that allows a customer of higher priority to interrupt the service of another customer.

preference matrix A table that allows the manager to rate an alternative according to several performance criteria.

present value of an investment The amount that must be invested now to accumulate to a certain amount in the future at a specific interest rate.

presourcing A level of supplier involvement in which suppliers are selected early in a product's concept development stage and are given significant, if not total, responsibility for the design of certain components or systems of the product.

prevention costs Costs associated with preventing defects before they happen.

priority rule A rule that selects the next customer to be served by the service facility.

priority sequencing rule A rule that specifies the job or customer processing sequence when several jobs are waiting in line at a workstation.

process Any activity or group of activities that takes one or more inputs, transforms them, and provides one or more outputs for its customers.

process analysis The documentation and detailed understanding of how work is performed and how it can be redesigned.

process capability The ability of the process to meet the design specifications for a service or product.

process capability index, C_{pk} An index that measures the potential for a process to generate defective outputs relative to either upper or lower specifications.

process capability ratio, C_p The tolerance width divided by six standard deviations.

process chart An organized way of documenting all the activities performed by a person or group of people, at a workstation, with a customer, or on materials.

process choice A way of structuring the process by organizing resources around the process or organizing them around the products.

process divergence The extent to which the process is highly customized with considerable latitude as to how its tasks are performed.

process failure Any performance shortfall, such as error, delay, environmental waste, rework, and the like.

process improvement The systematic study of the activities and flows of each process to improve it.

process simulation The act of reproducing the behavior of a process, using a model that describes each step.

process strategy The pattern of decisions made in managing processes so that they will achieve their competitive priorities.

process structure A process decision that determines the process type relative to the kinds of resources needed, how resources are partitioned between them, and their key characteristics.

producer's risk (α) The risk that the sampling plan will fail to verify an acceptable lot's quality and, thus, reject it (a type I error).

product family A group of services or products that have similar demand requirements and common process, labor, and materials requirements.

production plan a manufacturing firm's sales and operations plan that centers on production rates and inventory holdings.

product-mix problem A one-period type of planning problem, the solution of which yields optimal output quantities (or product mix) of a group of services or products subject to resource capacity and market demand constraints.

productivity The value of outputs (services and products) produced divided by the values of input resources (wages, costs of equipment, and so on).

program An interdependent set of projects that have a common strategic purpose.

program evaluation and review technique (PERT) A network planning method created for the U.S. Navy's Polaris missile project in the 1950s, which involved 3,000 separate contractors and suppliers.

project An interrelated set of activities with a definite starting and ending point, which results in a unique outcome for a specific allocation of resources.

project management A systemized, phased approach to defining, organizing, planning, monitoring, and controlling projects.

projected on-hand inventory An estimate of the amount of inventory available each week after gross requirements have been satisfied.

protection interval The period over which safety stock must protect the user from running out of stock.

pull method A method in which customer demand activates production of the service or item.

purchased item An item that has one or more parents but no components because it comes from a supplier.

purchasing The activity that decides which suppliers to use, negotiates contracts, and determines whether to buy locally.

push method A method in which production of the item begins in advance of customer needs.

quality A term used by customers to describe their general satisfaction with a service or product.

quality at the source A philosophy whereby defects are caught and corrected where they were created.

quality circles Another name for problem-solving teams; small groups of supervisors and employees who meet to identify, analyze, and solve process and quality problems.

quality engineering An approach originated by Genichi Taguchi that involves combining engineering and statistical methods to reduce costs and improve quality by optimizing product design and manufacturing processes.

quality loss function The rationale that a service or product that barely conforms to the specifications is more like a defective service or product than a perfect one.

quality of life A factor that considers the availability of good schools, recreational facilities, cultural events, and an attractive lifestyle.

quantity discount A drop in the price per unit when an order is sufficiently large.

R-chart A chart used to monitor process variability.

radio frequency identification (RFID) A method for identifying items through the use of radio signals from a tag attached to an item.

random number A number that has the same probability of being selected as any other number.

range of feasibility The interval (lower and upper bounds) over which the right-hand-side parameter of a constraint can vary while its shadow price remains valid.

range of optimality The interval (lower and upper bounds) of an objective function coefficient over which the optimal values of the decision variables remain unchanged.

raw materials (RM) The inventories needed for the production of services or goods.

rectified inspection The assumption that all defective items in the lot will be replaced with good items if the lot is rejected and that any defective items in the sample will be replaced if the lot is accepted.

rectilinear distance The distance between two points with a series of 90-degree turns, as along city blocks.

reduced cost How much the objective function coefficient of a decision variable must improve (increase for maximization or decrease for minimization) before the optimal solution changes and the decision variable "enters" the solution with some positive number.

reengineering The fundamental rethinking and radical redesign of processes to improve performance dramatically in terms of cost, quality, service, and speed.

regular time Wages paid to employees plus contributions to benefits.

reorder point (R) The predetermined minimum level that an inventory position must reach before a fixed quantity Q of the SKU is ordered.

reorder point (ROP) system See continuous review (Q) system.

repeatability The degree to which the same work can be done again.

resource flexibility The ease with which employees and equipment can handle a wide variety of products, output levels, duties, and functions.

resource plan A plan that determines the requirements for materials and other resources on a more detailed level than the sales and operations plan.

resource planning A process that takes sales and operations plans; processes information in the way of time standards, routings, and other information on how services or products are produced; and then plans the input requirements.

revenue management Varying price at the right time for different customer segments to maximize revenues yielded by existing supply capacity.

reverse logistics The process of planning, implementing, and controlling the efficient, cost effective flow of products, materials, and information from the point of consumption back to the point of origin for returns, repair, remanufacture, or recycling.

risk-management plan A plan that identifies the key risks to a project's success and prescribes ways to circumvent them.

rotating schedule A schedule that rotates employees through a series of workdays or hours.

route planning An activity that seeks to find the shortest route to deliver a service or product.

SA8000:2008 A list of standards covering nine dimensions of ethical workforce management.

safety stock inventory Surplus inventory that a company holds to protect against uncertainties in demand, lead time, and supply changes.

sales and operations plan (S&OP) A plan of future aggregate resource levels so that supply is in balance with demand.

salesforce estimates The forecasts that are compiled from estimates of future demands made periodically by members of a company's salesforce.

salvage value The cash flow from the sale or disposal of plant and equipment at the end of a project's life.

sample size A quantity of randomly selected observations of process outputs.

sampling plan A plan that specifies a sample size, the time between successive samples, and decision rules that determine when action should be taken.

scatter diagram A plot of two variables showing whether they are related.

schedule A detailed plan that allocates resources over short time horizons to accomplish specific tasks.

scheduled receipts (SR) Orders that have been placed but have not yet been received.

SCOR model A framework that focuses on a basic supply chain of plan, source, make, deliver, and return processes, repeated again and again along the supply chain.

select time (t) The average observed time based only on representative times.

self-managed team A small group of employees who work together to produce a major portion, or sometimes all, of a service or product.

sensitivity analysis A technique for systematically changing parameters in a model to determine the effects of such changes.

sequencing Determining the order in which jobs or customers are processed in the waiting line at a workstation.

sequential-sampling plan A plan in which the consumer randomly selects items from the lot and inspects them one by one.

service blueprint A special flowchart of a service process that shows which steps have high customer contact.

service facility A person (or crew), a machine (or group of machines), or both necessary to perform the service for the customer.

service level The desired probability of not running out of stock in any one ordering cycle, which begins at the time an order is placed and ends when it arrives in stock.

service system The number of lines and the arrangement of the facilities.

setup cost The cost involved in changing over a machine or workspace to produce a different item.

setup time The time required to change a process or an operation from making one service or product to making another.

shadow price The marginal improvement in Z (increase for maximization and decrease for minimization) caused by relaxing the constraint by one unit.

shortest processing time (SPT) A priority sequencing rule that specifies that the job requiring the shortest processing time is the next job to be processed.

shortest route problem A problem whose objective is to find the shortest distance between two cities in a network or map.

simple moving average method A time-series method used to estimate the average of a demand time series by averaging the demand for the n most recent time periods.

simplex method An iterative algebraic procedure for solving linear programming problems.

simulation The act of reproducing the behavior of a system using a model that describes the processes of the system.

single-bin system A system of inventory control in which a maximum level is marked on the storage shelf or bin, and the inventor is brought up to the mark periodically.

single-digit setup The goal of having a setup time of less than 10 minutes.

single-dimension rules A set of rules that bases the priority of a job on a single aspect of the job, such as arrival time at the workstation, the due date, or the processing time.

single-sampling plan A decision to accept or reject a lot based on the results of one random sample from the lot.

Six Sigma A comprehensive and flexible system for achieving, sustaining, and maximizing business success by minimizing defects and variability in processes.

slack The amount by which the left-hand side of a linear programming constraint falls short of the right-hand side.

slack per remaining operations (S/RO) A priority sequencing rule that determines priority by dividing the slack by the number of operations that remain, including the one being scheduled.

social responsibility An element of sustainability that addresses the moral, ethical, and philanthropic expectations that society has of an organization.

sole sourcing The awarding of a contract for a service or item to only one supplier.

special-purpose teams Groups that address issues of paramount concern to management, labor, or both.

staffing plan A sales and operations plan for a service firm, which centers on staffing and other human resource-related factors.

standard deviation(σ) for forecasting A measurement of the dispersion of forecast errors.

standard deviation (σ) for statistical quality control The square root of the variance of a distribution.

standard time (ST) A measurement found by incorporating the normal time and allowances; $ST = NTC(1 + A)$, where A equals the proportion of the normal time added for allowances.

statistical process control (SPC) The application of statistical techniques to determine whether a process is delivering what the customer wants.

steady state The state that occurs when the simulation is repeated over enough time that the average results for performance measures remain constant.

stock-keeping unit (SKU) An individual item or product that has an identifying code and is held in inventory somewhere along the supply chain.

stockout An order that cannot be satisfied, resulting in a loss of the sale.

straight-line depreciation method The simplest method of calculating annual depreciation; found by subtracting the estimated salvage value from the amount of investment required at the beginning of the project, and then dividing by the asset's expected economic life.

subassembly An intermediate item that is *assembled* (as opposed to being transformed by other means) from more than one component.

suggestion system A voluntary system by which employees submit their ideas on process improvements.

supplier relationship process A process that selects the suppliers of services, materials, and information and facilitates the timely and efficient flow of these items into the firm.

supply chain An interrelated series of processes within and across firms that produces a service or product to the satisfaction of customers.

supply chain design Designing a firm's supply chain to meet the competitive priorities of the firm's operations strategy.

supply chain processes Business processes that have external customers or suppliers.

supply chain integration The effective coordination of supply chain processes through the seamless flow of information up and down the supply chain.

supply chain management The synchronization of a firm's processes with those of its suppliers and customers to match the flow of materials, services, and information with customer demand.

support process A process that provides vital resources and inputs to the core processes and therefore is essential to the management of the business.

surplus The amount by which the left-hand side of a linear programming constraint exceeds the right-hand side.

sustainability A characteristic of processes that are meeting humanity's needs without harming future generations.

swim lane flowchart A visual representation that groups functional areas responsible for different sub-processes into lanes.

takt time Cycle time needed to match the rate of production to the rate of sales or consumption.

tardiness See past due.

teams Small groups of people who have a common purpose, set their own performance goals and approaches, and hold themselves accountable for success.

technological forecasting An application of executive opinion to keep abreast of the latest advances in technology.

theoretical minimum (TM) A benchmark or goal for the smallest number of stations possible, where the total time required to assemble each unit (the sum of all work-element standard times) is divided by the cycle time.

theory of constraints (TOC) A systematic management approach that focuses on actively managing those constraints that impede a firm's progress toward its goal.

throughput time Total elapsed time from the start to the finish of a job or a customer being processed at one or more workcenters.

time-based competition A strategy that focuses on the competitive priorities of delivery speed and development speed.

time between orders (TBO) The average elapsed time between receiving (or placing) replenishment orders of Q units for a particular lot size.

time compression The feature of simulation models that allows them to obtain operating characteristic estimates in much less time than is required to gather the same operating data from a real system.

time series The repeated observations of demand for a service or product in their order of occurrence.

time-series analysis A statistical approach that relies heavily on historical demand data to project the future size of demand and recognizes trends and seasonal patterns.

time study A work measurement method using a trained analyst to perform four basic steps in setting a time standard for a job or process: selecting the work elements (or nested processes) within the process to be studied, timing the elements, determining the sample size, and setting the final standard.

time value of money The concept that a dollar in hand can be invested to earn a return so that more than one dollar will be available in the future.

tolerance An allowance above or below the nominal value.

top quality Delivering an outstanding service or product.

total inventory The sum of scheduled receipts and on-hand inventories.

total quality management (TQM) A philosophy that stresses three principles for achieving high levels of process performance and quality: (1) customer satisfaction, (2) employee involvement, and (3) continuous improvement in performance.

tracking signal A measure that indicates whether a method of forecasting is accurately predicting actual changes in demand.

transportation method A more efficient solution technique than the simplex method for solving transportation problems.

transportation method for location problems A quantitative approach that can help solve multiple-facility location problems.

transportation problem A special case of linear programming that has linear constraints for capacity limitations and demand requirements.

traveling salesman problem A problem whose objective is to find the shortest possible route that visits each city exactly once and returns to the starting city.

trend projection with regression A forecasting model that is a hybrid between a time-series technique and the causal method.

two-bin system A visual system version of the Q system in which a SKU's inventory is stored at two different locations.

type I error An error that occurs when the employee concludes that the process is out of control based on a sample result that falls outside the control limits, when in fact it was due to pure randomness.

type II error An error that occurs when the employee concludes that the process is in control and only randomness is present, when actually the process is out of statistical control.

uncontrollable variables Random events that the decision maker cannot control.

undertime The situation that occurs when employees do not have enough work for the regular-time workday or workweek.

usage quantity The number of units of a component that are needed to make one unit of its immediate parent.

utilization The degree to which equipment, space, or the workforce is currently being used, and is measured as the ratio of average output rate to maximum capacity (expressed as a percent).

value analysis A systematic effort to reduce the cost or improve the performance of services or products, either purchased or produced.

value stream mapping (VSM) A qualitative lean tool for eliminating waste or *muda* that involves a current state drawing, a future state drawing, and an implementation plan.

variable cost The portion of the total cost that varies directly with volume of output.

variables Service or product characteristics, such as weight, length, volume, or time that can be measured.

variety Handling a wide assortment of services or products efficiently.

vendor-managed inventories (VMI) A system in which the supplier has access to the customer's inventory data and is responsible for maintaining the inventory on the customer's site.

visual system A system that allows employees to place orders when inventory visibly reaches a certain marker.

volume flexibility Accelerating or decelerating the rate of production of services or products quickly to handle large fluctuations in demand.

waiting line One or more "customers" waiting for service.

warranty A written guarantee that the producer will replace or repair defective parts or perform the service to the customer's satisfaction.

weeks of supply An inventory measure obtained by dividing the average aggregate inventory value by sales per week at cost.

weighted-distance method A mathematical model used to evaluate layouts (of facility locations) based on proximity factors.

weighted moving average method A time-series method in which each historical demand in the average can have its own weight; the sum of the weights equals 1.0.

work breakdown structure (WBS) A statement of all work that has to be completed.

work elements The smallest units of work that can be performed independently.

work-in-process (WIP) Items, such as components or assemblies, needed to produce a final product in manufacturing or service operations.

work measurement The process of creating labor standards based on the judgment of skilled observers.

work sampling method A process that estimates the proportion of time spent by people or machines on different activities, based on observations randomized over time.

work standard The time required for a trained worker to perform a task following a prescribed method with normal effort and skill.

workforce scheduling A type of scheduling that determines when employees work.

x-chart A chart used to see whether the process is generating output, on average, consistent with a target value set by management for the process or whether its current performance, with respect to the average of the performance measure, is consistent with past performance.

Name Index

Subject Index

Page numbers followed by f have figures. Page numbers followed by t have tables.